Data Visualization

Exploring and Explaining with Data

Jeffrey D. Camm
Wake Forest University

James J. Cochran
University of Alabama

Michael J. Fry
University of Cincinnati

Jeffrey W. Ohlmann
University of Iowa

Australia • Brazil • Canada • Mexico • Singapore • United Kingdom • United States

Data Visualization: Exploring and Explaining with Data, **Second Edition**
Jeffrey D. Camm, James J. Cochran, Michael J. Fry, Jeffrey W. Ohlmann

SVP, Product Management: Cheryl Costantini

VP, Product Management: Mark Santee

Product Director: Joe Sabatino

Senior Portfolio Product Manager: Aaron Arnsparger

Product Assistant: Flannery Cowan

Senior Learning Designer: Brandon Foltz

Content Manager: Jennifer Ziegler, Ramkumar Palani

Digital Project Manager: Andrew Southwell

Marketing Director: Danae April

Product Marketing Manager: Colin Kramer

Content Acquisition Analyst: Rida Syed

Production Service: MPS Limited

Designer: Chris Doughman

Cover Image Source:
Dan Reynolds Photography/Moment/Getty Images

For product information and technology assistance, contact us at
**Cengage Customer & Sales Support, 1-800-354-9706
or support.cengage.com.**
For permission to use material from this text or product, submit all requests online at **www.copyright.com.**

Library of Congress Control Number: 2024902264

ISBN: 978-0-357-92976-6

Cengage
5191 Natorp Boulevard
Mason, OH 45040
USA

Cengage is a leading provider of customized learning solutions. Our employees reside in nearly 40 different countries and serve digital learners in 165 countries around the world. Find your local representative at **www.cengage.com.**

To learn more about Cengage platforms and services, register or access your online learning solution, or purchase materials for your course, visit **www.cengage.com.**

Printed at CLDPC, USA, 04-24

Brief Contents

Contents

About the Authors

Jeffrey D. Camm is Inmar Presidential Chair and Senior Associate Dean for Faculty and Research in the School of Business at Wake Forest University. Born in Cincinnati, Ohio, he holds a B.S. from Xavier University (Ohio) and a Ph.D. from Clemson University. Prior to joining the faculty at Wake Forest, he was on the faculty of the University of Cincinnati. He has also been a visiting scholar at Stanford University and a visiting professor of business administration at the Tuck School of Business at Dartmouth College.

Dr. Camm has published more than 45 papers in the general area of optimization applied to problems in operations management and marketing. He has published his research in *Science, Management Science, Operations Research, INFORMS Journal on Applied Analytics*, and other professional journals. Dr. Camm was named the Dornoff Fellow of Teaching Excellence at the University of Cincinnati, and he was the 2006 recipient of the INFORMS Prize for the Teaching of Operations Research Practice. A firm believer in practicing what he preaches, he has served as an operations research consultant to numerous companies and government agencies. From 2005 to 2010, he served as editor-in-chief of the *INFORMS Journal on Applied Analytics*. In 2016, Professor Camm received the George E. Kimball Medal for service to the operations research profession, and in 2017, he was named an INFORMS Fellow.

James J. Cochran is Professor of Applied Statistics, and the Mike and Kathy Mouron Research Chair at The University of Alabama. Born in Dayton, Ohio, he earned his B.S., M.S., and M.B.A. from Wright State University and his Ph.D. from the University of Cincinnati. He has been at The University of Alabama since 2014 and has been a visiting scholar at Stanford University, Universidad de Talca, the University of South Africa, and Pole Universitaire Leonard de Vinci.

Dr. Cochran has published more than 50 papers in the development and application of operations research and statistical methods. He has published in several journals, including *Management Science, The American Statistician, Communications in Statistics—Theory and Methods, Annals of Operations Research, European Journal of Operational Research, Journal of Combinatorial Optimization, INFORMS Journal on Applied Analytics*, and *Statistics and Probability Letters*. He received the 2008 INFORMS Prize for the Teaching of Operations Research Practice, the 2010 Mu Sigma Rho Statistical Education Award, and the 2016 Waller Distinguished Teaching Career Award from the American Statistical Association. Dr. Cochran was elected to the International Statistics Institute in 2005, named a Fellow of the American Statistical Association in 2011, and named a Fellow of INFORMS in 2017. He also received the Founders Award in 2014 and the Karl E. Peace Award in 2015 from the American Statistical Association, the INFORMS President's Award in 2019, and the William G. Hunter Award from the American Society for Quality in 2023.

A strong advocate for effective operations research and statistics education as a means of improving the quality of applications to real problems, Dr. Cochran has chaired teaching effectiveness workshops around the globe. He has served as an operations research consultant to numerous companies and not-for-profit organizations. He served as editor-in-chief of *INFORMS Transactions on Education* and is on the editorial board of *INFORMS Journal on Applied Analytics, International Transactions in Operational Research*, and *Significance*.

Michael J. Fry is Professor of Operations, Business Analytics, and Information Systems (OBAIS), Lindner Research Fellow, and Managing Director of the Center for Business Analytics in the Carl H. Lindner College of Business at the University of Cincinnati. Born in Killeen, Texas, he earned a B.S. from Texas A&M University and M.S.E. and Ph.D. degrees from the University of Michigan. He has been at the University of Cincinnati since 2002, where he previously served as Department Head. He has also been a visiting professor at Cornell University and at the University of British Columbia.

Professor Fry has published more than 25 research papers in journals such as *Operations Research, Manufacturing and Service Operations Management, Transportation Science, Naval Research Logistics, IIE Transactions, Critical Care Medicine,* and *Interfaces.* He serves on editorial boards for journals such as *Production and Operations Management, INFORMS Journal on Applied Analytics,* and *Journal of Quantitative Analysis in Sports.* His research interests are in applying analytics to the areas of supply chain management, sports, and public-policy operations. He has worked with many different organizations for his research, including Dell, Inc., Starbucks Coffee Company, Great American Insurance Group, the Cincinnati Fire Department, the State of Ohio Election Commission, the Cincinnati Bengals, and the Cincinnati Zoo and Botanical Gardens. In 2008, he was named a finalist for the Daniel H. Wagner Prize for Excellence in Operations Research Practice, and he has been recognized for both his research and teaching excellence at the University of Cincinnati. In 2019, he led the team that was awarded the INFORMS UPS George D. Smith Prize on behalf of the OBAIS Department at the University of Cincinnati.

Jeffrey W. Ohlmann is Associate Professor of Business Analytics and Huneke Research Fellow in the Tippie College of Business at the University of Iowa. Born in Valentine, Nebraska, he earned a B.S. from the University of Nebraska and M.S. and Ph.D. degrees from the University of Michigan. He has been at the University of Iowa since 2003.

Professor Ohlmann's research on the modeling and solution of decision-making problems has produced more than two dozen research papers in journals such as *Operations Research, Mathematics of Operations Research, INFORMS Journal on Computing, Transportation Science,* and *European Journal of Operational Research.* He has collaborated with organizations such as Transfreight, LeanCor, Cargill, the Hamilton County Board of Elections, and three National Football League franchises. Because of the relevance of his work to industry, he was bestowed the George B. Dantzig Dissertation Award and was recognized as a finalist for the Daniel H. Wagner Prize for Excellence in Operations Research Practice.

Data Visualization: Exploring and Explaining with Data 2e is designed to introduce best practices in data visualization to undergraduate and graduate students. This is one of the first books on data visualization designed for college courses. The book contains material on effective design, choice of chart type, effective use of color, how to explore data visually, how to build data dashboards, and how to explain concepts and results visually in a compelling way with data. In an increasingly data-driven economy, these concepts are becoming more important for analysts, natural scientists, social scientists, engineers, medical professionals, business professionals, and virtually everyone who needs to interact with data. Indeed, the skills developed in this book will be helpful to all who want to influence with data or be accurately informed by data.

The book is designed for a semester-long course at either the undergraduate or graduate level. The examples used in this book are drawn from a variety of functional areas in the business world, including accounting, finance, operations, and human resources as well as from sports, politics, science, medicine, and economics. The intention is that this book will be relevant to students at either the undergraduate or graduate level in a business school as well as to students studying in other academic areas.

Data Visualization: Exploring and Explaining with Data 2e is written in a style that does not require advanced knowledge of mathematics or statistics. The first five chapters cover foundational issues important to constructing good charts. Chapter 1 introduces data visualization and how it fits into the broader area of analytics. A brief history of data visualization is provided as well as a discussion of the different types of data and examples of a variety of charts. Chapter 2 provides guidance on selecting an appropriate type of chart based on the goals of the visualization and the type of data to be visualized. Best practices in chart design, including discussions of preattentive attributes, Gestalt principles, and the data-ink ratio, are covered in Chapter 3. Chapter 4 discusses the attributes of color, how to use color effectively, and some common mistakes in the use of color in data visualization. Chapter 5 covers the important topic of visualizing and describing variability that occurs in observed values. Chapter 5 also introduces the visualization of frequency distributions for categorical and quantitative variables, measures of location and variability, and confidence intervals and prediction intervals.

Chapters 6 and 7 cover how to explore and explain with data visualization in detail with examples. Chapter 6 discusses the use of visualization in exploratory data analysis. The exploration of individual variables as well as the relationship between pairs of variables is considered. The organization of data to facilitate exploration is discussed as well as the effect of missing data. The special considerations of visualizing time series data and geospatial data are also presented. Chapter 7 provides important coverage of how to explain and influence with data visualization, including knowing your message, understanding the needs of your audience, and using preattentive attributes to better convey your message. Chapter 8 is a discussion of how to design and construct data dashboards, collections of data visualizations used for decision making. Chapter 9 covers the responsible use of data visualization to avoid confusing or misleading your audience, addresses the importance of understanding your data to best convey insights accurately, and discusses how design choices in a data visualization affect the insights conveyed to the audience. Finally, the data wrangling appendix provides an overview of approaches for exploring, cleaning, and wrangling data to make the data more amenable for data visualization and other analyses.

This textbook can be used by students who have previously taken a basic statistics course as well as by students who have not had a prior course in statistics. The two most technical chapters, Chapters 5 (Visualizing Variability) and 6 (Exploring Data Visually), do not assume a previous course in statistics. All technical concepts are gently introduced. For students who have had a previous statistics class, the statistical coverage in these chapters provides a good review within a treatment where the focus is on visualization. The book offers complete coverage for a full course in data visualization, but it can also support a basic statistics or analytics course. The following table gives our recommendations for chapters to use to support a variety of courses.

	Chapter 1	Chapter 2	Chapter 3	Chapter 4	Chapter 5	Chapter 6	Chapter 7	Chapter 8	Chapter 9
	Intro	Chart Type	Design	Color	Variability	Exploring	Explaining	Dashboards	Truth
Full Data Visualization Course	●	●	●	●	●	●	●	●	●
Data Visualization Course Focused on Presentation	●	●	●	●			●		●
Part of a Basic Statistics Course		●	●	●	●	●			●
Part of an Analytics Course		●	●	●	●	●			●

Updates in the Second Edition

Based on feedback from users of our first edition of *Data Visualization, Exploring and Explaining with Data*, we have made several significant updates to this second edition. As in the first edition, the main text depends only on Excel to construct visualizations. However, the job market indicates that other dedicated data visualization software skills are valued by employers. Therefore, we have added appendices with step-by-step instructions for how to construct data visualizations using two leading data visualization software packages: Microsoft Power BI and Tableau. Other feedback suggested that coverage of data preparation for visualization will help students be better prepared to develop impactful visualizations. Therefore, we have added an appendix on data wrangling to introduce techniques that can be used to prepare data for visualization. Additionally, it was suggested that students would benefit from additional exercises that require knowledge from multiple chapters in the textbook. Therefore, we have added multi-chapter cases that require the application of methods and tools from multiple chapters. Specifically, our updates include the following:

Power BI Appendices: We have added appendices on how to use Microsoft Power BI, one of the market-leading software packages for constructing data visualizations. These appendices provide detailed step-by-step instructions on how to build data visualizations for Chapters 1 through 6 and Chapter 8, using Power BI.

Tableau Appendices: Similar to the Power BI appendices, we have added step-by-step instructions on how to use Tableau, another leading data visualization software package for topics covered in Chapters 1 through 6 and Chapter 8.

Data Wrangling Appendix: This new appendix, *Data Wrangling: Preparing Data for Visualization*, provides instructions on how to prepare messy data for visualization. Topics covered include, among others, how to access and format data, how to handle missing data and identify errors, and data validation.

Multi-Chapter Cases: We have created four new cases that cover various topics across chapters. They are designed to provide students with an opportunity to apply concepts and tools from multiple chapters in the textbook and are more open-ended than the typical end-of-chapter problems. The cases cover applications in healthcare, operations, economics, and finance.

Continued Features and Pedagogy

The style and format of this textbook are similar to our other textbooks. Some of the specific features that we use in this textbook are listed here.

- **Data Visualization Makeover:** With the exception of Chapter 1, each chapter contains a Data Visualization Makeover. Each of these vignettes presents a real visualization that can be improved using the principles discussed in the chapter. We present the original data visualization and then discuss how it can be improved. The examples are drawn from many different organizations in a variety of areas including government, retail, sports, science, politics, and entertainment.

- **Learning Objectives:** Each chapter has a list of the learning objectives of that chapter. The list provides details of what students should be able to do and understand once they have completed the chapter.

- **Software:** Because of its widespread use and ease of availability, we have chosen Microsoft Excel as the software to illustrate the best practices and principles contained herein. Excel has been thoroughly integrated throughout this textbook. Whenever we introduce a new type of chart or table, we provide detailed step-by-step instructions for how to create the chart or table in Excel. (As previously noted, we do also include appendices on how to use Power BI and Tableau.)

- **Notes and Comments:** At the end of many sections, we provide Notes and Comments to give the student additional insights about the material presented in that section. Additionally, margin notes are used throughout the textbook to provide insights and tips related to the specific material being discussed.

- **End-of-Chapter Problems:** Each chapter contains at least 15 problems to help the student master the material presented in that chapter. The problems are separated into Conceptual and Applications problems. Conceptual problems test the student's understanding of concepts presented in the chapter. Applications problems are hands-on and require the student to construct or edit charts or tables.

- **DATAfiles and CHARTfiles:** All data sets used as examples and in end-of-chapter problems are Excel files designated as DATAfiles and are available for download by the student. The names of the DATAfiles are called out in margin notes throughout the textbook. Similarly, some Excel files with completed charts are available for download and are designated as CHARTfiles.

MindTap

MindTap is a customizable digital course solution that includes an interactive eBook, auto-graded exercises and problems from the textbook with solutions feedback, interactive visualization applets with quizzes, chapter overview and problem walk-through videos, and more! Contact your Cengage account executive for more information about MindTap.

Instructor and Student Resources

Additional instructor and student resources for this product are available online. Instructor assets include an Instructor's Manual, Educator's Guide, PowerPoint® slides, a Solutions and Answers Guide, and a test bank powered by Cognero®. Student assets include data sets. Sign up or sign in at **www.cengage.com** to search for and access this product and its online resources.

Acknowledgments

We would like to acknowledge the work of reviewers who have provided comments and suggestions for improvement of this text. Thanks to:

Randy Bulriss
Grand Canyon University

Xiaohui Chang
Oregon State University

Wei Chen
York College of Pennsylvania

Anjee Gorkhali
Susquehanna University

Rita Kumar
Cal Poly Pomona

Barin Nag
Towson University

Andy Olstad
Oregon State University

Vivek Patil
Gonzaga University

Nolan Taylor
Indiana University

Kylene Wesner
Texas A&M University

We are also indebted to the entire team at Cengage who worked on this title: Senior Portfolio Product Manager, Aaron Arnsparger; Senior Learning Designer, Brandon Foltz; Digital Project Manager, Andrew Southwell; Content Managers, Jennifer Ziegler and Ramkumar Palani; Subject Matter Expert, Deb Cernauskas, Program Manager, Maya Whelan, Designer Chris Doughman, and our Senior Project Manager at MPS Limited, Shruti Negi, for their editorial counsel and support during the preparation of this text.

The following Technical Content Developers worked on the MindTap content for this text: Christopher Krut, Philip Bozarth, Keri Pecora, Lisa Watson, and Matthew Holmes. Our thanks to them as well.

Jeffrey D. Camm
James J. Cochran
Michael J. Fry
Jeffrey W. Ohlmann

Chapter 1

Introduction

Contents

Learning Objectives

After completing this chapter, you will be able to

LO 1 Define analytics and describe the different types of analytics

LO 2 Describe the different types of data and give an example of each

LO 3 Describe various examples of data visualization used in practice

LO 4 Identify the various charts defined in this chapter

You need a ride to a concert, so you select the Uber app on your phone. You enter the location of the concert. Your phone automatically knows your location, and the app presents several options with prices. You select an option and confirm with your driver. You receive the driver's name, license plate number, make and model of vehicle, and photographs of the driver and the car. A map showing the location of the driver and the time remaining until arrival is updated in real time.

Without even thinking about it, we continually use data to make decisions in our lives. How the data are displayed to us has a direct impact on how well we understand the data and how much effort we must expend to utilize the data. In the case of Uber, we enter data (our destination), and we are presented with data (prices) that allow us to make an informed decision. We see the result of our decision with an indication of the driver's name, make and model of vehicle, and license plate number that makes us feel more secure. Rather than simply displaying the time until arrival, seeing the progress of the car on a map gives us some indication of the driver's route. Watching the driver's progress on the app removes some uncertainty and, to some extent, can divert our attention from how long we have been waiting. Which data are presented and how they are presented has an impact on our ability to understand the situation and make better-informed decisions.

A weather map, an airplane seating chart, the dashboard of your car, a chart of the performance of the Dow Jones Industrial Average, your fitness tracker—all of these involve the visual display of data. **Data visualization** is the graphical representation of data and information using displays such as charts, graphs, and maps. Our ability to process information visually is strong. For example, numerical data that have been displayed in a chart, graph, or map allow us to more easily see relationships between variables in our data set. Trends, patterns, and the distributions of data are more easily comprehended when data are displayed visually.

This book is about how to effectively display data to both discover and describe the information it contains. We provide best practices in the design of visual displays of data, the effective use of color, and chart type selection. The goal of this book is to instruct you how to create effective data visualizations. Through the use of examples (using real data when possible), this book presents visualization principles and guidelines for gaining insight from data and conveying an impactful message to the audience.

Because of its widespread availability, we use Microsoft Excel to demonstrate the techniques and best practices within each chapter of this book. We also provide instructions for two other leading software packages, Power BI and Tableau. End-of-chapter appendices cover the step-by-step procedures for using Power BI and Tableau to implement the data visualization techniques presented in the chapter.

With the increased use of analytics in business, industry, science, engineering, and government, data visualization has increased dramatically in importance. We begin with a discussion of analytics and data visualization's role in this rapidly growing field.

1.1 Analytics

Analytics is the scientific process of transforming data into insights for making better decisions.[1] Three developments have spurred the explosive growth in the use of analytics for improving decision making in all facets of our lives, including business, sports, science, medicine, and government:

- Incredible amounts of data are produced by technological advances such as point-of-sale scanner technology; e-commerce and social networks; sensors on all kinds of mechanical devices such as aircraft engines, automobiles, thermometers, and farm machinery enabled by the so-called Internet of Things; and personal electronic devices such as cell phones. Businesses naturally want to use these data to improve the efficiency and profitability of their operations, better understand their customers, and price their products more effectively and competitively. Scientists and engineers use these data to invent new products, improve existing products, and make new basic discoveries about nature and human behavior.

---

[1]We adopt the definition of analytics developed by the Institute for Operations Research and the Management Sciences (INFORMS).

- Ongoing research has resulted in numerous methodological developments, including advances in computational approaches to effectively handle and explore massive amounts of data, as well as faster algorithms for data visualization, machine learning, optimization, and simulation.
- The explosion in computing power and storage capability through better computing hardware, parallel computing, and cloud computing (the remote use of hardware and software over the Internet) enable us to solve larger decision problems more quickly and more accurately than ever before.

In summary, the availability of massive amounts of data, improvements in analytical methods, and substantial increases in computing power and storage have enabled the explosive growth in analytics, data science, and artificial intelligence.

Analytics can involve techniques as simple as reports or as complex as large-scale optimizations and simulations. Analytics is generally grouped into three broad categories of methods: descriptive, predictive, and prescriptive analytics.

Descriptive analytics is the set of analytical tools that describe what has happened. This includes techniques such as data queries (requests for information with certain characteristics from a database), reports, descriptive or summary statistics, and data visualization. Descriptive data mining techniques such as cluster analysis (grouping data points with similar characteristics) also fall into this category. In general, these techniques summarize existing data or the output from predictive or prescriptive analyses.

Predictive analytics consists of techniques that use mathematical models constructed from past data to predict future events or better understand the relationships between variables. Techniques in this category include regression analysis, time series forecasting, computer simulation, and predictive data mining. As an example of a predictive model, past weather data are used to build mathematical models that forecast future weather. Likewise, past sales data can be used to predict future sales for seasonal products such as snowblowers, winter coats, and bathing suits.

Prescriptive analytics are mathematical or logical models that suggest a decision or course of action. This category includes mathematical optimization models, decision analysis, and heuristic or rule-based systems. For example, solutions to supply network optimization models provide insights into the quantities of a company's various products that should be manufactured at each plant, how much should be shipped to each of the company's distribution centers, and which distribution center should serve each customer to minimize cost and meet service constraints.

Data visualization is mission-critical to the success of all three types of analytics. We discuss this in more detail with examples in the next section.

1.2 Why Visualize Data?

We create data visualizations for two reasons: exploring data and communicating/explaining a message. Let us discuss these uses of data visualization in more detail, examine the differences in the two uses, and consider how they relate to the types of analytics previously described.

Data Visualization for Exploration

Data visualization is a powerful tool for *exploring* data to more easily identify patterns, recognize anomalies or irregularities in the data, and better understand the relationships between variables. Our ability to spot these types of characteristics of data is much stronger and quicker when we look at a visual display of the data rather than a simple listing.

In chapter 2, we introduce a variety of different chart types and how to construct charts in Excel, Power BI, and Tableau.

As an example of data visualization for exploration, let us consider the zoo attendance data shown in Table 1.1 and Figure 1.1. These data on monthly attendance at a zoo can be found in the file *zoo*. Comparing Table 1.1 and Figure 1.1, observe that the pattern in the data is more detectable in the column chart of Figure 1.1 than in the table. A **column chart** shows numerical data by the height of the column for a variety of categories or time periods. In the case of Figure 1.1, the time periods are the different months of the year.

Table 1.1	Zoo Attendance Data					
Month	Jan	Feb	Mar	Apr	May	Jun
Attendance	5422	4878	6586	6943	7876	17843
Month	July	Aug	Sept	Oct	Nov	Dec
Attendance	21967	14542	8751	6454	5677	11422

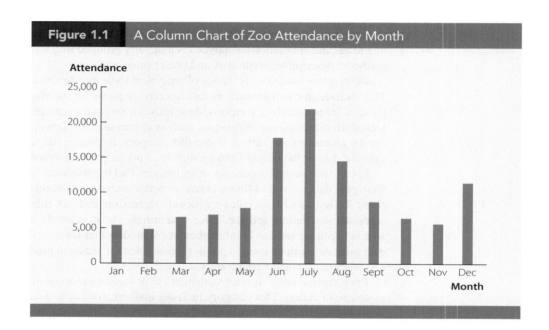

Figure 1.1   A Column Chart of Zoo Attendance by Month

Our intuition and experience tells us that we would expect zoo attendance to be highest in the summer months when many school-aged children are out of school for summer break. Figure 1.1 confirms this, as the attendance at the zoo is highest in the summer months of June, July, and August. Furthermore, we see that attendance increases gradually each month from February through May as the average temperature increases, and attendance gradually decreases each month from September through November as the average temperature decreases. But why does the zoo attendance in December and January not follow these patterns? It turns out the zoo has an event known as the "Festival of Lights" that runs from the end of November through early January. Children are out of school during the last half of December and early January for the holiday season, and this leads to increased attendance in the evenings at the zoo despite the colder winter temperatures.

Visual data exploration is an important part of descriptive analytics. Data visualization can also be used directly to monitor key performance metrics, that is, to measure how an organization is performing relative to its goals. A **data dashboard** is a data visualization tool that gives multiple outputs and may update in real time. Just as the dashboard in your car measures the speed, engine temperature, and other important performance data as you drive, corporate data dashboards measure performance metrics such as sales, inventory levels, and service levels relative to the goals set by the company. These data dashboards alert management when performances deviate from goals so corrective actions can be taken.

Data dashboards are discussed in more detail in Chapter 8.

Visual data exploration is also critical for ensuring that model assumptions hold in predictive and prescriptive analytics. Understanding the data before using that data in modeling builds trust and can be important in determining and explaining which type of model is appropriate.

As an example of the importance of exploring data visually before modeling, we consider two data sets provided by statistician Francis Anscombe.[2] Table 1.2 contains these two data sets, each of which contains 11 *X-Y* pairs of data. Notice in Table 1.2 that both data sets have the same average values for *X* and *Y*, and both sets of *X* and *Y* also have the same standard deviations. Based on these commonly used summary statistics, these two data sets are indistinguishable.

Figure 1.2 shows the two data sets visually as scatter charts. A **scatter chart** is a graphical presentation of the relationship between two quantitative variables. One variable is shown on the horizontal axis, and the other is shown on the vertical axis. Scatter charts are used to better understand the relationship between the two variables under consideration. Even though the two different data sets have the same average values and standard deviations of *X* and *Y*, the respective relationships between *X* and *Y* are different.

A scatter chart is often referred to as a scatter plot.

One of the most commonly used predictive models is linear regression, which involves finding the best-fitting line for the data. In the graphs in Figure 1.2, we show the best-fitting lines for each data set. Notice that the lines are the same for each data set. In fact, the measure of how well the line fits the data is the same. This is shown by a statistic labeled R^2, which indicates that 67% of the variation in the data is explained by the line. Yet, as we can see because we have graphed the data, in Figure 1.2a, fitting a straight line looks appropriate for the data set. However, as shown in Figure 1.2b, a line is not appropriate for data set 2. We will need to find a different, more appropriate mathematical equation for data set 2. The line shown in Figure 1.2 for data set 2 would likely dramatically overestimate values of *Y* for values of *X* less than 5 or greater than 14.

Hence, before applying predictive and prescriptive analytics, it is always best to visually explore the data to be used. This helps the analyst avoid misapplying more complex techniques and reduces the risk of poor results.

Table 1.2	Two Data Sets from Anscombe			
	Data Set 1		Data Set 2	
	X	*Y*	*X*	*Y*
	10	8.04	10	9.14
	8	6.95	8	8.14
	13	7.58	13	8.74
	9	8.81	9	8.77
	11	8.33	11	9.26
	14	9.96	14	8.1
	6	7.24	6	6.13
	4	4.26	4	3.10
	12	10.84	12	9.13
	7	4.82	7	7.26
	5	5.68	5	4.74
Average	9	7.501	9	7.501
Standard Deviation	3.317	2.032	3.317	2.032

[2]Anscombe, F. J., "The Validity of Comparative Experiments," *Journal of the Royal Statistical Society*, Vol. 11, No. 3, 1948, pp. 181–211.

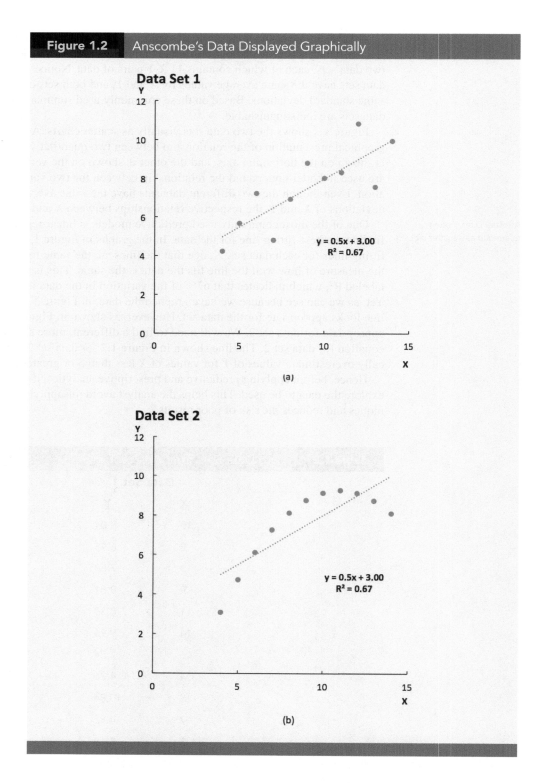

Figure 1.2   Anscombe's Data Displayed Graphically

DATA*file*

anscombe

Data Visualization for Explanation

Data visualization is also important for *explaining* relationships found in data and for explaining the results of predictive and prescriptive models. More generally, data visualization is helpful in communicating with the audience and ensuring that the audience understands and focuses on your intended message.

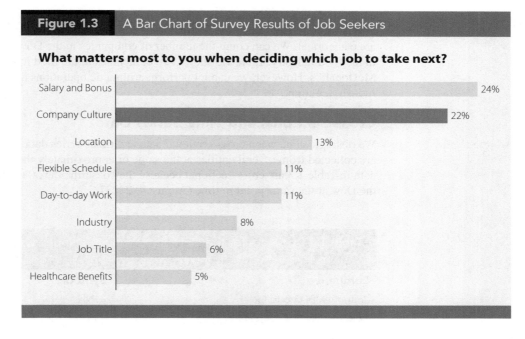

Figure 1.3 A Bar Chart of Survey Results of Job Seekers

What matters most to you when deciding which job to take next?

- Salary and Bonus 24%
- Company Culture 22%
- Location 13%
- Flexible Schedule 11%
- Day-to-day Work 11%
- Industry 8%
- Job Title 6%
- Healthcare Benefits 5%

The effective use of color is discussed in more detail in Chapter 4.

Let us consider the article, "Check Out the Culture Before a New Job," which appeared in *The Wall Street Journal*.[3] The article discusses the importance of finding a good cultural fit when seeking a new job. Difficulty in understanding a corporate culture or misalignment with that culture can lead to job dissatisfaction. Figure 1.3 is a re-creation of a bar chart that appeared in this article. A **bar chart** shows a summary of categorical data using the length of horizontal bars to display the magnitude of a quantitative variable.

The chart shown in Figure 1.3 shows the percentage of the 10,002 survey respondents who listed a factor as the most important in seeking a job. Notice that our attention is drawn to the dark blue bar, which is "Company culture" which is the focus of the article. We immediately see that only "Salary and Bonus" is more frequently cited than "Company Culture." When you first glance at the chart, the message that is communicated is that corporate culture is the second most important factor cited by job seekers. And as a reader, based on that message, you then decide whether the article is worth reading.

1.3 Types of Data

Different types of charts are more effective than others for certain types of data. For that reason, let us discuss the different types of data you might encounter.

The Dow Jones Industrial Average is a stock market index. It was created in 1896 by Charles Dow. The 30 companies that are included in the Dow change periodically to reflect changes in major corporations in the United States.

Table 1.3 contains information on the 30 companies that make up the Dow Jones Industrial Index (DJI). The table contains the company name, the stock symbol, the industry type, the share price, and the volume (number of shares traded). We will use the data contained in Table 1.3 to facilitate our discussion.

Quantitative and Categorical Data

Quantitative data are data for which numerical values are used to indicate magnitude, such as how many or how much. Arithmetic operations, such as addition, subtraction, multiplication, and division, can be performed on quantitative data. For instance, because Volume is a quantitative variable, we can sum the values for Volume in Table 1.3 to calculate a total volume of all shares traded by companies included in the Dow.

Categorical data are data for which categories of like items are identified by labels or names. Arithmetic operations cannot be performed on categorical data. We can summarize

[3]Lublin, J. S. "Check Out the Culture Before a New Job," *The Wall Street Journal*, January 16, 2020.

categorical data by counting the number of observations or computing the proportions of observations in each category. For instance, the data in the Industry column in Table 1.3 are categorical. We can count the number of companies in the Dow that are, for example, in the food industry. Table 1.3 shows two companies in the food industry: Coca-Cola and McDonald's. However, we cannot perform arithmetic operations directly on the data in the Industry column.

Cross-Sectional and Time Series Data

We distinguish between cross-sectional data and times series data. **Cross-sectional data** are collected from several entities at the same or approximately the same point in time. The data in Table 1.3 are cross-sectional because they describe the 30 companies that comprise the Dow at the same point in time (August 4, 2023).

DATA*file*

dow30

Table 1.3	Data for the Dow Jones Industrial Index Companies (August 4, 2023)	
Company	**Symbol**	**Price**
Unitedhealth Group Inc	UNH	503.40
Goldman Sachs Group Inc	GS	352.73
Home Depot Inc	HD	326.45
Microsoft Corp	MSFT	327.69
Mcdonald S Corp	MCD	287.16
Caterpillar Inc	CAT	276.27
Visa Inc	V	239.13
Boeing Co	BA	231.34
Amgen Inc	AMGN	240.95
Salesforce Inc	CRM	214.55
Apple Inc	AAPL	182.04
Honeywell International Inc	HON	189.36
Johnson & Johnson	JNJ	168.82
Travelers Cos Inc	TRV	169.21
American Express Co	AXP	165.46
Chevron Corp	CVX	159.75
Walmart Inc	WMT	158.22
Procter & Gamble Co	PG	155.19
Jpmorgan Chase & Co	JPM	154.01
Intl Business Machines Corp	IBM	144.23
Nike Inc Cl B	NKE	108.75
3m Co W/d	MMM	105.47
Merck & Co. Inc.	MRK	105.02
Walt Disney Co	DIS	86.26
Coca Cola Co	KO	60.75
Dow Inc	DOW	55.01
Cisco Systems Inc	CSCO	52.71
Intel Corp	INTC	35.10
Verizon Communications Inc	VZ	32.65
Walgreens Boots Alliance Inc	WBA	29.94

Time series data are data collected over several points in time (minutes, hours, days, months, years, etc.). Graphs of time series data are frequently found in business, economic, and science publications. Such graphs help analysts understand what happened in the past, identify trends over time, and project future levels for the time series. For example, the graph of the time series in Figure 1.4 shows the DJI value from January 2013 to August 2023. The graph shows the upward trend of the DJI value from 2013 to 2020, when there was a steep decline in value due to the economic impact of the COVID-19 pandemic. Although there is variation, the graph also shows the overall upward trend of the DJI value over time.

Big Data

There is no universally accepted definition of big data. However, probably the most general definition of **big data** is any set of data that is too large or too complex to be handled by standard data-processing techniques using a typical desktop computer. People refer to the four Vs of big data:

- volume—the amount of data generated
- velocity—the speed at which the data are generated
- variety—the diversity in types and structures of data generated
- veracity—the reliability of the data generated

Volume and velocity can pose a challenge for processing analytics, including data visualization. Special data management software such as Hadoop and higher capacity hardware or cloud computing may be required. The variety of the data is handled by converting video, audio, and text data to numerical data, to which we can then apply standard data visualization techniques.

In summary, the type of data you have will influence the type of graph you should use to convey your message. The zoo attendance data in Figure 1.1 are time series data. We used a column chart in Figure 1.1 because the numbers are the total attendance for each month, and we wanted to compare the attendance by month. The height of the columns allows us to easily compare attendance by month. Contrast Figure 1.1 with Figure 1.4, which is also

dji

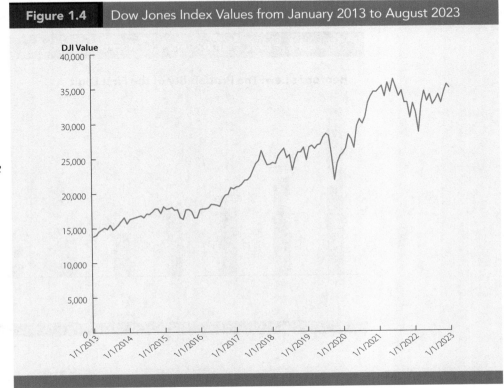

| **Figure 1.4** | Dow Jones Index Values from January 2013 to August 2023 |

*How to select an effective
chart type is discussed in more
detail in Chapter 2.*

time series data. Here, we have the value of the Dow Jones Index. These data are a snapshot of the current value of the DJI on the first trading day of each month. They provide what is essentially a time path of the value, so we use a line graph to emphasize the continuity of time.

1.4 Data Visualization in Practice

Data visualization is used to explore and explain data and to guide decision making in all areas of business and science. Even the most analytically advanced companies such as Google, Uber, and Amazon rely heavily on data visualization. Consumer goods giant Procter & Gamble (P&G), the maker of household brands such as Tide, Pampers, Crest, and Swiffer, has invested heavily in analytics, including data visualization. P&G has built what it calls the Business Sphere™ in more than 50 of its sites around the world. The Business Sphere is a conference room with technology for displaying data visualizations on its walls. The Business Sphere displays data and information P&G executives and managers can use to make better-informed decisions. Let us briefly discuss some ways in which the functional areas of business, engineering, science, and sports use data visualization.

Accounting

Accounting is a data-driven profession. Accountants prepare financial statements and examine financial statements for accuracy and conformance to legal regulations and best practices, including reporting required for tax purposes. Data visualization is a part of every accountant's tool kit. Data visualization is used to detect outliers that could be an indication of a data error or fraud. As an example of data visualization in accounting, let us consider Benford's Law.

Benfords Law, also known as the First-Digit Law, gives the expected probability that the first digit of a reported number takes on the values one through nine. Benford's Law is based on many real-life numerical data sets such as company expense accounts. A column chart displaying Benford's Law is shown in Figure 1.5. We have rounded the probabilities to four digits. We see, for example, that the probability of the first digit being a 1 is 0.3010. The probability of the first digit being a 2 is 0.1761, and so forth.

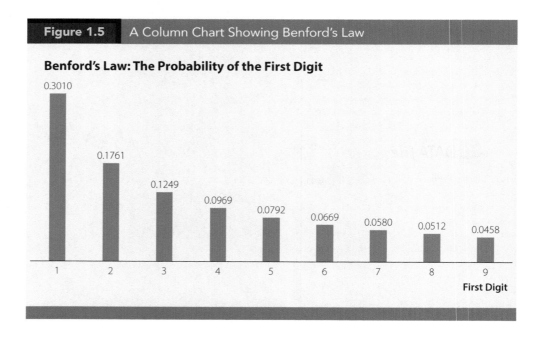

Figure 1.5   A Column Chart Showing Benford's Law

Benford's Law: The Probability of the First Digit

Accounts payable is the amount of money owed to the company.

Benford's Law can be used to detect fraud. If the first digits of numbers in a data set do not conform to Bedford's Law, then further investigation of fraud may be warranted. Consider the accounts payable for Tucker Software. Figure 1.6 is a clustered column chart, also known as a side-by-side column chart. A **clustered column chart** is a column chart that shows multiple variables of interest on the same chart, with the different variables usually denoted by different colors or shades of a color. In Figure 1.6, the two variables are Benford's Law probability and the first digit data for a random sample of 500 of Tucker's accounts payable entries. The frequency of occurrence in the data is used to estimate the probability of the first digit for all of Tucker's accounts payable entries. It appears that there are an inordinate number of first digits of 5 and 9 and a lower than expected number of first digits of 1. These might warrant further investigation by Tucker's auditors.

Finance

Like accounting, the area of business known as finance is numerical and data-driven. Finance is the area of business concerned with investing. Financial analysts, also known as "quants," use massive amounts of financial data to decide when to buy and sell certain stocks, bonds, and other financial instruments. Data visualization is useful in finance for recognizing trends, assessing risk, and tracking actual versus forecasted values of metrics of concern.

We discuss High-Low-Close Stock charts in more detail in Chapter 2.

Yahoo! Finance and other websites allow you to download daily stock price data. As an example, the file *verizon* has five days of stock prices for telecommunications company Verizon Wireless. Each of the five observations includes the date, the high share price for that date, the low share price for that day, and the closing share price for that day. Excel has several charts designed for tracking stock performance with such data. Figure 1.7 displays these data in a **high-low-close stock chart**, a chart that shows the high value, low value,

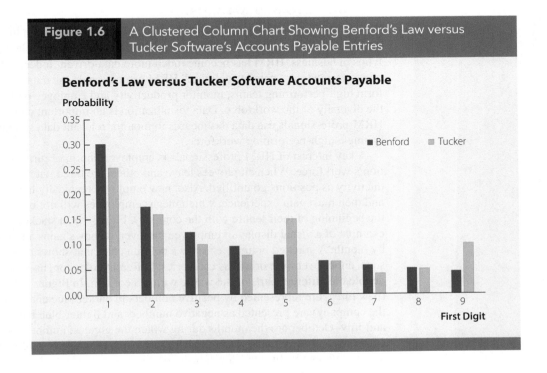

Figure 1.6   A Clustered Column Chart Showing Benford's Law versus Tucker Software's Accounts Payable Entries

Benford's Law versus Tucker Software Accounts Payable

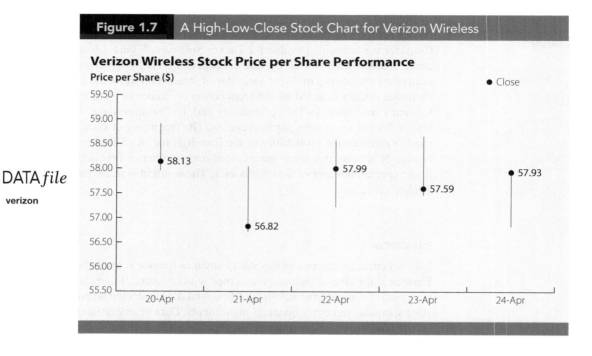

Figure 1.7   A High-Low-Close Stock Chart for Verizon Wireless

DATA*file*

verizon

and closing value of the price of a share of stock over time. For each date shown, the bar indicates the range of the stock price per share on that day, and the labeled point on the bar indicates closing price per share for that day. The chart shows how the closing price is changing over time and the volatility of the price on each day.

Human Resource Management

Human resource management (HRM) is the part of an organization that focuses on an organization's recruitment, training, and retention of employees. With the increased use of analytics in business, HRM has become much more data-driven. Indeed, HRM is sometimes now referred to as "people analytics." HRM professionals use data and analytical models to form high-performing teams, monitor productivity and employee performance, and ensure the diversity of the workforce. Data visualization is an important component of HRM, as HRM professionals use data dashboards to monitor relevant data supporting their goal of having a high-performing workforce.

A key interest of HRM professionals is employee churn, or turnover in an organization's workforce. When employees leave and others are hired, there is often a loss of productivity as positions go unfilled. Also, new employees typically have a training period and then must gain experience, which means employees will not be fully productive at the beginning of their tenure with the company. Figure 1.8, a stacked column chart, is an example of a visual display of employee turnover. It shows gains and losses of employees by month. A **stacked column chart** is a column chart that shows part-to-whole comparisons, either over time or across categories. Different colors or shades of color are used to denote the different parts of the whole within a column. In Figure 1.8, gains in employees (new hires) are represented by positive numbers in darker blue and losses (people leaving the company) are presented as negative numbers and lighter blue bars. We see that January and July–October are the months during which the greatest numbers of employees left the company, and the months with the highest numbers of new hires are April through June. Visualizations like Figure 1.8 can be helpful in better understanding and managing workforce fluctuations.

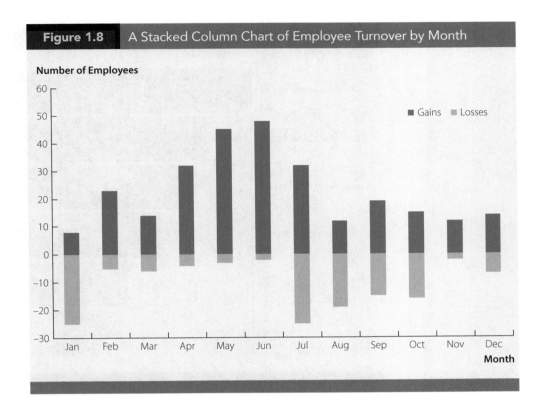

Figure 1.8 A Stacked Column Chart of Employee Turnover by Month

Marketing

Marketing is one of the most popular application areas of analytics. Analytics is used for optimal pricing, markdown pricing for seasonal goods, and the optimal allocation of the marketing budget. Sentiment analysis using text data such as tweets, social networks to determine influence, and website analytics for understanding website traffic and sales are just a few examples of how data visualization can be used to support more effective marketing.

Funnel charts are discussed in more detail in Chapter 2.

Let us consider a software company's website effectiveness. Figure 1.9 shows a funnel chart of the conversion of website visitors to subscribers and then to renewal customers. A **funnel chart** is a chart that shows the progression of a numerical variable for various categories from larger to smaller values. In Figure 1.9, at the top of the funnel, we track 100% of the first-time visitors to the website over some period of time, for example, a six-month period. The funnel chart shows that of those original visitors, 74% return to the website one or more times after their initial visit. Sixty-one percent of the first-time visitors downloaded a 30-day trial version of the software, 47% eventually contacted support services, 28% purchased a one-year subscription to the software, and 17% eventually renewed their subscription. This type of funnel chart can be used to compare the conversion effectiveness of different website configurations, the use of bots, or changes in support services.

Operations

Like marketing, analytics is used heavily in managing the operations function of business. Operations management is concerned with the management of the production and distribution of goods and services. It includes responsibility for planning and scheduling, inventory planning, demand forecasting, and supply chain optimization. Figure 1.10 shows time series data for monthly unit sales for a product (measured in thousands of units sold). Each

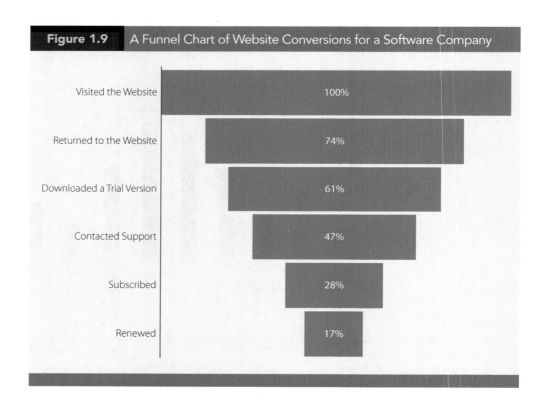

Figure 1.9 A Funnel Chart of Website Conversions for a Software Company

period corresponds to one month. To be able to develop a cost-effective production schedule, an operations manager might have responsibility for forecasting the monthly unit sales for the next 12 months (periods 37–48). In looking at the time series data in Figure 1.10, it appears that there is a repeating pattern, and units sold might also be increasing slightly

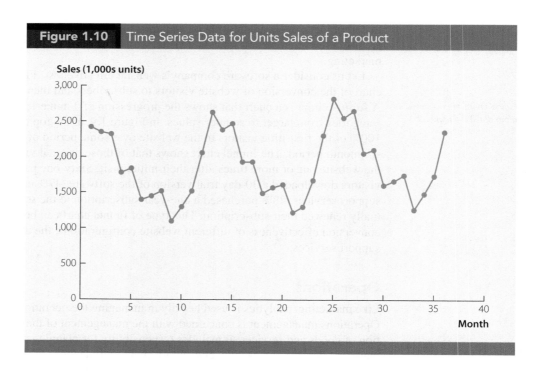

Figure 1.10 Time Series Data for Units Sales of a Product

over time. The operations manager can use these observations to help select the forecasting techniques to generate reasonable forecasts for periods 37–48.

Engineering

Engineering relies heavily on mathematics and data. For example, industrial engineers monitor the production process to ensure that it is "in control" or operating as expected. A **control chart** is a graphical display that is used to help determine if a production process is in control or out of control. A variable of interest is plotted over time relative to lower and upper control limits. Consider the control chart for the production of 10-pound bags of dog food shown in Figure 1.11. Every minute, a bag is diverted from the line and automatically weighed. The result is plotted along with lower and upper control limits obtained statistically from historical data. When the points are between the lower and upper control limits, the process is considered to be in control. When points begin to appear outside the control limits with some regularity and/or when large swings start to appear as in Figure 1.11, this is a signal to inspect the process and make any necessary corrections.

Sciences

The natural and social sciences rely heavily on the analysis of data and data visualization for exploring data and explaining the results of analysis. In the natural sciences, data are often geographic, so maps are used frequently. For example, the weather, pandemic hot spots, and species distributions can be represented on a geographic map. Geographic maps are not only used to display data, but also to display the results of predictive models. An example of this is shown in Figure 1.12. Predicting the path a hurricane will follow is a complicated problem. Numerous models, each with its own set of influencing variables, also known as model features, yield different predictions. Displaying the results of each model on a map gives a sense of the uncertainty in predicted paths across all models and

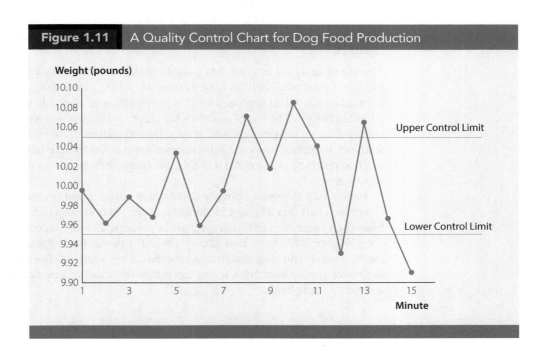

Figure 1.11   A Quality Control Chart for Dog Food Production

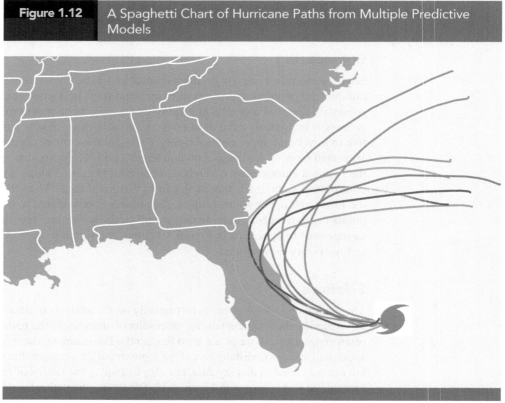

Figure 1.12 A Spaghetti Chart of Hurricane Paths from Multiple Predictive Models

Source: clickorlando.com

expands the alert to a broader range of the population than relying on a single model. Because the multiple paths resemble pieces of spaghetti, this type of map is sometimes referred to as a "spaghetti chart." More generally, a **spaghetti chart** is a chart depicting possible flows through a system using a line for each possible path.

Sports

The use of analytics in sports has gained considerable notoriety since 2003 when Michael Lewis published his book *Moneyball*. Lewis's book tells how the Oakland Athletics used an analytical approach for player evaluation to assemble a competitive team using a limited budget. The use of analytics for player evaluation and on-field strategy is now common throughout professional sports. Data visualization is a key component of how analytics is applied in sports. It is common for coaches to have tablet computers on the sideline that they use to make real-time decisions such as calling plays and making player substitutions.

Figure 1.13 shows an example of how data visualization is used in basketball. A **shot chart** is a chart that displays the location of the shots attempted by a player during a basketball game with different symbols or colors indicating successful and unsuccessful shots. Figure 1.12 shows shot attempts by NBA player Chris Paul, with a blue dot indicating a successful shot and an orange x indicating a missed shot (source: *Basketball-Reference.com*). Other NBA teams can utilize this chart to help devise strategies for defending Chris Paul.

| **Figure 1.13** | A Shot Chart for NBA Player Chris Paul |

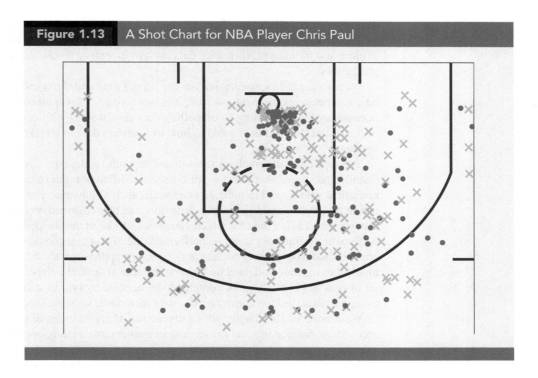

Notes + Comments

Chart is considered a more general term than *graph*. For example, charts encompass maps, bar charts, but graphs generally refer to a chart of the type shown in Figure 1.4 (a line chart). In this text, we use the terms *chart* and *graph* interchangeably.

Summary

This introductory chapter began with a discussion of analytics, the scientific process of transforming data into insights for making better decisions. We discussed the three types of analytics: descriptive, predictive, and prescriptive. Descriptive analytics describes what has happened and includes tools such as reports, data visualization, data dashboards, descriptive statistics, and some data-mining techniques. Predictive analytics consists of techniques that use past data to predict future events or understand the relationships between variables. These techniques include regression, data mining, forecasting, and simulation. Prescriptive analytics uses input data to suggest a decision or course of action. This class of analytical techniques includes rule-based models, simulation, decision analysis, and optimization. Descriptive and predictive analytics can help us better understand the uncertainty and risk associated with our decision alternatives.

This text focuses on descriptive analytics and, in particular, on data visualization. Data visualization can be used for exploring data and for explaining data and the output of analyses. We explore data to more easily identify patterns, recognize anomalies or irregularities in the data, and better understand relationships between variables. Visually displaying data enhances our ability to identify the characteristics of data. Often, we put various charts and tables of several related variables into a single display called a data dashboard. Data dashboards are collections of tables, charts, maps, and summary statistics that are updated as new data become available. Many organizations and businesses use data dashboards to explore and monitor performance data such as inventory levels, sales, and the quality of production.

We also use data visualization for explaining data and the results of data analyses. As business becomes more data-driven, it is increasingly important to be able to influence decision making by telling a compelling data-driven story with data visualization. Much of the rest of this text is devoted to how to visualize data to clearly convey a compelling message.

The type of chart, graph, or table to use depends on the type of data you have and your intended message. Therefore, we discussed the different types of data. Quantitative data are numerical values used to indicate magnitude, such as how many or how much. Arithmetic operations, such as addition and subtraction, can be performed on quantitative data. Categorical data are data for which categories of like items are identified by labels or names. Arithmetic operations cannot be performed directly on categorical data. Cross-sectional data are collected from several entities at the same or approximately the same point in time, and time series data are collected on a single variable at several points in time. Big data is any set of data that is too large or complex to be handled by typical data-processing techniques using a typical desktop computer. Big data includes text, audio, and video data.

We concluded the chapter with a discussion of applications of data visualization in accounting, finance, human resource management, marketing, operations, engineering, science, and sports, and we provided an example for each area. Each of the remaining chapters of this text will begin with a real-world application of a data visualization. Each *Data Visualization Makeover* is a real visualization we discuss and then improve by applying the principles of the chapter.

Glossary

Analytics The scientific process of transforming data into insights for making better decisions.

Bar chart A chart that shows a summary of categorical data using the length of horizontal bars to display the magnitude of a quantitative variable.

Big data Any set of data that is too large or complex to be handled by standard data-processing techniques using a typical desktop computer. Big data includes text, audio, and video data.

Categorical data Data for which categories of like items are identified by labels or names. Arithmetic operations cannot be performed on categorical data.

Clustered column chart A column chart showing multiple variables of interest on the same chart, with the different variables usually denoted by different colors or shades of a color with the columns side by side.

Column chart A chart that shows numerical data by the height of a column for a variety of categories or time periods.

Control chart A graphical display in which a variable of interest is plotted over time relative to lower and upper control limits.

Cross-sectional data Data collected from several entities at the same or approximately the same point in time.

Data dashboard A data visualization tool that gives multiple outputs and may update in real time.

Data visualization The graphical representation of data and information using displays such as charts, graphs, and maps.

Descriptive analytics The set of analytical tools that describe what has happened.

Funnel chart A chart that shows the progression of a numerical variable to typically smaller values through a process, for example, the percentage of website visitors who ultimately result in a sale.

High-low-close stock chart A chart that shows three numerical values: high value, low value, and closing value for the price of a share of stock over time.

Predictive analytics Techniques that use models constructed from past data to predict future events or better understand the relationships between variables.

Prescriptive analytics Mathematical or logical models that suggest a decision or course of action.

Quantitative data Data for which numerical values are used to indicate magnitude, such as how many or how much. Arithmetic operations, such as addition, subtraction, multiplication, and division, can be performed on quantitative data.

Scatter chart A graphical presentation of the relationship between two quantitative variables. One variable is shown on the horizontal axis, and the other is shown on the vertical axis.

Shot chart A chart that displays the location of shots attempted by a basketball player during a basketball game with different symbols or colors indicating successful and unsuccessful shots.

Spaghetti chart A chart depicting possible flows through a system using a line for each possible path.

Time series data Data collected over several points in time (minutes, hours, days, months, years, etc.).

Problems

1. **Types of Analytics.** Indicate which type of analytics (descriptive, predictive, or prescriptive analytics) each of the following represents. **LO 1**
   a. a data dashboard
   b. a model that finds the production schedule that minimizes overtime
   c. a model that forecasts sales for the next quarter
   d. a bar chart
   e. a model that allocates your financial investments to achieve your financial goal

2. **Transportation Planning**. An analytics professional is asked to plan the shipment of a product for the next quarter. She employs the following process:
   Step 1. For each of the 12 distribution centers, she plots the quarterly demand for the product over the last three years.
   Step 2. Based on the plot for each distribution center, she develops a forecasting model to forecast demand for next quarter for each distribution center.
   Step 3. She takes the forecast for next quarter for each distribution center and inputs those forecasts, along with the capacities of the company's four factories and transportation rates from each factory to each distribution center, into an optimization model. The optimization model suggests a shipping plan that minimizes the cost of satisfing the forecasted demand from the company's four different factories to the distribution centers.

   Describe the type of analytics being utilized in each of the three steps outlined above. **LO 1**

3. *Wall Street Journal* **Subscriber Characteristics**. A *Wall Street Journal* subscriber survey asked a series of questions about subscriber characteristics and interests. State whether each of the following questions provides categorical or quantitative data. **LO 2**
   a. What is your age?
   b. Are you male or female?
   c. When did you first start reading the *WSJ*? High school, college, early career, mid-career, late career, or retirement?
   d. How long have you been in your present job or position?
   e. What type of vehicle are you considering for your next purchase? Nine response categories for this question include sedan, sports car, SUV, minivan, and so on.

4. **Comparing Smartwatches.** *Consumer Reports* provides product evaluations for its subscribers. The following table shows data from *Consumer Reports* for five smartwatches on the following characteristics:

Overall Score—a score awarded for a variety of performance factors

Price—the retail price

Recommended—does *Consumer Reports* recommend purchasing the smartwatch based on performance and strengths?

Best Buy—if *Consumer Reports* recommends purchasing the smartwatch, does it also consider it a "best buy" based on a blend of performance and value?

Make	Overall Score	Recommended	Best Buy	Price
Apple Watch Series 5	84	Yes	No	$395
Fitbit Versa 2	78	Yes	Yes	$200
Garmin Venu	77	Yes	No	$350
Fitbit Versa Lite	65	No	No	$100

For each of the four pieces of data, indicate whether the data are quantitative or categorical and whether the data are cross-sectional or time series. **LO 2**

5. **House Price and Square Footage.** Suppose we want to better understand the relationship between house price and the square footage of the house, and we have collected the house price and square footage for 75 houses in a particular neighborhood of Cincinnati, Ohio, from the Zillow website on January 3, 2021. **LO 2, 3**
   a. Are these data quantitative or categorical?
   b. Are these data cross-sectional or times series?
   c. Which of the following type of chart would provide the best display of these data? Explain your answer.
      i. Bar chart
      ii. Column chart
      iii. Scatter chart

6. **Netflix Subscribers.** The following chart displays the total number of Netflix subscribers from 2010 to 2019. **LO 1, 2, 3**
   a. Are these data quantitative or categorical?
   b. Are these data cross-sectional or time series?
   c. What type of chart is this?

Netflix Subscribers (millions)

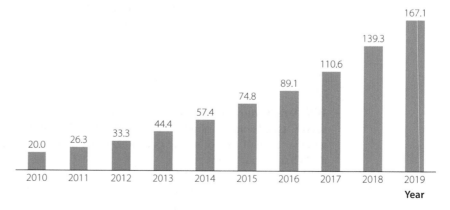

7. **U.S. Netflix Subscribers.** Refer to the previous problem. Suppose that in addition to the total number of Netflix subscribers, we have the number of those subscribers by year for the years 2010–2019 who live in the United States. Our message is to

emphasize how much of the growth is coming from the United States. Which of the following types of charts would best display the data? Explain your answer. **LO 2, 3**

  i.   Bar chart
 ii.   Clustered column chart
iii.   Stacked column chart
 iv.   Stock chart

8. **How Data Scientists Spend Their Day.** *The Wall Street Journal* reported the results of a survey of data scientists. The survey asked the data scientists how they spend their time. The following chart shows the percentage of respondents who answered less than five hours per week or at least five hours per week for the amount of time they spend on exploring data and on presenting analyses. **LO 2, 3, 4**

What Data Scientists Do: Exploring versus Presenting

a. Are these data quantitative or categorical?
b. Are these data cross-sectional or time series?
c. What type of chart is this?
d. What conclusions can you make based on this chart?

9. **Industries in the Dow Jones Industrial Index.** Refer to the data on the Dow Jones Industrial Index given in Table 1.3. The following chart displays the number of companies in each industry that make up this index. **LO 3**

a. What type of chart is this?
b. Which industry has the highest number of companies in the Dow Jones Industrial Index?

Number of Companies by Industry

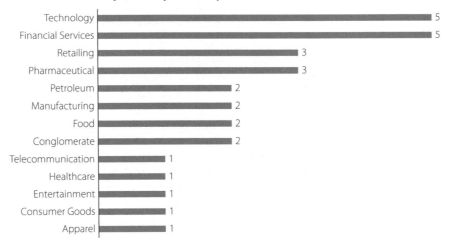

10. **Job Factors.** The following chart is based on the same data used to construct Figure 1.3. The data are percentages of respondents to a survey who listed various factors as most important when making a job decision. LO 3, 4
    a. What type of chart is this?
    b. What is the fifth most-cited factor?

What matters most to you when deciding which job to take next?

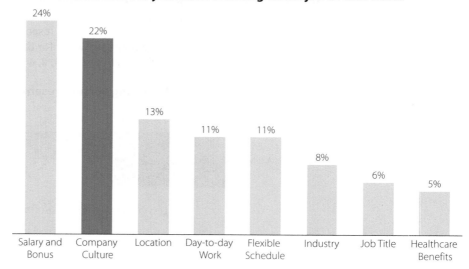

11. **Retirement Financial Concerns.** The results of the American Institute of Certified Public Accountants' *Personal Financial Planning Trends Survey* indicated 48% of clients had concerns about outliving their money. The top reasons for these concerns and the percentage of respondents who cited the reason were as follows. LO 3, 4

Concerns for Retirement

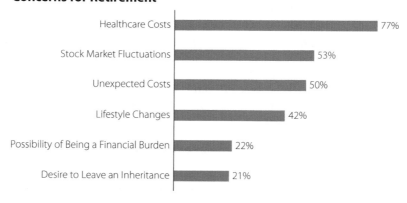

    a. What type of chart is this?
    b. Only 48% of the survey respondents had financial concerns about retirement (outliving their money). What percentage of the total people surveyed had retirement healthcare cost concerns?

12. **Master's Degree Program Recruiting.** The recruiting process for a full-time master's program in data science consists of the following steps. The program director obtains e-mail addresses of undergraduate seniors who have taken the Graduate Record Exam (GRE) and expressed an interest in data science. An e-mail inviting the students to an

online information session is sent. At the information session, faculty discuss the program and answer questions. Students apply through a web portal. An admissions committee makes an offer of admission (or not) along with any financial aid. If the person is admitted, the person either accepts or rejects the offer. Consider the following chart. **LO 3, 4**

Master's Degree in Data Science Recruiting

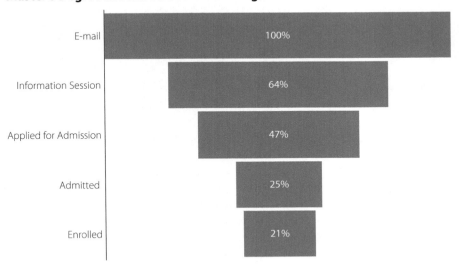

a. What type of chart is this?
b. Which of the following is the correct interpretation of the 21% for Enrolled?
   i. Of those who were sent an e-mail, 21% enrolled.
   ii. Of those who were admitted, 21% enrolled.
   iii. Of those who applied for admission, 21% enrolled.
   iv. None of the above
13. **Chemical Process Control.** The following chart is a quality control chart of the temperature of a chemical manufacturing process. What observations can you make about the process? **LO 3**

Temperature (degrees Fahrenheit)

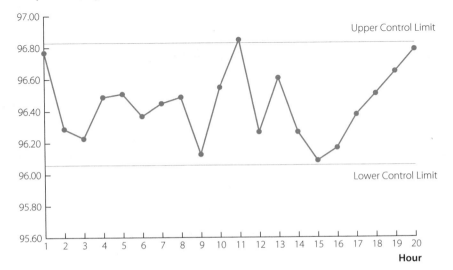

14. **Buying a Used Car.** The following chart shows data for a sample of 18 used cars of the same brand, model, and year. LO 2, 3, 4
    a. Are these data quantitative or categorical?
    b. What type of chart is this?
    c. How might you use this chart to find a used car to purchase?

Price (in $000)

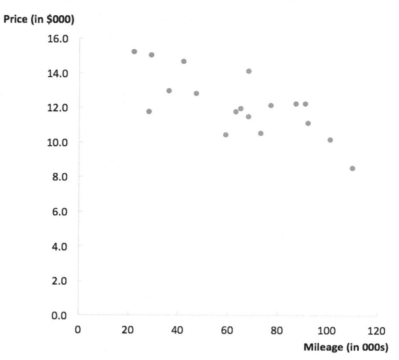

Mileage (in 000s)

15. **Tracking Stock Prices.** The following high-low-close stock chart gives the stock price for Exxon Mobile Corporation over a 12-month period. The data are the low, high, and closing price per share on the first trading day of the month. What can you say about the stock price and volatility of the stock price over this 12-month period? LO 3

Price ($ per share)

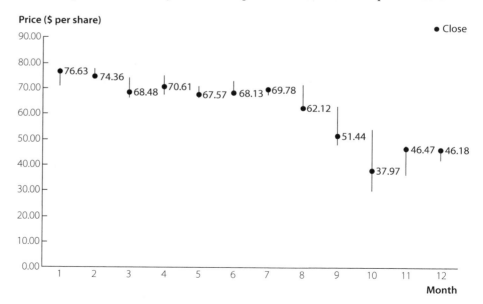

Month

Chapter 1 Appendix

Appendix 1.1 Introduction to Data Visualization with Power BI

Power BI is business intelligence software developed by Microsoft Corporation. It integrates with various data sources and provides users with an easy-to-use interface to create reports, numerous types of charts and graphs, and interactive data dashboards. In this Power BI Appendix and those in other chapters of this textbook, we use Power BI Desktop version 2.119.986.0 (July 2023).

Connecting to a Data File

Figure P1.1 shows the screen you will see when you open Power BI Desktop. Similar to Excel, the Ribbon at the top contains tabs, and each tab presents different groups. When you open Power BI, you will be on the **Home** tab in the **Report view**. In the left margin, there are three buttons that designate (from top to bottom) Report view 📊, Table view 🧮, and Model view 🗄.

The Report view allows you to import data. Power BI can connect with many different types of data files and sources for use in creating data visualizations. In the middle section in Figure P1.1, there are four alternatives for connecting to data: Import data from Excel, Import data from SQL Server, Paste data into a blank table, and Try a sample dataset. We will use the **Import data from Excel** option in this text.

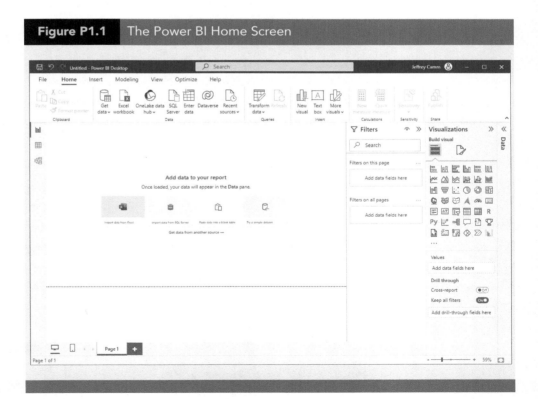

Figure P1.1   The Power BI Home Screen

Next, we provide the steps on how to import data from an Excel file into Power BI using the file *zoo*, which contains data on the monthly attendance numbers at a zoo.

DATA *file*

ZOO

Step 1. Click the **Import data from Excel** button (leftmost button). When the **Open** dialog box appears, navigate to where the file *zoo* is stored, click on the file *zoo*, and click **Open**

Step 2. When the **Navigator** dialog box appears (see Figure P1.2), select the checkbox next to **Data** and click **Load**. Once the data has loaded, click on the **Table view** in the left margin, and you will see the data as shown in Figure P1.3

Notice that in Figure P1.3, we see 12 months and the attendance for each month. Also, notice in Figure P1.3 that the **Table tools** tab is selected in the Ribbon. Items in the **Calculations** group of the **Table tools** allow you to add a new column to the existing table as well as create a new table of data that could then be joined to the existing table. As we will discuss in later Power BI appendices, we can create new columns based on existing data using a formula. The table of data shown is always the basis for creating charts, which will be accomplished in the Report view.

In Appendix 2.1, we discuss how to create charts in Power BI.

Another way to import data from an Excel file is to click the **Excel workbook** button in the **Data** group under the **Home** tab as shown in Figure P1.1. Once you click on the **Excel workbook** button, the procedure is the same as described in steps 1 and 2.

The **Get data** drop-down button in the **Data** group from the **Home** tab lists the numerous sources and types of data that can be imported into Power BI. These are shown

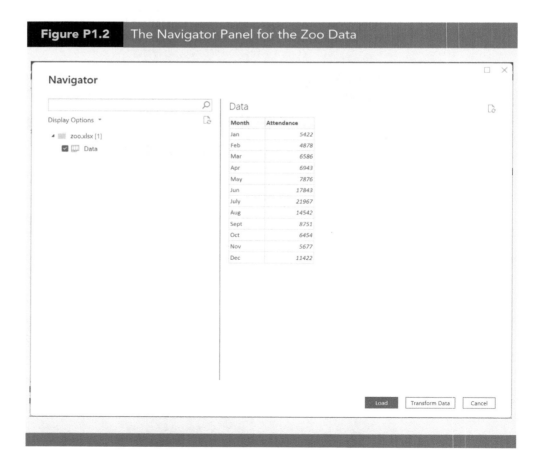

Figure P1.2   The Navigator Panel for the Zoo Data

Navigator

Display Options ▾

▲ zoo.xlsx [1]
   ☑ Data

Data

Month	Attendance
Jan	5422
Feb	4878
Mar	6586
Apr	6943
May	7876
Jun	17843
July	21967
Aug	14542
Sept	8751
Oct	6454
Nov	5677
Dec	11422

Load   Transform Data   Cancel

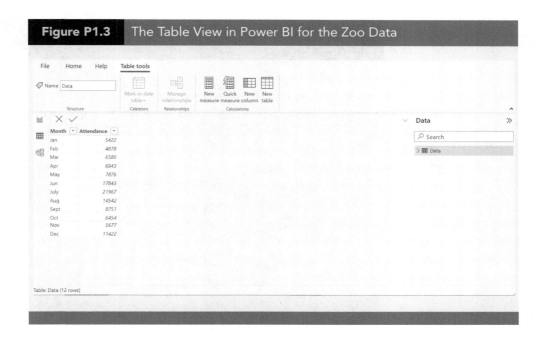

Figure P1.3 The Table View in Power BI for the Zoo Data

in Figure P1.4. Clicking on any of these options allows you to bring in the data from the specified type of source.

Types of Data in Power BI

Power BI supports a variety of data types, including Whole Number, Decimal Number, Fixed Decimal Number, Date/Time, Date, Time, Text, True/False, and Binary. Click **Table tools** in the **Ribbon** to continue with our example using the zoo attendance data (see Figure P1.3). Clicking on the **>** next to **Data** in the **Data pane** on the right side of the Power BI window expands the list of variables. Selecting **Month** invokes the **Column tools** tab as shown in Figure P1.5. In the **Structure** group of the **Column tools** tab, we see that the Name box gives the name of the selected variable, in this case, *Month*. The name of the variable can be changed by editing the text in the **Name** box. The second box gives the variable's data type; in this case, the month abbreviations have been stored as text data. The data type of the variable can be changed by selecting the drop-down menu to the right of the **Data type** box and selecting a data type.

We note that in the zoo example, the variable Month is text and cannot be converted to the Date format. This has implications for sorting and displaying the data that are discussed in Appendix 2.1.

The **Formatting** group of the **Column tools** tab determines how the variable values are displayed in Power BI. Here, the month abbreviations are displayed as text as indicated next to the Format box. The display format of the variable can be changed by selecting the drop-down menu on the right of the **Format** box and selecting a different format.

Figure P1.6 shows the result when we select the variable *Attendance*. We see in the **Structure** group of the **Column tools** tab that the variable name is *Attendance*, and the variable type is Whole Number. In the **Formatting** group, the format of the variable *Attendance* is a Whole number with 0 places to the right of the decimal place. We can display the variable values with a comma by clicking on the comma button **,**, which results in the display shown in Figure P1.7.

Notice that in the **Data** pane, there is a Σ before the *Attendance* variable. This is an indication that Power BI has summed the variable across categories or time periods. In this case, since there are unique months, there is no impact on the data. However, it is possible to undo the summarization of the data. The following steps will undo the summation.

Step 1. In the Data pane, select **Σ Attendance.** This invokes the **Column tools** tab as shown in Figure P1.7

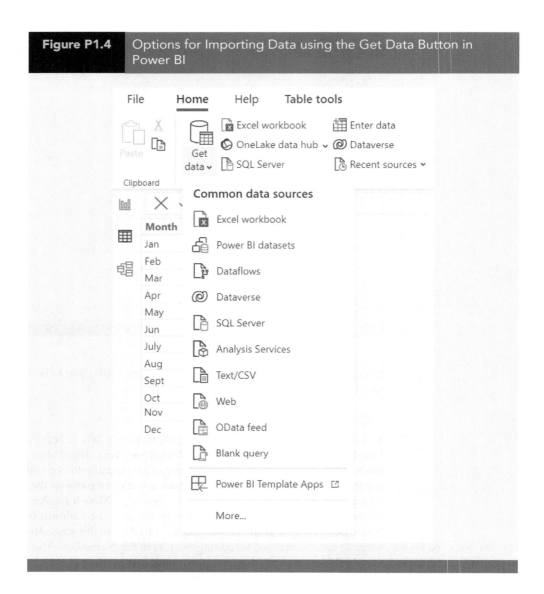

Figure P1.4 Options for Importing Data using the Get Data Button in Power BI

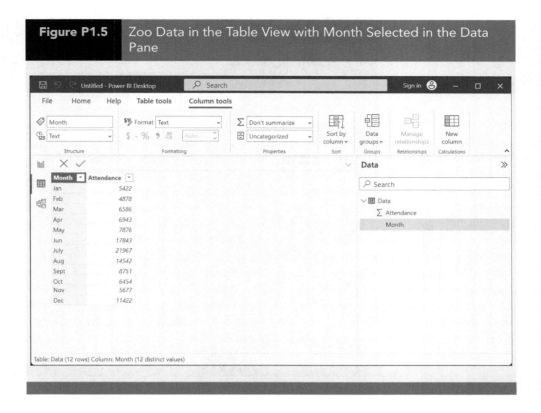

Figure P1.5   Zoo Data in the Table View with Month Selected in the Data Pane

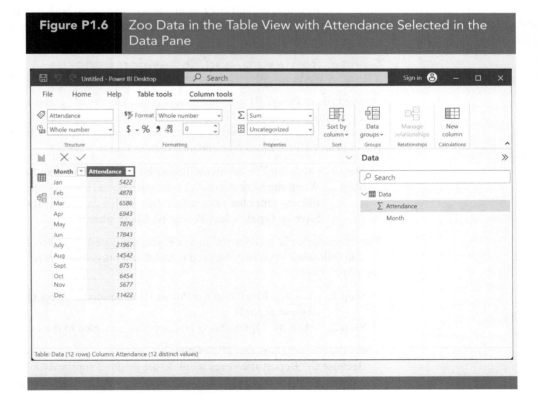

Figure P1.6   Zoo Data in the Table View with Attendance Selected in the Data Pane

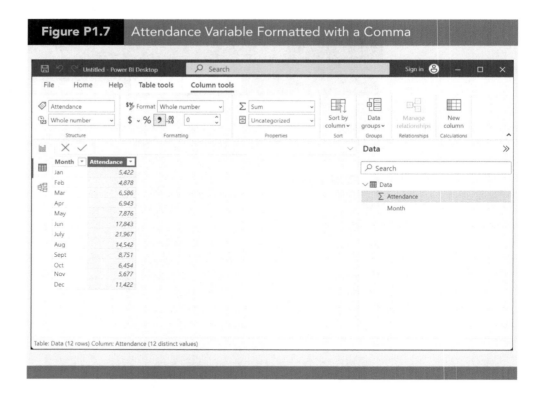

Figure P1.7   Attendance Variable Formatted with a Comma

Step 2. In the **Properties** group, expand the drop-down menu in the Σ Summarization box, and select **Don't Summarize**. The result is shown in Figure P1.8. Notice that the Σ is now removed from the variable *Attendance*

Saving, Retrieving, and Refreshing Report Files in Power BI

A saved file in Power BI is called a Report and has the file extension .pbix. A Report file saves not only the data used in the session but also any charts, graphs, or tables. Power BI also saves a link to the source data file. The following steps may be used to save a Report file in Power BI for the zoo attendance data in Figure P1.8.

Step 1. Click the **File** tab in the Power BI Ribbon and select **Save as**

Step 2. When the **Save As** dialog box appears, navigate to where you want to save the file and enter the name of the file, in this case, *zoo*, in the **File name:** box. For **Save as type:**, select **Power BI file (*.pbix)**

The file *zoo.pbix* is saved to the location you navigated to in step 2.

The following steps may be used to retrieve a previously saved report file, in this case, *zoo.pbix*.

Step 1. Click the **File** tab in the Power BI Ribbon and select **Open report**. Click **Browse reports**

Step 2. When the **Open** dialog box appears, navigate to the location of the *zoo.pbix* file

Select the *zoo.pbix* file, and click **Open**

Because the Report file saves a link to the original source data location, it is easy to update the Power BI Report file whenever the data in the source file is updated.

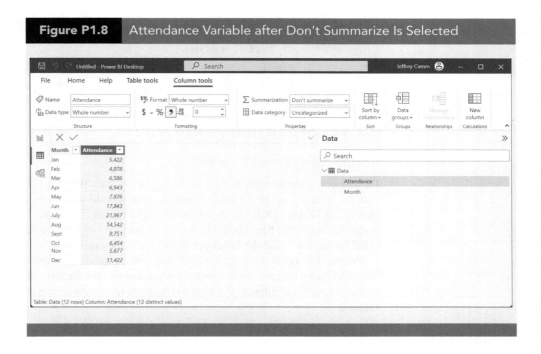

Figure P1.8 Attendance Variable after Don't Summarize Is Selected

For example, if the zoo data were updated to include two years' worth of attendance data by month, retrieving the file as just outlined and then clicking the **Home** tab in the Ribbon and then clicking the **Refresh** button Refresh in the **Queries** group will update the contents of the Report file.

Appendix 1.2 Introduction to Data Visualization with Tableau

Tableau is one of the leading data visualization software tools. It is an easy-to-use software tool that can create many different data visualizations and can also be used to explore and modify data. In this appendix, we explain how Tableau can be used to connect to a data file for further analysis and to create visualizations. For all the Tableau appendices in this textbook, we use Tableau Desktop version 2023.2.

Connecting to a Data File

Tableau can connect with many different types of data files for use in creating data visualizations. When you open Tableau Desktop, you should see a screen similar to Figure T1.1. This is the Tableau Desktop Home Screen. The Connect section allows you to connect to many different data file types. The Open section allows you to open sample data sets provided by Tableau, and the Discover section provides information on ways to use Tableau.

Tableau can open different types of data files, including Excel files, text files, database files, and many others. We will use the steps below and the file *zoo*, which contains data on the monthly attendance at a zoo, to illustrate how we can connect to an Excel file in Tableau.

DATA *file*

ZOO

Step 1. Click the **File** tab in the Tableau Ribbon and select **Open…**
Step 2. When the **Open** dialog box appears, navigate to the location of the *zoo* file
Select the *zoo* file, and click **Open**

Steps 1 and 2 above will open the Tableau Data Source screen shown in Figure T1.2. This screen shows a preview of the data file to which Tableau is currently connected. From the top right portion of Figure T1.2, we see that Tableau is connected to the data file *zoo* using a Live Connection. This means that as the data file is updated, these updates will be reflected in any visualizations created using Tableau. Alternatively, Tableau can use an

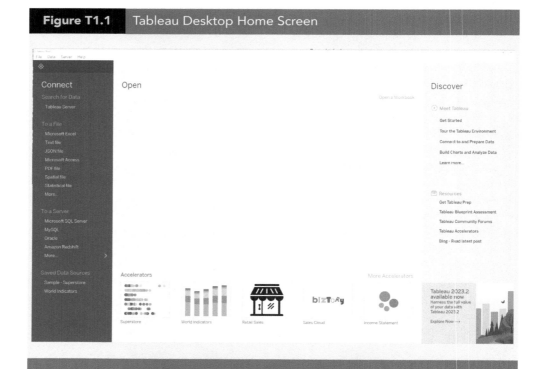

Figure T1.1   Tableau Desktop Home Screen

Figure T1.2   Tableau Data Source Screen for Zoo Attendance Data

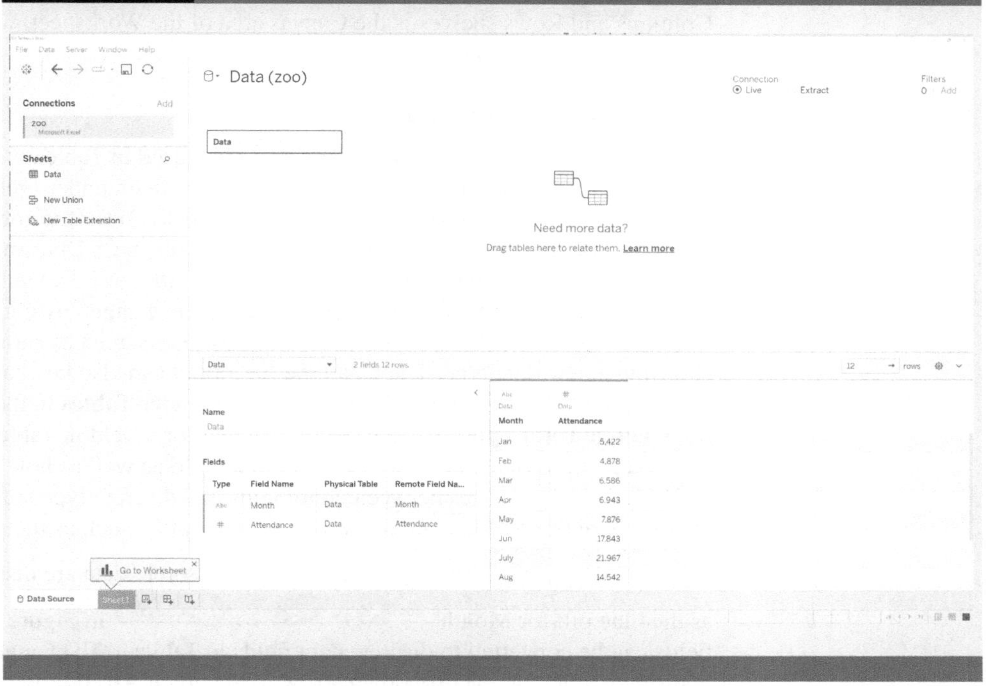

Extract Connection, in which case all data from the file would be extracted, and any visualizations created in Tableau would not be updated as the data in the file changes. Tableau can also link multiple data sources to each other by dragging each table to the portion of the screen in Figure T1.2 that shows "Need more data?" The lower portion of the Tableau Data Source screen shows a preview of the data file to which Tableau is connected. From Figure T1.2, we see the columns from the file *zoo* are titled "Month" and "Attendance," and we see the observations for months "Jan" through "Aug."

When you connect to a data file, Tableau also creates a Worksheet where visualizations can be created. The Worksheet can be accessed by clicking on **Sheet 1** as shown at the bottom left portion of Figure T1.2 with the note "Go to Worksheet." Clicking on **Sheet 1** opens the Worksheet view shown in Figure T1.3.

The Tableau Worksheet includes the Data pane on the left with tabs labeled Data and Analytics. Clicking the **Data** tab displays the Tables and Fields contained in the linked data set. Most visualizations are built in Tableau by dragging the field names, called "pills," to specific areas within the Tableau worksheet known as "cards" and "shelves." In Figure T1.3, the blue pill for Month Abc Month is visible under Tables in the Data pane on the left-hand side of the Worksheet view. The cards shown in Figure T1.3 include the Color Color , Size Size , Text Text , Detail Detail , and Tooltip Tooltip cards. The cards that appear in the Marks area depend on the type of data being used and the visualization being created. Therefore, the cards that appear in the Marks area will change. Other cards that may appear here include Label Label , Path Path , and Shape Shape .

The two long areas just above Sheet 1 in Figure T1.3 are called shelves. The shelves shown in Figure T1.3 include Columns ⅲ Columns and Rows ☰ Rows. Below the Columns and Rows shelves is the Canvas area of the Worksheet, where the visualization will appear once it is being built.

Types of Data in Tableau

There are several different data types that can be used in Tableau for a field, each of which is indicated by a specific icon in the Data Source screen under Fields (see Figure T1.2) and in the Data tab in the Worksheet view (see Figure T1.3) for the zoo attendance data. These data types include Text (string) values Abc, Date values 📅, Date and Time values 📅⊙, Number values (both decimal and whole) #, Boolean (true or false) values T|F, and Spatial (geographic) values ⊕. The data type for a field can be changed by clicking on **Type** displayed in the **Fields** table at the bottom of the **Data Source** screen as shown in Figure T1.2 and choosing a new data type. The data type for a field can also be changed in the **Worksheet** view by right clicking on the field name shown under **Tables** in the **Data** pane and selecting **Change Data Type**. The data type assigned for a field in Tableau can affect the types of visualizations that can be created using the field as well as how the data are displayed.

Tableau differentiates between continuous and discrete types of data for building visualizations. Continuous data are displayed as green pills, such as the green pill for Attendance # Attendance in Figure T1.3. Discrete data are displayed as blue pills, such as the blue pill for Month Abc Month in Figure T1.3. Continuous data fields can be converted to discrete data fields in Tableau. To change the Attendance field to discrete, click on the dropdown arrow in the green **Attendance** pill in the **Data** pane of the **Worksheet** view shown in Figure T1.3, and select **Convert to Discrete**. Tableau treats continuous data differently than discrete data for many types of visualizations.

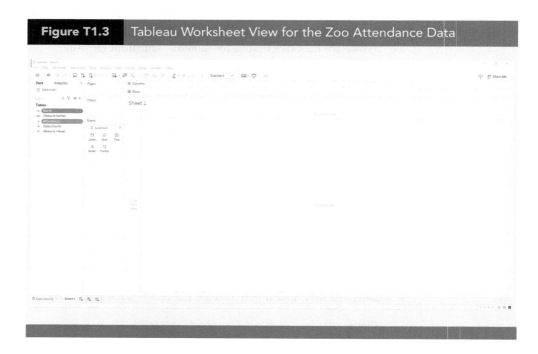

Figure T1.3 — Tableau Worksheet View for the Zoo Attendance Data

Notes + Comments

1. To update the visualizations created in Tableau from a Live Connection, first save any changes in the original data file. Then click **Data** in the Ribbon and select **Refresh Data Source**.

2. Additional worksheets can be created in Tableau to create multiple visualizations in the same Tableau environment. To create a new worksheet in Tableau, click **Worksheet** in the Ribbon of the Worksheet view of Tableau and select **New Worksheet**.

3. To connect multiple data sources to a visualization in Tableau, click **Data** in the Ribbon of the Worksheet view of Tableau and select **New Data Source**.

4. Tableau saves files as Tableau Workbooks with the file extension .twb or as Tableau Packaged Workbooks with the file extension .twbx. Workbooks of type .twb contain a link to the data file being used. Packaged Workbooks with the .twbx extension also contain the data source files. Workbooks of type .twb are useful because the visualizations can be updated when the source data file is updated. However, if the data source file is moved, the link becomes broken, and the visualizations are no longer produced. For this textbook, we provide Tableau files as Packaged Workbooks so they include the data source file and can be opened without reconnecting to the data file.

5. To save a file in Tableau as either a Tableau Workbook or a Tableau Packaged Workbook, click the **File** tab in the Ribbon, select **Save As**…, enter the name of the file for **File name:**, and select either **Tableau Workbook (*.twb)** or **Tableau Packaged Workbook (*.twbx)** for **Save as type:**.

Chapter 2

Selecting a Chart Type

Contents

Learning Objectives

After completing this chapter, you will be able to

LO 1 Create charts and graphs using Excel

LO 2 Modify charts and graphs using Excel

LO 3 Identify an appropriate chart type for a given goal and data type

LO 4 Interpret insights from charts and graphs

LO 5 Recognize which chart types should be avoided and explain why

Data Visualization Makeover

The New York City Comptroller

The New York City (NYC) comptroller's office has roughly 800 employees. Accountants, economists, engineers, investment analysts, information technology support, and administrative support all help the mission of the NYC Comptroller, which is to ensure the fiscal health of New York City. The Comptroller's office is responsible for auditing performance and efficiency, ensuring integrity in city contracting, managing assets to protect pensions, resolving claims against the city and risk management, managing city bonds, enforcing labor rights, and promoting fiscal health and a sound budget for New York City.

In its work, the comptroller's office generates a variety of annual reports including the Annual Audit Report, Annual Analysis of NYC Agency Contracts, Annual Claims Report, and the Annual Report on Capital Debt and Obligations. The pie chart in Figure 2.1 is from the Annual Report on Capital Debt and Obligations. It shows the amounts (in millions of dollars) allocated to each of

10 spending categories. For each of the 10 categories, it also expresses the respective spending allocation as a percentage of the total $70.24 billion dollar budget for fiscal years 2020–2023.[1]

The audience for the report is the public and most likely New York City residents who pay taxes and are interested in how the city allocates its budget. People with a passion for a particular cause might also be interested in this chart. For example, an advocate for parks and recreation might want to know how much money has been allocated to that cause and how much it is relative to other spending categories.

Figure 2.2 is a horizontal bar chart that displays the budget allocation amounts. Most data visualization experts suggest that pie charts should be avoided in favor of bar charts. There are several reasons for this. First, science has shown that we are better at assessing differences in length than angle and area. Glancing at the pie chart in Figure 2.1 and comparing the Other City Operations

Figure 2.1 A Pie Chart Showing the Allocation of New York City Funds

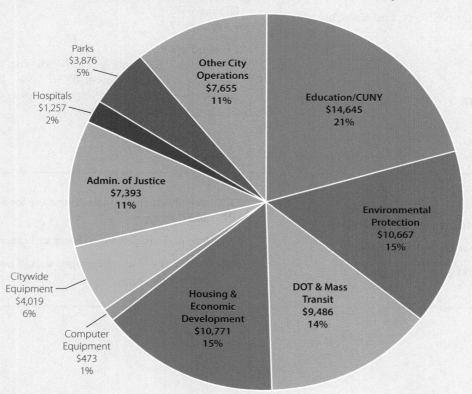

Source: NYC office of Management and Budget, FY 2020 Adopted Capital Commitment Plan, October 2019.

---

[1]Note that because of rounding, percentages do not add up to 100%.

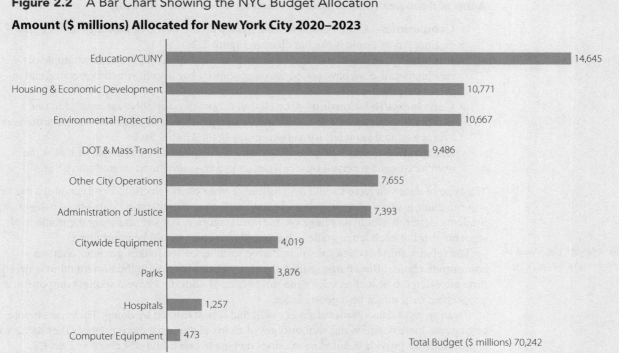

Figure 2.2 A Bar Chart Showing the NYC Budget Allocation

Amount ($ millions) Allocated for New York City 2020–2023

category with the Administration of Justice category, it is difficult to tell which has a larger allocation. Indeed, the allocations for these two categories are very close. However, in Figure 2.2, because we have sorted by amount allocated, we can see that the bar for Other City Operations is longer (also, it appears higher up in the list). Second, notice that in Figure 2.2, we do not need to use different colors to distinguish categories. Color is not necessary to distinguish each category in this bar chart because the length of the bars is used to distinguish the allocations by category. Third, we use a horizontal bar chart rather than a vertical bar chart so the category labels, a few of which are rather lengthy, are easier to read. Finally, we use the actual allocations and drop the percentages that appear in Figure 2.1. We could add the percentages, but it would make the bar chart more crowded. Instead, we opt to use only amounts because the bar lengths indicate the relative allocations, and a reader interested in the percentages can calculate them from the given allocation amounts.

In this chapter, we discuss in more detail how to select the right chart type to most effectively convey a message to your audience. In the case of the NYC Comptroller, we are comparing the amounts allocated by category, so the constituents of New York City can compare the spending categories and assess for themselves the budget allocation. A bar chart is appropriate for comparison.

There are numerous types of charts available, each designed for a purpose. Understanding the different types of charts and why some charts are more appropriate for certain purposes will make you a better data analyst and a better communicator with data. In this chapter, we describe some of the most commonly used types of charts and when they should be used. We also discuss some more advanced charts, as well as charts to be avoided.

2.1 Defining the Goal of Your Data Visualization

Selecting an Appropriate Chart

How do you choose an appropriate chart? If the goal of your chart is to explain, then the answer to this question depends on the message you wish to convey to your audience. If you are exploring data, the best chart type depends on the question you are asking and hope to answer from the data. Also, the type of data you have may influence your chart selection. A few of the more common goals for charts are to show the following:

- **Composition**—Composition is what makes up the whole of an entity under consideration. An example is the bar chart in Figure 2.2.
- **Ranking**—Ranking is the relative order of items. Figure 2.2 is also an example of ranking because we have sorted the categories by bar length, which is proportional to the amounts allocated.
- **Correlation/Relationship**—Correlation is how two variables are related to one another. An example of this is the relationship between average low temperature and average annual snowfall for various cities in the United States.
- **Distribution**—Distribution is how items are dispersed. An example of this is the number of calls received by a call center in a day, measured on an hourly basis.

The type of data you have should also influence your chart selection. For example, a bar or column chart is often an appropriate chart when we are summarizing data about categories. Students' letter grades in a college course are categories. For summarizing the number of students earning each letter grade, a bar or column chart would be appropriate.

The different types of data are discussed in Chapter 1.   The relationship between two quantitative variables often makes a scatter chart an appropriate choice. Bar charts, scatter charts, and line charts with the horizontal axis being time are often the best choice for time series data. If your data have a spatial component, a geographic map might be a good choice.

Creating great data visualizations is a skill that is best learned by doing. Therefore, before getting into more detail on the various types of charts and in what circumstances they are most appropriate, we provide detailed instructions on how to create and edit charts in Excel.

2.2 Creating and Editing Charts in Excel

In this section, we discuss how to create and edit a chart in Excel. Let us begin with how to create the chart of the zoo attendance data discussed in Chapter 1. The data, zoo attendance by month, are shown in Figure 2.3. We create a column chart using these data in the following steps.

DATA *file*

ZOO

Figure 2.3	Data in File *zoo*

◢	A	B
1	**Month**	**Attendance**
2	Jan	5422
3	Feb	4878
4	Mar	6586
5	Apr	6943
6	May	7876
7	Jun	17843
8	July	21967
9	Aug	14542
10	Sept	8751
11	Oct	6454
12	Nov	5677
13	Dec	11422

Creating a Chart in Excel

The following steps show how to create a column chart in Excel using the data in the file *zoo*.

Step 1. Select cells A1:B13
Step 2. Click the **Insert** tab on the Ribbon
Step 3. Click the **Insert Column or Bar Chart** button  in the **Charts** group
When the list of column and bar chart subtypes appears, click the
Clustered Column button

The chart created in the preceding steps appears in Figure 2.4. We can improve the appearance of the column chart in Figure 2.4 by following the steps below to delete the horizontal grid lines, make the axes better defined, add axis labels, and remove the border of the chart. This will improve the chart by making it simpler and better-defined.

Editing a Chart in Excel

CHART *file*

zoo_chart

Here, we give step-by-step instructions on how to edit the chart shown in Figure 2.4, included in the file zoo_chart, so it appears as shown in Figure 2.5. These steps for editing will be used throughout the following chapters in this book to improve the formatting of most charts created in Excel.

Step 1 removes the horizontal grid lines, and Step 2 edits the title.

*The **Chart Elements** button is not available in Mac versions of Excel. See the Notes + Comments at the end of this section for a description of how to access these features on a Mac.*

Step 1. Click anywhere on the chart, then click on the border of the chart title and press the **Delete** key
Click the **Chart Elements** button
Deselect the check box for **Gridlines**, and select the check box for **Axis Titles**
Step 2. Click the **Chart Title** text box above the chart and replace "Chart Title" with
Zoo Attendance by Month
Inside the text box, highlight "*Zoo Attendance by Month*"
Click the **Home** tab on the Ribbon, and in the **Font** group, select
Calibri 16 pt Bold
To change the position of the title, click on the border of the title box and slide the text box to the left so the title is above the vertical axis.

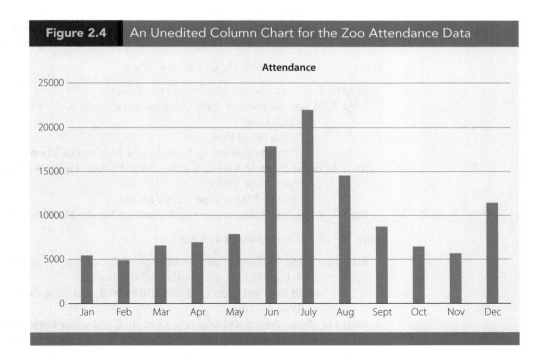

Figure 2.4   An Unedited Column Chart for the Zoo Attendance Data

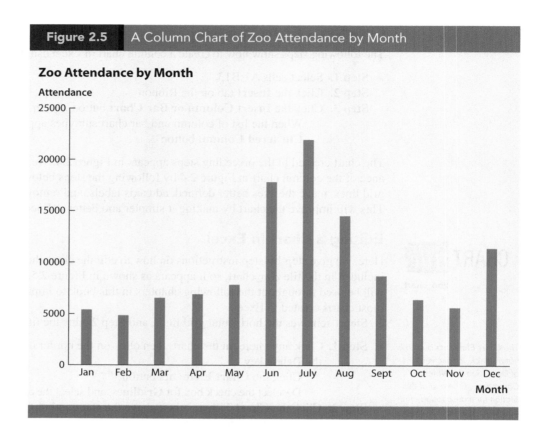

Figure 2.5   A Column Chart of Zoo Attendance by Month

Steps 3–5 format the horizontal axis and axis labels.

Step 3. Double click any label of the horizontal axis

Step 4. When the **Format Axis** task pane appears, click the **Fill & Line** button ⬦
Click **Line**
Select **Solid line**
In the drop down to the right of **Color**, under **Theme Colors**, select **Black**

Step 5. Click the **Home** tab on the Ribbon, and in the **Font** group, select **Calibri 10.5**

Steps 6–9 format the vertical axis and axis labels.

Step 6. Double click any label of the vertical axis

Step 7. When the **Format Axis** task pane appears, click the **Fill & Line** button ⬦
Click **Line**
Select **Solid line**
In the drop down to the right of **Color**, under **Theme Colors**, select **Black**

Step 8. In the **Format Axis** task pane, click the **Axis Options** button ▥
Click **Tick Marks**
Next to **Major type**, select **Inside**

Step 9. Click the **Home** tab on the Ribbon, and in the **Font** group, select **Calibri 10.5**

Steps 10–11 add and format axis titles.

Step 10. Select the horizontal axis title, place the cursor over the border of the text box, and drag it to the right to the end of the axis.
In the **Font** group, select **Calibri 10.5**, and click the **Bold** B button.
Type *Month*

Step 11. Select the vertical axis title, right click and select **Format Axis Title**, and click the **Size & Properties** ▦ button. Click **Alignment**, and next to **Text direction**, from the drop-down menu, select **Horizontal**. Place the cursor over the border, and drag it to the top of the vertical axis aligned above the axis labels.

In the **Font** group, select **Calibri 10.5**, and click the **Bold** Β button.

Type *Attendance*

Steps 12–13 eliminate the border of the chart.

In Step 12, if you click inside the rectangular area delimited by the horizontal and vertical axes, the **Format Plot Area** *task pane will be activated instead of the* **Format Chart Area** *task pane.*

Step 12. Click the Chart Area of the chart anywhere outside of the rectangular area delimited by the horizontal and vertical axes of the chart

Step 13. In the **Format Chart Area** task pane, click **Chart Options**

Click the **Fill & Line** button ◇

Click **Border**

Click **No line**

These steps produce the chart shown in Figure 2.5. In later chapters, we will introduce additional design elements that can be used to further improve charts.

Notes + Comments

1. The **Chart Elements** button ⊞ is not available in Excel for Mac. To access the features of **Chart Elements** in Excel for Mac, double click the chart, click the **Chart Design** tab, and click **Add Chart Element** from the **Chart Layouts** group.

2. When selecting data in Excel to populate a chart, the leftmost column of data is generally represented by the horizontal axis on the chart. The assignment of data to the horizontal and vertical axes can be switched by right-clicking on the chart, choosing **Select Data Source**, and on the **Select Data Source** dialog box, clicking **Switch Row/Column**.

3. To create a chart using nonadjacent columns of data in Excel, select the leftmost column you wish to include in the chart, press and hold down the control key (**Ctrl**), and select the other columns of data you wish to include.

4. The **Chart Elements** button offers a variety of features, including the ability to add or delete axes and axis titles, a chart title, data labels, gridlines, a legend, and a trendline.

5. An axis title can also be created using a text box by clicking **Insert** on the Ribbon, clicking **Text**, and then selecting where you want the axis title to appear.

6. The **Chart Styles** button ▧ allows you to change the style of the chart type you have selected as well the color scheme of the chart. The **Chart Styles** button is not available in Excel for Mac. To access the features of **Chart Styles** in Excel for Mac, double click the chart, click the **Chart Design** tab, and click on style from the **Chart Styles** group. To change the color scheme, click the **Change Colors** button in the **Chart Styles** group.

2.3 Scatter Charts and Bubble Charts

When exploring data, we are often interested in the relationship between two quantitative variables. For example, we might be interested in the square footage of a house and the cost of the house, or the age of a car and its annual maintenance costs. A **scatter chart** is a graphical presentation of the relationship between two quantitative variables. One variable is shown on the horizontal axis, the other is shown on the vertical axis, and a symbol is used to plot ordered pairs of the quantitative variable values. A scatter chart is appropriate for better understanding the relationship between two quantitative variables. As we shall also see, a bubble chart is an appropriate chart when trying to show relationships with more than two quantitative variables.

Scatter Charts

The file *snow* contains the average low temperature in degrees Fahrenheit and the average annual snowfall in inches for 51 major cities in the United States. A portion of the data are shown in Figure 2.6. These averages are based on 30 years of data. Suppose we are interested in the relationship between these two variables. Intuition tells us that the higher the average low temperature, the lower the average snowfall, but what is the nature of this relationship?

Figure 2.6	A Portion of the Data in File *snow*

	A	B	C	D
1	City	State	Average Low Temperature	Average Snowfall
2	Atlanta	Georgia	53	2.9
3	Austin	Texas	59	0.6
4	Baltimore	Maryland	45	20.2
5	Birmingham	Alabama	53	1.6
6	Boston	Massachusetts	44	43.8
7	Buffalo	New York	40	94.7
8	Charlotte	North Carolina	49	4.3
9	Chicago	Illinois	41	36.7
10	Cincinnati	Ohio	43	11.2
11	Cleveland	Ohio	43	68.1
12	Columbus	Ohio	44	27.5
13	Dallas	Texas	57	1.5
14	Denver	Colorado	36	53.8
15	Detroit	Michigan	42	42.7
16	Hartford	Connecticut	40	40.5

DATA*file*

snow

The data are plotted in Figure 2.7. This scatter chart is created using the following steps.

Step 1. Select cells C1:D52

Step 2. Click the **Insert** tab on the Ribbon

Step 3. Click the **Insert Scatter (X,Y) or Bubble Chart** button  in the **Charts** group

When the list chart subtypes appear, click the **Scatter** button

Then, edit the chart as outlined in Section 2.2

Each point on the chart in Figure 2.7 represents a *pair* of numbers. In this case, we have a pair of measurements for each of 51 cities. The measurements are average low temperature in degrees Fahrenheit and average annual amount of snowfall in inches. We can see from the chart that the average annual amount of snowfall intuitively levels off at zero for warm-weather cities.

Scatter charts are among the most useful charts for exploring pairs of quantitative data. But, what if you wish to explore the relationships between more than two quantitative variables? When exploring the relationships between three quantitative variables, a bubble chart may be useful.

Bubble Charts

A **bubble chart** is a scatter chart that displays a third quantitative variable using different sized dots, which we refer to as bubbles.

The file *airportdata* contains data on a sample of 15 airports. These data are shown in Figure 2.8. For each airport, we have the following quantitative variables: average wait time in the nonpriority Transportation Security Authority (TSA) queue measured in minutes, the cheapest on-site daily rate for parking at the airport measured in dollars, and the number of enplanements in a year (the number of passengers who board, including transfers) measured in millions of passengers.

DATA*file*

airportdata

Figure 2.7	A Scatter Chart for the Data in File *snow*

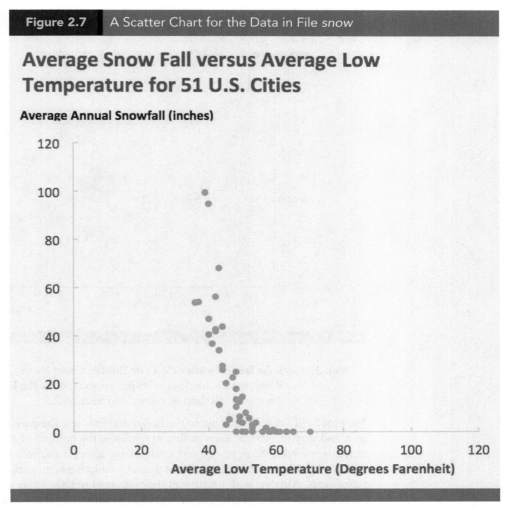

Average Snow Fall versus Average Low Temperature for 51 U.S. Cities

The data are plotted as a bubble chart in Figure 2.9. This chart was created using the following steps:

Step 1. Select cells B1:D16
Step 2. Click the **Insert** tab on the Ribbon

Figure 2.8	Data in File *airportdata*

	A	B	C	D
1	Airport Code	TSA wait time (minutes)	Cheapest on-site parking cost ($ per day)	Annual Enplanements (millions of passengers)
2	ATL	10.30	$14.00	49.06
3	CLT	9.45	$7.00	22.19
4	DEN	8.35	$8.00	27.02
5	AUS	5.30	$8.00	5.80
6	STL	4.80	$7.00	6.25
7	SMF	7.30	$10.00	4.60
8	RDU	6.75	$6.50	4.80
9	EWR	9.90	$18.00	18.80
10	SFO	7.25	$18.00	24.00
11	LAX	6.40	$12.00	36.10
12	SLC	4.50	$10.00	10.80
13	SAN	8.80	$15.00	9.70
14	MSY	4.60	$16.00	5.30
15	IAD	3.0	$10.00	10.70
16	BNA	2.50	$12.00	5.60

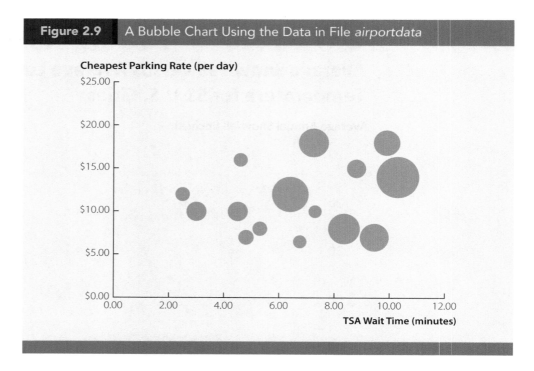

Figure 2.9   A Bubble Chart Using the Data in File *airportdata*

Step 3. Click the **Insert Scatter (X,Y) or Bubble Chart** button ⊡ ⌄ in the **Charts** group
When the list of chart subtypes appears, click the **Bubble** button ⬢
Then edit the chart as outlined in Section 2.2.

We plot the TSA wait time along the horizontal axis and the parking rate along the vertical axis and vary the size of each bubble to represent the number of enplanements. We see that airports with fewer passengers tend to have lower wait times than those with more passengers. There seems to be less of a relationship between parking rate and number of passengers. Airports with lower wait times do tend to have lower parking rates.

In a bubble chart, you might wish to change which variables correspond to the x (horizontal) values, the y (vertical) values, and the bubble sizes. Once the chart has been created in Excel, the following steps can be used to change these assignments.

Step 1. Right click any bubble and choose **Select Data...**
Step 2. When the **Select Data Source** dialog box appears, click the **Edit** button under **Legend Entries (Series)**
Step 3. Enter the location of the data you want to correspond to the horizontal values in the **Series X values:** box (see Figure 2.10). Do not include column headers
Step 4. Repeat Step 3 for **Series Y Values:** box and the **Series bubble size:** box
Click **OK**

2.4 Line Charts, Column Charts, and Bar Charts

In this section, we consider the line chart, a natural extension of a scatter chart discussed in the previous section. We also introduce column and bar charts, which are useful for displaying categorical data.

Line Charts

A line chart uses a point to represent a pair of quantitative variable values, one value along the horizontal axis and the other on the vertical axis, with a line connecting the points. Line charts are very useful for time series data (data collected over a period of time: minutes, hours, days, years, etc.). As an example, let us consider Cheetah Sports. Cheetah sells running shoes and has retail stores in shopping malls throughout the United States.

Figure 2.10 The Edit Series Dialog Box

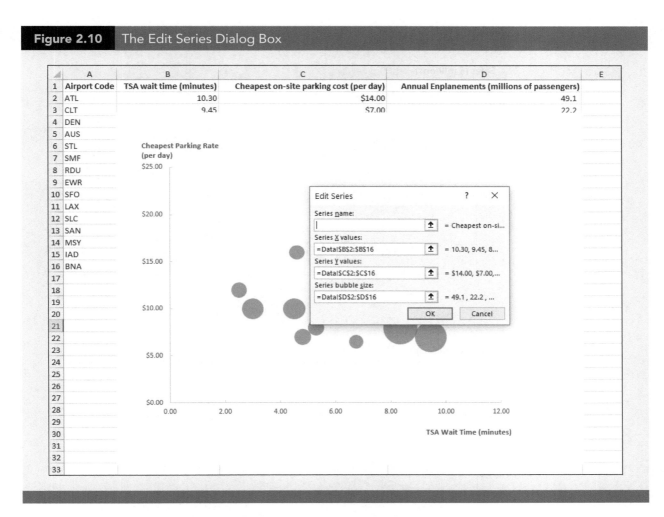

The file *cheetah* contains the last 10 years of sales for Cheetah Sports, measured in millions of dollars. These data are shown in Figure 2.11. Figure 2.12 displays a scatter chart and a line chart created in Excel for these sales data.

Figure 2.11 Data in the File *cheetah*

DATA *file*

cheetah

	A	B
1	Year	Sales ($ millions)
2	1	87
3	2	90
4	3	110
5	4	145
6	5	170
7	6	154
8	7	177
9	8	175
10	9	183
11	10	195

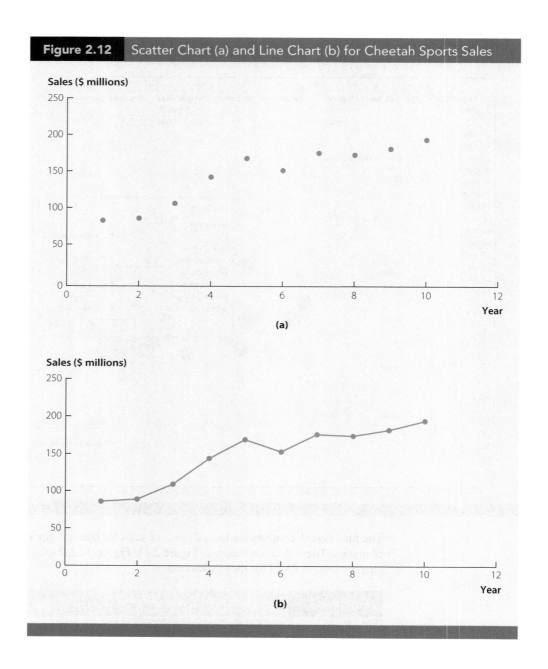

Figure 2.12   Scatter Chart (a) and Line Chart (b) for Cheetah Sports Sales

The following steps create the line chart of the Cheetah Sports sales data shown in Figure 2.12b.

Step 1. Select cells A1:B11
Step 2. Click the **Insert** tab on the Ribbon
Step 3. In the **Charts** group, click the **Insert Scatter (X,Y) or Bubble Chart** button
              Select **Scatter with Straight Lines and Markers**
              Edit the chart as described in Section 2.2

Comparing Figure 2.12b with Figure 2.12a, the addition of lines between the points suggests continuity and makes it is easier for the reader to see and interpret changes that have occurred over time.

Figure 2.13	The Data in the File *cheetahregion*		

	A	B	C	D
1	Year	Eastern Sales	Western Sales	Total Sales ($ millions)
2	1	59	28	87
3	2	57	33	90
4	3	68	42	110
5	4	91	54	145
6	5	109	61	170
7	6	96	58	154
8	7	110	67	177
9	8	72	103	175
10	9	63	120	183
11	10	65	130	195

DATA *file*

cheetahregion

Let us consider a second example that illustrates multiple lines on a single chart. Consider the file *cheetahregion*. Cheetah Sports has two sales regions: the eastern region and the western region. The file breaks down the total sales for the 10-year period by region as shown in Figure 2.13.

Cheetah Sports sales by region are shown in Figure 2.14. To create the line chart shown in Figure 2.14, select cells A1:C11 (do not select D1:D11) in the file *cheetahregion* and follow Steps 2 and 3 previously outlined for constructing a line chart. In addition to the chart editing from Section 2.2, we have also changed the color scheme to **Monochromatic Palette 1** (using the **Chart Styles** option as described in the Notes + Comments at the end of Section 2.2).

We can see from Figure 2.14 that sales in the Western region have increased over the last three years of this 10-year period, while sales in the Eastern region have dropped substantially since year 7.

Figure 2.14	Line Chart for Cheetah Sports Sales by Region

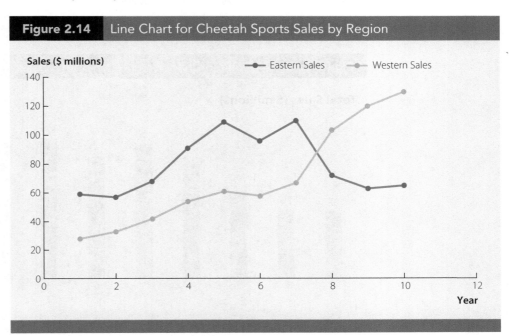

DATA *file*

cheetah

Column Charts

A **column chart** displays a quantitative variable by category or time period using vertical bars to display the magnitude of a quantitative variable. We have seen an example of a column chart in the zoo attendance data, where the categories are months of the year and the quantitative variable is zoo attendance. Let us elaborate more about when to use a column chart by continuing the Cheetah Sports annual sales example shown in Figure 2.11.

The following steps create the column chart of the Cheetah Sports sales data shown in Figure 2.15.

Step 1. Select cells A1:B11
Step 2. Click the **Insert** tab on the Ribbon
Step 3. In the **Charts** group, click the **Insert Column or Bar Chart** button
Select **Clustered Column**

Excel displays the year as if it is a quantitative variable. To correct this, we need the following steps:

Step 4. Right click the chart and select **Change Chart Type…**
Step 5. When the **Change Chart Type** task pane appears, select the **Cluster Column** type that plots the appropriate number of variables (in this case, the single variable Sales plotted with 10 monochromatic columns), and click **OK**
Edit the chart as outlined in Section 2.2

The next step adds data labels to the bars.

Step 6. Click the **Chart Elements** button ⊞ and select **Data Labels**

The line chart in Figure 2.12b and the column chart in Figure 2.15 are both good displays of the Cheetah Sports annual sales. The line chart, with its connected lines, makes it easier to see how sales are changing over time. The column chart, with its data labels, is preferred if it is important for the audience to know the value of sales in each year. Moreover, adding data labels to a line chart generally makes the chart too cluttered. On the other hand, if there are numerous categories or time periods, the line chart (without data labels) would be preferred over the column chart with data labels because the column chart would appear too cluttered, and labels would not be readable.

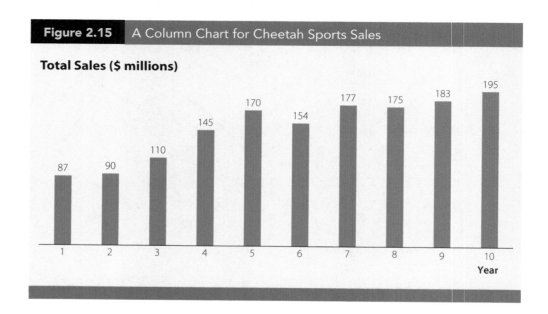

Figure 2.15   A Column Chart for Cheetah Sports Sales

DATA *file*

cheetahregion

Clustered column charts with multiple variables are also called side-by-side column charts.

Let us now reconsider the regional data for Cheetah Sports in the file *cheetahregion*. Using these data, let us construct a clustered column chart and compare it to the line chart in Figure 2.14. A **clustered column chart** displays multiple quantitative variables by categories or time periods with different colors, with the height of the columns denoting the magnitude of the quantitative variable.

To create the clustered column chart in Figure 2.16, select cells A1:C11 in the file *cheetahregion* as shown in Figure 2.13 (do not select cells D1:D11). Follow Steps 2–5 previously outlined for a column chart. In addition to the chart editing from Section 2.2, we have also changed the color scheme to **Monochromatic Palette 1** (using the **Chart Styles** option as described in the Notes + Comments at the end of Section 2.2).

Comparing Figures 2.14 and 2.16, we see that the changes in sales within a region over time are more apparent in the line chart. The clustered column chart in Figure 2.16 appears cluttered, and the changes in sales are not as obvious as in Figure 2.14. Adding data labels to Figure 2.16 would make the clustered column chart even more cluttered.

While Figure 2.14 is preferred over Figure 2.16 for the regional sales data for Cheetah Sports, neither of these charts convey that the Eastern and Western regions make up the total sales. It is difficult to tell how total sales are changing. We make this more obvious by using a stacked column chart. A **stacked column chart** is a column chart that uses color to denote the contribution of each subcategory to the total.

To create a stacked column chart for Cheetah Sports, we select cells A1:C11 in the file *cheetahregion*, and repeat Steps 2–5 previously outlined for a column chart—except in Step 3, we click the **Insert Column or Bar Chart** in the **Charts** group and select **Stacked Column** . After chart editing, we obtain the stacked column chart shown in Figure 2.17. This chart shows the combination of Eastern and Western region sales by year, and the total height of the column indicates the level of total sales.

The Cheetah Sports example with regional sales data demonstrates the important principle that the appropriate chart depends not only on the type of data, but also the goal of the analysis and needs of the audience. If demonstrating the change in sales over time within each region is a key point, then a line chart in this case is a good choice. If representing the total sales level and how each region contributes to total sales over time is important, then a stacked column chart is a good choice.

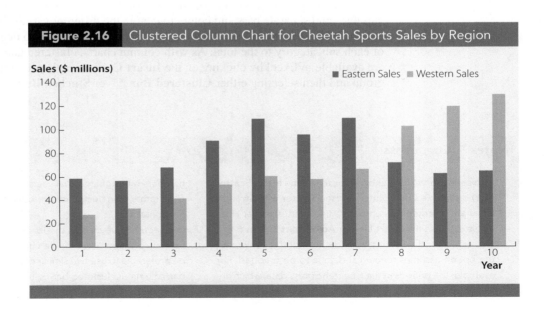

Figure 2.16 Clustered Column Chart for Cheetah Sports Sales by Region

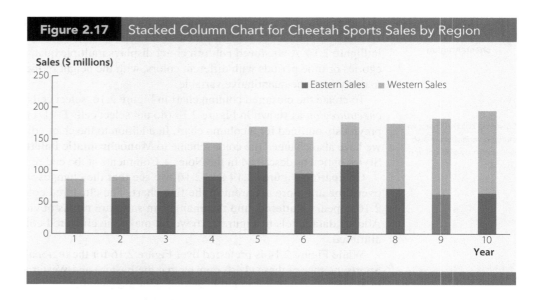

Figure 2.17   Stacked Column Chart for Cheetah Sports Sales by Region

Bar Charts

A **bar chart** shows a summary of categorical data using the length of horizontal bars to display the magnitude of a quantitative variable. That is, a bar chart is a column chart turned on its side. Like column charts, bar charts are useful for comparing categorical variables and are most effective when you do not have too many categories. Figure 2.2 in the Data Visualization Makeover of the Allocation of Funds in New York City is a good example. As shown in that example, a bar chart can be a good substitute for a pie chart when showing composition. Sorting the data as in Figure 2.2 makes the rank order of the components by the magnitude of the quantitative variable more obvious. A bar chart is preferred over a column chart if there are lengthy category names because it is easier to display the names horizontally (for improved legibility). However, for time series data, a column chart is better as it is more natural to display the passage of time from left to right horizontally.

A **clustered bar chart** displays multiple quantitative variables for categories or time periods using the length of horizontal bars to denote the magnitude of the quantitative variables and separate bars and colors to denote the different variables. Like a stacked column chart, a **stacked bar chart** is a bar chart that uses color to denote the contribution of each subcategory to the total. As with column charts, clustered and stacked bar charts are available in Excel by clicking on the **Insert Column or Bar** button in the **Charts** group and then selecting either **Clustered Bar** or **Stacked Bar** .

Notes + Comments

1. In this section, we have shown how to use the **Insert Scatter (X,Y) or Bubble Chart** button and the **Scatter with Straight Lines and Markers** to construct a line chart. Another alternative is to use the **Insert Line or Area Chart** button . This works for time series data (dates, months, years), but the option assumes numerical data is to be graphed. For example, the periods in the Cheetah Sports data, which are numbers rather than actual years, show up as a line on the chart rather than being interpreted as the categories for the horizontal axis.

2. In Chapter 3, we discuss the issue of trying to present too much information on a single chart. In some cases, it may be preferable to use two similar charts rather than a stacked bar/column or clustered bar/column chart.

2.5 Maps

In this section, we introduce three types of maps used to display various types of data. You are most likely familiar with geographic maps, which are very useful for displaying data that have a spatial or geographic component. We will also discuss heat maps and treemaps. Each is available in Excel.

Geographic Maps

A **geographic map** is generally defined as a chart that shows characteristics and the arrangement of the geography of our physical reality. A geographic map of the United States shows state borders and how the states are arranged. A **choropleth map** is a geographic map that uses shades of a color, unique colors, or symbols to indicate quantitative or categorical variables by geographic region or area.

Let us consider creating a choropleth map of the United States for which color shading is used to denote the population of each state. A darker shade will indicate a higher population, and a lighter shade will indicate a lower population.

The population data for the 50 states can be found in the file *statepopulation*. A portion of the data set is shown in Figure 2.18. The 50 states in the United States are listed in column A, and the corresponding estimated population of each state is in column B.

The following steps will create a choropleth map using shading to denote the size of the population for each state.

Step 1. Select cells A1:B51
Step 2. Click the **Insert** tab on the Ribbon
Step 3. In the **Charts** group, click the **Maps** button Maps
            Select **Filled Map**

After selecting Filled Map, you may need to allow Excel to send your request to the Bing search engine to complete the appropriate map.

After editing the chart title as outlined in Section 2.2, we obtain the map in Figure 2.19. The map shows that the states with the highest populations are California, Texas, Florida, and New York.

As an example of a choropleth map with categorical data, let us consider how Amazon is able to deliver packages so quickly to its U.S. customers. Amazon distributes customer orders from fulfillment centers that stock most of the products Amazon sells. The file *amazonfulfill* contains categorical data by state. For each state, "Yes" or "No" is provided to denote whether that state has at least one Amazon fulfillment center. A portion of the Amazon fulfillment data set is shown in Figure 2.20.

DATA *file*

statepopulation

Figure 2.18	A Portion of the State Population Data

	A	B
1	State	Estimated 2020 Population
2	California	39,937,489
3	Texas	29,472,295
4	Florida	21,992,985
5	New York	19,440,469
6	Pennsylvania	12,820,878
7	Illinois	12,659,682
8	Ohio	11,747,694
9	Georgia	10,736,059
10	North Carolina	10,611,862

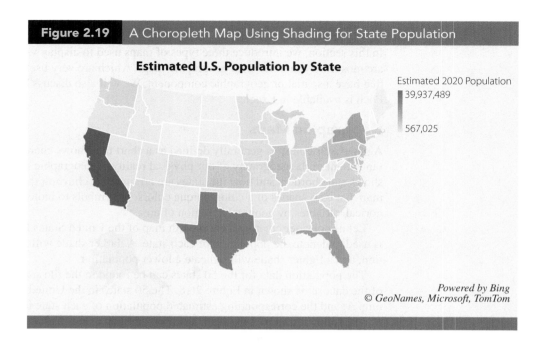

Figure 2.19   A Choropleth Map Using Shading for State Population

Estimated U.S. Population by State

Estimated 2020 Population

39,937,489

567,025

Powered by Bing
© GeoNames, Microsoft, TomTom

Selecting cells A1:B51 and following Steps 2–3 listed in the state population example results in the map shown in Figure 2.21. Amazon has at least one fulfillment center in 38 of the 50 states. The states without a fulfillment center tend to be either relatively sparsely populated or a geographic outlier. Clearly, Amazon has a lot of fulfillment centers to ensure quick customer delivery times for many of the products it sells.

Next, we consider two useful types of maps that are not required to be geographic.

DATA *file*

amazonfulfill

Figure 2.20   A Portion of the Amazon Fulfillment Data

◢	A	B
1	**State**	**Amazon Fullfillment Center**
2	Alabama	Yes
3	Alaska	No
4	Arizona	Yes
5	Arkansas	Yes
6	California	Yes
7	Colorado	Yes
8	Connecticut	Yes
9	Delaware	Yes
10	Florida	Yes

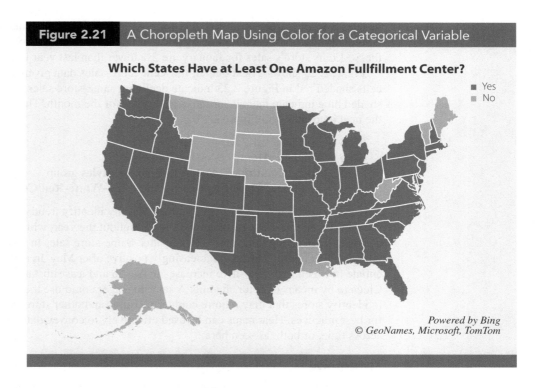

Figure 2.21   A Choropleth Map Using Color for a Categorical Variable

Which States Have at Least One Amazon Fullfillment Center?

■ Yes
■ No

Powered by Bing
© GeoNames, Microsoft, TomTom

Heat Maps

DATA *file*

samestoresales

A **heat map** is a two-dimensional (2D) graphical representation of data that uses different shades of color to indicate magnitude. Let us consider the data in the file *samestoresales*. The data are shown in Figure 2.22. The rows of this data set correspond to store locations, and the columns are the months of the year. The percentages given indicate the change

Figure 2.22   Same-Store-Sales Data in the File *samestoresales*

	A	B	C	D	E	F	G	H	I	J	K	L	M
1		JAN	FEB	MAR	APR	MAY	JUN	JUL	AUG	SEP	OCT	NOV	DEC
2	St. Louis	-2%	-1%	-1%	0%	2%	4%	3%	5%	6%	7%	8%	8%
3	Phoenix	5%	4%	4%	2%	2%	-2%	-5%	-8%	-6%	-5%	-7%	-8%
4	Albany	-5%	-6%	-4%	-5%	-2%	-5%	-5%	-3%	-1%	-2%	-1%	-2%
5	Austin	16%	15%	15%	16%	18%	17%	14%	15%	16%	19%	18%	16%
6	Cincinnati	-9%	-6%	-7%	-3%	3%	6%	8%	11%	10%	11%	13%	11%
7	San Francisco	2%	4%	5%	8%	4%	2%	4%	3%	1%	-1%	1%	2%
8	Seattle	7%	7%	8%	7%	5%	4%	2%	0%	-2%	-4%	-6%	-5%
9	Chicago	5%	3%	2%	6%	8%	7%	8%	5%	8%	10%	9%	8%
10	Atlanta	12%	14%	13%	17%	12%	11%	8%	7%	7%	8%	5%	3%
11	Miami	2%	3%	0%	1%	-1%	-4%	-6%	-8%	-11%	-13%	-11%	-10%
12	Minneapolis	-6%	-6%	-8%	-5%	-6%	-5%	-5%	-7%	-5%	-2%	-1%	-2%
13	Denver	5%	4%	1%	1%	2%	3%	1%	-1%	0%	1%	2%	3%
14	Salt Lake City	7%	7%	7%	13%	12%	8%	5%	9%	10%	9%	7%	6%
15	Raleigh	4%	2%	0%	5%	4%	3%	5%	5%	9%	11%	8%	6%
16	Boston	-5%	-5%	-3%	4%	-5%	-4%	-3%	-1%	1%	2%	3%	5%
17	Pittsburgh	-6%	-6%	-4%	-5%	-3%	-3%	-1%	-2%	-2%	-1%	-2%	-1%

in sales over the same month last year for a given store. This percentage change metric is commonly used in the retail industry and is referred to as "same-store-sales." For example, the St. Louis store's sales for January are 2% lower than last year in January.

Figure 2.23 shows a heat map of the same-store-sales data given in Figure 2.22. The cells shaded red in Figure 2.23 indicate declining same-store sales for the month, and cells shaded blue indicate increasing same-store sales for the month. The following steps create the heat map shown in Figure 2.23.

Step 1. Select cells B2:M17
Step 2. Click the **Home** tab on the Ribbon.
Step 3. Click **Conditional Formatting** in the **Styles** group
Select **Color Scales**, and click **Blue-White-Red Color Scale**

The heat map in Figure 2.23 helps the reader easily identify trends and patterns. We can see that Austin has had positive increases throughout the year, while Pittsburgh has had consistently negative same-store sales results. Same-store sales in Cincinnati started the year negative but then became increasingly positive after May. In addition, we can differentiate between strong positive increases in Austin and less substantial positive increases in Chicago by means of color shading. A sales manager could use the heat map in Figure 2.23 to identify stores that may require countermeasures and other stores that may provide ideas for best practices. Heat maps can be used effectively to convey data over different areas, across time, or both, as seen here.

Treemaps

A **treemap** is a chart that uses the size, color, and arrangement of rectangles to display the magnitudes of a quantitative variable for different categories, each of which are further decomposed into subcategories. The size of each rectangle represents the magnitude of the quantitative variable within a category/subcategory. The color of the rectangle represents the category, and all subcategories of a category are arranged together.

Categorical data that is further decomposed into subcategories are called hierarchical data. **Hierarchical data** can be represented with a tree-like structure, where the branches of the tree lead to categories and subcategories. As an example, let us consider the top 10

Figure 2.23   A Heat Map for Same-Store Sales

	A	B	C	D	E	F	G	H	I	J	K	L	M
1		JAN	FEB	MAR	APR	MAY	JUN	JUL	AUG	SEP	OCT	NOV	DEC
2	St. Louis	-2%	-1%	-1%	0%	2%	4%	3%	5%	6%	7%	8%	8%
3	Phoenix	5%	4%	4%	2%	2%	-2%	-5%	-8%	-6%	-5%	-7%	-8%
4	Albany	-5%	-6%	-4%	-5%	-2%	-5%	-5%	-3%	-1%	-2%	-1%	-2%
5	Austin	16%	15%	15%	16%	18%	17%	14%	15%	16%	19%	18%	16%
6	Cincinnati	-9%	-6%	-7%	-3%	3%	6%	8%	11%	10%	11%	13%	11%
7	San Francisco	2%	4%	5%	8%	4%	2%	4%	3%	1%	-1%	1%	2%
8	Seattle	7%	7%	8%	7%	5%	4%	2%	0%	-2%	-4%	-6%	-5%
9	Chicago	5%	3%	2%	6%	8%	7%	8%	5%	8%	10%	9%	8%
10	Atlanta	12%	14%	13%	17%	12%	11%	8%	7%	7%	8%	5%	3%
11	Miami	2%	3%	0%	1%	-1%	-4%	-6%	-8%	-11%	-13%	-11%	-10%
12	Minneapolis	-6%	-6%	-8%	-5%	-6%	-5%	-5%	-7%	-5%	-2%	-1%	-2%
13	Denver	5%	4%	1%	1%	2%	3%	1%	-1%	0%	1%	2%	3%
14	Salt Lake City	7%	7%	7%	13%	12%	8%	5%	9%	10%	9%	7%	6%
15	Raleigh	4%	2%	0%	5%	4%	3%	5%	5%	9%	11%	8%	6%
16	Boston	-5%	-5%	-3%	4%	-5%	-4%	-3%	-1%	1%	2%	3%	5%
17	Pittsburgh	-6%	-6%	-4%	-5%	-3%	-3%	-1%	-2%	-2%	-1%	-2%	-1%

Figure 2.24   Data in the file *brandvalues*

DATA *file*

brandvalues

⬜	A	B	C
1	**Industry**	**Brand**	**Value ($ billions)**
2	Technology	Apple	205.5
3	Technology	Google	167.7
4	Technology	Microsoft	125.3
5	Technology	Amazon	97.0
6	Technology	Facebook	88.9
7	Beverages	Coca-Cola	59.2
8	Technology	Samsung	53.1
9	Leisure	Disney	52.2
10	Automotive	Toyota	44.6
11	Restaurants	McDonald's	43.8

---

brand values given in the file *brandvalues* (source: *Forbes.com*). The data appear in the file as shown in Figure 2.24. Each observation consists of an industry, a brand within an industry, and the value of the brand.

Figure 2.25 shows how these data have a hierarchical or tree structure. The base of the tree is the top 10 brand values. The category is the industry of each company, the subcategory is the brand name, and the value of the brand is the quantitative variable.

Figure 2.26 is an example of a treemap for the brand values data. The following steps are used to create a treemap in Excel using the data in the file *brandvalues*.

Step 1. Select cells A1:C11
Step 2. Sort the data by Industry by using the following steps:
        Click **Data** on the Ribbon
        Click the **Sort** button in the **Sort & Filter** group
        In the **Sort** dialog box, select **Industry** from the drop-down menu
        From the **Order** drop-down menu, select **A to Z**

Figure 2.25   The Hierarchical Tree Structure of the Top 10 Brand Values Data

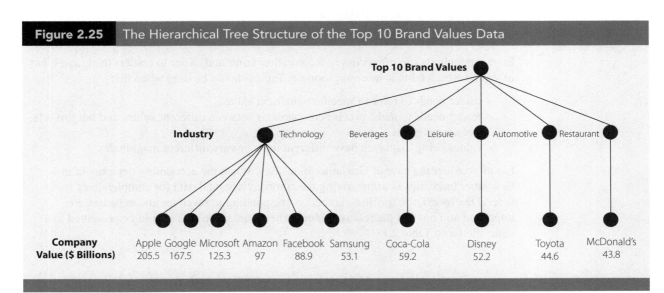

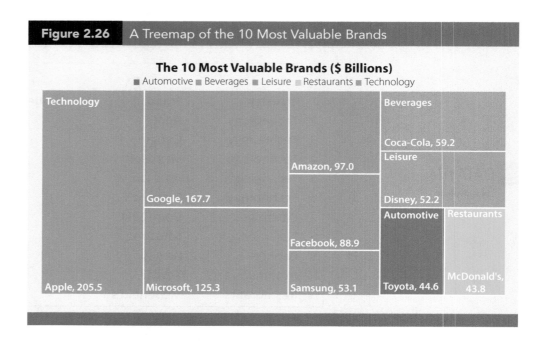

Figure 2.26   A Treemap of the 10 Most Valuable Brands

Step 3. Click **Insert** on the Ribbon.
　　　　　Click the **Insert Hierarchy Chart** button in the **Charts** group
　　　　　Select **Treemap** from the drop-down menu

To display the brand values:

Step 4. Click any brand label, and then right click
　　　　　Select **Format Data Labels…** from the drop-down menu
　　　　　Select **Text Options**, **Label Options**, and select **Value**

The colors in the treemap shown in Figure 2.26 correspond to industries. Each of the rectangles represents a brand, and the size of the rectangles indicates the size of the brand's value. We see that the technology industry has six brands in the top 10. Apple, Google, and Microsoft are the three highest brand values.

2.6 When to Use Tables

Tables versus Charts

In general, charts can often convey information faster and easier to readers than tables, but in some cases, a table is more appropriate. Tables should be used when the:

- reader needs to refer to specific numerical values.
- reader needs to make precise comparisons between different values and not just relative comparisons.
- values being displayed have different units or very different magnitudes.

Let us consider the case of Gossamer Industries. When the accounting department of Gossamer Industries is summarizing the company's annual data for completion of its federal tax forms, the specific numbers corresponding to revenues and expenses are important and not just the relative values. Therefore, these data should be presented in a table similar to Table 2.1.

Table 2.1	Table Showing Exact Values for Costs and Revenues by Month for Gossamer Industries						
	Month						
	Jan	**Feb**	**Mar**	**Apr**	**May**	**June**	**Total**
Costs ($)	48,123	56,458	64,125	52,158	54,718	50,985	326,567
Revenues ($)	64,124	66,125	67,125	48,178	51,785	55,678	353,015

DATA file

gossamer

Table design is discussed in Chapter 3.

We construct the chart-table combination using a line chart because this option is not available for a scatter chart. Excel does not support integration of charts and tables for all chart types.

Similarly, if it is important to know exactly by how much revenues exceed expenses each month, then this would also be better presented as a table rather than as a line chart as seen in Figure 2.27. Notice that it is very difficult to determine the monthly revenues and costs in Figure 2.27. We could add these values using data labels, but they would clutter the figure. A preferred solution is to combine the chart with the table into a single figure, as in Figure 2.28, to allow the reader to easily see the monthly changes in revenues and costs while also being able to refer to the exact numerical values.

Using the data in the file *gossamer*, the following steps show how to create the line chart accompanied with a table as shown in Figure 2.28.

Step 1. Select cells A2:G4

Step 2. Click the **Insert** tab on the Ribbon

Step 3. Click the **Insert Line or Area Chart** button in the **Charts** group

Step 4. When the list of column and bar charts subtypes appears, click the **Line** button

Step 5. Click anywhere on the chart

Click the **Chart Elements** button

Select the check box for **Data Table**

Edit the chart as outlined in Section 2.2

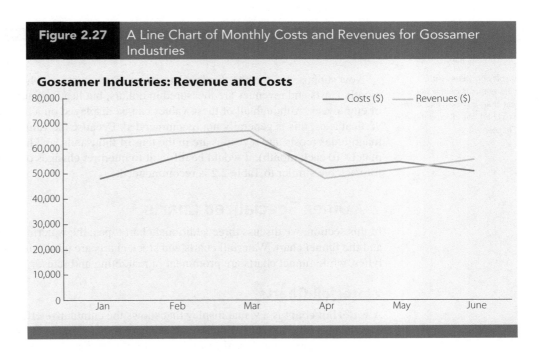

Figure 2.27	A Line Chart of Monthly Costs and Revenues for Gossamer Industries

Gossamer Industries: Revenue and Costs

—— Costs ($)   —— Revenues ($)

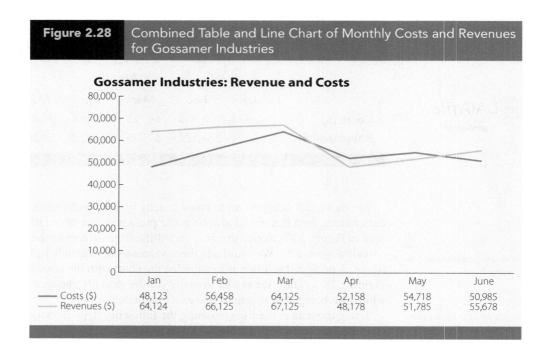

Figure 2.28	Combined Table and Line Chart of Monthly Costs and Revenues for Gossamer Industries

Gossamer Industries: Revenue and Costs

	Jan	Feb	Mar	Apr	May	June
— Costs ($)	48,123	56,458	64,125	52,158	54,718	50,985
— Revenues ($)	64,124	66,125	67,125	48,178	51,785	55,678

Table 2.2	Table Displaying Head Count, Costs, and Revenues for Gossamer Industries

	Month						
	Jan	Feb	Mar	Apr	May	June	Total
Head Count	8	9	10	9	9	9	
Costs ($)	48,123	56,458	64,125	52,158	54,718	50,985	326,567
Revenues ($)	64,124	66,125	67,125	48,178	51,785	55,678	353,015

Displaying values with different units on the same line chart is known as a dual-axis chart. We discuss these in Chapter 9.

Now suppose we wish to display data on revenues, costs, and head count for each month. Costs and revenues are measured in dollars, but head count is measured in number of employees. Although all of these values can be displayed on a line chart using multiple vertical axes, this is generally not recommended. Because the values have widely different magnitudes (costs and revenues are in the tens of thousands, and head count is approximately 10 each month), it would be difficult to interpret changes on a single chart. Therefore, a table similar to Table 2.2 is recommended.

2.7 Other Specialized Charts

In this section, we discuss three additional chart types: the waterfall chart, the stock chart, and the funnel chart. Waterfall charts and stock charts are used primarily in financial analytics, while funnel charts are prominent in marketing and sales.

Waterfall Charts

A **waterfall chart** is a visual display that shows the cumulative effect of positive and negative changes on a variable of interest. The changes in a variable of interest are reported for a series of categories (such as time periods), and the magnitude of each change is represented by a column anchored at the cumulative height of the changes in the preceding categories.

Figure 2.29   Gossamer Data on Costs, Revenues, and Gross Profit

	A	B	C	D	E	F	G	H
1					**Month**			
2		**Jan**	**Feb**	**Mar**	**Apr**	**May**	**June**	**Total**
3	**Costs ($)**	48,123	56,458	64,125	52,158	54,718	50,985	326,567
4	**Revenues ($)**	64,124	66,125	67,125	48,178	51,785	55,678	353,015
5	**Gross Profit ($)**	16,001	9,667	3,000	-3,980	-2,933	4,693	26,448
6								

Continuing with the Gossamer Industries example from Section 2.6, consider the data in the file *gossamergp*. The data are shown in Figure 2.29. Gross profit is the difference between revenue and variable costs.

The following steps are used to create the waterfall chart of gross profit shown in Figure 2.30.

Step 1.   Select cells A2:H2. Hold down the control key (**Ctrl**) and also select cells A5:H5
Step 2.   Click the **Insert** tab on the Ribbon
Step 3.   Click the **Insert Waterfall, Funnel, Stock, Surface or Radar Chart** button 📊 ⌄ in the **Charts** group
         When the list of subtypes appears, click the **Waterfall** button 📊

In the initial chart, notice that the Total has been treated like another month. The following steps will make the total appear as in Figure 2.30.

Step 4.   Double-click the column Total to activate the **Format Data Series** task pane, and then click the column of data again to activate the **Format Data Point** task pane
Step 5.   When the **Format Data Point** task pane appears, click the **Series Options** button ▮▮▮
         Select the check box for **Set as total**
         Then, edit the chart as outlined in Section 2.2

Figure 2.30   A Waterfall Chart for the Gossamer Gross Profit Data

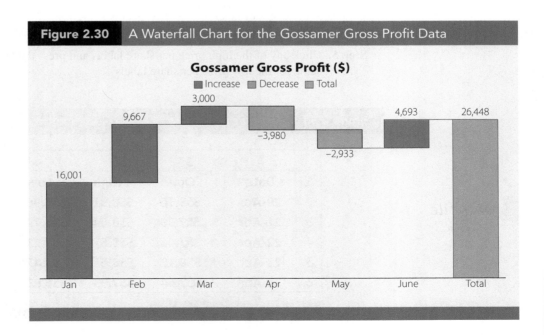

Figure 2.30 shows the gross profit by month, with blue indicating a positive gross profit and orange indicating a negative gross profit. The upper or lower level of the bar indicates the cumulative level of gross profit. For positive changes, the upper level of the bar is the cumulative level, and for negative changes, the lower end of the bar is the cumulative level. Here, we see that the cumulative level of gross profit rises from January to March, drops in April and May, and then increases in June to the cumulative gross profit of $26,448 for the six-month period.

Stock Charts

A **stock chart** is a graphical display of stock prices over time. Let us consider the stock price data for the telecommunication company Verizon Communications given in the file *verizon*. As shown in Figure 2.31, this data set lists, for five trading days in April, the date, opening price per share (price per share at the beginning of the trading day), the high price (highest price per share observed during the trading day), the low price (the lowest price per share observed during the trading day), and the closing price (the price per share at the end of the trading day).

Excel also provides an open-high-low-close stock chart, a volume-high-low-close stock chart, and a volume-open-high-low-close chart. These charts add data on a stock's opening price and trading volume to the basic high-low-close stock chart.

Excel provides four different types of stock charts. We illustrate the simplest one here, the high-low-close stock chart. A **high-low-close stock chart** is a chart that shows the high value, low value, and closing value of the price of a share of a stock at several points in time. The difference between the highest and lowest share prices for each point in time is represented by a vertical bar, and the closing share price by a marker on the bar.

The following steps are used to create Figure 2.32, the high-low-close stock chart for the Verizon stock price data.

Step 1. Select cells A1:A6. Hold down the control key (**Ctrl**), and also select cells C1:E6

Step 2. Click the **Insert** tab on the Ribbon

Step 3. Click the **Insert Waterfall, Funnel, Stock, Surface or Radar Chart** button in the **Charts** group

When the list of subtypes appears, click the **High-Low-Close** button

Edit the chart using the steps outlined in Section 2.2

The following steps add the closing price labels and markers.

Step 4. Click the **Chart Elements** button and select **Data Labels**

Step 4 places three sets of labels on each vertical bar (highest, closing, and lowest price per share). The following steps clean up the display.

Step 5. Click any of the high price per share labels and press the **Delete** key. Do the same for the low price per share labels

verizon

Figure 2.31	Stock Price Data for Verizon Communications

	A	B	C	D	E
1	Date	Open	High	Low	Close
2	20-Apr	$58.10	$58.91	$57.96	$58.13
3	21-Apr	$57.39	$58.04	$56.72	$56.82
4	22-Apr	$57.41	$58.57	$57.23	$57.99
5	23-Apr	$58.12	$58.66	$57.47	$57.59
6	24-Apr	$57.64	$57.99	$56.83	$57.93

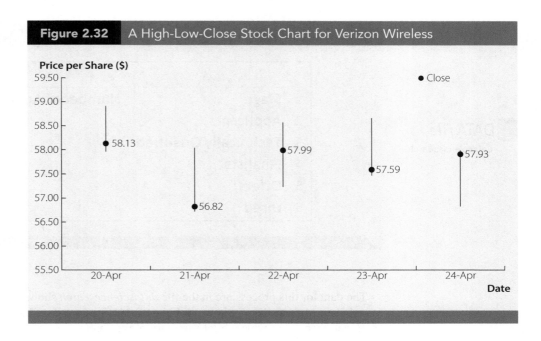

Figure 2.32 A High-Low-Close Stock Chart for Verizon Wireless

Step 6. On one of the vertical lines, click a data point directly next to one of the closing price labels

Step 7. When the **Format Data Series** task pane appears, click the **Fill & Line** button , then click **Marker**

Under **Fill**, select **Solid fill**, and to the right of **Color**, select **Black** from the drop down menu

Under **Border**, select **Solid line**, and to the right of **Color**, select **Black** from the drop down menu

To the right of **Width**, select **3 pt**

While typically used to display stock price data over time, a high-low-close stock chart can also be used to display the maximum, minimum, and mean (or median) of a variable of interest measured over a set of categories.

As shown in Figure 2.32, the closing prices per share over the five days are given. We see that on April 20, 21, and 23, the price closed near the low end of the trading price range. On April 24, the closing price was near the highest price of the day. On April 22, the closing price was near the middle of the trading price range.

Funnel Charts

Another specialized chart is a funnel chart. A **funnel chart** shows the progression of a quantitative variable for various categories from larger to smaller values. A funnel chart is often used to show the progression of sales leads that are converted through a series of steps to an eventual sale, but any progression of larger values to smaller values over a series of nested categories can be illustrated with a funnel chart. As an illustration, let us consider a company whose goal is to grow the number of well-qualified members on its data science team. The hiring process involves the following steps: (1) post the job ad; candidates apply and are then referred to as applicants, (2) applicants are given a technical test; those who pass are deemed technically qualified, (3) the technically qualified set of applicants are invited to do Zoom interviews, and based on the Zoom interviews, a subset of the technically qualified applicants are deemed finalists and are invited for on-site interviews, (4) based on test scores and the on-site interviews, a subset of the finalists are offered employment, and (5) those who accept are hired.

Figure 2.33 Data for Data Scientist Hiring

DATA *file*
datasciencesearch

	A	B
1	**Stage**	**Number of Applicants**
2	Applicants	51
3	Technically Qualified	37
4	Finalists	12
5	Offers	7
6	Hired	4

The data for this process are in the file *datasciencesearch* shown in Figure 2.33. A funnel chart of these data is shown in Figure 2.34. First, we give the steps for creating this chart, and then we provide a brief summary of the chart.

The following steps are used to create the funnel chart shown in Figure 2.34.

Step 1. Select cells A1:B6
Step 2. Click the **Insert** tab on the Ribbon
Step 3. Click the **Insert Waterfall, Funnel, Stock, Surface or Radar Chart** button 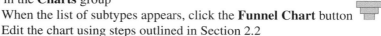 in the **Charts** group
When the list of subtypes appears, click the **Funnel Chart** button
Edit the chart using steps outlined in Section 2.2

The funnel chart shows the narrowing of the field of applicants as the process progresses. We see that the process started with 51 applicants and ended with 4 new hires. Specifically, we observe that the Zoom interviews narrowed the field from 37 technically qualified applicants to 12 finalists who were invited to interview on-site.

Figure 2.34 A Funnel Chart for Data Scientist Hiring

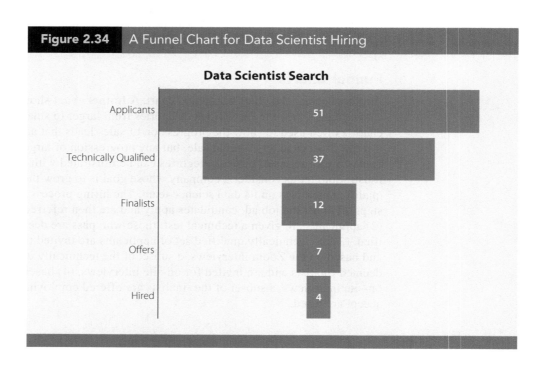

2.8 A Summary Guide to Chart Selection

In this section, we conclude the chapter with a discussion summarizing guidelines for chart selection.

Guidelines for Selecting a Chart

Recognizing that there are often exceptions to rules and that there are often disagreements even among data visualization experts, we provide general recommendations based on the goal of the visualization and the type of data being analyzed.

Goal: To Show a Relationship

scatter   bubble   line   stock   column   bar   heat map

To show a relationship between two quantitative variables, we recommend a scatter chart. An example is the temperature and snowfall data shown in a scatter chart in Figure 2.7. When dealing with three quantitative variables, a bubble chart can be used. Line charts can be used to emphasize the pattern across consecutive data points and are commonly used to display relationships over time. Stock charts show the relationship between time and stock price. Column charts, bar charts, and heat maps can be used to show the relationships that exist between categories.

Goal: To Show Distribution

scatter   bubble   column   bar   choropleth map

In addition to being useful for showing the relationships between quantitative variables, scatter and bubble charts can be useful for showing how the quantitative variable values are distributed over the range for each variable. For example, from the scatter chart in Figure 2.7, we can see that only 2 of the 51 cities have an average annual snowfall greater than 80 inches.

Other chart types useful for showing how data are distributed that rely on more advanced statistical concepts are discussed in Chapter 5.

Column and bar charts can be used to show the distribution of a variable of interest over discrete categories or time periods. For example, Figure 2.5 shows the distribution of zoo attendance by time (month). As previously mentioned, column charts rather than bar charts should be used for distribution over time, as it is more natural represent the progression of time from left to right. A choropleth map shows the distribution of a quantitative or categorical viable over a geographic space. Figures 2.19 and 2.21 are examples of these.

Goal: To Show Composition

bar   stacked bar   stacked column   treemap   waterfall   funnel

When the goal is to show the composition of an entity, a good choice is a bar chart, sorted by contribution to the whole. An example is the New York City budget in Figure 2.2. A stacked bar chart is appropriate for showing the composition of different categories, and a stacked column chart is good for showing composition over a time series. Figure 2.17, the sales for Cheetah Sports by region, is a good example of a stacked column chart with time series data.

While the goal of a pie chart is to show composition, for reasons discussed in the next section, we do not recommend the use of pie charts.

A treemap shows composition in a situation where there is a hierarchical structure among categorical variables. In Figure 2.26, we see the brand values (the quantitative variable of interest) for companies within industry sectors. For example, the technology sector is composed of six brands in the top 10. All other sectors are composed of only a single brand.

A waterfall chart shows the composition of a quantitative variable of interest over time or category. For example, Figure 2.30 shows the composition of the final value of gross profit over time. A funnel chart also shows composition in the sense that going from the bottom of the funnel to the top gives the composition of the original set at the top of the funnel. The funnel chart for the hiring process in Figure 2.34 is an example.

Goal: To Show Ranking

bar   column

Bar charts and column charts, sorted on the cross-sectional quantitative data of interest across categories, can be used to effectively show the rank order of categories on the quantitative variable. An example is the 10 categories ranked by spending allocation in the New York City budget shown in Figure 2.2.

When trying to select a chart type, we recommend starting with understanding the needs of the audience to determine the goal of the chart, understanding the types of data you have, and then selecting a chart based on the guidance provided in this section. Like most analytics tools, it is important to experiment with different approaches before arriving at a final decision on your data visualization.

Some Charts to Avoid

In this section, we discuss some charts that should be avoided. There are charts that many data visualization experts agree should be avoided. Usually, this is because a chart is overly cluttered or takes too much effort for most audiences to interpret the chart quickly and accurately. Here, we provide some guidance on charts we believe should be avoided in favor of other types of charts.

As we have already discussed in the data visualization makeover at the beginning of this chapter, many experts suggest that pie charts should be avoided. Instead of a pie chart, consider using a bar chart. This is because science has shown that we are better at assessing differences in length than angle and area. Small differences can be better detected in length than area, especially when sorted by length. Also, using a bar chart simplifies the chart in that there is no longer a need for a different color for each category. Figures 2.1 and 2.2 show the difference between the pie chart and the bar chart and illustrate why the latter is preferred.

A radar chart is also referred to as a spider chart or a web chart.

Another chart to be avoided is a radar chart. A **radar chart** is a chart that displays multiple quantitative variables on a polar grid with an axis for each variable. The quantitative values on each axis are connected with lines for a given category. Multiple categories can be overlaid on the same radar chart.

Let us consider data on four suppliers of a component needed by Newton Industries. Newton manufactures high-performance desktop computers and has started to vet four possible suppliers of one of the components needed for its computers. Newton's management needs to select a supplier to provide the component and has collected data on the percentage of late shipments, the percentage of defective components delivered, and the cost per unit each supplier would charge. These data are in the file *newtonsuppliers* and are shown in Figure 2.35. Figure 2.36 is the radar chart created from these data.

newtonsuppliers

Figure 2.35	Supplier Performance Data for a Component for Newton Industries

	A	B	C	D
1	Supplier	% Late	% Defective	Cost per Unit ($)
2	Ace	7	3	3.00
3	Beaty	10	4	3.00
4	Foster	3	1	3.00
5	Rolf	11	3	3.00

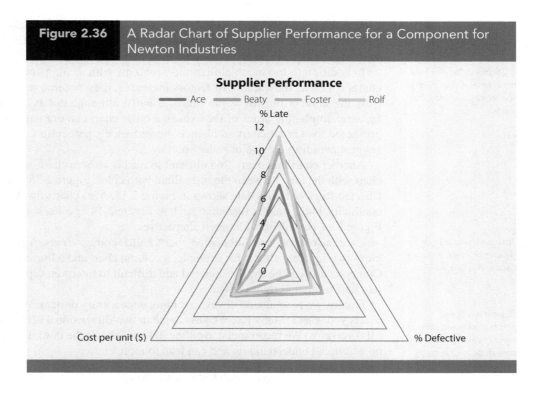

Figure 2.36   A Radar Chart of Supplier Performance for a Component for Newton Industries

The radar chart in Figure 2.36 has three axes corresponding to the three columns of data in Figure 2.35. Luckily, the three variables are of roughly the same magnitude. Variables of very different scales can distort a radar chart. The four suppliers each have their own color, and their data are connected by lines. Since Newton presumably wants low values for percentage late, percentage of defective components, and cost per unit, a dominant supplier's rectangle would be completely inside its competitors. It appears from Figure 2.36 that the supplier Foster might be the best choice, but it is difficult to distinguish the cost per unit. Even with this very small data set, the radar chart is quite busy and difficult for an audience to interpret.

Perhaps a better choice is the clustered column chart shown in Figure 2.37. Here, we can see that Foster is clearly better on percentage late and percentage defective and

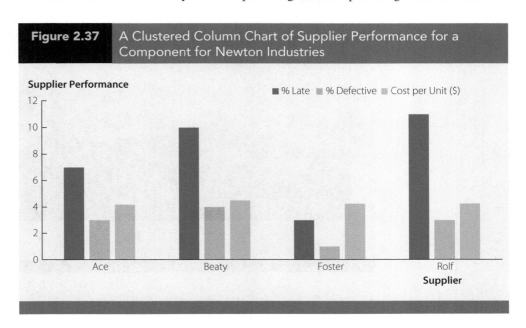

Figure 2.37   A Clustered Column Chart of Supplier Performance for a Component for Newton Industries

competitive on price. We do note that for more suppliers, even the clustered column chart will become cluttered. Not surprisingly, manufacturers will often develop a scoring model so a single score can be computed and used to compare suppliers.

In Chapter 3, we provide a more detailed discussion of how to remove clutter from charts.

In addition to too much clutter and problems with scaling, another criticism of radar charts is that as the number of factors increases, they become more circular and suffer from the same criticisms as pie charts. Finally, although not as obvious in our three-factor example, the order of the axes in a radar chart can dramatically alter the picture presented by a radar chart and hence the audience's perception. For these reasons, we suggest avoiding the use of radar charts.

Another chart that many find difficult to read is an area chart. An **area chart** is a line chart with the area between the lines filled with color. Figure 2.38 is an area chart of the Cheetah Regional sales data shown in Figure 2.13. Area charts display volume and convey continuity, but a simpler line chart such as Figure 2.14 or a stacked column chart such as Figure 2.17 provide less cluttered alternatives.

Dual-axis charts are one form of a combo chart; these are discussed in Chapter 9.

Excel also provides combination charts called combo charts. A **combo chart** combines two separate charts, for example, a column chart and a line chart, on the same chart. Combo charts can be overly cluttered and difficult to interpret, especially when they contain both a left and right vertical axis.

Unnecessary use of dimensionality and other chart design issues are discussed in more detail in Chapter 3.

Finally, we recommend always avoiding unnecessary dimensionality on any of the charts you select. Many Excel charts come in two-dimensional (2D) and three-dimensional (3D) versions. We recommend avoiding 3D versions as the third dimension typically adds no additional understanding and can lead to more clutter.

Excel's Recommended Charts Tool

Excel provides guidance for chart selection through its Recommended Charts tool. The **Recommended Charts** button is found in the **Charts** group of the **Insert** tab on the Ribbon. The following steps demonstrate the use of the Recommended Charts tool using the zoo attendance data in the file *zoo* shown in Figure 2.3.

DATA*file*

zoo

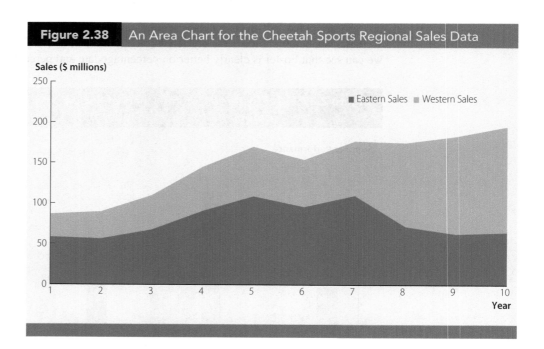

Figure 2.38   An Area Chart for the Cheetah Sports Regional Sales Data

Step 1. Select cells A1:B13
Step 2. Click the **Insert** tab on the Ribbon
Step 3. Click the **Recommended Charts** button   in the **Charts** group

The **Insert Chart** dialog box appears as shown in Figure 2.39. Four different chart types are recommended, a column chart (also shown to the right), a bar chart, a funnel chart, and a combination (combo) chart. Clicking on any of the four charts on the left will display that chart enlarged and to the right in the same way the column chart is displayed on the right in Figure 2.39. This allows you to see an enlarged version of the chart before committing to the chart.

Step 4. Select the **Clustered Column** chart and click **OK**
Edit the chart as outlined in Section 2.2

Figure 2.39   The Insert Chart Task Pane for the Zoo Attendance Data

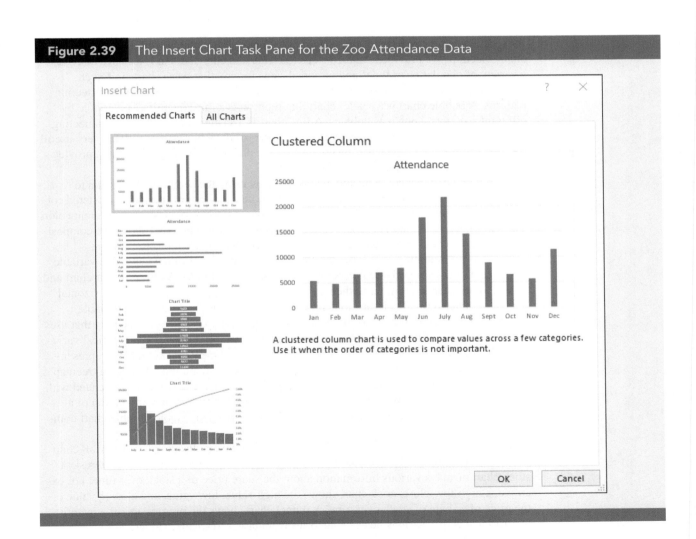

Notes + Comments

1. After clicking the **Recommended Charts** button, observe that selecting the **All Charts** tab from the **Insert Chart** task pane generates a listing of all available chart types. Selecting any of the listed charts provides a preview of the selected chart. Hence, an alternative to navigating the **Charts** group on the **Insert** tab on the Ribbon is to click the **Recommended Charts** button, select the **All Charts** tab and select from the list.

2. The Recommended Charts tool does not always recommend chart types consistent with the advice in this chapter. Indeed, sometimes chart types that we would not recommend show up as choices under Recommended Charts. Two examples are apparent in the last two choices shown in Figure 2.39. Using a funnel chart for the zoo attendance is a poor choice as there is no natural progression from high values to low values. Likewise, notice the combo chart sorts the months by decreasing order of attendance, which is not likely to be useful for these time series data if the goal is to better understand the pattern of attendance over time.

Summary

In this chapter, we discussed how the goal of the analysis and the type of data should inform chart selection. We provided detailed steps to create and edit charts in Excel. We discussed a variety of popular chart types and provided steps for creating these charts in Excel.

A scatter chart displays pairs of quantitative variables and is very useful for detecting patterns. A bubble chart is a scatter chart that represents a third quantitative variable by different size dots, known as bubbles. A line chart is a scatter chart with lines connecting the points. A line chart, like a scatter chart, is good for detecting patterns and is very useful for time series data. Line charts, by connecting the dots representing data points, provide more of a sense of continuity than scatter charts.

A column chart displays a quantitative variable by using the height of the column to denote the magnitude of the quantitative variable by category or time period. A clustered column chart is a column chart that displays multiple quantitative variables using different colors and side-by-side columns. A stacked column chart is a column chart that shows the composition for each column by using color to denote subcategory contributions to the total.

Similar to a column chart, a bar chart displays the magnitude of a quantitative variable using length but uses horizontal bars rather than vertical columns. A clustered bar chart and a stacked bar chart are similar to their column-chart counterparts, but they use horizontal bars rather than vertical columns to denote the magnitude of the quantitative variable.

We also discussed three types of maps. A choropleth map is a geographic map that uses shades of a color, different colors, or symbols to indicate quantitative or categorical variables by geographic region or area. A heat map is a two-dimensional graphical representation of data that uses different shades of color to indicate magnitude. Finally, a treemap uses different-sized rectangles and color to display quantitative data that is associated with hierarchical categories. We briefly discussed when to use a table or a combination of a table and a chart rather than a chart. If exact values are needed, a table or table/chart combination might be the best choice.

Three specialized charts, waterfall, stock, and funnel were discussed. A waterfall chart shows the cumulative effect of positive and negative changes on a variable of interest. A stock chart displays various information about the share price of a stock over time. For example, a high-low-close stock chart shows the high value, low value, and closing value of the price of a share of stock over time. A funnel chart shows the progression of a quantitative variable across various nested categories from larger to smaller values.

We provided guidance on how to select an appropriate chart based on the goal of the chart and the type of data being displayed. We also discussed some chart types to avoid. We concluded the chapter with a discussion of the Recommended Charts tool in Excel.

Glossary

Area chart A line chart with the area between the lines filled with color.

Bar chart A chart that displays a quantitative variable by category using the length of horizontal bars to display the magnitude of a quantitative variable.

Bubble chart A scatter chart that displays a third quantitative variable using different sized dots, which we refer to as bubbles.

Choropleth map A geographic map that uses shades of a color, different colors, or symbols to indicate quantitative or categorical variables by geographic region or area.

Clustered bar chart A chart that displays multiple quantitative variables for categories or time periods using the length of horizontal bars to denote the magnitude of the quantitative variables and separate bars and colors to denote the different categories.

Clustered column chart A chart that displays multiple quantitative variables for categories or time periods with different colors, with the height of the columns denoting the magnitude of the quantitative variable.

Column chart A chart that displays a quantitative variable by category or time period using vertical bars to display the magnitude of a quantitative variable.

Combo chart A chart that combines two separate charts, for example, a column chart and a line chart, on the same chart.

Funnel chart A chart that shows the progression of a quantitative variable for various nested categories from larger to smaller values.

Geographic map A chart that shows the characteristics and arrangement of the geography of our physical reality.

Heat map A two-dimensional graphical representation of data that uses different shades of color to indicate magnitude.

Hierarchical data Data that can be represented with a tree-like structure, where the branches of the tree lead to categories and subcategories.

High-low-close stock chart A chart that shows the high value, low value, and closing value of the price of a share of stock over time.

Line chart A chart that uses a point to represent a pair of quantitative variable values, one value along the horizontal axis and the other on the vertical axis, with a line connecting the points.

Radar chart A chart that displays multiple quantitative variables on a polar grid with an axis for each variable. The quantitative values on each axis are connected with lines for a given category.

Scatter chart A graphical presentation of the relationship between two quantitative variables. One variable is shown on the horizontal axis, the other is shown on the vertical axis, and a symbol is used to plot ordered pairs of the quantitative variable values.

Stacked bar chart A bar chart that uses color to denote the contribution of each subcategory to the total.

Stacked column chart A column chart that shows part-to-whole comparisons, either over time or across categories. Different colors, or shades of color, are used to denote the different parts of the whole within a column.

Stock chart A graphical display of stock prices over time.

Treemap A chart that uses the size, color, and arrangement of rectangles to display the magnitudes of a quantitative variable for different categories, each of which are further decomposed into subcategories. The size of each rectangle represents the magnitude of the quantitative variable within a category/subcategory. The color of the rectangle represents the category, and all subcategories of a category are arranged together.

Waterfall chart A visual display that shows the cumulative effect of positive and negative changes on a variable of interest. The basis of the changes can be time or categories, and changes are represented by columns anchored at the previous time or category's cumulative level.

Problems

Conceptual

1. **Sales by Region.** Consider the following data for percentage of sales by region. **LO 3**

Sales Region	Percentage of Total Sales
East	28%
North	14%
South	36%
West	22%

    a. Should a bar chart or a pie chart be used to display these data? Explain.
    b. List two ways to enhance the formatting of the chart to improve interpretability.

2. **Academic Makeup of Departments.** You are conducting an analysis of the makeup of the departments in your firm. Your goal is to compare the departments' mixes of academic backgrounds. You have defined the following categories for academic background: Business, Engineering, and Other. You have the percentage of employees in each category for each of the four departments as shown in the table below. **LO 3**

Department	Business	Engineering	Other
A	84%	0%	16%
B	45%	43%	12%
C	48%	20%	32%
D	17%	68%	15%

What type of chart is best suited to display these data?

3. **Charts of Gasoline Prices.** The following charts both show the average price (in dollars) per gallon of gasoline in the United States for 36 consecutive months. Consider the following charts. The first is a line chart and the second is a column chart. **LO 3**

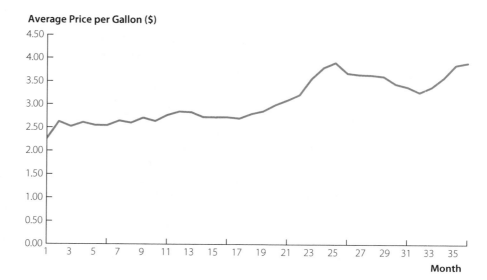

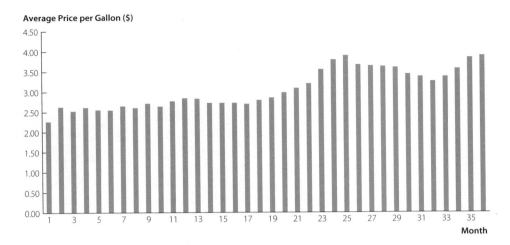

Which better displays the data? Why?

   i. Line chart

  ii. Column chart

4. **Pickup Truck Sales.** The following charts display the sales of pickup trucks in the United States by manufacturer for one year (source: *The Wall Street Journal*). You must choose one of these charts to edit to produce the final chart for your presentation to management. **LO 3, 5**

Which chart is best for displaying these data? Explain your answer.

   i. Column chart

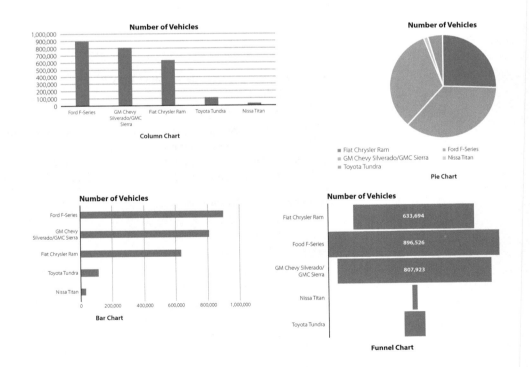

  ii. Pie chart

 iii. Bar chart

 iv. Funnel chart

5. **NCAA Women's Basketball.** Since 1994, the NCAA Division I women's basketball tournament has had a starting field of 64 teams and, over the course of 63 single-elimination games, a champion is determined. The following two charts (a funnel chart and a bar chart) show how the tournament progresses from the starting field of 64 teams. **LO 3**

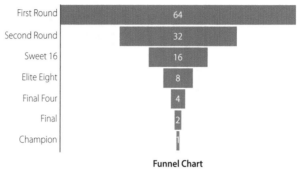

Funnel Chart

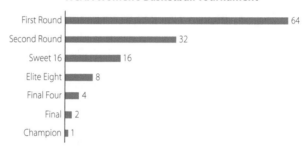

Bar Chart

Which chart best conveys these data? Why?
   i. Funnel chart
   ii. Bar chart

6. **Worldwide Robot Supply.** The International Federation of Robotics estimates the worldwide supply of industrial robots each year. The charts below show estimates of the worldwide supply of industrial robots for the years 2009–2021. The data are shown in two different charts below; the first is a line chart, and the second is a column chart. **LO 3**

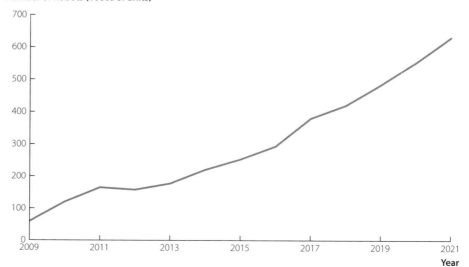

Industrial Robot Supply (1000s of units)

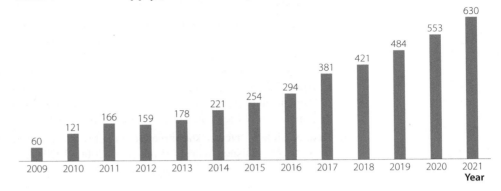

Which chart best displays these data? Why?
  i. Line chart
  ii. Column chart

7. **R&D Project Portfolio.** The Ajax Company uses a portfolio approach to manage their research and development (R&D) projects. Ajax wants to keep a mix of projects to balance the expected return and risk profiles of their R&D activities. Consider a situation in which Ajax has six R&D projects as characterized in the following table.

   Each project is given an expected rate of return and a risk assessment, which is a value between 1 and 10, where 1 is the least risky and 10 is the riskiest. Ajax would like to visualize their current R&D projects to keep track of the overall risk and return of their R&D portfolio. **LO 3**

Project	Expected Rate of Return (%)	Risk Estimated	Capital Invested ($ millions)
1	12.6	6.8	6.4
2	14.8	6.2	45.8
3	9.2	4.2	9.2
4	6.1	6.2	17.2
5	21.4	8.2	34.2
6	7.5	3.2	14.8

Which of the following chart types would be the most appropriate for these data? Explain your answer.
  i. Stacked bar chart
  ii. Line chart
  iii. Bubble chart
  iv. Funnel chart

8. **E-Marketing Campaign.** Gilbert Furniture has initiated a new marketing campaign for its high-end desk lamp. The analyst for e-commerce, Lauren Stevens, has been tracking the progress of the campaign and has collected the following data based on an email sent to the customer list: 68% opened the email, 29% clicked on the web link in the email, 11% added the desk lamp to their cart, and 9% purchased the lamp. **LO 3**

Which of the following is the most appropriate chart for these data?
  i. Funnel chart
  ii. Stacked bar chart

   iii. Line chart

   iv. Bubble chart

9. **Choosing the Best Chart Type.** Choose the most appropriate chart type (bar chart, bubble chart, choropleth map, line chart) for each data set described below. Use each chart type exactly once. **LO 3**
   a. Advertising budget, number of salespeople, percent of market share for 10 products
   b. Annual demand for potato chips (in tons) in the United States by state
   c. Annual sales in millions of dollars for seven regional salespeople
   d. Population of the United States for each year 1900–2020

10. **Disney Ticket Prices.** The three charts below show the price of a general admission ticket to Walt Disney World for the years 2000–2020. The first is a bar chart, the second is an area chart, and the third is a scatter chart. **LO 3**

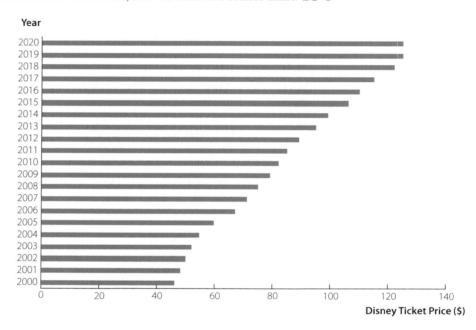

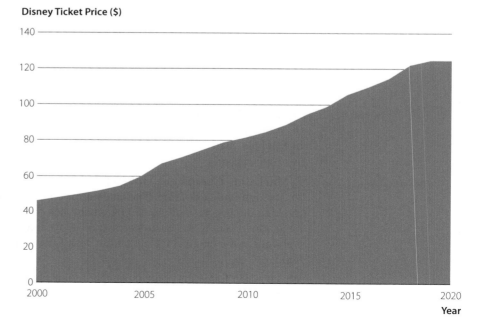

Disney Ticket Price ($)

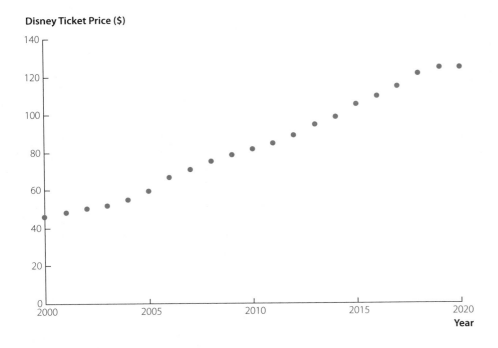

Which type of chart best displays these data? Why?
  i. Bar chart
  ii. Area chart
  iii. Scatter chart

11. **Exploring Private Colleges.** For a sample of 103 private colleges, data have been collected on year founded, tuition and fees (not including room and board), and the percentage of undergraduates who obtained their degree within six years (source: *The World Almanac*). The following two charts plot tuition versus year founded and graduation rate versus year founded, respectively. **LO 4**

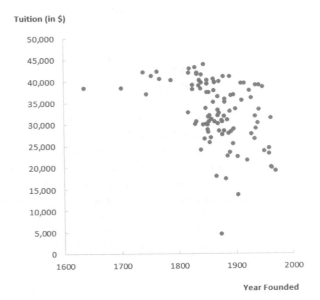

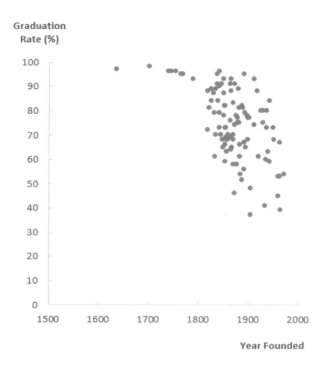

a. The two charts are the same type of chart. What type of chart are these?
   i. Line chart
  ii. Scatter chart
 iii. Stock chart
 iv. Waterfall chart

b. Which of the following statements best describes the relationship between tuition and year founded?
   i. Private colleges founded before 1800 are expensive, but there are greater differences in tuition for private colleges founded after 1800.
  ii. There is no apparent relationship between year founded and tuition for private colleges.
 iii. The newer the private college, the higher the tuition.

c. Which of the following best describes the relationship between graduation rate and year founded?
   i. There is no apparent relationship between year founded and graduation for private colleges.
  ii. The newer the private college, the higher the graduation rate.
 iii. Private colleges founded before 1800 have high graduation rates, but there are greater differences in graduation rates for private colleges founded after 1800.

12. **Vehicle Production Data.** The International Organization of Motor Vehicle Manufacturers (officially known as the Organisation Internationale des Constructeurs d'Automobiles, OICA) provides data on worldwide vehicle production by manufacturer. The following three charts, a line chart, a line chart with a table, and a clustered column chart, show vehicle production numbers for four different manufacturers for five recent years. **LO 3**

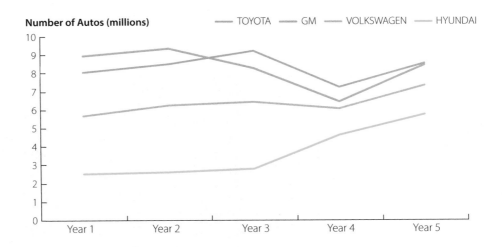

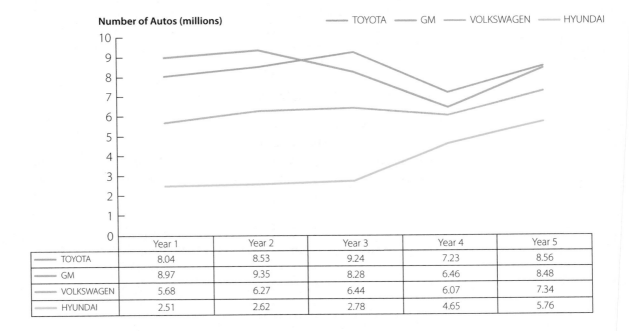

	Year 1	Year 2	Year 3	Year 4	Year 5
TOYOTA	8.04	8.53	9.24	7.23	8.56
GM	8.97	9.35	8.28	6.46	8.48
VOLKSWAGEN	5.68	6.27	6.44	6.07	7.34
HYUNDAI	2.51	2.62	2.78	4.65	5.76

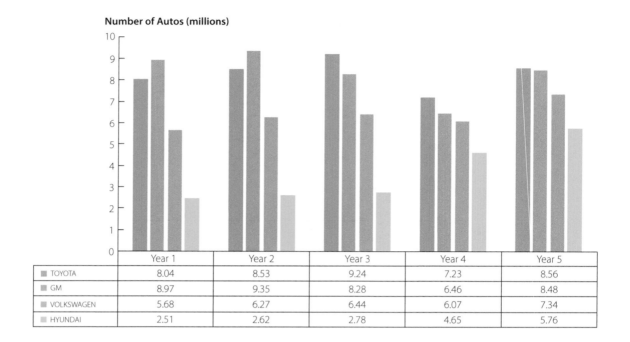

Number of Autos (millions)

	Year 1	Year 2	Year 3	Year 4	Year 5
▪ TOYOTA	8.04	8.53	9.24	7.23	8.56
▪ GM	8.97	9.35	8.28	6.46	8.48
▪ VOLKSWAGEN	5.68	6.27	6.44	6.07	7.34
▪ HYUNDAI	2.51	2.62	2.78	4.65	5.76

Which type of chart best displays these data? Why?
  i. Line chart
 ii. Line chart with table
iii. Clustered column chart with table

13. **Smartphone Ownership in Emerging Countries.** Suppose we have the following
survey results regarding smartphone ownership by age in emerging countries.
LO 3, 4

Age Category	Smartphone (%)	Other Cell Phone (%)	No Call Phone (%)
18–24	49	46	5
25–34	58	35	7
35–44	44	45	11
45–54	28	58	14
55–64	22	59	19
65+	11	45	44

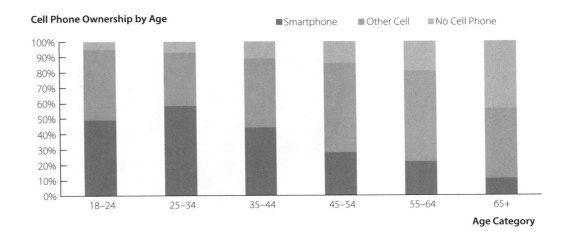

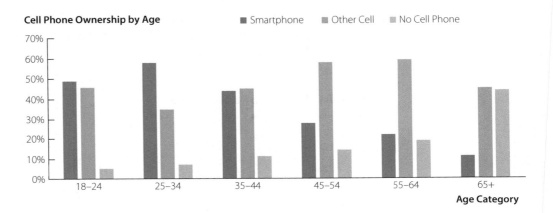

a. Which of the following charts best displays these data?
  i. Stacked column
  ii. Clustered column
b. Is the following statement true or false? Older people are less likely to own a smart-phone than a different type of cell phone compared to younger people.

14. **Home Goods Demand.** In supply chain planning, demand is often measured in pounds shipped. The following choropleth map shows the demand for home goods, measured in millions of pounds shipped for each state in the United States.
LO 4
a. Which five states have the highest demand?
b. Compare this map with Figure 2.19, which shows estimates of state population.

Does the demand for home goods appear to be related to population? Explain.

Home Goods Demand

Demand (in millions of pounds shipped)

87.6

3.7

Powered by Bing
© GeoNames, Microsoft, TomTom

15. **Coca-Cola Stock Prices.** The following stock chart shows stock price performance for Coca-Cola over a two-week period. Note that May 16 and May 17 are a Saturday and a Sunday and are nontrading days. **LO 4**

Coca-Cola Stock Price Performance

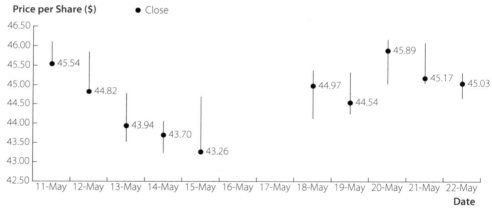

a. What type of chart is this?
b. Which day seems to have the most intra-day price variability?
c. What is the closing price on May 22?
d. If you bought 100 shares at the closing price on May 19 and sold all of those shares at the closing price on May 22, how much did you gain or lose (ignoring any transaction fees)?

16. **Day Trading.** In addition to the high, low, and closing price, an open-high-low-close stock chart uses the opening price per share to give an indication of the net change in the stock price from open to close on a given day. This is designated by a box inside the high-low range. The range of the box is determined by the opening and closing price per share. A black box indicates a loss, and a white box indicates a gain for that day. The length of the box indicates the magnitude of the loss or gain in share price. The following chart is an open-high-low-close chart for a two-week period for Coca-Cola. Note that May 16 and May 17 are a Saturday and a Sunday and are nontrading days.

Day trading is the practice of purchasing and then selling stock within the same day. As a novice day trader, your strategy is to buy at the start of the day and sell at the end of the day. **LO 4**

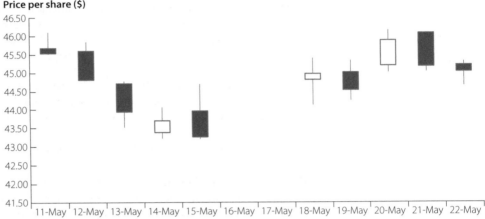

Coca-Cola Stock Price Performance

For which days would you have a gain, and for which would you have taken a loss (ignoring transaction costs) for the Coca-Cola data shown in the chart?

Applications

DATA *file*

smartspeaker

17. **Smart Speaker Usage.** Futuresource Consulting conducted a survey of owners of smart speakers to better understand how they use these devices (source: *The Wall Street Journal*). The file *smartspeaker* contains the percentage of the respondents who use their smart speaker for each of 11 activities. **LO 1, 2, 4**
    a. Construct a bar chart that shows the percentage of respondents by category. Use "How People Use Their Smart Speakers" for the chart title. Edit the chart to make it easier to interpret. Add data labels.
    b. Sort the data so percentages are ordered from smallest to largest, and note the differences in the corresponding chart.
    c. Of the categories in the survey, which is the most popular use of a smart speaker? Which is the least popular use?

DATA *file*

rideshare

18. **Age and Ridesharing.** A Gallup Poll showed that 30% of all Americans regularly use a ride-sharing service such as Lyft or Uber. The file *rideshare* contains the survey results by age category. **LO 1, 2, 4**
    a. Construct a column chart that shows the percentage of respondents who use a ride share by age category. Use "Who Uses Rideshare?" as the chart title and "Age (years)" as the horizontal axis title. Edit the chart to make it easier to interpret. Add data labels.
    b. Comment on the results.

DATA *file*

colleges

19. **Exploring Private Colleges (Revisited).** In this problem, we revisit the charts in Problem 11 showing the relationships between tuition and year founded and graduation rate and year founded. The two charts are similar. Consider the data in the file *colleges*. The file contains the following data for the sample of 102 private colleges: year founded, tuition and fees (not including room and board), and the percentage of undergraduates who obtained their degree within six years (source: *The World Almanac*). **LO 1, 2, 4**

a. Create a scatter chart to explore the relationship between tuition and percent who graduate. Use "Graduation Rate versus Tuition" as the chart title, "Tuition" as the horizontal axis title, and "Graduation Rate (%)" as the vertical axis title.

b. Comment on any apparent relationship.

20. **Top Management.** The Drucker Institute ranks corporations for managerial effectiveness based on a composite score derived from the following five factors: customer satisfaction, employee engagement and development, innovation, financial strength, and social responsibility. The file *managementtop25* contains the top 25 companies in the Institute's ranking based on the composite score (source: *The Wall Street Journal*). For each company, the industry sector, the company name, and the composite score are given. **LO 1, 2, 4**

managementtop25

a. Create a treemap chart using these data with the sector being the category, company being the subcategory, and the composite score being the quantitative variable. Use "Management Top 25" for the chart title. *Hint: Be sure to first sort the data by sector.*

b. In the sector with the most companies in the top 25, which company has the highest composite score?

21. **Biodiversity Preservation.** Ecologists often measure the biodiversity of a region by the number of distinct species that exist in the region. Nature reserves are lands specifically designated by the government to help maintain biodiversity. Care must be taken when setting up a network of nature reserves so the maximum number of species can exist in the network. Geography matters as well, as putting reserves too close together might subject the entire network to risks, such as devastation from wildfires. The initial step in this type of planning usually involves mapping the number of species that exist in each region. The file *species* contains the number of unique species that exist in each of the 50 states in the United States. **LO 1, 2, 4**

species

a. Create a choropleth map that displays number of species by state. Use "Number of Species per State" for the chart title. Add data labels.

b. Comment on the distribution of species over the United States. Which regions of the United States have relatively many species? Which regions have relatively few species?

c. Which two states have the most species?

22. **Disney Ticket Prices (Revisited).** In this problem, we revisit Problem 10, which displays the price of a general admission ticket to Walt Disney World for the years 2000–2020. However, these prices did not factor in inflation over these years. The file *disneypricesadjusted* gives the general admission price and the general admission price adjusted for inflation for the years 2000–2020. **LO 1, 2, 4**

disneypricesadjusted

a. Create a line chart that shows the price of admission and the adjusted price of admission for the years 2000–2020.

b. Explain what the adjusted ticket price data series shows that the nominal ticket price data series did not.

23. **Bubble Chart Labels.** The following bubble chart shows TSA wait time (in minutes) on the horizontal axis, cheapest daily parking rate on the vertical axis, and the size of each bubble is the number of enplanements in a year (measured in millions). The file *airportbubble_chart* contains this chart. **LO 2, 4**

airportbubble_chart

a. Using the following steps, add labels to the bubbles so the airport codes are easily identifiable with each bubble.

Step 1. Click anywhere on the chart

Step 2. Click the **Chart Elements** button ⊞ and select **Data Labels**
This puts the value of enplanements in each bubble

Step 3. Click the **Chart Elements** button ⊞ and move the cursor over **Data Labels**, and then select the black triangle on the right ☑ Data Labels ▶

Cheapest Parking Rate

TSA Time

to open a drop-down menu

From this drop-down menu, select **Other Options** to reveal the **Format Data Labels** task pane

Step 4. When the **Format Data Labels** task pane appears, under **Label Contains**, select **Value from Cells** and click the **Select Range…**button

When the **Data Label Range** dialog box opens, select cells A2:A16 in the worksheet

Click **OK**

Step 5. In the **Format Data Labels** task pane, deselect **Y Value** under **Label Contains**

   b. Which airport has the lowest TSA wait time?
   c. Which airport has the most enplanements?

24. **Regional Gains and Losses in Population.** The U.S. Census Bureau tracks shifts in population by each state and region in the United States. The net migration rate is an indicator of the movement of people from one area to another. A positive net migration rate means more people moved into the area than moved away, and a negative net migration rate means more people left the area than moved into the area. Mathematically, the net migration rate N is defined as follows:

$$N = \frac{(I - E)}{M} \times 1000$$

Where

I = number of people moving into the area in the year under consideration,

E = the number of people moving away from the area in the year under consideration, and

M = the mid-year population of the area.

The file *netmigration* contains net migration rates for four regions of the United States.
LO 1, 4

   a. Create a heat map using conditional formatting with the **Blue-White-Red Color Scale**.
   b. Which regions are losing population? Which regions are gaining population?

DATA*file*

netmigration

DATA_file_

bellevuebakery

25. **Income Statement.** An income statement is a summary of a company's revenues and costs over a given period of time. The data in the file *bellevuebakery* is an example of an income statement. It contains the revenues and costs for the last year for Bellevue Bakery. Revenues include gross sales and other income. Costs include returns, cost of goods sold, advertising, salaries/wages, other operating expenses, and taxes. In the income statement, there are intermediate calculations:

Net Sales = Gross Sales − Returns

Gross Profit = Net Sales − Other Income − Cost of Goods Sold

Net Income Before Taxes = Gross Profit − Advertising − Salaries/Wages − Other Operating Expenses

Net Income = Net Income Before taxes − Taxes

Create a waterfall chart of the income statement for Bellevue Bakery. Use "Bellevue Bakery Income Statement" for the chart title. Click the column associated with each of the calculations above and select **Set as Total**. Edit the chart to make it easier to interpret. **LO 1, 2**

26. **Marathon Records.** The file *marathonrecords* contains marathon world records for ages 6 to 90 for women and men (records for ages 9 and 10 are missing). **LO 1, 2, 4**

DATA_file_

marathonrecords

   a. Create a scatter chart with age on the horizontal axis and the women's marathon records on the vertical axis. Use "Female Marathon Records (in minutes)" as the vertical axis title and "Age (years)" as the horizontal axis title. Edit the chart to improve interpretation.

   b. Create a scatter chart with age on the horizontal axis and the men's marathon records on the vertical axis. Use "Male Marathon Records (minutes)" as the vertical axis title and "Age (years)" as the horizontal axis title. Edit the chart to improve interpretation.

   c. Create a scatter chart that plots both the women's records versus age and the men's records versus age. Select **Scatter with Straight Lines**. Use "Marathon Records (minutes)" as the vertical axis title and "Age (years)" as the horizontal axis title. Edit the chart to improve interpretation.

   d. Based on the charts in parts a, b, and c, what observations can you make regarding the women's and men's marathon records?

Chapter 2 Appendix

Appendix 2.1 Creating and Modifying Charts with Power BI

In this appendix, we discuss in detail how to create and modify a chart in Power BI.

Column and Bar Charts

The file *zoo* contains attendance at a zoo for 12 months. We demonstrate how to create a column chart of these data in Power BI.

DATA *file*

ZOO

Step 1. Following the steps outlined in Appendix 1.1, connect Power BI to the file *zoo*. Once the data are loaded, select Σ **Attendance**

In some of the steps described in this appendix, we give instructions to expand or collapse certain sections of Power BI. A section can be expanded by clicking on ❭ next to the section title. To collapse a section, click on ⌄ next to the section title.

Step 2. Click **Report view** on the left side of the Power BI window
In the **Visualizations pane** on the right side of the Power BI window, click on the **Build visual** icon to display the **Build visual matrix** of available charts
Select **Clustered column chart**
In the Data pane on the right side of the Power BI window, expand **Data** to display the variables
Drag **Month** from the **Data** pane to the **X-axis** box in the **Visualizations** pane
Drag Σ **Attendance** from the **Data** pane to the **Y-axis** box in the **Visualizations** pane
Increase the size of the chart by grabbing the bottom right corner and expanding it

The resulting chart is shown in Figure P2.1. Notice that Power BI has sorted by the values of *Attendance*. As can be verified by clicking on **Month** and Σ **Attendance** in the **Data** pane, the *Month* variable is a text data type, and the *Attendance* variable is a whole number data type. Next, we describe how to modify the chart to be in chronological order and how to edit the axis labels.

To be able to sort the data chronologically by *Month*, we need to create a new variable that gives the month number. For example, January is month 1, February is month 2, etc. The following steps are one way to create the month number:

Step 3. Click on **Table view** in the left margin. In the **Home** tab on the Ribbon, in the **Queries** group, click on the **Transform data** button and select **Transform data**
Click on the **Add Column** tab
In the **General** group, click on **Index Column** Index Column ▾ and select **From 1** from the drop-down menu
Click on the **Home** tab
Click on **Close & Apply** Close & Apply ▾ in the **Close** group on the far left side of the Ribbon

Figure P2.1   Column Chart for the Zoo Attendance Data

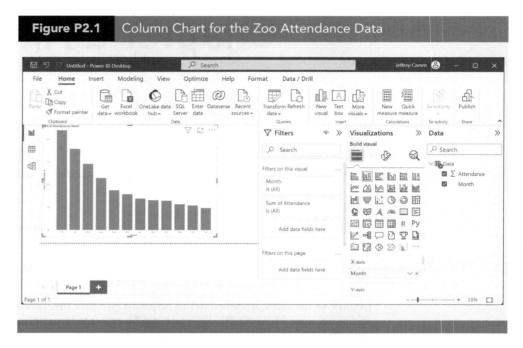

Step 4. Right click on the header **Index**, select **Rename**, type *MonthNumber*, and press **Enter**

The data should now appear as shown in Figure P2.2.

Step 5. Click on **Report view** 📊 and click on the column chart
Drag **Sum of MonthNumber** from the **Data** pane to the **Tooltips** box
In the upper right-hand corner of the chart, click on **More options** ⋯
Select **Sort axis, and** select **Sum of MonthNumber**
Click **More options** ⋯, select **Sort axis**, and select **Sort ascending**

Figure P2.2   Zoo Attendance Data with *Date* and *MonthNumber Variables Created*

Month	Attendance	Date	MonthNumber
Jan	5422	1 Jan 2023	1
Feb	4878	1 Feb 2023	2
Mar	6586	1 Mar 2023	3
Apr	6943	1 Apr 2023	4
May	7876	1 May 2023	5
Jun	17843	1 Jun 2023	6
July	21967	1 July 2023	7
Aug	14542	1 Aug 2023	8
Sept	8751	1 Sept 2023	9
Oct	6454	1 Oct 2023	10
Nov	5677	1 Nov 2023	11
Dec	11422	1 Dec 2023	12

`1 MonthNumber = MONTH([Date])`

Table: Data (12 rows) Column: MonthNumber (12 distinct values)

Step 5 results in the months appearing in chronological order from left to right.

Step 6. In the **Visualizations** pane, click on the **Format visual** button. To edit the
horizontal axis title and values, click **Visual** in the **Visualizations** pane
        Expand **X-axis**, scroll down to **Title**, and expand it.
        Select **Calibri** as the **Font** and **16** as the font size. Click on the **Bold** button B
        Collapse **Title** and expand **Values**.
        Select **Calibri** as the **Font** and **14** as the font size
        Collapse **Values**
        Collapse **X-axis**

Step 7. Expand **Y-axis**. Next to **Title**, toggle the **On** button to **Off** to hide the
vertical axis title
        Expand **Values**. Select **Calibri** as the **Font** and **14** as the font size
        Collapse **Values**.
        Expand **Range** and enter *25000* in the **Maximum** box
        Collapse **Range**. Collapse **Y-axis**. Next to **Legend**, toggle the **On** button
        to **Off** to turn off the legend
        Collapse **Legend**

Step 8. In the **Visualizations** pane, to the right of **Visuals**, click on **General**
        Expand **Title**.
        Edit the **Text** box to read *Attendance*. Select **Calibri** as the **Font** and **16** as
        the font size. Click on the **Bold** button B
        Collapse **Title**

Step 9. To remove the faint gridlines in the chart, click on **Visual** in the **Visualizations**
pane.
        Expand **Gridlines**
        Next to **Horizontal**, toggle the **On** button to **Off** to hide the horizon-
        tal grid lines
        Collapse **Gridlines**

Steps 5 through 9 produce the column chart shown in Figure P2.3.

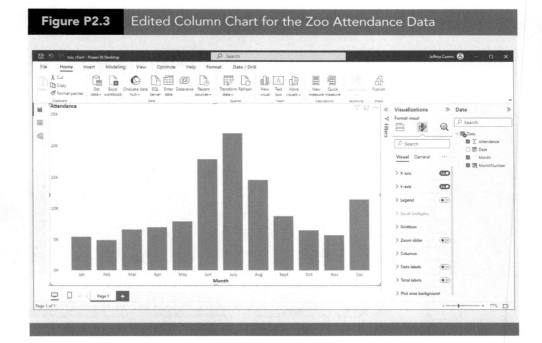

Figure P2.3 Edited Column Chart for the Zoo Attendance Data

CHART *file*

zoo_chart.pbix

*It is possible to export the chart as a PDF file by clicking **File** in the Ribbon, clicking **Export**, and then selecting **Export to PDF**.*

Power BI Desktop does not directly allow for copying the chart to place it in a Word or Power Point document. Instead, you will need to size the chart as desired (using the edges of the figure) and then use another tool such as the Snipping Tool that is available in Windows to copy and paste the chart into Word or Power Point. Figure P2.4 shows the chart of the zoo attendance data after editing and being copied with the Sniping Tool.

Scatter Charts

The file *snow* contains the average low temperature in degrees Fahrenheit and the average annual snow in inches for 51 major cities in the United States. We demonstrate how to create a scatter chart of these data in Power BI.

Step 1. Following the steps outlined in Appendix 1.1, connect Power BI to the file *snow*

DATA*file*
snow

In some of the steps described in this appendix, we give instructions to expand or collapse certain sections of Power BI. A section can be expanded by clicking on ❯ next to the section title. To collapse a section, click on ﹀ next to the section title.

Step 2. In the **Data** pane, expand **Data** to display the variables

*For scatter charts, you need to convert the variables to **Don't Summarize** to plot the individual data points.*

Click on Σ **Average Low Temperature** (not the checkbox but the variable name so it is highlighted)

Click the **Column tools** tab in the Ribbon.

In the **Properties** group, click the Σ **Summarization** box and select **Don't Summarize**

Step 3. Click on Σ **Average Snowfall** (not the checkbox but the variable name so it is highlighted)

Click the **Column tools** tab in the Ribbon.

In the **Properties** group, click the Σ **Summarization** box and select **Don't Summarize**

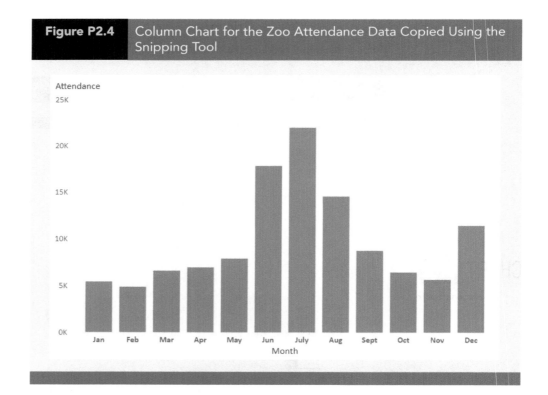

| **Figure P2.4** | Column Chart for the Zoo Attendance Data Copied Using the Snipping Tool |

Step 4. Click **Report** view on the left side of the Power BI window

In the **Visualizations** pane on the right side of the Power BI window, click

on the **Build visual** icon to display the **Build visual** matrix of available charts

Select **Scatter chart**

Drag **Average Low Temperature** from the **Data** pane to the **X-Axis** box in the **Visualizations** pane

Drag **Average Snowfall** from the **Data** pane to the **Y-Axis** box in the **Visualizations** pane

Increase the size of the chart by grabbing the bottom right corner and expanding

Step 5. In the **Visualizations** pane, click on the **Format visual** button

To edit the horizontal axis title and values, click **Visual** in the **Visualizations** pane, expand **X-axis**, scroll down to **Title**, and expand it

Select **Calibri** as the **Font** and **16** as the font size.

Click on the **Bold** button B

Collapse **Title** and expand **Values.**

Select **Calibri** as the **Font** and **14** as the font size

Collapse **Values**

Collapse **X-axis**

Step 6. Expand **Y-axis.** Next to **Title**, toggle the **On** button to **Off** to hide the vertical axis title

Expand **Values.**

Select **Calibri** as the **Font** and **14** as the font size

Collapse **Values**

Collapse **Y-axis**

Step 7. In the **Visualizations** pane, to the right of **Visuals**, click on **General**. Expand **Title**

Edit the **Text** box to read *Average Snowfall.*

Select **Calibri** as the **Font** and **16** as the font size. Click on the **Bold** button B

Collapse **Title**

Step 8. To remove the faint gridlines in the chart, click on **Visual** in the **Visualizations** pane

Expand **Gridlines**

Next to **Horizontal**, toggle the **On** button to **Off** to hide the horizontal grid lines

Next to **Vertical**, toggle the **On** button to **Off** to hide the vertical grid lines

Collapse **Gridlines**

Steps 1–8 result in the chart shown in Figure P2.5. Notice that some of the dots in the scatter plot appear cut off by the horizontal axis and by the top edge of the chart under the title. This can be remedied by expanding the range of the axes using the following steps.

Step 9. Click on the chart. In the **Visualizations** pane, click on the **Format your visual** button , and click **Visual**

Expand **Y-axis**, and then expand **Range**

In the **Minimum** box, type −*1*, and in the **Maximum**, box type *101*

Collapse **Range**

Collapse **Y-axis**

Figure P2.5   Scatter Chart for the Snowfall Data

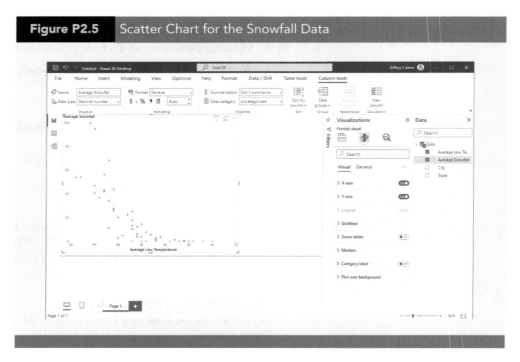

Step 10. In the **Visualizations** pane, expand **X-axis**, and then expand **Range**
In the **Minimum** box, type *30*, and in the **Maximum** box, enter *75*.
Collapse **Range**
Collapse **X-axis**

CHART *file*

snow_chart.pbix

Figure P2.6 shows the resulting chart after completing steps 9 and 10.

Figure P2.6   Completed Scatter Chart for the Snowfall Data after Adjusting the Axes Ranges

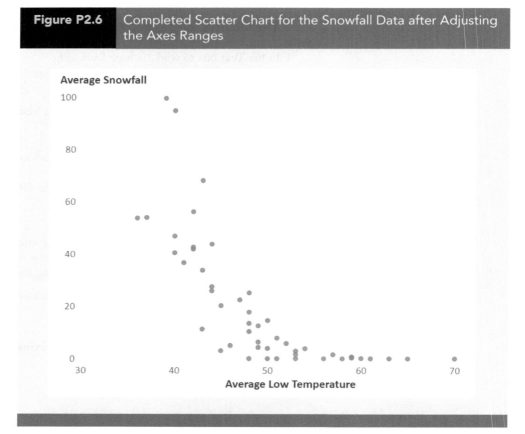

Bubble Charts

Next, we demonstrate how to create a bubble chart. The file *airportdata* contains data on a sample of 15 airports. The file contains the following quantitative variables: average wait time in the nonpriority Transportation Security Authority (TSA) queue (measured in minutes), the cheapest on-site daily rate for parking at the airport (measured in dollars), and the number of enplanements in a year, which is defined as the number of passengers who board, including transfers (measured in millions of passengers). The following steps will create a bubble chart.

airportdata

> **Step 1.** Following the steps outlined in Appendix 1.1, connect Power BI to the file *airportdata*

In some of the steps described in this appendix, we give instructions to expand or collapse certain sections of Power BI. A section can be expanded by clicking on > next to the section title. To collapse a section, click on ⌄ next to the section title.

> **Step 2.** In the **Data** pane, expand **Data** to display the variables
> Click on Σ **TSA wait time (minutes)** (not the checkbox but the variable name so it is highlighted) in the **Data** pane
> Click **Column tools** in the Ribbon
> In the **Properties group**, select **Don't summarize** from the drop-down menu in the **Summarization** box

For bubble charts, convert the variables for the X and Y axes to Don't Summarize *to plot the individual data points.*

> **Step 3.** Click on Σ **Cheapest on-site parking cost (per day)** (the variable name not the check box) in the **Data** pane
> Click **Column tools** in the Ribbon
> In the **Properties group**, select **Don't summarize** from the drop-down menu in the **Summarization** box

> **Step 4.** Click **Report** view 📊 on the left side of the Power BI window
> In the **Visualizations** pane on the right side of the Power BI window, click on the **Build visual** icon ▦ to display the **Build visual** matrix of available charts
> Select **Scatter chart** 📈
> In the Data pane, expand **Data** to display the variables
> Drag **TSA Wait Time (minutes)** from the **Data** pane to the **X-Axis** box in the **Visualizations** pane
> Drag **Cheapest on-site parking cost (per day)** from the **Data** pane to the **Y-Axis** box in the **Visualizations** pane
> Drag **Annual Enplanements (millions of passengers)** from the **Data** pane to the **Size** box in the **Visualizations** pane
> Increase the size of the chart by grabbing the bottom right corner and expanding

Figure P2.7 shows the result, which is a bubble chart with TSA wait time (minutes) on the horizontal axis, cheapest on-site parking (per day) on the vertical axis, and the size of the bubble indicates the annual enplanements (millions of passengers).

The following steps edit the chart.

> **Step 5.** In the **Visualizations** pane, click on the **Format visual** button 🖌
> To edit the horizontal axis title and values, click **Visual**, expand **X-axis**, and expand **Title**
> Select **Calibri** as the **Font** and **16** as the font size.
> Click on the **Bold** button B
> Collapse **Title** and expand **Values**
> Select **Calibri** as the font and **14** as the font size
> Collapse **Values**
> Collapse **X-axis**

Figure P2.7   Bubble Chart of the Airport Data Before Editing

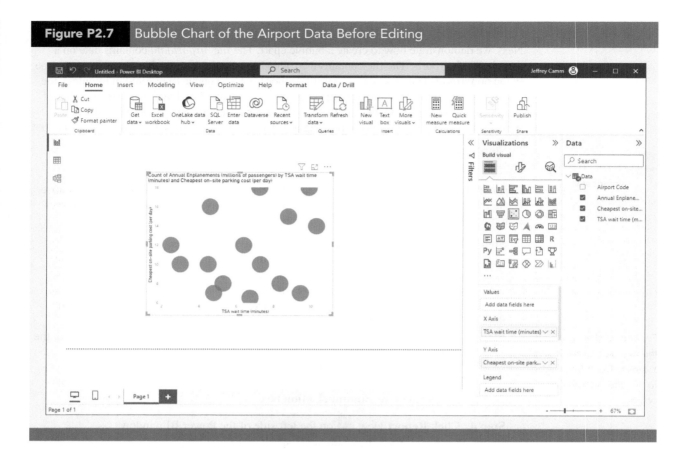

Step 6. Expand **Y-axis**, and expand **Title**
  Select **Calibri** as the font and **16** as the font size.
  Click on the **Bold** button Β Collapse **Title**, and expand **Values**
  Select **Calibri** as the **Font** and **14** as the font size
  Collapse **Values**, and expand **Range**
  Type *0* in the **Minimum** box
  Type *20* in the **Maximum** box
  Collapse **Range**, and collapse **Y-axis**

Step 7. To remove the faint gridlines in the chart, click on **Visual** in the **Visualizations** pane
  Expand **Gridlines**
  Next to **Horizontal**, toggle the **On** button to **Off** to hide the horizontal grid lines
  Next to **Vertical**, toggle the **On** button to **Off** to hide the vertical grid lines
  Collapse **Gridlines**

Step 8. In the **Visualizations** pane, to the right of **Visuals**, click on **General**. Expand **Title**
  Edit the **Text** box to read *Size is proportional to enplanements (millions of passengers).*
  Select **Calibri** as the **Font** and **16** as the font size. Click on the **Bold** button Β
  Under Horizontal alignment, click **Center**
  Collapse **Title**

The resulting chart is shown in Figure P2.8.

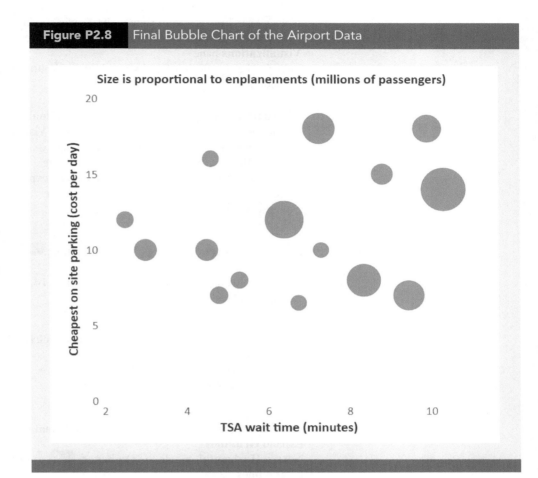

Figure P2.8   Final Bubble Chart of the Airport Data

CHART *file*

airportdata_chart.pbix

Line Charts

As an example of how to create a line chart in Power BI, let us consider Cheetah Sports. Cheetah sells running shoes and has retail stores in shopping malls throughout the United States. The file *cheetah* contains the last 10 years of sales for Cheetah Sports, measured in millions of dollars. The following steps create a line chart.

DATA *file*

cheetah

> **Step 1.** Following the steps outlined in Appendix 1.1, connect Power BI to the file
> *cheetah*

In some of the steps described in this appendix, we give instructions to expand or collapse certain sections of Power BI. A section can be expanded by clicking on ❯ next to the section title. To collapse a section, click on ⌄ next to the section title.

> **Step 2.** Click **Report** view 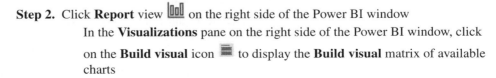 on the right side of the Power BI window
> In the **Visualizations** pane on the right side of the Power BI window, click
> on the **Build visual** icon  to display the **Build visual** matrix of available
> charts

Select **Line chart** 〰️
In the Data pane, expand **Data** ＞ ▦ Data to display the variables
Drag Σ **Year** from the **Data** pane to the **X-axis** box in the **Visualizations** pane
Drag Σ **Sales ($millions)** from the **Data** pane to the **Y-axis** box in the **Visualizations** pane
Increase the size of the chart by grabbing the bottom right corner and expanding

Step 3. In the **Visualizations** pane, click on the **Format visual** button 🖒
To edit the horizontal axis title and values, click **Visual** in the **Visualizations** pane, expand **X-axis,** scroll down to **Title**, and expand it
Select **Calibri** as the **Font** and **16** as the font size.
Click on the **Bold** button B, Collapse **Title**, and expand **Values**
Select **Calibri** as the font and **14** as the font size
Collapse **Values**
Collapse **X-axis**

Step 4. Expand **Y-axis**. Next to **Title**, toggle the **On** button `On ●` to **Off** to hide the vertical axis title
Expand **Values**. Select **Calibri** as the **Font** and **14** as the font size
Collapse **Values**
Collapse **Y-axis**

Step 5. In the **Visualizations** pane, to the right of **Visuals**, click on **General**. Expand **Title**
Edit the **Text** box to read *Sales ($ millions)*
Select **Calibri** as the **Font** and **16** as the font size.
Click on the **Bold** button B
Collapse **Title**

Step 6. To remove the faint gridlines in the chart, click on **Visual** in the **Visualizations** pane
Expand **Gridlines**
Next to **Horizontal**, toggle the **On** button `On ●` to **Off** to hide the horizontal grid lines
Next to **Vertical**, toggle the **On** button `On ●` to **Off** to hide the vertical grid lines
Collapse **Gridlines**

Steps 1–6 result in the line chart shown in Figure P2.9.

Next, we consider a line chart with multiple lines. Cheetah Sports has two sales regions: the eastern region and the western region. The file *cheetahregion* contain sales data for the two regions for a 10-year period. The following steps will create a line chart with multiple lines.

Step 1. Following the steps outlined in Appendix 1.1, connect Power BI to the file *cheetahregion*

DATA *file*

cheetahregion

In some of the steps described in this appendix, we give instructions to expand or collapse certain sections of Power BI. A section can be expanded by clicking on ＞ next to the section title. To collapse a section, click on ⌄ next to the section title.

Step 2. Click **Report** view 📊 on the left side of the Power BI window
In the **Visualizations** pane on the right side of the Power BI window, click on the **Build visual** icon ▤ to display the **Build visual** matrix of available charts
Select **Line chart** 〰️
In the Data pane, expand **Data** ＞ ▦ Data to display the variables
Drag Σ **Year** from the **Data** pane to the **X-axis** box in the **Visualizations** pane

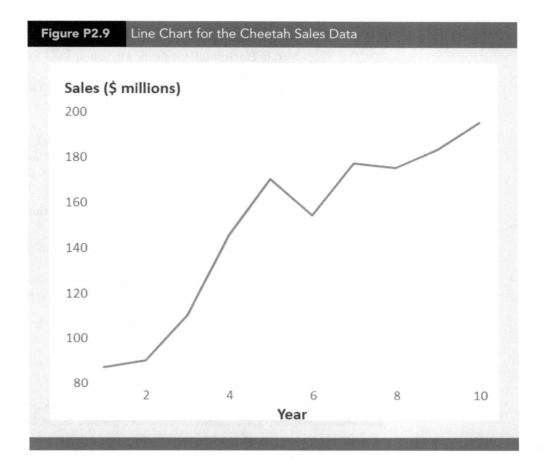

Figure P2.9   Line Chart for the Cheetah Sales Data

CHART *file*

cheetah_chart.pbix

Drag Σ **Eastern Sales** from the **Data** pane to the **Y-axis** box in the **Visualizations** pane

Drag Σ **Western Sales** from the **Data** pane to the **Y-axis** box in the **Visualizations** pane

Increase the size of the chart by grabbing the bottom right corner and expanding

Step 3. In the **Visualizations** pane, click on the **Format visual** button ✍

To edit the horizontal axis title and values, expand **X-axis**, and expand **Title**

Select **Calibri** as the **Font** and **16** as the font size.

Click on the **Bold** button B, Collapse **Title**, and expand **Values**

Select **Calibri** as the **Font** and **14** as the font size

Collapse **Values**

Collapse **X-axis**

Step 4. Expand **Y-axis**. Next to **Title**, toggle the **On** button `On●` to **Off** to hide the vertical axis title

Expand **Values.** Select **Calibri** as the **Font** and **14** as the font size

Collapse **Values**

Collapse **Y-axis**

Step 5. Expand **Legend** and expand **Text**

Select **Calibri** as the font and **12** as the font size. Collapse **Text**

To change the legend from circles to lines, expand **Options**, and in the **Style** drop-down menu, select **Line**

Collapse **Legend**

Step 6. To remove the faint gridlines in the chart, click on **Visual** in the **Visualizations** pane.
Expand **Gridlines**
Next to **Horizontal**, toggle the **On** button to **Off** to hide the horizontal grid lines
Next to **Vertical**, toggle the **On** button to **Off** to hide the vertical grid lines
Collapse **Gridlines**

Step 7. In the **Visualizations** pane, to the right of **Visuals**, click on **General**. Expand **Title**
Edit the **Text** box to read *Sales by Region ($ millions)*.
Select **Calibri** as the **Font** and **16** as the font size. Click on the **Bold** button B
Collapse **Title**

Step 8. To change the labels in the legend, in the **Visualizations** pane, click on the
Build visual icon
In the **Y-axis** box, right click on **Sum of Eastern States**, and select **Rename for this Visual**.
Type *Eastern States*, and press **Enter**
In the **Y-axis** box, right click on **Sum of Eastern States**, and select **Rename for this Visual**.
Type *Western States*, and press **Enter**

Steps 1–8 result in the chart shown in Figure P2.10.

CHART *file*

cheetah_mulitple_line_chart.pbix

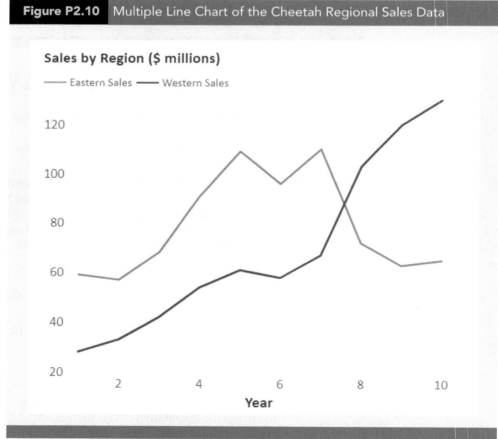

Figure P2.10   Multiple Line Chart of the Cheetah Regional Sales Data

Sales by Region ($ millions)
—— Eastern Sales —— Western Sales

Clustered and Stacked Column Charts

Next, we use the Cheetah regional sales data to illustrate how to construct a clustered column chart and a stacked column chart. The following steps will create a clustered column chart.

cheetahregion

> **Step 1.** Following the steps outlined in Appendix 1.1, connect Power BI to the file *cheetahregion*

In some of the steps described in this appendix, we give instructions to expand or collapse certain sections of Power BI. A section can be expanded by clicking on $>$ next to the section title. To collapse a section, click on $\vee$ next to the section title.

> **Step 2.** Click **Report** view on the left side of the Power BI window
>
> In the **Visualizations** pane on the right side of the Power BI window, click on the **Build visual** icon to display the **Build visual** matrix of available charts Select **Clustered column chart**
>
> In the **Data** pane, expand **Data** $>$ Data to display the variables
> Drag Σ **Year** from the **Data** pane to the **X-axis** box in the **Visualizations** pane
> Drag Σ **Eastern Sales** from the **Data** pane to the **Y-axis** box in the **Visualizations** pane
> Drag Σ **Western Sales** from the **Data** pane to the **Y-axis** box in the **Visualizations** pane
> Increase the size of the chart by grabbing the bottom right corner and expanding

> **Step 3.** In the **Visualizations** pane, click on the **Format visual** button
> To edit the horizontal axis title and values, expand **X-axis** and expand **Title**
> Select **Calibri** as the **Font** and **16** as the font size.
> Click on the **Bold** button B
> Collapse **Title** and expand **Values**
> Select **Calibri** as the **Font** and **14** as the font size
> Collapse **Values**
> Collapse **X-axis**

> **Step 4.** Expand **Y-axis**. Next to Title, toggle the **On** button to **Off** to hide the vertical axis title
> Expand **Values**
> Select **Calibri** as the **Font** and **14** as the font size.
> Collapse **Values**
> Collapse **Y-axis**

> **Step 5.** Expand **Legend** and expand **Text**
> Select **Calibri** as the font and **12** as the font size
> Collapse **Text**
> Collapse **Legend**

> **Step 6.** To remove the faint gridlines in the chart, click on **Visual** in the **Visualizations** pane
> Expand **Gridlines**
> Next to Horizontal, toggle the **On** button to **Off** to hide the horizontal grid lines
> Next to Vertical, toggle the **On** button to **Off** to hide the vertical grid lines
> Collapse **Gridlines**

Step 7. To change the text in the legend, in the **Visualizations** pane, click on the **Build visual** icon ▦

> In the **Y-axis** box, right click on **Sum of Eastern States**, select **Rename for this Visual**, type *Eastern States*, and press **Enter**
> In the **Y-axis** box, right click on **Sum of Eastern States**, select **Rename for this Visual**, type *Western States*, and press **Enter**

Step 8. In the **Visualizations** pane, click on the **Format visual** button 👆
> To the right of Visual, click on **General**
> Expand **Title**
> Edit the **Text** box to read *Sales by Region ($ millions)*.
> Select **Calibri** as the **Font** and **16** as the font size. Click on the **Bold** button B
> Collapse **Title**

Steps 1–8 result in the chart shown in Figure P2.11.

You can also change this clustered chart to a stacked chart by clicking on the **Build visual** icon ▦ and selecting the **Stacked column chart** icon ▥

CHART *file*

cheetahregion_cluster_chart.pbix

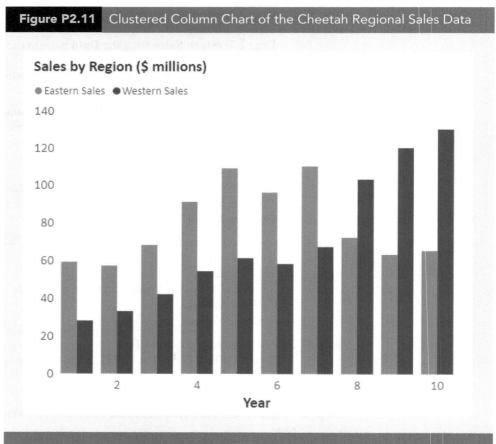

Figure P2.11   Clustered Column Chart of the Cheetah Regional Sales Data

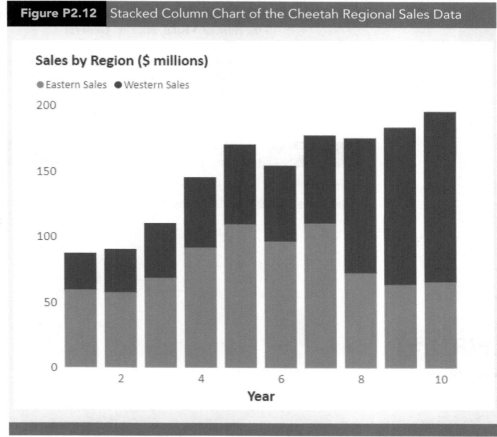

Figure P2.12   Stacked Column Chart of the Cheetah Regional Sales Data

CHART *file*

cheetahregion_stacked_chart.pbix

Choropleth Maps

In this section, we show how to create a choropleth map in Power BI. The file *statepopulation* contains populations for the 50 U.S. states.

DATA *file*

statepopulation

Step 1. Following the steps outlined in Appendix 1.1, connect Power BI to the file *statepopulation*

In some of the steps described in this appendix, we give instructions to expand or collapse certain sections of Power BI. A section can be expanded by clicking on 〉 next to the section title. To collapse a section, click on ⌄ next to the section title.

If the Shape map does not appear as an option, click on File, click on Option and settings, click on Options, select Preview features and select Shape map visual. You may have to restart Power BI for this change to take effect.

Step 2. Click **Report** view 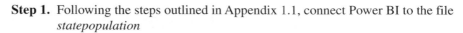 on the left side of the Power BI window
In the **Visualizations** pane on the right side of the Power BI window, click on the **Build visual** icon ▦ to display the **Build visual** matrix of available charts Select **Shape map** ⬡

Step 3. Click **Report** view 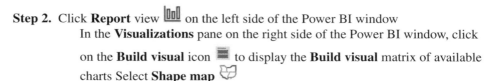 on the left side of the Power BI window
In the **Data** pane, expand **Data** 〉 ▦ Data to display the variables
Drag **State** from the **Data** pane to the **Location** box in the **Visualizations** pane
Drag **Σ Estimated 2020 Population** from the **Data** pane to the **Color Saturation** box in the **Visualizations** pane
Increase the size of the chart by grabbing the bottom right corner and expanding

Step 4. In the **Visualizations** pane, click on the **Format visual** button .
To the right of **Visual**, click on **General**
Expand **Title**
Edit the **Text** box to read *Estimated 2020 Population by State*.
Select **Calibri** as the **Font** and **16** as the font size. Click on the **Bold** button B
Collapse **Title**

Steps 1–4 result in the map shown in Figure P2.13

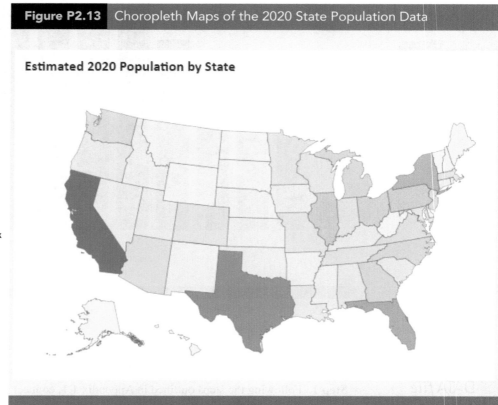

| **Figure P2.13** | Choropleth Maps of the 2020 State Population Data |

Estimated 2020 Population by State

CHART *file*

statepopulation_map_chart.pbix

Appendix 2.2 Creating and Modifying Charts with Tableau

In this appendix, we discuss in detail how to create and modify charts in Tableau.

Column and Bar Charts

Tableau refers to both vertical column charts and horizontal bar charts as "bar charts."

DATA *file*

zoo

The file *zoo* contains attendance at a zoo for 12 months. We demonstrate how to create a column chart of these data in Tableau.

Step 1. Following the steps outlined in Appendix 1.2, connect Tableau to the file *zoo*
Click the **Sheet 1** tab at the bottom of the Tableau Data Source screen to open the worksheet view

Step 2. In the worksheet view of Tableau, drag the pill for **Month** from the **Data** pane to the **Columns** shelf. Drag the pill for **Attendance** from the **Data** pane to the **Rows** shelf

The resulting chart is shown in Figure T2.1.

To modify the axis titles in the column chart for the zoo attendance data, follow the steps below.

Step 3. To edit the vertical axis, right click on the vertical axis of the column chart in the Canvas and click **Edit Axis…**. When the **Edit Axis [Attendance]** dialog box appears:
To adjust the range of the axis, select **Custom** under **Range**, enter *0* for **Fixed start** and *25,000* for **Fixed end**
To modify the vertical axis title, select **Custom** under **Axis Titles** and type *Zoo Attendance*
Click ✕ to close the **Edit Axis [Attendance]** dialog box

The Format pane can also be opened by clicking on the pill for SUM(Attendance) in the Rows shelf and selecting Format….

Step 4. To modify the format of the vertical axis, right click on the vertical axis and select **Format…**. When the **Format SUM(Attendance)** pane appears:
To adjust the font size, click next to **Font:** under **Default**, and change the font size to **11**

| **Figure T2.1** | Column Chart of the Zoo Attendance Data |

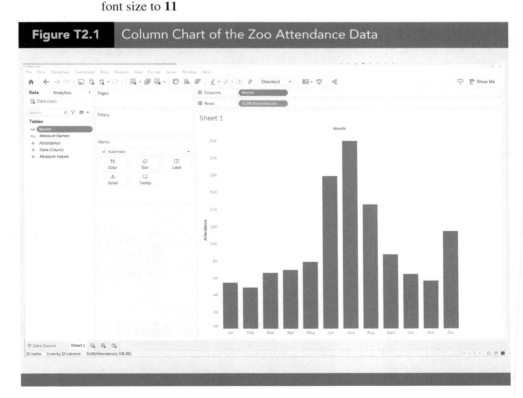

To adjust the format of the vertical axis labels, click next to **Numbers:** under **Scale**, and select **Number (Standard)**
   Click ✕ to close the **Format SUM(Attendance)** dialog box

Step 5. To hide the horizontal axis title of "Month" that appears at the top of the column chart, right click on **Month** and select **Hide Field Labels for Columns**

Step 6. To modify the format of the horizontal axis, right click on the horizontal axis and select **Format....** When the **Format Month** pane appears:
   To adjust the font size, click next to **Font:** under **Default**, and change the font size to **11**

Step 7. To edit the title, right click on **Sheet 1** at the top of the column chart and select **Edit Title....** When the **Edit Title** dialog box appears:
   Replace **<Sheet Name>** with *Zoo Attendance Highest in Summer Months and December*
   Highlight the text of the title, then change the font size to **16** and click the **Bold** button Ḃ to make the title bold font
   Click **OK** to close the **Edit Title** dialog box

Step 8. To remove the unnecessary grid lines in the chart, right click on the column chart and select **Format....** When the **Format** task pane appears, click on the

   Lines button ☰ and select **None** next to **Grid Lines:**

The column chart in Tableau should now appear as shown in Figure T2.2.

CHART *file*

zoocolumn_chart.twbx

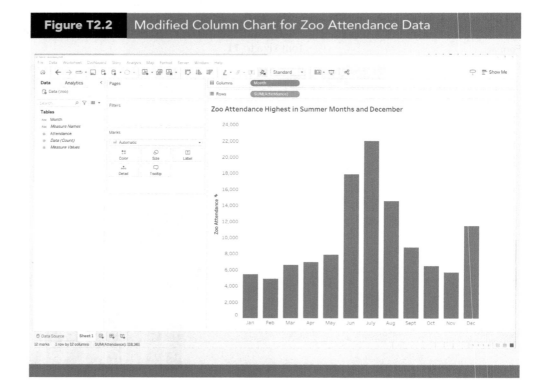

Figure T2.2   Modified Column Chart for Zoo Attendance Data

You can toggle to and from Presentation Mode in Tableau by pressing F7.

To view a larger version of the column chart, click **Window** in the Ribbon and select **Presentation Mode**. This will produce the column chart shown in Figure T2.3.

To create a bar chart rather than a column chart in Tableau, we just need to reverse the pills in the Columns and Rows shelves as demonstrated in the following step.

Step 9. Drag the **Month** pill from the **Columns** shelf to the **Rows** shelf, and drag the **SUM(Attendance)** pill from the **Rows** shelf to the **Columns** shelf

CHART *file*

zoobar_chart.twbx

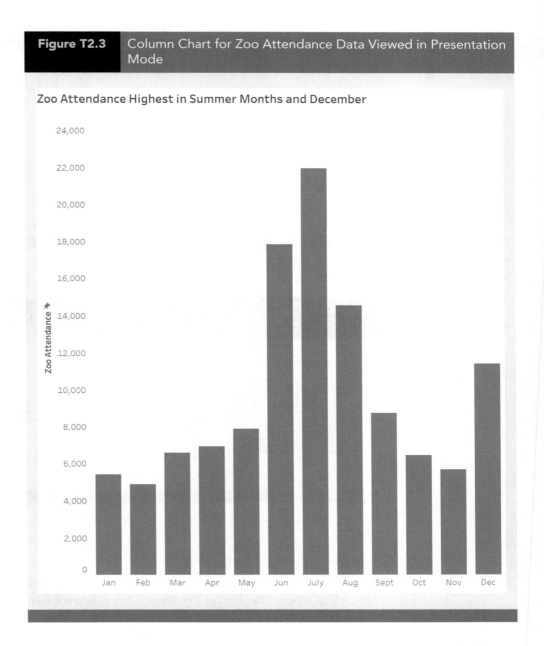

| Figure T2.3 | Column Chart for Zoo Attendance Data Viewed in Presentation Mode |

Step 9 creates the bar chart shown in Figure T2.4.

To view a larger version of the column chart, click **Window** in the Ribbon and select **Presentation Mode**. This will produce the bar chart shown in Figure T2.5.

Figure T2.4   Bar Chart for Zoo Attendance Data

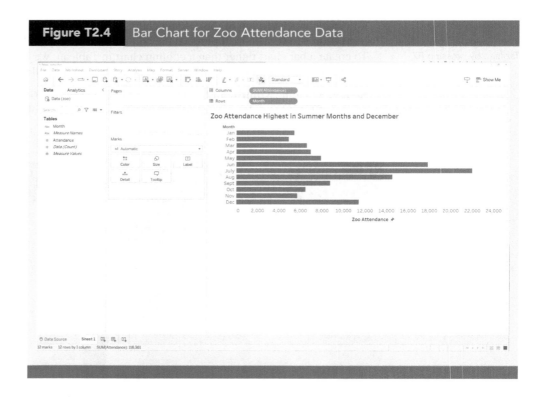

Figure T2.5   Bar Chart for Zoo Attendance Data Viewed in Presentation Mode

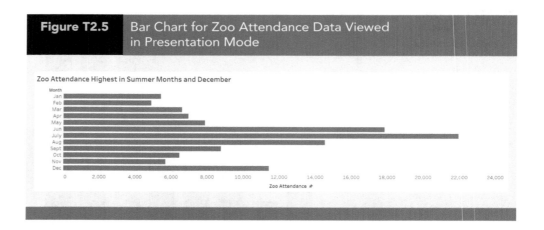

Scatter and Bubble Charts

To demonstrate the use of Tableau to create a scatter chart, we will use the data in the file *snow*, which contains the average low temperature in degrees Fahrenheit and the average annual snow in inches for 51 major cities in the United States.

DATA *file*

snow

Step 1. Following the steps outlined in Appendix 1.2, connect Tableau to the file *snow*
Click the **Sheet 1** tab at the bottom of the Tableau Data Source screen to open the worksheet view

Step 2. In the worksheet view of Tableau, drag the pill for **Average Low Tempera-ture** from the **Data** pane to the **Columns** shelf, and drag the pill for **Average Snowfall** to the **Rows** shelf

Steps 1 and 2 create the chart shown in Figure T2.6, which displays only a single point on the scatter chart because Tableau is using the sum of the average low temperature data and the sum of the average snowfall data, which results in a single data point. Step 3 indicates that the level of detail for this scatter chart is by city, which will break up this single point into points for the average low temperature and average snowfall for each city in the data set.

Step 3. Drag the pill for **City** to the **Detail** card Detail in the **Marks** area

Steps 1 through 3 create the scatter chart shown in Figure T2.7.
The following steps will modify the scatter chart to improve clarity.

Step 4. To edit the horizontal axis, right click on the horizontal axis and select **Edit Axis…**. When the **Edit Axis [Average Low Temperature]** dialog box appears:

> To modify the range of the horizontal axis, click **Custom** under **Range** and enter *30* for **Fixed start** and *75* for **Fixed end**
> To modify the title of the horizontal axis, select **Custom** under **Axis Titles** and enter *Average Low Temperature (degrees Fahrenheit)*
> Click ✕ to close the **Edit Axis [Average Low Temperature]** dialog box

Step 5. Right click the horizontal axis of the chart and select **Format…**. When the **Format SUM(Average Low Temperature)** pane appears:

> Click next to **Font:** under **Default** and change the font size to **11**

We enter −5 for the Fixed start value in step 6 so points corresponding to cities with 0 inches of average annual snowfall appear in the scatter chart.

Step 6. To edit the vertical axis, right click on the vertical axis and select **Edit Axis…**. When the **Edit Axis [Average Snowfall]** dialog box appears:

> To modify the range of the vertical axis, click **Fixed** under **Range** and enter *-5* for **Fixed start** and *105* for **Fixed end**

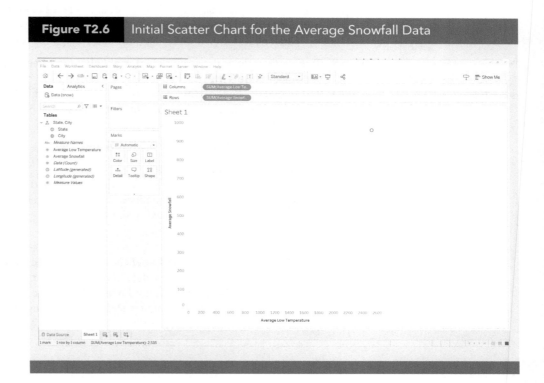

Figure T2.6   Initial Scatter Chart for the Average Snowfall Data

Figure T2.7 Scatter Chart for the Average Snowfall Data for Each City in Dataset

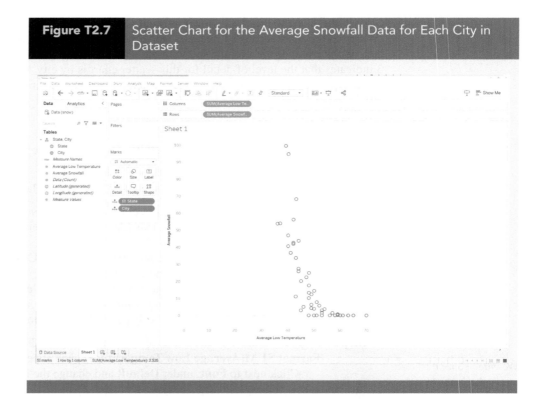

To modify the title of the vertical axis, select **Custom** under **Axis Titles** and enter *Average Annual Snowfall (inches)*
Click ✕ to close the **Edit Axis [Average Snowfall]** dialog box

Step 7. Right click the vertical axis of the chart and select **Format…**. When the **Format SUM(Average Snowfall)** pane appears:
Click next to **Font:** under **Default** and change the font size to **11**

To unhide a chart title, right-click the chart and select Title

Step 8. To hide the title of the scatter chart, right click on **Sheet 1** at the top of the chart and select **Hide Title**

Step 9. To remove the unnecessary grid lines in the chart, right click on the scatter chart and select **Format…**. When the **Format** task pane appears, click on the **Lines** button ☰, and select **None** next to **Grid Lines:**

The resulting chart is shown in Figure T2.8.

The following step adds labels to each point in the scatter chart to indicate city names. Note that Tableau automatically adjusts the placement of the data labels and does not display all city names to avoid overlapping text in the scatter chart.

Step 10. Drag the pill for **City** to the **Label** card Label in the **Marks** area

Step 11. To increase the font size of the data labels in the chart, right click in the scatter chart and select **Format…**. In the **Format Font** pane:
Click next to **Worksheet:** under **Default** and change the font size to **11**

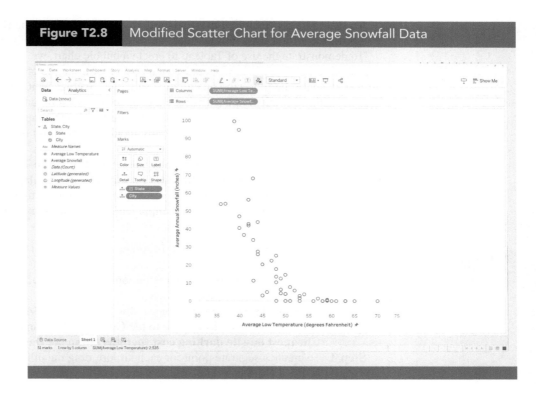

Figure T2.8   Modified Scatter Chart for Average Snowfall Data

These additional steps result in the scatter chart with labeled data points shown in Figure T2.9.

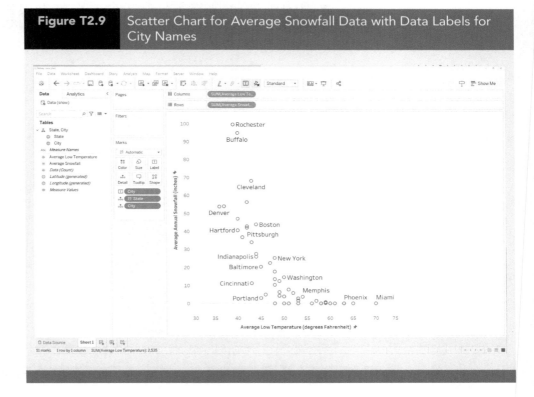

Figure T2.9   Scatter Chart for Average Snowfall Data with Data Labels for City Names

CHART *file*

snow_chart.twbx

To view a larger version of the scatter chart, click **Window** in the Ribbon and select **Presentation Mode**. This will produce the scatter chart shown in Figure T2.10.

To demonstrate the use of Tableau to create a bubble chart, we will use the data in the file *airportdata*. The file *airportdata* contains data for a sample of 15 airports. For each airport, we have the following quantitative variables: average wait time in the nonpriority Transportation Security Authority (TSA) queue measured in minutes, the cheapest on-site daily rate for parking at the airport measured in dollars, and the number of enplanements in a year (the number of passengers who board, including transfers) measured in millions of passengers.

The steps below demonstrate how to create a bubble chart in Tableau for the data in the file *airportdata* where TSA wait times (in minutes) are displayed on the horizontal axis, the cheapest parking rate (per day) is displayed on the vertical axis, and the size of each bubble corresponds to the annual enplanements (in millions of passengers) at that airport.

DATA *file*

airportdata

Step 1. Following the steps outlined in Appendix 1.2, connect Tableau to the file *airportdata*
Click the **Sheet 1** tab at the bottom of the Tableau Data Source screen to open the worksheet view

Step 2. In the worksheet view of Tableau, drag the pill for **TSA wait times (in minutes)** from the **Data** pane to the **Columns** shelf, and drag the pill for **Cheapest on-site parking cost (per day)** from the **Data** pane to the **Rows** shelf

Step 3. To create a separate point for each airport, drag the pill for **Airport Code** from the **Data** pane to the **Detail** card [Detail] in the **Marks** area

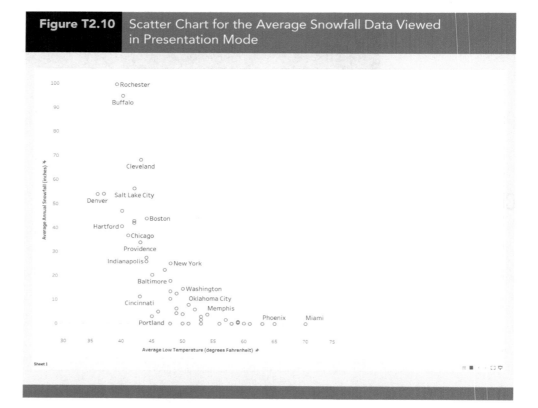

Figure T2.10   Scatter Chart for the Average Snowfall Data Viewed in Presentation Mode

Step 4. To make the size of each bubble correspond to the number of annual enplanements at each airport, drag the pill for **Annual Enplanements (millions of passengers)** from the **Data** pane to the **Size** card ⬡ Size in the **Marks** area

To increase the sizes of the bubbles, click on the **Size** card to reveal the size slider ▭, and move the slider to the right to increase the size of the bubbles

Step 5. To add labels to each bubble for the airport code, drag the pill for **Airport Code** from the **Data** pane to the **Label** card 🔤 Label in the **Marks** area

Steps 1 through 5 create the bubble chart shown in Figure T2.11.
The following steps modify the chart to improve the clarity of the bubble chart.

Step 6. Right click the vertical axis of the line chart and select **Format...**. When the **Format SUM(Cheapest on-site parking cost (per day))** pane appears:
Click next to **Font**: under **Default** and change the font size to **11**

Step 7. Right click the horizontal axis of the line chart and select **Format...**. When the **Format SUM(TSA wait time (minutes))** pane appears:
Click next to **Font:** under **Default** and change the font size to **11**

Step 8. To increase the font size of the data labels in the chart, right click in the bubble chart and select **Format...**. In the **Format** pane:
Click next to **Worksheet**: under **Default** and change the font size to **11**

Figure T2.11   Initial Bubble Chart Created for Airport Data

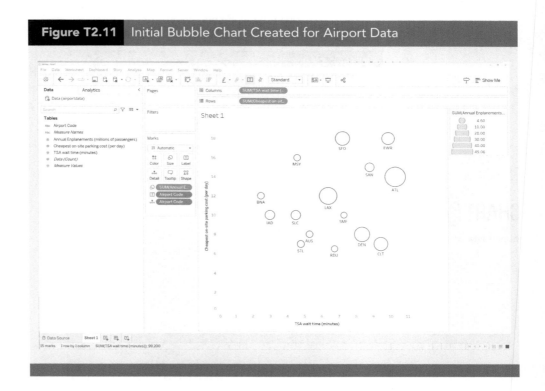

Step 9. To edit the legend for the chart, right click on the legend in the upper right corner of the chart and select **Format Legends…**. When the **Format Legends** pane appears:

Click next to **Font:** under **Body** and change the font size to **11**

Step 10. To edit the chart title, right click on **Sheet 1** at the top of the bubble chart and select **Edit Title…**. Replace **<Sheet Name>** with *Bubble Chart for Airport Data (size of bubble corresponds to annual enplanements),* change the font size to **16**, and change the font to bold by selecting the text and clicking on the Bold button

Step 11. To remove the unnecessary grid lines in the chart, right click on the bubble chart and select **Format…**. When the **Format** task pane appears:

Click on the **Lines** button 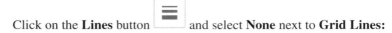 and select **None** next to **Grid Lines:**

The modified bubble chart appears in Figure T2.12.

To view a larger version of the bubble chart, click **Window** in the Ribbon and select **Presentation Mode**. This will produce the bubble chart shown in Figure T2.13.

Line Charts

As an example of how to create a line chart in Tableau, let us consider Cheetah Sports. Cheetah Sports sells running shoes and has retail stores in shopping malls throughout the United States. The file *cheetah* contains the last 10 years of sales for Cheetah Sports, measured in millions of dollars. The following steps will create a line chart.

cheetah

Step 1. Following the steps outlined in Appendix 1.2, connect Tableau to the file *cheetah*

Click the **Sheet 1** tab at the bottom of the Tableau Data Source screen to open the worksheet view

airportdata_chart.twbx

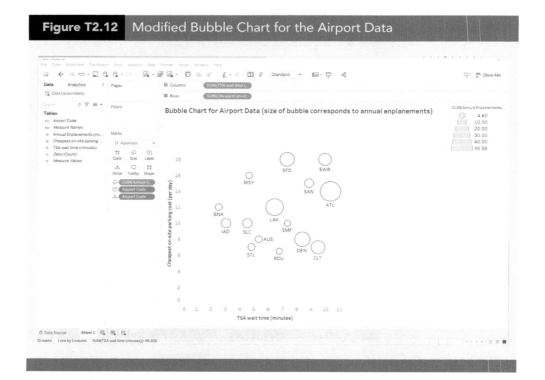

Figure T2.12   Modified Bubble Chart for the Airport Data

Figure T2.13 Modified Bubble Chart for the Airport Data Viewed in Presentation Mode

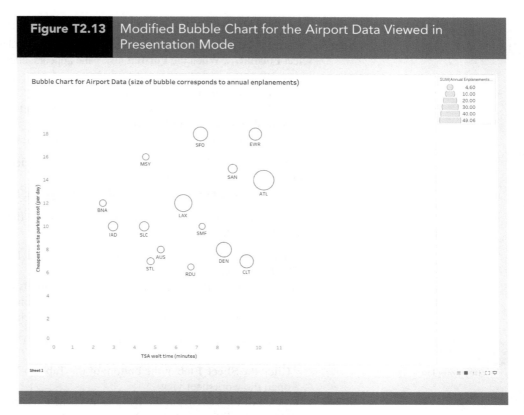

Step 2. In the worksheet view of Tableau, drag the pill for **Year** from the **Data** pane to the **Columns** shelf, and drag the pill for **Sales ($ millions)** from the **Data** pane to the **Rows** shelf

Steps 1 and 2 create the line chart shown in Figure T2.14.

Figure T2.14 Initial Line Chart for Cheetah Sports Sales Data

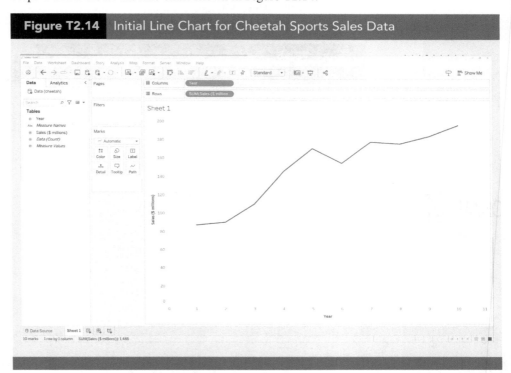

The following steps modify the line chart to improve readability.

Step 3. To remove the unnecessary grid lines in the chart, right click on the line chart and select **Format…**. When the **Format** task pane appears, click on the **Lines** button

≡ , and select **None** next to **Grid Lines:**

Step 4. Right click the vertical axis of the line chart and select **Format…**. When the **Format SUM(Sales ($ millions))** pane appears:
Click next to **Font:** under **Default** and change the font size to **11**

Step 5. Right click the horizontal axis of the line chart and select **Format…**. When the **Format Year** pane appears:
Click next to **Font:** under **Default** and change the font size to **11**

Step 6. To hide the title of the chart, right click on **Sheet 1** at the top of the chart and select **Hide Title**

These additional steps produce the line chart shown in Figure T2.15 when viewed using **Presentation Mode** in Tableau.

Next, we consider a line chart with multiple lines. Cheetah Sports has two sales regions: the eastern region and the western region. The file *cheetahregion* contain sales data for the two regions for a 10-year period. The following steps will create a line chart with multiple lines.

DATA *file*
cheetahregion

Step 1. Following the steps outlined in Appendix 1.2, connect Tableau to the file *cheetahregion*
Click the **Sheet 1** tab at the bottom of the Tableau Data Source screen to open the worksheet view

Step 2. Drag the pill for **Year** from the **Data** pane to the **Columns** shelf
Drag the pill for **Eastern Sales** from the **Data** pane to the **Rows** shelf
Drag the pill for **Western Sales** from the **Data** pane to the **Rows** shelf

Step 3. Click on the **Show Me** button ☰ Show Me in the top right corner of the worksheet view
Select the chart for **dual lines** 〰 (see Figure T2.16)

CHART *file*
cheetah_chart.twbx

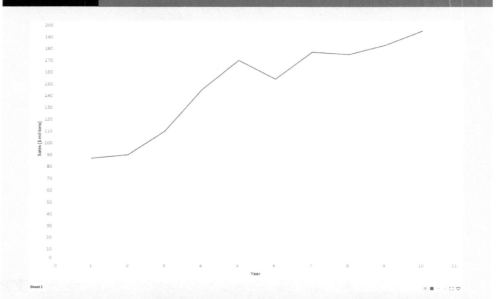

Figure T2.15 Completed Line Chart for Cheetah Sports Data Viewed in Presentation Mode

Figure T2.16 The Show Me Function to Create a Dual Axis Line Chart

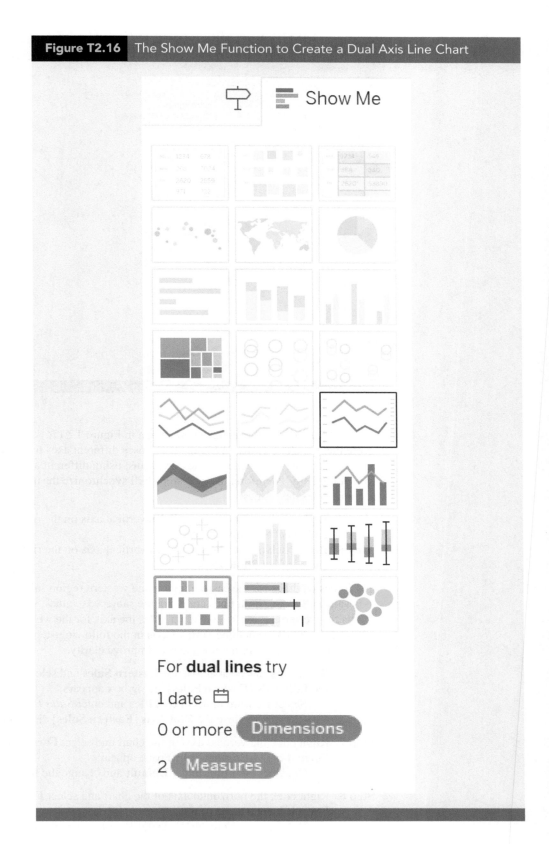

The Show Me button allows you to easily create many different standard charts in Tableau. It will also tell you the types of variables that are required to create each type of chart.

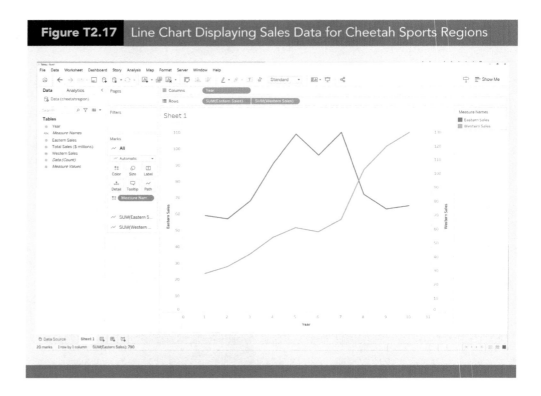

Figure T2.17   Line Chart Displaying Sales Data for Cheetah Sports Regions

Steps 1–3 create the dual axis line chart shown in Figure T2.17.

Note that the chart shown in Figure T2.17 uses different axes for the eastern region and western region sales. We generally advise against using different axes to compare values as we are doing here. Therefore, the next steps will synchronize the axes for the eastern and western region sales values.

Step 4. Right click on the **Western Sales** vertical axis on the right side of the line chart and select **Synchronize Axis**

Step 5. Right click on the **Western Sales** vertical axis on the right side of the line chart and deselect **Show Header**

Step 4 forces the lines for the eastern region and western region sales to use the same range of axis values. Because both lines are using the same axis values, we hide the unnecessary dual axis for western region sales. Step 5 hides the axis for the western region. We will modify the title of the remaining vertical axis in the following steps.

The following steps modify the line chart to improve clarity.

Step 6. Right click the vertical axis for **Eastern Sales** and select **Edit Axis…**. When the **Edit Axis [Eastern Sales]** dialog box appears:

Select **Custom** under **Axis Titles** and enter *Sales ($ millions)*
Click ✕ to close the **Edit Axis [Eastern Sales]** dialog box

Step 7. Right click the vertical axis of the chart and select **Format…**. When the **Format SUM(Eastern Sales)** pane appears:

Click next to **Font:** under **Default** and change the font size to **11**

Step 8. Right click the horizontal axis of the chart and select **Format…**. When the **Format Year** pane appears:

Click next to **Font:** under **Default** and change the font size to **11**

Step 9. To hide the unnecessary title of the chart, right click on **Sheet 1** at the top of the chart and select **Hide Title**

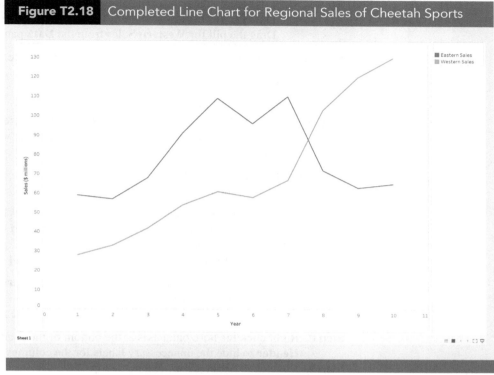

Figure T2.18 Completed Line Chart for Regional Sales of Cheetah Sports

CHART *file*

cheetahregionline_chart.twbx

Step 10. To edit the legend for the chart, right click on the legend in the upper right corner of the chart and select **Format Legends…..**. When the **Format Legends** pane appears:

Click next to **Font:** under **Body** and change the font size to **11**

To hide the unnecessary title of the legend, right click on the legend, and select **Title**

Step 11. To remove the unnecessary grid lines in the chart, right click on the line chart and select **Format….**. When the **Format** task pane appears, click on the **Lines** button ☰, and select **None** next to **Grid Lines:**

The completed line chart viewed in **Presentation Mode** showing the regional sales for Cheetah Sports appears in Figure T2.18.

Clustered and Stacked Column/Bar Charts

To demonstrate creating clustered and stacked columns/bar charts in Tableau, we will continue to use the Cheetah Sports regional sales data that contains 10 years of sales data at Cheetah Sports in the eastern region and western region.

DATA *file*

cheetahregion

Step 1. Following the steps outlined in Appendix 1.2, connect Tableau to the file *cheetahregion*

Click the **Sheet 1** tab at the bottom of the Tableau Data Source screen to open the worksheet view

Step 2. Click on the pill for **Year** under **Tables** in the **Data** pane and select **Convert to Discrete**

Step 2 is necessary because we want to create column/bar charts, so we need to designate the Year variable as a discrete variable.

Step 3. Drag the pill for **Year** from the **Data** pane to the **Columns** shelf

Drag the pill for **Eastern Sales** from the **Data** pane to the **Rows** shelf

Drag the pill for **Western Sales** from the **Data** pane to the **Rows** shelf

Step 4. Drag the pill for **Measure Names** from the **Data** pane to the **Color** card

in the **Marks** area

Step 5. Drag **SUM(Western Sales)** from the **Rows** shelf to the **Eastern Sales** vertical axis label of the column chart to put both eastern and western region sales on the same vertical axis (see Figure T2.19)

The resulting clustered column chart is shown in Figure T2.20.

The following steps modify the line chart to improve clarity.

Step 6. Right click the vertical axis and select **Edit Axis…**. When the **Edit Axis [Measure Values]** dialog box appears, select **Custom** under **Axis Titles** and enter *Sales ($ millions)*

Click × to close the **Edit Axis [Measure Values]** dialog box

Step 7. Right click the vertical axis of the chart and select **Format…**. When the **Format Measure Values** pane appears:

Click next to **Font:** under **Default** and change the font size to **11**

Step 8. Right click the horizontal axis at the bottom of the chart and select **Show Header** to hide the unnecessary labels for the columns

Step 9. Right click on the **Year** label at the top of the chart and select **Format…**. When the **Format Field Labels** pane appears:

Click next to **Font:** under **Default** and change the font size to **11**

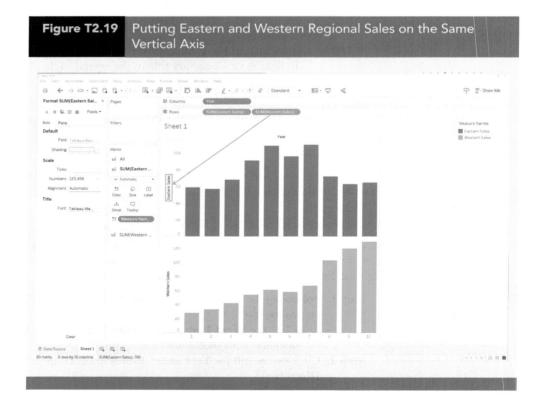

Figure T2.19 Putting Eastern and Western Regional Sales on the Same Vertical Axis

Figure T2.20	Initial Clustered Column Chart Created for the Cheetah Regional Sales Data

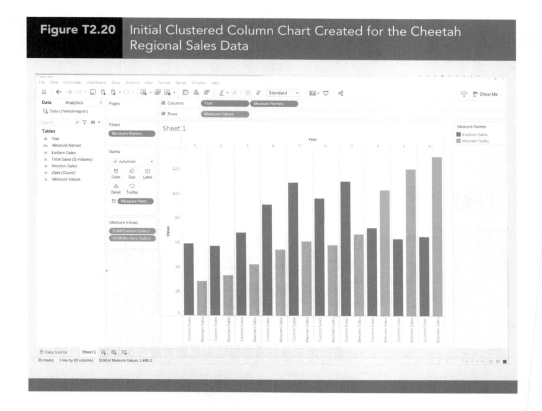

Step 10. Right click on year number labels at the top of the chart and select **Format…**. When the **Format Year** pane appears:
Click next to **Font:** under **Default** and change the font size to **11**

Step 11. To hide the unnecessary title of the chart, right click on **Sheet 1** at the top of the chart and select **Hide Title**

Step 12. To edit the legend for the chart, right click on the legend in the upper right corner of the chart and select **Format Legends…..** When the **Format Legends** pane appears:
Click next to **Font:** under **Body** and change the font size to **11**
To hide the unnecessary title of the legend, right click on the legend and select **Title**

Step 13. To remove the unnecessary grid lines in the chart, right click on the line chart and select **Format…**. When the **Format** task pane opens, click on the **Lines** button ▭, and select **None** next to **Grid Lines:**

Tableau refers to clustered charts as "side-by-side" charts.

The completed clustered column chart viewed in **Presentation Mode** showing the regional sales for Cheetah Sports appears in Figure T2.21.

The following step converts the clustered column chart shown in Figure T2.21 to the stacked column chart shown in Figure T2.22.

Step 14. Drag **Measure Names** from the **Columns** shelf back to the **Tables** area of the **Data** pane

| **Figure T2.21** | Completed Clustered Column Chart for the Cheetah Regional Sales Data |

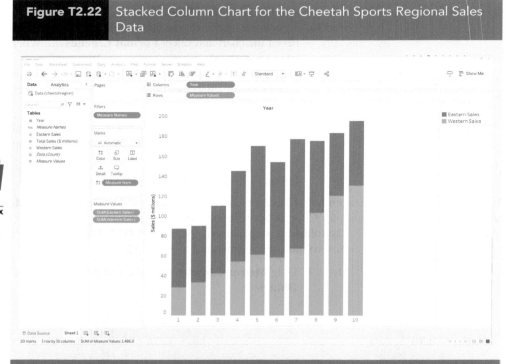

CHART *file*

**cheetahregionalclustered_
chart.twbx**

To create a bar chart rather than a column chart, you must reverse the variables assigned to the Columns shelf and the Rows shelf. For instance, in Figure T2.22, the stacked column chart can be changed to a stacked bar chart by moving the pill for **Year** to the **Rows** shelf and the pill for **Measure Values** to the **Columns** shelf as shown in Figure T2.23.

| **Figure T2.22** | Stacked Column Chart for the Cheetah Sports Regional Sales Data |

CHART *file*

**cheetahregionalstacked_
chart.twbx**

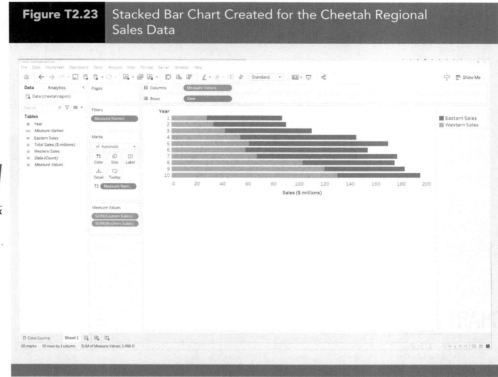

Figure T2.23 Stacked Bar Chart Created for the Cheetah Regional Sales Data

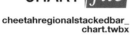

CHART *file*

**cheetahregionalstackedbar_
chart.twbx**

Choropleth Maps

In this section, we show how to create a choropleth map in Tableau. The file *statepopulation* contains populations for the 50 states in the United States.

DATA *file*

statepopulation

Step 1. Following the steps outlined in Appendix 1.2, connect Tableau to the file *statepopulation*

Click the **Sheet 1** tab at the bottom of the Tableau Data Source screen to open the Worksheet view

Step 2. Drag the pill for **Longitude (generated)** from the **Data** pane to the **Columns** shelf, and drag the pill for **Latitude (generated)** from the **Data** pane to the **Rows** shelf

Step 3. Drag the pill for **State** from the **Data** pane to the **Detail** card ⬚ Detail in the **Marks** area to show each state on the map

Step 4. Drag the pill for **Estimated 2020 Population** from the **Data** pane to the **Color** card ⬚ Color in the **Marks** area to shade each state in the map based on population

Step 5. To modify the title of the chart, click **Sheet 1** at the top of the map and select **Edit Title…**. When the **Edit Title** dialog box opens:

Replace **<Sheet Name>** with *Estimated United States Population by State*

Highlight the text of the title, then change the font size to **16** and click the

Bold button **B** to make the title bold font

Click **OK** to close the **Edit Title** dialog box

These steps produce the choropleth map shown in Figure T2.24.

Note that you can also generate the choropleth map shown in Figure T2.24 using the Tableau Show Me tool by dragging **State** to the Rows shelf, clicking the **Show Me** button

≣ Show Me , selecting the **Filled Map** icon 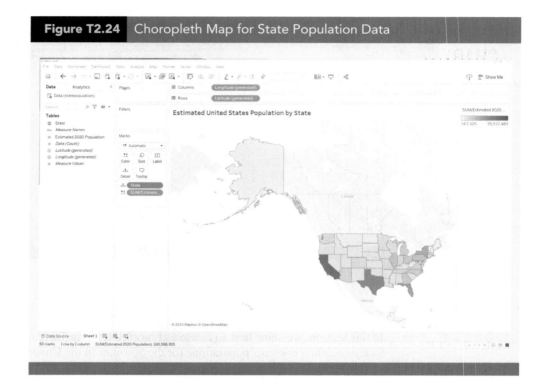, and then dragging the pill for **Estimated 2020 Population** from the **Data** pane to the **Color** card in the **Marks** area.

Figure T2.24   Choropleth Map for State Population Data

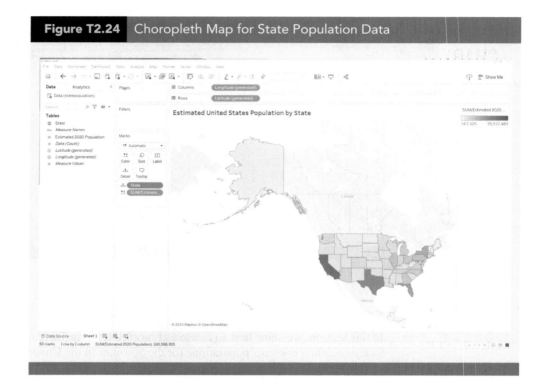

CHART *file*

**statepopulation_
chart.twbx**

Chapter 3

Data Visualization and Design

Contents

Learning Objectives

After completing this chapter, you will be able to

LO 1 Define the meaning of preattentive attributes and explain how preattentive attributes associated with color, form, spatial positioning, and movement are used in data visualizations

LO 2 Explain how the Gestalt principles of similarity, proximity, enclosure, and connection can be used to create effective data visualizations

LO 3 Define data-ink ratio and explain how increasing this ratio through decluttering can create data visualizations that are easier to interpret

LO 4 Create data visualizations that are easier for the audience to interpret by minimizing the required eye travel and applying the concepts of preattentive attributes, Gestalt principles, and decluttering

LO 5 Explain why certain types of font are preferred over others for use in text in data visualizations

LO 6 List several common mistakes in designing data visualizations and explain how these mistakes can be avoided

Data Visualization Makeover

Fast-Food Restaurant Sales

Charts for making comparisons with data are one of the most common types of data visualizations created by analysts. We create charts to compare corporate revenues, country populations, student test scores, rainfall amounts in different locations, etc. There are many ways to show comparisons within a chart, but we must design the chart appropriately so we do not confuse the audience or make the chart unnecessarily difficult to interpret.

Consider the chart shown in Figure 3.1. This chart compares the sales of several leading fast-food restaurants using the logo of each company to form something similar to a column chart. Using graphics and logos can make charts more visually appealing, but we should make sure their use does not distract the audience or make it difficult to correctly interpret the chart. Because each logo in Figure 3.1 is two-dimensional (each logo has a length and a width), it is natural to compare the sales values based on the overall size, or area, of each logo. However, this is not what is depicted in the chart. The height of each logo is what is actually being used for comparison. The width of each logo is not used to convey any meaningful information. To improve the clarity of this chart, it is better to remove the meaningless dimension of the width of the logo in the chart.

There are several other design elements that make this chart difficult to interpret. The gross domestic product (GDP) for the country of Afghanistan is shown here in an attempt to give a relative scale to the sales

of each fast-food restaurant. Giving a reference value can be effective because it can give the audience a context to frame the scale of values. However, using the shape of the country of Afghanistan here creates several problems. First, it again disguises what is being used for comparison since only the height of the shape and not the overall size of the shape corresponds to the GDP. Second, the shape is partially hidden by the logos for McDonald's and Burger King, making it difficult to see. Finally, it is debatable how familiar the audience will be with the actual shape of the country of Afghanistan, so it is unclear that including this shape provides any additional information or a helpful reference for context to the audience.

We also note that this chart shows the vertical axis on the right side of the chart, which is unusual. Audiences typically expect to see the vertical axis on the left side of the chart. The vertical axis title is also not located next to the axis. This requires the audience to move their eyes from place to place on the chart, which makes it more difficult for the audience to interpret.

Figure 3.2 displays the same data as Figure 3.1, but we have made several changes to the design of the chart to make it easier for the audience to interpret. We have changed the chart to a more typical column chart that uses the length of the columns rather than the logos to make relative comparisons among sales at the fast-food restaurants. We have moved the vertical axis to the left side of the chart, and we have repositioned the vertical axis label

Figure 3.1   Column Chart Using Logos to Compare Fast-Food Restaurant Sales

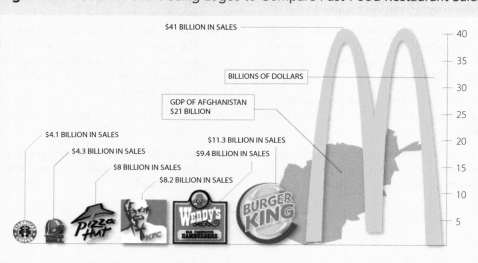

Source: http://www.princeton.edu/~ina/infographics/starbucks.html

(Continued)

above the vertical axis. This makes the chart easier for the audience to interpret. We have also used a horizontal line on the column graph to indicate the GDP of Afghanistan. We have made this final change because this value represents a different variable (GDP) than what is shown on the vertical axis (sales), and this makes it clear that this horizontal line is only intended to provide a reference for the scale of the other values. If including the fast-food restaurant logos makes the chart more visually appealing to the audience, then these could be included as the horizontal-axis labels for each column rather than using the actual names.

Figure 3.2 Improved Column Chart to Compare Fast-Food Restaurant Sales

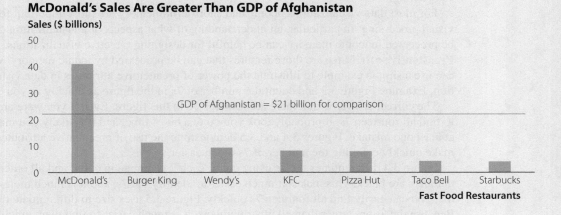

McDonald's Sales Are Greater Than GDP of Afghanistan

In this chapter, we discuss specific design elements that can help create effective data visualizations. However, a good data visualization is not simply created by following a series of steps. What makes a chart or table effective depends on how well it addresses the needs of the audience. Therefore, the first step in creating effective visualizations is understanding the purpose of the chart or table and the needs of the audience. The design elements covered in this chapter can then be used to most effectively achieve the designated purpose of the visualization and meet the needs of the audience.

We begin this chapter by discussing preattentive attributes, which are the visual properties that our minds process without conscious effort. We introduce Gestalt principles, which explain how people perceive the world around them. We then demonstrate how preattentive attributes and Gestalt principles can be used to improve data visualizations through decluttering and increasing the data-ink ratio. We also discuss the importance of minimizing the eye travel required by the audience and using appropriate fonts for the text in a data visualization to make the interpretation of visualizations as easy as possible for the audience. Finally, we conclude the chapter with a discussion of common mistakes made in data visualization design and how these mistakes can be avoided.

3.1 Preattentive Attributes

The act of "seeing" a chart or table used for data visualization involves a combination of our eyes and brains. Our eyes receive inputs as reflections of light from a visualization that our brains must differentiate and process. The process through which our brains interpret the reflections of light that enter our eyes is known as **visual perception**.

The process of visual perception is related to how memory works in our brain. At a very high level, there are three forms of memory that affect visual perception: iconic memory, short-term memory, and long-term memory. **Iconic memory** is the most quickly processed form of memory. Information stored in iconic memory is processed automatically, and the information is held there for less than a second. **Short-term memory** holds information for about a minute, and our minds accomplish this by chunking, or grouping, similar pieces of information together. Estimates vary somewhat, but it is believed that most people can hold about four chunks of visual information in their short-term memories. For instance, most people find it difficult to remember which color represents which category if more than four different colors/categories are used in a bar or column chart. **Long-term memory** is where we store information for an extended amount of time. Most long-term memories are formed through repetition and rehearsal, but they can also be formed through clever use of storytelling.

We discuss storytelling as it relates to data visualization in Chapter 7.

For most data visualizations, iconic and short-term memory are most important for visual processing. In particular, an understanding of what aspects of a visualization can be processed in iconic memory can be helpful for designing effective visualizations. **Preattentive attributes** are those features that can be processed by iconic memory. We can use a simple example to illustrate the power of preattentive attributes in data visualization. Examine Figure 3.3 and count the number of 7s in the figure as quickly as you can.

The correct answer is that there are fourteen 7s in this figure. Even if you were able to find all fourteen 7s, it probably took you quite a bit of time, and it is likely you made at least one mistake. Figures 3.4 and 3.5 demonstrate the use of preattentive attributes to make quickly counting the number of 7s much easier.

Figure 3.4 differentiates the 7s using color; each 7 is orange in color, and all other numbers are black. This makes it much easier to identify the 7s, and it is much more likely that you can easily find all fourteen 7s quickly. Figure 3.5 uses size to differentiate the 7s. Because the 7s are larger than all other numbers, it is much easier to find them quickly. Both color and size are preattentive attributes; we process these in our iconic memory and immediately differentiate between their values. This simple example shows the power of using preattentive attributes to convey meaning in data visualizations.

The proper use of preattentive attributes in a data visualization reduces the **cognitive load**, or the amount of effort necessary to accurately and efficiently process the information being communicated by a data visualization. This makes it easier for the audience to

Figure 3.3	Count the Number of 7s That Appear in This Figure

7	3	4	1	3	4	5	6	4	0
3	0	6	9	0	4	5	8	6	3
2	7	2	2	9	9	4	5	2	1
2	2	4	5	2	0	9	2	0	4
2	4	0	7	6	9	3	0	0	4
7	7	8	9	2	6	7	2	4	7
6	1	3	3	2	1	4	4	9	0
3	6	6	2	7	5	5	2	5	4
1	1	4	0	6	3	4	0	5	1
3	7	5	2	7	5	7	7	3	9
3	3	8	6	9	5	5	3	6	4
7	6	0	3	0	9	9	0	2	9
4	6	9	4	8	2	6	5	8	3
9	3	9	2	2	8	4	3	9	8
5	8	8	2	9	1	2	4	8	5
1	7	4	0	1	1	9	9	5	8

Figure 3.4	Count the Number of 7s Aided by the Preattentive Attribute of Color

7	3	4	1	3	4	5	6	4	0
3	0	6	9	0	4	5	8	6	3
2	7	2	2	9	9	4	5	2	1
2	2	4	5	2	0	9	2	0	4
2	4	0	7	6	9	3	0	0	4
7	7	8	9	2	6	7	2	4	7
6	1	3	3	2	1	4	4	9	0
3	6	6	2	7	5	5	2	5	4
1	1	4	0	6	3	4	0	5	1
3	7	5	2	7	5	7	7	3	9
3	3	8	6	9	5	5	3	6	4
7	6	0	3	0	9	9	0	2	9
4	6	9	4	8	2	6	5	8	3
9	3	9	2	2	8	4	3	9	8
5	8	8	2	9	1	2	4	8	5
1	7	4	0	1	1	9	9	5	8

Figure 3.5	Count the Number of 7s Aided by the Preattentive Attribute of Form (Specifically Size)

7	3	4	1	3	4	5	6	4	0
3	0	6	9	0	4	5	8	6	3
2	7	2	2	9	9	4	5	2	1
2	2	4	5	2	0	9	2	0	4
2	4	0	7	6	9	3	0	0	4
7	7	8	9	2	6	7	2	4	7
6	1	3	3	2	1	4	4	9	0
3	6	6	2	7	5	5	2	5	4
1	1	4	0	6	3	4	0	5	1
3	7	5	2	7	5	7	7	3	9
3	3	8	6	9	5	5	3	6	4
7	6	0	3	0	9	9	0	2	9
4	6	9	4	8	2	6	5	8	3
9	3	9	2	2	8	4	3	9	8
5	8	8	2	9	1	2	4	8	5
1	7	4	0	1	1	9	9	5	8

interpret the visualization with less effort. Preattentive attributes related to visual perception are generally divided into four categories: color, form (which includes size), spatial positioning, and movement. We will examine each of these preattentive attributes in detail to see how we can use them to reduce cognitive load and create effective data visualizations.

Color

In terms of data visualization, **color** includes the attributes of hue, saturation, and luminance. Figure 3.6 displays the difference between these aspects of color. **Hue** refers to what we typically think of as the basis of different colors, for example, red versus blue versus orange. In technical terms, the hue is defined by the position the light occupies on the visible light spectrum. **Saturation** refers to the intensity or purity of the color, which is defined as the amount of gray in the color. **Luminance** refers to the amount of black versus white within the color.

Hue, saturation, and luminance can each be used to draw the user's attention to specific parts of a data visualization and to differentiate among values in a visualization. Using differences in hue in a data visualization creates bold, stark contracts, while changing the saturation or luminance creates softer, less stark contrasts.

Color can be an extremely effective attribute to use to differentiate particular aspects of data in a visualization. However, one must be careful not to overuse color as it can become distracting in a visualization. It should also be noted that many people experience color-blindness, which affects their ability to differentiate between some colors.

Because color is used so extensively in data visualization, we discuss this preattentive attribute in much more detail in Chapter 4.

Form

Form includes the preattentive attributes of orientation, size, shape, length, and width. Each of these attributes can be used to call attention to a particular aspect of a data visualization. Figure 3.7 shows an example of each of these form-related preattentive attributes.

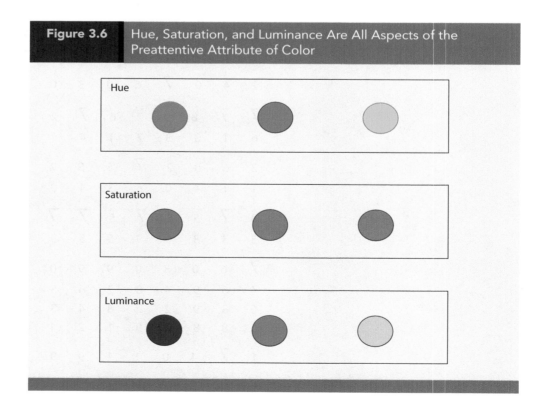

| Figure 3.6 | Hue, Saturation, and Luminance Are All Aspects of the Preattentive Attribute of Color |

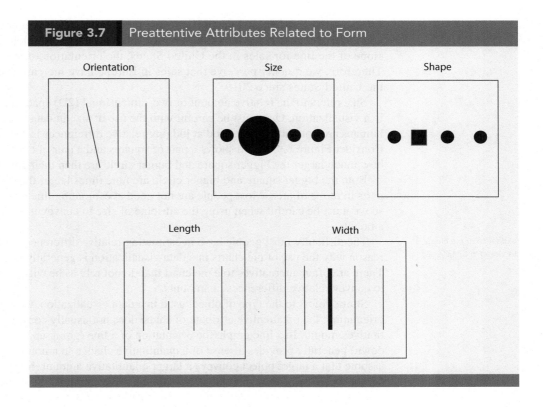

Figure 3.7 Preattentive Attributes Related to Form

Orientation refers to the relative positioning of an object within a data visualization. It is a common preattentive attribute present in line graphs. Consider the chart in Figure 3.8 that visualizes sales of a specific form of syringe that is used for administering insulin to patients with diabetes in Europe and the United States. The difference in the orientation of these lines makes it easy for the audience to perceive that sales in

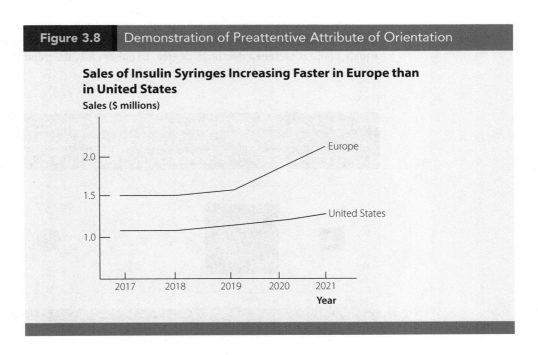

Figure 3.8 Demonstration of Preattentive Attribute of Orientation

Europe are increasing at a much faster rate than the United States for the years 2019 and 2020. Because the slope of the line for sales in Europe is much steeper than the slope of the line for sales in the United States, the orientation of these lines is different. Therefore, we quickly perceive that sales in Europe have increased much faster than in the United States since 2019.

Size refers to the relative amount of two-dimensional (2D) space an object occupies in a visualization. One must be careful with the use of size in data visualizations because humans are not particularly good at judging relative differences in the 2D sizes of objects. Consider Figure 3.9, which shows a pair of squares and a pair of circles. Try to determine how much larger the bigger square and bigger circle are than their smaller counterparts.

Both the bigger square and bigger circle are nine times larger than their smaller counterparts in terms of area. Most people are not good at estimating this relative size difference, so we must be careful when using the attribute of size to convey information about relative amounts.

Avoidance of pie charts is discussed in Chapter 2.

The difficulty most people have in estimating relative differences in 2D size is a major reason why the use of pie charts in a data visualization is generally not recommended. There are often alternatives to a pie chart that do not rely as heavily on the attribute of size to convey relative differences in amounts.

Shape refers to the type of object used in a data visualization. Contrary to size and orientation, the preattentive attribute of shape does not usually convey a sense of quantitative amount. In a line graph, the orientation of a line (going up, staying flat, or going down) generally provides a sense of a quantitative change in amount. For size, most people assume that a larger object conveys a larger quantitative amount. In general, most shapes do not specifically correspond to certain quantitative amounts. Nevertheless, shape can be effectively used to draw attention in a visualization or as a way to group common items and distinguish between items from different groups.

Figure 3.10 uses the attributes of color and shape to show how items are grouped. For example, suppose these 20 items represented 20 employees of a company. In Figure 3.10a we use the preattentive attribute of color to divide the items into three different groups or categories: orange, blue, and black. For example, color could represent the type of educational degree the corresponding employee has earned. Orange could represent a business degree, blue could represent an engineering degree, and black could represent any other degree. In Figure 3.10b, we use the preattentive attribute of shape to divide the items into three groups: circle, square, and triangle. For example, shape could represent the highest educational degree level that the corresponding employee has earned. A circle could represent a bachelor's degree, a triangle could represent a master's degree, and a square could represent a doctorate degree. In either case, the mind can quickly process

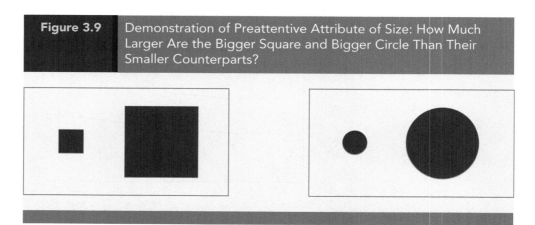

Figure 3.9   Demonstration of Preattentive Attribute of Size: How Much Larger Are the Bigger Square and Bigger Circle Than Their Smaller Counterparts?

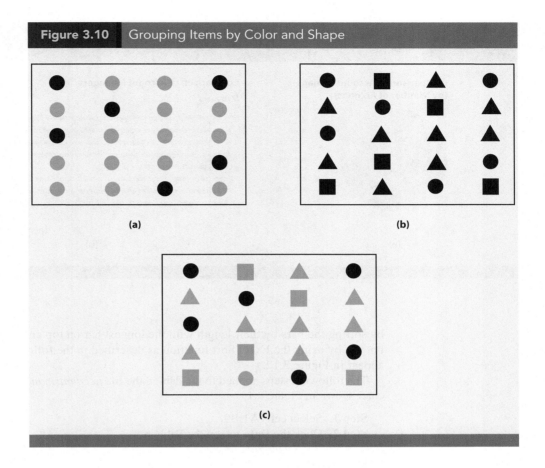

Figure 3.10 Grouping Items by Color and Shape

these visualizations and divide the items into their distinct groups. Figure 3.10c uses both attributes, color and shape, to group items into nine groups—each combination of color (degree type) and shape (degree level). It requires a much higher cognitive load here to determine which items are in the same group. This illustrates why we have to be careful not to overuse combinations of preattentive attributes or we will lose the ability of our mind to quickly recognize these.

Length and Width

When we refer to the preattentive attributes of length and width for data visualization, we are generally referring to their use with lines, bars, or columns. Therefore, **length** refers to the horizontal, vertical, or diagonal distance of a line or bar/column, while **width** refers to the thickness of the line or bar/column (see Figure 3.7). Length is useful for illustrating quantitative values because a longer line corresponds to a larger value. Length is used extensively in bar and column charts to visualize data. Because it is much easier to compare relative lengths than relative sizes, bar and column charts are often preferred to pie charts for visualizing data. Consider data on the number of accounts managed by eight account managers. Figure 3.11 displays these same data as a pie chart (using the size of the pie pieces to indicate the number of accounts and color to indicate the manager) and a bar chart (using the length of the bars to indicate the number of accounts and labels on the vertical axis to indicate the manager).

It is much easier to see that the manager with the most accounts managed is Elijah and that Kate manages the second-most accounts from the bar chart in Figure 3.11b than from the pie chart in Figure 3.11a. We could make the bar chart even easier to interpret

Figure 3.11 Using a Pie Chart (Size and Color) and a Bar Chart (Length) to Display the Accounts Managed Data

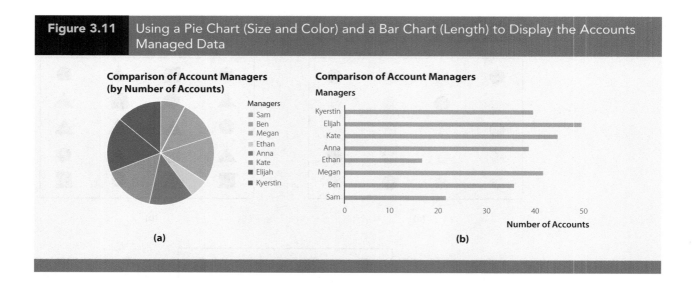

(a)

(b)

by sorting the bars by their length with the longest bar on top and the shortest bar on the bottom by using the Excel Sort function as described in the following steps. The data appear in Figure 3.12.

The following steps applied to the data in the file *accountsmanaged_chart* result in the chart shown in Figure 3.13.

Step 1. Select cells A1:B9
Step 2. Click the **Data** tab on the Ribbon
Select **Sort**
Step 3. When the **Sort** dialog box appears:
Select the check box for **My data has headers**
In the **Sort by** box, select **Number of Accounts,** and in the **Order** box, select **Smallest to Largest**
Click **OK**

Line width is used much less frequently in data visualizations. One of the more common uses of line width in data visualizations is the Sankey chart. A **Sankey chart** typically depicts the proportional flow of entities where the width of the line represents the relative

Figure 3.12 Data in File *accountsmanaged_chart*

CHART *file*

accountsmanaged_chart

⊿	A	B
1	**Manager**	**Number of Accounts**
2	Sam	21
3	Ben	35
4	Megan	41
5	Ethan	16
6	Anna	38
7	Kate	44
8	Elijah	49
9	Kyerstin	39

Figure 3.13 Sorted Bar Chart Comparing Number of Accounts Managed

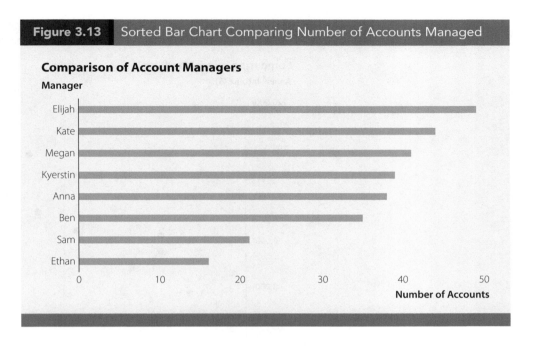

flow rate compared to the widths of the other lines. Figure 3.14 shows an example of a Sankey chart for the anticipated major and actual major at graduation for students in a liberal arts college. We can see in Figure 3.14 that most students who anticipate majoring in the Humanities graduate with a major in Humanities, but we also see that some planned Humanities majors switch to Social Science majors, and fewer switch to Natural Sciences/ Engineering and Interdisciplinary studies. It is relatively easy to interpret which graduation major is most popular for a particular anticipated major in Figure 3.14. However, because it is not easy to compare relative line widths, it is more difficult to compare the proportion of graduation majors from different anticipated majors. Sankey charts can often quickly become overwhelming and difficult to interpret, so one should be careful not to try to include too much information within this type of visualization.

Figure 3.14 Sankey Chart Demonstrating Use of Line Width Attribute

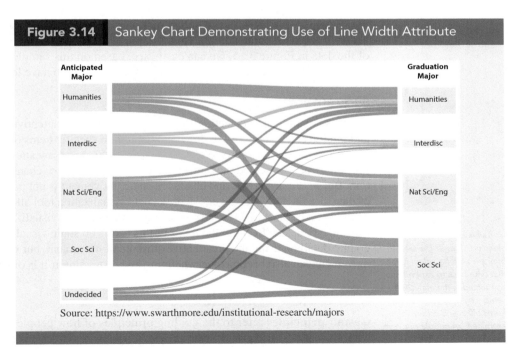

Source: https://www.swarthmore.edu/institutional-research/majors

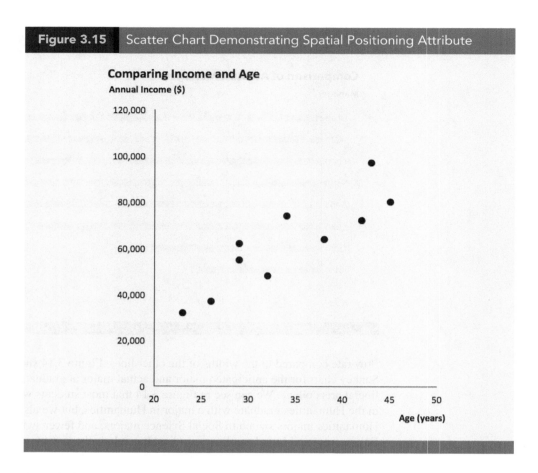

Figure 3.15 Scatter Chart Demonstrating Spatial Positioning Attribute

Spatial Positioning

Spatial positioning refers to the location of an object within some defined space. The spatial positioning most often used in data visualization is 2D positioning. Scatter charts are a common type of chart that make use of the preattentive attribute of spatial positioning. Figure 3.15 shows a scatter chart that provides information about the relationship between annual income and age for a sample of 10 people. Based on the spatial location of the dots in Figure 3.15, we can easily see, based on this sample, that older people tend to have higher annual incomes and younger people tend to have lower annual incomes.

Movement

Humans are attuned to detecting movement. Therefore, preattentive attributes such as flicker and motion can be effective at drawing attention to specific items or portions of a data visualization. **Flicker** refers to effects such as flashing to draw attention to something, while **motion** involves directed movement and can be used to show changes within a visualization. Because many tables and charts are static, movement is not possible in many contexts of data visualization. However, when the data visualization tool allows for the use of movement, it can be used to direct attention to certain areas of a visualization or to show changes over time or space. Because the focus of this text is on static visualizations, we will not go into detail on using the preattentive attribute of movement, but we should caution that movement can also become overwhelming and distracting if it is overused in a visualization.

Gestalt is a German word meaning "form." The Gestalt principles are based on ideas that date back to experiments conducted in the early 20th century by Max Wertheimer, Kurt Koffka, and others to examine how people perceive the world around them.

3.2 Gestalt Principles

Gestalt principles refer to the guiding principles of how people interpret and perceive what they see. These principles can be used in the design of effective data visualizations.

The principles generally describe how people define order and meaning in things they see. We will limit our discussion to the four Gestalt principles that are most closely related to the design of data visualizations: similarity, proximity, enclosure, and connection. An understanding of these principles can help in creating more effective data visualizations and help differentiate between clutter and meaningful design in data visualizations.

Similarity

The Gestalt principle of **similarity** states that people consider objects with similar characteristics as belonging to the same group. These characteristics could be color, shape, size, orientation, or any preattentive attribute. When a data visualization includes objects with similar characteristics, it is important to understand that this communicates to the audience that these objects should be seen as belonging to the same group. Figure 3.16 is a portion of what was shown in Figure 3.10, but here, we are using it to represent the Gestalt principle of similarity. The audience will perceive objects that are the same color or same shape as belonging to the same group. We need to understand this when we design a visualization and make sure that we only use similar characteristics for objects when they belong to the same group.

Proximity

The Gestalt principle of **proximity** states that people consider objects that are physically close to one another as belonging to a group. People will generally seek to collect objects that are near each other into a group and separate objects that are far from one another into different groups. The principle of proximity is apparent in many data visualization charts, including scatter charts.

Consider a firm that would like to perform a market segmentation analysis of its customers to learn more about the customers who purchase its products. The company has collected data on the ages and annual incomes of its customers. A simple scatter chart of the age and income of customers is shown in Figure 3.17. Here, our natural inclination is to view this as three distinct groups of customers based on the proximity of the points. This is an example of the Gestalt principle of proximity.

Enclosure

*To create enclosures such as the ones in Figure 3.18 in Excel, click **Insert** on the Ribbon, then click **Shapes** in the **Illustrations** group.*

The Gestalt principle of **enclosure** states that objects that are physically enclosed together are seen as belonging to the same group. We can illustrate this principle using two modified versions of Figure 3.17. First, we can simply reinforce the similarity principle by creating an enclosure of the points that are already in close proximity (see Figure 3.18a). Alternatively,

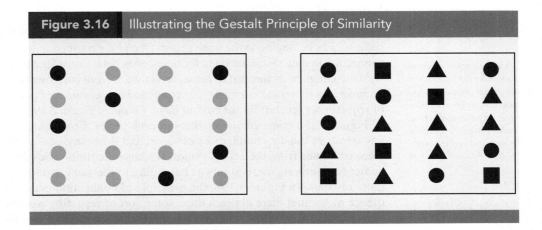

Figure 3.16   Illustrating the Gestalt Principle of Similarity

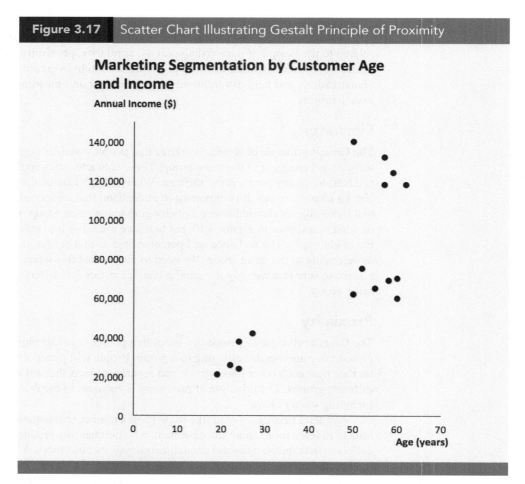

Figure 3.17   Scatter Chart Illustrating Gestalt Principle of Proximity

Marketing Segmentation by Customer Age and Income

suppose there is a third attribute of the customers other than annual income and age that can be used to group these customers, such as educational background. If we want to visually indicate certain customers that share this characteristic of having similar educational backgrounds, then we can use the principle of enclosure to illustrate this even when customers do not appear close together in the chart. This is shown in Figure 3.18b. Note that the enclosure can be indicated in multiple ways in a chart. In Figure 3.18a, we have used shaded areas to enclose points. In Figure 3.18b, we have used dashed boxes. In general, we only need to create a suggestion of enclosure for the audience to view the objects being enclosed as members of the same group.

Connection

The Gestalt principle of **connection** states that people interpret objects that are connected in some way as belonging to the same group. One of the most common uses of the principle of connection in data visualization is for time-series data. Consider a data center company that wants to compare its forecast to actual server loads from customers over the past 14 days. Figure 3.19a shows the company's forecasts and actual values of peak server loads (in terms of requests per second) for the past 14 days. Compare Figure 3.19a to Figure 3.19b.

Figure 3.19b connects the markers in each series. Connecting these markers makes any trends in the data much more obvious, and it becomes easier to separate the forecast values from the actual values. Because the time-series data are connected, the audience interprets these points as belonging to the same group, and patterns become more obvious. In Figure 3.19b, the principle of connection makes it easier for the audience to see that there appears to be some sort of repeating pattern in our data where server loads increase for several days and then decrease and also that our forecast is consistently over-forecasting peak demand on the days with the lowest demand.

Whether or not to retain the markers for the individual data points in a time-series chart is mostly a matter of preference. Here, we have retained the markers, but they could also be removed to show only the line.

Figure 3.18   Scatter Charts Illustrating Gestalt Principle of Enclosure

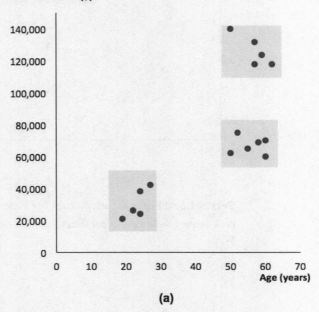

(a)

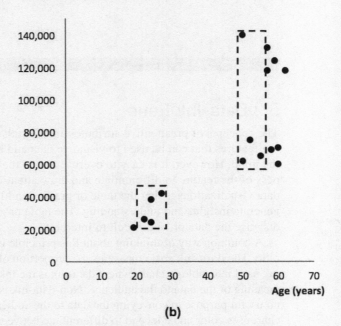

(b)

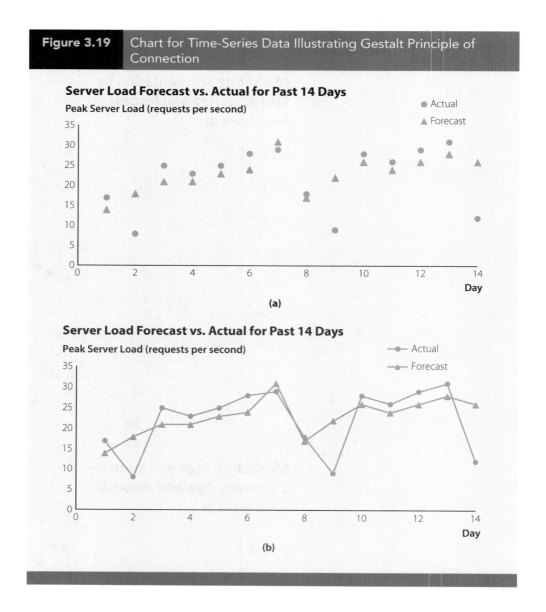

Figure 3.19 Chart for Time-Series Data Illustrating Gestalt Principle of Connection

3.3 Data-Ink Ratio

The concepts of preattentive attributes and Gestalt principles are valuable in understanding features that can be used to visualize data and how visualizations are processed by the mind. However, it is easy to overuse any of the features and diminish the effectiveness of the feature to differentiate and draw attention. A guiding principle for effective data visualizations is that the table or graph should illustrate the data to help the audience generate insights and understanding. The table or graph should not be so cluttered as to disguise the data or be difficult to interpret.

The data-ink ratio was introduced by Edward Tufte in his 1983 book The Visual Display of Quantitative Information.

A common way of thinking about this principle is the idea of maximizing the data-ink ratio. The **data-ink ratio** measures the proportion of "data-ink" to the total amount of ink used in a table or chart, where data-ink is the ink used that is necessary to convey the meaning of the data to the audience. Non-data-ink is ink used in a table or chart that serves no useful purpose in conveying the data to the audience. Note in Figure 3.11a that the pie chart uses color and a legend to differentiate between the eight managers. The bar chart in this figure communicates the same information without either of these features and so has a higher data-ink ratio.

Table 3.1	Example of Low Data-Ink Ratio Table		
Scarf Sales			
Day	**Sales (units)**	**Day**	**Sales (units)**
1	150	11	170
2	170	12	160
3	140	13	290
4	150	14	200
5	180	15	210
6	180	16	110
7	210	17	90
8	230	18	140
9	140	19	150
10	200	20	230

Let us consider the case of Diaphanous Industries, a firm that produces fine silk clothing products. Diaphanous is interested in tracking the sales of one of its most popular items, a particular style of scarf. Table 3.1 and Figure 3.20 provide examples of a table and chart with low data-ink ratios used to display sales of this style of scarf. The data used in this table and figure represent product sales by day. Both of these examples are similar to tables and charts generated with Excel using common default settings. In Table 3.1, most of the gridlines serve no useful purpose. Likewise, in Figure 3.20, the gridlines in the chart add little additional information. In both cases, most of these lines can be deleted without reducing the information conveyed. However, an important piece of information is missing from Figure 3.20: titles for axis. Generally, axes should always be labeled in a chart. There are rare exceptions to this where both the meaning and unit of measure are obvious, such as when the axis displays the names of months (i.e., "January," "February," "March"). For most charts, we recommend labeling the axes to avoid the possibility of misinterpretation by the audience and to reduce the cognitive load required by the audience.

Table 3.2 shows a modified table in which the gridlines have been deleted. Deleting the gridlines in Table 3.1 increases the data-ink ratio because a larger proportion of the ink in the table is used to convey the information (the actual numbers). Similarly, deleting the unnecessary horizontal and vertical gridlines in Figure 3.20 increases the data-ink ratio. Note that deleting these gridlines and removing (or reducing the size of) the markers at each data point can make it more difficult to determine the exact values plotted in the chart. Thus, understanding the needs of the audience is essential to defining what constitutes a good visualization for that audience. If the audience needs to know the exact sales values on different days, then it may be appropriate to add ink to the chart to label each data point or even to display the data as a table rather than as a chart.

In many cases, **white space**, the portion of a data visualization that is devoid of markings, can improve readability in a table or chart. This principle is similar to the idea of increasing the data-ink ratio. Consider Table 3.2 and Figure 3.21. Removing the unnecessary lines has increased the white space, making it easier to read both the table and the chart. The fundamental idea in creating effective tables and charts is to make them as simple as

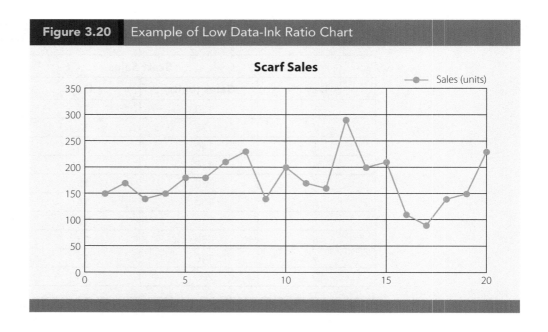

Figure 3.20 | Example of Low Data-Ink Ratio Chart

possible in conveying information to the reader. The following steps describe how to modify the chart in Figure 3.20 to appear as it does in Figure 3.21.

scarfsales_chart

The Chart Elements button is not available in Mac versions of Excel. See the Notes + Comments at the end of Section 2-2 for a description of how to access these features on a Mac.

Step 1. Click anywhere on the chart in the file *scarfsales_chart*
Click the **Chart Elements** button ⊞
Deselect the check box for **Gridlines**
Deselect the check box for **Legend**

Step 2. Double-click one of the data points in the chart
When the **Format Data Series** task pane appears, click the **Fill & Line** icon ◇
Select **Marker**, and under **Marker Options**, select **None**

Table 3.2 | Increasing the Data-Ink Ratio in a Table by Removing Unnecessary Gridlines

Scarf Sales

Day	Sales (units)	Day	Sales (units)
1	150	11	170
2	170	12	160
3	140	13	290
4	150	14	200
5	180	15	210
6	180	16	110
7	210	17	90
8	230	18	140
9	140	19	150
10	200	20	230

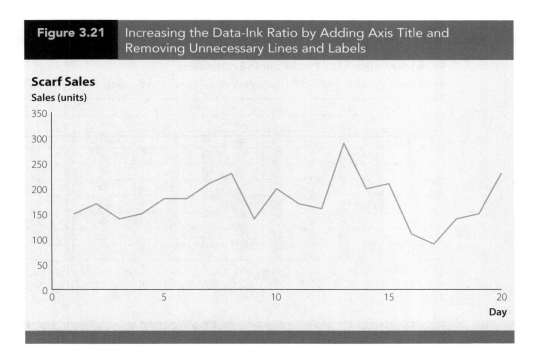

Figure 3.21   Increasing the Data-Ink Ratio by Adding Axis Title and Removing Unnecessary Lines and Labels

Step 3. Click the chart title "Scarf Sales"
Drag this text box to the left so it aligns with the vertical axis
Click the **Home** tab on the Ribbon, and select the **Align Left** button ≡ in the **Alignment** group to left justify the chart title
Click the chart title text box, type *Sales (units)* under the existing chart title, and change the font of this text to **Calibri 10.5 Bold** to create the vertical axis title (see Figure 3.21)
Step 4. Click the **Insert** tab on the Ribbon, and select **Text Box** from the **Text** group
Click on the chart just below the end of the horizontal axis to create a title for this axis
Type *Day* into the text box, and position it just below the end of the horizontal axis
Change the font for this text to **Calibri 10.5 Bold** to create the horizontal axis title (see Figure 3.21)

Comparing Figure 3.20 to Figure 3.21 also illustrates the importance of editing the default charts created in Excel. Without additional edits, most charts created in Excel will appear more like Figure 3.20 than Figure 3.21. It is important to spend the extra time to add axis titles where needed, remove unnecessary gridlines, and format the chart title to improve the data-ink ratio of charts created in Excel. This will greatly enhance the visual appeal of these charts and make them easier for the audience to interpret.

The process of increasing the data-ink ratio in charts is also known as decluttering. **Decluttering** refers to removing the clutter, or non-data-ink, in a chart. In Figure 3.20, the gridlines are considered clutter because they provide little value to the audience's ability to interpret the chart.

As another example of decluttering, consider Figure 3.22. This figure shows the course evaluations for Professor Bob Smith's Statistics (STAT) 7011 course, Introduction to Analytics. The chart shows Professor Smith's course evaluation score for the question, "How effective is this instructor?" which is scored on a scale of 1 = *Not effective* to 5 = *Extremely effective*. The historical average score over all

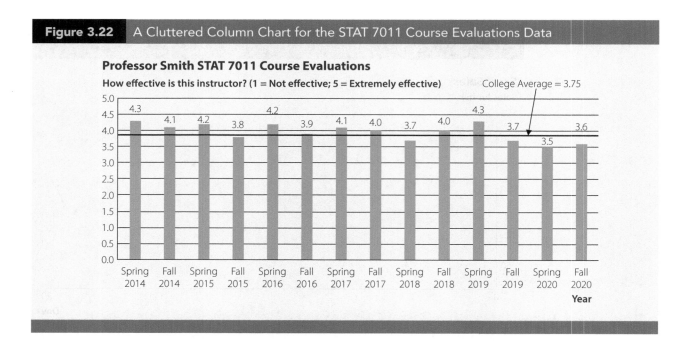

Figure 3.22   A Cluttered Column Chart for the STAT 7011 Course Evaluations Data

courses in the college for this question is 3.75, so this value is also indicated on the chart.

The chart in Figure 3.22 has a low data-ink ratio and is cluttered. We can improve the data-ink ratio and declutter the chart by removing aspects of the chart that are not helpful to the audience. We can remove the gridlines and simplify the horizontal axis. By adding a legend that specifies Fall Semester and Spring Semester, we can simplify the horizontal axis by only showing years. We can simplify the vertical axis by removing some of the markings to increase the use of white space. If our main goal for the chart is to compare Professor Smith's performance to the college average, we can also remove the data labels from each column to further declutter the chart.

The steps below show how to declutter this chart to improve the data-ink ratio. Because Excel is somewhat limited in the editing functions available for charts to create the most effective designs, we will manually adjust several elements of this chart using text boxes to declutter the chart.

coursevals_chart

Step 1. Click anywhere on the chart in the file *coursevals_chart*
Click the **Chart Elements** button ⊞
   Deselect the check box for **Gridlines**
   Deselect the check box for **Data Labels**
Step 2. Click anywhere on the chart
   Select the vertical axis
Step 3. When the **Format Axis** task pane appears:
   Change the entry in the **Major Box** under **Units** from 0.5 to *1.0* to remove the vertical-axis increments of 0.5
Step 4. Double-click the second column in the chart corresponding to "Fall 2014" so only this column is selected in the chart
   In the **Format Data Point** task pane, click the **Fill & Line** icon ◇

   Under **Fill**, select a darker blue color for this column 🖌▾
Step 5. Repeat Step 4 for each column corresponding to a Fall semester in the chart (see Figure 3.23)

Step 6. Click the semester labels below the horizontal axis and press the **Delete** key to remove the name of each column

Step 7. Delete the text in cells A2:A15 to remove the horizontal axis labels
Type *2014* in cell A2, *2015* in cell A4, *2016* in cell A6, *2017* in cell A8, *2018* in cell A10, *2019* in cell A12, and *2020* in cell A14 to add the years to the horizontal axis on the chart.

Step 8. Click the arrow in the chart pointing to the line for the college average evaluation score and press the **Delete** key

Step 9. Move the text box containing **College Average = 3.75** closer to the line that marks the college average evaluation score

Step 10. Click the **Insert** tab on the Ribbon

Click **Text Box** Text Box in the **Text** group, and click near the upper right of the chart
Click the **Home** tab in the Ribbon, and change the font type to **Wingdings 10.5**
Type *n* in the text box to create a square box
Change the font color of the square box to match the lighter blue columns in the chart
Change the font type back to **Calibri 10.5** and the font color back to black
Type *Spring Semester*, and press **Enter**
Click the **Home** tab in the Ribbon, and change the font type to **Wingdings 10.5**
Type *n* in the text box to create a square box
Change the font color of the square box to match the darker blue columns in the chart
Change the font type back to **Calibri 10.5** and the font color back to black
Type *Fall Semester* (see the legend in Figure 3.23)

Step 11. Line up any added elements of the chart that may have been moved in the editing process. See Figure 3.23 for how the finished chart should appear

Wingdings is a font that contains a variety of symbols that can be edited as text. The Wingdings font can be useful to create text that matches the symbols used in Excel for creating charts.

Figure 3.23 has a higher data-ink ratio and more white space than Figure 3.22, which makes it easier for the audience to interpret. The vertical and horizontal axis labels are now cleaner, and redundant information has been removed. By differentiating Fall Semester and Spring Semester using the preattentive attribute of color and manually creating a legend, we also make it easier for the audience to compare Fall Semester evaluation scores to each other and Spring Semester evaluation scores to each other.

Decluttering is also applicable to tables used in data visualization. In keeping with the principle of maximizing the data-ink ratio, for tables, this usually means avoiding vertical lines in a table unless they are necessary for clarity. Horizontal lines are generally only necessary for separating column titles from data values or when indicating that a calculation has taken place. Consider Figure 3.24, which compares several forms of a table displaying cost, revenue, and profit data for a company. Most people find Design D, with the fewest gridlines, easiest to read. In this table, gridlines are used only to separate the column headings from the data and to indicate that a calculation has occurred to generate the Profits row and the Total column.

In large tables, we can use vertical lines or light shading to help the audience differentiate the columns or rows. Table 3.3 displays revenue data by location for nine cities and shows 12 months of revenue and cost data. In Table 3.3, every other column has been lightly shaded. This helps the reader quickly scan the table to see which values correspond with each month. The horizontal line between the revenue for Academy and the Total row helps the audience differentiate the revenue data for each location and

Figure 3.23   Improved Column Chart through Decluttering for the STAT 7011 Course Evaluations Data

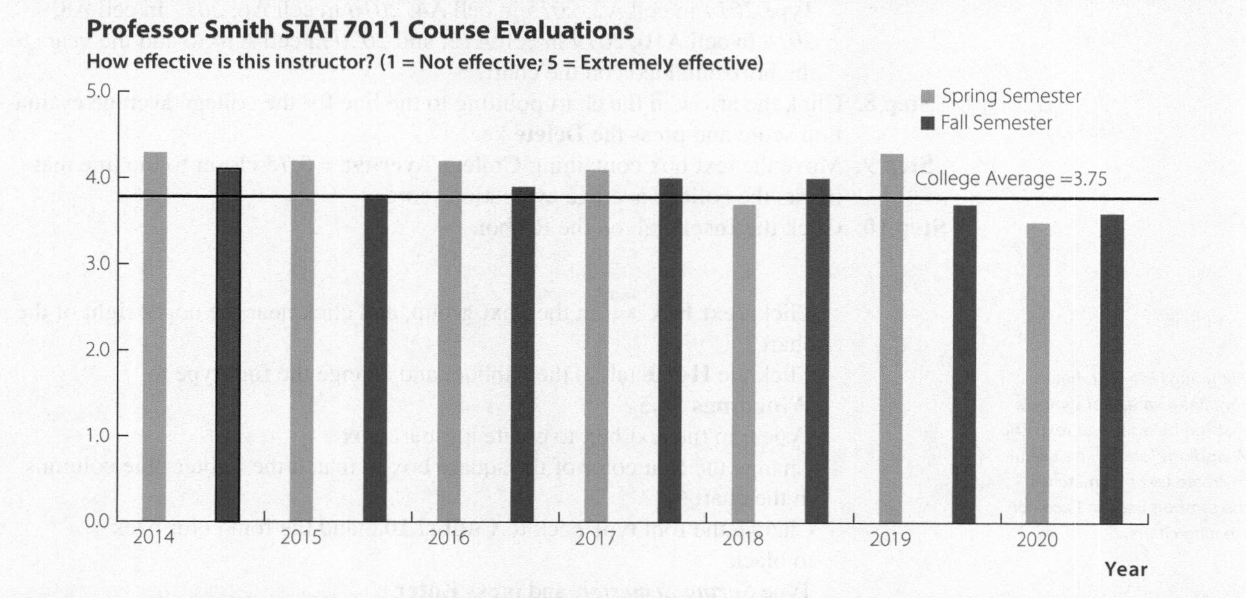

indicates that a calculation to generate the totals by month has been performed. If one wanted to highlight the differences between locations, we could shade every other row instead of every other column.

Notice also the alignment of the text and numbers in Table 3.3. Columns of numerical values in a table should usually be right-aligned; that is, the final digit of each number should be aligned in the column. This makes it easy to see differences in the magnitude of values. If you are showing digits to the right of the decimal point, all values should include the same number of digits to the right of the decimal. Also, use only the number of digits that are necessary to convey the meaning in comparing the values; including additional digits that are not meaningful for comparisons to the audience increases clutter.

Figure 3.24   Comparing Different Table Designs with Different Data-Ink Ratios

Design A:

	Month						
	1	2	3	4	5	6	Total
Costs ($)	48,123	56,458	64,125	52,158	54,718	50,985	326,567
Revenues ($)	64,124	66,128	67,125	48,178	51,785	55,687	353,027
Profits ($)	16,001	9,670	3,000	(3,980)	(2,933)	4,702	26,460

Design B:

	Month						
	1	2	3	4	5	6	Total
Costs ($)	48,123	56,458	64,125	52,158	54,718	50,985	326,567
Revenues ($)	64,124	66,128	67,125	48,178	51,785	55,687	353,027
Profits ($)	16,001	9,670	3,000	(3,980)	(2,933)	4,702	26,460

Design C:

	Month						
	1	2	3	4	5	6	Total
Costs ($)	48,123	56,458	64,125	52,158	54,718	50,985	326,567
Revenues ($)	64,124	66,128	67,125	48,178	51,785	55,687	353,027
Profits ($)	16,001	9,670	3,000	(3,980)	(2,933)	4,702	26,460

Design D:

	Month						
	1	2	3	4	5	6	Total
Costs ($)	48,123	56,458	64,125	52,158	54,718	50,985	326,567
Revenues ($)	64,124	66,128	67,125	48,178	51,785	55,687	353,027
Profits ($)	16,001	9,670	3,000	(3,980)	(2,933)	4,702	26,460

| Table 3.3 | Table Showing Revenues by Location for 12 Months of Data | | | | | | | | | | | | |

| Revenues by Location ($) | Month | | | | | | | | | | | | Total |
	1	2	3	4	5	6	7	8	9	10	11	12	
Temple	8,987	8,595	8,958	6,718	8,066	8,574	8,701	9,490	9,610	9,262	9,875	11,058	107,895
Killeen	8,212	9,143	8,714	6,869	8,150	8,891	8,766	9,193	9,603	10,374	10,456	10,982	109,353
Waco	11,603	12,063	11,173	9,622	8,912	9,553	11,943	12,947	12,925	14,050	14,300	13,877	142,967
Belton	7,671	7,617	7,896	6,899	7,877	6,621	7,765	7,720	7,824	7,938	7,943	7,047	90,819
Granger	7,642	7,744	7,836	5,833	6,002	6,728	7,848	7,717	7,646	7,620	7,728	8,013	88,357
Harker Heights	5,257	5,326	4,998	4,304	4,106	4,980	5,084	5,061	5,186	5,179	4,955	5,326	59,763
Gatesville	5,316	5,245	5,056	3,317	3,852	4,026	5,135	5,132	5,052	5,271	5,304	5,154	57,859
Lampasas	5,266	5,129	5,022	3,022	3,088	4,289	5,110	5,073	4,978	5,343	4,984	5,315	56,620
Academy	4,170	5,266	7,472	1,594	1,732	2,025	8,772	1,956	3,304	3,090	3,579	2,487	45,446
Total	64,124	66,128	67,125	48,178	51,785	55,687	69,125	64,288	66,128	68,128	69,125	69,258	759,079
Costs ($)	48,123	56,458	64,125	52,158	54,718	50,985	57,898	62,050	65,215	61,819	67,828	69,558	710,935

In many business applications, we report financial values, in which case we often round to the nearest dollar or include two digits to the right of the decimal when such precision is necessary. For extremely large numbers, we may prefer to display data rounded to the nearest thousand, ten thousand, or even million. For instance, if we need to include, say, $3,457,982 and $10,124,390 in a table when exact dollar values are not necessary, we could write these as 3.458 and 10.124 and indicate that all values in the table are in units of $1,000,000 (or $ millions).

It is generally most effective to left-align text values within a column in a table, as in the Revenues by Location (the first) column of Table 3.3. In some cases, you may prefer to center text, but you should do this only if the text values are all approximately the same length. Otherwise, aligning the first letter of each data entry promotes readability. Column headings should either match the alignment of the data in the columns or be centered over the values, as in Table 3.3.

3.4 Other Data Visualization Design Issues
Minimizing Eye Travel

Data visualizations should be easy to view and interpret by the audience. Charts and tables should reveal insights to the audience while minimizing the cognitive load required of the audience. We can minimize the cognitive load by using preattentive attributes and Gestalt principles as well as by increasing the data-ink ratio in our data visualizations. We can also minimize cognitive load by minimizing the eye travel required by the audience.

Consider the Office of Budget and Performance Improvement for the City of Springfield. This city office would like to compare the performance of the two police districts located in its city. One performance metric used by the city is clearance rate, which is the fraction of reported crimes that result in an arrest. Figure 3.25 compares the clearance rates for property crimes in Springfield's District 1 and District 2 over the last 6 months.

Figure 3.25 has several characteristics that increase the required eye travel for the audience. Many of these characteristics are typical of default charts created in Excel. First, the

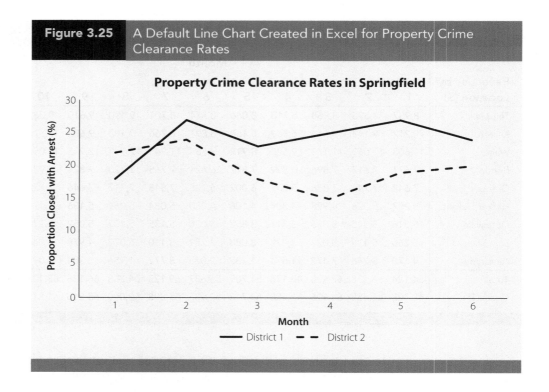

Figure 3.25   A Default Line Chart Created in Excel for Property Crime Clearance Rates

legend is located at the bottom of the chart. This requires the audience members to look at the legend at the bottom of the chart and then move their eyes up to the lines to match the line type from the legend with the correct line in the chart. We can greatly reduce the eye travel required of the audience by moving the legend closer to the lines or, even better, by directly labeling each line in the chart. Second, Excel also typically inserts vertical-axis title text as rotated 90 degrees from the chart title and horizontal-axis title. This requires the audience's eyes to move all around the chart to read the horizontal-axis title, the vertical-axis title, and the chart title. It is better to align the titles within a chart as much as possible so the audience can look at only a few places to quickly interpret the chart. The steps below demonstrate how we can improve Figure 3.25 to reduce the amount of eye travel required by the audience.

clearancerates_chart

Steps 4–6 add labels to the lines within the chart so a separate legend is not necessary to minimize eye travel.

Step 1. Click anywhere on the chart in the file *clearancerates_chart*

Click the **Chart Elements** button +

Deselect the check box for **Legend**

Step 2. Double-click the last data point, on the line in the chart for the District 1 data to select only that data point

Right click the selected data point, and select **Add Data Label** (this will add a data label with the value of this data point which is "24")

Change the "24" in this data label to *District 1*, and change the font to **Calibri 10.5**

Step 3. Double-click the last data point on the line in the chart for the District 2 data to select only that data point

Right click the selected data point, and select **Add Data Label** (this will add a data label with the value of this data point, which is "20")

Change the "20" in this data label to *District 2*, and change the font to **Calibri 10.5**

Step 4. Click the vertical-axis title "Proportion Closed with Arrest (%)"

Press the **Delete** key

Step 5. Click the chart title "Property Crime Clearance Rates in Springfield"

Drag this text box to the left so it aligns with the vertical axis

Click the **Home** tab on the Ribbon, and select the **Align Left** button ≡ in the **Alignment** group to left justify the chart title

Step 6. Click the **Insert** tab on the Ribbon

Click **Text Box** in the **Text** group, and click above the vertical axis to create a text box for the vertical axis title

Type *Proportion Closed with Arrest (%)* in the text box, and change the font to **Calibri 10.5 Bold** to create the vertical axis title (see Figure 3.26)

Step 7. Click the horizontal-axis title "Month," and drag the text box to the end of the horizontal axis so it lines up with the last label on the horizontal axis, in this case, the "6" (see Figure 3.26)

Excel's automatic axis title options only allow for limited formatting changes. There-fore, to create a vertical-axis title above the axis that mini-mizes eye travel, we manually create this with a text box.

Figure 3.26 reduces the eye travel required of the audience by aligning the chart title and vertical-axis title with the vertical axis, moving the line labels adjacent to the chart lines, and aligning the horizontal-axis label with the line labels and the end of the horizontal axis. This allows the audience to naturally view the chart by scanning from left to right and easily in-terpret all important information with a low cognitive load. This is the final form we will use for most charts in this textbook. The preceding steps require additional effort from what is easily created in Excel, but we recommend these steps when creating a final version of a data visualization to make it as easy as possible for the audience to interpret your chart.

Choosing a Font for Text

Text is an important part of any data visualization. It is used to label axes, fill in table val-ues, and call out important aspects of the visualization to the audience. Because text is such an important part of a data visualization, the font that is used to display the text is also an important consideration. Most data visualization software tools, including Excel, allow the user to choose from dozens, and even hundreds, of font options for displaying text.

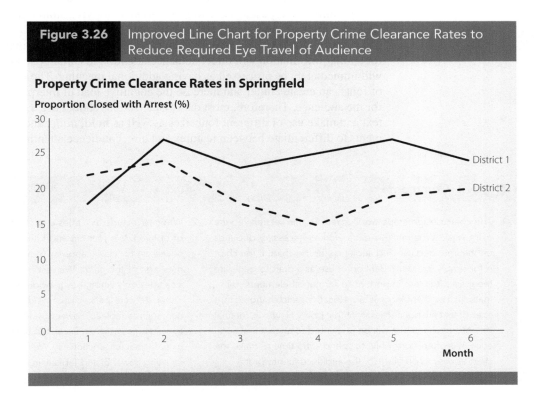

Figure 3.26   Improved Line Chart for Property Crime Clearance Rates to Reduce Required Eye Travel of Audience

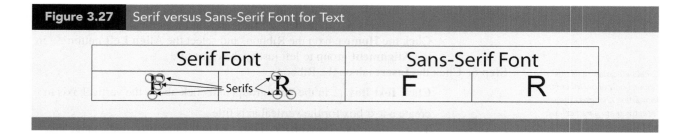

Figure 3.27   Serif versus Sans-Serif Font for Text

Serif Font	Sans-Serif Font

Not all data visualization experts agree on the preferred type of font to use for text in data visualizations, and often this choice may depend on the needs of the audience or on other design elements of the data visualization. However, most experts agree that some font types are generally preferred for text in a data visualization over others; for example, **sans-serif fonts** (fonts that do not contain serifs) are generally preferred over **serif fonts** (fonts that do contain serifs) for text in a data visualization. **Serifs** refer to the small end-of-stroke features that are visual in the characters created using serif fonts. Figure 3.27 illustrates the difference between sans-serif and serif fonts. Common serif fonts include Times, Times New Roman, and Courier. Common sans-serif fonts include Arial, Calibri, Myriad Pro and Verdana.

In general, serif fonts are preferred for printed work, and sans-serif fonts are preferred for text displayed digitally. Sans-serif fonts are also often more legible than serif fonts at small sizes. Because data visualizations are often viewed in both print form and digitally, and because data visualizations often contain fonts of many different sizes, sans-serif fonts are generally preferred over serif fonts for text in data visualizations. In this textbook, all charts provided in Excel use the sans-serif font Calibri because it is the default font in Excel. Most printed charts in the textbook use the sans-serif font Myriad Pro because it is legible at many different sizes, and it works well for both print and digital work. However, other sans-serif fonts, such as Arial and Verdana, are also usually acceptable for data visualization purposes.

Perhaps even more important than whether text in a data visualization uses serif or sans-serif font is that the choice of fonts is consistent and restrained. Generally, charts should use the same font type and same font size when conveying similar information to the audience. For instance, horizontal- and vertical-axis titles should generally have the same type and size of font. Because size is a preattentive attribute, the use of inconsistent font sizes for similar information will direct audience attention to certain parts of a visualization and will immediately be processed as having additional meaning. The use of too many types of fonts can create clutter and increase the cognitive load of interpreting the visualization for the audience. Therefore, most data visualizations should use a single type of font for text and make use of different font sizes as well as **bold**, *italic*, and possibly color enhancements to differentiate between features and direct audience attention.

Notes + Comments

1. The chart design steps we illustrate in this section require extra work. Whether this extra work is necessary depends on the intended use and audience for the chart. If the chart is for simply exploring data or for use as a draft to generate feedback, it is less important to format all elements; reformats such as changing axis label locations and changing font sizes of text are not necessary at that point. However, for final versions of charts that will be presented to an external audience, it is often worthwhile to spend extra time to make the chart as easy as possible for the audience to interpret.

2. When to include axis titles and chart titles is often a matter of opinion. We recommend having a chart title when it is necessary for clarification or to make explicit the intended message of the chart. We recommend omitting chart and axis titles only when they provide redundant information.

3. Other software packages commonly used for data visualization, such as Tableau, Power BI, and R, have more flexibility for formatting charts than Excel, but they also require more time to learn their full functionality. We include chapter appendices for using Power BI and Tableau in this textbook.

3.5 Common Mistakes in Data Visualization Design
Wrong Type of Visualization

The best type of chart or table to use for data visualization strongly depends on the audience that will view the visualization as well as the insights or story that is to be told through the visualization. Throughout this textbook, we provide best practices for designing effective data visualizations, but many of the decisions related to which chart to use and some aspects of the design will depend on the situation and goal of the visualization. In this section, we use the concepts presented in this chapter to discuss several situations for which one type of visualization is preferred over another. However, we must keep in mind that the most effective visualization depends on the needs of the audience and the message we are trying to convey.

Understanding the needs of the audience is discussed in more detail in Chapter 7.

If the goal of the visualization is to convey precise numerical values, then it is often preferable to use a table rather than a chart. Because it is more difficult for an audience to make relative comparisons on the preattentive attribute of shape than on the preattentive attribute of length, bar or column charts are generally preferred over pie charts. However, there are cases for which the most appropriate type of visualization depends on the goal of the visualization and is not always obvious.

Recommendations for when to use a table versus a chart and which type of chart to use are discussed in more detail in Chapter 2.

Consider the case of Stanley Consulting Group, a company that provides analytics consulting to nonprofit companies. Stanley Consulting Group has offices in Hartford, Stamford, and Providence. Each office has a similar number of consultants and similar performance expectations. Stanley Consulting Group would like to compare the performance of each office. It is mostly interested in comparing each office's performance relative to the quarterly goal and in identifying trends over time at each location. Figure 3.28 uses a clustered column chart to compare the performances of the offices in terms of quarterly booked revenue for the previous six quarters. The chart also compares this performance to the quarterly booked revenue goal of $600,000 that applies to each office.

The clustered column chart in Figure 3.28 is not necessarily inappropriate for any obvious reason, but we should try to visualize the same data with other charts to see if we can

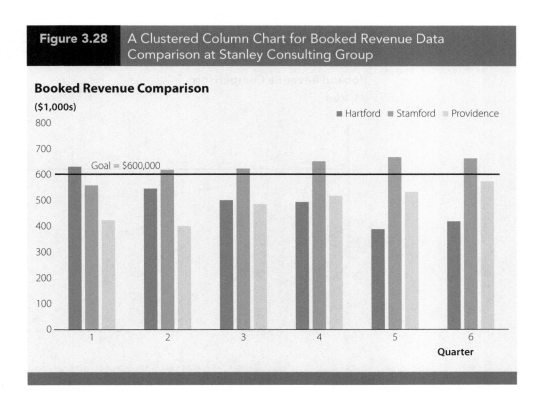

Figure 3.28 A Clustered Column Chart for Booked Revenue Data Comparison at Stanley Consulting Group

improve on this design. The steps below show how we can change the clustered column chart shown in Figure 3.28 to a line chart in Excel.

bookedrevenue_chart

Step 1. Right click anywhere on the chart in the file *bookedrevenue_chart*
      Select **Change Chart Type...**
Step 2. When the **Change Chart Type** dialog box appears
      Select [⋈] Line
      Click **OK**
Step 3. Click anywhere on the line chart
      Click the **Chart Elements** button [＋]
      Deselect the check box for **Legend**
Step 4. Double-click the last data point on the line in the chart for the Stamford data to select only this data point
      Right click the selected data point, and select **Add Data Label** (this will add a data label with the value of this data point, which is "665")
      Change the "665" in this data label to *Stamford*, and change the font to **Calibri 10.5**
Step 5. Double-click the last data point on the line in the chart for the Providence data to select only that data point
      Right click the selected data point, and select **Add Data Label** (this will add a data label with the value of this data point, which is "575")
      Change the "575" in this data label to *Providence,* and change the font to **Calibri 10.5**
Step 6. Double-click the last data point on the line in the chart for the Hartford data to select only that data point
      Right click the selected data point, and select **Add Data Label** (this will add a data label with the value of this data point, which is "420")
      Change the "420" in this data label to *Hartford,* and change the font to **Calibri 10.5**

Steps 4–6 add labels to the lines within the chart so a separate legend is not necessary to minimize eye travel.

These steps result in the line chart shown in Figure 3.29.

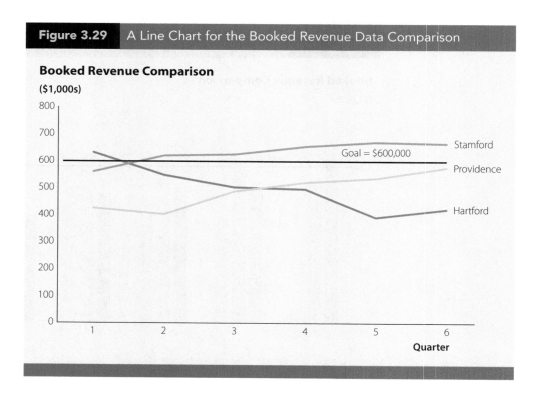

Figure 3.29   A Line Chart for the Booked Revenue Data Comparison

Using a line chart for these data in Figure 3.29 has several advantages. First, the Gestalt principle of connectedness in the line chart makes it much easier to see trends in booked revenue by office. From Figure 3.29, we see that Hartford exceeded the booked revenue goal in Quarter 1 but that it has fallen below the goal consistently after that, and its booked revenues are generally declining. Booked revenues at the Stamford office fell short of the goal in Quarter 1, but it has exceeded the goal in every subsequent quarter, and its booked revenues have been steady. Booked revenues have fallen short of the goal in each quarter for the Providence office, but its booked revenues have been steadily increasing. It is much more challenging to see these trends in Figure 3.28 because it is more difficult to group the booked revenues for a location together without taking advantage of the principle of connectedness. Figure 3.29 is also preferable because it reduces the eye travel required of the audience through the removal of the legend from Figure 3.28 and the labeling of each line.

Trying to Display Too Much Information

Another common mistake in building effective charts is trying to convey too much information on a single chart, which is a symptom of trying to communicate too many insights to the audience simultaneously.

Consider the case of Keeland Industries, an online company that provides replacement parts for automobiles. It provides both original-equipment manufacturer (OEM) replacement parts and replacement parts made by different manufacturers that are known as aftermarket replacement parts. Because Keeland sells the replacement parts online, it sells parts to customers throughout the United States. For sales tracking and performance measurement purposes, Keeland divides the United States into 12 regions. Keeland's management team is most interested in comparing the OEM sales across the 12 regions to see which are performing best for OEM sales and in comparing the Aftermarket sales across the 12 regions to see which are performing best for Aftermarket sales.

Figure 3.30 displays the OEM and Aftermarket sales by region as a clustered column chart. The clustered column chart makes it easy to compare OEM sales to Aftermarket

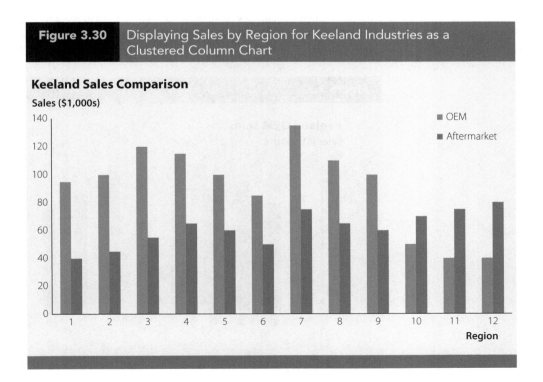

Figure 3.30   Displaying Sales by Region for Keeland Industries as a Clustered Column Chart

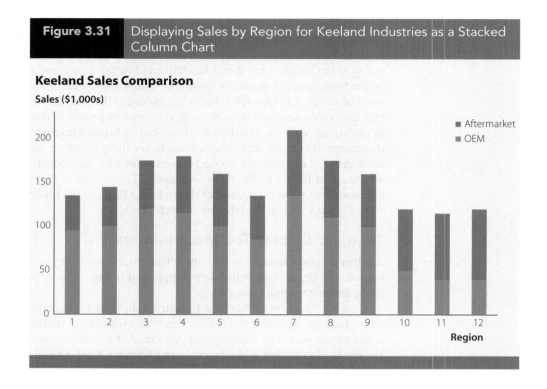

Figure 3.31   Displaying Sales by Region for Keeland Industries as a Stacked Column Chart

sales in each region. However, if the potential markets for these different types of parts are different in each region, that comparison is not particularly useful.

Figure 3.31 displays the OEM and Aftermarket sales by region as a stacked column chart. The stacked column chart makes it much easier to compare the total sales in the different regions. Therefore, a stacked column chart would be a good choice if the goal is to compare total sales (OEM plus Aftermarket) among the 12 regions. However, the stated goal of this visualization is to compare the OEM sales across regions separately from the Aftermarket sales. The best visualization to accomplish the stated goal is to use two separate column charts as shown in Figures 3.32 and 3.33.

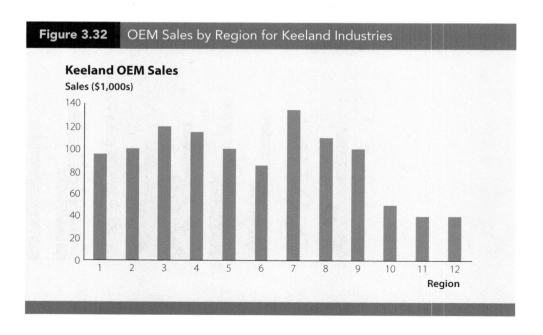

Figure 3.32   OEM Sales by Region for Keeland Industries

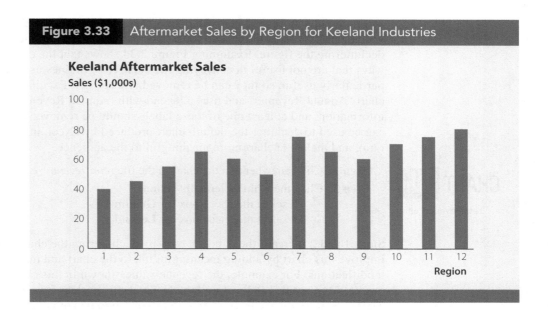

Figure 3.33   Aftermarket Sales by Region for Keeland Industries

Keeland Aftermarket Sales

Sales ($1,000s)

Using Excel Default Settings for Charts

Microsoft Excel allows for the creation of a variety of charts and tables to visualize data. However, a common mistake is to use the default output from Excel without considering changes to the design and format of the visualizations it produces. Excel's default settings are counter to many of the suggestions covered in this chapter (and the rest of this textbook) for creating good data visualizations. Consider Figure 3.34. This column chart, which was produced using Excel, shows revenues for eight retail store locations in Texas. The company is interested in comparing revenues by location and specifically in examining the relative performance of the store located in Laredo because this store has recently had a change in management.

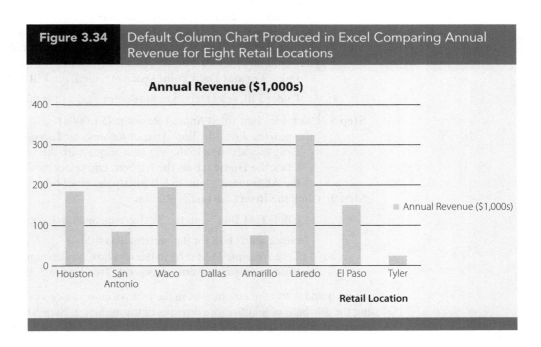

Figure 3.34   Default Column Chart Produced in Excel Comparing Annual Revenue for Eight Retail Locations

Annual Revenue ($1,000s)

Figure 3.34 suffers from several flaws that prevent it from being an effective data visualization. The data-ink ratio for Figure 3.34 is low, so we should consider ways of decluttering the figure. Examining Figure 3.34 shows that the chart uses ink in several ways that are not useful in conveying the data. The gridlines used in this chart are not particularly useful, so they can be removed. We see that Excel automatically titles the chart "Annual Revenue" and uses a legend with "Annual Revenue." This is redundant information, and at least one of these labels should be removed. The following steps can be used to declutter the default chart produced by Excel, increase the data-ink ratio, and make the chart more meaningful to the audience.

retailrevenue_chart

Step 1. Click anywhere on the chart in the file *retailrevenue_chart*
Step 2. Click the **Chart Elements** button ⊞
       Deselect the check box for **Gridlines**
       Deselect the check box for **Legend**

Steps 1 and 2 increase the data-ink ratio by decluttering the chart. We can further improve this chart by adding meaningful ink to the chart and making a few other modifications. For example, the revenue values shown in this chart are from the previous year and are in 1,000s of dollars. None of this is clear from the chart. To make it easier for the audience to compare the relative amounts of annual revenue by location, we can sort the columns in decreasing order. Finally, because the audience is particularly interested in annual sales at the Laredo location, we can change the color of the column associated with Laredo to draw the audience's attention to that part of the chart. The following steps create the finished column chart shown in Figure 3.35.

Step 3. Select cells A1:B9
       Click the **Data** tab on the Ribbon
       Click **Sort** in the **Sort & Filter** group
Step 4. When the **Sort** dialog box appears:
       Select the check box for **My data has headers**
       In the **Sort by** box, select **Annual Revenue,** and in the **Order** box, select **Largest to Smallest**
       Click **OK**
Step 5. Click the **Chart Elements** button ⊞
       Select the check box for **Data Labels**
Step 6. Click on the vertical axis labels and press the **Delete** key
Step 7. Double-click the second column in the chart corresponding to "Laredo" so only this column is selected in the chart
       In the **Format Data Point** task pane, click the **Fill & Line** icon ◇
       Under **Fill**, select a darker blue color 🎨 ▾ for this column
Step 8. Click the chart title "Annual Revenue ($1,000s)" and change this title to
       Comparing Previous Year Annual Revenue at Laredo to Other Locations
       Drag this text box to the left so it aligns with the vertical axis
       Click the **Home** tab on the Ribbon, and select the **Align Left** button ≡ in the **Alignment** group to left justify the chart title
Step 9. Click the **Insert** tab on the Ribbon
       Click **Text Box** 📝 in the **Text** group, and click above the vertical axis to create a text box for the vertical axis title
       Type *Revenue ($1,000s)* in the text box, and change the font to **Calibri 10.5 Bold** to create the vertical axis title (see Figure 3.35)

Steps 3 and 4 sort the columns to make relative comparisons of the revenue by location using the attribute of length more obvious to the audience. Step 5 adds data labels at the top of each column to give the exact value of revenues at that location. This should only be

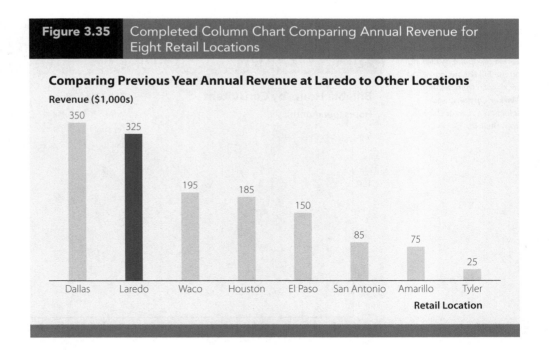

| **Figure 3.35** | Completed Column Chart Comparing Annual Revenue for Eight Retail Locations |

Comparing Previous Year Annual Revenue at Laredo to Other Locations

Revenue ($1,000s)

done when the audience may need to know the exact values shown in the chart. Because we have added data labels to each column, we remove the redundant vertical axis labels in Step 6. Step 7 uses the preattentive attribute of color to differentiate the column corresponding to Laredo to draw the audience's attention to this column. Finally, Steps 8 and 9 align the chart title and vertical-axis title with the vertical axis to minimize the required eye travel to interpret this chart.

Too Many Attributes

In Section 3-1, we discuss the importance of using preattentive attributes in data visualizations to make them easy to understand by the audience. However, using too many preattentive attributes in the same visualization can cause confusion for the audience. Consider again the case of Stanley Consulting Group. The company wants to examine how consultant characteristics such as job title, length of time with the company, and highest educational degree attained are related to the amount of billable hours filed by that consultant. Figure 3.36 attempts to show this information.

All of the information the company wants to consider is shown in Figure 3.36: the number of billable hours for each consultant (on the vertical axis), the length of time at the company (on the horizontal axis), the consultant's job title (indicated by the color of the marker in the chart), and the highest degree attained by the consultant (indicated by the shape of the marker in the chart). Figure 3.36 uses several preattentive attributes from Section 3-1, including spatial positioning, shape, and color. However, because we are using many different preattentive attributes, this chart is difficult for an audience to process. It requires the audience to scan back and forth between the markers in the chart, the legends, and the vertical and horizontal axes. Therefore, this is probably not a particularly useful chart.

Figure 3.36 can be an effective chart for the analyst who is exploring the data looking for relationships. However, it is probably not the most effective choice for presenting to an audience as a final version meant to explain the data.

A better chart than what is shown in Figure 3.36 would concentrate on examining fewer relationships and using fewer preattentive attributes. The exact choice of which features to show on the chart depends on the goals of the chart and needs of the audience. If it is more important to examine the relationship between billable hours, length of time at the company, and the job title of the consultant, then a chart such as the one shown in Figure 3.37 is preferred.

*The type of marker displayed on a chart in Excel can be changed in the **Format Data Series** task pane by clicking on the **Fill & Line** icon, clicking on **Marker**, then **Marker Options,** and selecting a marker shape from **Built-in.***

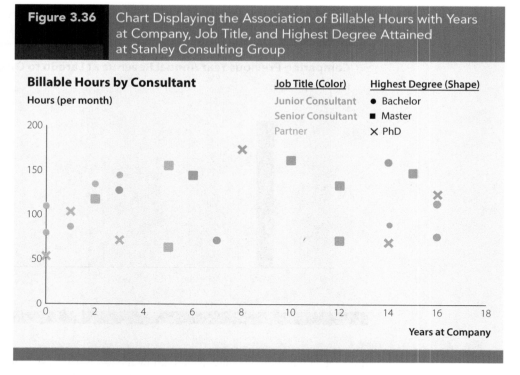

Figure 3.36	Chart Displaying the Association of Billable Hours with Years at Company, Job Title, and Highest Degree Attained at Stanley Consulting Group

Unnecessary Use of 3D

Three-dimensional (3D) charts are often difficult for an audience to understand. Many novice analysts will create 3D charts in Excel even when the third dimension does not provide any useful information. Consider the 3D column chart shown in Figure 3.38. This chart compares the billable hours for eight consultants who work for Stanley Consulting Group. Because the third dimension in Figure 3.38 is not used to display any useful information, it only serves to decrease the data-ink ratio of the chart and make it more difficult for the

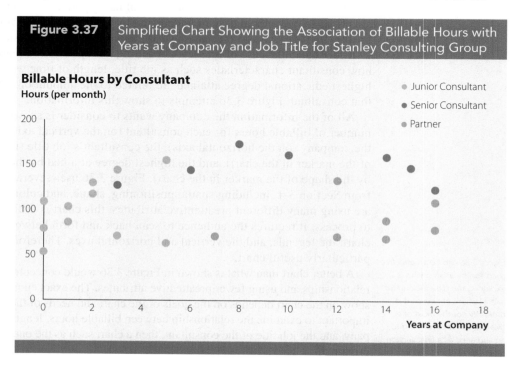

Figure 3.37	Simplified Chart Showing the Association of Billable Hours with Years at Company and Job Title for Stanley Consulting Group

Figure 3.38	A 3D Column Chart Displaying Billable Hours for Stanley Group Consultants Where the Third Dimension Provides No Useful Information

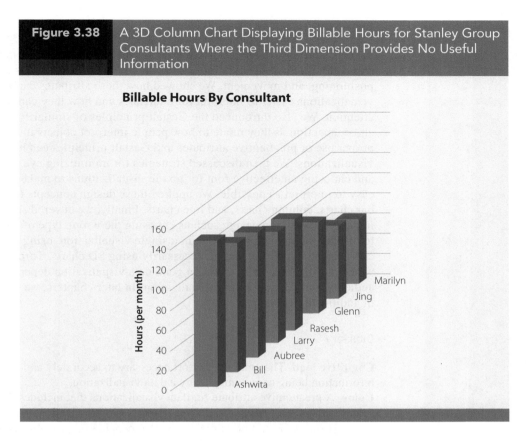

audience to interpret. Even if the third dimension is used to display unique information, 3D charts are difficult to interpret. Therefore, we generally recommend against the use of 3D charts for data visualization. In a better design for this column chart, we remove the third dimension and display the chart as the 2D column chart shown in Figure 3.39.

Figure 3.39	An Improved 2D Column Chart Displaying Billable Hours for Stanley Group Consultants

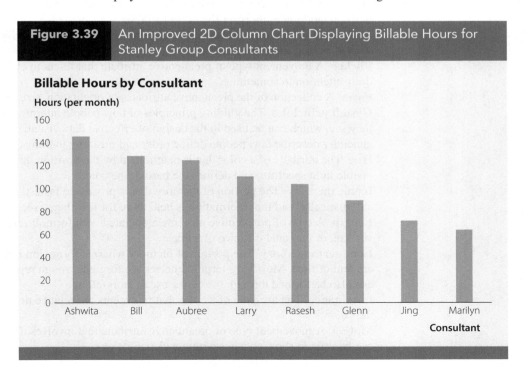

Summary

In this chapter, we have discussed how to use specific design elements to create effective data visualizations. We introduced the preattentive attributes of color, form, spatial positioning, and movement. We showed how these attributes can be used to make data visualizations easier to interpret for audiences and how they can direct the audience's attention. We also introduced the Gestalt principles of similarity, proximity, enclosure, and connection as they relate to how people interpret objects in a data visualization. The proper use of preattentive attributes and Gestalt principles can help create effective data visualizations. We then discussed strategies for minimizing eye travel for the audience and choosing an effective font for text in visualizations to make charts and tables as easy to interpret as possible. We applied these design concepts to tables, scatter charts, bar charts, column charts, and line charts. Finally, we covered some common mistakes in data visualization design such as choosing the wrong type of visualization, trying to display too much information in a single visualization, using the default format for charts created in Excel, and unnecessarily using 3D charts. Throughout the chapter, we emphasized that what makes a good data visualization depends on the needs of the audience and the goal of the visualization. In later chapters, we will cover these issues in additional detail.

Glossary

Cognitive load The amount of effort necessary to accurately and efficiently process the information being communicated by a data visualization.

Color A preattentive attribute for data visualizations that includes the attributes of hue, saturation, and luminance.

Connection A Gestalt principle stating that people interpret objects that are connected in some way as belonging to the same group.

Data-ink ratio Measures the proportion of "data-ink" to the total amount of ink used in a table or chart where data-ink is the ink used that is necessary to convey the meaning of the data to the audience.

Decluttering The act of removing the non-data-ink in the visualization that does not help the audience interpret the chart or table.

Enclosure A Gestalt principle stating that objects that are physically enclosed together are seen as belonging to the same group.

Flicker A movement type of preattentive attribute that refers to effects such as flashing to draw attention to something.

Form A collection of the preattentive attributes of orientation, size, shape, length, and width.

Gestalt principles The guiding principles of how people interpret and perceive things they see, which can be used in the design of effective data visualizations. The principles generally describe how people define order and meaning in things they see.

Hue The attribute of a color that is determined by the position the light occupies on the visible light spectrum and defines the base of the color.

Iconic memory The portion of memory that is processed fastest. It is processed automatically, and the information is held there for less than a second.

Length A type of preattentive attribute associated with form. It refers to the horizontal, vertical, or diagonal distance of a line.

Long-term memory The portion of memory where information is stored for an extended amount of time. Most long-term memories are formed through repetition and rehearsal but can also be formed through the clever use of storytelling.

Luminance The attribute of a color that represents the relative degree of black or white in the color.

Motion A movement type of preattentive attribute that involves directed movement and can be used to show changes within a visualization.

Orientation A type of preattentive attribute associated with form. It refers to the relative positioning of an object within a data visualization.

Preattentive attributes Features of a data visualization that can be processed by iconic memory. Preattentive attributes related to visual perception are generally divided into four categories: color, form, spatial positioning, and movement.

Proximity A Gestalt principle stating that people consider objects that are physically close to one another as belonging to a group.

Sankey chart A type of data visualization chart that typically depicts the proportional flow of entities where the width of the line represents the relative flow rate compared to the widths of the other lines.

Sans-serif font A style of text that does not include small end-of-stroke features on the characters. These types of fonts include Arial, Calibri, Myriad Pro, and Verdana and are generally preferred for text in data visualizations.

Saturation The attribute of a color that represents the amount of gray in the color and determines the intensity or purity of the hue in the color.

Serif font A style of text that includes small end-of-stroke features on the characters. These types of fonts include Times, Times New Roman, and Courier.

Serifs The small end-of-stroke features that are visible in the characters created using serif fonts.

Shape A type of preattentive attribute associated with form. It refers to the type of object used in a data visualization.

Short-term memory The portion of memory that holds information for about a minute. It utilizes chunking, or grouping things together, to hold about four chunks of visual information at one time.

Similarity A Gestalt principle stating that people consider objects with similar characteristics as belonging to the same group.

Size A type of preattentive attribute associated with form. It refers to the relative amount of 2D space that an object occupies in a visualization.

Spatial positioning A preattentive attribute that refers to the location of an object within some defined space.

Visual perception The process through which our brains interpret the reflections of light that enter our eyes.

White space The portion of a data visualization that is devoid of markings.

Width A type of preattentive attribute associated with form. It refers to the thickness of the line.

Problems

Conceptual

1. **Memory Used for Preattentive Attributes.** Which of the following types of memory is used to process preattentive attributes? **LO 1**
   i. Iconic memory
   ii. Short-term memory
   iii. Long-term memory
   iv. Random access memory

2. **Preattentive Attributes in a Data Visualization.** Which of the following statements about the use of preattentive attributes in a data visualization are true? (Select all that apply.) **LO 1**
   i. The use of preattentive attributes reduces the cognitive load required by the audience to interpret the information conveyed by a data visualization.
   ii. Preattentive attributes can be used to draw the audience's attention to certain parts of a data visualization.

iii. Overuse of preattentive attributes can lead to clutter and can be distracting to the audience.

iv. Preattentive attributes include attributes such as proximity and enclosure.

3. **Descriptions of Gestalt Principles.** For each description below, provide the name of the Gestalt principle that is being described. **LO 2**

a. Objects that are physically close to one another are seen as belonging to the same group.

b. Objects that are linked in some way are seen as belonging to the same group.

c. Objects that are physically bound together are seen as belonging to the same group.

d. Objects with like characteristics such as color, shape, size, etc. are seen as belonging to the same group.

4. **Scatter with Straight Lines and Markers Chart in Excel.** Using a Scatter with Straight Lines and Markers Chart in Excel makes use of which Gestalt principle? **LO 2**

i. Similarity

ii. Proximity

iii. Enclosure

iv. Connection

5. **Increasing the Data-Ink Ratio on a Chart.** Which of the following changes to a chart would increase the data-ink ratio? (Select all that apply.) **LO 3**

i. Removing unnecessary gridlines.

ii. Removing a legend on a bar chart where each bar is already labeled with the same information.

iii. Adding axis labels to a chart where the units used in each axis are not clear from the chart title.

iv. Adding data labels for each point on a scatter chart when the audience does not need to know exact values.

6. **Pie Charts versus Bar or Column Charts.** Which of the following reasons accurately describe why bar or column charts are often preferred to pie charts for a data visualization? (Select all that apply.) **LO 4**

i. Bar and column charts utilize the Gestalt principle of proximity, while pie charts use the Gestalt principle of connection.

ii. Using a legend for a pie chart creates unnecessary eye travel that can often be reduced by using a bar or column chart that does not require a legend.

iii. Bar and column charts use length rather than size to make comparisons, and length is much easier for the audience to interpret than size.

iv. Pie charts often use different colors to differentiate each piece of the pie, which can create unnecessary clutter compared to bar or column charts that can display the same information without the use of multiple colors.

7. **Market Segmentation for Brandience.** Brandience Marketing LLC provides marketing analytics consulting for clients. For one of its clients, Brandience has been asked to perform a market segmentation study for a business client that provides auditing services to manufacturing customers. The client believes there are two variables of importance that should be used to group similar customers into clusters: Years of Service with the Client and Total Assets. Brandience plans to use a clustering algorithm to group similar customers into different clusters, but before applying the algorithm, Brandience creates a simple scatter chart to plot each customer based on their Years of Service with the Client and Total Assets. The scatter chart created by Brandience follows. **LO 2**

Market Segmentation Analysis of Brandience Clients

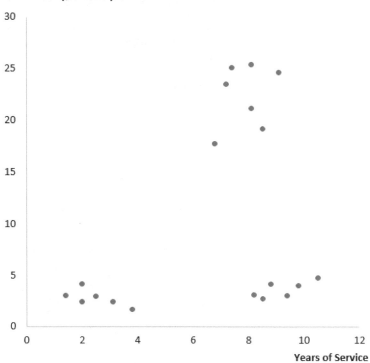

Total Assets ($ millions)

Years of Service

CHART *file*

brandience_chart

a. Based on the Gestalt principle of proximity, how many different groups of customers are shown in the scatter chart?

b. What other Gestalt principle could be used to reinforce the appearance of the different groups of customers for the audience?

8. **Philadelphia City Schools.** The following chart displays data related to the student enrollment at several schools located in the Philadelphia City School District. **LO 1, 4**

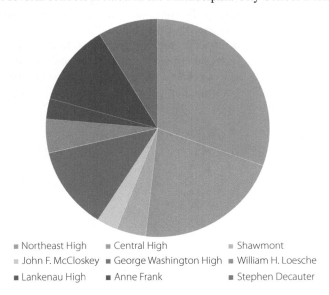

- Northeast High   - Central High   - Shawmont
- John F. McCloskey   - George Washington High   - William H. Loesche
- Lankenau High   - Anne Frank   - Stephen Decauter

a. Which preattentive attributes are being used in this chart?

b. What changes would you suggest to this chart to make it easier for the audience to interpret?

9. **Percentage of College Graduates and Median Monthly Rent in New York City.** The following scatter chart shows the relationship between the percentage of college graduates and the median monthly rent in different sub-boroughs (a description of an area within the city) of New York City. Each point in the scatter chart represents a different sub-borough in New York City. **LO 1**

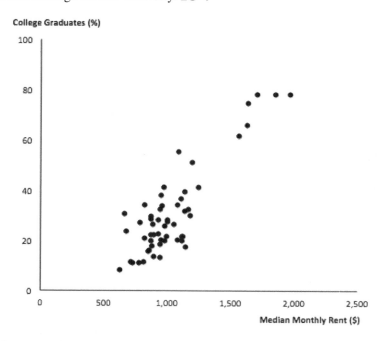

a. Which preattentive attribute is used in this scatter chart?

b. What can you say about the relationship between the percentage of college graduates and the median monthly rent in sub-boroughs of New York City?

10. **Patient Waiting Times at Scott & White.** The Scott & White Medical Center in Temple, Texas, is examining the mean waiting time for patients to receive common orthopedic surgeries at its facility. The medical administrators have collected data on patient waiting times. The mean patient waiting times (in days) for different orthopedic surgeries are shown in the chart below. The medical center is particularly interested in the wait times for anterior cruciate ligament (ACL) reconstruction surgeries because ACL reconstructions are the most common type of orthopedic surgery performed at its facility. **LO 1**

Comparing Patient Waiting Times at Scott & White Medical Center

Surgery Type

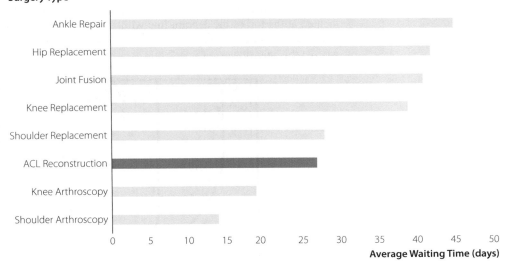

Average Waiting Time (days)

What types of preattentive attributes are used in this chart, and what information do these attributes convey to the audience?

11. **Comparing Managing Consultants at Platt Consulting.** Platt Consulting Services is interested in comparing the number of customer accounts managed by its consultants. In particular, the company needs to compare the number of accounts managed by Bernie Smith, Stanley Lucas, and Gracie Rogers because these three accountants started with the company at approximately the same time and have similar skills. The chart below is a default chart produced in Excel. **LO 1**

Number of Customer Accounts Managed

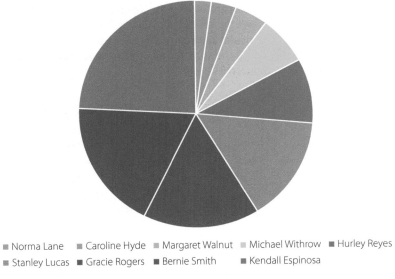

■ Norma Lane   ■ Caroline Hyde   ■ Margaret Walnut   ■ Michael Withrow   ■ Hurley Reyes
■ Stanley Lucas   ■ Gracie Rogers   ■ Bernie Smith   ■ Kendall Espinosa

a. Which preattentive attributes are used in the pie chart?
b. What preattentive attributes would you use in redesigning this chart to improve its clarity for the audience?

12. **Basketball Scouting Report.** Meg Lawson is an assistant coach for a high school basketball team. Meg has prepared a scouting report on her team's upcoming opponent, which is led by a star player who prefers to shoot from near the 3-point line. Meg has

created the following diagram to show this star player's shot selection from a recent game. Each × corresponds to a missed shot, and each ● corresponds to a made shot. Meg has noticed that the star player made most of her shots from the area on the court located at the top of the 3-point line while missing most of her shots from the corners. Meg wants to draw her team's attention to these areas so they can properly defend against this star player. **LO 1, 2**

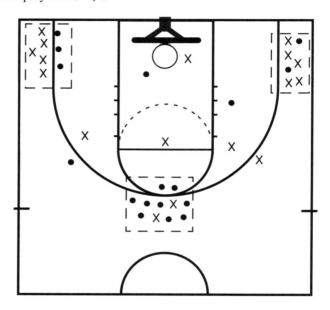

a. What preattentive attributes and Gestalt principles has Meg used in this diagram?
b. Are the preattentive attributes and Gestalt principles used in this diagram effective in communicating Meg's message to her audience? Why or why not?

13. **Revenues and Costs at a Manufacturing Firm.** A manufacturing firm would like to compare its monthly revenues and costs for the previous year. The following table shows the revenues and costs for the company in each month of the previous year. Of particular interest to the company is how the company's revenues and costs perform during the summer months because that is when the company's sales tend to be highest. **LO 3**

Month	Revenues ($1,000s)	Costs ($1,000s)
Jan	1,121	1,007
Feb	997	1,002
Mar	1,151	1,010
Apr	1,202	1,085
May	1,422	1,287
Jun	1,877	1,488
Jul	1,911	1,621
Aug	1,988	1,625
Sep	1,521	1,617
Oct	1,288	1,178
Nov	1,100	1,008
Dec	1,022	987

Previous Year Revenues and Costs

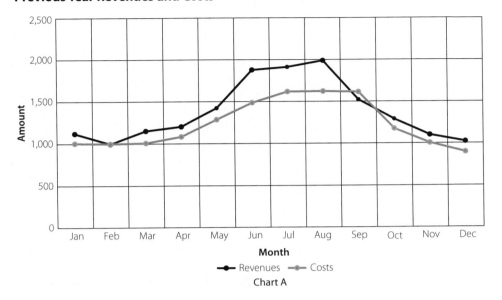

Chart A

Previous Year Revenues and Costs
($1,000s)

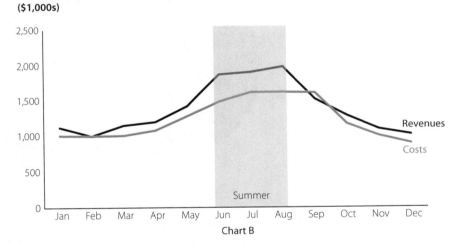

Chart B

   a. Compare the two charts above (Chart A and Chart B). Which chart has the higher data-ink ratio? Why?

   b. How does the chart with the higher data-ink ratio help the audience interpret the chart more effectively?

14. **Serif versus Sans-Serif Fonts.** Consider the fonts that are shown in the table that follows. **LO 5**

(1) A b c d 1 2 3	(4) A b c d 1 2 3	(7) A b c d 1 2 3
(2) *A b c d 1 2 3*	(5) A b c d 1 2 3	(8) A b c d 1 2 3
(3) A B C D 1 2 3	(6) A b c d 1 2 3	(9) **A b c d 1 2 3**

   a. Which of these fonts are considered serif fonts?

   b. If you are creating text for a data visualization that will mostly be viewed on smartphones and other small mobile devices, would you suggest using the serif fonts for text in the data visualization? Why or why not?

15. **Approval Voting Results.** Approval voting is a type of voting system in which voters can vote for any number of eligible candidates. A vote for a candidate in this type of system indicates that the voter "approves" of that candidate for the position the candidate is seeking. In the final tally of the election results, the total number of approval votes for each candidate is calculated. The candidate who receives the most approval votes is declared the winner. The figure below displays the results from an approval voting election in which there were four eligible candidates: C. Sittenfeld, A. Marshall, S. Keskin, and K. Nowak. A total of 1,218 voters participated in this election. The table below shows the number of votes received by each candidate as well as the proportion of voters who approved of each candidate. **LO 4, 6**

Candidate	Number of Votes Received	Proportion of Voters Who Approve of This Candidate
C. Sittenfeld	482	39.6%
A. Marshall	689	56.6%
S. Keskin	354	29.1%
K. Nowak	514	42.2%

Proportion of Voters Who Approve of Candidate

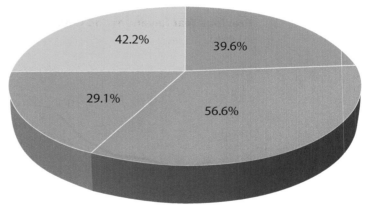

■ C. Sittenfeld   ■ A. Marshall   ■ S. Keskin   ■ K. Nowak

a. The figure displays the election result proportions as a 3D pie chart. What problems are associated with displaying the election results in this way?

b. Suggest an alternative type of chart for displaying these data that would be easier for the audience to interpret. Explain why this alternative type of chart would be easier to interpret.

16. **Headcount and Annual Revenues at BeFit Gyms.** BeFit Gyms operates four exercise gyms in the state of Michigan. The gyms are located in Saline, Tecumseh, Dexter, and Jackson. The gyms are different sizes, and they require different headcounts of staff to operate. The table below displays the headcount, in full-time equivalent (FTE) employees, and annual revenue ($1,000s) for each of the four locations. **LO 4, 6**

Gym Location	Headcount (FTE)	Annual Revenue ($1,000s)
Saline	18	787
Tecumseh	11	674
Dexter	9	784
Jackson	12	642

Comparing Headcount and Annual Revenue Across Locations

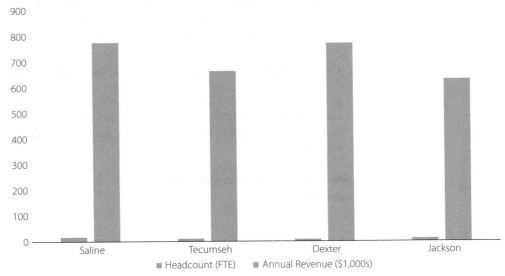

a. The clustered column chart displays the headcount and annual revenue for each location. What are the problems with displaying these data using this type of chart?
b. Would it be appropriate to display these data using a stacked column chart rather than a clustered column chart?

Applications

plattconsulting

17. **Comparing Managing Consultants at Platt Consulting (Revisited).** In this problem, we revisit the pie chart in Problem 11. Platt Consulting Services is interested in comparing the number of customer accounts managed by its managing consultants. In particular, the company needs to compare the number of accounts managed by Bernie Smith, Stanley Lucas, and Gracie Rogers because these three accountants started with the company at about the same time and have similar skill sets. The following chart is a default chart produced in Microsoft Excel. **LO 1, 6**

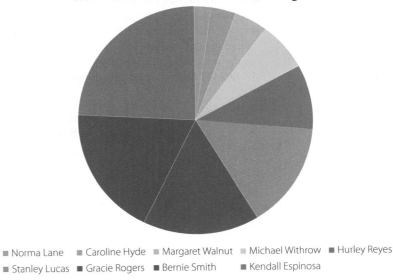

Use the data in the file *plattconsulting* to create a new data visualization that uses a different type of chart and demonstrates the proper use of preattentive attributes to allow for easier comparison of the number of accounts managed by each consultant.

CHART *file*

brandience_chart

18. **Market Segmentation for Brandience (Revisited).** In this problem, we revisit the scatter chart in Problem 7. Starting with the chart in the file *brandience_chart*, modify the chart by using an additional Gestalt principle to make it more obvious to the audience which clients are in each cluster. Which additional Gestalt principle did you use? **LO 2, 4**

19. **Comparing Direct and Indirect Costs at Sackenheim Compressors.** Sackenheim Compressors, Inc. manufactures air compressors for industrial use. The company is performing an analysis of its direct and indirect costs related to manufacturing a particular type of air compressor. It has gathered cost data for the previous 20 weeks, and it would like to identify any trends in the data. A scatter chart created using the data follows. **LO 2, 4**

Direct vs. Indirect Cost Comparison

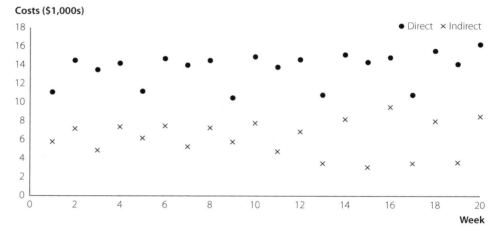

CHART *file*

sackenheim_chart

a. Which Gestalt principle should be used here to make it easier for the audience to identify trends in the data?

b. Using the chart included in the file *sackenheim_chart* as a starting point, create an improved version of this chart by applying the Gestalt principle from part a that makes any trends in the data more obvious to the audience.

20. **Sales Performance Bonuses.** A sales manager is trying to determine appropriate sales performance bonuses for her team this year. The following table contains the data relevant to determining the bonuses, but it is not easy to read and interpret. Reformat the table using the data in file *salesbonuses* to improve readability and help the sales manager make her decisions about bonuses. (*Hint*: It will also help the sales manager if the table is ordered from top-to-bottom by Total Sales.) **LO 3**

DATA *file*

salesbonuses

Salesperson	Total Sales ($)	Average Performance Bonus Previous Years ($)	Customer Accounts	Years with Company
Smith, Michael	325000.78	12499.3452	124	14
Yu, Joe	13678.21	239.9434	9	7
Reeves, Bill	452359.19	21987.2462	175	21
Hamilton, Joshua	87423.91	7642.9011	28	3
Harper, Derek	87654.21	1250.1393	21	4
Quinn, Dorothy	234091.39	14567.9833	48	9
Graves, Lorrie	379401.94	27981.4432	121	12
Sun, Yi	31733.59	672.9111	7	1
Thompson, Nicole	127845.22	13322.9713	17	3

21. **Gross Domestic Product Values over Time.** The following table shows an example of gross domestic product values for five countries over six years in equivalent U.S. dollars ($).
LO 2, 3

Gross Domestic Product (US $)

Country	Year 1	Year 2	Year 3	Year 4	Year 5	Year 6
Albania	7385937423	8105580293	9650128750	11592303225	10781921975	10569204154
Argentina	169725491092	198012474920	241037555661	301259040110	285070994754	339604450702
Australia	704453444387	758320889024	916931817944	982991358955	934168969952	1178776680167
Austria	272865358404	290682488352	336840690493	375777347214	344514388622	341440991770
Belgium	335571307765	355372712266	408482592257	451663134614	421433351959	416534140346

DATA *file*

gdp_years

a. How could you improve the readability of this table?
b. The file *gdp_years* contains sample data from Year 1 to Year 6 in US $. Create a table that provides all these data for an audience. Format the table to make it as easy to read as possible. *Hint:* It is generally not important for the audience to know GDP to an exact dollar figure. It is typical to present GDP values in millions or billions of dollars.

22. **Monthly Revenue Data at Tedstar, Inc.** The following table provides monthly revenue values for Tedstar, Inc., a company that sells valves to large industrial firms. The monthly revenue data have been graphed using a line chart in the following figure.
LO 3, 4

Month	Jan	Feb	Mar	Apr	May	Jun	Jul	Aug	Sep	Oct	Nov	Dec
Revenue ($)	145,869	123,576	143,298	178,505	186,850	192,850	134,500	145,286	154,285	148,523	139,600	148,235

DATA *file*

tedstar

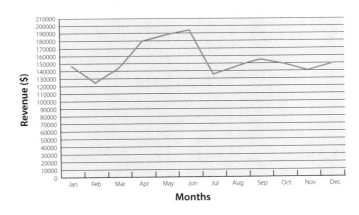

a. What characteristics of this line chart make it more difficult than necessary to interpret?
b. Using the data in the file *tedstar*, create a new line chart for the monthly revenue data at Tedstar, Inc. Format the chart to make it easy to read and interpret. Use the chart title "Tedstar, Inc. Revenue Analysis" and the vertical-axis title "Monthly Revenue ($)."

23. **Comparing Hoxworth Blood Center Locations.** Hoxworth Blood Center, located in Cincinnati, Ohio, is a leader in transfusion medicine. Founded in 1938, it is the second oldest blood bank in the United States. Hoxworth operates at seven locations in the Greater Cincinnati area where it collects blood from donors. Hoxworth is performing a comparison of the amount of blood donors serviced by each of its locations during the

CHART *file*

hoxworth_chart

month of October. Suppose that Hoxworth has a stated goal of each location servicing an average of 50 blood donors per day each month. The column chart that follows compares the average number of blood donors at each Hoxworth location. However, this chart is cluttered, and the data-ink ratio is low. Starting with the chart in the file *hoxworth_chart*, declutter the chart, and improve the data-ink ratio to produce an improved column chart. **LO 3, 4**

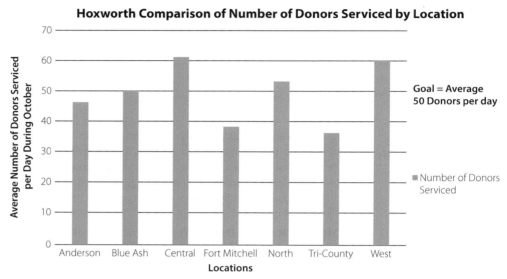

24. **Comparing Package Delivery Drivers.** Red Sky Delivery performs "last-mile" delivery services for online retailers such as Amazon. Red Sky employs delivery drivers who perform the "last-mile" of delivery service by delivering packages to individual residence and business locations. Red Sky measures several delivery driver performance metrics, including number of delivery stops completed per eight-hour shift. The table below provides data on nine Red Sky delivery drivers and the average number of packages delivered per shift over the previous 30 days. **LO 1, 3, 4**

redsky_deliveries

Delivery Driver	Average Number of Delivery Stops Completed (per shift)
Amy Urbaczewski	92.87
Sally Melouk	110.78
Brenda Barnes	114.20
Jonathan Payne	132.50
Bruce Wheeler	148.20
Cam Madsen	87.51
Sheila Stevens	139.82
Grant Inhara	154.23
Finn Helton	109.11

a. Using the data in the file *redsky_deliveries*, create a column chart to display the information in the table above. Format the column chart to best display the data. Use a chart title of "Comparing Red Sky Delivery Drivers" and a vertical-axis title of "Average number of deliveries per shift." Get rid of any unnecessary gridlines and add data labels that show the average number of delivery stops completed for each driver.

    b. Create a sorted column chart to make it easier for the audience to see which drivers have the highest and lowest average number of delivery stops per shift.

    c. Further investigation by Red Sky indicates that all of these delivery drivers except Amy Urbaczewski have similar delivery routes. Amy typically delivers in more rural areas, while all other drivers support more urban routes. Red Sky wants to draw attention to the fact that Amy's routes are different than the others. Modify the sorted column chart by changing the color of the column associated with Amy Urbaczewski to indicate that this column is different from the others.

25. **Inbound and Outbound Shipping Costs at Rainbow Camping.** Rainbow Camping makes outdoor equipment for camping and backpacking that it sells online. Because Rainbow Camping mails each of its sales from its distribution center direct to the consumer, it spends considerable funds each month on outbound shipping. Rainbow Camping also has costs related to inbound shipping to get its products from the manufacturers to its distribution center. Rainbow Camping would like to examine its outbound and inbound shipping expenses over the last 12 months (labeled months 1 through 12). These shipping costs are shown in the following table. **LO 4**

DATA *file*

rainbowcamping

| | Shipping Costs ($1,000s) | |
Month	Outbound	Inbound
1	478	324
2	524	274
3	628	224
4	787	292
5	648	348
6	612	309
7	598	378
8	641	287
9	546	292
10	476	345
11	378	304
12	512	298

    a. Using the data in the file *rainbowcamping*, create a single chart that displays both the outbound and inbound shipping costs for each month on the same chart. Use the title "Rainbow Camping Shipping Costs Analysis" for the chart title, "Costs ($1,000s)" for the vertical-axis title, and "Month" for the horizontal-axis title. Format the chart title and vertical-axis title to make these easy for the audience to interpret. Modify the Minimum and Maximum Bounds of the horizontal axis so this axis starts at 1 and ends at 12 (**Minimum** and **Maximum Bounds** can be found in the **Format Axis** task pane by clicking on the **Axis Options** icon and then under **Axis Options**). Remove the markers so only lines are displayed for each of these shipping costs. Delete any unnecessary gridlines in the chart.

    b. To further minimize the eye travel required by the audience, delete the default legend created with the chart and use text boxes to label the lines in the chart as "Outbound" and "Inbound."

26. **University of Michigan Enrollments over Time.** The University of Michigan was founded in 1817 as the first university in what was then the Northwest Territories of the United States. The university's nickname is the Wolverines and its main campus is located in Ann Arbor, Michigan. The file *michiganenrollment* contains enrollment data for students at the University of Michigan's Ann Arbor campus for Fall Semesters

DATA *file*

michiganenrollment

from 1966 to 2016 in five-year increments. Create a default chart for these data by clicking **Insert** in the Ribbon in Excel and then choosing **Scatter with Straight Lines and Markers**  from the **Charts** group. Use the principles of data-ink ratio and decluttering to improve this chart for the audience. **LO 3, 4**
In particular, you should:

- Create meaningful chart and vertical axis titles, and position them appropriately to minimize eye travel.
- Adjust the Minimum and Maximum Bounds of the horizontal axis to make it clear to the audience that the data points correspond to 1966, 1971, 1976, etc. (**Minimum** and **Maximum Bounds** can be found in the **Format Axis** task pane by clicking on the **Axis Options** icon ▮▮▮ and then under **Axis Options**).
- Create an appropriate horizontal-axis title to ensure the audience understands that these values correspond to Fall Semester enrollments and position this axis title to minimize eye travel.
- Remove the gridlines and adjust the vertical-axis units to increase the data-ink ratio.
- Make any other improvements to the chart you think would help the audience interpret this chart.

DATA *file*

cms

27. **Evaluating Marketing Strategies.** Cuero Marketing Services (CMS) is a marketing agency that designs marketing plans for companies. CMS is working with a large global corporation on new brand strategies. CMS formed seven different test groups to evaluate how people perceive two competing ideas for new brand strategies. Each test group is composed of 25 people. CMS collects all data from the test groups, and for each member of the test group, it creates an overall evaluation of whether the test group member has an overall good impression of the brand strategy or does not have an overall good impression of the brand strategy. To preserve confidentiality, CMS refers to the two competing brand strategies in all written documents as "Blue Triangle" and "Orange Square." The table below shows how many test group members from each test group had an overall good impression of the Blue Triangle and Orange Square brand strategies. CMS would like to create a simple data visualization to show these data. **LO 4, 6**

	Number of Positive Impressions	
Test Group Number	Blue Triangle	Orange Square
1	17	12
2	21	15
3	16	13
4	19	14
5	23	17
6	26	18
7	20	16

a. Using the data in the file *cms*, create a scatter chart that shows both data series in a single chart. Use the test group number on the horizontal axis and the number of test group members who had an overall good impression on the vertical axis. Use "Test Group Analysis for Brand Strategies" as the chart title, "Number of Members with Overall Good Impression of Strategy (out of 25)" as the vertical-axis title, and "Test Group" as the horizontal-axis title. Format the title to minimize eye travel and remove any unnecessary gridlines.

b. To make the chart more intuitive for the audience, CMS would like to display markers that match the name of each brand strategy. To do this, remove the default legend from chart and replace the markers for the Blue Triangle brand strategy with blue triangles and use orange squares for the markers of the Orange Square brand strategy. (*Hint*: The markers on a chart can be changed in the **Format Data**

Series task pane by clicking on the **Fill & Line** icon , clicking on **Marker**, then **Marker Options** and selecting a marker shape from **Built-in**.)

c. Change the type of chart used to display these data to a clustered column chart. Do you think the scatter chart or the clustered column chart would be most effective for displaying these results to an audience? Why?

malaria_chart

28. **Affinity and Capacity of Donors for Malaria No More.** Nonprofits often score potential donors on multiple dimensions, including affinity and capacity. Affinity attempts to measure how passionate and engaged the potential donor is regarding the nonprofit's cause. Capacity attempts to measure the donor's available wealth and ability to donate to the nonprofit. Malaria No More is a nonprofit that focuses on eradicating malaria across the world. Suppose that Malaria No More measures the affinity and capacity of potential donors on scales of 1–100 where 1 corresponds to little affinity or capacity and 100 corresponds to extreme affinity or capacity. The file *malaria_chart* contains a scatter chart showing a sample of 50 potential donors to Malaria No More, including their affinity and capacity scores. **LO 2, 4**

a. Starting with the scatter chart in the file *malaria_chart*, improve the design of this chart to increase its effectiveness. Change the title of this chart to "Evaluating Potential Donors for Malaria No More." Add a vertical-axis title of "Capacity Score" and a horizontal-axis title of "Affinity Score." Format the chart title and axis titles to minimize eye travel.

b. Malaria No More would like to improve this chart to convey a specific message to its audience. It wants to focus the audience's attention on those potential donors with capacity and affinity scores greater than or equal to 80 because it believes these are the best donor prospects. Use the Gestalt principle of enclosure to highlight the potential donors on the chart. (*Hint*: To create an enclosure in Excel, click Insert on the Ribbon, then click **Shapes** Shapes in the **Illustrations** group.)

29. **Funstate Carnivals Staffing Analysis.** Funstate Carnivals operates four large amusement parks, all located in California. Funstate would like to examine the staffing across these four amusement parks. It is most interested in comparing the total number of staff employed at each park, but it is also interested in comparing the gender breakdown of the staffing at each park. The table below shows the total number of staff employed at each park, broken out by gender. **LO 4**

funstate

	Total Number of Staff	
Location	Male	Female
Fresno	72	84
Sacramento	89	61
Long Beach	65	84
Oakland	48	51

a. Using the data in the file *funstate*, create a stacked bar chart to display these data. Use different colors for Male and Female. Use the chart title "Funstate Carnivals Staffing Analysis," choose appropriate axis titles, and include a chart legend to identify Male versus Female in the bar chart. Format the chart to minimize eye travel, and remove any unnecessary gridlines to increase the data-ink ratio.

b. Funstate would like to show the exact numbers of Male and Female staff at each location on the chart. Add data labels to the stacked bar chart to display the number of Male and number of Female staff at each location. Format the data labels so they are easy for the audience to read.

c. Because of decreased revenues, Funstate wants to implement a policy of no more than 125 total staff members at each location. Draw a line and use a text box to indicate "Staffing Goal = 125" on the stacked bar chart to show this limit.

(*Hint*: Click **Insert** on the Ribbon, then click **Shapes** ◇ in the **Illustrations** group

Shapes

to add a line and text box.) Which locations currently exceed this staffing limit?

approvalvoting

30. **Approval Voting Results (Revisited).** In this problem, we revisit the data from Problem 15 on the results of an election using approval voting. The original figure in Problem 15 used a pie chart to display the results from an approval voting election in which there were four eligible candidates: C. Sittenfeld, R. Manley, S. Keskin, and K. Nowak. A total of 1218 voters participated in this election. **LO 3, 4**

a. Using the data in the file *approvalvoting*, create a sorted bar chart that displays the proportion of voters who approve of each candidate. Choose appropriate titles for the chart and axes. Sort the bars so the candidate who received the most votes is at the top. Use data labels to display the proportion of votes received by each candidate. Format the chart title to minimize eye travel, and remove any unnecessary gridlines to increase the data-ink ratio. Which candidate should be declared the winner of this election?

b. Create a sorted bar chart that displays the number of votes received by each candidate. Choose appropriate titles for the chart and axes. Sort the bars so the candidate who received the most votes is at the top. Use data labels to display the number of votes received by each candidate. Format the chart title to minimize eye travel, and remove any unnecessary gridlines to increase the data-ink ratio. Which candidate should be declared the winner of this election?

c. Do you think the sorted bar chart in part a or in part b is more effective for communicating the results of the election to an audience? Why?

31. **Headcount and Annual Revenues at BeFit Gyms (Revisited).** In this problem, we revisit the data from Problem 16 on staff headcount and annual revenues for BeFit Gyms. Recall that each gym is a different size. To support larger headcounts, larger gyms are expected to generate greater annual revenue. BeFit is interested in identifying the incremental revenue a location should expect from a larger headcount. In Problem 16, a clustered column chart was used to display these data. However, we would like to make it easier for the audience to make comparisons from these data and generate insights about the relation between headcount and annual revenue. **LO 3, 4, 6**

befit

a. Using the data in the file *befit*, create two different column charts to display the headcount and annual revenue data for BeFit Gyms: one chart that displays the headcount for each location and one chart that displays the annual revenue for each location. Make sure to create a meaningful chart title for each chart and create vertical-axis titles that clearly define the units of measurement. Remove unnecessary and redundant information to increase the data-ink ratio. Why might these two charts be easier for the audience to generate insights from the data than the original clustered column chart in Problem 16?

b. Recall that the audience is most interested in identifying the incremental revenue a location should expect from a larger headcount. Create a single column chart using these data that would compare each location based on both headcount and annual revenue. (*Hint*: You can create a new metric for each location that measures the annual revenue per FTE.) Which location generates the greatest annual revenue per headcount?

Chapter 3 Appendix

Appendix 3.1 Data Visualization and Design with Power BI

In this appendix, we discuss in more detail how to edit a chart in Power BI to make it more effective at conveying your message to the audience.

Editing a Chart to Increase the Data-Ink Ratio

Power BI's default options for visualizations are often effective with regard to the data-ink ratio. However, you may want to edit the default charts created in Power BI to improve their appearance by making them easier to interpret, increasing the data-ink ratio, or tailoring them for a specific audience or message. In this appendix, we discuss basic steps for editing visualizations in Power BI.

To demonstrate the use of Power BI to edit visualizations, we use the data in the file *scarf*. This file contains monthly sales data for Diaphonous Industries, a company that produces fine silk clothing products. The file *scarf* contains 20 days of sales data (measured in units sold) for a particular style of scarf. To create a line chart displaying daily sales values, use the following steps.

DATA *file*

scarf

    Step 1. Following the steps outlined in Appendix 1.1, connect Power BI to the file *scarf*

In some of the steps that follow, we give instructions to expand or collapse certain sections of Power BI. A section can be expanded by clicking > next to the section title. To collapse a section, click ⌄ next to the section title.

    Step 2. Click **Report** view ⬛ on the left side of the Power BI window
        In the **Visualizations** pane on the right side of the Power BI window, click the **Build visual** icon ⬛ to display the **Build visual** matrix of available charts

        Select **Line Chart** 📈
        In the **Data** pane on the right side of the Power BI window, expand **Data** to display the list of variables
        Drag Σ **Day** from the **Data** pane to the **X-axis** box in the **Visualizations** pane
        Drag Σ **Sales (units)** from the **Data** pane to the **Y-axis** box in the **Visualizations** pane

        Increase the size of the chart by grabbing the bottom right corner and expanding it

This creates the default line chart shown in Figure P3.1.

We can improve the effectiveness of the line chart shown in Figure P3.1 by editing the chart title, axis titles, and axis values, and by adding data labels using steps 3–6. We note that in steps 3–6, we will give instructions to expand or collapse certain sections of Power BI.

    Step 3. In the **Visualizations** pane, click the **Format visual** button 🖉
        To edit the horizontal axis title and values, click **Visual** in the **Visualizations** pane, and expand the **X-axis.**
        Scroll down to **Title**, and expand it
        Select **Calibri** from the **Font** drop-down list and **16** as the font size.
        Click the **Bold** button **B**

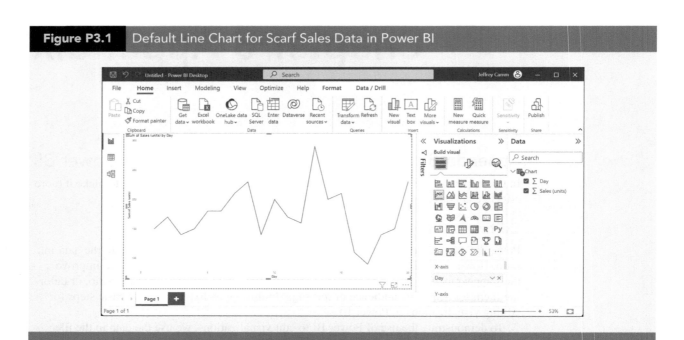

Figure P3.1   Default Line Chart for Scarf Sales Data in Power BI

> Collapse **Title**, and expand **Values**
> Select **Calibri** as the **Font** and **14** as the font size
> Collapse **Values**
> Collapse **X-axis**

We will add data labels that will eliminate the need for the vertical axis. The following steps hide the vertical axis values and the vertical axis title.

Step 4. In the **Visualizations** pane, expand the **Y-axis**
> Next to the **Y-axis**, toggle the **On** button ⬤ to **Off** to hide the vertical axis values
> Next to **Title**, toggle the **On** button ⬤ to **Off** to hide the vertical axis title

Step 5 adds data labels to the line chart and edits the labels for readability.

Step 5. With the **Y-axis** expanded in the Visualizations pane, scroll down to **Data labels** and expand it
> Next to **Data labels**, toggle the **Off** button ⬤ to **On** to display data labels
> Scroll down to **Value**, and expand it
> Select **Calibri** as the **Font** and **14** as the font size
> Collapse **Value**
> Collapse **Data labels**
> Collapse **Y-axis**

Finally, we edit the chart title for readability and remove the unnecessary grid lines to increase the data-ink ratio.

Step 6. Next to **Visual** in the **Visualizations** pane, click **General**
> Expand **Title**
> Edit the **Text** box to read *Scarf Sales (in units)*
> Select **Calibri** as the **Font** and **16** as the font size. Click the **Bold** button **B**
> Collapse **Title**

Figure P3.2	Edited Line Chart for the Scarf Sales Data

Step 7. To remove the faint gridlines in the chart, click **Visual** in the **Visualizations** pane

Expand **Gridlines**

Next to Vertical, toggle the **On** button to **Off** to hide the vertical grid lines

Collapse **Gridlines**

Steps 1 through 7 produce the line chart shown in Figure P3.2.

We can easily change the type of chart being displayed in Power BI. The following step changes the line chart to a column chart for the scarf sales data.

Step 8. Click **Report** view on the left side of the Power BI window

In the Visualizations pane on the right side of the Power BI window, click

the **Build visual** icon to display the Build visual matrix of available charts

Select **Clustered column chart**

Step 8 produces the column chart shown in Figure P3.3.

Creating a Sorted Bar/Column Chart

Sorted column (or bar) charts can be very effective data visualizations. We illustrate how to create a sorted column chart in Power BI using annual revenue data for eight different retail store locations in the state of Texas. These data are available in the file *retailrevenue*. The following steps create a sorted column chart for these data. The sorted column chart more clearly shows which locations are generating the most revenue and which locations have the least revenue.

Step 1. Following the steps outlined in Appendix 1.1, connect Power BI to the file *retailrevenue*

In some of the steps that follow, we give instructions to expand or collapse certain sections of Power BI. A section can be expanded by clicking ⟩ next to the section title. To collapse a section, click ⌄ next to the section title.

CHART *file*

scarfline_chart.pbix

DATA *file*

retailrevenue

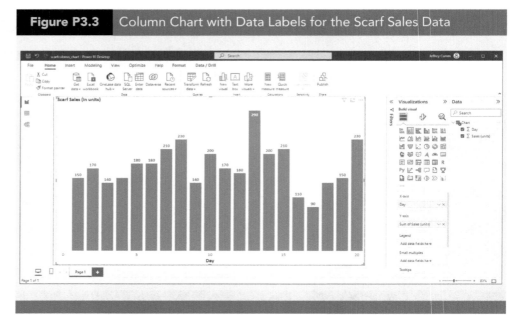

Figure P3.3   Column Chart with Data Labels for the Scarf Sales Data

CHART *file*

scarfcolumn_chart.pbix

Step 2. Click **Report** view on the left side of the Power BI window

In the **Visualizations** pane on the right side of the Power BI window, click

on **Build visual** to display the matrix of available charts

Select **Stacked column chart**

In the **Data** pane on the right side of the Power BI window, click **Data** to expand the list of variables

Drag **Location** from the **Data** pane to the **X-axis** box in the **Visualizations** pane

Drag Σ **Annual Revenue ($1,000s)** from the **Data** pane to the **Y-axis** box in the **Visualizations** pane

Increase the size of the chart by grabbing the bottom right corner and expanding it

The resulting column chart is shown in Figure P3.4. Notice that Power BI has automatically sorted the data by **Annual Revenue ($1,000s)**. This is because the variable *Location* is text data. We note that this did not happen in the previous example because the variable *Day* was numerical and so remained sorted by day.

As we did in the previous example, we can improve the effectiveness of the column chart shown in Figure P3.4 by editing the chart title, axis titles, and axis values and by adding data labels using the following steps.

Step 3. In the Visualizations pane, click the **Format visual** button

To edit the horizontal axis title and values, click **Visual** in the Visualizations pane

Expand **X-axis**, scroll down to **Title**, and expand it

Select **Calibri** as the **Font** and **16** as the font size.

Click the **Bold** button **B**

Collapse **Title** and expand **Values**

Select **Calibri** as the **Font** and **14** as the font size.

Click the **Bold** button **B**

Collapse **Values**

Collapse **X-axis**

Figure P3.4 The Retail Revenue Data Shown in Decreasing Order of Revenue

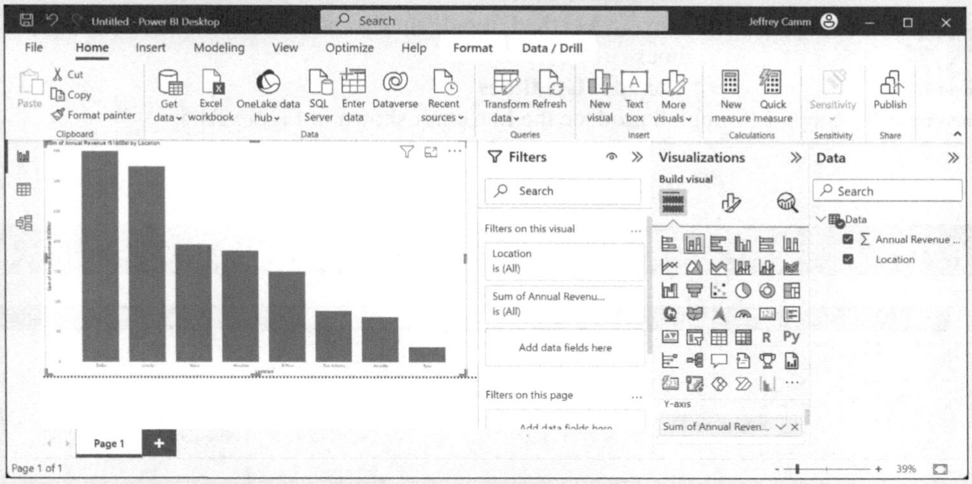

We will add data labels that will eliminate the need for the vertical axis. The following steps hide the vertical axis values and the vertical axis title.

Step 4. Scroll to **Y-axis** in the Visualizations pane, and expand it

Next to Values, toggle the **On** button ⬤ to **Off** to hide the vertical axis values

Next to Title, toggle the **On** button ⬤ to **Off** to hide the vertical axis title

Collapse **Y-axis**

The following steps add data labels to the chart and edit the labels for readability.

Step 5. In the **Visualizations** pane, scroll down to **Data labels** and expand it

Next to **Data labels**, toggle the **Off** button ⬤ to **On** to display data labels

Scroll to **Value** and expand it

Select **Calibri** as the **Font** and **16** as the font size

Collapse **Value**

Collapse **Data labels**

Step 6. In the **Visualizations** pane, expand **Y-axis** and expand **Range**

In the **Maximum** box, enter *400*

Collapse **Range**

Collapse **Y-axis**

Finally, we edit the chart title for readability and to remove the unnecessary grid lines to increase the data-ink ratio.

Step 7. Next to **Visual** in the **Visualizations** pane, click **General**

Expand **Title**

Edit the **Text** box to read *Annual Revenue ($1,000s)*.

Select **Calibri** as the **Font** and **16** as the font size.

Click the **Bold** button **B**

Collapse **Title**

Step 8. To remove the faint gridlines in the chart, click **Visual** in the **Visualizations** pane

Expand **Gridlines**

Next to **Vertical**, toggle the **On** button to **Off** to hide the vertical grid lines

Collapse **Gridlines**

Steps 1 through 8 produce the line chart shown in Figure P3.5.

CHART *file*

retailrevenue_chart.pbix

Figure P3.5 | Sorted Column Chart with Data Labels for the Retail Sales Data

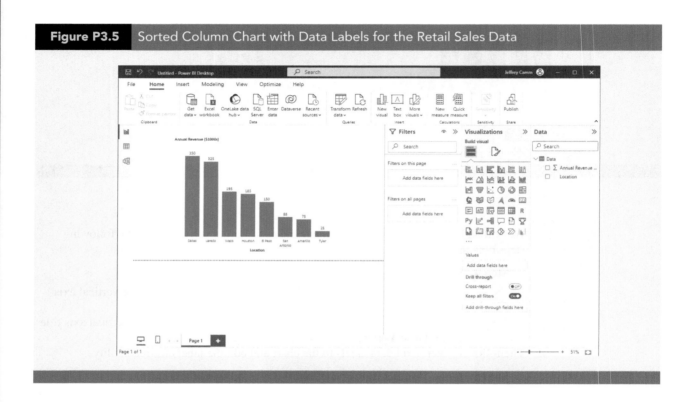

Appendix 3.2 Data Visualization and Design with Tableau
Editing a Chart to Increase the Data-Ink Ratio

Tableau's default options for visualizations are often effective. However, you may want to edit the default charts created in Tableau to improve their appearance by increasing the data-ink ratio or tailor them for a specific audience or purpose. This appendix introduces the basic functions for editing visualizations in Tableau.

We will demonstrate the use of Tableau to edit visualizations using the data in the file *scarf*. This file contains monthly sales data for Diaphonous Industries, a company that produces fine silk clothing products. The file *scarf* contains daily sales data for a particular style of scarf produced by Diaphonous Industries. To create a default line chart displaying daily sales values, use the following steps.

DATA *file*

scarf

Step 1. Following the steps outlined in Appendix 1.2, connect Tableau to the file *scarf*
Click the **Sheet 1** tab at the bottom of the Tableau Data Source screen to open the worksheet view
Step 2. In the worksheet view of Tableau, drag the pill for **Day** from the **Data** pane to the **Columns** shelf. Drag the pill for **Sales (units)** from the **Data** pane to the **Rows** shelf

This creates the default line chart shown in Figure T3.1.

We can improve the effectiveness of the line chart shown in Figure T3.1 by adding a chart title and axis titles and deleting unnecessary gridlines as outlined in the following steps.

Step 3. To add a title for the chart, right click on **Sheet 1** at the top of the canvas and select **Edit Title…**
When the **Edit Title** dialog box opens, replace **<Sheet Name>** with *Scarf Sales*, highlight the title text, and change the font size to **16** and the font type to **Bold**
Click **OK** to close the **Edit Title** dialog box

When you right click on ***Sheet 1****, you can also choose to* ***Hide Title*** *to delete the chart title.*

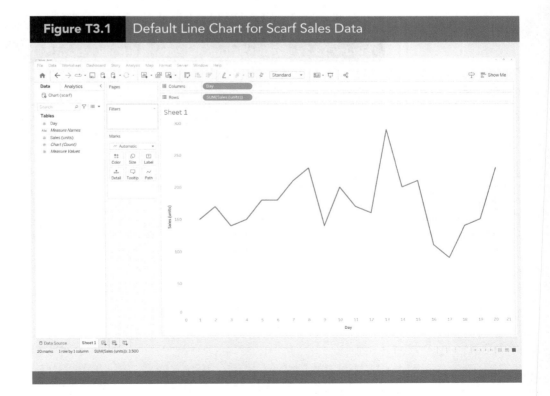

Figure T3.1   Default Line Chart for Scarf Sales Data

Step 4. To edit the horizontal axis labels and title, right click on the horizontal axis at the bottom of the chart and select **Format…**

When the **Format Day** task pane opens, select the **Axis** tab, click on **Font:** under **Default**, and change the font size to **11** to change the size of the horizontal axis labels to 11 point. Click on **Font:** under **Title**, and change the font size to **11** to change the size of the horizontal axis title to 11 point

You can also bring up the **Format** *task pane by clicking on the pill for a variable in the* **Columns** *or* **Rows** *shelf and selecting* **Format….**

Step 5. To edit the vertical axis label and title, right click on the vertical axis on the right of the chart and select **Format…**

When the **Format SUM(Sales(units))** task pane opens, select **Font:** under **Default** and change the font size to **11** to change the size of the vertical axis labels to 11 point. Click on **Font:** under **Title** and change the font size to **11** to change the size of the vertical axis title to 11 point.

Step 6. To edit the range of the vertical axis, click on the vertical axis on the left of the chart and select **Edit Axis…**

When the **Edit Axis [Sales (units)]** dialog box appears, click on the **General** tab, select **Custom** under **Range**, enter *0* for **Fixed start**, and enter *350* for **Fixed end**

Click ✕ to close the **Edit Axis [Sales(units)]** dialog box

Step 6 changes the vertical axis to have a range between 0 and 350. Note that you can also edit the axis title in the **Edit Axis** dialog box by clicking on the axis title next to **Custom** under **Axis Titles**. You can then change this axis title to another title or delete the title completely by deleting the existing text next to **Custom**.

Step 7. To delete the unnecessary gridlines, right click on the chart and select **Format…**

In the **Format** task pane, click the **Lines** button ≡ , and select **None** for **Grid Lines:**

Click ✕ to close the **Format** task pane

Steps 1 through 7 produce the line chart shown in Figure T3.2.

CHART *file*

scarfline_chart.twbx

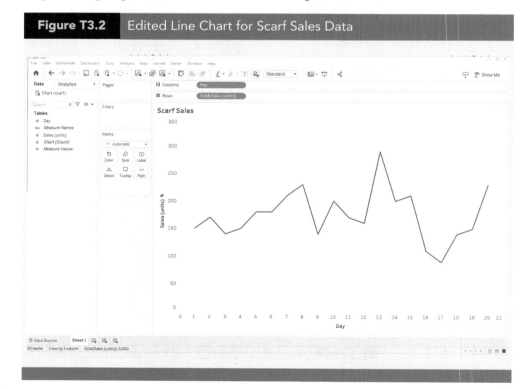

Figure T3.2   Edited Line Chart for Scarf Sales Data

We can add data labels to a chart by using the **Label** card in the **Marks** area. Step 8 adds data labels to the line chart for the scarf sales data.

> **Step 8.** Drag the **Sales (units)** pill from the **Tables** area to the **Label** card  in the **Marks** area

Because we have added data labels, the vertical axis becomes somewhat redundant, and you may wish to remove the labels on this axis to increase the data-ink ratio. To remove the vertical axis, right click on the vertical axis and deselect **Show Header**. This produces the chart shown in Figure T3.3 (note that we have also added "(in units)" to the chart title so the audience knows what units of measure are being displayed).

Tableau refers to both vertical column charts and horizontal bar charts as "bar charts."

Tableau tries to produce a chart that best visualizes the data based on the number of variables being visualized and the type of data (discrete or continuous, etc.). We can change the type of chart being displayed in Tableau by clicking on **Automatic** in the **Marks** area and selecting a different chart type. Step 9 changes the line chart to a column chart for the scarf sales data as shown in Figure T3.4.

> **Step 9.** Click on **Automatic** in the **Marks** area, and select **Bar**

Creating a Sorted Bar/Column Chart

Sorted column (or bar) charts can be very effective data visualizations. To illustrate how to create a sorted column chart in Tableau, we will use the previous year's retail revenue data for eight different store locations in the state of Texas. These data are available in the file *retailrevenue*. The steps below create a sorted column chart for these data that clearly

DATA*file*

retailrevenue

CHART *file*

scarflinelabels_chart.twbx

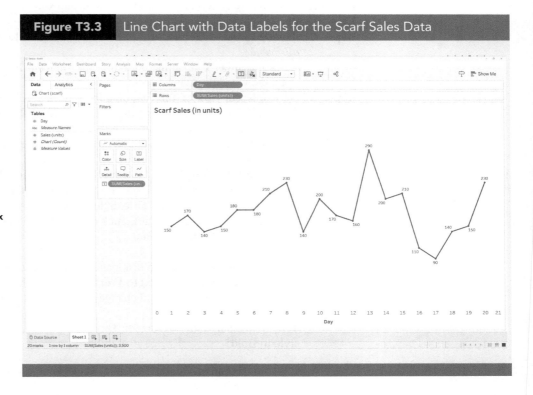

Figure T3.3   Line Chart with Data Labels for the Scarf Sales Data

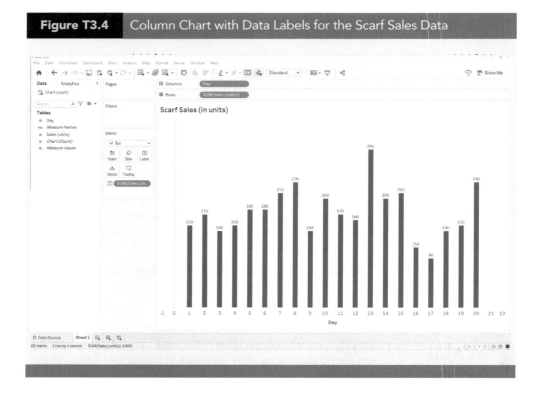

Figure T3.4   Column Chart with Data Labels for the Scarf Sales Data

CHART *file*

scarfcolumn_chart.twbx

shows which locations are generating the most revenue and which locations are generating the least revenue.

Step 1. Following the steps outlined in Appendix 1.2, connect Tableau to the file *retailrevenue*

Click the **Sheet 1** tab at the bottom of the Tableau Data Source screen to open the worksheet view

Step 2. In the worksheet view of Tableau, drag the pill for **Location** from the **Data** pane to the **Columns** shelf. Drag the pill for **Annual Revenue ($1,000s)** from the **Data** pane to the **Rows** shelf

Step 3. To add a title for the chart, right click on **Sheet 1** at the top of the canvas, and select **Edit Title…**

When the **Edit Title** dialog box opens, replace **<Sheet Name>** with *Comparing Previous Year Annual Revenues by Store Location*

Click **OK** to close the **Edit Title** dialog box

When you right click on Sheet 1, you can also choose to Hide Title to delete the chart title.

Step 4. To edit the formatting of the chart, click on the pill for **Location** in the **Columns** shelf and select **Format…**

When the **Format Location** task pane opens, select the **Font** button [A], then under **Default** click next to **Worksheet:** and change the font size to **11**, click next to **Header:** and change the font size to **14**, then click next to **Title:** and change the font size to **16**, and click the **B** to change the font style to Bold

Click on the **Lines** button [≡], and select **None** next to **Grid Lines:** to remove the grid lines in the chart

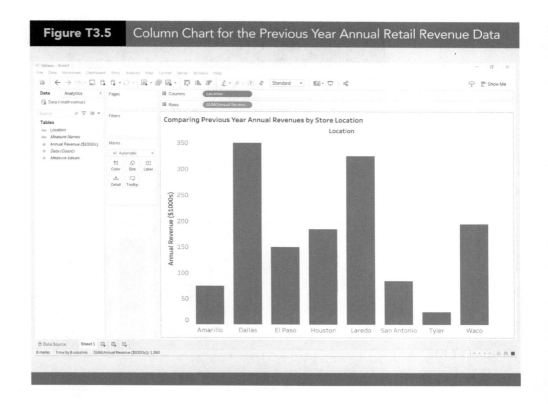

Figure T3.5   Column Chart for the Previous Year Annual Retail Revenue Data

Steps 1 through 4 produce the column chart shown in Figure T3.5. To make it more obvious which locations have the highest annual revenue values and which have the lowest annual revenue values, we can sort the column chart as shown in the following step.

Step 5. To sort the columns in the chart, click on the pill for **Location** in the **Columns** shelf, and select **Sort…**

When the **Sort [Location]** dialog box appears, select **Field** for **Sort By**, **Descending** for **Sort Order**, **Annual Revenue ($1,000s)** for **Field Name**, and **Sum** for **Aggregation** (see Figure T3.6)

Click ✕ to close the **Sort [Location]** dialog box

Step 5 creates the sorted column chart shown in Figure T3.6 that clearly shows Dallas has the highest previous year annual revenue, and Tyler has the smallest.

Note that we can view additional details regarding the underlying data for visualizations created with Tableau through the Tooltip. Hovering your pointer over a column will display the location of the store and the annual revenue for that location. Clicking on a data value in a visualization in Tableau will highlight that data value and display the Tooltip. For instance, Figure T3.7 shows the result of clicking on the column corresponding to Laredo.

You can change the information contained in the Tooltip by clicking on the **Tooltip** card ⬜ Tooltip in the **Marks** area, which will display the **Edit Tooltip** dialog box (see Figure T3.8 for the Edit Tooltip dialog box corresponding to the previous year's annual retail revenue data).

Figure T3.6	Sorted Column Chart for the Previous Year Annual Retail Revenue Data

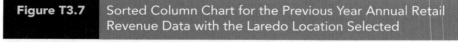

CHART *file*

retailrevenue_sorted_chart.twbx

Figure T3.7	Sorted Column Chart for the Previous Year Annual Retail Revenue Data with the Laredo Location Selected

*Clicking **Keep Only** in the popup that appears after clicking the column for Laredo will use only the data for that column in the visualization. Clicking **Exclude** will ignore this data in creating the visualization. To return to the full visualization after selecting Keep Only or Exclude, click the left arrow **Undo** button in the Ribbon ← .*

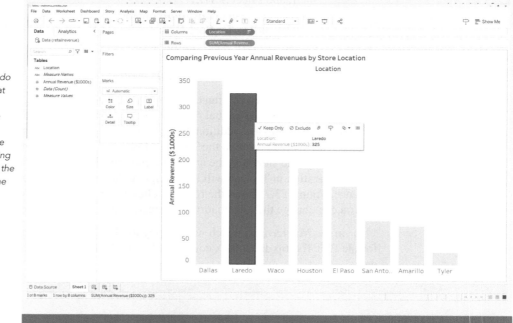

Figure T3.8   Edit Tooltip Dialog Box for the Previous Year Annual Retail Revenue Data

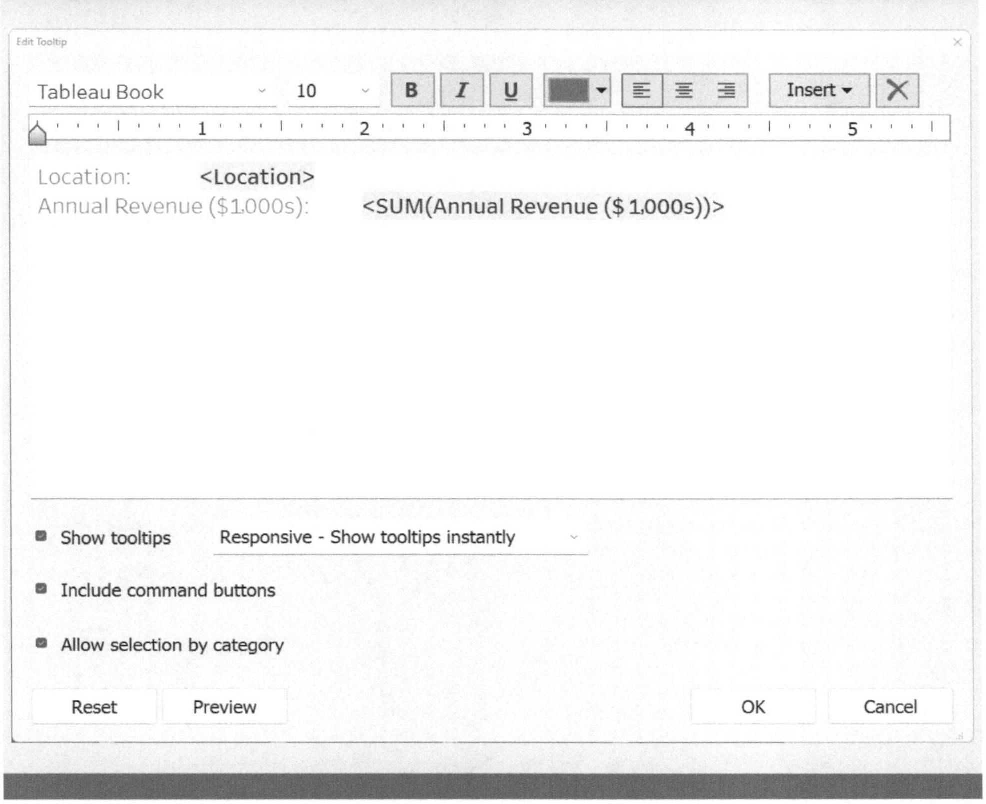

Edit Tooltip   ×

| Tableau Book | ⌄ | 10 | ⌄ | **B** | *I* | U̲ | ▣ ▾ | ☰ ☰ ☰ | Insert ▾ | ✕ |

Location: **\<Location\>**
Annual Revenue ($1.000s):   **\<SUM(Annual Revenue ($ 1.000s))\>**

☑ Show tooltips   Responsive - Show tooltips instantly   ⌄

☑ Include command buttons

☑ Allow selection by category

| Reset | Preview | | OK | Cancel |

Chapter 4

Purposeful Use of Color

Contents

Learning Objectives

After completing this chapter, you will be able to

LO 1 Describe and differentiate between hue, saturation, and luminance

LO 2 Describe the differences between color psychology and color symbolism and explain how each can be used effectively

LO 3 Design color schemes that are appropriate for categorical data, ordered data, and quantitative data with meaningful reference values

LO 4 Use the hue, saturation, luminance (HSL) system to define colors in data visualization software

LO 5 Employ color to create data visualizations that are easier for the audience to interpret

LO 6 List common mistakes made when using color in data visualizations and know how to avoid them

The Science of Hitting

Ted Williams played left field for the Boston Red Sox from 1939 to 1960, with interruptions for military service during World War II and the Korean War. Williams was a 19-time All-Star, a 6-time American League batting champion, and Major Leagues Baseball's last .400 hitter. He won the American League Most Valuable Player Award twice. He finished his playing career with a .344 batting average and 521 home runs, and his lifetime .482 on-base percentage is the highest of all time. Williams is widely regarded as one of the greatest hitters in baseball history.

In 1970, Williams published the influential book *The Science of Hitting*. In this book, he wrote about his approach to hitting. The original cover art (shown in Figure 4.1a) features Williams in his batting stance with his adjacent strike zone divided into 11 rows and seven columns of nonoverlapping circles representing baseballs. Each circle contains Williams's estimate of his batting average (proportion of at bats in which he got a hit) on pitches in that location. By adding colors to these circles to indicate Williams's relative batting average in each pitch location, the book created one of the earliest visual displays of a baseball player's performance.

Through the original cover art, we can see that Williams achieved his highest batting averages on pitches that are around belt-high and across the middle of home plate (indicated in red and orange), and he achieved his lowest batting averages on pitches that are below his belt and on the outside far-right portion of home plate (indicated in gray).

The original cover art communicates the pitch locations for which Williams achieved his highest and lowest batting averages, and it changed the way many baseball professionals thought about hitting. However, with a few small changes, the original cover art could communicate more efficiently and effectively.

The original cover art of *The Science of Hitting* features a single variable—Williams's estimated batting average—for different pitch locations in his strike zone. It also uses several different colors to indicate his batting averages in various pitch locations. As the batting average drops, the colors used move from red for the highest batting average to orange to yellow to green to blue to purple and finally to gray for the lowest batting averages. These colors do not naturally

lead the viewer to an understanding of the graphical display; if the batting averages were not included in the circles at the various pitch locations, it would be impossible to discern which pitch locations were most favorable for Williams.

The purpose of the cover art is to show the progression of a single variable (batting average) from high to low, so using a single color and creating a gradient effect to define the scale would be more effective. In our initial revision of the cover art (shown in Figure 4.1b), we replace the various colors used in the circles of the original cover art with red, and we use a gradient of red in a manner that corresponds with the batting averages. The circles corresponding to the highest batting averages are relatively dark, and the circles corresponding to the lowest batting averages are relatively light. The resulting revised display more effectively and efficiently communicates Williams's performance on pitches in various locations.

Our first revision differs from the original cover art in another subtle but important way. The top and bottom halves of circles in four pitch locations in the original cover art have different colors. Since we are only given Williams's estimated batting average for the entire circle in each pitch location (and not the distinct batting averages in the top and bottom halves of these locations), this is potentially confusing. Therefore, we have made each of these circles a single color that is consistent with the batting average for pitches in this zone.

Although our first revision is superior to the original cover art, the values of Williams's estimated batting averages that are given in each of the pitch locations are difficult to read. Further, they convey the same information as the gradient of the color, so we removed the numerical batting averages in our second revision (Figure 4.1c). Our choice of Figure 4.1b or Figure 4.1c depends on how critical it is for the audience to know the exact value of the estimated batting averages in the pitch locations.

Although the original *The Science of Hitting* cover art was groundbreaking and helped readers understand how Ted Williams performed on pitches in various locations in the strike zone, the revisions are easier to interpret and understand. By observing some basic principles of the use of color and simplifying the original display, we have created revised displays that communicate the message more effectively and efficiently. In this chapter, we will elaborate on these and other guidelines for the effective use of color in charts.

Figure 4.1 Versions of Cover Art for Ted Williams's *The Science of Hitting*

(a) Original Cover Art   (b) First Revision   (c) Second Revision

Color is one of the preattentive attributes discussed in Chapter 3.

Color is the property of an object that results from the way the object reflects or emits light. It is a ubiquitous characteristic, sometimes natural and sometimes by human design, of virtually every object around us. Color can catch and hold someone's attention, communicate, and evoke memories and emotional reactions. This makes color a powerful tool that can enhance the meaning and clarity of data visualizations, but to use color effectively, we must understand how color works and what color can and cannot do well. In this chapter, we provide the basis for understanding color and using it to create more effective charts.

4.1 Color and Perception

One of the strengths of color as a means of communicating through charts is its ability to evoke emotions and reactions, create moods, and attract attention to key aspects of the chart. Understanding how color is perceived enables us to use it to more effectively deliver our message. Failure to understand how color is perceived can lead to its misuse, which can result in confusion, unnecessary clutter, and miscommunication. In this section, we discuss important considerations in the use of color to effectively communicate through charts.

Attributes of Color: Hue, Saturation, and Luminance

Other color models include Red, Yellow, Blue (RYB) and Cyan, Magenta, Yellow (CMY).

One of the three attributes of a color is its **hue**, which is the base of a color. The **primary hues** are the three hues that cannot be mixed or formed by any combination of other hues, and all other hues are derived from these three hues. Excel uses the red, green, blue (RGB) color model with primary hues red, green, and blue. Combinations of these hues create

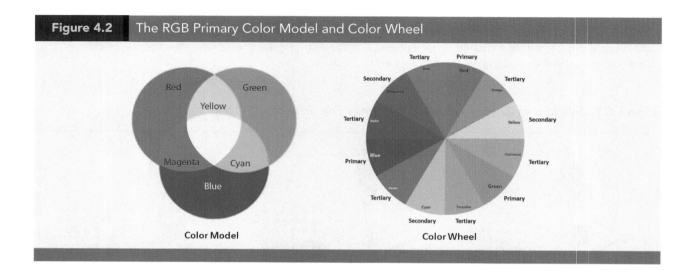

Figure 4.2   The RGB Primary Color Model and Color Wheel

other secondary colors, such as orange, yellow, and violet, and various tertiary colors. The relationships between primary, secondary, and tertiary colors are commonly displayed on a **color wheel**. Figure 4.2 shows the RGB model and RGB color wheel.

In addition to hue, colors are commonly distinguished by saturation and luminance. **Saturation** refers to the amount of gray in a color and determines the intensity or purity of the hue in the color. A completely pure hue has no grayness and is referred to as 100% saturated. As the saturation level decreases, the hue becomes less intense and more grayish. At 0% saturation, all hues become gray. Figure 4.3 shows the primary hues in the RGB primary color model at various levels of saturation.

Luminance measures the relative degree of black or white in a color. Adding white to a hue creates a lighter color, and adding black to a hue creates a darker color. Greater differences in luminance of a color create greater contrast between them, so luminance is a good way to indicate hierarchy or degree. However, it is important to note that the human eye can only discern about 6 or 7 degrees of luminance in a color. At 100% luminance, all hues become white; at 0% luminance, all hues become black. Figure 4.4 shows the primary hues in the RGB primary color model at various levels of luminance.

Combinations of hue, luminance, and saturation determine the base, brightness, and grayness of a color. As we will see later in this chapter, Excel allows you to control the hue, saturation, and luminance of the color of an Excel object.

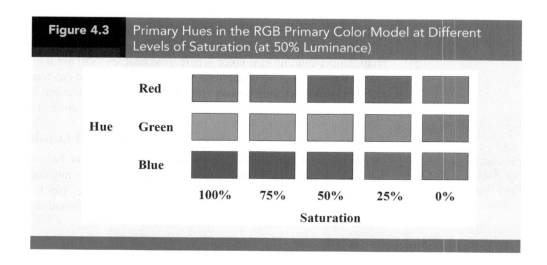

Figure 4.3   Primary Hues in the RGB Primary Color Model at Different Levels of Saturation (at 50% Luminance)

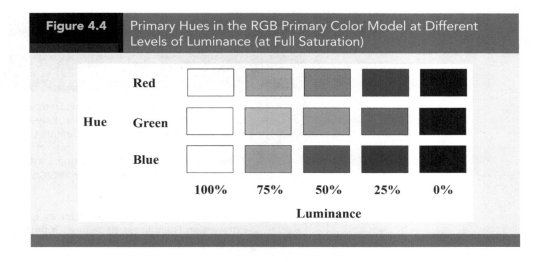

Figure 4.4 Primary Hues in the RGB Primary Color Model at Different Levels of Luminance (at Full Saturation)

Color Psychology and Color Symbolism

Color psychology is the study of the innate relationships between color and human be-havior. Although human psychological reactions to various colors is not uniform, research suggests that people react with a high degree of consistency to various colors. For example, blue skies are thought to make us happier and more energized, while gray skies are thought to make us sadder and more lethargic.

The psychological categorization of colors as warm and cool is thought to be of particular importance. **Cool hues** are considered to be soothing, calming, and reassur-ing. On the other hand, **warm hues** evoke energy, passion, and danger. Purple, blue, and green hues are generally considered to be cool, and yellow, orange, and red hues are generally considered to be warm.

Color symbolism refers to the cultural meanings and significance associated with color. Although they are similar and it is sometimes difficult to discern between them, color psychol-ogy and color symbolism are distinct types of stimuli. Color psychology deals with instinc-tive relationships between color and human behavior, and color symbolism refers to learned relationships between color and human behavior. This implies that color symbolism can differ much more across cultures and can change over time. For example, blue typically symbolizes masculinity in Europe and North America, but it often symbolizes femininity in China. People associate green with envy in the United States, but yellow symbolizes envy to many people from France and Germany. Yellow is associated with success and power in many African cultures, and it symbolizes refinement to the Japanese. The relationships between color and human behavior that are due to color psychology are much more pervasive and reliable than the relationships between color and human behavior that are due to color symbolism, and we must be careful when using color symbolism in selecting the color palette for a chart.

Although color psychology and color symbolism are distinct, their ramifications are similar. When selecting colors for a visual display, it is important to recognize that color can enhance or change audience perception, so you should give careful thought to the consistency of the traits associated with the various colors you are considering with your message. Figure 4.5 provides a summary of various traits that have been associated with different colors.[1]

Perceived Color

We do not perceive color in an absolute manner; that is, we may perceive a color differently depending on the other colors currently in our field of vision. Although the wavelengths of light our eyes receive from an object do not change, we perceive the color of the object in contrast to the colors adjacent to the object. In the rounded

---

[1]Source: nickkolenda.com

Figure 4.5	Traits Frequently Associated with Various Colors

COLOR	MEANINGS AND ASSOCIATIONS
Red	Anxiety, Arousing, Daring, Dominant, Energy, Excitement, Health, Life, Love, Passion, Power, Protection, Spirited, Stimulating, Strength, Up-To-Date
Orange	Abundance, Arousing, Comfort, Daring, Excitement, Extraversion, Fun, Happiness, Lively, Security, Sensuality, Spirited, Warmth
Yellow	Arousing, Cheerful, Confidence, Creativity, Excitement, Extraversion, Friendliness, Happiness, Optimism, Self-Esteem, Sincerity, Smiley, Spirited
Green	Calm, Comfort, Equilibrium, Harmony, Health, Hope, Nature, Outdoorsy, Peace, Prosperity, Relaxation, Security, Serenity, Soothing, Tender
Blue	Calm, Comfort, Competence, Coolness, Dignified Duty, Efficiency, Intelligence, Logic, Peace, Reflection, Relaxation, Reliability, Security, Serenity, Soothing, Successful, Tender, Tranquility, Trust
Purple	Authenticity, Charming, Dignified, Exclusive, Luxury, Quality, Regal, Sensuality, Sophistication, Spiritual, Stately, Upper Class
Pink	Charming, Cheerful, Feminine, Gentle, Nurturing, Sincerity, Soft, Sophistication, Tranquility, Warmth
Brown	Nature, Outdoorsy, Reliability, Ruggedness, Security, Support, Tough
Black	Dignified, Efficiency, Elegance, Emotional Safety, Glamour, Power, Richness, Ruggedness, Security, Sophistication, Stately, Substance, Tough, Upper Class
White	Calm, Clarity, Cleanness, Down-to-Earth, Happiness, Heavens, Honest, Hygiene, Innocence, Peace, Purity, Serenity, Sincerity, Soothing, Tender

rectangle in the upper left corner of Figure 4.6, the background is a gradient of blue that progressively darkens from left to right. This rounded rectangle also contains five squares of the same blue color placed horizontally across the progressive blue gradient. Although the five squares in this rounded rectangle are the same hue, saturation, and luminance, the squares appear darker against the lighter portions of the progressive gradient blue background, and they appear lighter against the darker portions of the progressive gradient blue background. We perceive the colors this way because of the changes in the contrast between the consistently colored squares and the progressively darkening background. As Figure 4.6 demonstrates, this phenomenon is not a unique

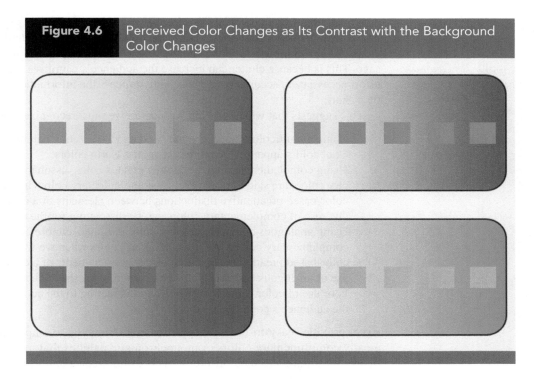

Figure 4.6 Perceived Color Changes as Its Contrast with the Background Color Changes

characteristic of shades of blue. Using a white, gray, or light-colored background mitigates this phenomenon and is why a white or gray background is most commonly used for charts.

Note in Figure 4.6 that as the cool-colored (blue and green) backgrounds become darker, the squares appear to advance into the foreground of the image. Similarly, as the warm-colored (red and orange) backgrounds become lighter, the squares appear to recede into the background of the image. This is because the warmth of a color has an effect on how close objects appear; warmer colors appear to be nearer and tend to advance into the foreground. Cooler colors appear more distant and tend to recede into the background. The same effect can occur when adjacent objects are different colors as well. Saturation and luminance can also either enhance or diminish the effects of cool and warm colors on human reactions and behavior.

This effect can be amplified through the use of colors that are directly opposite each other on the color wheel; such color pairs are known as **complementary colors**. Complementary colors create color dissonance; such colors appear stark and create strong contrast when overlaid or adjacent to each other in a chart. Complementary colors are useful when you want particular objects in a display to stand out, but overuse of complementary colors can be distracting for the audience. As shown in Figure 4.2, examples of complementary colors in the RGB primary color model include blue and yellow, green and magenta, and chartreuse and violet.

Colors that are directly adjacent to each other on a color wheel are called **analogous colors**. Because of the underlying similarities in their hues, analogous colors appear softer and smoother than complementary colors when used together. Note that the nearer colors are to each other on a color wheel, the more analogous they are considered. Analogous colors appear less stark and create less contrast when overlaid or adjacent to each other in a data visualization than complementary colors, but their overuse can still be distracting for the audience. An example of analogous colors in the RGB color wheel shown in Figure 4.2 is blue and azure or violet; another example is orange and red or yellow.

Cognitive load is discussed in Chapter 3.

Not all use of color on charts is effective, and sometimes color is pointless, distracting, or confusing. Unnecessary use of color creates clutter and is potentially detrimental to charts as it can interfere with the audience's ability to interpret and understand the message. This is because clutter can increase the audience's **cognitive load**, or the amount of effort necessary to accurately and efficiently process the information being communicated by a chart.

This suggests that when working with color, we must recognize that:

- Using a multicolored background for data visualization can be distracting.
- Cool colors appear to be more distant that warm colors.
- Using complementary colors together creates color dissonance. That is, complementary colors are said to clash. We use complementary colors to make strong, color-based preattentive distinctions between elements of a data visualization. Overuse of complementary colors can be distracting for the audience.
- Using analogous colors creates less color dissonance/more color harmony than complementary colors. We use analogous colors when we want to make moderate color-based preattentive distinctions between elements of a data visualization. Overuse of analogous colors can also be distracting for the audience.
- Poor use of color can be confusing and distracting to the audience and can increase the audience's cognitive load.

Excel provides easy-to-use color palettes that allow you to emphasize contrast using mostly complimentary colors or monochromatic palettes that provide less contrast by using a single hue with different levels of luminance and saturation. Other software that is used to produce data visualization displays, such as Tableau and Power BI, also provide color palettes that allow the user to customize the colors on the display.

4.2 Color Schemes and Types of Data

The **color scheme** is the set of colors (hues, saturations, and luminances) that are to be used in a data visualization or a series of related data visualizations. The color scheme that we select for a visualization should result from strong consideration of the nature of the data we want to represent with color and the message we want to convey to the audience. For example, color can be used in different ways to represent a categorical variable depending on whether its values represent unordered or ordered groups. When considering a quantitative variable, the way to use color depends on whether we want to express the magnitudes of the values or convey how far the values are below or above a predefined reference value (such as 32° Fahrenheit for temperature). In this section, we consider color strategies for representing categorical variables with unordered groups, variables with values that can be ordered, and quantitative variables for which we want to show deviations from a reference value.

Categorical Color Schemes

Categorical variables are discussed in Chapter 1.

Because the values of a categorical variable represent discrete groups, displays of a categorical variable are generally used to communicate information about the absolute or relative frequency for each group. When the groups of the categorical variable have no inherent ascending or descending order, the variable is well suited for representation by a distinct color for each of its unique groups. This type of color scheme is referred to as a **categorical color scheme** or a qualitative color scheme.

Because the color assigned to each unique group must appear distinct to the audience, we generally limit the categorical color scheme to six or fewer colors. When we exceed six colors, the audience may find distinguishing between groups by the associated color to be challenging. Figure 4.7 shows examples of categorical color palettes available in Excel.

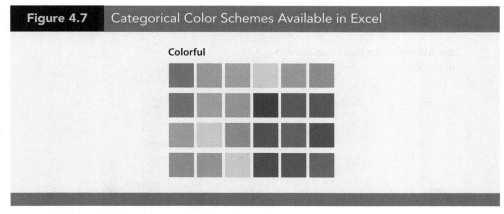

Figure 4.7   Categorical Color Schemes Available in Excel

Colorful

*A number of color palettes useful for categorical data are available in Excel. To set the **Colorful** palette shown in Figure 4.7, click on the **Page Layout** tab, click on the Colors drop-down menu in the **Themes** group, and select the **Office** theme.*

We can use color to add information on categorical variables to many types of charts. Consider the data shown in Figure 4.8. The data are zoo attendance by month in two categories, children and adults. We display these data using a stacked column chart as shown in Figure 4.9.
The following steps maybe used to create this chart.

Step 1. Select cells A1:C13
Click the **Insert** tab on the Ribbon
Step 2. Click the **Insert Column or Bar Chart** button in the **Charts** group
Step 3. When the list of column and bar chart subtypes appears, click the **Stacked Column** button

After some editing, the stacked column chart is as it appears in Figure 4.9. The first palette shown in Figure 4.7 was used by default and uses blue and orange, two relatively complementary colors, to clearly distinguish between the two categories of adult and children attendance. To change to another row of the **Colorful** palette shown in Figure 4.7, click the chart, click the **Chart Design** tab and select **Change Colors** in the **Chart Styles** group, and choose the desired palette.

Change
Colors˅

DATA *file*

zooattendance

Figure 4.8   Data in the File *zooattendance*

	A	B	C
1	**Month**	**Children**	**Adults**
2	Jan	1,681	3,741
3	Feb	1,805	3,073
4	Mar	2,964	3,622
5	Apr	3,541	3,402
6	May	4,253	3,623
7	Jun	9,814	8,029
8	July	13,180	8,787
9	Aug	8,289	6,253
10	Sept	4,901	3,850
11	Oct	3,550	2,904
12	Nov	3,179	2,498
13	Dec	3,883	7,539

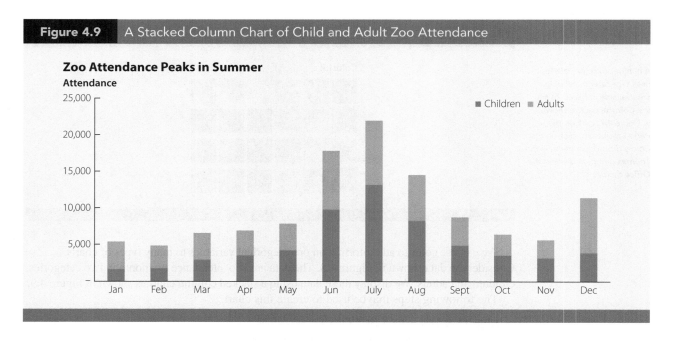

Figure 4.9 A Stacked Column Chart of Child and Adult Zoo Attendance

As we see in Figure 4.9, total zoo attendance is highest in the summer months of June, July, and August. There is a rather large increase in attendance from November to December, which is composed of more adults than children. The zoo celebrates its Festival of Lights, which caters to an adult audience, in December.

Sequential Color Schemes

When the values of a variable can be arranged in ascending or descending order, a **sequential color scheme** (or sequential color palette) should be used. In a sequential color scheme, the relative degree of saturation or luminance of a single hue is used to create a gradient that represents the relative value of the variable. Although either the relative degree of saturation or luminance can be used to create a sequential color scheme, luminance is most frequently used for this purpose. In Figure 4.10, we show examples of sequential color palettes available in Excel.

As an example of the use of sequential color, let us consider the average annual temperature in degrees Fahrenheit for each of the 50 states in the United States. These data are in the file *avgtemp*, a portion of which appears in Figure 4.11.

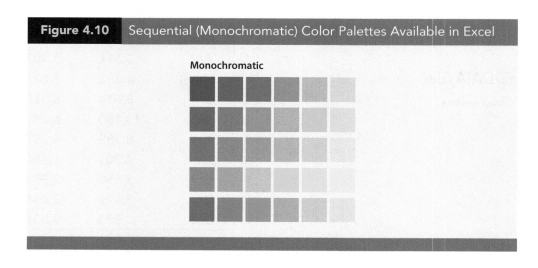

Figure 4.10 Sequential (Monochromatic) Color Palettes Available in Excel

Figure 4.11   A Portion of the Data in file *avgtemp*

DATA*file*

avgtemp

	A	B
1	**State**	**Avg. Temp**
2	Alabama	62.8
3	Alaska	26.6
4	Arizona	60.3
5	Arkansas	60.4
6	California	59.4
7	Colorado	45.1
8	Connecticut	49.0
9	Delaware	55.3

In older versions of Excel, the Map Chart function may not exist. You can create a somewhat similar chart using Excel's Power Map function.

The following steps create the choropleth map of the average temperatures shown in Figure 4.12.

Step 1. Select cells A1:B51
Step 2. Click the **Insert** tab on the Ribbon
Step 3. Click the **Insert Map Chart** button in the **Charts** group and click on **Filled Map**
Step 4. Click **Chart Title** and enter *Average Temperature by State* using font Calibri 16 pt. bold

Figure 4.12   Choropleth Map of Average Annual Temperature by State Using Blue

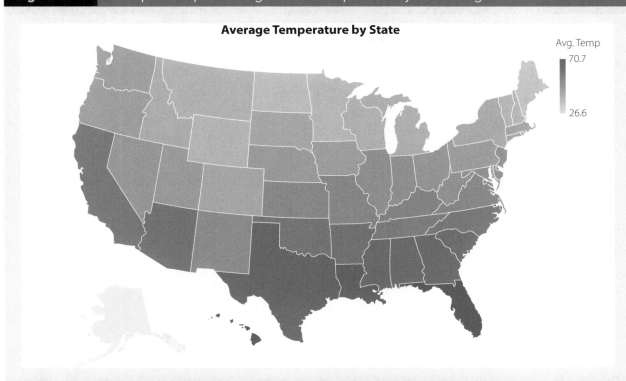

If you have set the Theme to Office, the default of blue will appear (as it is the first row in Figure 4.10 ▮▮▮▮▮▮). Here, darker blue signifies higher average temperature. Since blue is a cool color, we might want to switch to a warmer color to help the audience's intuition. The following steps allow us to change the color using the **Monochromatic** colors displayed in Figure 4.10 to produce the map shown in Figure 4.13.

Step 1. Click on the map
Step 2. Click the **Chart Design** tab on the Ribbon
Step 3. Click the **Change Colors** drop-down menu in the **Chart Styles** group
Select the second row in the **Monochromatic** themes (brown ▮▮▮▮▮▮)
as shown in Figure 4.10

In Figure 4.13, we see that higher average temperatures exist in the south where the darkest color exists. In the lower left, we see that Alaska on the left has a low average temperature and Hawaii on the right has a high average temperature.

Diverging Color Schemes

When working with a quantitative variable for which there is a meaningful reference value, such as a target value or the mean, a **diverging color scheme** (or diverging color palette) should be used. A diverging color scheme is essentially a gradient formed by the combination of two sequential color schemes with a shared endpoint at the reference value. These color schemes use two hues, one of which is associated with values below the reference value and the other of which is associated with values above the reference value. As the value of the variable increases, the luminance of the hue associated with values below the reference value progressively increases and the color becomes lighter until we cross the reference point. At that point, the luminance of the hue associated with values above the reference point progressively decreases and the color becomes darker.

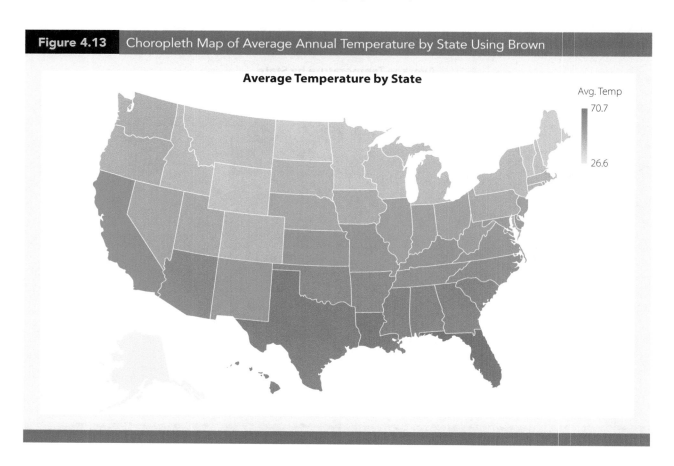

Figure 4.13   Choropleth Map of Average Annual Temperature by State Using Brown

Table 4.1		Monthly Mean Daily Low Temperatures for Indianapolis 2010–2019										
	Jan	Feb	Mar	Apr	May	Jun	Jul	Aug	Sep	Oct	Nov	Dec
2010	18	20	36	49	57	67	70	69	58	46	34	19
2011	17	25	35	45	55	65	72	66	57	45	41	31
2012	26	29	46	44	58	63	72	64	56	44	31	32
2013	22	23	28	42	56	63	65	65	59	45	31	23
2014	11	14	25	42	53	64	61	65	55	45	28	28
2015	15	11	30	44	57	64	66	63	60	47	39	36
2016	21	26	40	43	53	65	68	70	62	51	39	24
2017	28	33	35	49	53	62	67	63	59	49	35	22
2018	17	29	30	37	62	66	68	67	63	47	31	29
2019	20	26	29	44	55	62	69	65	63	46	30	29

Thus, the hue communicates the direction of deviation from the reference point, and the luminance conveys the relative deviation from the reference point. For this reason, the hues used on each side of the reference point in a diverging color scheme are typically distinctive; primary hues are often used to make it easier to distinguish the direction and degree of deviation from the reference point.

Diverging color schemes are most effective when highlighting both extremes (high and low values) of a variable. Continuing with another temperature example, consider the monthly mean daily low Fahrenheit temperatures for Indianapolis for each year from 2010–2019 in Table 4.1.[2]

We can use the following steps to build a heat map of these data in Excel using the file *indlowtemps.*

indlowtemps

Step 1. Select cells B2:M11

Step 2. Click the **Home** tab on the Ribbon and click **Conditional Formatting** in the **Styles** group

Step 3. Click **Color Scales** and select **More Rules**

Step 4. When the **New Formatting Rule** dialog box opens, in the **Edit the Rule Description** box

Select **3-Color Scale** from the **Format Style** drop-down menu

Select a blue hue to be associated with values below the reference point from the **Color** drop-down menu in the **Minimum** column

Select **Number** from the **Midpoint** drop-down menu for **Type**, enter *32* in the **Value** box, and select white to be associated with values near the reference point from the **Color** drop-down menu

Select a red hue to be associated with values above the reference point from the **Color** drop-down menu in the **Maximum** column

Check the **Preview** bar to ensure you have created the diverging color gradient you desire

Click **OK**

This creates a heat map with the values in the cells. To format the values so they do not appear in the cells:

*Entering the semicolon (;) in the **Type** box formats the values in the highlighted cells so they do not appear in the cells.*

Step 5. With cells B2:M11 still selected, right click any cell in B2:M11 and select **Format Cells...**

Click the **Number** tab, then click **Custom** in the **Category** box

Enter *;* in the **Type** box

Click **OK**

These steps produce the heat map with a diverging color scheme shown in Figure 4.14.

[2] Data from https://www.usclimatedata.com/climate/indianapolis/indiana/united-states

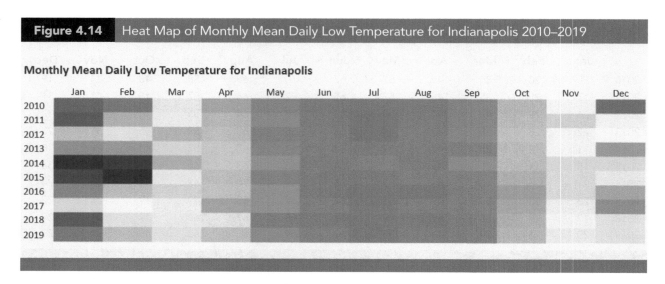

Figure 4.14 Heat Map of Monthly Mean Daily Low Temperature for Indianapolis 2010–2019

Note that we have considered color psychology by selecting red for warmer temperatures and blue for cooler temperatures when selecting the hues for this heat map.

In the heat map in Figure 4.14, the reference value is 32° Fahrenheit, blue is the hue associated with temperatures below the reference value, and red is the hue associated with temperatures above the reference value. As expected, the coldest months (those months shaded in the most intense blue) are January, February, and December, and the warmest months (those months shaded in the most intense red) are June, July, and August. We also see that March and November are apparently transition months; in a few years the mean low temperatures in March or November were below the reference point (shaded blue), and in a few other years the mean low temperatures in March or November were above the reference point (shaded red).

Notes + Comments

Diverging color schemes can be difficult to interpret near the reference point in grayscales. The high levels of luminance of the two colors on opposite sides of the reference point can also be indistinguishable when the chart is displayed in grayscale (as is often the case in printed material).

4.3 Custom Color Using the HSL Color System

In the previous examples, we used Excel's color palettes to demonstrate the various types of color schemes. However, it is also possible to customize the colors used in a chart. We can directly control the hue, saturation, and luminance (HSL) in Excel through the Colors dialog box, which allows for control of each of these three color characteristics in the following ways.

Hue: The color's hue is expressed as an integer in the range 0 to 255. The primary and secondary colors of the RGB primary color mode using fixed values for saturation and luminance are:

Color	Hue
Red	0
Yellow	40
Green	80
Cyan	120
Blue	160
Magenta	200

In Figure 4.15, we illustrate changing hues with fixed levels of saturation and luminance in the Colors dialog box.

Figure 4.15 Setting the Hue Parameter Using the Colors Dialog Box

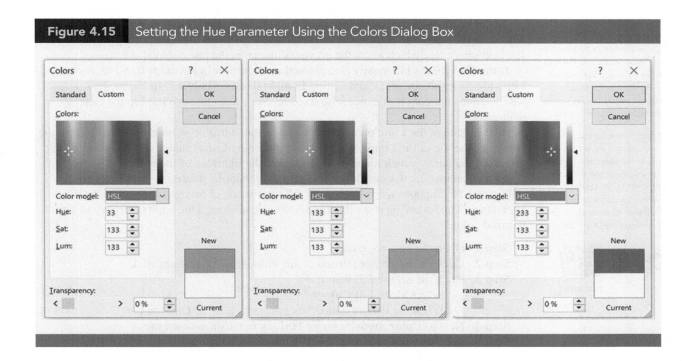

As the value of the Hue parameter increases, the indicator ⬚ moves horizontally from left to right across the color spectrum control in the Colors dialog box to indicate the selected hue.

Sat: The color's saturation is expressed as an integer in the range 0 to 255. Higher Sat: values correspond with more intense or pure color, and lower Sat: values produce increasingly gray shades. Setting Sat: to 0 results in a gray tone regardless of the hue and luminance settings. In Figure 4.16, we illustrate changing saturation with fixed levels of hue and luminance in the Colors dialog box.

*You can alter the value of Hue: by entering a value from 0 to 255 in the **Hue:** box, adjusting the value with the arrow keys adjacent to the **Hue:** box, or using your cursor to drag the indicator ⬚ horizontally across the color spectrum control.*

Figure 4.16 Setting the Sat Parameter Using the Colors Dialog Box

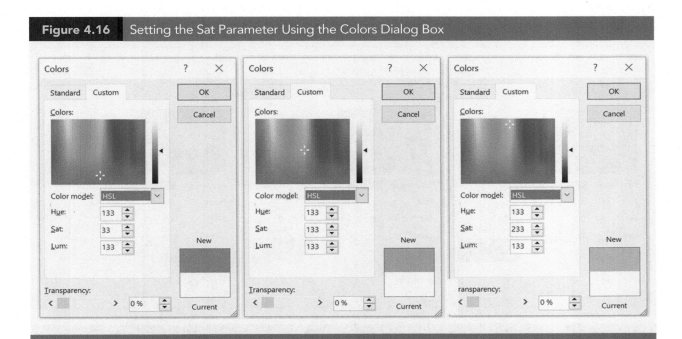

*You can alter the value of Sat: by entering a value from 0 to 255 in the **Sat:** box, adjusting the value with the arrow keys adjacent to the **Sat:** box, or using your cursor to drag the indicator ▭ vertically across the color spectrum control.*

*You can alter the value of Lum: by entering a value from 0 to 255 in the **Lum:** box, adjusting the value with the arrow keys adjacent to the **Lum:** box, or using your cursor to drag the indicator ◄ vertically across the luminosity slide control.*

zoo_chart

As the value of the Sat parameter increases, the indicator ▭ moves vertically from the bottom to the top of the color spectrum control in the Colors dialog box to indicate the selected saturation, which alters the grayness/increases the purity of the color.

Lum: The color's luminosity is expressed as an integer in the range 0 to 255. Setting Lum: to 255 results in white, and setting Lum: to 0 results in black. In Figure 4.17, we illustrate changing luminance with fixed levels of hue and saturation in the Colors dialog box.

As the value of the Lum: parameter increases, the indicator ◄ moves vertically from the bottom to the top of the Luminosity slide control in the Colors dialog box to indicate the selected luminance, which reduces and increases the lightness of the color.

As an example, let us consider again the zoo attendance stacked column chart shown in Figure 4.18. Suppose we wish to use a different shade of orange to represent the adult attendance. The following steps illustrate how we can change the adults category to a customized color.

Step 1. Open the file *zoo_chart*
Step 2. Click on the orange portion of any column and then right click
Step 3. Click the **Shape Fill** button 🖌˅
           Select **More Fill Colors…**
           When the **Colors** dialog box appears, click the **Custom** tab
Step 4. Next to **Color model:** choose **HSL** from the drop-down menu
Step 5. Set **Hue** to *21*, **Sat** to *238,* and **Lum** to *182*
Step 6. Click **OK**

The zoo data with the lighter shade of orange is shown in Figure 4.18.

In some instances, you may want to replicate a color used in an existing image. You can use the Eyedropper, a tool in Microsoft PowerPoint that determines the HSL settings for colors used in an image. For example, consider an analyst who is creating a presentation to give to the management of Grappenhall Publishers and wants to use the color scheme of the company's logo (shown in Figure 4.19) in creating this presentation.

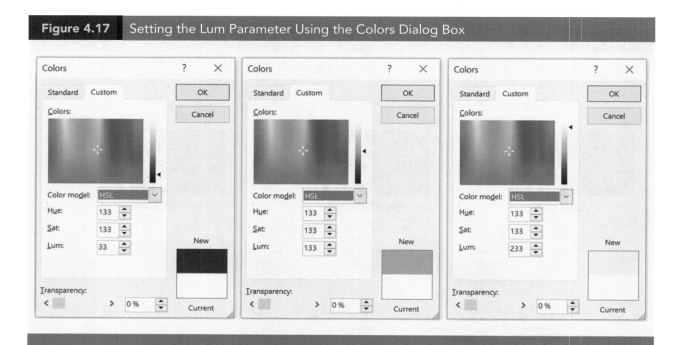

Figure 4.17   Setting the Lum Parameter Using the Colors Dialog Box

Figure 4.18 A Stacked Column Chart of Children and Adult Zoo Attendance with Lighter Orange

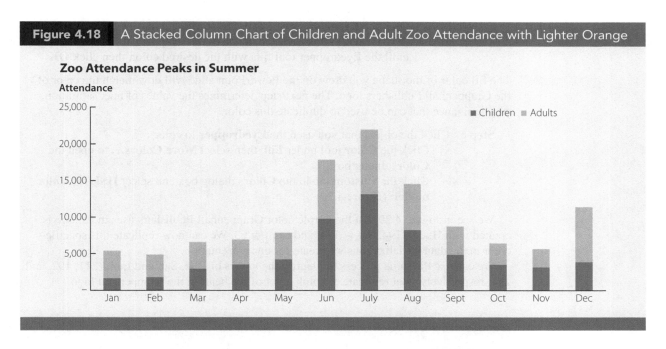

The following steps explain how to use the Eyedropper tool in PowerPoint to determine the values of hue, saturation, and luminance that create the distinctive purple color of the Grappenhall Publishers logo in Figure 4.19.

Step 1. Open a new PowerPoint document presentation

Step 2. Paste a copy of the image of interest into a blank slide

Step 3. Click the **Insert** tab on the Ribbon

Click the **Shapes** button in the **Illustrations** group, select any shape icon, and use the cursor to draw the shape into the same slide

Step 4. Right click the shape you have drawn and select **Format Shape** to open the **Format Shape** task pane

On the **Format Shape** task pane:

Click the **Fill & Line** icon

Under **Fill**, select **Solid Fill**

Click the **Color** tool under **Fill**, then select **Eyedropper** to open the **Eyedropper** tool

Figure 4.19 Grappenhall Publishers Logo

Drag the **Eyedropper** tool over the object that has the color you want to replicate (in this case, the image of the Grappenhall Publishers logo) until the Eyedropper tool fills with the desired color, then click **OK**

The fill color of the shape you drew on the PowerPoint slide will now match the color of the Grappenhall Publishers logo. The next step determines the values of hue, saturation, and luminance that can be used to duplicate this color.

Step 5. Click the object that you used the **Eyedropper** to color
Click the **Color** tool under **Fill**, then select **More Colors...** to open the **Colors** dialog box
Click the **Custom** tab in the **Colors** dialog box and select **HSL** for **Color model:** (Figure 4.20)

We see in Figure 4.20 that the purple color Grappenhall Publishers uses in its logo is created with Hue = 194, Sat = 174, and Lum = 63. We can now replicate this specific color in the data visualizations we create for our presentation.

We can use the same process to identify the values of Hue, Sat, and Lum (211, 192, and 154, respectively) that replicate the pink color of the heart in the Grappenhall logo.

Figure 4.20   Colors Dialog Box Showing the Values of Hue, Saturation, and Luminance Used in the Grappenhall Publishers Logo

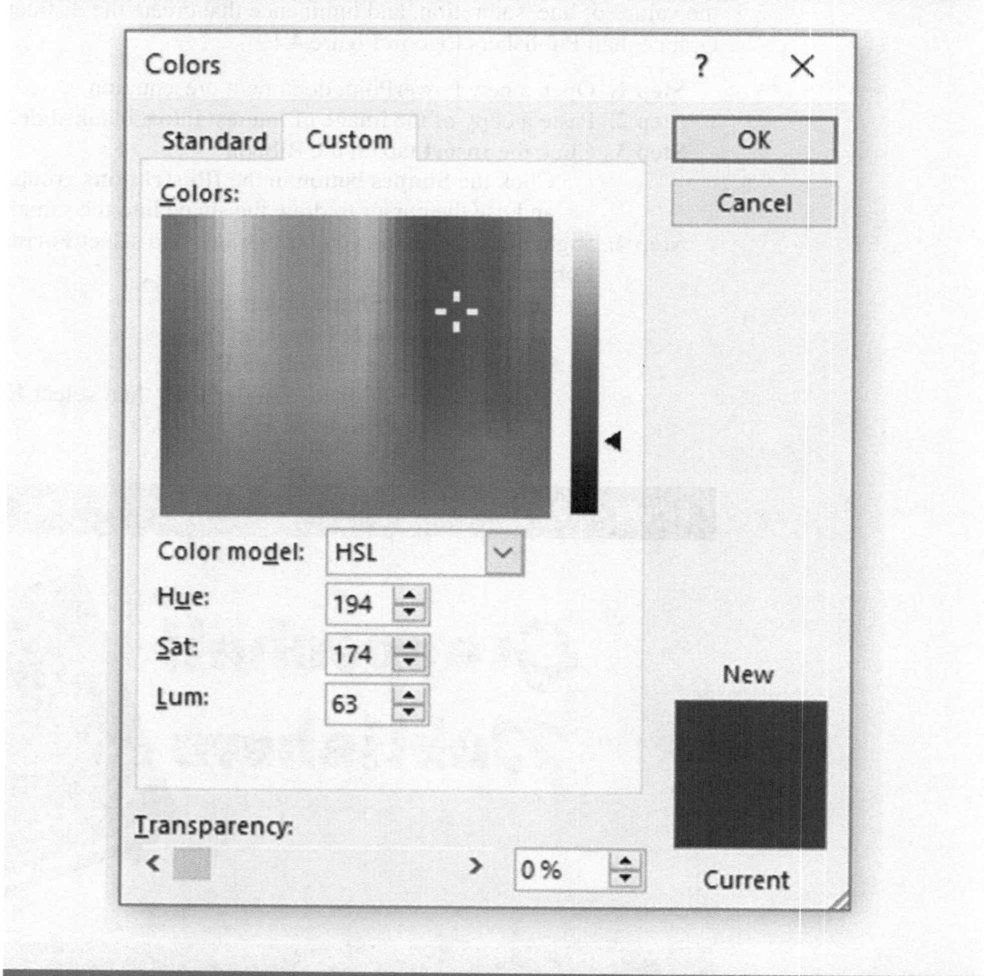

Notes + Comments

1. In addition to the HSL color scheme, Excel has the Red, Green, Blue (RGB) color scheme available corresponding to the Red, Green, Blue color wheel. You may access this by selecting RGB from the **Color model:** drop-down menu in the **Colors** dialog box.

2. The **Standard** tab in the **Colors** dialog box allows the user to modify color in Excel's RGB color model. Clicking on a particular hexagon invokes the associated color that appears on the **New-Current** box in the lower right of the dialog box. Clicking **OK** will change the object to the new color.

3. In Excel's RGB color model, the **Transparency** slider in the **Colors** dialog box controls how much you can see through a color. You can drag the **Transparency** slider or enter a number between 0 and 100 in the **Transparency** slider box adjacent to the slider. You can vary the percentage of transparency from 0 (fully opaque, the default setting) to 100% (fully transparent).

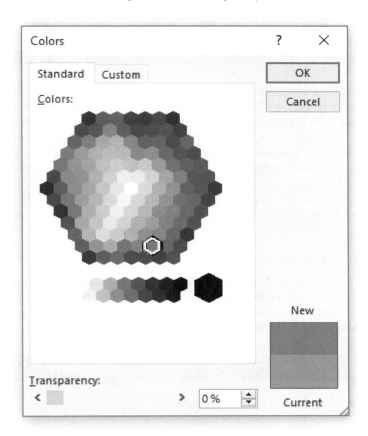

4.4 Common Mistakes in the Use of Color in Data Visualization

Although color is a powerful tool for communicating with charts, it is often misused. When misused, it may distort the intended message or distract the audience. In this section, we discuss several common mistakes committed when using color in a data visualization.

Unnecessary Color

Data visualization experts agree that color should only be used when it communicates something that no other aspect of a chart communicates to the audience. Figure 4.21 shows the number of units sold (in thousands) for seven top-selling midsize sedans.

In this chart, the audience can discern which column corresponds to each of the models through the colors of the columns and the legend. Although this communicates the data,

CHART *file*

sedansales_chart

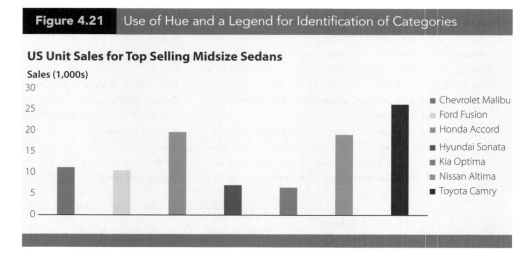

Figure 4.21   Use of Hue and a Legend for Identification of Categories

US Unit Sales for Top Selling Midsize Sedans

we can accomplish the same communication with a chart that creates less cognitive load by avoiding the use of multiple colors. If we clearly label the columns on the horizontal axis, then there is no need for a different color for each model of sedan.

The chart shown in Figure 4.22 uses only horizontal-axis labels to communicate the association between the columns and the models. The audience now does not have to look back and forth between the columns and the legend to make these associations in this chart, which reduces the audience's cognitive load.

Note that one could produce a chart that includes both the colors and legend of Figure 4.21 and the horizontal-axis labels of Figure 4.22, but this would embed redundant information in the chart and further decrease its data-ink ratio.

Excessive Color

There is a limit to the amount of information that can be communicated to the audience using color. Suppose you are analyzing quarterly house-price indexes from 1992 to 2019 for each state and the District of Colombia, and you want to emphasize the western-most states in the continental United States (Arizona, California, Nevada, Oregon, and

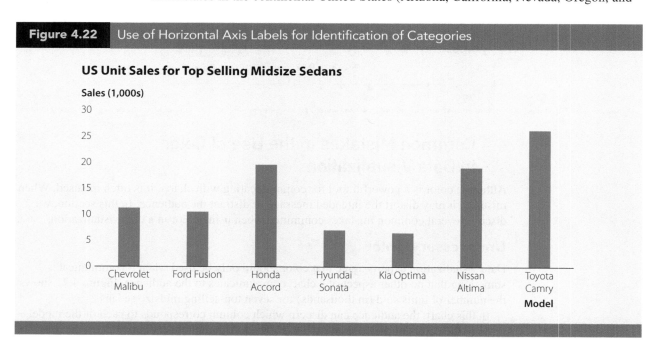

Figure 4.22   Use of Horizontal Axis Labels for Identification of Categories

US Unit Sales for Top Selling Midsize Sedans

statehousingindices_chart

Washington). The chart in Figure 4.23 shows the quarterly house-price index from 1992 to 2019 for each state and the District of Colombia.[3] The chart captures information on house-price index by state for each quarter of the 28-year period (112 quarters). It enables the audience to quickly see that house prices increased steadily on a national level until around 2004, when the rate of increase accelerated dramatically until sometime around 2007. The audience can also see that the housing market then crashed, and house prices generally fell for about four to five years until they began to increase again sometime around 2010.

You can re-create the chart in the file *statehousingindices_chart* using the file *statehousingindices* and the following steps:

statehousingindices

Step 1. Open the file *statehousingindices,* and select the data for AK in cells A2:D85
Use the **Recommended Charts** button in the **Charts** group on the **Insert** tab of the Ribbon to create a line chart using these data

Step 2. Right click the chart, then select **Select Data** to open the **Select Data Source** dialog box (shown in Figure 4.24)
Click Series1 in the **Legend Entries (Series)** area and click the **Remove** button ✕ Remove to remove this series from the chart
Click Series2 in the **Legend Entries (Series)** area
Click the **Edit** button 📝 Edit in the **Legend Entries (Series)** area to open the **Edit Series** dialog box for this series
Click the **Series name:** box, then select cell A2 to use the contents of this cell (AK) for the series name
Click **OK** to close the **Edit Series** dialog box
Click **OK** to close the **Select Data Source** dialog box

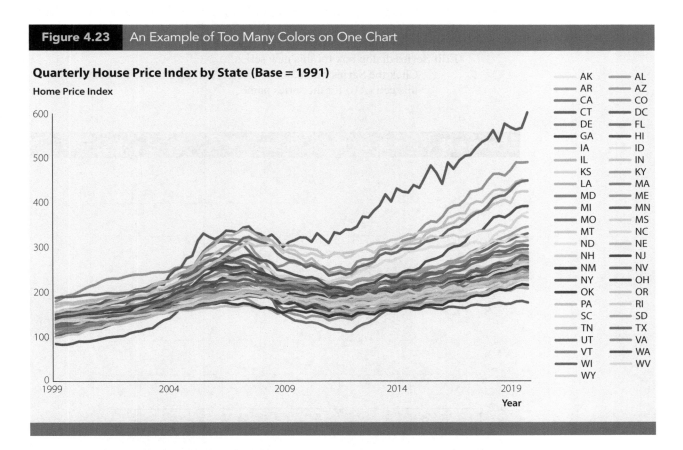

Figure 4.23	An Example of Too Many Colors on One Chart

Quarterly House Price Index by State (Base = 1991)

³ Data from https://www.fhfa.gov/DataTools/Downloads/Pages/House-Price-Index-Datasets.aspx

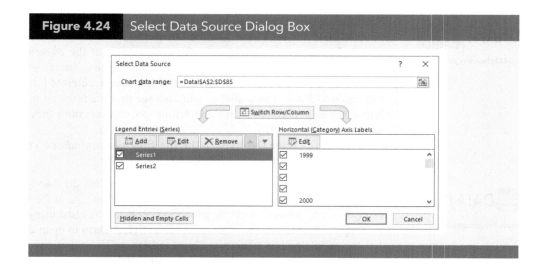

Figure 4.24   Select Data Source Dialog Box

Step 2. Right click the legend at the bottom of the chart, then click **Format Legend…** to open the **Format Legend** pane

      Click **Legend Options**, then click the **Legend Options** button █▐█ and select **Right**

This produces the chart in Figure 4.25.

    To add the next state in the data (AL) to the chart:

Step 3. Right click the chart and select **Select Data…** to open the **Select Data Source** dialog box

      Click the **Add** button ▦ Add in the **Legend Entries (Series)** area to open the **Edit Series** dialog box for this new series

            Click the **Series name** box and select cell A86 to use the contents of this cell (AL) for the series name

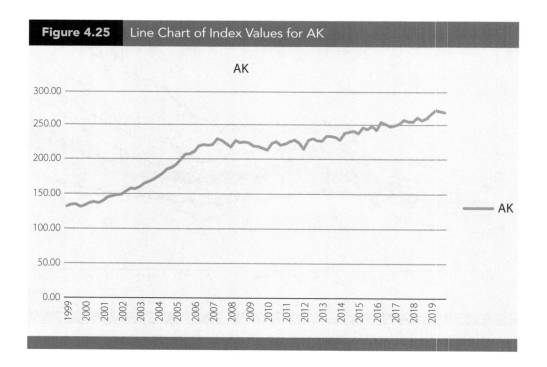

Figure 4.25   Line Chart of Index Values for AK

Click the **Series values** box and select cells D86:D169 to use the contents of these cells for this new series (AL)
Click **OK**
Click the **Edit** button 📝 Edit in the **Horizontal (Category) Axis Labels** area to open the **Axis Labels** dialog box
Click the **Axis label range** box and select cells B86:B169
Click **OK**
Click **OK**

This produces the chart in Figure 4.26.
   To add the remaining states and the District of Columbia to the chart:

Step 4. Repeat Step 3 for each remaining state and the District of Columbia

This and some editing produces the chart in Figure 4.23.
   Comparing housing prices across states with this chart is difficult because there are 51 categories/colors on this chart. The human brain can only process a few distinct colors simultaneously. The use of a legend in Figure 4.23 also creates additional eye travel for the audience.
   We can make it easier for the audience to find the westernmost states in the continental United States (Arizona, California, Nevada, Oregon, and Washington) on this chart by applying a different color for each of these states and using gray for all other states. We can also remove the legend and add a label for each of the five westernmost states in the continental United States to the end of their respective lines. The following steps detail how to produce the chart that results from these modifications.

statehousingindices_chart

Step 1. Open the file *statehousingindices_chart* (or use the chart that you created with the file *statehousingindices*)
Step 2. Double click **AZ** in the legend of the chart to select this series and open the **Format Legend Entry** task pane (make sure you have selected only "AZ" and not the entire legend)
Step 3. When the **Format Legend Entry** task pane opens
Click the **Fill & Line** icon 🖌
Select **Solid Line** in the **Border** area
From the drop-down **Color** menu, click **More Colors...**

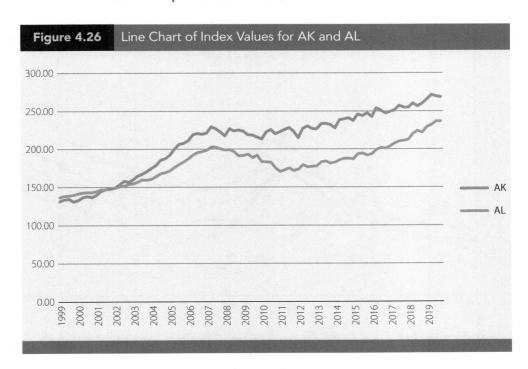

Figure 4.26   Line Chart of Index Values for AK and AL

In the **Colors** dialog box, click on the **Custom** tab

From the **Color model:** drop-down menu, select **HSL**

Change the value of color of the line associated with AZ (Figure 4.27 uses Hue = 32, Sat = 255, Lum = 128)

Step 4. Repeat Steps 2–3 for

CA (Figure 4.27 uses Hue = 155, Sat = 133, Lum = 132)

NV (Figure 4.27 uses Hue = 0, Sat = 255, Lum = 128)

OR (Figure 4.27 uses Hue = 112, Sat = 173, Lum = 71)

WA (Figure 4.27 uses Hue = 222, Sat = 230, Lum = 92)

Step 5. Repeat Steps 2–3 for each other state and DC using the same shade of gray (the chart in Figure 4.24 uses Hue = 0, Sat = 5, Lum = 207)

Step 6. Right click **AZ** in the legend of the chart to select this series and select **Format Data Series…**

When the **Format Data Series** task pane opens, click the **Series Options** icon ▮▮▮

Select **Secondary Axis** to put the AZ series on a secondary vertical axis that will be located on the right side of the chart and may overlap the legend

Step 7. Repeat Step 7 for each of the CA, NV, OR, and WA series

Step 8. Click the legend and press **Delete**

Step 9. Click the secondary legend to open the **Format Axis** task pane

Click the **Axis Options** icon ▮▮▮

Enter *600* for **Maximum** under **Bounds** in the **Axis Options** area so the scales are the same on the primary and secondary vertical axes

Step 10. Click the secondary vertical axis and press **Delete**

Using a secondary axis in Steps 7–10 brings the lines associated with the states in which we have an interest to the forefront of the chart.

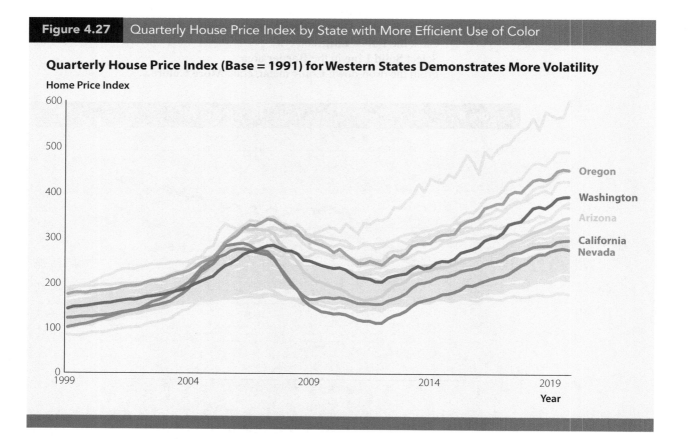

Figure 4.27   Quarterly House Price Index by State with More Efficient Use of Color

Step 11. Click any area in the chart

Click the **Insert** tab on the Ribbon

Click the **Text box** button ⬚ in the **Text** group, use the cursor to draw the shape into the same slide adjacent to the AZ line, and enter *Arizona* into the text box

Click the text box and format its contents (the chart in Figure 4.24 uses **Calibri 9pt** font with Hue = 32, Sat = 255, Lum = 128)

Step 12. Repeat Step 11 for the CA, NV, OR, and WA series (entering *California, Nevada, Oregon,* and *Washington* in the respective textboxes). Use **Calibri 10.5pt** font with the values of hue, sat, and lum for each of these states that is given in Step 4

It is much easier to see in Figure 4.27 that the five westernmost states experienced more rapid growths in housing prices than most other states immediately prior to the 2007 housing market collapse, and the drops in housing prices in these states during the 2007 housing market collapse were steeper than most other states. The chart also shows that the states in this region have experienced an average, or stronger than average, post-housing market collapse recovery.

Insufficient Contrast

When using color to distinguish between elements of a chart, it is important that the audience can easily distinguish between the selected colors. If the colors assigned to different chart elements are difficult to differentiate, the audience can become confused or may have to work harder than necessary to understand the chart's message.

In a story on the change in the portion of England's public services budget devoted to the country's National Health Service (NHS) over a 60-year period, the British Broadcasting Company (BBC) included the pie charts originally produced by the Institute for Fiscal Studies as shown in Figure 4.28. The charts use color to differentiate between spending on the NHS (hue = 127, sat = 241, lum = 40) and the remainder of the public services budget (hue = 127, sat = 241, lum = 53). The use of green hues takes advantage of the color's common symbolic association with finance and economics, but these colors only differ slightly in luminance. This difference is not sufficient to allow the audience to easily discern which slice is associated with spending on the National Health Service and which slice is associated with the remainder of the public services budget in each of these pie charts.

A simple adjustment to the color used to represent the remainder of the budget will make these pie charts far easier for the audience to process with less cognitive load. In Figure 4.29, we show the charts re-created in Excel using a hue level of 127 and saturation level of 241 for both categories and a luminance level of 131 for the NHS and 53 for the rest of the budget to increase the visual contrast between the categories.

The most extreme and most confusing form of insufficient contrast is redundancy, which occurs when the same color is associated with two unrelated categories or variables in a chart or series of charts.

Because we have increased the contrast between the two slices of each pie chart by increasing the difference in the luminance, the audience can more easily differentiate between the NHS portion of the budget and the rest of the budget for each time period in the display. The use of a higher luminance for the NHS portion of the budget also focuses the attention on that portion of the budget.

Inconsistency across Related Charts

Data dashboards are discussed in Chapter 8.

When creating several charts for a single report, a presentation, an ongoing analysis, or a data dashboard, it is critical that color is used consistently. Using different color schemes or using different colors to represent categories on different charts will confuse the audience and dramatically increase its cognitive load.

Consider the zoo attendance data shown in Figure 4.8, shown again here in Figure 4.30. The column chart uses orange and blue, two complementary colors, to distinguish between

As discussed in Chapters 2 and 3, the use of pie charts is generally discouraged.

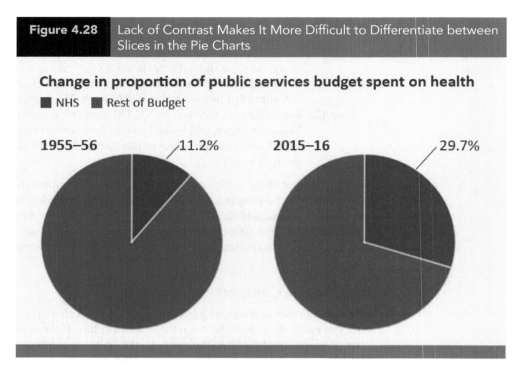

Figure 4.28 Lack of Contrast Makes It More Difficult to Differentiate between Slices in the Pie Charts

Change in proportion of public services budget spent on health
■ NHS   ■ Rest of Budget

1955–56   11.2%   2015–16   29.7%

adults and children. Now, suppose as part of a presentation to the Zoo Board, you have Figure 4.30 on a slide, and it will be followed by a second slide that shows adult versus child December ticket revenue for the last five years. Consistency in the use of color across slides will make it easier for the audience to comprehend. So, rather than use different colors, it is helpful to use the same orange and blue to represent other factors related to adults and children. Figure 4.31 shows a chart of the December revenue data. The consistency in the use of color will help the audience's comprehension of the data presented across the series of slides.

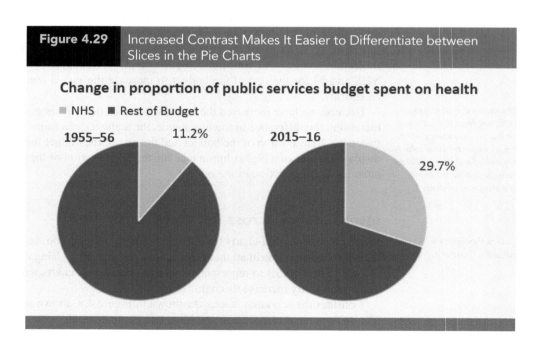

Figure 4.29 Increased Contrast Makes It Easier to Differentiate between Slices in the Pie Charts

Change in proportion of public services budget spent on health
■ NHS   ■ Rest of Budget

1955–56   11.2%   2015–16   29.7%

Figure 4.30   A Stacked Column Chart of Children and Adult Zoo Attendance

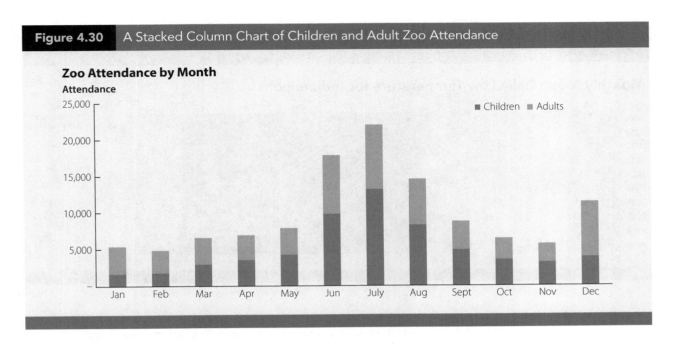

Neglecting Colorblindness

Consider the monthly mean daily low temperatures for Indianapolis 2010–2019 in Table 4.1. If we had used green to represent temperatures below freezing in the gradient we developed for Figure 4.14, the result would look like the chart in Figure 4.32.

Although green may not be as appealing in this chart because it is not as closely associated with cold as is blue, many people can still interpret the heat map in Figure 4.32 with relative ease. That is, unless a member of the audience is red-green colorblind, in which case the resulting heat map may look like the chart in Figure 4.33.

Figure 4.31   A Line Chart of Ticket Revenue for the Month of December

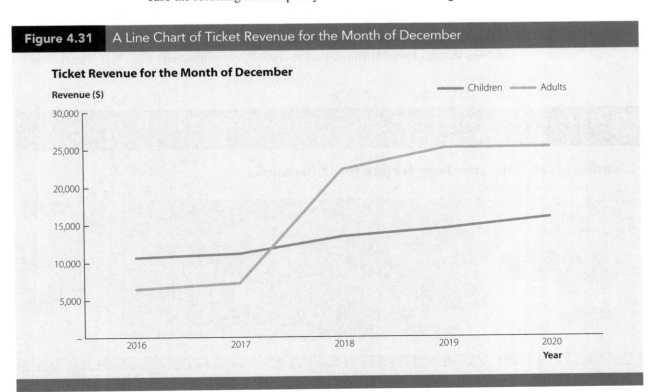

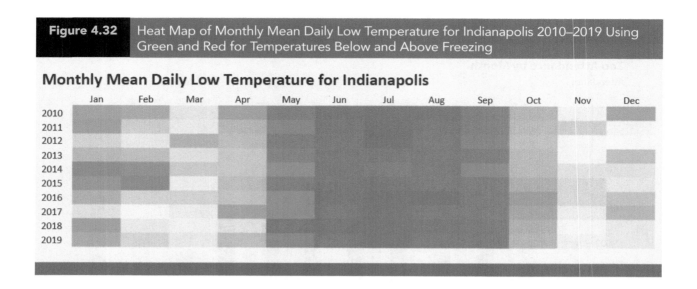

Figure 4.32   Heat Map of Monthly Mean Daily Low Temperature for Indianapolis 2010–2019 Using Green and Red for Temperatures Below and Above Freezing

Some of the blocks representing the cold months of December, January, and February in Figure 4.32 appear to be identical to some of the blocks representing the hot months June, July, and August for someone who is red-green colorblind, so this chart has little meaning for those members of the audience who have difficulty differentiating red from green.

Colorblindness, or a reduced ability to accurately perceive some colors, occurs when at least one of the three types of cones in a retina is insensitive to the wavelength of light it is responsible for sensing. The most common form of colorblindness is red-green colorblindness, which affects approximately 8% of all men and approximately 0.5% of all women. People with red-green colorblindness cannot perceive, to some degree, differences between red and green. Blue-yellow colorblindness is far less common, occurring in approximately .01% of the population. These individuals cannot perceive, to some degree, differences between blue and yellow. The 0.003% of the population that is completely colorblind see only in shades of gray. If you neglect to consider color-blindness when you select colors

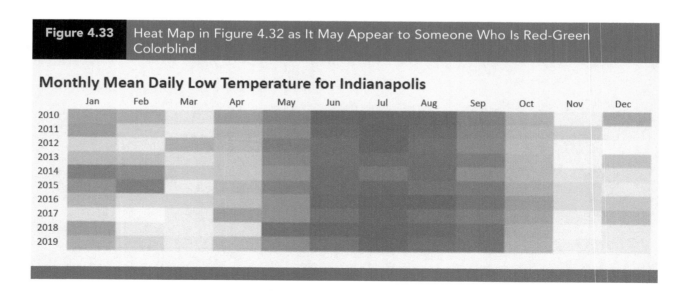

Figure 4.33   Heat Map in Figure 4.32 as It May Appear to Someone Who Is Red-Green Colorblind

for your charts, you risk making it more difficult for some members of the audience to understand your message.

Not Considering the Mode of Delivery

Color works differently in print and projection. Projected presentations will be seen from a distance, and the audience will generally have relatively little time to review specific aspects of a projected presentation. Use of thick lines, color contrast, and relatively high saturation and luminance in this medium is critical. Use sharp outlines and saturated contrasting colors when creating a presentation that is to be projected. On the other hand, the audience will generally be close to printed presentations and will have more time to review specific aspects of a printed report, so you do not need to rely as extensively on thick lines, color contrast, and relatively high saturation and luminance in this medium. Use softer outlines with colors with less saturation, lower luminance, and less contrast when creating a presentation that is to be printed.

Colors will also vary from monitor to monitor, projector to projector, and monitor to projector. When possible, go through your entire presentation in advance with the projection equipment that will you use when giving the actual presentation, and make necessary adjustments iteratively until you are satisfied with the projected colors. If this is not possible, avoid extremely bright colors in your color scheme as those often differ most between the appearance on the monitor you use when creating the presentation and the appearance on the screen with the projection system you will ultimately use.

Similarly, colors vary from printer to printer and from monitor to printer. Consider creating a test page that includes each of the colors you use in your report on the printer you will ultimately use to print your report. Print this single page, review the results, adjust as necessary, and repeat the process until you are satisfied with the printed colors.

Notes + Comments

1. It is a good idea to view your data visualizations in grayscale to ensure that the levels of saturation and luminance used provide sufficient basis for colorblind members of the audience to understand the intended message. This can be done in Excel by selecting the **Grayscale** setting in the Print menu and viewing the result in the **Print Preview** window.

2. Several colorblind-friendly color schemes have been developed such as the one developed by David Nichols (https://davidmathlogic.com/colorblind/).

Summary

In this chapter, we have discussed specific aspects of the preattentive attribute color and how to use color to create effective data visualizations. We defined the roles of hue, saturation, and luminance in defining a color. We discussed the differences between color psychology and color symbolism and how each can be used effectively. We then described how to design color schemes that are appropriate for categorical variables, ordered variables, and quantitative variables with meaningful reference values. We discussed the HSL system for defining colors in data visualization software, and we demonstrated how to use the HSL system in Excel. We concluded with a discussion of various common mistakes made when using color in data visualizations, including neglecting to consider colorblindness when creating data visualizations. And throughout the chapter, we provided examples and step-by-step instructions on how to address the issues discussed in this chapter across a wide variety of chart types.

Glossary

Analogous colors Colors that are directly adjacent to each other on a color wheel.

Categorical color scheme A set of colors used to describe a categorical variable when the categories have no inherent ascending or descending order. Also called a categorical color palette.

Color symbolism The cultural meanings and significance associated with color.

Cognitive load The amount of effort necessary to accurately and efficiently process the information being communicated by a chart.

Color A preattentive attribute for data visualizations that includes the attributes hue, saturation, and luminance.

Color psychology The study of the innate relationships between color and human behavior.

Color scheme A set of colors used in a chart or in a series of related charts. Also called a color palette.

Color wheel A common chart used to show the relationships between primary, secondary, and tertiary hues for a primary color model.

Colorblindness An inability to accurately detect some colors.

Complementary colors Colors that are directly opposite each other on a color wheel.

Cool hues Hues that are thought to be soothing, calming, and reassuring. Blues, purples, and greens are generally considered to be cool hues.

Diverging color scheme A set of colors used in a chart or in a series of related charts to describe values of a quantitative variable for which there is a meaningful reference value, such as a target value or the mean. Also called a diverging color palette.

Hue The attribute of a color that is determined by the position the light occupies on the visible light spectrum and defines the base of the color.

Luminance The attribute of a color that represents the relative degree of black or white in the color.

Primary hues The three hues in a primary color model that cannot be mixed or formed by any combination of other hues. All other hues in a primary color model are derived from these three hues.

Saturation The attribute of a color that represents the amount of gray in the color and determines the intensity or purity of the hue in the color.

Sequential color scheme A set of colors used to describe the values of a quantitative variable or a categorical variable when the categories have an inherent ascending or descending order. Also called a sequential color palette.

Warm hues Hues that are thought to evoke energy, passion, and danger. Yellows, oranges, and reds are generally considered to be warm hues.

Problems

Conceptual

1. **Understanding Hue, Saturation, and Luminance.** For each of the following statements, indicate whether hue, saturation, or luminance is being described. **LO 1**
   a. The amount of gray in a color
   b. The position the light occupies on the visible light spectrum
   c. The intensity or purity of a color
   d. The relative degree of black or white in the color

huesatlum_chart

2. **Differentiating Between Hue, Saturation, and Luminance.** Each of the following pairs of colors differ on a single characteristic of color (hue, saturation, or luminance). Each pair of shapes provided in parts a through f is also provided in worksheets of the same names (*a, b, c, d, e,* and *f*) in the file *huesatlum_chart*. Use this file and the Colors dialog box to determine whether each pair of colors differs on hue, saturation, or luminance and explain your answer. **LO 1**

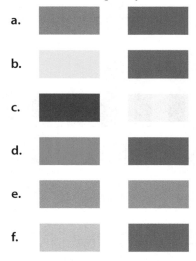

a.

b.

c.

d.

e.

f.

q1sales_chart

3. **Using Hue, Saturation, and Luminance to Differentiate Categories.** The charts in parts a, b, and c each show 2019 and 2020 quarter 1 sales for nine popular midsize sedans. These charts are included in worksheets of the same names (*a*, *b*, and *c*) in the file *q1sales_chart*. Use the Colors dialog box to determine whether hue, saturation, or luminance is used to differentiate the Honda Accord from the other eight models in each chart. **LO 1**

a.

Midsize Sedans Quarter 1 Unit Sales

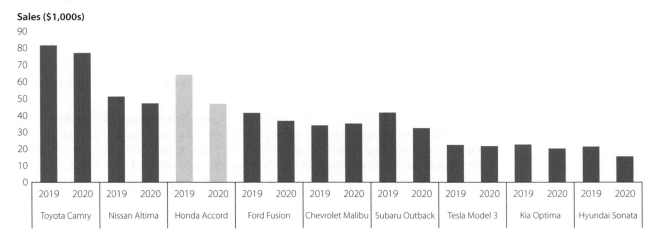

b.

Midsize Sedans Quarter 1 Unit Sales

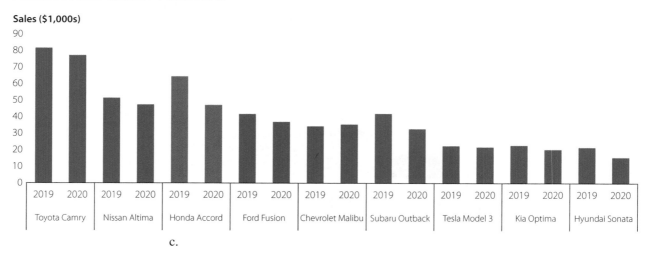

c.

Midsize Sedans Quarter 1 Unit Sales

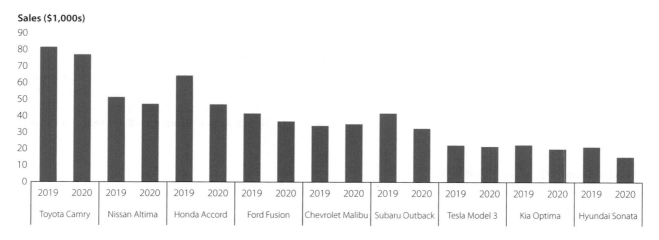

d. Which of the charts in parts a, b, and c is *least* effective in differentiating between the Honda Accord and the other models? Why?

4. **Using Categorical Color Schemes, Sequential Color Schemes, and Diverging Color Schemes.** Identify whether a categorical color scheme, a sequential color scheme, or a diverging color scheme should be applied in each of the following examples. In each instance, explain why this is the appropriate color scheme. **LO 2**

a. You have been given the following data on a popular regional product's unit sales and net profit for several markets.

City	Sales (units)	Net Profit
Amarillo	99,299	$122,619
Ft. Worth	112,219	−$132,762
El Paso	117,893	$169,500
Dallas	139,486	−$136,332
Houston	143,721	$63,646
San Antonio	157,241	$115,632
Austin	175,555	$80,707

From these data, you have created the following bar chart to show the number of units sold by market. You now want to add the information on net profit to the bars on this chart to show the profit or loss earned in each market.

Market

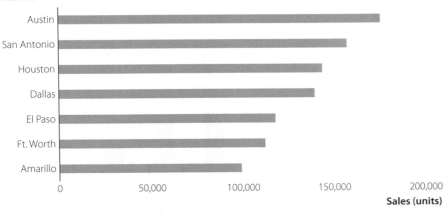

b. You have been given the following data on mean daily high temperature for a city and the number of cups of hot chocolate a chain of coffee shops sold in that city by month.

Month	Mean Daily High Temperature in Fahrenheit	Unit Sales
Jan	27	144,908
Feb	32	120,032
Mar	43	103,917
Apr	50	90,866
May	62	60,110
Jun	74	36,357
Jul	83	16,002
Aug	77	29,445
Sep	62	63,523
Oct	53	81,847
Nov	40	112,818
Dec	33	130,423

From these data, you have created the following column chart to show the mean daily high temperature by month for this city. You now want to add the information to this chart to show the number of cups of hot chocolate that were sold each month.

Mean Daily High Temperature by Month

Temperature (degrees Fahrenheit)

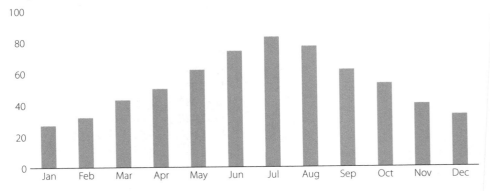

c. You want to add information on the continent of the nation in which headquarters for the top 50 companies in an industry are located to the following column chart that shows the number of these headquarters by nation.

Number of Top 50 Firm Headquarters by Nation

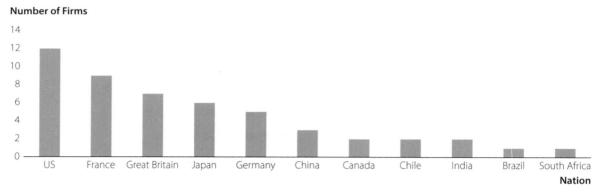

d. You have been asked by a real estate agent to use the following data to create a chart that provides insight into the nature of the relationship between the sales price and number of days on the market for homes she has recently sold.

Sales Price	Days on the Market	Neighborhood
$247,412	58	East Highland
$249,787	60	Sebastian
$194,955	34	Hargrove Hills
$173,612	55	Hargrove Hills
$171,299	55	Sebastian
$281,197	62	Sebastian
$264,477	25	Hargrove Hills
$264,838	50	East Highland
$261,819	30	East Highland
$293,953	42	East Highland
$296,002	32	East Highland
$167,136	38	Hargrove Hills
$334,063	33	Hargrove Hills
$332,340	32	Manafort Falls
$264,066	47	Manafort Falls
$255,070	55	Manafort Falls
$185,572	29	East Highland
$314,198	31	East Highland
$256,183	42	Manafort Falls
$230,741	63	Sebastian
$274,552	38	Manafort Falls
$262,332	45	Manafort Falls
$219,969	39	Hargrove Hills
$253,708	41	East Highland
$245,114	55	Sebastian
$296,920	49	Manafort Falls
$295,866	25	Hargrove Hills
$270,353	59	Manafort Falls
$202,422	55	Sebastian
$214,206	53	East Highland

You have created the following scatter chart. The real estate agent has asked you to add the information on the neighborhood in which each of these homes is located to the scatter chart you have created.

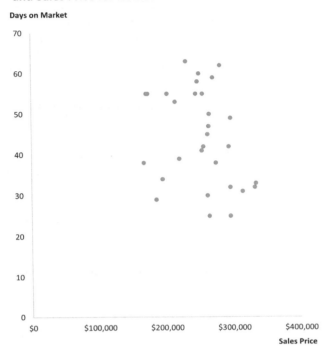

Relationship Between Days on the Market and Sales Price for Homes

e. You have been given the following data on monthly change in the number of subscribers to several online publications devoted to popular hobbies. You have now been asked to add color to this display to indicate whether the number of subscribers is increasing or decreasing each month.

	Jan	Feb	Mar	Apr	May	Jun	Jul	Aug	Sep	Oct	Nov	Dec
Sporting Goods	0.9%	−0.7%	−0.1%	0.2%	0.2%	0.5%	−0.3%	1.6%	1.2%	0.3%	−0.8%	0.9%
Philatelist Quarterly	0.5%	0.1%	0.3%	−0.1%	0.5%	0.5%	−0.9%	−0.1%	0.1%	−0.4%	−1.2%	0.3%
American Spelunker	0.2%	−1.6%	0.6%	1.6%	−1.4%	0.0%	−0.1%	0.6%	−1.3%	−1.2%	−0.8%	0.4%
Home Cooks	0.5%	−0.9%	0.2%	1.2%	0.8%	−0.3%	1.2%	0.5%	0.6%	−1.4%	−0.6%	0.3%
Classic Literature Digest	0.5%	0.2%	−0.1%	0.4%	0.0%	0.4%	1.2%	0.0%	−0.7%	−1.4%	−0.1%	1.4%
Numismatics Magazine	−0.1%	0.0%	0.5%	0.4%	0.0%	1.0%	−0.7%	1.4%	0.1%	1.2%	1.3%	1.4%
Gardening World	0.7%	−0.5%	0.5%	−1.8%	1.5%	−0.6%	0.8%	−1.2%	0.9%	1.6%	0.9%	1.0%
Knitting News	1.1%	1.2%	−1.0%	−1.2%	−0.3%	1.5%	−0.3%	0.6%	−0.2%	−0.5%	1.2%	1.1%
Online Gamer	1.1%	1.2%	0.7%	0.5%	1.8%	1.1%	0.2%	0.1%	0.4%	1.0%	1.4%	2.1%
Popular Photographer	−0.6%	0.3%	−0.9%	0.1%	0.8%	1.4%	−0.1%	−1.0%	−0.4%	−0.7%	0.7%	0.8%

5. **Considering Colorblindness in the Design of a Chart.** Four design artists (Frances Bittinger, Dorian Martin, Bill Zander, and Mariana Knoop) of a regional marketing research firm's graphic arts department have each designed a chart for use in a presentation to a team of Happy Lawn landscaping service executives, two of whom are colorblind. Each has designed a heat map showing the relative percentage change in the number of customers using various lawn care services over the past year in several Midwestern states: Illinois (IL), Indiana (IN), Michigan (MI), Minnesota (MN), Ohio (OH), and Wisconsin (WI).

Explain why each of these charts may or may not be difficult for the colorblind members of the team of Happy Lawn landscaping service executives to visually process. **LO 6**

Percentage Change in Customers (by Frances Bittinger)

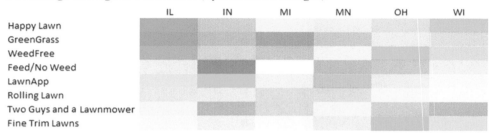

Percentage Change in Customers (by Dorian Martin)

Percentage Change in Customers (by Bill Zander)

	IL	IN	MI	MN	OH	WI
Happy Lawn	-6.0%	10.2%	4.4%	5.1%	7.7%	-3.8%
GreenGrass	-6.3%	11.9%	16.0%	10.3%	5.7%	7.8%
WeedFree	-5.5%	8.5%	11.2%	3.8%	-4.1%	-2.7%
Feed/No Weed	4.7%	-7.6%	1.0%	11.9%	10.6%	4.8%
LawnApp	-2.0%	-4.0%	4.7%	-4.5%	5.8%	2.7%
Rolling Lawn	6.1%	5.4%	8.0%	7.6%	3.4%	2.2%
Two Guys and a Lawnmower	3.6%	12.3%	8.4%	3.6%	9.9%	12.2%
Fine Trim Lawns	2.7%	-1.3%	2.3%	5.1%	-4.5%	-2.4%

Percentage Change in Customers (by Mariana Knoop)

6. **Identifying Mistakes in the Use of Color in a Column Chart.** According to *USA Today*, the headquarters of over one-third of all Fortune 500 (F500) companies are located in one of six U.S. metropolitan areas: Chicago, Dallas-Ft. Worth, Houston, Minneapolis-St. Paul, New York, and San Francisco. The following chart displays the number of F500 headquarters for each of these metropolitan areas. **LO 6**

Metropolitan Areas with the Highest Number of Fortune 500 (F500) Headquarters

Number of F500 Headquarters

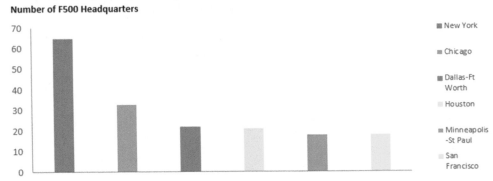

Explain what color is being used to uniquely communicate in this chart, what aspects of the use of color in this chart are ineffective, and how the weakness(es) in the use of color in this chart could be corrected. Also, indicate all other revisions you would make to improve this chart.

7. **Identifying Mistakes in the Use of Color in a Bar Chart.** The most widely grown lawn turf grasses in the southeastern United States are warm-season grasses: bahiagrass, bermudagrass, centipedegrass, St Augustinegrass, and zoysia. Dana Tanner, crew chief with Holiday Grass lawn care service in Birmingham, Alabama, is now planning her resource needs for the upcoming summer. Each of these grasses has different fertilizer and direct sunlight needs, drought and heat tolerance, growth rate, and disease and weed resistance. Therefore, it is important that Ms. Tanner understand the number of lawns of each grass in her district when planning her resource needs for the upcoming summer. To develop a better understanding of the number of lawns of each grass in her district, she observes and records the type of lawn for a random sample of 500 homes in her district, and she summarizes her results in the following chart. **LO 6**

Grasses Grown on Birmingham Area Lawns

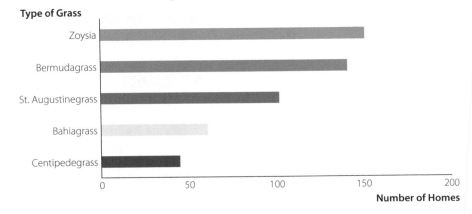

Explain what information color is being used to uniquely communicate in this chart, what aspects of the use of color in this chart are ineffective, and how the weakness(es) in the use of color in this chart could be corrected.

f500metros_chart

Application

8. **Comparing the Number of Fortune 500 Headquarters in Six U.S. Metropolitan Areas.** Consider the number of Fortune 500 (F500) headquarters in the six U.S. metropolitan areas (Chicago, Dallas-Ft. Worth, Houston, Minneapolis-St. Paul, New York, and San Francisco) that are home to the greatest numbers of F500 headquarters. Modify the following column chart (from Problem 6) displaying these data, which is provided in the file *f500metros_chart*, so it uses color more effectively. Also, make all other necessary revisions to improve this chart. Explain why the changes you have made produce a chart that is superior to the original bar chart from Problem 6. **LO 5**

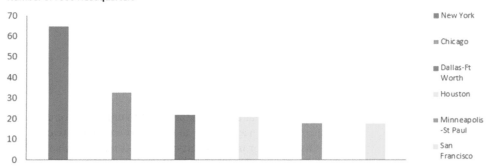

9. **Frequency of Types of Grass.** Consider the number of lawns from a sample of 500 Birmingham, Alabama, homes that have various types of warm-season grasses (bahiagrass, bermudagrass, centipedegrass, St Augustinegrass, and zoysia) in their lawns. The following bar chart of these data (from Problem 7) is provided in the file *holidaygrass_chart*. **LO 5**

holidaygrass_chart

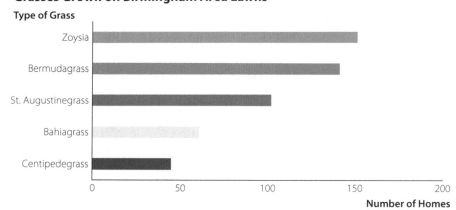

a. Modify this bar chart, which is provided in the file *holidaygrass_chart*, so it uses color more effectively. Also, declutter the chart where possible. Explain why the changes you made produce a chart that is superior to the original bar chart in the file *holidaygrass_chart*.

b. Modify the bar chart in part a to highlight Bermudagrass.

gpgc_chart

10. **T-Shirt Sales over Time.** You have been asked to prepare a line chart that shows monthly sales for the past year for the four colors of slub cotton t-shirts that are manufactured and marketed by the Great Plains Garment Company (GPGC). GPGC sells all of its products online. You obtain the data from GPGC's sales department and produce the following chart in Excel.

GPGC Monthly Slub T-Shirt Sales

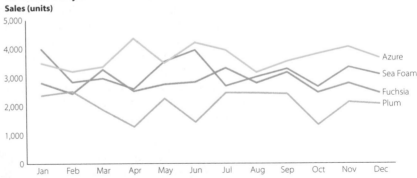

Upon reviewing your chart, you realize that you could make it more effective through appropriate use of color symbolism. After deciding to use the color of each t-shirt for its line on the chart, you obtain the following image showing the four colors of GPGC's slub t-shirts from its website collection. The data, the original chart, and the following image (which can be cut out of the Excel spreadsheet and pasted into PowerPoint) are included in the file *gpgc_chart*. **LO 2**

SEA FOAM   FUCHSIA   PLUM   AZURE

a. Use PowerPoint and the Eyedropper tool to determine the hue, saturation, and luminance of the predominant color of each t-shirt. List the values of the hue, saturation, and luminance of each color.

b. Revise the line chart in the file *gpgc_chart* so the color of each line corresponds to the color of the associated slub t-shirt from part a. Also, change the color of the text in the label at the end of each line to match the color of the corresponding slub t-shirt.

attendwins_chart

11. **The Relationship between Wins and Attendance in Baseball.** In doing an analysis of the economics of baseball in your state, you collect data on annual home game attendance and number of wins from 2000 to 2019 for the state's two baseball teams, the Komodos and the Condors. To communicate the nature of the relationship between annual home game attendance and number of wins for the two teams over that period, you produce the following scatter chart in Excel.

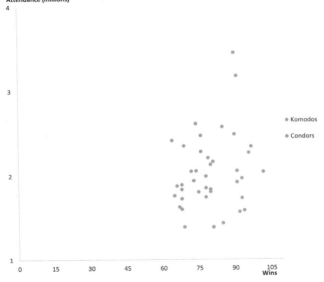

The chart shows a mildly positive relationship between annual home game attendance and number of wins for each team. The chart also shows the Condors have routinely won more games than the Komodos but have generally had lower attendance. However, you see a way to improve this chart by using the predominant color of each team's uniform instead of the Excel default colors for the points that represent the two teams.

You obtain the following images of the two team's home jerseys from their respective websites and paste them into the file *attendwins_chart* that also contains the data and your original chart. **LO 4**

a. Use PowerPoint and the Eyedropper tool to determine the hue, saturation, and luminance of the predominant color of each jersey. List the values of the hue, saturation, and luminance of each color. Images of the two jerseys are included in the file *attendwins_chart* and can be cut and pasted into PowerPoint.
b. Revise the scatter chart in the file *attendwins_chart* so the color of each series corresponds to the color of the corresponding team's jersey from part a.

brmc_chart

12. **Composition of Boise Regional Medical Center Nursing Staff.** Boise Regional Medical Center (BRMC) is completing its annual report for the Idaho Board of Trustees. One section of this report is devoted to an analysis of the composition of the BRMC nursing staff. The current draft of this report includes the following bar chart that shows the percentage of the nursing staff by classification. This chart is included in the file *brmc_chart*.

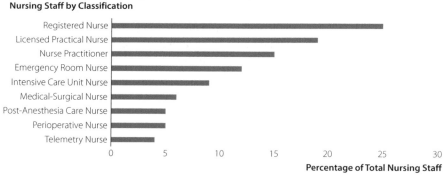

Composition of Boise Regional Medical Center
Nursing Staff by Classification

In its review of the draft report, management has noted that some audience members may consider the color of the bars in this chart to be inappropriate for BRMC because red is often associated with anxiety. Management has requested that the chart be revised using a color that is more calming. Revise this chart using a color for the bars that is generally considered to be comforting and calming. Refer to Figure 4.13 to identify the hue you will use. **LO 2**

ohhighered_chart

13. **Relationship between University Enrollment and Changes in Mean Faculty Salary.** The Ohio Board of Regents (OBR) is preparing its five-year report on the state of higher education in Ohio. The current draft of the report includes a scatter chart of enrollment and the percentage five-year change in average faculty salary for the 16 largest four-year institutions in the state. The scatter chart that is included in the current draft of the report follows and is provided in the file *ohhighered_chart*.

Enrollment and Five-Year Change in Mean Faculty Salary for Universities in Ohio

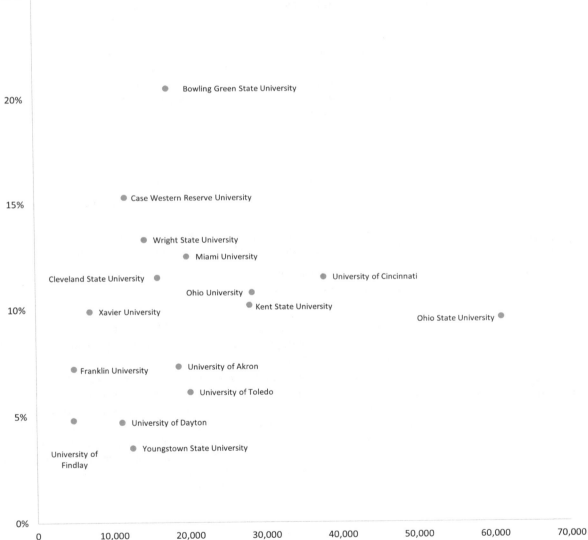

On reviewing the current draft, one of the members of the OBR has asked that you add an indication of which of these universities is private to this scatter chart. Use color to distinguish the private universities (Case Western Reserve University, University of Dayton, Xavier University, Franklin University, University of Findlay) on the scatter chart from the public universities. What does this additional information tell you? **LO 3**

14. **Viewership of Top Rated Scripted Television Shows.** The 18–49 age group is an extremely lucrative demographic for television networks. Advertisers pay a premium to reach consumers in this age group with their advertising. The following column chart shows the number of viewers in millions that the top 10 scripted series averaged during the 2019–2020 television season.

Number of 18–49 Year Old Viewers for Scripted Television Series

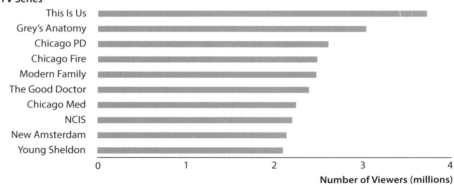

It is also important for this graph to show which television network (ABC, CBS, FOX, NBC) broadcasts each show. The networks that broadcast these shows are:

top10tv2020_chart

ABC: *The Good Doctor, Modern Family, Grey's Anatomy*
CBS: *Young Sheldon, NCIS*
NBC: *New Amsterdam, Chicago Med, Chicago Fire, Chicago PD, This Is Us*

Use color to add this information to the original bar chart, which is provided in the file *top10tv2020_chart*. Will your chart be difficult for colorblind audience members to visually process? Explain. **LO 3**

cd_chart

15. **Relationship between Estimated and Actual Time to Complete a Housepainting Job.** Charlene & Daughters (C&D) employ 20 crews of interior house painters that work throughout the northwest United States. The leader of each crew is responsible for visiting potential job sites and developing an estimate of the number of hours it will take to complete a job based on a C&D formula that considers the square footage of the surfaces to be painted, the amount and type of trim, and whether ceilings are to be painted. The crew leader also has the latitude to make subjective adjustments based on other factors that are not considered by the formula.

C&D is now assessing the accuracy of its estimates of the time it will take to complete jobs. It has collected the estimated and actual times to complete each of the 10 most recent jobs for each crew, and it has entered these data into the file *cd_chart*. A portion of the data, which includes the name of the crew leader, the estimated time to complete the job, and the actual time to complete the job, follows.

Repair Person	Estimated Hours	Actual Hours
Briggs	25.8	29.4
Briggs	62.5	66.3
Briggs	75.6	50.9
Briggs	75.7	77.0
Briggs	61.9	74.8
Briggs	6.1	5.8
Briggs	38.2	36.3
Briggs	52.2	55.3
Briggs	63.1	69.3
Briggs	66.9	77.5
Cobb	37.1	32.6
Cobb	45.0	46.6
⋮	⋮	⋮
Taubee	6.8	6.0
Taubee	54.1	62.5
Vincent	25.7	20.3
Vincent	80.9	93.6
Vincent	20.8	20.6
Vincent	24.8	25.7
Vincent	74.4	84.7
Vincent	18.3	18.3
Vincent	74.6	81.2
Vincent	58.7	52.9
Vincent	37.5	41.1
Vincent	68.7	56.0

C&D has also used these data to produce a scatter chart, and it has used color to differentiate between the crews on this chart. The chart, which follows, is also included in the file *cd_chart*. Note that the legend identifies each crew by the name of its crew leader. **LO 3**

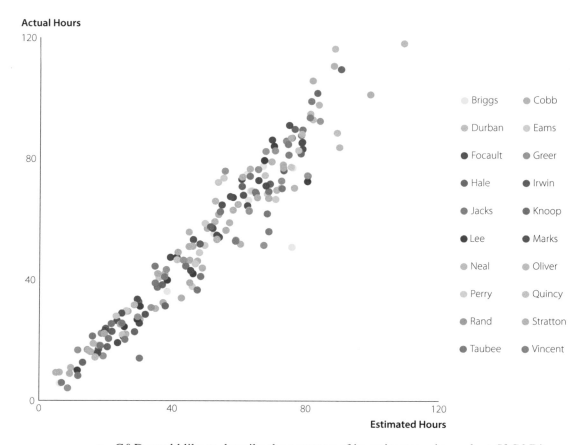

a. C&D would like to describe the accuracy of its estimates using a chart. If C&D's estimated hours matched the actual hours perfectly, then all points in this scatter chart would lie on a diagonal line that is 45° from the origin. Draw a diagonal line at 45° from the origin through the chart to help you assess the accuracy of C&D's estimates. To draw this 45° line, draw a line that passes through the points (0,0); (40,40); (80,80); and (120,120) on the chart. Would you advise that C&D incorporate this line into its scatter chart? Why or why not?

b. Revise the chart so all of the points are blue (Hue = 148, Sat = 151, Lum = 152). Is the use of color in this chart more effective than the use of color in the chart in part a? Why or why not?

c. C&D has indicated some concern over recent estimates of the crew headed by Cobb. Use color on the scatter chart to draw attention to the jobs completed by the crew headed by Cobb and interpret the results.

16. **Production of Laptop Computer Screens.** CrystalClear, Inc. manufactures low-resolution 15-inch screens for inexpensive laptop computers at plants in five states (California, Nebraska, North Carolina, North Dakota, and Texas). The number of units produced by each plant is provided in the following table and is provided in the file *crystalclear*.

Plant Location	Units Produced
Texas	54,210
North Dakota	61,002
California	75,143
Nebraska	79,210
North Carolina	82,157

CrystalClear, Inc. management suspects that its larger plants are producing the greatest number of units. The square footage for each plant follows and is also provided in the file *crystalclear*.

Plant Location	Sq Ft
Texas	47,000
North Dakota	53,000
California	65,000
Nebraska	63,000
North Carolina	70,000

Provide a scatter chart of the plant data to provide insight into the nature of the relationship between units produced and size of the plant for the five plants and highlight the Nebraska plant. **LO 4**

DATA *file*

catsanddogs

17. **Pet Food Sales by State.** Pet Fare, Inc. produces high-end refrigerated pet food and ships it anywhere in the United States. Total Pet Fare sales of cat food and dog food by state for the previous year are given in separate worksheets in the file *catsanddogs*. **LO 5**

   a. Create a geographic information system (GIS) map that uses a sequential color scheme to represent total Pet Fare cat food sales by state. Use orange for the color for this choropleth map. What information does this chart convey to the audience?

   b. Create a geographic information system (GIS) map that uses a sequential color scheme to represent total Pet Fare dog food sales by state. Use blue for the color for this choropleth map. What information does this chart convey to the audience?

   c. Create a scatter chart that enables the audience to better understand the relationship between total cat food sales and total dog food sales for the states. What does this chart tell you about the relationship between total cat food sales and total dog food sales?

   d. Use color to highlight Wyoming in the scatter chart from part c. What does this chart tell you about total cat food sales and total dog food sales in Wyoming relative to the other states?

   e. What inherent weaknesses do you see in the analysis performed in parts a–c? How would you address these issues? (*Hint*: Consider the disparities in the sizes of the statewide markets.)

DATA *file*

alabamaunemployment

18. **Alabama Unemployment Rate by County.** The Labor Market Information Division of the Alabama Department of Labor is preparing its monthly report on unemployment, and it would like to include a choropleth map that shows unemployment rate by county. Use the unemployment rate for each of Alabama's 77 counties provided in the file *alabamaunemployment* to create this choropleth map. What does this map tell you about where the highest rates of unemployment are in Alabama? **LO 5**

DATA *file*

ledbulbs

19. **Life Expectancy of LED Bulbs.** Capital Electrics (CE) advertises that the life expectancy of the LED bulbs it produces is 28,000 hours. The electrical engineering team at CE has designed a test to assess the impact of ambient temperature on the LED light bulbs CE manufactures. Using strict temperature controls, the engineers set up rooms starting at 0° Fahrenheit in 10-degree increments to 160° Fahrenheit. They then put a bulb at each wattage from 7 watts to 25 watts in a light fixture in each room, turn on the fixtures, and record the number of hours until each bulb fails. The data they have collected are provided in the file *ledbulbs*.

Use these data to create a heat map of the life of the LED bulbs by their wattage and the ambient temperature of the room in which they are placed. In the **New Formatting Rule** dialog box of **Conditional Formatting**, enter *3-Color Scale* for **Format Style**, enter *Number* in the **Type:** box of the **Midpoint** column, enter *28000* in the **Value:** box of the **Midpoint** column, and in the **Color:** row, use orange (Hue = 17, Sat = 255, Lum = 115) for values below 28,000, white for the Midpoint, and blue (Hue = 156, Sat = 255, Lum = 48) for values above 28,000. Mask the cell values and create a legend that tells the audience that orange corresponds to low bulb lives less than 28,000 hours, blue corresponds to bulb lives greater than 28,000 hours, and the color grows darker as the deviation of the bulb life from 28,000 increases in either direction. **LO 5**

DATA *file*

bayside

20. **Comparing Regional Market Shares.** Bay Side Manufacturing produces small leather goods such as wallets, travel organizers, toiletry kits, briefcases, and folios. The company has a 16% share in the U.S. travel organizers market, but management is concerned that its market share in the southeastern United States lags behind its national share. Bay Side's monthly share of the travel organizers market for the past year in 15 major cities in the southeastern United States is provided in the file *bayside*. A portion of the data is shown in the following table.

	Market Share						
	Jan	Feb	Mar	Apr		Nov	Dec
Atlanta	0.142	0.145	0.137	0.152	...	0.132	0.152
Baltimore	0.172	0.199	0.177	0.189	...	0.181	0.185
Baton Rouge	0.133	0.084	0.137	0.123	...	0.144	0.097
Birmingham	0.087	0.105	0.105	0.096	...	0.118	0.121
Charlotte	0.088	0.112	0.094	0.100	...	0.069	0.077
Jacksonville	0.188	0.188	0.190	0.173	...	0.197	0.185
Louisville	0.217	0.214	0.164	0.190	...	0.189	0.192
Memphis	0.107	0.115	0.132	0.111	...	0.125	0.115
Miami	0.162	0.158	0.158	0.157	...	0.180	0.169
Nashville	0.053	0.054	0.074	0.081	...	0.083	0.099
New Orleans	0.129	0.161	0.159	0.189	...	0.194	0.155
Raleigh	0.156	0.188	0.162	0.150	...	0.190	0.191
Richmond	0.178	0.156	0.183	0.157	...	0.158	0.145
Tampa	0.119	0.115	0.108	0.145	...	0.144	0.110
Virginia Beach	0.172	0.174	0.129	0.166	...	0.164	0.191
Washington	0.232	0.241	0.204	0.191	...	0.207	0.243

Use these data to create a heat map of Bay Side's monthly share of the travel organizers market for these 15 southeastern U.S. cities. In the **New Formatting Rule** dialog box of **Conditional Formatting**, enter *3-Color Scale* for **Format Style**, enter *Number* in the **Type:** box of the **Midpoint** column, enter *0.16* in the **Value:** box of the **Midpoint** column, and in the **Color:** row, use orange (Hue = 17, Sat = 214, Lum = 143) for values below 0.16 and blue (Hue = 156, Sat = 255, Lum = 48) for values above 0.16. Mask the cell values and create a legend that tells the audience that orange corresponds to market shares less than 14%, blue corresponds to market shares greater than 14%, and the color grows darker as the deviation of the market share from 14% increases in either direction.

What message will this map communicate to an audience? Will this chart be difficult for colorblind audience members to visually process? Explain. **LO 5**

Chapter 4 Appendix

Appendix 4.1 Using Color in Data Visualization with Power BI

In this appendix, we discuss in more detail how to edit a chart in Power BI and use color to make it more effective at conveying your message to your audience.

Using Categorical Color

The file *zooattendance* contains attendance at a zoo for children and adults for twelve months. We demonstrate how to create a stacked column chart that uses categorical color for these data in Power BI.

DATA *file*
zooattendance

Step 1. Following the steps outlined in Appendix 1.1, connect Power BI to the file *zooattendance*

In some of the steps that follow, we give instructions to expand or collapse certain sections of Power BI. A section can be expanded by clicking $>$ next to the section title. To collapse a section, click $\vee$ next to the section title.

Step 2. Click **Report** view ![icon], and in the **Visualizations** pane, click **Build visual** ![icon] to display the **Build visual** matrix of available charts

Select **Stacked column chart** ![icon]

In the **Data** pane, expand **Data** $>$![icon] Data to display the variables

Drag **Month** from the **Data** pane to the **X-axis** box in the **Visualizations** pane
Drag **Σ Children** from the **Data** pane to the **Y-axis** box in the **Visualizations** pane
Drag **Σ Adults** from the **Data** pane to the **Y-axis** box in the **Visualizations** pane
Increase the size of the chart by grabbing the bottom right corner and expanding it

The resulting chart is shown in Figure P4.1. Notice that Power BI has sorted by the values of *Children*. The *Month* variable is text, and the *Children* variable is a whole number. Next, we describe how to modify the chart to be in chronological order and edit the axis labels.

To be able to sort the data chronologically by *Month*, we need to create a new variable that gives the month number. For example, January is month 1, February is month 2, etc. The following steps are one way to create the month number:

Step 3. Click **Table view** ![icon] in the left margin.

In the Home tab on the ribbon, in the **Queries** group, click the **Transform data** button ![Transform data icon] and select **Transform data**
Click the **Add Column** tab
In the **General** group, click on the arrow on the **Index Column** ![Index Column icon] and select **From 1** from the drop-down menu
Click the **Home** tab
Click **Close & Apply** ![Close & Apply icon] in the Close group on the far left side of the Ribbon

Step 4. Right click the header **Index**, select **Rename**, type *MonthNumber*, and press **Enter**

Figure P4.1   A Stacked Column Chart of the Zoo Attendance Data Sorted by Children

The data should now appear as shown in Figure P4.2.

Step 5. Click **Report view** 📊 and click the column chart
Drag Σ **MonthNumber** from the **Data** pane to the **Tooltips** box
In the upper right-hand corner of the chart, click **More options** ⋯
Select **Sort axis**, and select **Sum of MonthNumber**
Click **More options** ⋯, select **Sort axis**, and select **Sort ascending**

Figure P4.2   The Zoo Attendance with Month Number

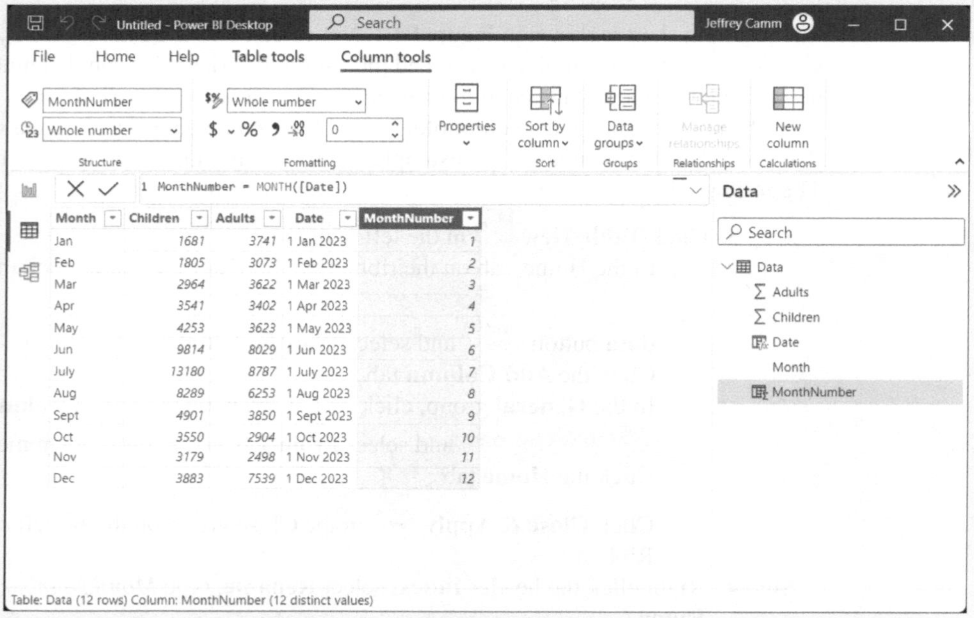

Month	Children	Adults	Date	MonthNumber
Jan	1681	3741	1 Jan 2023	1
Feb	1805	3073	1 Feb 2023	2
Mar	2964	3622	1 Mar 2023	3
Apr	3541	3402	1 Apr 2023	4
May	4253	3623	1 May 2023	5
Jun	9814	8029	1 Jun 2023	6
July	13180	8787	1 July 2023	7
Aug	8289	6253	1 Aug 2023	8
Sept	4901	3850	1 Sept 2023	9
Oct	3550	2904	1 Oct 2023	10
Nov	3179	2498	1 Nov 2023	11
Dec	3883	7539	1 Dec 2023	12

Table: Data (12 rows) Column: MonthNumber (12 distinct values)

Step 6. In the **Visualizations** pane, click the **Format visual** button ✍
>To edit the horizontal axis title and values, click **Visual** in the **Visualization** pane
>Expand **X-axis**, and expand **Title**
>Select **Calibri** as the **Font** and **16** as the font size
>Click the **Bold** button B
>Collapse **Title**, and expand **Values**
>Select **Calibri** as the **Font** and **14** as the font size
>Collapse **Values**, and collapse **X-axis**

Step 7. Expand **Y-axis.** Next to **Title**, toggle the **On** button `On●` to **Off** to hide the vertical axis title
>Expand **Values**
>Select **Calibri** as the **Font** and **14** as the font size
>Collapse **Values**, and expand **Range**
>Type *25000* in the **Maximum** box
>Collapse **Range,** and collapse **Y-axis**

Steps 8–12 edit the legend, including removing the **Sum of MonthNumber**, which is not needed in the chart, changing the colors, and changing the font and size of the text.

Step 8. In the **Visualizations** pane, click **Build visual** ▦
>In the **Y-axis box**, right click **Sum of Children**, select **Rename for this visual**, and type *Children*
>In the **Y-axis** box, right click **Sum of Adults**, select **Rename for this visual**, and type *Adults*
>In the **Tooltips** box, right click **Sum of MonthNumber**, select **Rename for this visual**, and type a blank space (this will cause the variable to not appear in the legend)

Step 9. In the **Visualizations** pane, click **Format visual** ✍
>Expand **Legend**, and expand **Text**
>Select **Calibri** as the **Font** and **12** as the font size
>Collapse **Text**, and collapse **Legend**

Step 10. Expand **Columns**, and expand **Color**
>Under **Apply settings to**, select **Children** from the **series** drop-down menu
>Change the **Children** color to dark blue
>Under **Apply settings to**, select **Adult** from the **series** drop-down menu
>Change the **Adult** color to dark orange
>Collapse **Colors**, and collapse **Columns**

Step 11. To remove the faint gridlines in the chart, click the chart
>In the **Visualizations** pane, expand **Gridlines**
>Next to **Horizontal**, toggle the **On** button `On●` to **Off** to hide the horizontal grid lines
>Collapse **Gridlines**

Step 12. In the **Visualizations** pane to the right of **Visual**, click **General**
>Expand **Title**.
>Edit the **Text** box to read *Zoo Attendance*
>Select **Calibri** as the **Font** and **16** as the font size
>Click on the **Bold** button B
>Collapse **Title**

Steps 1–12 create the stacked bar chart shown in Figure P4.3.

Figure P4.3	A Stacked Column Chart of the Zoo Attendance Data in Chronological Order

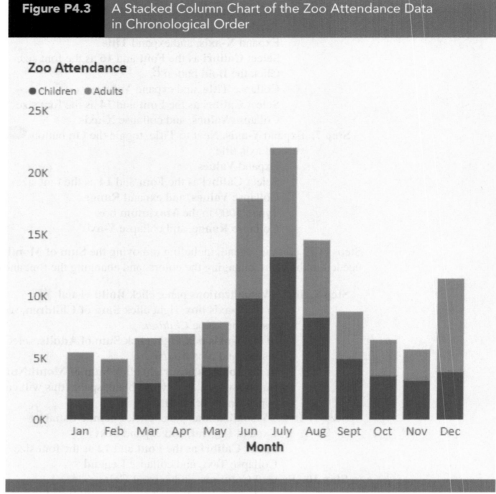

CHART *file*

zooattendance_chart.pbix

Using Sequential Color

As an example of the use of sequential color, let us consider the average annual temperature in degrees Fahrenheit for each of the 50 states in the United States. These data are in the file *avgtemp*.

DATA *file*

avgtemp

*If the Shape map does not appear as an option, click on **File**, click on **Option and Settings**, click on **Options**, select **Preview features**, and select the check box for **Shape map visual**.*

Step 1. Following the steps outlined in Appendix 1.1, connect Power BI to the file *avgtemp*

Step 2. Click **Report** view, and in the **Visualizations** pane, click **Build visual** to display the **Build visual** matrix of available charts

Select **Shape map**

Step 3. In the **Data** pane on the right, expand **Data** > Data to display the variables
Drag **State** from the **Data** pane to the **Location** box in the **Visualizations** pane
Drag **Σ Avg. Temp** from the **Data** pane to the **Color Saturation** box in the **Visualizations** pane
Increase the size of the chart by grabbing the bottom right corner and expanding it

Step 4. In the **Visualizations** pane, click **Format visual**, and click on **General**

Figure P4.4   Choropleth Map of Annual Average Temperature by State

CHART *file*

avgtemp_chart.pbix

Expand **Title**, and type *Avg. Temp by State* in the Text box
Select **Calibri** as the **Font** and **16** as the font size
Click on the **Bold** button B
Collapse **Title**

Figure P4.4 shows the resulting choropleth map.

Although the meaning of color may vary by culture, in the United States, blue is most often used to indicate coolness, while red indicates hotness. In a choropleth map, darker indicates intensity. The data indicate the average temperature for southern states is higher than for northern states, so using blue could be misinterpreted (implying that southern states are cooler). To clarify this, let us change the color used in the map from blue to red.

Step 5. Click on the chart. In the **Visualization** pane, click on **Format visual**

Click on **Visual**, and expand **Fill colors**
In the Minimum box, expand the options, and click on **More colors**
More colors...
Select light red
In the Maximum box, expand the options, and click on **More colors**
More colors...
Select dark red

The finished map appears in Figure P4.5.

Figure P4.5 A Choropleth Map of Annual Average Temperature by State Using Red to Indicate Hotness

Avg. Temp by State

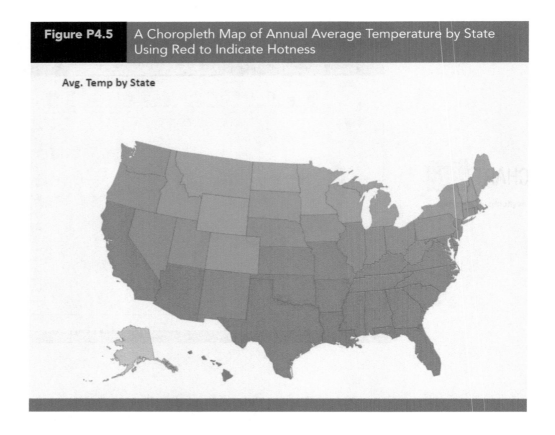

Figure P4.6 The Color Option Panel

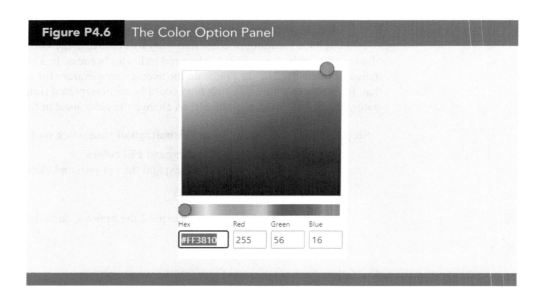

Notes + Comments

In step 5, we entered data to get the desired color. You may also use an interactive slider as shown in Figure P4.6. This is shown under More colors More colors... and can be activated by sliding the dots shown to arrive at an acceptable color.

Using Diverging Color

indlowtemps_stacked

As an example of the use of divergent color, we use another example based on temperature. The file *indlowtemps_stacked* contains the monthly average daily low temperature in degrees Fahrenheit for the city of Indianapolis. The file contains the variables *Year*, *Month*, *MonthNumber*, and *Average Low Temp*. We will use *MonthNumber* for sorting purposes.

Step 1. Following the steps outlined in Appendix 1.1, connect Power BI to the file *indlowtemps_stacked*

Step 2. Click **Report** view , and in the **Visualizations** pane, click **Build visual** to display the **Build visual** matrix of available charts

Select **Matrix**

Grab the lower right corner of the matrix, and drag to increase the size

Step 3. In the **Data** pane on the right, expand **Data** > Data to display the variables
Drag Σ **Year** from the **Data** pane to the **Rows** box in the **Visualizations** pane
Drag **Month** from the **Data** pane to the **Columns** box in the **Visualizations** pane
Drag Σ **Average Low Temp** from the **Data** pane to the **Values** box in the **Visualizations** pane

Notice that after Step 3, the months (columns) are in alphabetical rather than chronological order. Step 6 will place the months in chronological order.

Step 4. In the **Data** pane, select **Month** (click **Month**, not the checkbox)
In the Ribbon, click **Column tools** and **Sort by Column** in the **Sort** group
Select **MonthNumber**

Step 5. In the **Visualizations** pane, click the **Format visual** button
Click **Visual**
Next to **Column subtotals**, toggle the **On** button to **Off** to turn off the **Total** column
Next to **Row subtotals**, toggle the **On** button to **Off** to turn off the **Total** row
Expand **Grid**, and expand **Options**
Change the **Global font size** to **16**
Collapse **Options**, and collapse **Grid**

The matrix should now appear as shown in Figure P4.7.

The values of 10 and 80 are chosen for the minimum and maximum because these are below/above the lowest/ highest temperatures in the data.

Step 6. In the **Visualizations** pane, click the **Format visual** button and expand **Cell elements**
Next to **Background color**, toggle the **Off** button to **On**
Click the **Conditional formatting** button fx under Background color
When the **Background** color dialog box appears:
Under **Minimum**, select **Custom**, and enter *10* in the **Enter a value** box
To the right of Custom, choose a dark blue color
Under **Maximum**, select **Custom**, and enter *80* in the **Enter a value** box
To the right of **Custom**, choose a dark red color
Click **OK**

Steps 1–8 result in the Heat Map Table that uses blue and red as diverging colors as shown in Figure P4.8.

Figure P4.7   Matrix of Average Daily Low Temperatures in Indianapolis

Figure P4.8   Heat Map Table that Uses Blue and Red as Diverging Colors.

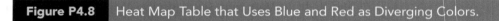

**indlowtemps_stacked
_chart.pbix**

Year	January	February	March	April	May	June	July	August	September	October	November	December
2010	18	20	36	49	57	67	70	69	58	46	34	19
2011	17	25	35	45	55	65	72	66	57	45	41	31
2012	26	29	46	44	58	63	72	64	56	44	31	32
2013	22	23	28	42	56	63	65	65	59	45	31	23
2014	11	14	25	42	53	64	61	65	55	45	28	28
2015	15	11	30	44	57	64	66	63	60	47	39	36
2016	21	26	40	43	53	65	68	70	62	51	39	24
2017	28	33	35	49	53	62	67	63	59	49	35	22
2018	17	29	30	37	62	66	68	67	63	47	31	29
2019	20	26	29	44	55	62	69	65	63	46	30	29

Appendix 4.2 Using Color in Data Visualization with Tableau

In this appendix, we discuss the use of color for data visualizations created using Tableau. Specifically, we discuss the use of categorical, sequential, and diverging color schemes using Tableau.

Using Categorical Color

A stacked column or bar chart commonly uses a categorical color scheme to differentiate between categories within each column or bar. The file *zooattendance* contains attendance at a zoo for children and adults for twelve months. We demonstrate how to create a stacked column chart that uses categorical color for these data in Tableau.

DATA *file*

zooattendance

Step 1. Following the steps outlined in Appendix 1.2, connect Tableau to the file *zooattendance*
  Click the **Sheet 1** tab at the bottom of the Tableau Data Source screen to open the worksheet view

Step 2. In the worksheet view of Tableau, drag the pill for **Month** from the **Data** pane to the **Columns** shelf
  Drag the pill for **Adults** from the **Data** pane to the **Rows** shelf
  Drag the pill for **Children** from the **Data** pane to the **Rows** shelf

Step 3. Drag the pill for **Measure Names** from the **Data** pane to the **Color** card 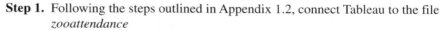 in the **Marks** area

Step 4. Drag **SUM(Children)** from the **Rows** shelf to the **Adults** vertical axis label of the column chart to put both Adults and Children on the same vertical axis (see Figure T4.1)

Figure T4.1	Putting Adult and Children Attendance on the Same Vertical Axis

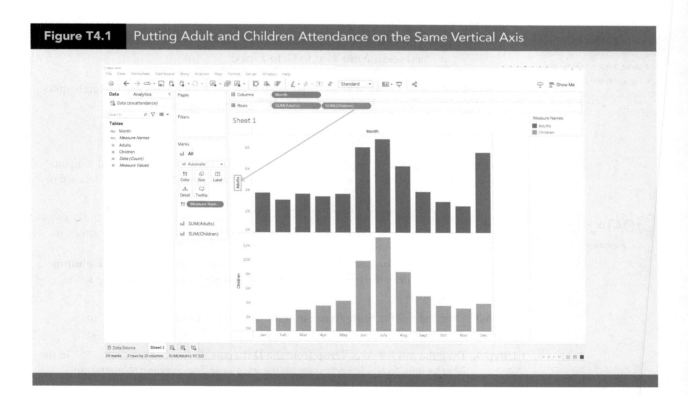

Step 5. Drag **Measure Names** from the **Columns** shelf back to the **Tables** area of the **Data** pane to change the clustered column chart to a stacked column chart

The following steps modify the chart to improve clarity.

Step 6. Right click the vertical axis and select **Edit Axis…**. When the **Edit Axis [Measure Values]** dialog box appears, select **Custom** under **Axis Titles** and type *Attendance*
      Click ✕ to close the **Edit Axis [Measure Values]** dialog box

Step 7. Right click the vertical axis of the chart and select **Format…**. When the **Format Measure Values** pane appears:
      Click next to **Font:** under **Default** and change the font size to **11**

Step 8. Right click the horizontal axis at the bottom of the chart and select **Format…**. When the **Format Month** pane appears:
      Click next to **Font:** under **Default** and change the font size to **11**

Step 9. Right click on the **Month** label at the top of the chart, and select **Hide Field Labels for Columns** to remove the unnecessary label

Step 10. To edit the title of the chart, right click on **Sheet 1** at the top of the chart, and select **Edit Title…**. When the Edit Title dialog box appears:
      Replace **<Sheet Name>** with title *Zoo Attendance Peaks in Summer*
      Highlight the text of the title, then change the font size to **16** and click the **Bold** button ß to make the title bold font
      Click **OK** to close the **Edit Title** dialog box

Step 11. To edit the legend for the chart, right click on the legend in the upper right corner of the chart and select **Format Legends…**. When the **Format Legends** pane appears:
      Click next to **Font:** under **Body**, and change the font size to **11**
      To hide the unnecessary title of the legend, right click on the legend and deselect **Title**

*If the legend is not visible, it may be behind the Show Me pane. To close the Show Me pane, click on **Show Me** ☰ Show Me in the upper right corner.*

Step 12. To remove the unnecessary grid lines in the chart, right click on the chart and select **Format…**. When the **Format** task pane opens, click on the **Lines** button ☰ and select **None** next to **Grid Lines:**

The completed stacked column chart using categorical colors for adult and children attendance to the zoo viewed in **Presentation Mode** appears in Figure T4.2.

Using Sequential Color

As an example of the use of sequential color, let us consider the average annual temperature in degrees Fahrenheit for each of the 50 states in the United States. These data are in the file *avgtemp*.

DATA *file*
avgtemp

Step 1. Following the steps outlined in Appendix 1.2, connect Tableau to the file *avgtemp*
      Click the **Sheet 1** tab at the bottom of the Tableau Data Source screen to open the worksheet view

Step 2. Drag the pill for **Longitude (generated)** from the **Data** pane to the **Columns** shelf, and drag the pill for **Latitude (generated)** from the **Data** pane to the **Rows** shelf

Step 3. Drag the pill for **State** from the **Data** pane to the **Detail** card 〔Detail〕 in the **Marks** area to show each state on the map

Step 4. Drag the pill for **Avg. Temp** from the **Data** pane to the **Color** card 〔Color〕 in the **Marks** area to shade each state on the map based on average temperature

Figure T4.2   Stacked Column Chart for the Zoo Attendance Data Using Categorical Colors for Adult and Children Attendance

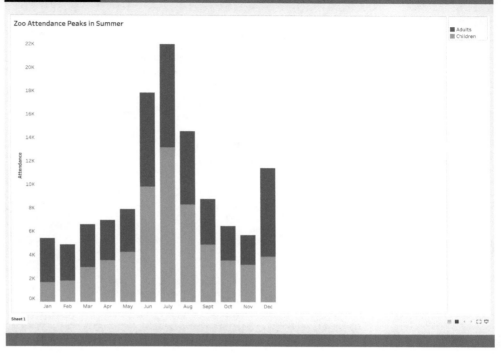

zooattendance_chart.twbx

Step 5. To modify the title of the chart, right click **Sheet 1** at the top of the map and select **Edit Title…**. When the **Edit Title** dialog box opens:

Replace **<Sheet Name>** with *Average Temperature by State*

Highlight the text of the title, then change the font size to **16**, and click the **Bold** button Β to make the title bold font

Click **OK** to close the **Edit Title** dialog box

Step 6. To modify the title of the legend for the chart, click the ◀ next to the legend title in the upper right corner of the chart and select **Edit Title…**. When the **Edit Legend Title** dialog box appears, replace **SUM(Avg. Temp)** with *Avg. Temp*

These steps produce the choropleth map using sequential colors shown in Figure T4.3.

Although the meaning of color can vary by culture, in the United States, blue is most often used to indicate coolness, while red indicates hotness. In a choropleth map, darker indicates intensity. The data indicate the average temperature for southern states is higher than for northern states, so using blue could be misinterpreted (implying that southern states are cooler). To clarify this, let us change the color used in the map from blue to red.

Step 7. Click the ◀ next to the legend title, and select **Edit Colors…**. When the **Edit Colors [Avg. Temp]** dialog box appears:

Change the option for **Palette:** to **Red**

Click **OK** to close the **Edit Colors [Measure Values]** dialog box

Step 7 changes the choropleth map to what is shown in Figure T4.4.

Figure T4.3	Choropleth Map using Sequential Colors to Display Average Annual Temperature by State

Figure T4.4	Choropleth Map Using Sequential Colors changed to Red to Display Average Annual Temperature by State

CHART *file*

avgtemp_chart.twbx

Using Diverging Color

As an example of the use of divergent color, we use another example based on temperature. The file *tempstacked* contains the monthly mean daily low temperature in degrees Fahrenheit for the city of Indianapolis. Note that this file contains data in stacked form. Each row represents an observation for the mean daily low temperature in Indianapolis for a particular month of a particular year.

DATA *file*

tempstacked

Step 1. Following the steps outlined in Appendix 1.2, connect Tableau to the file *tempstacked*

> Click the **Sheet 1** tab at the bottom of the Tableau Data Source screen to open the worksheet view

Step 2. Right click on the pill for **Year** in the **Tables** area of the **Data** pane and select **Convert to Discrete**

Step 3. Drag the pill for **Month** from the **Data** pane to the **Columns** shelf, and drag the pill for **Year** from the **Data** pane to the **Rows** shelf

Step 4. Drag the pill for **Temperature** from the **Data** pane to the **Color** card Color in the **Marks** area

Step 5. Right click the Legend in the top right of the chart and select **Edit Colors…**. When the **Edit Colors[Temperature]** dialog box appears:

> Change the **Palette:** to **Red-Blue Diverging**
> Select the checkbox for **Reversed**
> Click **OK** to close the **Edit Colors [Temperature]** dialog box

Step 6. To modify the title of the chart, right click **Sheet 1** at the top of the map and select **Edit Title…**. When the **Edit Title** dialog box opens:

> Replace **<Sheet Name>** with *Monthly Mean Daily Low Temperature for Indianapolis*
> Highlight the text of the title, then change the font size to **16**, and click the **Bold** button Β to make the title bold font
> Click **OK** to close the **Edit Title** dialog box

Step 7. To hide the unnecessary label at the top of the chart, right click **Month** and select **Hide Field Labels for Columns**

Step 8. To modify the title of the legend for the chart, click the ◀ next to the legend title in the upper right corner of the chart and select **Edit Title…**. When the **Edit Legend Title** dialog box appears, replace **SUM(Temperature)** with *Temperature*

The completed heat map using diverging colors appears in Figure T4.5.

| Figure T4.5 | Heat Map of Monthly Mean Daily Low Temperature for Indianapolis 2010–2019 |

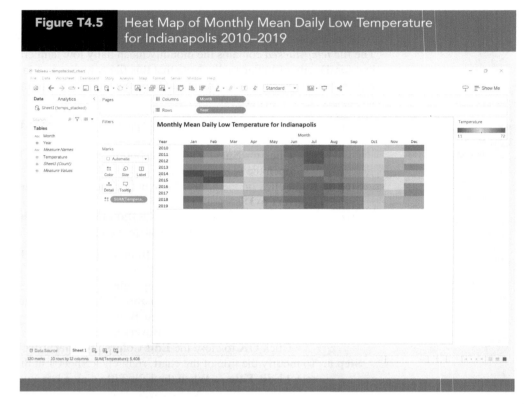

tempstacked_chart.twbx

Chapter 5

Visualizing Variability

Contents

Learning Objectives

After completing this chapter, you will be able to

LO 1 Create and interpret charts used to visualize the frequency distribution of a categorical variable

LO 2 Create and interpret histograms and frequency polygons to visualize the distribution of a quantitative variable

LO 3 Create and interpret visualizations comparing the distributions of two or more variables

LO 4 Create and interpret strip charts, recognize situations in which to use them, and employ techniques to improve their clarity

LO 5 Describe basic statistical measures of central location, variability, and distribution shape

LO 6 Create and interpret a box and whisker chart

LO 7 Create and interpret visualizations that depict the uncertainty resulting from sampling error

LO 8 Create and interpret charts that depict the uncertainty in predictions from simple regression models and time series models

Data Visualization Makeover

Age Distribution of U.S. Gymnasts

An article by *The Washington Post* examined the age range of U.S. Olympic athletes in recent Summer Games. To summarize the analysis, *The Washington Post* used a chart similar to what is shown in Figure 5.1 for U.S. Olympic gymnasts. This chart has a visual similarity to a stacked bar chart, but unfortunately this similarity contributes to confusion when interpreting the chart. In a stacked bar chart, different colors correspond to different quantities, and an increasing length of a colored bar segment corresponds to an increase in the number or proportion of a respective quantity. However, in Figure 5.1, the length of a bar does not convey the same information as a stacked bar chart. Figure 5.1 depicts an overlapping range bar chart. In a range bar chart, the endpoints correspond to the smallest and largest values of a variable. In Figure 5.1, the smallest value is 15 and the largest value is 30.

After referring to the chart legend, we realize that two of the colors correspond to male and female athletes, respectively, while the third color depicts when the age ranges of male and female athletes overlap. That is, the third color does not correspond to a third quantity, but it must be used in conjunction with the colors of the male and female athletes to make appropriate conclusions about the age ranges. This use of color is not intuitive and increases the cognitive load of the audience. In this case, one can determine the age range for female gymnasts to be 15 years to 26 years by considering the left end of the pink bar and right end of the purple bar. Similarly, one can determine the age range for male gymnasts to be 17 years to 30 years by considering the left end of the purple bar and right end of the blue bar. However, there is no information

conveyed in this chart to show how male and female gymnasts are distributed over their respective ranges.

We can find several opportunities for improving the design of the chart in Figure 5.1. We can ease the cognitive load and communicate more information about the age distributions of U.S. Olympic athletes if we use a different type of chart. A chart known as a frequency polygon, which will be discussed in this chapter, more effectively communicates insights from these data to the audience.

Figure 5.2 displays a pair of shaded frequency polygons, one for male gymnasts and one for female gymnasts. In addition to the age range of female and male gymnasts, the shaded frequency polygons displayed in Figure 5.2 provide other information on the age distributions of male and female gymnasts. The curve representing female gymnasts is highest for younger ages and the curve representing male gymnasts is highest for older ages. This indicates that the age distribution for female gymnasts is more heavily weighted toward younger ages, while the age distribution for male gymnasts is weighted toward older ages. The curve for female gymnasts peaks at 16, while the peak for male gymnasts is at 26. This indicates that the most common age for a female gymnast is 16 and the most common age for a male gymnast is 26. While the overlap in the shaded polygons in Figure 5.2 creates a third color as in Figure 5.1, the use of color in Figure 5.2 is more straightforward as the continuity of the curves allows the audience to distinguish between male and female gymnasts. If this shading is undesirable, unshaded frequency polygons can be displayed.

Figure 5.1   Overlapping Range Bar Chart for Ages of U.S. Olympic Gymnasts

Male   Female   Both

Age Range of U.S. Gymnasts in the Four Most Recent Summer Games

Age   15   20   25   30   35   40   45   50   55   60

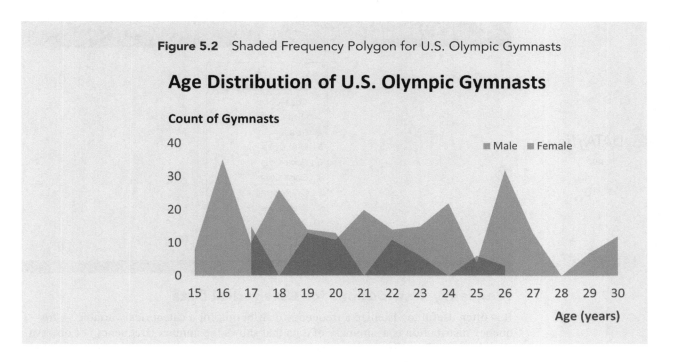

Figure 5.2   Shaded Frequency Polygon for U.S. Olympic Gymnasts

Age Distribution of U.S. Olympic Gymnasts

In this chapter, we address how to visualize the deviations in observed values of data. These deviations may occur among the values of a variable, such as the age of women Olympic gymnasts discussed in the *Data Visualization Makeover*. We describe different types of charts used to display the distribution of a variable's values and discuss how the type of data (categorical or quantitative), the amount of data, and the number of variables to compare affect the choice of visualization. As an aid in interpreting charts displaying a variable's distribution, we define and describe some basic statistical measures of location and variability. We conclude the chapter with discussions on how to visually convey the variability in sample statistics and prediction estimates.

5.1 Creating Distributions from Data

Practically every challenge an organization or individual faces is concerned with the impact the possible values of relevant variables will have on an outcome of interest. Thus, we are concerned with how the value of a variable can vary; **variation** is the difference in a variable measured over observations (time, customers, items, etc.). This variation is often uncertain; we do not perfectly know its magnitude or timing due to factors beyond our control. In general, a quantity whose values are not known with certainty is called a **random variable**.

When we collect data, we are gathering past observed values, or realizations, of a random variable. The role of descriptive analytics is to analyze and visualize data to gain a better understanding of variation and its impact. The **frequency distribution** of a variable describes which values were observed and how often those values appear in the data being analyzed. A frequency distribution can be created for both a categorical variable and a quantitative variable. For a **categorical variable**, data consist of labels or names that cannot be arithmetically manipulated. For a **quantitative variable**, data consist of numerical values that can be arithmetically manipulated.

In most cases, it is not feasible to collect data from the entire **population** of all elements of interest. In such instances, we collect data from a subset of the population known as a **sample**. In the analysis of this chapter, we assume we are dealing with a sample of data representative of the population so generalizations about the entire population can be made.

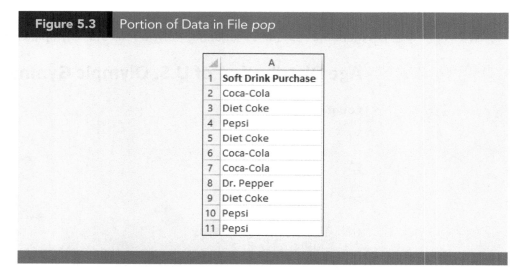

Figure 5.3   Portion of Data in File *pop*

	A
1	**Soft Drink Purchase**
2	Coca-Cola
3	Diet Coke
4	Pepsi
5	Diet Coke
6	Coca-Cola
7	Coca-Cola
8	Dr. Pepper
9	Diet Coke
10	Pepsi
11	Pepsi

DATA *file*

pop

Frequency Distributions for Categorical Data

It is often useful to visualize a frequency distribution for a categorical variable. A frequency distribution is a summary of data that shows the number (frequency) of observations in each of several nonoverlapping classes, typically referred to as **bins**. Consider 500 soft drink purchases. Figure 5.3 displays a portion of these data. Each purchase is for one of five popular soft drinks, which define the five bins: Coca-Cola, Diet Coke, Dr. Pepper, Pepsi, and Sprite.

We can use Excel to calculate the frequency of categorical observations occurring in a data set and then display the frequency distribution. The following steps show how to create a column chart in Excel using the data in the file *pop*.

Step 1. Select cells A1:A501
Step 2. Click the **Insert** tab on the Ribbon
Step 3. Click the **Recommended Charts** button ⏹? ₍Recommended Charts₎ in the **Charts** group
Step 4. When the **Insert Chart** dialog box appears:
Select **Clustered Column**
Click **OK**
Step 5. Click any of the columns in the chart that appears. While the columns are selected, right click a column, then select **Sort** and **Sort Largest to Smallest**

The chart in Figure 5.4 (and all figures in this chapter) has been edited using steps described in Chapters 2 and 3.

Figure 5.4 displays the output of Steps 1 through 5, which generate a PivotTable to summarize the data with a frequency distribution and a PivotChart to visualize the frequency distribution. As Figure 5.4 shows, Coca-Cola appears 190 times, Pepsi appears 130 times, Diet Coke appears 80 times, Sprite appears 50 times, and Dr. Pepper appears 50 times. This frequency distribution provides a summary of how the 500 soft drink purchases are distributed across the five soft drinks. The frequency distribution shows that Coca Cola is the leader, Pepsi is second, Diet Coke is third, and Sprite and Dr. Pepper are tied for fourth. The frequency distribution thus summarizes information about the popularity of the five soft drinks.

We discuss PivotTables and PivotCharts in more detail in Chapter 6.

In Step 5, we ordered the data from largest to smallest to facilitate the comparison of the different soft drink types. This reordering of the data is acceptable because there is no ordinal relationship between soft drinks. However, if an ordinal relationship exists between bin categories, then it would not be appropriate to sort the bins by the number of observations in each bin. Instead, the bins should be ordered according to their ordinal relationship.

If an analyst prefers not to use the Recommended Charts approach to construct a PivotTable and PivotChart to display a frequency distribution for categorical data, Excel functions and a column chart can be used to do so in a more manual fashion as we explain next.

Referring again to the data in the file *pop*, we count the number of times each soft drink appears using the COUNTIF function. Figure 5.5 shows a portion of the 500 soft

Figure 5.4   PivotTable and PivotChart of Frequency Distribution of Soft Drink Purchase Data

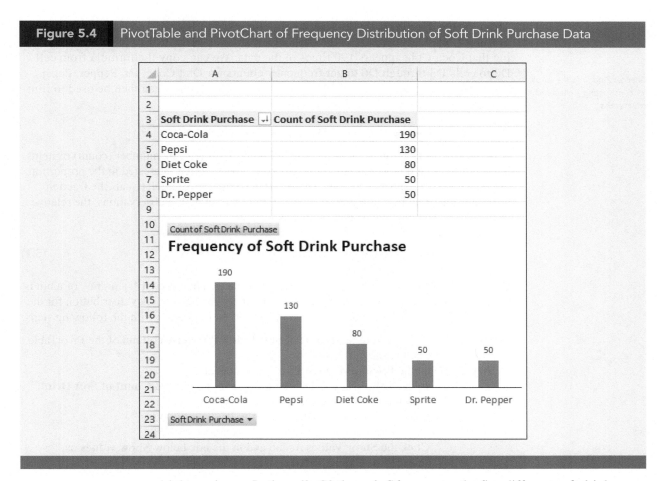

drink purchases. In the cells C2 through C6, we enter the five different soft drinks as the bin labels. In cell D2, we enter the formula $=COUNTIF(A:A, C2)$, where A:A refers to the column range containing the data and C2 is the bin label (Coca-Cola) that we are trying to match. The COUNTIF function in Excel counts the number of times a

Figure 5.5   Creating a Frequency Distribution for Categorical Data Using COUNTIF Function

	A	B	C	D	E
1	Soft Drink Purchase		Bin	Frequency	Percent Frequency
2	Coca-Cola		Coca-Cola	=COUNTIF(A:A,C2)	=D2/SUM($D$2:$D$6)
3	Diet Coke		Diet Coke	=COUNTIF(A:A,C3)	=D3/SUM($D$2:$D$6)
4	Pepsi		Dr. Pepper	=COUNTIF(A:A,C4)	=D4/SUM($D$2:$D$6)
5	Diet Coke		Pepsi	=COUNTIF(A:A,C5)	=D5/SUM($D$2:$D$6)
6	Coca-Cola		Sprite	=COUNTIF(A:A,C6)	=D6/SUM($D$2:$D$6)
7	Coca-Cola				

	A	B	C	D	E
1	Soft Drink Purchase		Bin	Frequency	Percent Frequency
2	Coca-Cola		Coca-Cola	190	38%
3	Diet Coke		Diet Coke	80	16%
4	Pepsi		Dr. Pepper	50	10%
5	Diet Coke		Pepsi	130	26%
6	Coca-Cola		Sprite	50	10%
7	Coca-Cola				

Chapter 2 outlines the steps for constructing a clustered column chart.

certain value appears in the indicated range. In this case we want to count the number of times Coca-Cola appears in the data. The result is a value of 190 in cell D2, indicating that Coca-Cola appears 190 times in the data. We can copy the formula from cell D2 to cells D3 through D6 to get frequency counts for Diet Coke, Dr. Pepper, Pepsi, and Sprite. Using the data in C2:D6, a clustered column chart can then be used to illustrate the distribution of soft drink purchases.

Relative Frequency and Percent Frequency

A frequency distribution, such as the one in Figure 5.4, shows the number (count) of items in each of several nonoverlapping bins. However, we are often interested in the proportion, or percentage, of items in each bin. The **relative frequency** of a bin equals the fraction or proportion of items belonging to a class. For a data set with n observations, the relative frequency of each bin can be determined as follows:

$$\text{Relative frequency of a bin} = \frac{\text{Frequency of the bin}}{n} \tag{5.1}$$

Often, a relative frequency is expressed as a percentage. The **percent frequency** of a bin is the relative frequency multiplied by 100. To obtain a percent frequency distribution for the data in the file *pop*, we continue from the PivotTable in Figure 5.4 with the following steps:

Step 1. Select any cell in the **Count of Soft Drink Purchase** column of the PivotTable (any cell in range B3:B8)
Step 2. When the **PivotTable Fields** task pane appears:
In the **Values** area, select the triangle to the right of **Count of Soft Drink Purchase** `Count of Soft Drink Purchase ▼`
Select **Value Field Settings…** from the list of options
Step 3. When the **Value Field Settings** dialog box appears:
Click the **Show Values As** tab and in the box below **Show values as,** select **% of Grand Total**

A percent frequency distribution can be manually constructed in the spreadsheet in Figure 5.5 by implementing equation (5.1) as a spreadsheet formula in the range E2:E6, respectively.

Figure 5.6 shows the result of the preceding steps. The percent frequency for Coca-Cola is 190/500 = 0.38 = 38%, the percent frequency for Pepsi is 130/500 = 0.26 = 16%, and so on. We can also note that 38% + 26% + 16% = 80% of the purchases were the top three soft drinks.

A percent frequency distribution can be used to provide estimates of the relative likelihoods of different values for a random variable. So, by constructing a percent frequency distribution from observations of a random variable, we can estimate the **probability distribution** that characterizes its variability. For example, suppose a concession stand has determined it will procure a total of 12,000 ounces of soft drinks for an upcoming concert, but it is uncertain how to divide this total over the individual soft drink types. However, if the data in the file *pop* are representative of the concession stand's customer population, the manager can use this information to determine appropriate volumes of each type of soft drink. For example, the data suggest that the manager should procure 12,000 × 0.38 = 4,560 ounces of Coca-Cola.

A prominent example of a relative frequency distribution often used in accounting and finance is **Benford's Law**, which states that in many data sets, the proportion of observations in which the first digit is 1, 2, 3, 4, 5, 6, 7, 8, or 9, respectively, follows the distribution in Figure 5.7. Benford's Law applies to a variety of naturally occurring data sets, including item prices, utility bills, street addresses, corporate expense reports, city populations, and river lengths. It tends to be most applicable in data sets governed by a **power law**, in which a variable of interest experiences a proportional change in response to a change in one or more other variables. When dealing with data in an application that typically obeys Benford's Law, if the relative frequency distribution of the first digits of these data deviates substantially from the relative frequency distribution in Figure 5.7, then there may be systemic errors in the data or the data may be fraudulent.

Figure 5.6   Percent Frequency Distribution of Soft Drink Purchase Data

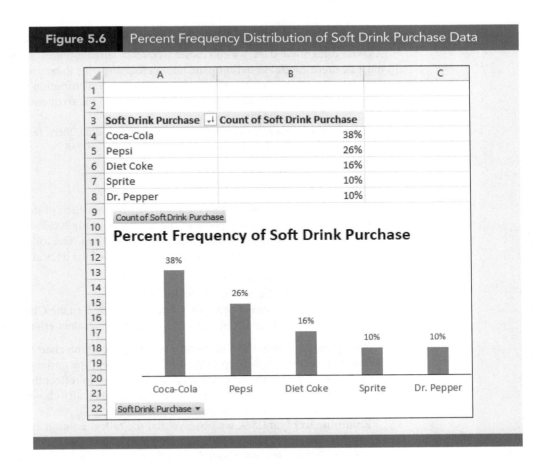

Figure 5.7 indicates that, according to Benford's Law, approximately 30% of the values in an applicable data set would begin with a digit of 1, while only about 4.6% of the values would begin with a digit of 9. This is different than if we assumed that the first digits of the values would all be equally likely, in which case we would expect $1/9 \approx 11.1\%$ of the values in a data set to start with each digit.

Figure 5.7   Relative Frequency Distribution of Data Obeying Benford's Law

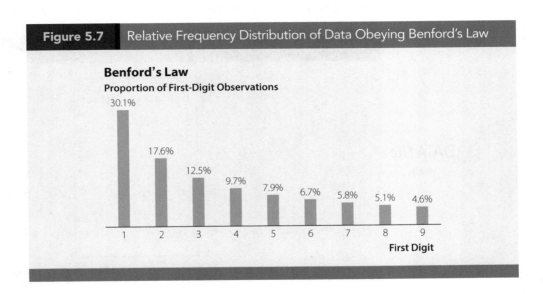

Visualizing Distributions of Quantitative Data

As with categorical data, we can create frequency distributions for quantitative data, but we must be more careful in defining the nonoverlapping bins to be used in the frequency distribution. Recall that for categorical data, a frequency distribution's bins are based on the different categories. For quantitative data, each bin in the frequency distribution is based on the range of values the bin contains.

To create a frequency distribution for quantitative data, three features need to be defined:

1. The number of nonoverlapping bins
2. The width (numerical range) of each bin
3. The range spanned by the set of bins

Excel possesses functionality that automatically defines each of these features. To demonstrate, consider a data set that contains the age at death for 700 individuals. Figure 5.8 displays a portion of this data, contained in the file *death*. The following steps construct the **histogram** in Figure 5.9, illustrating the distribution of the ages at death.

Step 1. Select cells A1:A701
Step 2. Click the **Insert** tab on the Ribbon
Step 3. Click the **Insert Statistic Chart** button in the **Charts** group
When the list of statistic charts appears, select **Histogram**

As Figure 5.9 illustrates, a histogram is simply a column chart with no spaces between the columns whose heights represent the frequencies of the corresponding bins. Eliminating the space between the columns allows a histogram to reflect the continuous nature of the variable of interest. For this data set, Excel automatically chose to use 16 bins, each spanning 7 years, traversing the range from 0 to 112.

Returning to Figure 5.9, we observe that the tallest column corresponds to the bin (77, 84]. To interpret this bin, we note that a square bracket indicates that the end value is included in the bin, and a round parenthesis indicates the end value is excluded. So the most common ages at death occur in the range greater than 77 years old and less than or equal to 84 years old. Furthermore, we observe the data are highly skewed left, with most individuals dying at relatively old ages but small numbers of individuals dying at young ages.

The choice of number of bins and bin width can strongly affect a histogram's display of a distribution. If an analyst prefers not to use the automatic histogram generated by Excel's Charts functionality, more user control is possible by using the Excel function FREQUENCY and a column chart to construct a histogram. Again, we will use the 700 observations in the file *death* to manually create a histogram. The first step in

Figure 5.8	Portion of Data in File *death*

DATA *file*

death

	A
1	Age at Death (Years)
2	83
3	76
4	78
5	74
6	35
7	78
8	73
9	84
10	55
11	73

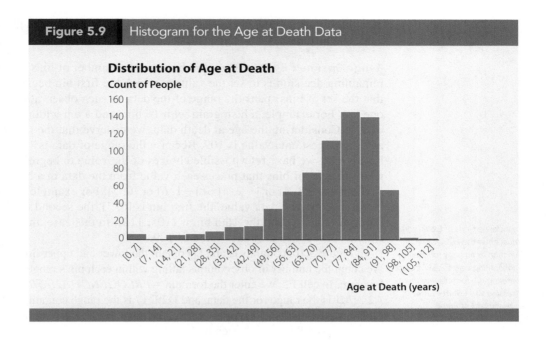

Figure 5.9 Histogram for the Age at Death Data

manually creating a histogram is determining the number of bins, the width of the bins, and the range spanned by the bins.

Number of Bins Bins are formed by specifying the ranges used to group the data. As a general guideline, we recommend using from 5 to 20 bins. Using too many bins results in a histogram in which many bins contain only a few observations. With too many bins, the histogram does not capture generalizable patterns in the distribution and instead may appear jagged and "noisy." Using too few bins results in a histogram that aggregates observations with too wide of a range of values into the same bins. With too few bins, the histogram fails to accurately capture the variation in the data and presents only blurred, high-level patterns. For a small number of observations, as few as five or six bins may be used to summarize the data. For a larger number of observations, more bins are usually required. The determination of the number of bins is an inherently subjective decision, and the notion of a "best" number of bins depends on the subject matter and goal of the analysis. Because the number of observations in the file *death* is relatively large ($n = 700$), we should choose a larger number of bins. We will use 16 bins to match Figure 5.9.

Width of the Bins As a general guideline, we recommend that the width be the same for each bin. Thus, the choices of the number of bins and the width of bins are not independent decisions. A larger number of bins means a smaller bin width and vice versa. To determine an approximate bin width, we begin by identifying the largest and smallest data values. Then, with the desired number of bins specified, we can use the following expression to determine the approximate bin width.

$$\text{approximate bin width} = \frac{\text{largest data value} - \text{smallest data value}}{\text{number of bins}} \tag{5.2}$$

The approximate bin width given by Equation (5.2) can be rounded to a more convenient value based on the preference of the person developing the frequency distribution. For example, using Equation (5.2) supplies an approximate bin width of $(109 - 0)/16 = 6.8125$. We round this number up to obtain a bin width of 7. By rounding up, we assure that 16 bins of width 7, with the first bin starting from the smallest data value, will cover the range of values in the data.

Range Spanned by Bins Once we have set the number of bins and the bin width, the remaining decision is to set the value at which the first bin begins. We must ensure that the set of bins spans the range of the data so each observation belongs to exactly one bin. For example, a histogram with 16 bins and a bin width of 7 will cover a range of 112. Considering the age at death data, we observe that the smallest data value is 0 and the largest data value is 109. Because the range of data is 109 but the range of the bins is 112, we have four possible choices of the value to begin the first bin that would result in a set of bins that places each value from the data in a bin. We can define the first bin as $[-3, 4]$ or $[-2, 5]$ or $[-1, 6]$ or $[0, 7]$. For example, if we begin the first bin at the smallest data value, the first bin is $[0, 7]$, the second bin is $(7, 14]$, the third bin is $(14, 21]...$, and the 16th bin is $(105, 112]$. In this case, the 16th bin's range extends past the largest data value of 109.

*In older versions of Excel, you must enter the FREQUENCY function as an array function by highlighting cells E2:E17 before entering the formula and then pressing **Ctrl+Shift+Enter** rather than just Enter.*

In Figure 5.10, columns C and D contain the lower and upper limits defining the bins. We count the number of observations falling within each bin's range using the FREQUENCY function. In cell E2, we enter the formula $=FREQUENCY(A2:A701, D2:D17)$, where A2:A701 is the range for the data, and D2:D17 is the range containing the upper limits for each bin. After pressing Enter in cell E2, the range E2:E18 is populated with the number of observations falling within each bin's range.

In older versions of Excel, the CONCAT function may not exist and you must use the CONCATENATE function instead.

Using the data in D2:E17, a clustered column chart can then be used to illustrate the distribution of ages at death. In column F, we use the Excel CONCAT function to create a set of bin labels that we will use for the horizontal axis. The CONCAT function simply combines elements from different cells and/or different text strings into the same cell.

DATAfile

deathfrequency

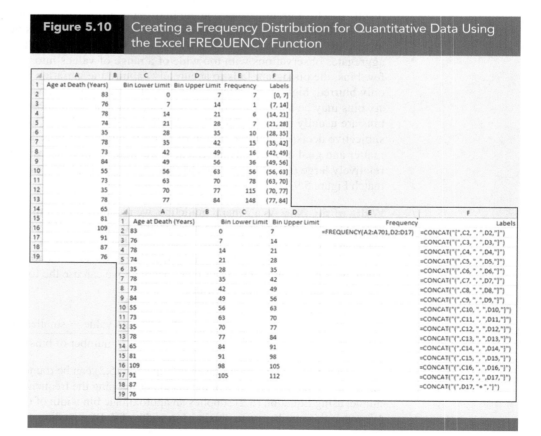

| Figure 5.10 | Creating a Frequency Distribution for Quantitative Data Using the Excel FREQUENCY Function |

Step 1. Select cells D2:E17

Step 2. Click the **Insert** tab on the Ribbon

Step 3. Click the **Insert Column or Bar Chart** button ⬛ˇ in the **Charts** group

When the list of column and bar chart subtypes appears, click the **Clustered Column** button ⬛

Steps 1 through 3 result in plotting both Bin Upper Limit and Frequency. To correct this, we need the following steps:

Step 4. Right click the chart and select **Change Chart Type…**

Step 5. When the **Change Chart Type** task pane appears, select the **Cluster Column** type that plots the appropriate number of variables (in this case, the single variable Frequency plotted with 16 columns ⬛) and click **OK**

Step 6. Right click one of the columns in the chart and select **Format Data Series…**

When the **Format Data Series** task pane opens, click the **Series Options** button ⬛ and set the **Gap Width** to 0%

Click the **Fill &Line** button ⬥ , under **Border** select **Solid line**, and to the right of **Color**, select white from the drop down menu

Step 7. Right click the chart and select **Select Data…**

When the **Select Data Source** dialog box appears, click **Edit** under **Horizontal (Category) Axis Labels**. In the **Axis Labels** dialog box, enter *=Data!F2$F$17* in the box below **Axis label range:** and click **OK**

Click **OK** to close the **Select Data Source** dialog box

Further editing will result in a histogram that matches Figure 5.9.

We note that the choice of the number of bins (and the corresponding bin width) may change the shape of the histogram (particularly for small data sets). Therefore, it is common to determine the number of bins and the appropriate bin width by trial and error. Once a possible number of bins is chosen, Equation (5.2) is used to find the approximate bin width. The process can be repeated for several different numbers of bins.

To illustrate the impact of varying the number of bins and bin width on the shape of the histogram, we consider 30 observations in the file *death30*, a subset of the data in the file *death*. Figure 5.11 depicts three histograms, one using 5 bins with width 12, one using 8 bins with width 8, and one using 10 bins with width 6. As Figure 5.11 illustrates, the choice of binning parameters can affect the shape of the histogram's distribution. The histogram with 5 bins and the histogram with 10 bins both suggest that the bin containing the oldest age range is the most likely. However, the histogram with 8 bins suggests that the bin containing the second oldest age range is most likely, and the oldest age range is the third-most likely. An inspection of the data reveals that 6 out of the 30 observations had an age at death of 87 years, making the display of the distribution highly sensitive to the bin that contains 87.

One of the most important uses of a histogram is to provide information about the shape, or form, of a distribution. **Skewness**, or the lack of symmetry, is an important characteristic of the shape of a distribution. Figure 5.12 contains four histograms constructed from relative frequency distributions that exhibit different patterns of skewness. Figure 5.12a shows a histogram for a set of data moderately skewed to the left. A histogram is said to be skewed to the left if its tail extends farther to the left than to the right. This histogram is typical for exam scores, with no scores above 100%, most of the scores above 70%, and only a few really low scores.

Figure 5.12b shows a histogram for a set of data moderately skewed to the right. A histogram is said to be skewed to the right if its tail extends farther to the right than to the left. An example of this type of histogram would be for data such as housing prices; a few expensive houses create the skewness in the right tail.

DATA *file*

death30

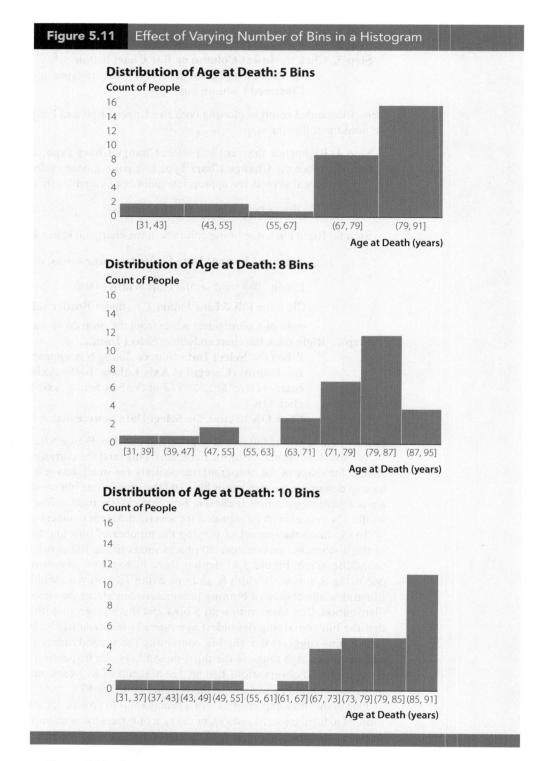

Figure 5.11   Effect of Varying Number of Bins in a Histogram

Distribution of Age at Death: 5 Bins

Count of People

Age at Death (years)

Distribution of Age at Death: 8 Bins

Count of People

Age at Death (years)

Distribution of Age at Death: 10 Bins

Count of People

Age at Death (years)

Figure 5.12c shows a symmetric histogram, in which the left tail mirrors the shape of the right tail. Histograms for data found in applications are rarely perfectly symmetric, but the histograms for many applications are roughly symmetric. Data for standardized test scores, the heights and weights of people, and so on lead to histograms that are roughly symmetric.

Figure 5.12d shows a histogram highly skewed to the right. This histogram was constructed from data on the amount of customer purchases in one day at an apparel store. Data from applications in business and economics often lead to histograms that are skewed

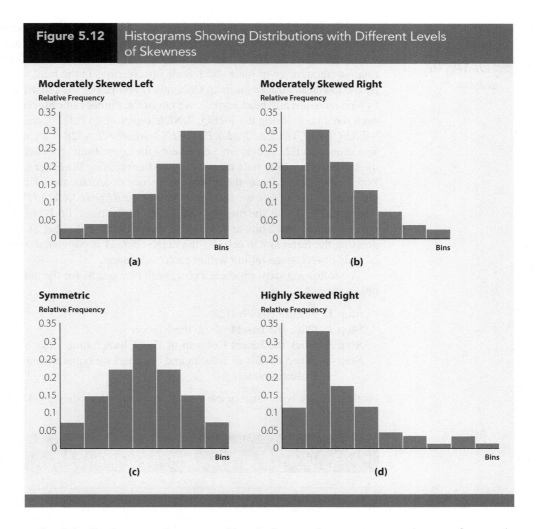

Figure 5.12   Histograms Showing Distributions with Different Levels of Skewness

to the right. For instance, data on wealth, salaries, purchase amounts, and so on often result in histograms skewed to the right.

As we have shown, column charts and histograms can be effective ways to visualize the distribution of a variable. However, when comparing the distribution of two or more variables, these columnar displays become cluttered. Next, we present a visualization tool that is particularly helpful for visualizing the distributions of multiple variables.

A **frequency polygon** is a visualization tool useful for comparing distributions, particularly for quantitative variables. Like a histogram, a frequency polygon plots frequency counts of observations in a set of bins. However, a frequency polygon uses lines to connect the counts of different bins in contrast to a histogram, which uses columns to depict the counts in different bins.

To demonstrate the construction of histograms and frequency polygons for two different variables, we consider the data in the file *deathtwo*, which supplements the age at death information for the 700 individuals in the file *death* with the sex assigned at birth of each of these individuals. Similar to how we constructed the frequency distribution for all 700 observations, we must create separate frequency distributions for the female and male observations, respectively. However, when comparing frequency distributions, it is a good practice to use relative frequency calculations because the total number of observations in the two distributions may not be the same. For instance, in the file *deathtwo*, there are 327 female observations and 373 male observations, so comparing just the count of observations in the bins may distort the comparison.

DATA *file*

deathtwo

In Figure 5.13, we compute the number of female and male observations by entering the formula =*COUNTIF(B2:B701, "Female")* in cell F3 and the formula =*COUNTIF(B2:B701, "Male")* in cell G3. We use these counts to compute the relative frequencies of male and female observations in the bins, which are defined by the lower and upper limits in Columns D and E. For the female and male observations (which have already been sorted), we count the number of observations falling within each bin's range using the FREQUENCY function. In cell F6, we enter the formula =*FREQUENCY(A2:A328, E6:E21)/$F$3*, where A2:A328 is the range for the female observations, E6:E21 is the range containing the upper limits for each bin, and cell F3 contains the total number of female observations. After pressing the Enter key in cell F6, the range F6:F22 is populated with the relative frequency of female observations falling within each bin's range. In cell G6, we enter the formula =*FREQUENCY(A329:A701, E6:E21)/$G$3*, where A329:A701 is the range for the male observations, E6:E21 is the range containing the upper limits for each bin, and cell G3 contains the total number of male observations. After pressing the Enter key in cell G6, the range G6:G21 is populated with the relative frequency of male observations falling within each bin's range.

The following steps produce a chart with histograms for the male and female observations.

Step 1.   Select cells F6:G21
Step 2.   Click the **Insert** tab on the Ribbon
Step 3.   Click the **Insert Column or Bar Chart** button in the **Charts** group
Step 4.   When the list of column and bar chart subtypes appears, click the **Clustered Column** button

Further editing will result in the clustered column chart displayed in Figure 5.14a.

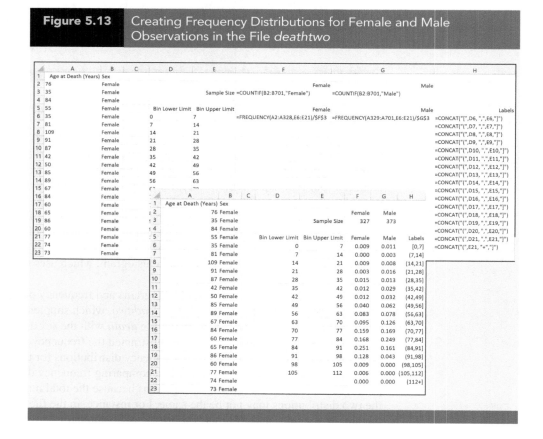

Figure 5.13   Creating Frequency Distributions for Female and Male Observations in the File *deathtwo*

DATA *file*

deathtwofrequency

To display the age at death distributions for female and male observations as a frequency polygon, we execute the following steps.

Step 1. Select cells F6:G21
Step 2. Click the **Insert** tab on the Ribbon
Step 3. Click the **Insert Line or Area Chart** button 〽 ⌄ in the **Charts** group
> When the list of line and area chart subtypes appears, click the **Line** button 〽

Further editing will result in the frequency polygons displayed in Figure 5.14b.

When plotting a distribution with respect to two variables, shading the respective polygons may improve the interpretability of the chart. To display the age at death distributions for female and male observations as a shaded frequency polygon as depicted in Figure 5.14c, we execute the following steps.

Step 1. Select cells F6:G21
Step 2. Click the **Insert** tab on the Ribbon
Step 3. Click the **Insert Line or Area Chart** button 〽 ⌄ in the **Charts** group
> When the list of line and area chart subtypes appears, click the **Area** button 〽
Step 4. Right click on the area chart corresponding to the Male data, and select **Format Data Series...**
> When the **Format Data Series** pane opens, click the **Fill & Line** button ◇ , and under **Fill**, select **Solid fill**, for **Color**, select blue from the drop down menu, and for **Transparency**, set the slider bar to *50%*
Step 5. With the **Format Data Series** pane still open, click on the area chart corresponding to the Female data
> In the **Format Data Series** pane, click the **Fill & Line** button ◇ , and under **Fill**, select **Solid fill**, for **Color**, select orange from the drop down menu, and for **Transparency**, set the slider bar to *50%*
> Close the **Format Data Series** pane

As Figure 5.14 illustrates for the age at death distributions for males and females, the use of lines in the frequency polygons preserves the continuity of each distribution's shape, while the use of a clustered column chart provides a disrupted visualization of the distributions. While frequency polygons provide for a more transparent comparison of two or more distributions, for a single distribution they do not support the magnitude comparison of different bins as well as a histogram. Therefore, histograms are typically preferred for the visualization of a single variable's distribution.

When comparing many distributions (three or more), frequency polygons plotted on the same chart can become cluttered. For shape comparisons of multiple distributions, an arrangement of individual visualizations in a **trellis display** can be helpful. A trellis display is a vertical or horizontal arrangement of individual charts of the same type, size, scale, and formatting that differ only by the data they display. Figure 5.15 contains a vertical trellis display of the length of stay distributions of three hospitals using histograms. This trellis display facilitates distribution shape comparisons, but it is not as useful for magnitude comparisons.

One shortcoming of both histograms and frequency polygons is the specific values of the smallest and largest values are difficult to discern from the visualization due to the binning of values. If we want to display a small set of values in a manner that shows the individual values, a visualization known as a **strip chart** can be useful.

| Figure 5.14 | Comparing Frequency Polygon Display to Clustered Column Display |

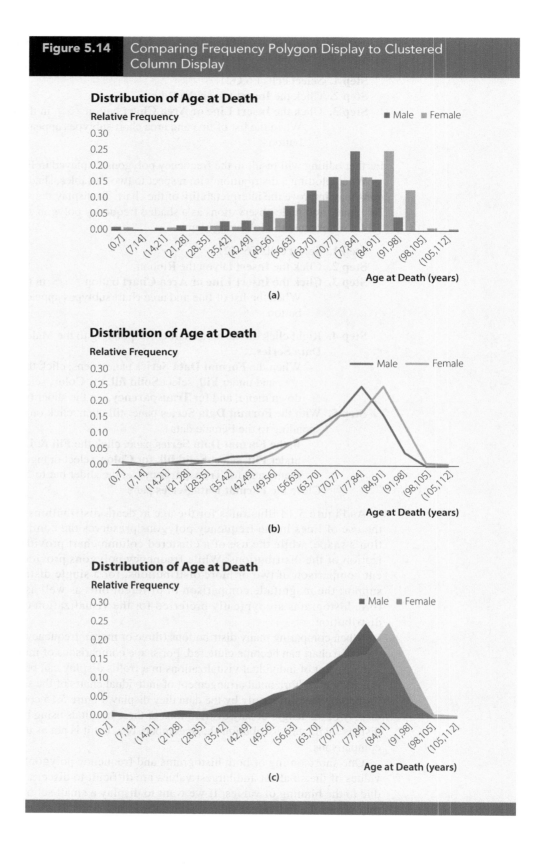

Figure 5.15   Trellis Display of Length of Stay Distributions for Three Hospitals

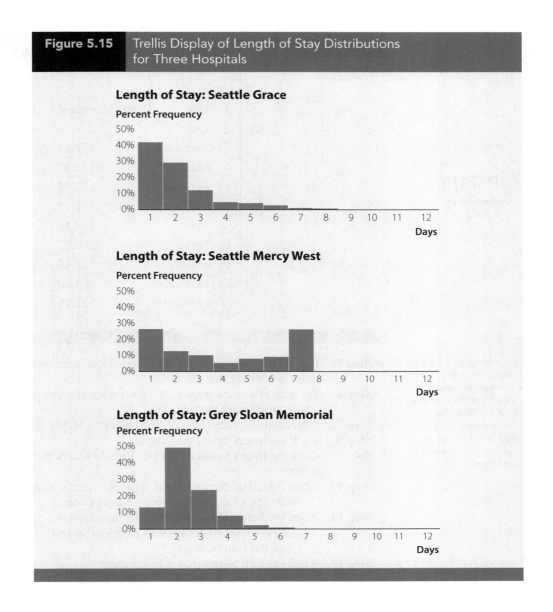

To demonstrate a strip chart, consider the data in the file *halfmarathon*, which contains times for a collection of runners in a competitive half-marathon race. Figure 5.16 displays a portion of these data. The following steps construct horizonal strip charts displaying the times for the male and female runners, respectively.

Step 1.   Select cells A1:B54
Step 2.   Click the **Data** tab on the Ribbon
Step 3.   Click the **Sort** button in the **Sort & Filter** group
Step 4.   When the **Sort** dialog box appears, select the check box for **My data has headers**
In the **Sort by** row, select **Sex** for the **Column** entry, **Cell Values** for the **Sort on** entry, and **Z to A** for the **Order** entry
Click **Add Level**
In the **Then by** row, select **Time (Minutes)** for the **Column** entry, **Cell Values** for the **Sort on** entry, and **Smallest to Largest** for the **Order** entry
Click **OK**

Figure 5.16   Portion of the Data in File *halfmarathon*

◢	A	B
1	Sex	Time (Minutes)
2	Male	148.70
3	Female	122.62
4	Male	127.98
5	Female	122.48
6	Female	111.22
7	Male	108.18
8	Female	189.27
9	Male	128.40
10	Female	153.88
11	Female	121.25

In a horizontal strip chart, the vertical axis has no meaning. In this example, we plot male half-marathon times at a height of 10 and female half-marathon times at a height of 20 to create visual separation, but these values are arbitrary.

Step 5. For each cell in the range C2:C23 (each cell corresponding to a Male finishing time), enter the value *10*

Step 6. For each cell in the range C24:C54 (each cell corresponding to a Female finishing time), enter the value *20*

Step 7. Select cells B2:C23 (cells corresponding to Male finishing times)

Step 8. Click the **Insert** tab on the Ribbon

Step 9. Click the **Insert Scatter (X,Y) or Bubble Chart** button in the **Charts** group

Step 10. When the list of chart subtypes appears, click the **Scatter** button
Right click the chart and select **Select Data…**

Step 11. When the **Select Data Source** dialog box appears:
Select **Series1** under **Legend Entries (Series)**
Click the **Edit** button

Step 12. When the **Edit Series** dialog box appears:
Enter *Male* in the box under **Series name:**
Click **OK** to close the **Edit Series** dialog box

Step 13. In the **Select Data Source** dialog box, click the **Add** button

Step 14. When the **Edit Series** dialog box appears:
Enter *Female* in the box under **Series name:**
Enter *=Data!$B$24:$B$54* in the box under **Series X values:**
Enter *=Data!$C$24:$C$54* in the box under **Series Y values:**
Click **OK** to close the **Edit Series** dialog box
Click **OK** to close the **Select Data Source** dialog box

After editing, these steps produce the strip chart in Figure 5.17. Figure 5.17 displays each half-marathon time for males and females, respectively, and we can see the fastest and slowest times for each sex. However, this strip chart fails to clearly show the relative density of half-marathon times over the range like a histogram or frequency polygon because the vertical axis in the strip chart has no meaning. Furthermore, as the number of values to plot increases and when there are multiple values that are the same or nearly the same, a strip chart suffers from occlusion. **Occlusion** is the inability to distinguish some individual data points because they are hidden behind others with the same or nearly the same value. Occlusion in strip charts can be mitigated by (1) plotting hollow dots rather than filled dots and (2) jittering the observation. **Jittering** an observation involves slightly adjusting the value of one or more of the variables comprising the observation.

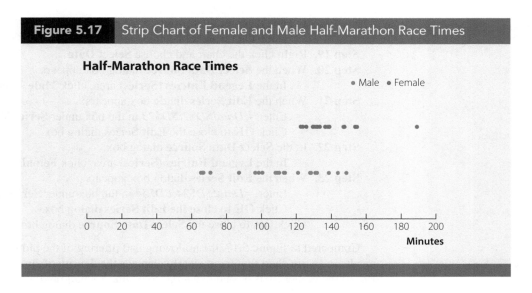

Figure 5.17   Strip Chart of Female and Male Half-Marathon Race Times

To address the occlusion in Figure 5.17, starting from this chart, we execute the following steps.

Step 15. Right click the **Female** data series in the chart and select **Format Data Series…**

Step 16. When the **Format Data Series** task pane appears:
Click the **Fill & Line** button
Click **Marker Fill**
Under **Fill**, select **No fill**

Step 17. Leaving the **Format Data Series** task pane open, click the **Male** data series in the chart
Click the **Fill & Line** button
Click **Marker Fill**
Under **Fill**, select **No fill**

Steps 15–17 plot the half-marathon times using hollow dots. To jitter the observations vertically, we execute steps 18–23 to produce Figure 5.18. Specifically, in steps 18 and 19, we jitter by adding a small random number between zero and one to the height at which male and female half-marathon times are plotted.

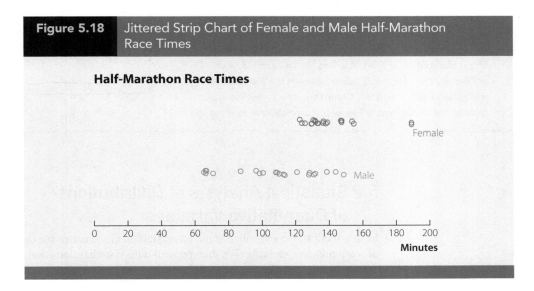

Figure 5.18   Jittered Strip Chart of Female and Male Half-Marathon Race Times

Step 18. In cell D2, enter the formula $=C2+RAND()$
  Copy the formula in cell D2 to cells D3:D54
Step 19. Right click the chart and choose **Select Data...**
Step 20. When the **Select Data Source** dialog box appears:
  In the **Legend Entries (Series)** area, click **Male** and then click **Edit**
Step 21. When the **Edit Series** dialog box appears:
  Enter $=Data!\$D\$2:\$D\$23$ in the box under **Series Y values:**
  Click **OK** to close the **Edit Series** dialog box
Step 22. In the **Select Data Source** dialog box:
  In the **Legend Entries (Series)** area, click **Female** and then click **Edit**
Step 23. When the **Edit Series** dialog box appears:
  Enter $=Data!\$D\$24:\$D\$54$ in the box under **Series Y values:**
  Click **OK** to close the **Edit Series** dialog box
  Click **OK** to close the **Select Data Source** dialog box

Compared to Figure 5.17, the hollowing and jittering of the plotted values in Figure 5.18 results in a strip chart that more clearly displays the density of similar half-marathon times. Recall the vertical axis has no meaning, so adding a small random value between zero and one to the *y*-series values does not alter the interpretation of the chart at all, but it allows the audience to visually discern between similar half-marathon times. If necessary, we could have also jittered the *x*-series values by adding and subtracting relatively small values to the half-marathon times without qualitatively changing the insight derived from the chart, but that was not necessary in this case.

Notes + Comments

1. When jittering the data points of a chart, it may be necessary to add or subtract values more extreme than random values between zero and one. In these cases, the Excel formula $=a+RAND()*(b-a)$ can be used to generate a random value between *a* and *b* to be added to a data point. For example, $=-5+RAND()*(5-(-5))$ generates a random value between -5 and 5.

2. A **kernel density chart** is a "continuous" alternative to histograms designed to overcome the reliance of histograms on the choice of number of bins and bin width. Kernel density charts employ a smoothing technique known as kernel density estimation to generate a more robust visualization of the distribution of a set of values. As an example, a kernel density chart for the 30 observations in the file *death30* is displayed with this note. Comparing the kernel density chart to the histograms in Figure 5.11, we observe that the

kernel density chart smooths the extremes of the histograms in an attempt to generalize the patterns in the data. Excel does not have built-in functionality to construct a kernel density chart (which is not the same as a frequency polygon), but many statistical software packages such as R do.

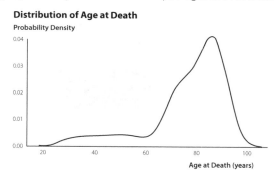

Distribution of Age at Death

5.2 Statistical Analysis of Distributions of Quantitative Variables

In this section, we introduce some basic statistical measures for describing the distribution of a quantitative variable. We then present data visualizations that utilize these statistical measures.

Measures of Location

A measure of (central) location identifies a single value of a variable that in some manner best characterizes the entire set of values. In this sense, a measure of location is a measure of a variable's center around which other values are distributed. In this section, we present different measures of location and discuss their relative advantages and disadvantages.

A common measure of central location is the **mean**, or average value, for a variable. To illustrate the computation of the mean of a set of sample values, consider the 12 home sales in a Cincinnati, Ohio, suburb listed in the file *cincysales* and displayed in Figure 5.19. The mean of these 12 values is

$$\frac{456,400 + 298,000 + \cdots + 108,000}{12} = \$219,950$$

The mean of a variable can be found in Excel using the AVERAGE function. In Figure 5.19, the formula *=AVERAGE(A2:A13)* in cell D2 calculates the mean home sale value of $219,950.

The **median**, another measure of central location, is the value in the middle when the data are arranged in ascending order (smallest to largest value). With an odd number of observations, the median is the middle value. An even number of observations has no

Figure 5.19   Measures of Location for Cincinnati Home Sales Data

	A	B	C	D
1	**Selling Price**			
2	108000		Mean:	=AVERAGE(A2:A13)
3	138000		Median:	=MEDIAN(A2:A13)
4	138000		Mode 1:	=MODE.MULT(A2:A13)
5	142000		Mode 2:	
6	186000			
7	199500			
8	208000			
9	254000			
10	254000			
11	257500			
12	298000			
13	456400			

	A	B	C	D
1	**Selling Price**			
2	$108,000		Mean:	$219,950
3	$138,000		Median:	$203,750
4	$138,000		Mode 1:	$138,000
5	$142,000		Mode 2:	$254,000
6	$186,000			
7	$199,500			
8	$208,000			
9	$254,000			
10	$254,000			
11	$257,500			
12	$298,000			
13	$456,400			

DATA*file*

cincysales

single middle value. In this case, we define the median as the average of the values for the middle two observations. The median of the 12 Cincinnati home sales is the average of the sixth and seventh observations as computed by

$$\frac{\$208{,}000 + \$199{,}500}{2} = \$203{,}750$$

The median of a variable can be found in Excel using the function MEDIAN. In Figure 5.19, the formula $=MEDIAN(A2{:}A13)$ in cell D3 calculates the median home sale value of $203,750.

Although the mean is a commonly used measure of central location, its calculation is influenced by outlying values—extremely small and extremely large values. Therefore, the median is often the preferred measure of central location as its calculation is resistant to outlying values. Notice that the median is smaller than the mean in Figure 5.19. This is because the one large value of $456,400 in our data set inflates the mean but does not affect the median. Notice also that the median would remain unchanged if we replaced the $456,400 with a sales price of $1.5 million. In this case, the median selling price would remain $203,750, but the mean would increase to $306,916.67. If you were looking to buy a home in this suburb, the median gives a better indication of the central selling price of the homes there. We can generalize, saying that whenever a data set contains extreme values or is severely skewed, the median is the preferred measure of central location; this is particularly true for data sets with relatively few observations.

A third measure of location, the **mode**, is the value that occurs most frequently in a data set. Occasionally, the greatest frequency occurs at two or more different values, in which case more than one mode exists. If no value in the data occurs more than once, we say the data have no mode. In the Cincinnati home sales data, there are two values that each occur twice and all other values occur just once. Therefore, the two modes are $254,000 and $138,000. All modes of a variable can be found in Excel using the function MODE.MULT. In Figure 5.19, the formula $=MODE.MULT(A2{:}A13)$ in cell D4 calculates the two modes of $254,000 and $138,000 and places them in cells D4 and D5, respectively.

*In older versions of Excel, the MODE.MULT function must be executed by pressing **Ctrl+Shift+Enter** rather than just Enter.*

The mode can be a useful measure of central location for variables that have a relatively small set of distinct values. For variables with many possible values, such as the value of home sales in the file *cincysales* or the race times in the file *halfmarathon*), the frequency that defines the mode will either be small or the mode may not exist. For variables with many possible values, it may be best to construct a histogram and apply the notion of the mode to refer to the bin (range of values) with the most observations. That is, the bin in a histogram with the most observations (the tallest column) may then be referred to as the mode.

Measures of Variability

While measures of location provide a single central value that in some sense is most characteristic for a sample of a variable's values, these measures fail to convey any information regarding the variability in the values. For instance, the median home sale value of $203,750 for the Cincinnati home sales data provides no information on how spread out the set of 12 home sale values are. So, in addition to measures of location, it is often desirable to consider measures of variability, or dispersion.

The simplest measure of variability is the **range**. The range can be found by subtracting the smallest value from the largest value in a data set. For the Cincinnati home sales data, the range is

$$\$456{,}400 - \$108{,}000 = \$348{,}400$$

Excel does not offer a range function, but the range of a variable can be found in Excel using the MAX and MIN functions. In Figure 5.20, the formula $=MAX(A2{:}A13) - MIN(A2{:}A13)$ in cell D7 calculates the range of home sale values to be $348,400.

Figure 5.20	Measures of Variability for Cincinnati Home Sales Data

	A	B	C	D
1	**Selling Price**			
2	108000		Mean:	=AVERAGE(A2:A13)
3	138000		Median:	=MEDIAN(A2:A13)
4	138000		Mode 1:	=MODE.MULT(A2:A13)
5	142000		Mode 2:	
6	186000			
7	199500		Range:	=MAX(A2:A13) - MIN(A2:A13)
8	208000		Standard Deviation:	=STDEV.S(A2:A13)
9	254000			
10	254000		25th Percentile:	=PERCENTILE.EXC(A2:A13,0.25)
11	257500		50th Percentile:	=PERCENTILE.EXC(A2:A13,0.5)
12	298000		75th Percentile:	=PERCENTILE.EXC(A2:A13,0.75)
13	456400			
14			IQR:	=D12-D10

	A	B	C	D
1	**Selling Price**			
2	$108,000		Mean:	$219,950
3	$138,000		Median:	$203,750
4	$138,000		Mode 1:	$138,000
5	$142,000		Mode 2:	$254,000
6	$186,000			
7	$199,500		Range:	$348,400
8	$208,000		Standard Deviation:	$95,100
9	$254,000			
10	$254,000		25th Percentile:	$139,000
11	$257,500		50th Percentile:	$203,750
12	$298,000		75th Percentile:	$256,625
13	$456,400			
14			IQR:	$117,625

Although the range communicates a notion of variability by supplying how much the largest value differs from the smallest value, it is seldom relied upon as the only measure of variability. This is because the range is based on only two of the observations and thus is highly influenced by extreme values. For example, in the Cincinnati home sales data, range provides no notion of how close or how far apart the other 10 home sale values are; it only tells us that the largest home sale and smallest home sale are $348,400 apart.

Another common measure of variability is **standard deviation**, which is based on how much each observation's value deviates from the mean. The standard deviation of a sample of a variable's values can be viewed as the average amount that an observation in the sample deviates from the sample mean. For the Cincinnati home sales data, the standard deviation is computed by

$$\sqrt{\frac{(\$456{,}400 - \$219{,}950)^2 + (\$298{,}000 - 219{,}950)^2 + \cdots + (\$108{,}000 - 219{,}950)^2}{12 - 1}}$$

$$= \$95{,}100$$

The sample standard deviation can be calculated in Excel using the STDEV.S function. In Figure 5.20, the formula =*STDEV.S(A2:A13)* in cell D8 calculates the standard deviation of home sale values to be $95,100.

Standard deviation (st. dev.) is a reliable measure of variability when the values of a variable resemble the histogram in Figure 5.21, in which values are distributed symmetrically around a single mode. For such bell-shaped distributions, we can use the standard deviation to describe the variability of the distribution using intervals. Specifically,

- ≈ 68% of data values lie in the interval [mean − st. dev., mean + st. dev.]
- ≈ 95% of data values lie in the interval [mean − 2 × st. dev., mean + 2 × st. dev.]
- > 99% of data values lie in the interval [mean − 3 × st. dev., mean + 3 × st. dev.]

However, because its calculation relies on the mean, the standard deviation can also be heavily influenced by extreme values. For skewed distributions, the standard deviation cannot be reliably used to provide an interpretable measure of the variability of a set of values.

Another way to describe the variability of a set of values is with percentiles. A **percentile** is the value of a variable that a specified (approximate) percentage of observations are below. The pth percentile tells us the point in the data where approximately $p\%$ of the observations have values less than the pth percentile; hence, approximately $(100 - p)\%$ of the observations have values greater than the pth percentile.

A percentile can be computed for any value between 0% and 100%, but common percentiles are the 25th, 50th, and 75th percentiles, which are also known as the first quartile, second quartile, and third quartile, respectively. The 25th, 50th, and 75th percentiles are called **quartiles** because they divide the data into four parts or quarters. The difference between the third and first quartiles (the 75th and 25th percentiles) is often referred to as the **interquartile range**, or IQR. The interquartile range spans the middle 50% of the distribution of a variable's values and is sometimes used as a measure of variation.

To calculate the value of the pth percentile for a data set, we first compute its position among the set of ordered values and then perform any necessary interpolation. To demonstrate, consider the 25th percentile for the 12 values in the Cincinnati home sales data. The position of the 25th percentile is computed by

$$\frac{25}{100} \times (12 + 1) = 3.25$$

The position of 3.25 for the 25th percentile means that it lies between 25% of the way between the value of the third smallest and fourth smallest values. The third smallest value is $138,000 and the fourth smallest value is $142,000, so we compute the value of the 25th percentile as

$$\$138,000 + (3.25 - 3) \times (\$142,000 - \$138,000) = \$139,000$$

There are many different ways to calculate the percentile for a data set. The method described here matches the method used by Excel, but other software packages may have slightly different ways of calculating percentiles.

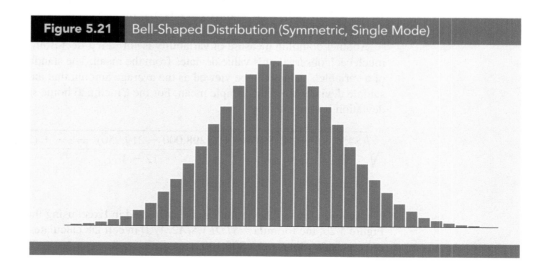

Figure 5.21   Bell-Shaped Distribution (Symmetric, Single Mode)

Similarly, for the 50th percentile, the position is

$$\frac{50}{100} \times (12 + 1) = 6.5$$

The position of 6.5 for the 50th percentile means that it lies between 50% of the way between the value of the sixth smallest and seventh smallest values. The sixth smallest value is $199,500, and the seventh smallest value is $208,000, so we compute the value of the 50th percentile as

$$\$199,500 + (6.5 - 6) \times (\$208,000 - \$199,500) = \$203,750$$

Notice that the 50th percentile and the median have the same value. That is, 50% of the observations have values less than the median, which matches the definition of the median.

For the 75th percentile, the position is

$$\frac{75}{100} \times (12 + 1) = 9.75$$

The position of 9.75 for the 75th percentile means that it lies between 75% of the way between the value of the ninth smallest and tenth smallest values. The ninth smallest value is $254,00 and the tenth smallest value is $257,500, so we compute the value of the 75th percentile as

$$\$254,000 + (9.75 - 9) \times (\$257,500 - \$254,000) = \$256,625$$

The pth percentile can be calculated in Excel using the function PERCENTILE.EXC. In Figure 5.20, the formula $=PERCENTILE.EXC(A2:A13, 0.25)$ in cell D10 calculates the 25th percentile of home sale values to be $139,000. Similarly, the 50th percentile and 75th percentile are computed with the formulas $=PERCENTILE.EXC(A2:A13, 0.5)$ and $=PERCENTILE.EXC(A2:A13, 0.75)$ in cells D11 and D12, respectively. Finally, the interquartile range (IQR) is computed in cell D14 with the formula $=D12-D10$ to obtain a value of $117,625.

The use of percentiles and the interquartile range to measure variability has advantages over the range and standard deviation. First, extreme values do not distort the value of percentiles. Second, percentiles do not require a variable's distribution to be bell-shaped to accurately convey its variability.

Box and Whisker Charts

Box and whisker charts are also known as box plots.

A **box and whisker chart** is a graphical summary of the distribution of data. A box and whisker chart is developed from the quartiles (the 25th, 50th, and 75th percentiles) of a set of values. The following step-by-step directions illustrate how to create a box and whisker chart in Excel using the file *cincysales*.

cincysales

Step 1. Select cells A1:A13
Step 2. Click the **Insert** tab on the Ribbon
Step 3. Click the **Insert Statistic Chart** button ▥ ⌄ in the **Charts** group
When the list of statistic charts appears, select **Box and Whisker** ▯

Further editing will result in a box and whisker chart similar to Figure 5.22. For explanatory purposes, we have added labels for the parts of the box and whisker chart, but these are not necessary if the audience is familiar with the chart. As Figure 5.22 illustrates, a box is drawn with the vertical ends of the box located at the first and third quartiles. For this data, the first quartile is $139,000 and the third quartile is $256,625. This box contains the middle 50% of the data. A horizontal line is drawn in the box at the location of the median ($203,750). An "X" marks the location of the mean ($219,950).

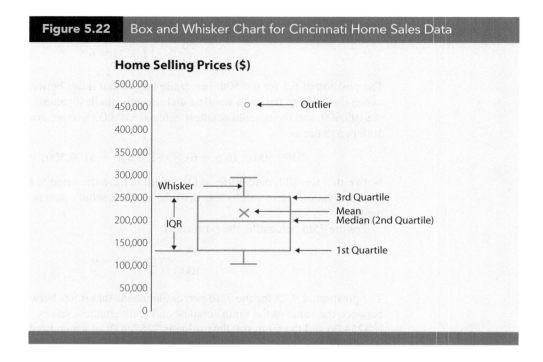

Figure 5.22   Box and Whisker Chart for Cincinnati Home Sales Data

Vertical lines, called whiskers, extend from the top and bottom sides of the box. The top whisker is drawn up to the largest value in the data that is less than or equal to (third quartile $+1.5 \times$ IQR). For this data, the top whisker extends to \$298,000, which is the largest value less than or equal to \$433,062.5 ($= \$256,625 + 1.5 \times \$117,625$).

The bottom whisker is drawn down to the smallest value in the data that is greater than or equal (first quartile $-1.5 \times$ IQR). For this data, the bottom whisker extends to \$108,000, which is the smallest value greater than or equal to $-\$37,437.5$ ($= \$139,000 - 1.5 \times \$117,625$).

There is no single accepted definition for what constitutes an outlier in a data set. Therefore, different software packages may define outliers slightly differently.

A value outside the range [first quartile $- 1.5 \times$ IQR; third quartile $+ 1.5 \times$ IQR] is considered an **outlier**. For this data, only one value (\$456,400) lies outside the range [$-\$37,437.5$; \$433,062.5]. This value is plotted in the box and whisker chart in Figure 5.22 to identify it as an outlier.

With their use of statistical measures, box and whisker charts support the detailed comparison of the distributions of multiple variables. We will use the file *salescomparison* to demonstrate the construction of box and whisker charts for multiple variables in Figure 5.23.

DATA*file*

salescomparison

Step 1. Select cells B1:F11
Step 2. Click the **Insert** tab on the Ribbon
Step 3. Click the **Insert Statistic Chart** button ▥ ∨ in the **Charts** group
           When the list of statistic charts appears, select **Box and Whisker**

Further editing will result in the visualization in Figure 5.23.

From the box and whisker charts in Figure 5.23, we can make several observations about the distributions of home selling price in these five locations. Shadyside has the highest home selling prices—the middle 50% of its price distribution is larger than all the selling prices in Groton and Hamilton (and larger than almost every selling price in Fairview). The median home selling price is nearly the same in Groton and Irving. However, Irving's houses have high variability in selling price, while Groton's houses have low variability in selling price. Irving's selling price distribution is skewed right (positively skewed) by large selling prices that extend to the largest over all five locations. Groton's houses have

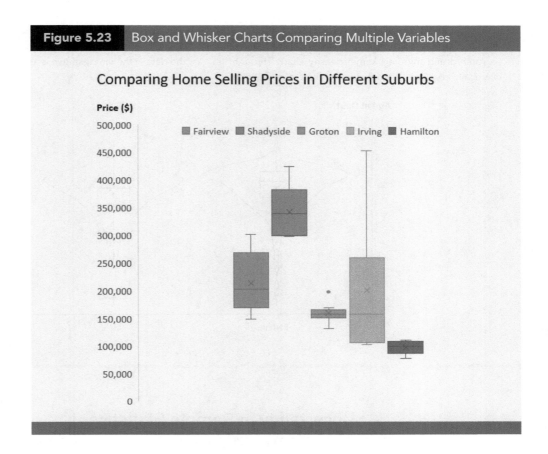

Figure 5.23   Box and Whisker Charts Comparing Multiple Variables

Comparing Home Selling Prices in Different Suburbs

relatively similar selling prices, but there is one selling price in Groton that is an outlier due to its relatively large value. The selling prices in Hamilton are generally the smallest over all five locations. Hamilton's selling price distribution demonstrates relatively little variability and is nearly symmetric around its mean and median (which are the smallest of the five locations).

Notes + Comments

1. In our discussion of statistical measures of a variable's distribution, we have implicitly assumed that we have a *sample* of values that is a subset of the *population* of values. In almost every application, it is not possible (or necessary) to collect data on the entire set of values of a variable.

2. For a set of n values, $x_1, x_2, \ldots x_n$, the formula for computing the sample mean is

$$\bar{x} = \frac{x_1 + x_2 + \cdots + x_n}{n}$$

3. For a set of n values, $x_1, x_2, \ldots x_n$, the formula for computing the sample standard deviation is

$$s = \sqrt{\frac{(x_1 - \bar{x})^2 + (x_2 - \bar{x})^2 + \cdots + (x_n - \bar{x})^2}{n - 1}}$$

4. For a set of n values ordered from smallest to largest, $x_{(1)}, x_{(2)}, \ldots x_{(n)}$, the formula for computing the location, L_p, of the pth percentile is

$$L_p = \frac{p}{100} \times (n + 1)$$

Let $\lfloor L_p \rfloor$ be the largest integer less than or equal to L_p. Let $\lceil L_p \rceil$ be the smallest integer greater than or equal to L_p. Let $x_{(\lfloor Lp \rfloor)}$ be the variable value at position $\lfloor L_p \rfloor$ when variables are ordered from smallest to largest. Let $x_{(\lceil Lp \rceil)}$ be the variable value at position $\lceil L_p \rceil$ when variables are ordered from smallest to largest. Then, the value of the pth percentile is then given by

$$p\text{th percentile} = x_{(\lfloor L_p \rfloor)} + (L_p - \lfloor L_p \rfloor) \times (x_{(\lceil L_p \rceil)} - x_{(\lfloor L_p \rfloor)})$$

5. A **violin chart** is an advanced visualization that combines the statistical descriptors of a box and whisker chart with a rotated and mirrored kernel density chart. Through its vertically displayed kernel density chart, the violin chart provides a clearer picture of the distribution shape than the box and whisker chart. As an example, the violin chart for the data in the file *deathtwo* is as follows.

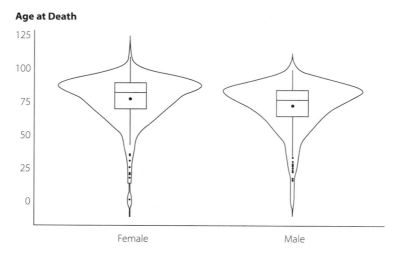

Age at Death

5.3 Uncertainty in Sample Statistics

In the first two sections of this chapter, we presented methods for visualizing the distribution of values for one or more variables. In this section, we discuss the visualization of the variability that results from statistical sampling. The process of using sample data to make estimates of or draw conclusions about one or more characteristics of a population is called **statistical inference**.

A common example of statistical inference is political polling. Consider an example in which members of a political party in Texas are considering the support of a particular candidate for election to the U.S. Senate, and party leaders want to estimate the proportion of registered voters in the state that favor the candidate. Suppose a sample of 400 registered voters in Texas is selected, and 160 of those voters indicate a preference for the candidate. Thus, an estimate of the proportion of the population of registered voters who favor the candidate is 160/400 = 0.40. However, because this sample of 400 is only a portion of the voter population of Texas, some error or deviation is to be expected between the sample proportion and the population proportion that we are estimating. That is, there is uncertainty in how close the sample proportion is to the population proportion.

Another example of statistical inference arises in market research. Consider the situation where a sample of weekly grocery bills is collected to estimate the average amount of money spent on groceries by a target population of potential customers of a grocery delivery service. Suppose a sample of 100 weekly grocery bills is selected, and the sample mean is $102.70. However, because this sample of 100 is only a portion of possible weekly grocery bills by potential customers, some error or deviation between the sample mean and the population mean that we are estimating is to be expected. That is, there is uncertainty in how close the sample mean is to the population mean.

In this section, we will discuss how to portray the uncertainty in sample-based estimates of proportions and means. Failure to appropriately convey the inherent uncertainty in these estimates may lead the audience to develop a false sense of confidence in these point estimates. We want to construct visualizations that help the audience comprehend these sample-based estimates as intervals rather than points.

Displaying a Confidence Interval on a Mean

Because the sample mean cannot be expected to provide the exact value of the population mean, a **confidence interval** is computed by adding and subtracting a value, called the **margin of error**, to the sample mean:

$$\text{sample mean} \pm \text{margin of error}$$

The purpose of a confidence interval is to provide information about how close the sample mean may be to the value of the population mean. While the derivation of the formula for the margin of error for a confidence interval on a mean is beyond the scope of this book, we note that it is dependent on three factors: (1) the sample size, (2) how variable the sample values are (as measured by the sample standard deviation), and (3) with how much confidence we want to claim that the population mean lies within the interval. As the sample size increases, the margin of error decreases. This is intuitive because as we collect more data, we should be able to better estimate the mean. As the sample standard deviation increases, the margin of error increases. This is intuitive because as the values in the data demonstrate more variation, it becomes more difficult to estimate the mean. Finally, as the required confidence level increases, the margin of error increases. If we must state an interval with more confidence, then we must be more conservative with that interval and increase its width. Common levels of confidence are 95% and 99%.

We provide an overview of the formula for computing the margin of error for a 95% confidence interval on a mean in the Notes+Comments at the end of this section.

Using the file *deathage_chart*, we demonstrate the calculations of the margin of error for a 95% confidence interval on a mean. In Figure 5.24, we compute the sample mean, the sample standard deviation, and sample size for the female and male observations in the cell range E2:F4 using the appropriate Excel functions. In cells E5 and F5, we compute the margin of error on the mean for the female and male samples, respectively, using the CONFIDENCE.T function. The CONFIDENCE.T formula requires three input arguments, =CONFIDENCE.T(*significance level, std dev, sample size*). For a 95% confidence interval, the first argument of the CONFIDENCE.T function is $1 - 0.95 = 0.05$, and is called the level of significance. The second and third arguments of the CONFIDENCE.T function are the sample standard deviation and the sample size, respectively.

The 95% confidence interval on the mean age at death for females is $76.56 \pm 1.85 = [74.71, 78.41]$. We are 95% confident that the overall female population's mean age at death is in this interval. That is, if we collected 100 different samples of 327 females and constructed confidence intervals on each of these 100 samples, we would expect 95 of the 100 confidence intervals to contain the overall female population's mean age at death.

Similarly, the 95% confidence interval on the mean age at death for males is $70.85 \pm 1.81 = [69.04, 72.66]$. We are 95% confident that the overall male population's mean age

Figure 5.24 Calculations for Confidence Interval on Mean Using the File *deathage_chart*

▲	A	B	C	D	E	F
1	Age at Death (Years)	Sex			Female	Male
2	76	Female		Sample Mean	=AVERAGE(A2:A328)	=AVERAGE(A329:A701)
3	35	Female		Sample Standard Deviation	=STDEV.S(A2:A328)	=STDEV.S(A329:A701)
4	84	Female		Sample Size	=COUNT(A2:A328)	=COUNT(A329:A701)
5	55	Female		95% C.I. Margin of Error	=CONFIDENCE.T(0.05,E3,E4)	=CONFIDENCE.T(0.05,F3,F4)
6	35	Female				

▲	A	B	C	D	E	F
1	Age at Death (Years)	Sex			Female	Male
2		76	Female	Sample Mean	76.56	70.85
3		35	Female	Sample Standard Deviation	17.04	17.75
4		84	Female	Sample Size	327.00	373.00
5		55	Female	95% C.I. Margin of Error	1.85	1.81
6		35	Female			

at death is in this interval. That is, if we collected 100 different samples of 373 males and constructed confidence intervals on each of these 100 samples, we would expect 95 of the 100 confidence intervals to contain the overall male population's mean age at death.

With the value of the margin of error computed, we can use Excel to display the confidence intervals around a sample mean. Starting with the column chart in the file *deathage_chart*, the following steps show how to visualize a confidence interval for a mean.

deathage_chart

Step 1. Click the column chart
Step 2. Click the **Chart Elements** button ⊞ and select **Error Bars**
Click the black triangle ▶ to the right of **Error Bars**, and select **More Options...**
Step 3. When the **Format Error Bars** task pane appears:
Click **Error Bar Options** ▮▮
In the **Error Amount** area, select **Custom**
Click the **Specify Value** button to the right of **Custom**
In the **Custom Error Bars** dialog box, enter =*Data!$E$5:$F$5* in both the **Positive Error Value** box and **Negative Error Value** box

Figure 5.25a displays the column chart for the mean age of death for females and males with the vertical axis starting at zero. In most cases, starting the vertical axis at zero is recommended as this prevents distortion and misleading the audience. However, as the objective of this column chart is to compare the difference (and not the absolute value of the mean ages), starting the vertical axis at a non-zero value as in Figure 5.25b facilitates this comparison. As Figure 5.25b illustrates, the sample-based estimate of the average age at death for females and males exhibits some uncertainty, but because the computed confidence intervals do not overlap for this sample, one can claim with at least 95% confidence that, on average, females live longer than males.

Displaying a Confidence Interval on a Proportion

Similar to the process of constructing a confidence interval around the sample mean, the degree of uncertainty in the sample proportion can be expressed with a confidence interval formed by adding and subtracting a margin of error. This confidence interval can be generally expressed as:

$$\text{sample proportion} \pm \text{margin of error}$$

The purpose of a confidence interval is to provide information about how close the sample proportion may be to the value of the population proportion. The calculation of the margin of error for a confidence interval on a proportion is different than the analogous calculation for a confidence interval on a mean. While the derivation of the formula for the margin of error is beyond the scope of this book, we note that it can be estimated using the sample size, the sample proportion, and the confidence with which we want to claim that the population proportion lies within the interval. A common level of confidence is 95%.

We provide an overview of the formula for computing the margin of error for a 95% confidence interval on a proportion in the Notes+Comments at the end of this section.

Using the file *incumbent*, we demonstrate the calculations of the margin of error for a 95% confidence interval on a proportion (as displayed in Figure 5.26). The file *incumbent* contains the yes or no response for 900 surveyed citizens on whether or not they support the incumbent president. In cell D2, we compute the sample size using the function COUNTA to count all the text responses in the range A2:A901. In cell D3, we compute the sample proportion as the ratio of "Yes" responses (counted with the Excel formula =*COUNTIF(A2:A901, "Yes")*) and the sample size. Cell D4 contains the formula for the margin of error for a 95% confidence interval on a proportion.

The 95% confidence interval on the proportion of citizens who support the incumbent president is $0.440 \pm 0.032 = [0.408, 0.472]$. We are 95% confident that the overall citizen population proportion of incumbent supporters is in this interval. That is, if we collected 100 different samples of 900 citizens and constructed confidence intervals on each of these 100 samples, we would expect 95 of the 100 confidence intervals to contain the overall population's proportion of incumbent supporters.

| **Figure 5.25** | Column Charts with Error Bars for Mean Age at Death: Vertical Axis Starting at 0 Versus Vertical Axis Starting at 64 |

The legends labeling the error bars in Figure 5.25 as a 95% confidence intervals were inserted manually as a text boxes.

*By right-clicking the vertical axis and selecting **Format Axis** and then **Axis Options**, we edited the minimum value of the bound on the vertical axis.*

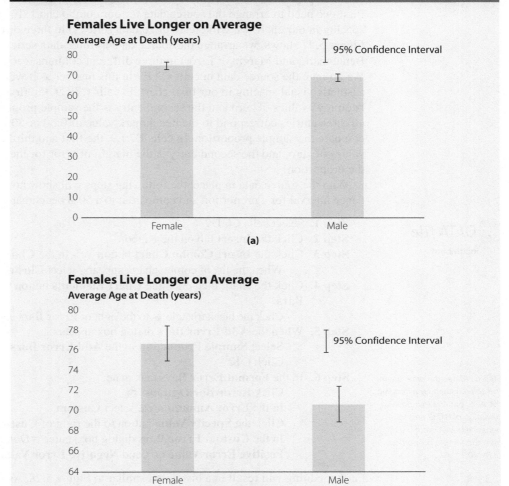

| **Figure 5.26** | Calculations for Confidence Interval on Proportion Using the File *incumbent* |

	A	B	C	D
1	Support Incumbent?			
2		Yes	Sample Size	=COUNTA(A2:A901)
3		No	Sample Proportion of "Yes"	=COUNTIF(A2:A901,"Yes")/D2
4		Yes	95% C.I. Margin of Error	=ABS(NORM.S.INV((1-0.95)/2))*SQRT((D3*(1-D3))/D2)
5		Yes		

	A	B	C	D
1	Support Incumbent?			
2		Yes	Sample Size	900
3		No	Sample Proportion of "Yes"	0.440
4		Yes	95% C.I. Margin of Error	0.032
5		Yes		

To create a visualization that accounts for the margin of error in the sample of 900 to illustrate whether we are 95% confident that less than 50% of citizens support the incumbent president, we will employ the calculations in Figure 5.26 within a combo chart. First, we need to arrange the source data for our combo chart. To create aesthetic visual spacing in our chart, we will create three data series () in three different columns. As Figure 5.27 shows, we arrange the source data as three data series (Sample Proportion, Benchmark, and Margin of Error) in three different columns, each with three entries. We arrange the source data in cells C7:E9 in this manner as it will allow us to create an aesthetic visual spacing in our final chart. In cells C7:C9, the first and third entries are "dummy" values of zero and the second entry is the sample proportion. In cells D7:D9, all three entries correspond to the benchmark value of 0.50 or 50% to which we want to compare the sample proportion. In cells E7:E9, the first and third entries are "dummy" values of zero, and the second entry is the margin of error for the confidence interval on the proportion.

With the source data in place, the following steps will show how to visualize a confidence interval for a proportion and compare it to a 50% benchmark.

DATA*file*

incumbent

Step 1. Select cells C6:D9
Step 2. Click the **Insert** tab on the Ribbon
Step 3. Click the **Insert Combo Chart** button 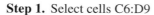 ˅ in the **Charts** group
    When the list of combo charts appears, select **Clustered Column - Line**
Step 4. Click the chart, then click the **Chart Elements** button ＋, and select **Error Bars**
    Click the black triangle ▶ to the right of **Error Bars** and select **More Options**
Step 5. When the **Add Error Bars** dialog box appears:
    Select **Sample Proportion** in the **Add Error Bars based on Series:** box
    Click **OK**

Step 6 creates the error bar for the column chart by extending the error bar line to a positive deviation of 0.032 and to a negative deviation of 0.032 from the sample proportion of 0.440.

Step 6. In the **Format Error Bars** task pane:
    Click **Error Bar Options** ▐▮
    In the **Error Amount** area, select **Custom**
    Click the **Specify Value** button to the right of **Custom**
    In the **Custom Error Bars** dialog box, enter =*Data!$E$7:$E$9* in both the **Positive Error Value** box and **Negative Error Value** box

Further editing will result in a histogram similar to Figure 5.28. As Figure 5.28 shows, the 95% confidence interval on the proportion does not contain 0.50. Therefore, even accounting for the margin of error in the sample proportion, we are 95% confident that less than 50% of citizens support the incumbent president.

| **Figure 5.27** | Arranging Source Data for Chart Comparing Sample Proportion to a Benchmark |

	A	B	C	D	E
1	Support Incumbent?				
2		Yes	Sample Size	900	
3		No	Sample Proportion of "Yes"	0.440	
4		Yes	95% C.I. Margin of Error	0.032	
5		Yes			
6		No	Sample Proportion	Benchmark	Margin of Error
7		No	0.000	0.500	0.000
8		No	0.440	0.500	0.032
9		Yes	0.000	0.500	0.000

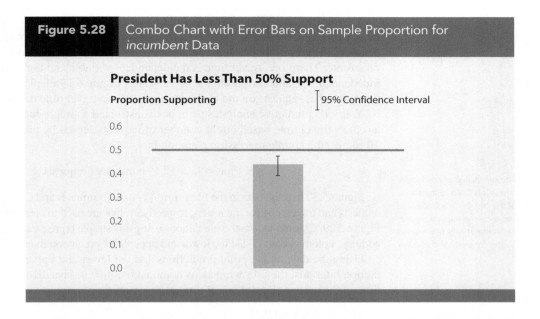

Figure 5.28   Combo Chart with Error Bars on Sample Proportion for *incumbent* Data

Notes + Comments

1. For a set of n values where $\bar{x}$ is the sample mean and s is the sample standard deviation, the formula for computing a 95% confidence interval on the mean is approximately:

$$\bar{x} \pm 1.96\frac{s}{\sqrt{n}}$$

2. For a set of n values where $\bar{p}$ is the sample proportion, the formula for computing a 95% confidence interval on the proportion is approximately:

$$\bar{p} \pm 1.96\frac{\sqrt{\bar{p}(1-\bar{p})}}{\sqrt{n}}$$

3. Determining whether a statistically significant difference between two means exists by checking for overlap is not as precise as computing a single confidence interval on the difference between the means. However, comparing the confidence intervals on the respective means is visually appealing and will not result in stating a claim that is not true at the specified level of confidence.

5.4 Uncertainty in Predictive Models

Predictive analytics consists of techniques that use models constructed from past data to predict the value of future observations. For example, past data on product sales may be used to construct a mathematical model to predict future sales. This model can factor in the product's growth trajectory and seasonality based on past patterns.

In this section, we consider predictive models that provide point estimates of future observations. Similar to the sample-based estimates of statistical inference discussed in Section 5.3, it is unrealistic to expect that these predicted point estimates have no error. That is, there is uncertainty in how close a predicted point estimate will be to the corresponding future observation.

The uncertainty in a model's predicted values of future observations can be expressed using a **prediction interval**. A prediction interval for a future observation is conceptually similar to a confidence interval on a population mean or proportion but is computed using a different formula. In this section, we consider the visualization of prediction intervals for two different types of predictive models: simple linear regression and time series models.

Illustrating Prediction Intervals for a Simple Linear Regression Model

Simple linear regression approximates the relationship between two variables with a straight line. The variable being predicted is called the **dependent variable** (y). The dependent variable is plotted on the vertical axis. The variable being used to predict or explain the dependent variable is called the **independent variable** (x). The independent variable is plotted on the horizontal axis.

The dependent variable is also sometimes referred to as the response or target variable.

Yourier LLC is a home delivery service that picks up items from stores and delivers them to customers. To assess the effectiveness of its process of routing customer requests, Yourier is interested in predicting the travel time of a route based on the number of requests on a route. Therefore, travel time is the dependent variable and the number of requests is the independent variable. For a sample of 10 routes, Figure 5.29 displays a scatter chart with the number of requests on the horizontal axis (x) and travel time on the vertical axis (y).

Yourier's predictive analytics team has constructed a simple regression model to predict a route's travel time based on the number of requests served by the route. Based on these 10 routes, the simple regression equation is

$$\text{travel time} = 0.2852 \times \text{number of requests} + 1.356$$

The calculation of prediction intervals is beyond the scope of this book. Many dedicated statistical software packages will automatically provide this output for prediction models.

Figure 5.30 lists the data in the file *yourier_chart*. Columns B and C contain the number of requests and travel time for the routes, respectively, that are used to create the scatter chart in Figure 5.29. Column D lists the predictions using this simple regression equation for the routes. In addition, columns E and F list the lower and upper 95% prediction interval limits for the routes.

Using the data on the point predictions and the lower and upper limits of the 95% prediction intervals, the following steps demonstrate how to visualize this prediction information on the scatter chart of travel time versus number of requests.

CHART *file*

yourier_chart

Step 1. Right click the chart and select **Select Data…**
Step 2. When **Select Data Source** dialog box appears, click the **Add** button ⊞ Add
Step 3. In the **Edit Series** dialog box:
          Enter =*Data!$D$1* in the box under **Series name:**
          Enter =*Data!$B$2:$B$13* in the box under **Series X values:**
          Enter =*Data!$D$2:$D$13* in the box under **Series Y values:**
          Click **OK**
Step 4. In the **Select Data Source** dialog box, click the **Add** button ⊞ Add
Step 5. In the **Edit Series** dialog box:
          Enter =*Data!$E$1* in the box under **Series name:**
          Enter =*Data!$B$2:$B$13* in the box under **Series X values:**
          Enter =*Data!$E$2:$E$13* in the box under **Series Y values:**
          Click **OK**

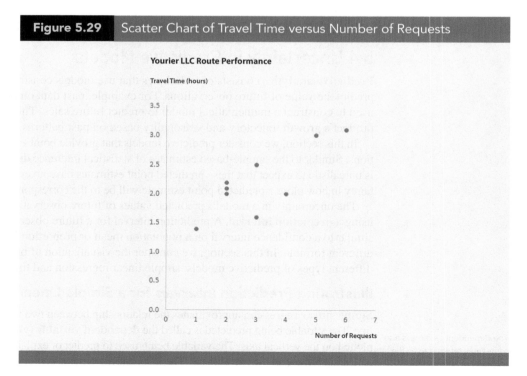

Figure 5.29   Scatter Chart of Travel Time versus Number of Requests

Figure 5.30	Simple Regression Predictions and 95% Prediction Interval Limits for Yourier Data

▲	A	B	C	D	E	F
1	Route	Requests	Travel Time	Prediction	Lower 95% P.I.	Upper 95% P.I.
2		0		1.356	0.336	2.376
3	1	1	1.4	1.641	0.706	2.577
4	2	2	2.2	1.926	1.047	2.806
5	3	2	2.1	1.926	1.047	2.806
6	4	2	2	1.926	1.047	2.806
7	5	3	1.6	2.211	1.354	3.069
8	6	3	2.5	2.211	1.354	3.069
9	7	3	2.5	2.211	1.354	3.069
10	8	4	2	2.497	1.625	3.369
11	9	5	3	2.782	1.860	3.704
12	10	6	3.1	3.067	2.065	4.069
13		7		3.352	2.247	4.457

Step 6. In the **Select Data Source** dialog box, click the **Add** button ⊞ Add

Step 7. In the **Edit Series** dialog box:

Enter *=Data!$F$1* in the box under **Series name:**

Enter *=Data!$B$2:$B$13* in the box under **Series X values:**

Enter *=Data!$F$2:$F$13* in the box under **Series Y values:**

Click **OK**

Click **OK** to close **Select Data Source** dialog box

At this stage, the visualization consists of four series of data plotted as scatter charts as in Figure 5.31.

Figure 5.31	Scatter Chart Display of Observations, Predictions, and Prediction Interval Limits

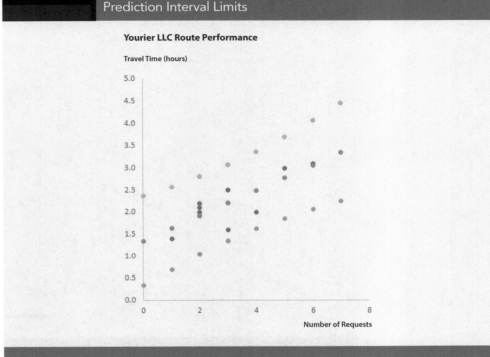

The next steps modify the visualization to display the point predictions and prediction interval limits with lines rather than points.

Step 8. Click a data series corresponding to either the point predictions or the prediction interval limits. With this data series selected, right click, and then select **Change Series Chart Type…** from the menu

Step 9. When the **Change Chart Type** dialog box appears, click **XY Scatter** ⁝⁚ XY (Scatter)
Select **Scatter with Smooth Lines** on the **All Charts** tab
Click **OK**

Make sure that only the blue line is selected.

Step 10. Click the blue line representing the observed travel times. Right click this line and select **Format Data Series…**

Step 11. In the **Format Data Series** task pane, click the **Fill & Line icon** 🖋
Click **Line** and select **No Line**
Click **Marker,** and under **Marker Options,** select **Automatic**

Step 12. Select the chart, click the **Chart Elements** button ➕, and select **Legend**
Click the black triangle ▶ to the right of **Legend** and select **Top**

Further editing will result in a chart similar to Figure 5.32. We use color to differentiate between the past observations (blue data points), point estimates from the regression model (solid orange line), and the limits of the prediction intervals (dashed orange lines).

The 95% prediction interval corresponds to the range that we are 95% confident will contain the value of the independent variable in a future observation with a specified value of the dependent variable. For instance, for a future route servicing three requests, the simple regression model predicts a travel time of 2.211 hours and is 95% confident that the route's travel time will be between 1.354 hours and 3.069 hours (a width of 1.715 hours).

Now consider a future route servicing six requests. The simple regression model predicts a travel time of 3.067 hours and is 95% confident that the route's travel time will be between 2.065 hours and 4.069 hours (a width of 2.004 hours). Intuitively, the simple regression model predicts that a route with more requests will require more travel time. In addition, notice that the simple regression model is more confident in its travel time predictions for routes with three requests than for routes with six requests. We can observe this in Figure 5.32 by noting that the dotted lines corresponding to the prediction interval limits are not straight lines.

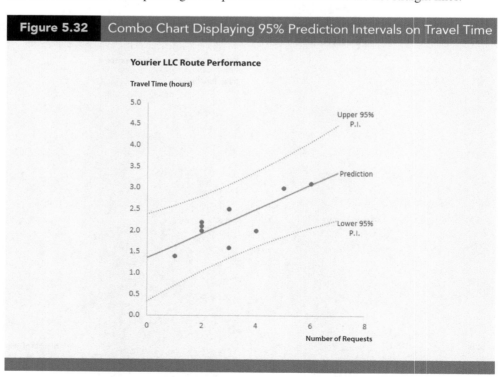

Figure 5.32 Combo Chart Displaying 95% Prediction Intervals on Travel Time

Instead, these lines are slightly curved to depict that the width of the prediction interval is the narrowest near the mean value of the number of requests. That is, the width of the prediction interval depends on the value of the independent variable for the observation being predicted.

Illustrating Prediction Intervals for a Time Series Model

Time series data is a sequence of observations on a variable measured at successive points in time. The measurements may be taken every hour, day, week, month, year, or at any other regular interval. To display a time series chart, a special type of line chart called a **time series chart** is typically used. In a time series chart, the time unit is represented on the horizontal axis and the values of the variable are shown on the vertical axis. Connecting the consecutive observations with line segments in a time series chart accentuates the temporal nature of the data and the inherent relationship between consecutive time periods.

Bundaberg Brewed Drinks is a company that makes craft brewed sodas. Premium Australian root beer is an integral part of its product portfolio, and Bundaberg is interested in forecasting its sales in future quarters. Figure 5.33 displays a time series chart of Bundaberg's sales of root beer measured over the past 17 quarters. From this time series chart, the seasonal nature of root beer sales is evident. Sales peak in quarters 3, 7, 11, and 15, while sales are lowest in quarters 1, 5, 9, 13, and 17. That is, the seasonal pattern for root beer sales repeats itself every fourth quarter. In addition, the time series chart suggests that there is no meaningful trend in root beer sales. That is, apart from seasonal variation, quarterly sales do not appear to exhibit any upward or downward change. This can be seen by comparing the sales from every fourth quarter and observing that there is no upward or downward pattern.

Bundaberg's forecasting team has constructed a time series model that accounts for the seasonality to predict root beer sales over the next eight quarters. Figure 5.34 lists the data in the file *bundaberg_chart*. Column C contains the point estimates for root beer sales for the next eight quarters. Columns D and E list the lower and upper 95% prediction interval limits for these eight predictions.

Using the data on the point predictions (in column C) and the lower and upper limits of the 95% prediction intervals (in columns D and E), the following steps demonstrate how to visualize this prediction information on the time series chart of quarterly root beer sales.

The calculation of predictions and prediction intervals from time series models is beyond the scope of this book. Many dedicated statistical software packages will automatically provide this output for prediction models.

bundaberg_chart

In step 1, we set the prediction for quarter 17 to be the same as the actual sales in order to create a connected line between the actual sales and the forecasted sales.

Step 1. In cell C18, enter =*B18*

Step 2. Right click the chart and select **Select Data...**

Step 3. When the **Select Data Source** dialog box appears, click the **Add** button

Step 4. In the **Edit Series** dialog box:

Enter =*Data!$C$1* in the box under **Series name:**

Enter =*Data!$C$2:$C$26* in the box under **Series values:**

Click **OK**

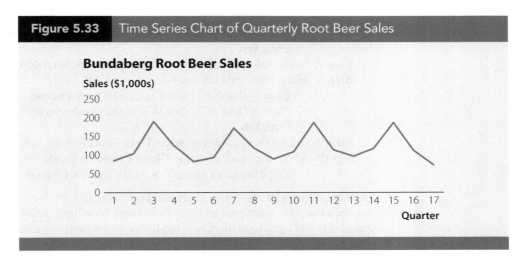

Figure 5.33   Time Series Chart of Quarterly Root Beer Sales

Figure 5.34	Time Series Data and Predictions for Quarterly Root Beer Sales

	A	B	C	D	E
1	Quarter	Sales	Prediction	Lower 95% P.I.	Upper 95% P.I.
2	1	86			
3	2	105			
4	3	191			
5	4	127			
6	5	83			
7	6	94			
8	7	173			
9	8	120			
10	9	90			
11	10	110			
12	11	188			
13	12	115			
14	13	98			
15	14	119			
16	15	188			
17	16	114			
18	17	74			
19	18		119.0	81.1	156.9
20	19		188.0	150.1	225.9
21	20		114.0	76.1	151.9
22	21		74.0	36.1	111.9
23	22		119.0	65.4	172.6
24	23		188.0	134.4	241.6
25	24		114.0	60.4	167.6
26	25		74.0	20.4	127.6

Step 5. In the **Select Data Source** dialog box, click the **Add** button ⊞ Add

Step 6. In the **Edit Series** dialog box:

Enter =*Data!$D$1* in the box under **Series name:**

Enter =*Data!$D$2:$D$26* in the box under **Series values:**

Click **OK**

Step 7. In the **Select Data Source** dialog box, click the **Add** button ⊞ Add

Step 8. In the **Edit Series** dialog box:

Enter =*Data!$E$1* in the box under **Series name:**

Enter =*Data!$E$2:$E$26* in the box under **Series values:**

Click **OK**

Step 9. Click **OK** to close the **Select Data Source** dialog box

Step 10. Select the chart, click the **Chart Elements** button ⊞, and select **Legend**

Click the black triangle ▶ to the right of **Legend**, and select **Top**

Further editing will result in a chart similar to Figure 5.35. We use color to differentiate between the sales from past quarters (solid dark blue line), point estimates for future quarters (solid light blue line), and the limits of the prediction intervals (dashed light blue lines).

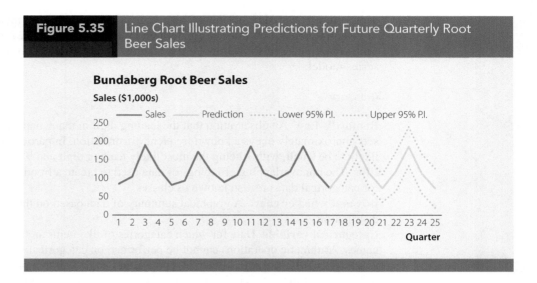

Figure 5.35 Line Chart Illustrating Predictions for Future Quarterly Root Beer Sales

As Figure 5.35 illustrates, the predictions for root beer sales in the next eight quarters reflect the seasonal nature of this product. In general, a 95% prediction interval corresponds to the range that we are 95% confident will contain the time series variable value for the specified future time period. For instance, the time series model predicts root beer sales of $119,000 in quarter 18 and is 95% confident that sales will be between $81,100 and $156,900 (a width of $75,800).

Now consider the forecast for quarter 22. As quarter 22 is in the same season as quarter 18 and past sales do not exhibit any upward or downward trend, the time series model again predicts root beer sales to be $119,000 (same as its prediction for quarter 18). However, the 95% prediction interval on quarter 22 sales is $20,400 to $127,600 (a width of $107,200), which is wider than the prediction interval for quarter 18. To maintain a level of 95% confidence, the time series model must quote a wider prediction interval as it makes predictions further into the future. That is, the width of the prediction interval for a time series model depends on how far into the future the prediction is. This is reflected by the growing distance between the lower and upper limits of the 95% prediction interval in Figure 5.35 for predictions further in the future.

Summary

In this chapter, we have discussed how to visualize the variation in the values of a variable of interest. We introduced the notion of a frequency distribution as measured by counts and relative (percent) frequency. Then, we showed how to use Excel to visualize a frequency distribution for a categorical variable.

We introduced several ways to visualize a frequency distribution for a quantitative variable. We demonstrated how to use the columnar display of histograms to analyze the shape of a distribution and defined the measure of skewness to formally describe distribution shape. As an alternative to a histogram, we explained how to use a line chart to create a frequency polygon to illustrate the shape of variable's distribution. For small data sets, we introduced strip charts and how to use hollow dots and jittering to avoid occlusion.

We defined formal statistical measures of central location such as the mean, median, and mode. Then, we defined formal statistical measures of variability such as the range, standard deviation, and interquartile range. We showed how to construct a box and whisker chart and interpret the statistical measures utilized by this chart.

In the final two sections, we discuss how to convey the uncertainty that arises in statistical inference and predictive analytics. Specifically, we describe how to use error bars to portray the margin of error in sample-based estimates of a mean or a proportion. For predictions based on a simple linear regression model, we explain how to visualize prediction intervals generated by this causal model. Finally, we consider time series data and show how to display prediction intervals on forecasts from a time series model.

Glossary

Benford's Law An observation that the leading digit in many naturally occurring data sets approximately obeys a known frequency distribution. In particular, the leading digit is likely to be small, with 1 being the most likely leading digit and 9 the least likely.

Bins The nonoverlapping groupings of data used to create a frequency distribution. Bins for categorical data are also known as classes.

Box and whisker chart A graphical summary of data based on the quartiles of a distribution.

Categorical variable Data for which categories of like items are identified by labels or names. Arithmetic operations cannot be performed on categorical variables.

Confidence interval An estimate of a population parameter that provides an interval of the form point estimate ± margin of error, believed to contain the value of the parameter with a specified confidence. For example, if an interval estimation procedure provides intervals such that 95% of the intervals formed using the procedure will include the population parameter, the interval estimate is said to be constructed at the 95% confidence level.

Dependent variable The variable that is being predicted or explained. It is generally plotted on the vertical axis. Also sometimes referred to as the response variable or target variable.

Frequency distribution A summary of data that shows the number (frequency) of observations in each of several nonoverlapping bins (classes).

Frequency polygon A chart used to display a distribution by using lines to connect the frequency values of each bin.

Histogram A columnar presentation of a frequency distribution, relative frequency distribution, or percent frequency distribution of quantitative data constructed by placing the bin intervals on the horizontal axis and the frequencies, relative frequencies, or percent frequencies on the vertical axis.

Independent variable The variable used for predicting the values of the dependent variable. It is generally plotted on the horizontal axis.

Interquartile range The difference between the third and first quartiles.

Jittering The process of slightly altering the actual values of one or more variables in the observations of a data set so identical observations occupy slightly different positions when plotted.

Kernel density chart A chart for visualizing the distribution that smooths the bin frequency values of a histogram representation by using kernel density estimation.

Margin of error The value added to and subtracted from a point estimate to develop a confidence interval for a population parameter.

Mean A measure of central location computed by summing the data values and dividing by the number of observations.

Median A measure of central location provided by the value in the middle when the data are arranged in ascending order. The median is the 50th percentile.

Mode A measure of central location defined as the value (or range of values) that occurs with the greatest frequency.

Occlusion The inability to distinguish some individual data points because they are hidden behind others with the same or nearly the same value.

Outlier An unusually small or unusually large data value.

Percent frequency A frequency measure in a distribution analysis that computes the percentage of observations in each of several nonoverlapping bins (classes).

Percentile A value such that approximately $p\%$ of the observations have values less than the pth percentile; hence, approximately $(100 - p)\%$ of the observations have values greater than the pth percentile.

Population The set of all elements of interest in a particular study.

Power law An observation that in some data, the relative change in one variable results in a proportional relative change in another variable.

Prediction interval An interval estimate of the prediction of a future value of the dependent variable such that there is a specified confidence that this interval will contain the future value of the dependent variable.

Predictive analytics Techniques that use models constructed from past data to predict the future or to ascertain the impact of one variable on another.

Probability distribution A description of the range and relative likelihood of possible values of a random variable.

Quantitative variable Data for which numerical values are used to indicate magnitude, such as how many or how much. Arithmetic operations such as addition, subtraction, and multiplication can be performed on a quantitative variable.

Quartile The 25th, 50th, and 75th percentiles, referred to as the first quartile, second quartile, and third quartile, respectively. The quartiles can be used to divide a set of data values into four parts, with each part containing approximately 25% of the values.

Random variable A quantity whose values are not known with certainty.

Range A measure of variability defined to be the largest value minus the smallest value.

Relative frequency A frequency measure in a distribution analysis that computes the fraction or proportion of observations in each of several nonoverlapping bins (classes).

Sample A subset of the population.

Simple linear regression A statistical procedure predicting the value of one dependent variable with the value of one independent variable through a linear equation.

Skewness A measure of the lack of symmetry in a distribution.

Standard deviation A measure of variability that captures how much a set of values deviates from the mean.

Statistical inference The process of making estimates and drawing conclusions about one or more characteristics of a population (the value of one or more parameters) through the analysis of sample data drawn from the population.

Strip chart A chart consisting of sorted variable values along either the horizontal or vertical axis.

Time series chart A chart where a measure of time is represented on the horizontal axis and a variable of interest is shown on the vertical axis. Temporally consecutive data points are generally connected with straight lines.

Time series data Data that are collected at intervals over time.

Trellis display A vertical or horizontal arrangement of individual charts of the same type, size, scale, and formatting that differ only by the data they display.

Variation Differences in values of a variable over observations.

Violin chart A graphical method that encases the elements of a box and whisker chart inside a rotated and mirrored kernel density chart.

Problems

Conceptual

1. **Histogram Bin Widths for Boating Customers.** Based on a survey of 1,046 individuals who recently took a boat cruise on Lake Havasu, Rochambeau Boating is analyzing the percent frequency distribution of its customers' ages. An analyst has created four histograms by varying the bin size. Rochambeau seeks a visualization of the customer age distribution that captures general trends in the data but does not blur patterns by grouping customers with disparate ages (and therefore behaviors) into the same bins.

Which histogram would you recommend that the analyst use to describe the customer age distribution? **LO 2**

i.

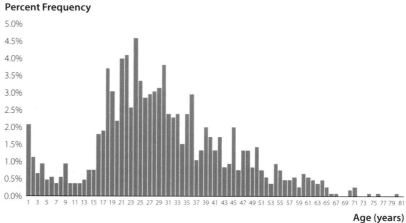

ii.

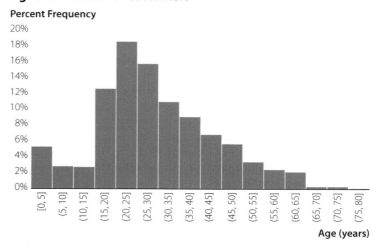

iii.

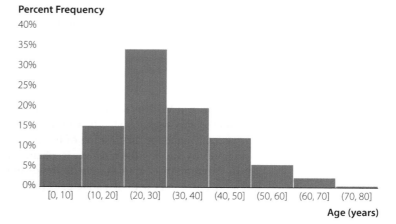

iv.

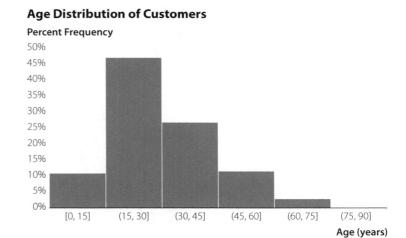

Age Distribution of Customers

Percent Frequency

2. **Stacked Column Chart for Boating Customers.** Based on a survey of 1,046 individuals who recently took a boat cruise on Lake Havasu, Rochambeau Boating is analyzing the demographics of its customers. It is believed that the sample (388 females and 658 males) is representative of Rochambeau's overall customer population. An analyst has created the following chart depicting the age and sex distribution of the survey respondents. **LO 3**

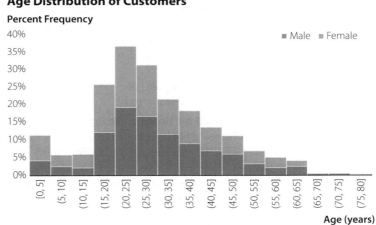

Age Distribution of Customers

Percent Frequency

Which of the following statements accurately assess this stacked column chart? (Select all that apply.)
   i. The use of color is unnecessary and distracting.
   ii. The stacked orientation makes it difficult to compare the shape of the age distributions of male and female customers.
   iii. A strength of this chart is how the stacked orientation visualizes the overall age distribution and how the number of customers in each age bin are split into male and female categories.
   iv. It would be better to orient this chart vertically as a stacked bar chart.

3. **Clustered Column Chart for Boating Customers.** Based on a survey of 1,046 individuals who recently took a boat cruise on Lake Havasu, Rochambeau Boating is analyzing the demographics of its customers. It is believed that the sample (388 females and 658 males) is representative of Rochambeau's overall customer

population. An analyst has created the following chart depicting the age and sex distribution of the survey respondents. **LO 2, 3**

Age Distribution of Customers

a. Which of the following statements accurately criticizes this clustered column chart?
   i. There are too few bins.
   ii. The alternating male and female frequency columns cast a disrupted visualization of the distributions.
   iii. The use of color is unnecessary and distracting.
   iv. A stacked column chart would compare females and males better.
b. Which of the following is a better way to visualize these data to facilitate the comparison of the age distributions of female and male customers?
   i. Stacked column chart
   ii. Strip chart
   iii. Frequency polygon
   iv. Stem and leaf chart

4. **Age Pyramid for Boating Customers.** Based on a survey of 1,046 individuals who recently took a boat cruise on Lake Havasu, Rochambeau Boating is analyzing the demographics of its customers. Treating the sample of 388 females and 658 males separately, an analyst is interested in comparing how the ages of the female customers are distributed as a percentage of the 388 females surveyed and how the ages of the male customers are distributed as a percentage of the 658 males surveyed. An analyst has created the following chart depicting the age and sex distribution of the survey respondents. **LO 3**

Age Distribution of Customers

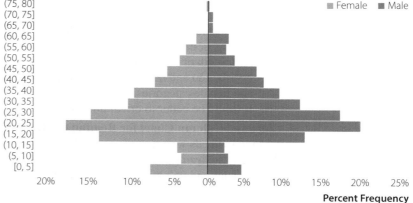

a. Which of the following statements accurately criticizes this chart?
   i. Orienting the frequency bars for females and males end-to-end makes it harder to visually compare their magnitudes.
   ii. There are too many bins.
   iii. The use of color is unnecessary and distracting.
   iv. Rotating the chart by 90 degrees would allow for better binwise comparison of females and males.
b. Which of the following is a better way to visualize these data to facilitate the comparison of the age distributions of female and male customers?
   i. Clustered column chart
   ii. Strip chart
   iii. Violin chart
   iv. Frequency polygon

5. **Distribution Deviation Chart for Boating Customers.** Based on a survey of 1,046 individuals who recently took a boat cruise on Lake Havasu, Rochambeau Boating is analyzing the demographics of its customers. Treating the sample of 388 females and 658 males separately, an analyst is interested in comparing how the ages of the female customers are distributed as a percentage of the 388 females surveyed and how the ages of the male customers are distributed as a percentage of the 658 males surveyed. An analyst has created the following chart computing the difference in these percentages for each age bin. **LO 3**

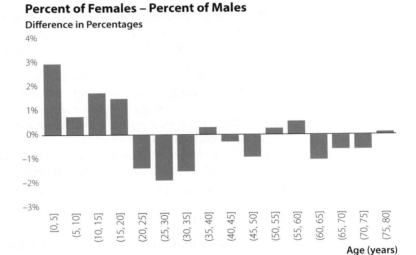

Percent of Females – Percent of Males
Difference in Percentages

a. Which of the following statements accurately criticizes this chart?
   i. There are too few bins.
   ii. There are too many bins.
   iii. The chart needs to use color differentiation.
   iv. This chart provides no insight on the shape of the age distributions for female and male customers, and the differences computed are highly dependent on the bins used.
b. Which of the following is a better way to visualize these data to facilitate the comparison of the age distributions of female and male customers?
   i. Kernel density chart
   ii. Clustered column chart
   iii. Frequency polygon
   iv. Strip chart

6. **Daily Temperature Strip Charts.** Aspiring meteorologist Jesse Kosch has collected data on the daily high temperature in Valentine, Nebraska, over an entire year. Jesse then used a strip chart to display each day's high temperature by month. **LO 4**

a. Which of the following statements accurately criticizes this chart?
   i. It is not clear what each data point represents.
   ii. The chart suffers from occlusion as there is not a distinct data point for each day in each month.
   iii. A line chart would better display this data.
   iv. The chart needs to use color differentiation.
b. How could Jesse best improve this visualization?
   i. Differentiate each month with a different color
   ii. Jitter each data point vertically
   iii. Change horizontal axis to day of year and plot as time series chart
   iv. Use hollow dots instead of solid dots and horizontally jitter each data point

7. **Histogram for Assessed Home Values.** Chris Fultz, a realtor at Betelgeuse Realty, is conducting research on assessed home values in a local suburb. Chris has constructed the following histogram. **LO 2, 5, 6**

Distribution of Assessed Home Values

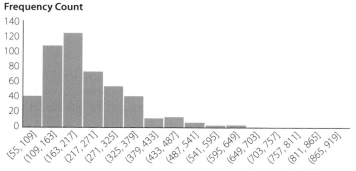

Which box and whisker chart corresponds to the histogram?

i.

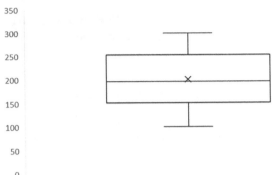

ii.

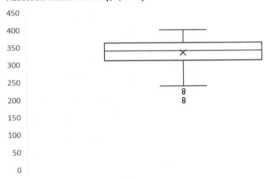

iii.

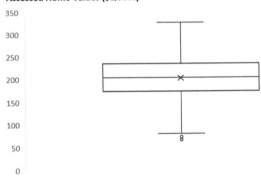

iv.

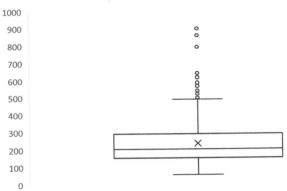

8. **Frequency Polygon for Assessed Home Values.** Abbie Aburizek, a realtor at Alamo Acres, is conducting research on assessed home values in a local suburb. Abbie has constructed the following frequency polygon. **LO 2, 5, 6**

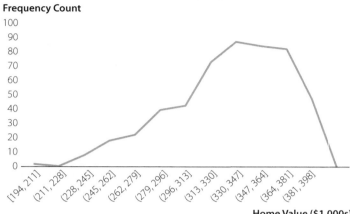

Which box and whisker chart corresponds to the frequency polygon?

i.

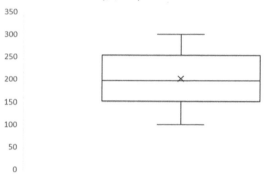

ii.

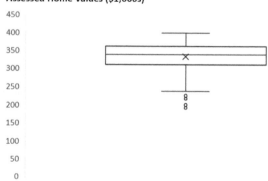

iii.

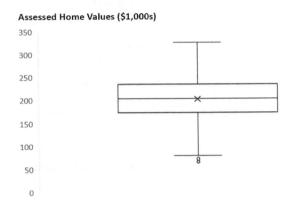

iv.

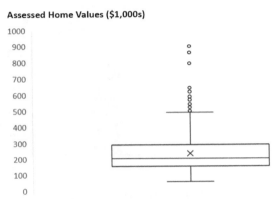

9. **Life Insurance Analysis.** Josh Bell, an actuarial scientist for Yolo Life Insurance, has created the following box and whisker charts of the age at death for a randomly drawn sample representative of potential clients. **LO 6**

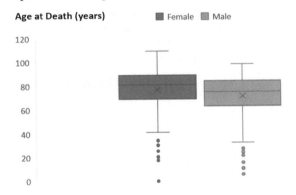

Which of the following assessments are true?
   i. The distributions are positively skewed; females live longer on average.
   ii. The distributions are negatively skewed with several outliers of extremely small values; females live longer on average.
   iii. The distributions are symmetric; the mean and median values are the same.
   iv. There are no outliers in either sample; both the female and male distributions have the same shape.

10. **Restaurant Delivery Times.** A foodie blog has gathered data on the delivery times for four various restaurant delivery services (CHOMP, Uber Eats, DoorDash, GrubHub). Blog editor Auguste Gusteau has been analyzing the distribution of delivery times for each of these delivery companies and is contemplating how to visually compare the four delivery time distributions. Which of the following would you recommend? **LO 3**

   i. Plotting all four delivery time distributions on a clustered column chart.
   ii. Using a trellis display arranging the four frequency polygons vertically.
   iii. Using a collection of six charts each displaying a different pair of delivery time distributions with frequency polygons.
   iv. Plotting all four delivery time distributions with frequency polygons.

11. **Call Center Response Times.** Skylar Diggins is reviewing the performance of four call centers under her management. Twelve observations of the amount of time it took to process refund requests have been collected from each of the four call centers. Based on these observations, the following column chart displays the average service time of each call center. **LO 7**

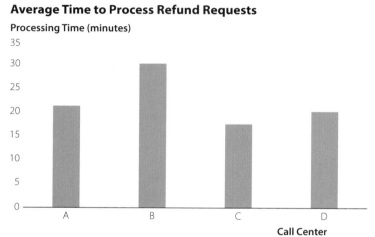

Average Time to Process Refund Requests

Processing Time (minutes)

Call Center

  a. Why may the interpretation of the average service time from this column chart be misleading?
  b. How can this chart be improved to provide a more accurate comparison of the average service times at the call centers?

12. **Vision Insurance.** Before including vision insurance in the benefits package for its 10,000 employees, Valmont Industries wants to confirm that it is desired by a majority of employees. Valmont has taken an employee survey and out of the 100 survey respondents, 55 employees said they would opt into the coverage. An analyst has displayed the results in the following column chart. **LO 7**

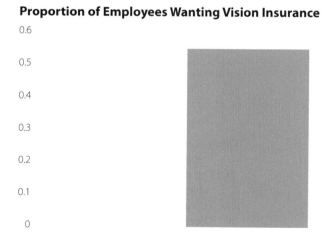

Proportion of Employees Wanting Vision Insurance

  a. Why may the results of the sample proportion in this chart be misleading in terms of interpreting the proportion of all 10,000 employees who want vision insurance?
  b. How can this chart be changed to convey the survey results more accurately?

13. **Restaurant Franchising.** A restaurant chain particularly popular with college students has collected data on the relationship between the quarterly sales of existing restaurants and the size of the college student population in the respective restaurant's immediate region. Janice Moore, director of franchising, has constructed a simple linear regression model using quarterly sales as the dependent variable (y) and college student population as the independent variable (x). The data and simple linear regression model are displayed in the chart below.

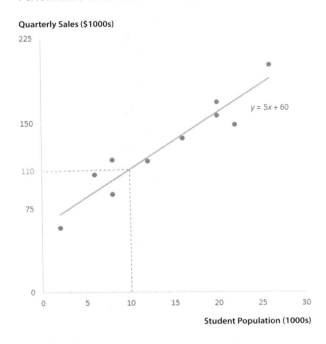

Performance of Restaurant Locations

The development team has identified a promising location for a new franchise that has 10,000 college students living nearby. Based on her simple regression model, Janice predicts that this new franchise would experience quarterly sales of $y = 5x + 60 = (5 \times 10) + 60 = 110$, or \$110,000. Janice has highlighted this prediction on her chart. **LO 8**

a. Why may the results of this chart be misleading?

b. How can this chart be changed to convey the survey results more accurately?

14. **Forecasting Stock Price.** To inform his day trading, Jorge Belfort has gathered historical stock price data on Nile Inc., a green energy company he has been researching. Jorge has constructed the following time series chart to display the stock prices as well as his forecasts of the stock price over the next few days.

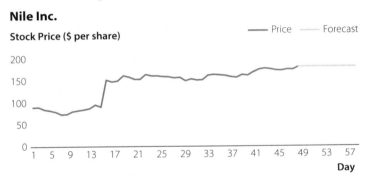

How can Jorge modify this chart to further communicate any uncertainty associated with his forecast for this stock? **LO 8**

Applications

websites

15. **Most Visited Websites.** In a recent report, the top five most-visited English-language websites were google.com (GOOG), facebook.com (FB), youtube.com (YT), yahoo.com (YAH), and wikipedia.com (WIKI). The file *websites* contains a sample of the favorite website for 50 Internet users. **LO 1**
    a. Using a column chart, visualize the frequency distribution for these data.
    b. On the basis of the sample, which website is listed most frequently as the favorite website for Internet users? Which is second?

travelexpenses

16. **Auditing Travel Expense Reports.** Courtney Boyce is currently auditing a sample of the travel expense reports submitted by company employees over the past year. **LO 1**
    a. Using the data in the file *travelexpenses*, create a percent frequency distribution of the first digit of the expense reported in each report.
    b. Assessing this distribution with Benford's Law, does Courtney have any reason to suspect reporting error or fraud? *Hint:* Treat the first digit of the expense amount as a categorical variable (text) rather than as a numerical value.

endowments

17. **University Endowments.** University endowments are financial assets that are donated by supporters to be used to provide income to universities. There is a large discrepancy in the size of university endowments. The file *endowments* provides a listing of many of the universities that have the largest endowments as reported by the National Association of College and University Business Officers. **LO 2, 5**
    a. Construct a histogram of the frequency counts.
    b. Comment on the shape of the distribution displayed by the histogram.

airports

18. **Busiest North American Airports.** Based on the total passenger traffic, the airports in the file *airports* are among the busiest in North America. **LO 2, 5**
    a. Construct a histogram of the frequency counts using a bin width of 10 with the first bin starting at a value of 30 million.
    b. What is the most common passenger traffic range based on this histogram?
    c. Describe the shape of the histogram.

xfl

19. **Television Viewership of Football Games.** Companies considering purchasing ads during televised XFL football games are interested in the viewership of games as a way of estimating the exposure their ads get. The file *xfl* contains a sample of viewership numbers for XFL games televised on Friday and Saturday nights, respectively. **LO 6**
    a. Construct box and whisker charts on the same chart that compares the viewership distribution of Friday night XFL games to the viewership distribution of Saturday night XFL games.
    b. Use the box and whisker charts to compare the two distributions.
    c. Use the box and whisker chart of the Friday night XFL games to describe this distribution.
    d. Use the box and whisker chart of the Saturday night XFL games to describe this distribution.

ceotime

20. **CEO Time in Meetings.** A study was conducted to examine how chief executive officers (CEOs) spend their work days. The file *ceotime* contains a sample of data from this study, which tracked the minutes per day various CEOs spent in meetings. **LO 4, 5**
    a. Construct a strip chart displaying the data, making sure to employ techniques to avoid occlusion.
    b. What is the median amount of time a CEO spends in meetings per day?
    c. What is the mean amount of time a CEO spends in meetings per day?
    d. What is the most common amount of time a CEO spends in meetings per day?

teachers

21. **Number of Hours Worked per Week by Teachers.** According to the National Education Association (NEA), teachers generally spend more than 40 hours each week working on instructional duties. The file *teachers* contains data on the number of hours

worked per week for a sample of high school science teachers and English teachers. **LO 4, 5**

a. Construct a strip chart comparing the number of hours worked per week for high school science teachers to the number of hours worked per week for English teachers. Be sure to employ techniques to mitigate occlusion.

b. Compute the 25th, 50th, and 75th percentiles of the data for the high school science teachers and for high school English teachers.

c. Comment on the differences in the number of hours worked per week for high school science teachers and English teachers.

DATAfile
fedtaxerrors

22. **Average Tax Payment Error.** A sample of 10,001 Federal income tax returns with errors has been collected, and the amount of payment error for each is provided in the file *fedtaxerrors*. A positive value indicates the taxpayer underpaid and a negative value indicates that the taxpayer overpaid. **LO 5, 7**

a. What is the sample mean tax payment error made on these erroneous Federal income tax payments?

b. What is the sample standard deviation in payment error amount?

c. What is the margin of error for a 95% confidence interval on the mean payment error amount?

d. Construct a column chart displaying the sample mean tax payment error with error bars depicting a 95% confidence interval.

e. Can we conclude with 95% confidence that the mean tax payment error is positive (a taxpayer underpayment)?

DATAfile
fedtaxerrors

23. **Proportion of Tax Underpayment.** A sample of 10,001 Federal income tax returns with errors has been collected, and the amount of payment error for each is provided in the file *fedtaxerrors*. A positive value indicates the taxpayer underpaid and a negative value indicates that the taxpayer overpaid. **LO 7**

a. What is the sample proportion of erroneous income tax returns that correspond to tax underpayments?

b. What is the margin of error for a 95% confidence interval on the proportion of erroneous tax returns corresponding to tax underpayments?

c. Construct a column chart displaying the sample proportion of tax underpayments with error bars depicting a 95% confidence interval. Construct the chart to explicitly compare the sample proportion and confidence interval to a 50% proportion benchmark.

d. Can we conclude with 95% confidence that more than 50% of tax payment errors correspond to tax underpayments?

DATAfile
restaurant_chart

24. **Restaurant Franchising (Revisited).** In this problem, we revisit the simple linear regression model from Problem 13 for predicting a restaurant's quarterly sales with the size of the nearby student population. The chart and associated data are contained in the file *restaurant_chart*. **LO 8**

a. Modify the chart to convey the uncertainty related to the predictions corresponding to the simple linear regression model.

b. For approximately what value of the student population is the regression model the most accurate?

DATAfile
daytrading_chart

25. **Forecasting Stock Price (Revisited).** In this problem, we revisit the chart from Problem 14 displaying historical price and forecasted price for a stock. The chart and associated data are contained in the file *daytrading_chart*. **LO 8**

a. Modify the chart to convey the uncertainty related to the forecasts of the stock prices in future days.

b. What can be said about the prediction of the stock price one day in the future versus the prediction of the stock price 10 days in the future?

Chapter 5 Appendix

Appendix 5.1 Visualizing Variability with Power BI

In this appendix, we discuss in more detail how to visualize variability with Power BI, including frequency distributions for categorical variables and box and whisker charts.

Frequency Distributions for Categorical Variables

The file *pop* contains a sample of 500 soft drink purchases including Coca-Cola, Pepsi, Diet Coke, Sprite, and Dr. Pepper. We demonstrate how to create frequency chart of these purchases.

DATA*file*

pop

Step 1. Click the **Import data from Excel** button (leftmost button).
When the **Open** dialog box appears, navigate to where the file *pop* is stored, click the file *pop*, and click **Open**

Step 2. When the **Navigator** dialog box appears, select the checkbox next to **Data**

Notice that the text "Soft Drink Purchase" is in the second row, and the column of data has the header "**Column1**". This is because all of the data are text, and Power BI cannot distinguish Soft Drink Purchase from the other data. We will need to transform the data to ensure that "Soft Drink Purchase" is treated as a column header.

Step 3. In the **Navigator** dialog box, click **Transform Data**. Note that this will send you to the **Power Query Editor** as shown in Figure P5.1

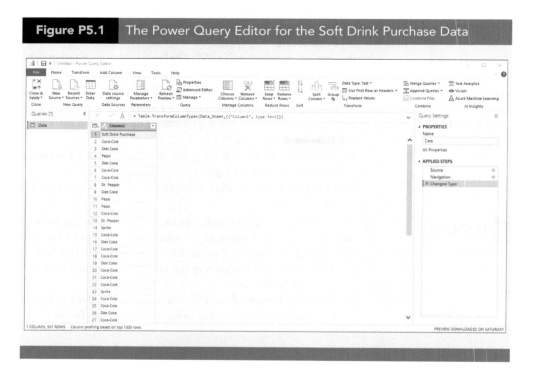

Figure P5.1 The Power Query Editor for the Soft Drink Purchase Data

Click the **Home** tab on the Ribbon, and in the **Transform** group, select **Use First Row as Headers** ▦ Use First Row as Headers ▾

On the far left, in the **Close** group, click **Close & Apply** _{Close & Apply ▾}

Completing step 3 will take you back to Power BI, and the data will now have the header "Soft Drink Purchase."

In some of the steps that follow, we give instructions to expand or collapse certain sections of Power BI. A section can be expanded by clicking on ❯ next to the section title. To collapse a section, click ﹀ next to the section title.

Step 4. Click **Report** view 📊, and in the **Visualizations** pane, click **Build visual** ▦ to display the **Build visual** matrix of available charts

Select **Table** ▦
In the **Data** pane, expand **Data** ❯ ▦ Data
Drag **Soft Drink Purchases** from the **Data** pane to the **Columns** box in the **Visualizations** pane

Next, we need to create a new measure that will give the count (frequency of purchase) for each soft drink in the data.

Step 5. Click the **Home** tab in the Ribbon In the **Calculations** group,

click **New measure** _{New measure}

Next to "Measure =" in the formula bar, type *count* and select **COUNT** from the dropdown menu
Edit the text so it reads *COUNT(Data[Soft Drink Purchase])*, and press **Enter**

Upon completion of step 5, **Measure** will appear under **Data** in the **Data** pane.

Step 6. Drag **Measure** from the **Data** pane to the **Columns** box in the **Visualizations** pane
Right click **Measure** in the **Data** pane, and select **Rename**
Type *Count*
Increase the size of the table by grabbing the bottom right corner and expanding it.

Step 7. In the **Visualizations** pane, click the **Format visual** button 🖊
Click **Visual**
Expand **Grid**, and expand **Options**
Change the **Global font size** to 16
Collapse **Options**, and collapse **Grid**

The table should now appear as shown in Figure P5.2.
We will keep this table and make a copy that we will then change to a frequency chart.

Step 8. Right click the table, select **Copy** and **Copy visual**
Click the **Home** tab in the Ribbon
In the far left **Clipboard** group, click **Paste**

The copy of the table will be placed directly over the original. Click the table and slide it to a new position. Be sure to keep the copy selected.

Figure P5.2	Table of Soft Drink Purchases with Count

Soft Drink Purchase	Count
Coca-Cola	190
Diet Coke	80
Dr. Pepper	50
Pepsi	130
Sprite	50
Total	**500**

Step 9. Click **Report** view ▦, and in the **Visualizations** pane, click **Build visual** ▤ to display the **Build visual** matrix of available charts

Click **Stacked column chart** ▥

Step 10. In the **Visualizations** pane, click the **Format visual** button ✎
To edit the horizontal axis title and values, click **Visual** in the **Visualizations** pane
Expand **X-axis**
Next to Title, toggle the **On** button (On ●) to **Off** turn off the x-axis title
Expand **Values**
Select **Calibri** as the **Font** and **14** as the font size
Collapse **Values**, and collapse **X-axis**

Step 11. In the **Visualizations** pane, expand **Y-axis**
Next to Y-axis, toggle the **On** button (On ●) to **Off**

Next to Title, toggle the **On** button (On ●) to **Off** to hide the vertical axis and the title
Collapse **Y-axis**

Step 12. In the **Visualizations** pane, scroll down to **Data labels**, and toggle the **Off** button (● Off) to **On** to turn on data labels
Expand **Data labels**
Expand **Values**
Select **Calibri** as the **Font** and **14** as the font size
Collapse **Values**, and collapse **Data labels**

Step 13. In the **Visualizations** pane, to the right of **Visuals**, click **General**
Expand **Title**
Edit the **Text** box to read *Frequency of Soft Drink Purchase*
Select **Calibri** as the **Font** and **16** as the font size.
Click **Bold** button ⌗B⌗
Collapse **Title**

The resulting table and chart appear in Figure P5.3.

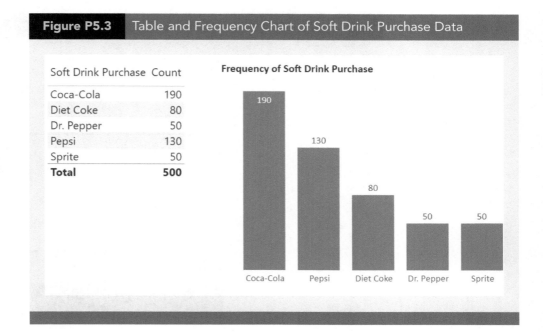

Figure P5.3   Table and Frequency Chart of Soft Drink Purchase Data

Soft Drink Purchase	Count
Coca-Cola	190
Diet Coke	80
Dr. Pepper	50
Pepsi	130
Sprite	50
Total	**500**

Frequency of Soft Drink Purchase

CHART *file*

pop_chart.pbix

Distributions for Quantitative Variables Using a Box and Whisker Plot

The file *cincysales* contains the selling price of 12 homes in Cincinnati, Ohio. We demonstrate how to create a box and whisker plot of these selling price data in Power BI.

DATA *file*

cincysales

*You may need to add the Box and Whisker by MAQ Software to the build matrix of charts. To do so, click **Build visual** in the **Visualizations** pane, and click the three dots at the bottom of the matrix. Click **Get more visuals**, and select the **Box and Whisker chart by MAQ Software** (you can search by name for the app in the **Search** box). When the **AppSource** pane appears, click the **Add** button.*

> **Step 1.** Following the steps outlined in Appendix 1.1, connect Power BI to the file *cincysales*

In some of the steps that follow, we give instructions to expand or collapse certain sections of Power BI. A section can be expanded by clicking on ❯ next to the section title. To collapse a section, click ❮ next to the section title.

> **Step 2.** Click **Report** view , and in the **Visualizations** pane, click **Build visual** to display the **Build visual** matrix of available charts.
>
> > Select **Box and Whisker by MAQ Software**
> > In the **Data** pane on the right, expand **Data** ❯ ▦ Data to display the variables
> > Drag Σ **Selling Price** from the **Data** pane to the **Value** box in the **Visualizations** pane
> > Drag Σ **Selling Price** from the **Data** pane to the **Axis** box in the **Visualizations** pane
> > Right click **Sum of Selling Price** in the **Value** box, and select **Average**
> > Increase the size of the chart by grabbing the bottom right corner and expanding it

After completing steps 1 and 2, the chart should appear as shown in Figure P5.4.

We can edit the chart in Figure P5.4 to be more descriptive. Make sure the chart is selected before proceeding with the following steps.

> **Step 3.** In the **Visualization** Pane, click **Format your visual** ✍ and click **Visual**
> > Expand **Box options**
> > Select **< 1.5 IQR** for **Whisker type**
> > Select a light blue color for **Upper box color**

Figure P5.4   Box and Whisker Plot of the Cincinnati House Sales Data

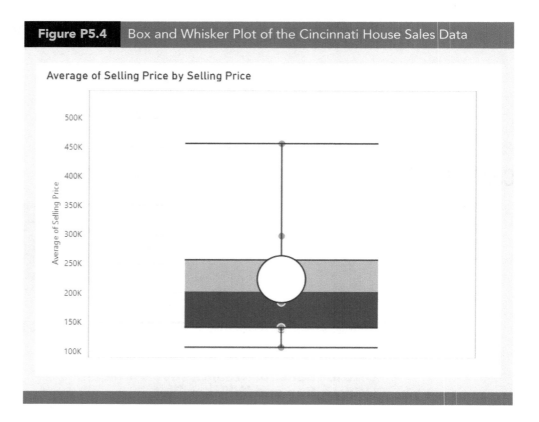

Average of Selling Price by Selling Price

          Select a dark blue color for the **Lower box color**

          Collapse **Box options**

Step 4. Expand **Mean**

          Select **Square** for **Mean shape**

          Select **Small** for **Mean width**

          Collapse **Mean**

Step 5. Expand **Y-axis** and type *0* in the **Start** box

          Next to **Show title**, toggle the **On** button On● to **Off** to hide the title of the Y-axis

          Select **14** as the **Text size** and **Calibri** as the font for **Labels font family**

          Collapse **Y-axis**

Step 6. In the **Visualizations** pane, click **General**

          Expand **Title**

          Edit the text in the **Text** box to read *Home Selling Price ($)*

          Select **Calibri** as the **Font** and **16** as the font size

          Collapse **Title**

After completing steps 1–6, the chart should appear as shown in Figure P5.5.

As a second example of creating box and whisker charts in Power BI, we use data in the file *salescomparison_stacked*. The file contains the selling price of 10 homes in each of five different suburbs.

Figure P5.5	The Finished Box and Whisker Plot for the Cincinnati Home Sales Data

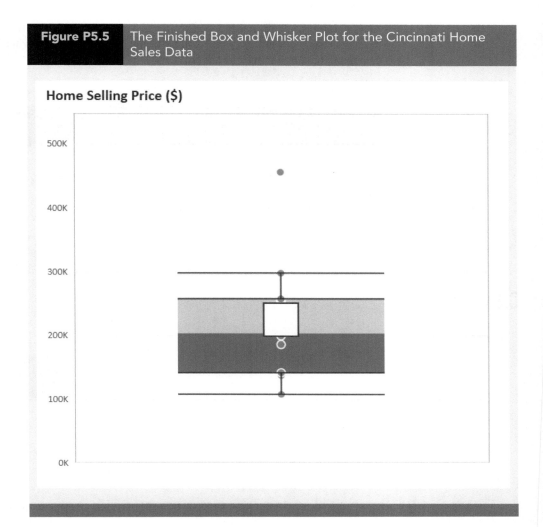

Home Selling Price ($)

CHART *file*

cincysales_chart.pbix

DATA *file*

salescomparison_stacked

Step 1. Following the steps outlined in Appendix 1.1, connect Power BI to the file *salescomparison_stacked*

In some of the steps that follow, we give instructions to expand or collapse certain sections of Power BI. A section can be expanded by clicking on ⟩ next to the section title. To collapse a section, click ⌄ next to the section title.

Step 2. Click **Report** view 📊, and in the Visualizations pane, click **Build visual** ▦ to display the **Build visual** matrix of available charts.

Select **Box and Whisker by MAQ Software** ⊡

In the **Data** pane on the right, expand **Data** ⟩ ▦ Data to display the variables

Drag **Σ Selling Price** from the **Data** pane to the **Axis** box in the **Visualizations** pane

Drag **Suburb** from the **Data** pane to the **Axis category l** box in the **Visualizations** pane

Drag **Σ Selling Price** from the **Data** pane to the **Value** box in the **Visualizations** pane

Right click **Sum of Selling Price** in the **Value** box, and select **Average**

After editing the chart in a similar fashion as described previously in steps 3–6 but leaving the mean as a medium circle and turning of the dots, the box and whisker chart for these data appear as shown in Figure P5.6.

Figure P5.6   The Finished Box and Whisker Plot Comparison for the Suburb Home Sales Data

salescomparison_stracked_chart.pbix

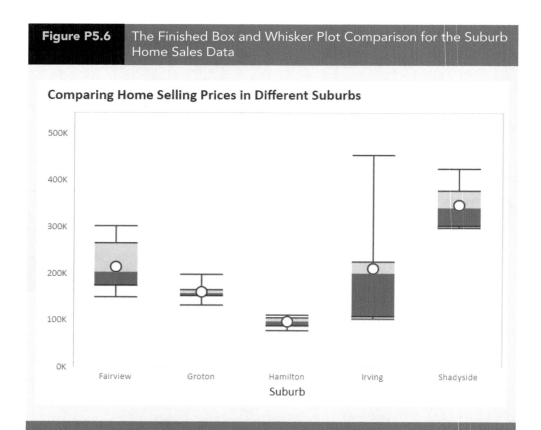

Appendix 5.2 Visualizing Variability with Tableau

In this appendix, we discuss in more detail how to visualize variability in Tableau, including frequency distributions for categorical variables, histograms, and box and whisker charts.

Frequency Distributions for Categorical Variables

The file *pop* contains data on 50 soft drink purchases. Each purchase is of one of five popular soft drinks: Coca-Cola, Diet Coke, Dr. Pepper, Pepsi, and Sprite. The steps below create a histogram for these categorical data using Tableau.

DATA*file*

pop

Step 1. Following the steps outlined in Appendix 1.2, connect Tableau to the file *pop*
Click the **Sheet 1** tab at the bottom of the Tableau Data Source screen to open the worksheet view

Step 2. Drag the pill for **Soft Drink Purchase** from the **Data** pane to the **Columns** shelf and drag the pill for **Data (Count)** from the **Data** pane to the **Rows** shelf

Step 3. To sort the columns based on purchase frequency, right click the pill for **Soft Drink Purchase** in the Columns shelf and select Sort…. When the **Sort [Soft Drink Purchase]** dialog box appears:
Change **Sort By** to **Field**
Select **Descending** for **Sort Order**
Select **Data** for **Field Name**
Click ✕ to close the **Sort [Soft Drink Purchase]** dialog box

Step 4. To add data labels to the columns, drag **Data (Count)** from the **Data** pane to the **Label** card ⊤ Label in the **Marks** area

The following steps modify the chart to improve clarity.

Step 5. To hide the unnecessary vertical axis, right click the vertical axis and deselect **Show Header**

Step 6. To remove the unnecessary label at the top of the chart, right click **Soft Drink Purchase** at the top of the chart and select **Hide Field Labels for Columns**

Step 7. To modify the title of the chart, right click on **Sheet 1** at the top of the chart, and select **Edit Title…**. When the **Edit Title** dialog box appears:
Replace **<Sheet Name>** with title *Frequency of Soft Drink Purchases*
Highlight the text of the title, then change the font size to **16**, and click the
Bold button **B** to make the title bold font
Click **OK** to close the **Edit Title** dialog box

Step 8. Right click the horizontal axis at the bottom of the chart, and select **Format…**. When the **Format Soft Drink Purchase** pane appears:
Click next to **Font:** under **Default** and change the font size to **11**

Step 9. Right click on one of the data labels at the top of a column and select **Format…** When the **Format** pane appears:
Click next to **Worksheet:** under **Default**, and change the font size to **11**

Step 10. To remove the unnecessary grid lines in the chart, right click on the chart, and select **Format…**. When the **Format** task pane opens, click on the **Lines** button
≡ and select **None** next to **Grid Lines:**

Step 11. Hover between any two horizontal axis labels and when the ⬌ appears, click and slide it right or left to widen or narrow the columns.

The completed categorical frequency distribution chart for the soft drink data appears in Figure T5.1.

Figure T5.1	Frequency Distribution Chart for the Soft Drink Data

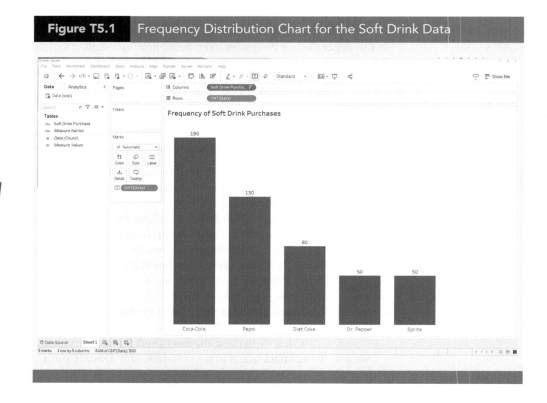

CHART *file*

pop_chart.twbx

Frequency Distributions for Quantitative Variables

The file *death30* contains data on 30 observations of the age of death. The steps below create a histogram for these quantitative data using Tableau.

DATA *file*

death30

Step 1. Following the steps outlined in Appendix 1.2, connect Tableau to the file *death30*

　　　　Click the **Sheet 1** tab at the bottom of the Tableau Data Source screen to open the worksheet view

Step 2. In the worksheet view of Tableau, drag the pill for **Age at Death (Years)** from the **Data** pane to the **Rows** shelf

Step 3. Click the **Show Me** button 📊 Show Me in the far upper right, and select the

　　　　Histogram icon ▪▫▪▫▪ to generate a default histogram

　　　　Click the **Show Me** button 📊 Show Me to close the **Show Me** panel

These steps create the default histogram for the age at death data shown in Figure T5.2. The following steps modify the chart to improve clarity.

Step 4. To modify the vertical axis, right click the vertical axis, and select **Edit Axis…**.
　　　　When the **Edit Axis [Count of Age at Death (Years)]** dialog box appears:
　　　　　　Select **Custom** for **Title**, and change the title to *Count of People*
　　　　　　Click ✕ to close the **Edit Axis [Count of Age at Death (Years)]** dialog box

Step 5. Right click the vertical axis of the chart and select **Format…**. When the **Format CNT(Age at Death (Years))** pane appears:
　　　　　　Click next to **Font:** under **Default** and change the font size to **11**

Figure T5.2   Default Histogram for the Age at Death Data

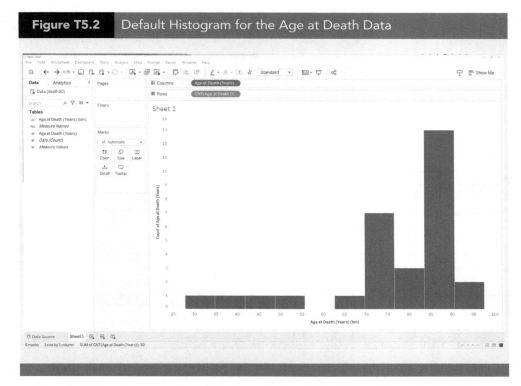

Step 6. Right click the horizontal axis, and select **Edit Axis…**. When the **Edit Axis [Age at Death (Years) (bin)]** dialog box appears, select **Custom** under **Axis Titles** and enter *Age at Death (Years)*

   Click ✕ to close the **Edit Axis [Age at Death (Years) (bin)]** dialog box

Step 7. Right click the horizontal axis of the chart and select **Format…**. When the **Format Age at Death (Years) (bin)** pane appears:

   Click next to **Font:** under **Default** and change the font size to **11**

Step 8. To modify the title of the chart, right click on **Sheet 1** at the top of the chart, and select **Edit Title…**. When the Edit Title dialog box appears:

   Replace **<Sheet Name>** with the title *Distribution of Age at Death*

   Highlight the text of the title, then change the font size to **16**, and click the

   Bold button **B** to make the title bold font

   Click **OK** to close the **Edit Title** dialog box

Step 9. To remove the unnecessary grid lines in the chart, right click on the chart, and select **Format…**. When the **Format** task pane opens, click on the **Lines** button

   ☰ , and select **None** next to **Grid Lines:**

   Click ✕ to close the **Format** task pane

These steps create the modified histogram shown in Figure T5.3.

   We can adjust the appearance of the histogram by changing the sizes of the bins as demonstrated in the following steps.

Step 10. Right click the pill for **Age at Death (Years)** bin in the **Tables** area of the **Data** pane, and select **Edit…**. When the **Edit Bins [Age at Death (Years)]** dialog box appears:

   Enter *12* as the **Size of bins:**

   Click **OK**

Figure T5.4 shows a histogram viewed in Presentation Mode for the age at death data with a bin size equal to 12 years, and Figure T5.5 shows a histogram for the age at death data with a bin size equal to 8.

| Figure T5.3 | Modified Histogram for the Age at Death Data (Bin Size = 5) |

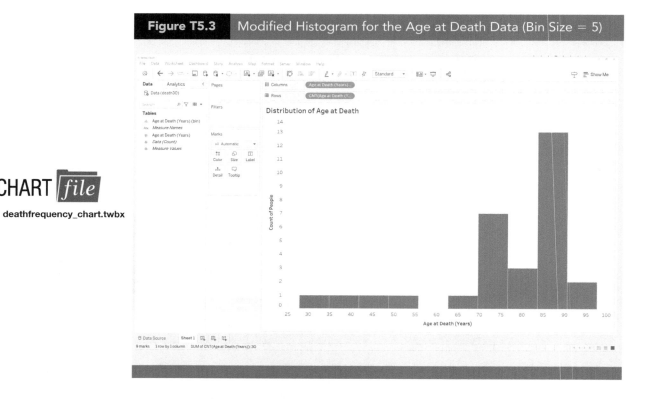

| Figure T5.4 | Modified Histogram for the Age at Death Data (Bin Size = 12) |

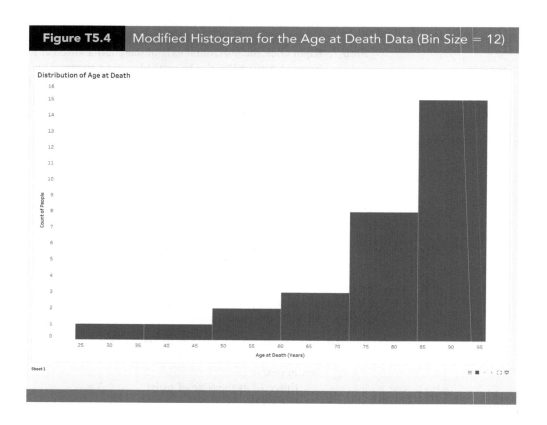

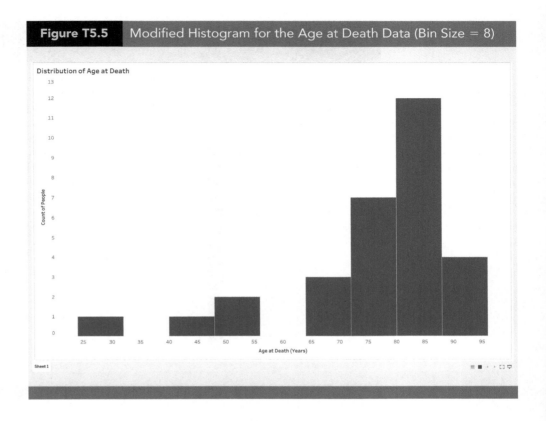

Figure T5.5   Modified Histogram for the Age at Death Data (Bin Size = 8)

Box and Whisker Charts

The file *homesales_stacked* contains the selling prices of 50 different homes as well as the size (in square feet), the location, and the type of home (either detached or condo). The steps below create a box and whisker chart for these data using Tableau. Note that the file *homesales_stacked* contains the data in a stacked form where each row corresponds to a single home sale.

DATA*file*

homesales_stacked

Step 1. Following the steps outlined in Appendix 1.2, connect Tableau to the file *homesales_stacked*
Click the **Sheet 1** tab at the bottom of the Tableau Data Source screen to open the worksheet view

Step 2. In the worksheet view of Tableau, drag the pill for **Selling Price ($)** from the **Data** pane to the **Rows** shelf

Steps 1 and 2 create the column chart shown in Figure T5.6. To create a box and whisker chart, we need to disaggregate the data in step 3.

Step 3. Click the **Analysis** tab in the Ribbon, and deselect **Aggregate Measures** to disaggregate the Selling Price ($) values (see Figure T5.7)

Step 4. Click the **Show Me** button ⊟ Show Me, and select the **box and whisker plots** icon ⊞ to generate the default box and whisker chart
Click the **Show Me** button ⊟ Show Me to close the **Show Me** panel

Step 5. Drag the pill for **Location** from the **Data** pane to the **Columns** shelf to create multiple box and whisker charts based on the suburb where the home is located

Step 6. Drag the pill for **Type** from the **Data** pane to the **Color** card ⠿ Color in the **Marks** area

Figure T5.6   Results of Steps 1 and 2 for Creating Box and Whisker Charts for the Homesales Data

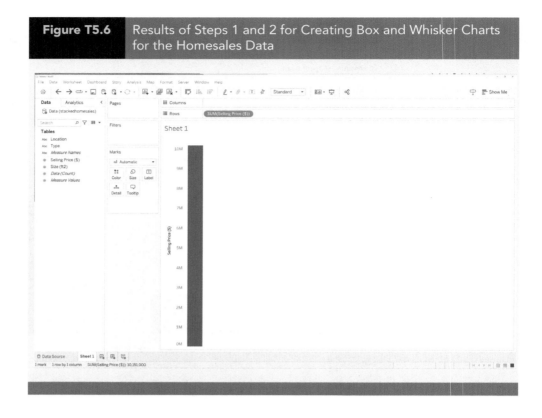

Figure T5.7   Result of Disaggregating the Homesales Data to Create Box and Whisker Charts

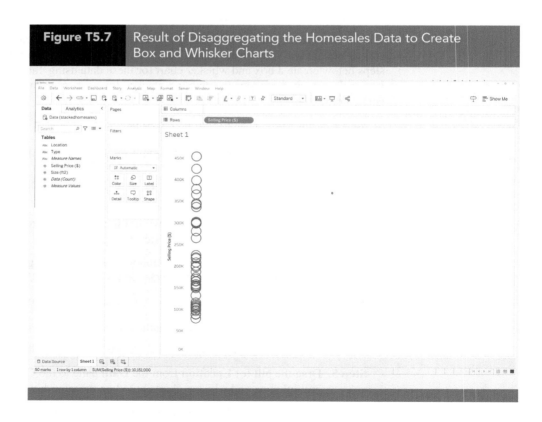

The following steps modify the chart to improve clarity.

Step 7. Right click the vertical axis of the chart and select **Format…**. When the **Format Selling Price ($)** pane appears:

Click next to **Font:** under **Default**, and change the font size to **11**

Step 8. Right click the horizontal axis of the chart and select **Format…**. When the **Format Location** pane appears:

Click next to **Font:** under **Default**, and change the font size to **11**

Step 9. To remove the unnecessary label at the top of the chart, right click on **Location** at the top of the chart and select **Hide Field Labels for Columns**

Step 10. To modify the title of the chart, right click on **Sheet 1** at the top of the chart, and select **Edit Title…**. When the **Edit Title** dialog box appears:

Replace **<Sheet Name>** with the title *Comparing Home Selling Prices in Different Suburbs*

Highlight the text of the title, then change the font size to **16**, and click

the **Bold** button **B** to make the title bold font

Click **OK** to close the **Edit Title** dialog box

Step 11. To remove the unnecessary grid lines in the chart, right click on the chart, and select **Format…**. When the **Format** task pane opens, click on the **Lines**

button ☰, and select **None** next to **Grid Lines:**

Step 12. Hover between any two horizontal axis labels and when the ⟺ appears, click and slide it right or left to widen or narrow box and whisker charts

The completed box and whisker charts for the selling prices of homes in each location where the individual data points are differentiated based on color depending on whether the home is a condo or detached type is shown in Figure T5.8.

CHART *file*

homesales_chart.twbx

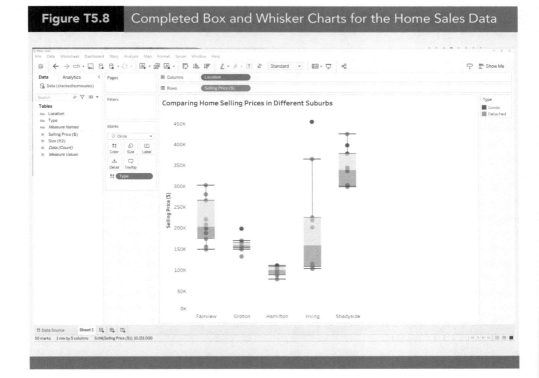

Figure T5.8   Completed Box and Whisker Charts for the Home Sales Data

Chapter 6

Exploring Data Visually

Contents

Learning Objectives

After completing this chapter, you will be able to

LO 1   Organize and arrange data to facilitate data exploration and visualization

LO 2   Create and interpret visualizations to explore the distributions of individual variables

LO 3   Construct crosstabulations and their related charts to explore patterns in data involving multiple variables

LO 4   Select an appropriate chart type for exploring patterns based on the type of data and analysis goals

LO 5   Create and compare visualizations that display the association between two quantitative variables

LO 6   Define correlation and how to estimate its strength on a scatter chart

LO 7   Define the types of missing data and understand the implications on how to address missing data

LO 8   Create visualizations for time series data and identify temporal patterns

LO 9   Explain the strengths and weaknesses of choropleth maps and cartograms for exploring data

Arctic Sea Ice Volume

The visualization of data sets can be helpful in generating insights from data. However, it can also be challenging to choose the best type and format of visualization to best generate insights from data exploration. The Polar Science Center affiliated with the University of Washington is a custodian of several data sets monitoring the oceanography, climatology, meteorology, biology, and ecology of the ice-covered regions on Earth. One of the Polar Science Center's studies involves the volume of ice covering the Arctic Sea. Figure 6.1 displays a chart similar to that constructed by Haveland-Robinson Associates that plots the monthly average Arctic Sea ice volume from 1979 to 2014.

As Figure 6.1 shows, this chart corresponds to a lot of data points. However, the spherical nature of the chart makes it difficult for the audience to quickly determine insights from the data. Other than facilitating the pithy title of "Arctic Death Spiral," the circular orientation of the chart does not lend itself well to displaying the data. Often a circular display such as this is used when data are repeating over a period of time (days of week, months), but years do not repeat, and to add an additional year's data to this chart would require entirely redrawing the chart (most likely dropping off the oldest year's worth of data). The chart also heavily relies on gridlines, which decreases the chart's data-ink ratio. Because the months are plotted based on their corresponding ice-volume values, the chart does not display months in chronological order as most audiences would expect. This makes the choice to show the ice-volume values by month more confusing than helpful for the audience.

Figure 6.1   Radar Chart of Monthly Ice Volume Observations

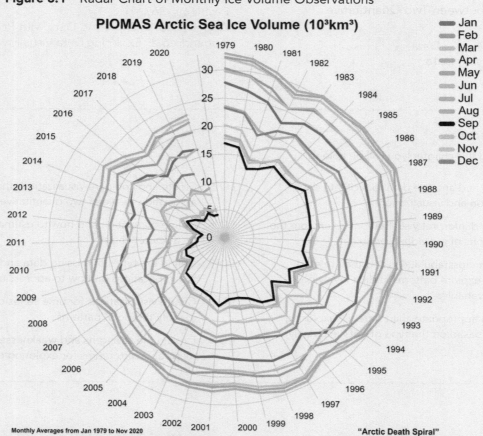

An alternative approach to visualizing these data is to remove the individual month values from the chart. Instead, the analyst could still use the monthly average data but present it in a manner that conveys the general pattern in the data, which in this case is a decrease in the ice volume. Figure 6.2 contains a sequence of box and whisker plots, each based on 12 monthly averages from the corresponding year. Each box and whisker plot provides statistical summaries of the year's observations, such as the first and third quartile, the median, and the mean. Perhaps more importantly, the long-term decrease in ice volume in terms of these statistical measures is clearly displayed.

An additional benefit of the box and whisker plot is that data at the most granular level could be used rather than monthly averages. In this case, the Polar Science Center has daily observations of the Arctic Sea ice volume. These daily observations can be used as the basis of each year's box and whisker plot if the analyst determines that the audience is interested in exploring the variation at the daily level.

Figure 6.2   Annual Box and Whisker Plots of Monthly Ice Volume Observations

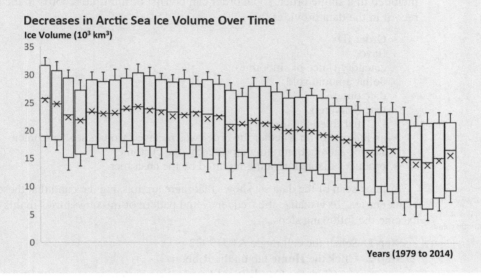

In this chapter, we describe the role of data visualization in exploring data. Data are often said to be "dirty" and "raw" before they have been put in a form that is best suited for in-depth analysis. We describe how to leverage data visualization during the examination of missing data and unusual values in the **data cleansing** process. We demonstrate how to use different types of charts to search for patterns within a single variable, such as the decreasing ice volume discussed in the *Data Visualization Makeover*. Then, we introduce the use of crosstabulation and scatter charts to investigate patterns between two or more variables. We conclude the chapter with specific considerations when exploring time series data and geospatial data.

6.1 Introduction to Exploratory Data Analysis

As a first step in an analytical study, it is critical to examine and explore the data. This **exploratory data analysis (EDA)** makes heavy use of descriptive statistics and visualization to gain an initial understanding of the data. The objectives of EDA include (1) detection of errors, missing values, and any other unusual observations; (2) characterization of the distribution of the values for the individual variables; and (3) identification of patterns and relationships between variables. Visual display is an essential principle of EDA as it allows the analyst to translate the information contained in the rows and columns of data into charts, providing "first looks at the data" that achieve the EDA objectives.

To understand the challenges in exploring data, we consider its structural dimensions. **Tall data** occurs when the number of records (rows) is large. **Wide data** occurs when the number of variables (columns) is large. As data grow taller or wider, the possibility of data errors and missing values increases. In addition, wide data becomes increasingly arduous to explore because there are a large number of possible combinations of variables to examine.

Espléndido Jugo y Batido, Inc. Example

Let us consider an example involving Espléndido Jugo y Batido, Inc. (EJB), a company that manufactures bottled juices and smoothies. EJB produces its products in five fruit flavors (apple, grape, orange, pear, and tomato) and four vegetable flavors (beet, carrot, celery, and cucumber), and it ships these products from distribution centers (DCs) in Idaho, Mississippi, Nebraska, New Mexico, North Dakota, Rhode Island, and West Virginia.

EJB management has retrieved data on each order it has received over the past three years and stored it in the file *ejb* (partially displayed in Figure 6.3). Each record in the data corresponds to the amount of one product (a combination of category and flavor) included in a single order, so an order can consist of multiple records in the data. Each record in the data provides the

- Order ID
- flavor
- category (juice or smoothie)
- dollar amount sold
- date ordered
- date delivered
- DC that filled the order
- an indication on whether the order was received from a new customer
- service satisfaction rating reported by the customer
- product satisfaction rating reported by the customer

Missing data entries may be coded in a variety of ways, such as blank entries, "NA" entries, or entries with unrealistic values such as -9999.

A quick scan of the data set shows that there are missing data and that these appear as blank entries. To visualize the frequency and pattern of missing entries in this data set, we execute the following steps.

Step 1. Select the cell range A1:J19932
Step 2. Click the **Home** tab on the Ribbon
Click the **Conditional Formatting** button 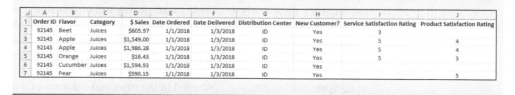 in the **Styles** group
Select **New Rule...**
Step 3. When the **New Formatting Rule** dialog box appears:
In the **Select a Rule Type:** area, select **Format only cells that contain**
In the **Edit the Rule Description:** area:
In the leftmost box under **Format only cells with:**, select **Blanks**
Click the **Format** button, and when the **Format Cells** dialog box appears:
On the **Fill** tab, select the black color rectangle from the **Background Color:** gallery
Click **OK** to close the **Format Cells** dialog box
Click **OK** to close the **New Formatting Rule** dialog box

Figure 6.3   A Portion of Espléndido Jugo y Batido, Inc. Data in the File *ejb*

ejb

	A	B	C	D	E	F	G	H	I	J
1	Order ID	Flavor	Category	$ Sales	Date Ordered	Date Delivered	Distribution Center	New Customer?	Service Satisfaction Rating	Product Satisfaction Rating
2	92145	Beet	Juices	$605.97	1/1/2018	1/3/2018	ID	Yes	3	
3	92145	Apple	Juices	$1,549.00	1/1/2018	1/3/2018	ID	Yes	5	4
4	92145	Apple	Juices	$1,986.28	1/1/2018	1/3/2018	ID	Yes	5	4
5	92145	Orange	Juices	$16.43	1/1/2018	1/3/2018	ID	Yes	5	3
6	92145	Cucumber	Juices	$1,594.93	1/1/2018	1/3/2018	ID	Yes		
7	92145	Pear	Juices	$590.15	1/1/2018	1/3/2018	ID	Yes		5

*Changing the **Zoom** setting of the spreadsheet on the **View** tab of the Ribbon allows you to view more or less of the data set and view the pattern of missing data at a more or less granular level.*

Figure 6.4 shows the result of the preceding steps. Cells with missing data are colored black to visually emphasize the frequency and pattern of the missing entries. For the EJB data, we see that the only variables with missing entries are the Service Satisfaction Rating and the Product Satisfaction Rating. Presumably, some customers neglect to provide these voluntary ratings when solicited. Later in this chapter, we will investigate the nature of these missing data more closely.

Organizing Data to Facilitate Exploration

In this section, we introduce the functionality of Excel's Table object to facilitate exploration of a data set. The following steps show how to create a Table object in Excel using the data in the file *ejb*.

We execute the steps to create the Excel Table on a version of the EJB data that does not have the missing cell entries highlighted in black.

Step 1. Click the **Insert** tab on the Ribbon
Click the **Table** button ⊞ in the **Tables** group

Step 2. When the **Create Table** dialog box appears:
Enter *=$A$1:$J$19932* in the **Where is the data for your table?** box
Select the **My table has headers** box
Click **OK**

Figure 6.5 displays a portion of the table that results from these steps. In addition to the distinctive banded formatting that an Excel Table has by default, we can recognize that data in Excel are in a Table object because of the presence of the Table Design tab in the Ribbon when selecting any cell in the range of the data. By default, the Table containing the data is named Table1, but we rename the table with the following steps.

Figure 6.4	A Portion of the EJB Data Conditionally Formatted to Display the Pattern of Missing Data

	A	B	C	D	E	F	G	H	I	J
1	Order ID	Flavor	Category	$ Sales	Date Ordered	Date Delivered	Distribution Center	New Customer?	Service Satisfaction Rating	Product Satisfaction Rating
2	92145	Beet	Juices	605.97	1/1/2018	1/3/2018	ID	Yes	3	
3	92145	Apple	Juices	1549.00	1/1/2018	1/3/2018	ID	Yes	5	4
4	92145	Apple	Juices	1986.28	1/1/2018	1/3/2018	ID	Yes	5	4
5	92145	Orange	Juices	16.43	1/1/2018	1/3/2018	ID	Yes	5	3
6	92145	Cucumber	Juices	1594.93	1/1/2018	1/3/2018	ID	Yes		
7	92145	Pear	Juices	590.15	1/1/2018	1/3/2018	ID	Yes		5
8	92146	Beet	Juices	1764.92	1/1/2018	1/3/2018	MS	Yes	3	
9	92146	Pear	Juices	428.46	1/1/2018	1/3/2018	MS	Yes	5	
10	92146	Cucumber	Smoothies	138.92	1/1/2018	1/3/2018	MS	Yes		3
11	92146	Orange	Juices	6.50	1/1/2018	1/3/2018	MS	Yes		4
12	92147	Beet	Juices	872.00	1/1/2018	1/3/2018	ND	No	3	
13	92147	Orange	Smoothies	1437.94	1/1/2018	1/3/2018	ND	No	3	
14	92150	Grape	Juices	1366.97	1/1/2018	1/3/2018	NE	Yes	3	5
15	92151	Apple	Juices	1786.11	1/1/2018	1/3/2018	NE	Yes	5	
16	92152	Orange	Smoothies	63.72	1/1/2018	1/3/2018	NM	Yes	3	3
17	92152	Tomato	Smoothies	1971.52	1/1/2018	1/3/2018	NM	Yes	3	
18	92153	Carrot	Smoothies	1366.25	1/1/2018	1/3/2018	NM	No	5	
19	92737	Orange	Juices	920.78	3/10/2018	3/12/2018	NE	No	3	
20	92974	Orange	Juices	81.29	3/29/2018	3/31/2018	RI	No	4	
21	92156	Orange	Juices	312.87	1/1/2018	1/3/2018	RI	Yes		4
22	93205	Orange	Juices	543.54	4/19/2018	4/21/2018	MS	No	3	
23	92199	Apple	Juices	1128.87	1/5/2018	1/7/2018	MS	No		
24	92199	Orange	Smoothies	1629.45	1/5/2018	1/7/2018	MS	No		
25	92245	Pear	Smoothies	1982.27	1/10/2018	1/12/2018	MS	Yes		
26	92246	Tomato	Smoothies	1624.45	1/10/2018	1/12/2018	ND	No	4	
27	92247	Carrot	Juices	411.28	1/10/2018	1/12/2018	ND	No	4	5
28	92247	Orange	Smoothies	443.48	1/10/2018	1/12/2018	ND	No		
29	92252	Celery	Juices	215.24	1/10/2018	1/12/2018	WV	No	4	
30	92252	Pear	Juices	1431.32	1/10/2018	1/12/2018	WV	No	4	
31	92253	Cucumber	Juices	1212.89	1/10/2018	1/12/2018	WV	No	4	
32	92253	Tomato	Juices	1730.99	1/10/2018	1/12/2018	WV	No	4	
33	92265	Grape	Smoothies	36.91	1/12/2018	1/14/2018	ID	No	5	2
34	92282	Beet	Juices	1602.19	1/13/2018	1/15/2018	WV	No	4	
35	92282	Tomato	Juices	797.25	1/13/2018	1/15/2018	WV	No	4	2
36	93213	Orange	Juices	1013.00	4/19/2018	4/21/2018	NE	No	3	
37	92298	Cucumber	Juices	928.99	1/16/2018	1/18/2018	ND	Yes	1	5
38	92298	Carrot	Smoothies	303.48	1/16/2018	1/18/2018	ND	Yes	1	2

Figure 6.5	A Portion of the EJB Data Formatted as an Excel Table

	A	B	C	D	E	F	G	H	I	J
1	Order ID	Flavor	Category	$ Sales	Date Ordered	Date Delivered	Distribution Center	New Customer?	Service Satisfaction Rating	Product Satisfaction Rating
2	92145	Beet	Juices	605.97	1/1/2018	1/3/2018	ID	Yes	3	
3	92145	Apple	Juices	1549.00	1/1/2018	1/3/2018	ID	Yes	5	4
4	92145	Apple	Juices	1986.28	1/1/2018	1/3/2018	ID	Yes	5	4
5	92145	Orange	Juices	16.43	1/1/2018	1/3/2018	ID	Yes	5	3
6	92145	Cucumber	Juices	1594.93	1/1/2018	1/3/2018	ID	Yes		
7	92145	Pear	Juices	590.15	1/1/2018	1/3/2018	ID	Yes		5

Step 3. Select any cell in the range of the data, for example, cell A1

Step 4. Click the **Table Design** tab on the Ribbon

In the **Properties** group, enter *EJBData* in the box below **Table Name:**

As the Filter Arrow ▼ next to each column heading in Figure 6.5 suggests, when an Excel Table is created, the data set is automatically prepared to filter with respect to a variable's value. To demonstrate this functionality, suppose we are interested only in viewing the records corresponding to beet smoothies. To filter the data to list only this flavor and category combination, we execute the following steps.

Step 1. Click the **Filter Arrow** ▼ in cell B1 next to **Flavor**

Deselect the box next to (**Select All**)

Select the box next to **Beet**

Click **OK**

Step 2. Click the **Filter Arrow** ▼ in cell C1 next to **Category**

Deselect the box next to (**Select All**)

Select the box next to **Smoothies**

Click **OK**

The result is a display of only the records that were part of orders for beet smoothies (see Figure 6.6).

Suppose now that we only want to view beet smoothie records that were greater than or equal to $1,500 in sales. To filter on a quantitative variable such as $ Sales, we execute the following steps.

Step 1. Click the **Filter Arrow** ▼ in cell D1 next to **$ Sales**

Step 2. Select **Number Filters** and then **Greater Than Or Equal To…**

Step 3. When the **Custom AutoFilter** dialog box appears:

In the top box on the left in the **Show rows where:** area, select **is greater than or equal to,** and enter *1500* in the adjacent box

Click **OK**

The result is a display of only the beet smoothie records of at least $1,500 in sales (see Figure 6.7).

Figure 6.6	A Portion of the EJB Data Filtered to Show Only Beet Smoothie Records

	A	B	C	D	E	F	G	H	I	J
1	Order ID	Flavor	Category	$ Sales	Date Ordered	Date Delivered	Distribution Center	New Customer?	Service Satisfaction Rating	Product Satisfaction Rating
41	92301	Beet	Smoothies	1180.36	1/16/2018	1/18/2018	NE	No	1	
51	92311	Beet	Smoothies	1441.67	1/16/2018	1/18/2018	WV	No	1	
54	92370	Beet	Smoothies	44.72	1/25/2018	1/27/2018	NE	No	3	4
118	92651	Beet	Smoothies	1315.08	3/2/2018	3/4/2018	NM	No	2	
263	93457	Beet	Smoothies	651.19	5/9/2018	5/11/2018	ID	No	5	4

Figure 6.7	A Portion of the EJB Data Filtered to Show Only Beet Smoothie Records with Sales ≥ $1500

	A	B	C	D	E	F	G	H	I	J
1	Order ID	Flavor	Category	$ Sales	Date Ordered	Date Delivered	Distribution Center	New Customer?	Service Satisfaction Rating	Product Satisfaction Rating
279	93588	Beet	Smoothies	1663.03	5/21/2018	5/23/2018	ND	No	5	
357	94056	Beet	Smoothies	1518.84	7/11/2018	7/13/2018	ND	No	2	
1529	100582	Beet	Smoothies	1740.09	1/10/2020	1/12/2020	ND	No	4	
1921	102392	Beet	Smoothies	1500.04	5/5/2020	5/7/2020	ND	No	5	
3368	94785	Beet	Smoothies	1620.61	9/27/2018	9/30/2018	ID	No	3	

We can further filter the data by choosing the Filter Arrow in other columns. We can make all the data visible again by clicking the Filter Arrow in each filtered column (as denoted by the ⌁ icon) and checking **(Select All)**. We can also undo all filtering by clicking **Clear** in the **Sort & Filter** group of the **Data** tab.

In addition to filtering records, the Filter Arrow for a column can be used to quickly sort data according to magnitude (for a **quantitative variable**), alphabetically (for a **categorical variable**), or chronologically (for a variable coded as a date). After removing all previous filters and making all data visible again, the following steps demonstrate how to sort a Table according to the Date Delivered variable chronologically from the oldest date to the newest date. Figure 6.8 shows a portion of the resulting table.

Step 1. Click the **Filter Arrow** ▼ in column F1 next to **Date Delivered**
Step 2. Select **Sort Oldest to Newest**

An Excel Table enables the creation of a new variable that is calculated from other variables in the data set. To demonstrate, the following steps add a new variable to the Table containing the EJB data called Time to Deliver.

Step 1. Click the top of column G, right click and select **Insert** from the drop-down menu
Step 2. In cell G1, enter *Time to Deliver*
Step 3. In cell G2, enter *=F2-E2*
Step 4. Select column G by clicking the top of the column
Step 5. In the **Home** tab of the Ribbon, within the **Number** group:
From the drop-down menu, select **Number**
Click the **Decrease Decimal** button twice
Step 6. In the **Home** tab of the Ribbon, within the **Alignment** group:
Click the **Align Right** ≡ button

Figure 6.9 shows the result of these steps. When pressing **Enter** to execute the formula in Step 3 above, entries for the entire column are automatically completed with the analogous calculations.

Figure 6.8	A Portion of the EJB Data Sorted Oldest Date Delivered to Newest Date Delivered

	A	B	C	D	E	F	G	H	I	J
1	Order ID	Flavor	Category	$ Sales	Date Ordered	Date Delivered	Distribution Center	New Customer?	Service Satisfaction Rating	Product Satisfaction Rating
2	92145	Beet	Juices	605.97	1/1/2018	1/3/2018	ID	Yes	3	
3	92145	Apple	Juices	1549.00	1/1/2018	1/3/2018	ID	Yes	5	4
4	92145	Apple	Juices	1986.28	1/1/2018	1/3/2018	ID	Yes	5	4
5	92145	Orange	Juices	16.43	1/1/2018	1/3/2018	ID	Yes	5	3
6	92145	Cucumber	Juices	1594.93	1/1/2018	1/3/2018	ID	Yes		

Figure 6.9   A Portion of the EJB Data after Insertion of Time to Deliver Variable

	A	B	C	D	E	F	G	H	I	J	K
1	Order ID	Flavor	Category	$ Sales	Date Ordered	Date Delivered	Time To Deliver	Distribution Center	New Customer?	Service Satisfaction Rating	Product Satisfaction Rating
2	92145	Beet	Juices	605.97	1/1/2018	1/3/2018	2	ID	Yes	3	
3	92145	Apple	Juices	1549.00	1/1/2018	1/3/2018	2	ID	Yes	5	4
4	92145	Apple	Juices	1986.28	1/1/2018	1/3/2018	2	ID	Yes	5	4
5	92145	Orange	Juices	16.43	1/1/2018	1/3/2018	2	ID	Yes	5	3
6	92145	Cucumber	Juices	1594.93	1/1/2018	1/3/2018	2	ID	Yes		

If you append a record to a row adjacent to an Excel Table or add a variable in a column adjacent to an Excel Table, the Table is automatically resized to include this new row or column. To ease analysis of the EJB data based on order date, it may help to decompose the Date Ordered variable into three new variables: Year Ordered, Month Ordered, and Day Ordered. The following steps create these new variables in the Excel Table (shown in Figure 6.10).

Step 1. In cell L1, enter *Year Ordered*
Step 2. In cell M1, enter *Month Ordered*
Step 3. In cell N1, enter *Day Ordered*
Step 4. In cell L2, enter *=YEAR(E2)*
Step 5. In cell M2, enter *=TEXT(E2,"mmm")*
Step 6. In cell N2, enter *=DAY(E2)*

In the Excel function TEXT, the second argument specifies the format of value (date) to be converted to text. TEXT(E2, "mmm") returns the abbreviated month corresponding to the date listed in cell E2.

An Excel Table supports the automatic calculation of summary statistics for each column (variable). For example, suppose we are interested in computing the average value of $ Sales for a set of filtered observations and comparing that to the average value of $ Sales for all observations. The following steps demonstrate this comparison for beet smoothies starting with the entire (unfiltered) table of observations in the file *ejb*.

Step 1. Select any cell in the range of the Table, for example, cell A2
Step 2. In the **Table Design** tab on the Ribbon, select **Total Row** in the **Table Style Options** group

Step 2 will append a row to the bottom of the Table with the label **Total** in the first column. The following steps execute the calculation of the average value of $ Sales.

*Inserting the Total Row in a Table automatically computes the Sum of the variable in the last column. This calculation can be removed by clicking on the drop-down menu arrow in this cell and selecting **None**.*

Step 3. In the Total row (row 19933), select the entry corresponding to the $ Sales column
Click the **Drop-down Menu Arrow** ▼ and select **Average** from the menu

Figure 6.11 shows that $894.18 is the average sales amount when considering all records. A convenient feature of an Excel Table is that this Total calculation updates appropriately for filtered records. Figure 6.12 shows that $706.05 is the average sales amount for records corresponding to beet smoothies.

Figure 6.10   A Portion of the EJB Data after Insertion of Year Ordered, Month Ordered, and Day Ordered Variables (Columns H through K Hidden

	A	B	C	D	E	F	G	L	M	N
1	Order ID	Flavor	Category	$ Sales	Date Ordered	Date Delivered	Time To Deliver	Year Ordered	Month Ordered	Day Ordered
2	92145	Beet	Juices	605.97	1/1/2018	1/3/2018	2	2018	Jan	1
3	92145	Apple	Juices	1549.00	1/1/2018	1/3/2018	2	2018	Jan	1
4	92145	Apple	Juices	1986.28	1/1/2018	1/3/2018	2	2018	Jan	1
5	92145	Orange	Juices	16.43	1/1/2018	1/3/2018	2	2018	Jan	1
6	92145	Cucumber	Juices	1594.93	1/1/2018	1/3/2018	2	2018	Jan	1

Figure 6.11	Calculation of Average $ Sales for All Records Using Table's Total Row

	Order ID	Flavor	Category	$ Sales	Date Ordered	Date Delivered	Time To Deliver	Distribution Center	New Customer?
19926	105012	Tomato	Juices	1889.96	10/16/2020	11/6/2020	21	ND	Yes
19927	105012	Beet	Smoothies	1111.82	10/16/2020	11/6/2020	21	ND	Yes
19928	105012	Cucumber	Juices	1576.28	10/16/2020	11/6/2020	21	ND	Yes
19929	105012	Apple	Juices	1743.86	10/16/2020	11/6/2020	21	ND	Yes
19930	105017	Beet	Juices	90.05	10/16/2020	11/6/2020	21	NE	No
19931	105017	Grape	Juices	1375.50	10/16/2020	11/6/2020	21	NE	No
19932	105029	Pear	Juices	1486.91	10/16/2020	11/6/2020	21	WV	No
19933	Total			894.18					

An Excel Table accommodates tall data by automatically replacing the column labels of A, B, C,… with the column headers in the first row (variable names) as you scroll down.

Figure 6.12	Calculation of Average $ Sales for Beet Smoothie Records Using Table's Total Row

	Order ID	Flavor	Category	$ Sales	Date Ordered	Date Delivered	Time To Deliver	Distribution Center	New Customer?
19791	104488	Beet	Smoothies	130.13	9/15/2020	9/26/2020	11	NM	No
19805	103559	Beet	Smoothies	1225.41	7/20/2020	8/4/2020	15	NE	No
19861	94183	Beet	Smoothies	196.77	7/24/2018	8/10/2018	17	MS	Yes
19873	95838	Beet	Smoothies	362.66	1/9/2019	1/26/2019	17	ID	Yes
19923	106068	Beet	Smoothies	939.72	12/27/2020	1/14/2021	18	NM	No
19927	105012	Beet	Smoothies	1111.82	10/16/2020	11/6/2020	21	ND	Yes
19933	Total			706.05					

In the next two sections, we will demonstrate how an Excel Table facilitates EDA and the construction of charts. When relevant and possible, we will perform the statistical summaries and visualization of EDA with a PivotTable and PivotChart. A PivotTable is an Excel tool that summarizes data for one or more variables. A PivotChart is an Excel charting tool connected with a PivotTable.

Notes + Comments

An Excel Table automatically names cell ranges using the column headers, so cells can be referenced with these names rather than cell column-row references (e.g., C7). If you are creating a cell formula by clicking on the cells involved, these cells in the Excel Table will automatically be referenced using the named range when selecting the cell range for the cell formula. Named ranges make Excel more dynamic by allowing a formula to reference ranges that are not fixed to column-row references that may change if new data are added to the spreadsheet.

6.2 Analyzing Variables One at a Time

In Chapter 5, we discuss the various charts used to analyze the distribution of a variable's values and provide step-by-step instructions on how to construct them.

As a general principle, it is almost always a good idea to first examine one variable at a time before exploring relationships between two or more variables. Examining one variable (column) of a data set is called **univariate analysis**. Univariate analysis focuses on the distribution of a variable's values. In this section, we discuss how to examine categorical and quantitative variables.

Exploring a Categorical Variable

We demonstrate the construction of charts displaying an individual categorical variable's distribution using Excel's PivotChart functionality. We will use the data from the EJB example, formatted using an Excel Table found in the file *ejb_table*.

ejb_table

Step 1. Select any cell in the range of the data, for example, cell A3
Step 2. Click the **Insert** tab on the Ribbon
In the **Charts** group, click the **PivotChart** button
PivotChart

Step 3. When the **Create PivotChart** dialog box appears:

> Under **Choose the data that you want to analyze**, choose **Select a table or range** and enter *EJBData* in the **Table/Range:** box
> Under **Choose where you want the PivotChart to be placed**, select **New Worksheet**
> Click **OK**

The resulting initial (empty) PivotTable and PivotChart are shown in Figure 6.13. With the PivotChart selected, the PivotChart task pane is activated. Each of the 14 columns (variables) is identified as a PivotChart Field by Excel. PivotChart Fields may be chosen to represent axes (categories), legends (series), filters, or values in a PivotChart. The following steps show how to use Excel's PivotChart Field List to assign Flavor to the horizontal axis and chart the percent frequency of Order IDs for each flavor.

When the PivotTable is selected, the PivotTable task pane will be activated instead of the PivotChart task pane. The PivotTable task pane is similar to the PivotChart task pane with the only differences being that a PivotTable has Rows and Columns areas instead of Axis (Categories) and Legend (Series) areas.

Step 4. In the **PivotChart Fields** task pane, under **Choose fields to add to report:**

> Drag the **Flavor** field to the **Axis (Categories)** area under **Drag fields between areas below:**
> Drag the **Order ID** field to the **Values** area

Step 5. Click **Sum of Order ID** in the **Values** area under **Drag fields between areas below:**

Step 6. Select **Value Field Settings...** from the list of options

Step 7. When the **Value Field Settings** dialog box appears:

> Click the **Summarize Values By** tab and under **Summarize value field by**, select **Count**
> Click the **Show Values As** tab and in the **Show values as** drop-down menu, select **% of Grand Total**
> Click **OK**

Step 8. Click any of the columns in the PivotChart. While the columns are selected, right click a column, then select **Sort** and **Sort Largest to Smallest**

Further editing will result in a chart that matches Figure 6.14. Figure 6.14 shows the percent frequency of records by flavor. We observe that orange is the most commonly

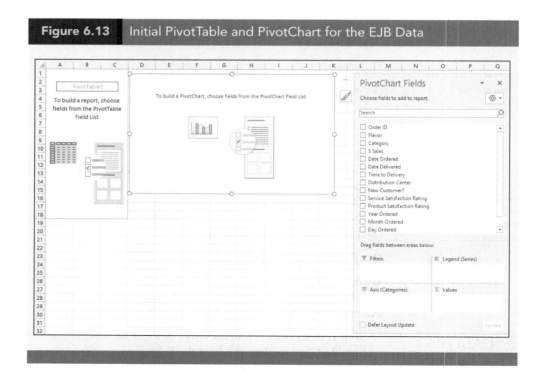

Figure 6.13   Initial PivotTable and PivotChart for the EJB Data

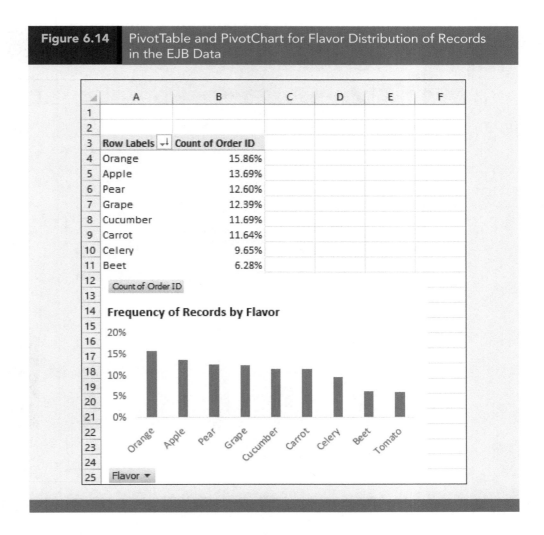

Figure 6.14 PivotTable and PivotChart for Flavor Distribution of Records in the EJB Data

ordered flavor (15.86% of all records) and tomato is the least commonly ordered flavor (6.20% of all records).

Similar frequency charts can be constructed for the other categorical variables in the EJB data (Category, Distribution Center, New Customer) for which there is no natural ordering of the categories.

In the EJB data, Service Satisfaction Rating and Product Satisfaction Rating are **ordinal variables**—categorical variables with a natural ordering. Frequency charts for ordinal variables can be constructed in a similar manner as frequency charts for general categorical variables, but one must be careful not to disrupt the natural ordering of the variable values with sorting. For example, Figure 6.15 displays the distribution of records by the Service Satisfaction Rating. Because there is a natural ordering of the values (1 is the lowest rating, 2 is the second lowest, etc.), it would be inappropriate to sort these values in order of increasing or decreasing frequency. Figure 6.15 shows that the most common service satisfaction rating was a 5 but also that 27.47% of the records were missing a service satisfaction rating response. In an upcoming section, we discuss ways to address missing data such as these.

Exploring a Quantitative Variable

We demonstrate the construction of charts displaying an individual quantitative variable's distribution using Excel's PivotTable and PivotChart functionality. We assume that a PivotTable and PivotChart using the data in the Table named EJBData have

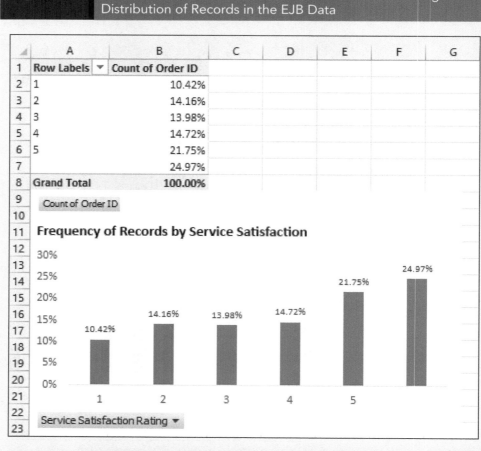

Figure 6.15   PivotTable and PivotChart for Service Satisfaction Rating Distribution of Records in the EJB Data

previously been created (corresponding to the analysis in Figure 6.14). In the following steps, we outline how to construct another PivotTable and PivotChart on the same source data, the Excel Table EJBData.

Step 1. Select the worksheet containing the previously constructed PivotTable and Pivot-Chart, and make a copy of this worksheet by right-clicking on the worksheet name, selecting **Move or Copy**, and when the **Move or Copy** dialog box appears:
Select the check box for **Create a copy**
Click **OK**

*If the PivotChart Fields task pane does not appear when you select the PivotChart, right click the chart and choose **Show Field List**.*

Step 2. Click the PivotChart in the new worksheet
When the **PivotChart Fields** task pane appears, clear the contents of the current PivotTable and PivotChart by deselecting the boxes next to the currently selected fields

The following steps show how to use Excel's PivotChart Field List to assign $ Sales to the horizontal axis and chart the percent frequency of Order IDs in the bins specified by a range of $ Sales values.

Step 3. In the **PivotChart Fields** task pane, under **Choose fields to add to report:**
Drag the **$ Sales** field to the **Axis (Categories)** area
Drag the **Order ID** field to the **Values** area
Step 4. Click **Sum of Order ID** in the **Values** area

Step 5. Select **Value Field Settings...** from the list of options

Step 6. When the **Value Field Settings** dialog box appears:

Click the **Summarize Values By** tab and under **Summarize value field by**, select **Count**

Click the **Show Values As** tab and in the **Show values as** drop-down menu, select **% of Grand Total**

Click **OK**

Step 7. Right click in cell A2 or any other cell containing a $ Value row label

Select **Group** from the list of options

Step 8. When the **Grouping** dialog box appears:

Enter *0* in the **Starting at:** box

Enter *2000* in the **Ending at:** box

Enter *100* in the **By:** box

Click **OK**

Further editing will result in a chart that matches Figure 6.16. Figure 6.16 displays the distribution of sales amounts at the product record level. We see that the records with smaller sales amounts are slightly more common and that the frequency of records with increasingly larger sales amounts gradually decreases.

In a similar manner, we can visualize the distribution of the Time to Deliver variable at the product record level. Figure 6.17 displays the corresponding PivotTable and PivotChart. We observe that the delivery time ranged from 2 days to 21 days with a most common delivery time of 3 days. The distribution of delivery times is skewed to the right by rare lengthy times to delivery.

Box and whisker plots are discussed in detail in Chapter 5. Box and whisker plots cannot be constructed through the PivotChart tool.

Another way to visualize the distribution of a quantitative variable is the box and whisker plot. The box and whisker plot summarizes the values of a variable by displaying various statistical measures: first quartile, second quartile (median), third quartile, mean, and interquartile range (IQR). The IQR is computed as the difference between the third quartile and the first quartile. Because the box and whisker plots use the median to measure the central location of a variable and the IQR to measure the deviation of a variable, their

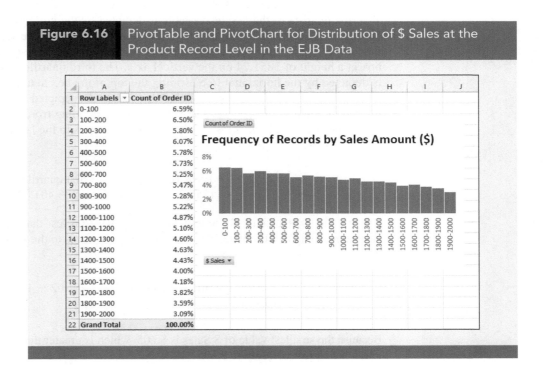

Figure 6.16 PivotTable and PivotChart for Distribution of $ Sales at the Product Record Level in the EJB Data

	A	B
1	Row Labels	Count of Order ID
2	0-100	6.59%
3	100-200	6.50%
4	200-300	5.80%
5	300-400	6.07%
6	400-500	5.78%
7	500-600	5.73%
8	600-700	5.25%
9	700-800	5.47%
10	800-900	5.28%
11	900-1000	5.22%
12	1000-1100	4.87%
13	1100-1200	5.10%
14	1200-1300	4.60%
15	1300-1400	4.63%
16	1400-1500	4.43%
17	1500-1600	4.00%
18	1600-1700	4.18%
19	1700-1800	3.82%
20	1800-1900	3.59%
21	1900-2000	3.09%
22	Grand Total	100.00%

Figure 6.17 PivotTable and PivotChart for Distribution of Time to Deliver at the Product Record Level in the EJB Data

	A	B
2		
3	Row Labels ▾	Count of Order ID
4	2	17.93%
5	3	27.55%
6	4	19.17%
7	5	12.20%
8	6	7.08%
9	7	5.65%
10	8	3.76%
11	9	2.13%
12	10	1.60%
13	11	1.00%
14	12	0.64%
15	13	0.34%
16	14	0.31%
17	15	0.17%
18	16	0.15%
19	17	0.18%
20	18	0.07%
21	19	0.03%
22	21	0.07%
23	Grand Total	100.00%

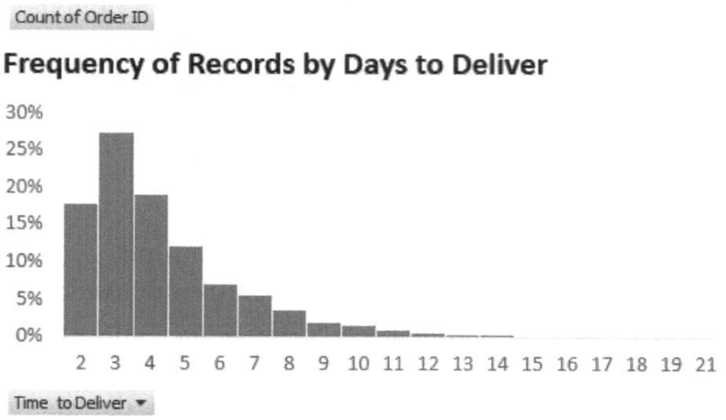

display is robust to the effects of extreme values, making them a valuable EDA visualization. The box and whisker plot is good at presenting information about a variable's central tendency, the symmetry or lack of symmetry in the distribution, and data points with extreme values.

For example, Figure 6.18 displays a box and whisker plot for the $ Sales variable. The first quartile of the $ Sales variable is depicted by the horizontal line forming the bottom of the box at a height of $401.02 on the vertical axis. The second quartile (the median) of the $ Sales variable is depicted by the horizontal line on the inside of the box at a height of $851.74 on the vertical axis. The third quartile of the $ Sales variable is depicted by the horizontal line forming the top of the box at a height of $1,355.08 on the vertical axis. The mean of the $ Sales variable is depicted by the X on the inside of the box at a height of $894.18. The vertical lines extending from the top and bottom of the box are called whiskers. The top whisker extends to the largest value of $ Sales that is less than or equal to

$$\text{third quartile} + 1.5 \times (\text{third quartile} - \text{first quartile})$$
$$= 1355.08 + 1.5 \times (1355.08 - 401.02) = \$2786$$

Because the largest value of $ Sales is $1,999.92, which is less than $2,786, the top whisker extends only to $1,999.92. The bottom whisker extends to the smallest value of $ Sales that is greater than or equal to

$$\text{first quartile} - 1.5 \times (\text{third quartile} - \text{first quartile}) = 401.02 - 1.5 \times (1355.08 - 401.02)$$
$$= -\$1030.07$$

Because the smallest value of $ Sales is $0.05, which is greater than −$1,030.07, the bottom whisker extends only to $0.05.

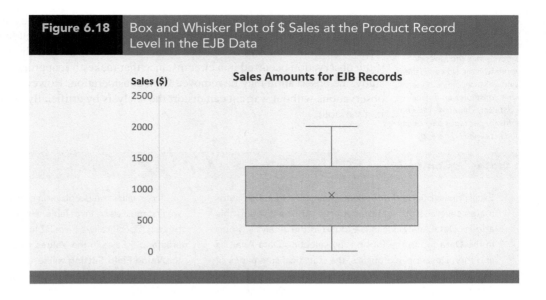

Figure 6.18 Box and Whisker Plot of $ Sales at the Product Record Level in the EJB Data

From the box and whisker plot of $ Sales in Figure 6.18, we can deduce that the distribution of $ Sales has a slight positive skew as the upper whisker is just a bit longer than the lower whisker. The mean being slightly larger than the median reinforces the implication of slight positive skew. All of these observations can be confirmed by referring to the histogram of the $ Sales variable in Figure 6.16.

Now consider the box and whisker plot for the Time to Deliver variable in Figure 6.19. We observe that the mean delivery time is larger than the median delivery time. Additionally, the bottom whisker is much shorter than the top whisker, suggesting that below there is a high concentration of delivery time observations over a narrow range of small values. The longer top whisker indicates delivery time observations above the median are spread out over a relatively wide range. The short lower whisker, long upper whisker, and mean value larger than the median value suggest that the delivery time distribution is positively skewed. Additionally, the presence of several **outliers** beyond the top whisker suggest that

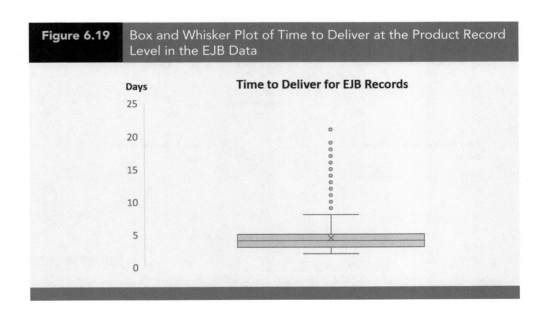

Figure 6.19 Box and Whisker Plot of Time to Deliver at the Product Record Level in the EJB Data

With respect to a box and whisker plot, an outlier is an observation that is more extreme than the lower or upper whisker. However, there is no universal definition for what constitutes an outlier in a data set. Therefore, different software packages may define outliers slightly differently.

the delivery time distribution has a long tail of relatively large values. It is a good idea to inspect the records corresponding to these outliers to confirm that these are accurately reported and not the result of an error. If the value of an outlier is the result of an error or if the observation occurred in a circumstance that makes it inappropriate for an analytical study, the observation may be removed from consideration. However, removing outlier observations without warrant can distort the analysis by artificially reducing the variation in a variable.

Notes + Comments

1. Excel comes bundled with a Data Analysis add-in that automates several statistical procedures. After activating this add-in, Data Analysis can be found in the Analysis group in the Data tab in the Ribbon. By selecting Data Analysis and then Descriptive Statistics, the statistical summaries of the quantitative variables can be calculated.

2. If **Data Analysis** does not appear in the **Analysis** group in the **Data** tab, you will have to load the Analysis Toolpak add-in into Excel. To do so, click the **File** tab in the Ribbon and click **Options**. When the **Excel Options** dialog box appears, click **Add-ins** from the menu. Next to **Manage:**, select **Excel Add-ins**, and click **Go...** at the bottom of the dialog box. When the **Add-Ins** dialog box appears, check the box next to **Analysis Toolpak,** and click **OK**.

3. The distribution analysis of the $ Sales and Time to Deliver variables in Figures 6.16, 6.17, 6.18, and 6.19 is based on record-level data. However, because some product records may be part of the same order (and share the same Order ID), it also may be insightful to visualize the distribution of the $ Sales and Time to Deliver variables at the order level.

To visualize the distribution of $ Sales at the order level, we first must use a PivotTable to aggregate the data appropriately. Specifically, a PivotTable with Order ID in the **Rows** area and $ Sales in the **Values** area with **Sum** selected as the **Value Field Setting** will result in a table of data listing each order with its corresponding sales amount. This data can then be copied and pasted outside the PivotTable and used as the basis for a histogram and box and whisker chart (see Figures (a) and (c) below).

To visualize the distribution of Time to Deliver at the order level, we first must use a PivotTable to aggregate the data appropriately. Specifically, a PivotTable with Order ID in the **Rows** area and Time to Deliver in the **Values** area with **Average** selected as the Value Field Setting will result in a table of data listing each order with its corresponding sales amount. Because all products in an order are delivered at the same time, the average time to deliver reflects the observed delivery time. This data can then be copied and pasted outside the PivotTable and used as the basis for a histogram and box and whisker chart (see Figures (b) and (d) below).

(a)

(b)

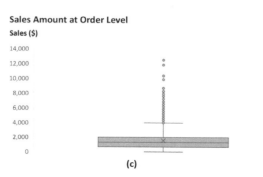

(c)

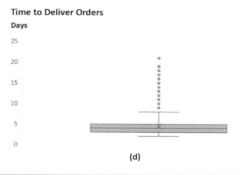

(d)

6.3 Relationships between Variables

After satisfactorily examining one variable at a time, the natural progression is to examine relationships between variables. Examining two or more variables at a time to explore relationships is called **multivariate analysis**. Generally, multivariate analysis involves pairs of variables (and thus is bivariate) but may involve three or more variables. Whether the variables of interest are categorical or quantitative dictates the statistical summary and visualization technique deployed. In this section, we first discuss a **crosstabulation**, which is a tabular summary of the statistical measure of a variable of interest with respect to two or more (typically categorical) variables. Then, we discuss the use of scatter charts to visualize the relationship between two quantitative variables.

Crosstabulation

In this section, we will demonstrate crosstabulation analysis of two or more variables and associated visualizations using Excel's PivotTable and PivotChart functionality. Suppose EJB is interested in investigating how the average sales amount of a record depends on the DC from which it was shipped and its product category. The following steps show how to construct a crosstabulation of Distribution Center as the variable in the table rows and Category (juices or smoothies) as the variable in the table columns. $ Sales is the variable to be summarized with respect to its average value in the corresponding cross-sections of Distribution Center and Category. We begin our steps from an empty PivotTable and PivotChart using the Excel Table EJBData as the source data as in Figure 6.13.

To clear the content of the PivotChart, click the Pivot-Chart. From the PivotChart Fields task pane, clear the contents of the current PivotTable and PivotChart by deselecting the boxes next to the currently selected fields.

Step 1. Select any cell in the range of the empty PivotTable, for example, cell A5
Step 2. When the **PivotTable Fields** task pane appears, under **Choose fields to add to report:**
> Drag the **$ Sales** field to the **Values** area
> Drag the **Distribution Center** field to the **Rows** area
> Drag the **Category** field to the **Columns** area
Step 3. Click **Sum of $ Sales** in the **Values** area
Step 4. Select **Value Field Settings…** from the list of options
Step 5. When the **Value Field Settings** dialog box appears:
> Click the **Summarize Values By** tab and under **Summarize value field by**, select **Average**
> Click **OK**

Further editing will result in a chart that matches Figure 6.20. Each entry in the Pivot-Table of Figure 6.20 corresponds to the average dollar sales per record computed over a corresponding cross-section of the data. For example, the value of 874.01 in cell B6 means that juice records shipped from the DC in Nebraska (NE) had an average sales amount of $874.01. The Grand Total amounts at the end of each column or row correspond to the average sales amounts over the corresponding column or row. For example, the value of 865.78 in cell D5 means that records shipped from the DC in North Dakota (ND) had an average sales amount of $865.78 (computed over both product categories). Analogously, the value of 887.19 in cell C10 means that smoothie records had an average sales amount of $887.19 (computed over all DCs).

From Figure 6.20, we observe several patterns in the average sales amount of a record relative to the DC and product category. First, the average sales amount for a juice record is larger than the average sales amount for a smoothie record for all DCs except Nebraska (NE) and West Virginia (WV). The largest average sales amounts for both juices and smoothies are associated with records shipped from Rhode Island (RI). The smallest average sales amount is associated with smoothie records shipped from Nebraska (NE).

While the variables used in the rows and columns of a PivotTable are typically categorical variables, it is possible to place a quantitative variable in the rows or columns of a

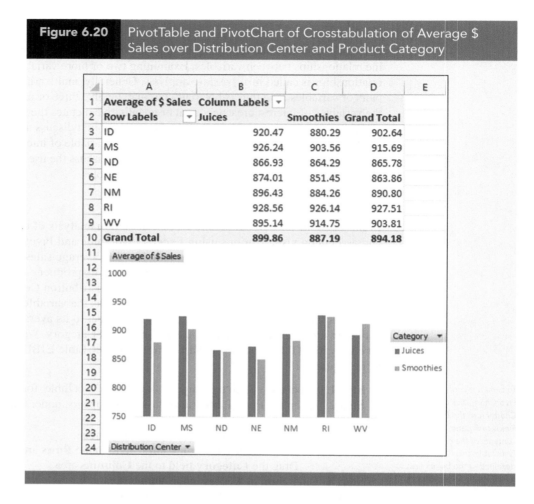

Figure 6.20 PivotTable and PivotChart of Crosstabulation of Average \$ Sales over Distribution Center and Product Category

PivotTable and then form bins by grouping consecutive values of the quantitative variable. Suppose EJB is interested in investigating how the distribution of the sales amount of a product record depends on whether a customer is new or existing. The following steps show how to construct a crosstabulation of \$ Sales as the variable in the table rows and New Customer as the variable in the table columns. As we are interested in the frequency distribution of records over the cross-section of \$ Sales and New Customer, we may select and count over any variable that is not missing values. We choose Order ID as the variable to be summarized with respect to its count value in the corresponding cross-sections of Distribution Center and Category. We begin our steps from an empty PivotTable and PivotChart using the Excel Table EJBData as the source data (as shown in Figure 6.13).

Step 1. Select any cell in the range of the empty PivotTable, for example, cell A5

Step 2. When the **PivotTable Fields** task pane appears, under **Choose fields to add to report:**

Drag the **Order ID** field to the **Values** area
Drag the **\$ Sales** field to the **Rows** area
Drag the **Category** field to the **Columns** area

Step 3. Click **Sum of Order ID** in the **Values** area

Select **Value Field Settings…** from the list of options

Step 4. When the **Value Field Settings** dialog box appears:

Click the **Summarize Values By** tab and under **Summarize value field by**, select **Count**
Click the **Show Values As** tab and in the **Show values as** drop-down menu, select **% of Column Total**
Click **OK**

Step 5. Right click in cell A5 or any other cell containing a $ Value row label

Select **Group** from the list of options

Step 6. When the **Grouping** dialog box appears:

Enter *0* in the **Starting at:** box

Enter *2000* in the **Ending at:** box

Enter *100* in the **By:** box

Click **OK**

Step 7. With the PivotChart selected, right click and select **Change Chart Type...**

In the **Change Chart Type** dialog box, select **Line**

Click **OK**

Further editing will result in a chart that matches Figure 6.21. Each entry in the PivotTable of Figure 6.21 corresponds to the percentage of the total number of records in a column that occur in a corresponding cross-section of the data. For example, the value of 6.54% in cell B4 means that 6.54% of all records corresponding to existing customers have sales amounts in the range (100, 200] (greater than $100 and less than or equal to $200). From Figure 6.21, we observe that for both existing and new customers, the frequency of records gradually decreases as the sales amount of the record increases. It does not appear that the customer status (existing or new) dramatically affects the sales amount of an record.

A PivotTable can be used to consider a crosstabulation of more than two variables. Suppose EJB is interested in examining total annual sales patterns over the years of 2018, 2019, and 2020, while also considering whether records originated from new customers and the DC from which the records were shipped. The following steps show how to construct a crosstabulation of Distribution Center and Year Ordered as the variables in the table rows and New Customer as the variable in the table columns. $ Sales is the variable to be summarized with respect to its sum value in the corresponding cross-sections. We begin our steps from an empty PivotTable and PivotChart using the Excel Table EJBData as the source data (as in Figure 6.13).

Step 1. Select any cell in the range of the empty PivotTable, for example, cell A5

Step 2. When the **PivotTable Fields** task pane appears, under **Choose fields to add to report:**

Drag the **$ Sales** field to the **Values** area

Drag the **Distribution Center** field to the **Rows** area

Drag the **Year Ordered** field to the **Rows** area

Drag the **New Customer?** field to the **Columns** area

Step 3. Click the PivotChart, right click and select **Change Chart Type...** from the menu

In the **Change Chart Type** dialog box, select **Column** from the list of charts and then select **Stacked Column** from the gallery

Click **OK**

You should confirm that $ Sales is being summarized by the Sum function as indicated by Sum of $ Sales in the Values area of the Pivot-Tables Fields task pane.

The next steps add an Excel feature called Slicers. An Excel Slicer provides a visual method for filtering the data considered by the PivotTable and PivotChart.

Step 4. With the PivotChart selected, in the **Insert** tab in the Ribbon, select **Slicer** in the **Filters** group

In the **Insert Slicers** dialog box, select **Distribution Center, New Customer?**, and **Year Ordered**

Click **OK**

The next two steps format the Slicers and PivotChart.

Step 5. Select the Slicer box for **Distribution Center** and in the **Slicer** tab in the Ribbon:

In the **Buttons** group, enter *7* in the **Columns:** box

Step 6. Select the Slicer box for **Years Ordered** and in the **Slicer** tab in the Ribbon:

In the **Buttons** group, enter *3* in the **Columns:** box

Step 7. Select the Slicer box for **New Customer?** and in the **Slicer** tab in the Ribbon:

In the **Buttons** group, enter *2* in the **Columns:** box

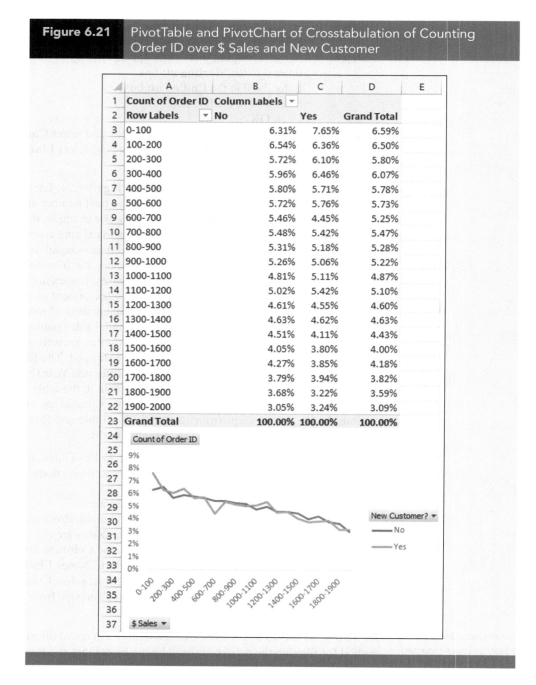

Figure 6.21	PivotTable and PivotChart of Crosstabulation of Counting Order ID over $ Sales and New Customer

After positioning the Slicer boxes adjacent to the PivotChart and sizing all boxes to create a seamless display, a single Excel object can be created with the following step. Further editing will result in a chart that matches Figure 6.22.

Step 8. Select the PivotChart and in the **PivotChart Analyze** tab in the Ribbon:
In the **Show/Hide** group, click the down arrow next to **Field Buttons**
Select **Hide All**

Step 9. Select the vertical axis labels, right click, select **Format Axis…**, and in the **Format Axis** task pane:
Select **Axis Options**, and in the drop-down menu next to **Display units:**
Select **Thousands**
Deselect the check box next to **Show display units label on chart**

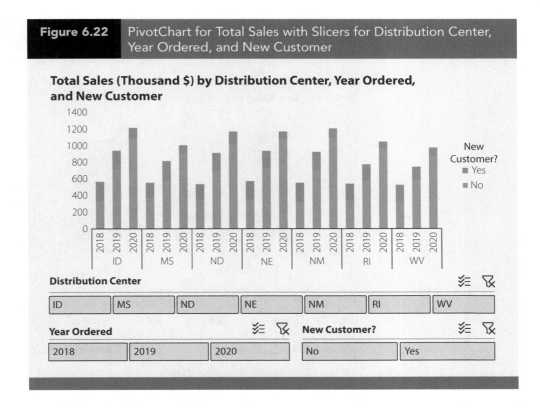

Figure 6.22 PivotChart for Total Sales with Slicers for Distribution Center, Year Ordered, and New Customer

Step 10. Holding the **Ctrl** key, select the three Slicer boxes and PivotChart
Right click any of the selected objects and select **Group**

We can remove the borders from a Slicer box by executing the following steps to create a new slicer style, which we can apply to any Slicer in the Excel workbook.

Step 11. With a Slicer box selected, click the **Slicer** tab on the Ribbon
Step 12. In the **Slicer Styles** group, right click the current style and select **Duplicate**
Step 13. When the **Modify Slicer Style** dialog box appears, select **Whole Slicer** from the **Slicer Element:** box and click **Format**
In the **Format Slicer Element** dialog box:
Click the **Border** tab and select **None** in the **Presets** area
Click **OK**
Click **OK** to close the **Modify Slicer Style** dialog box

Selecting Slicer boxes and applying the newly defined slicer style to these will remove the borders from them. Further editing will result in a chart that matches Figure 6.22.

The PivotChart in Figure 6.22 will allow the user to graphically display total dollar sales for any combination of years ordered, DCs, and new/existing customer status. For example, suppose we want to compare sales of new customers for the New Mexico and Rhode Island DCs in 2019 and 2020. We can create a chart for this purpose by selecting **NM** and **RI** in the **Distribution Center** slicer, **2019** and **2020** in the **Year Ordered** slicer, and **Yes** in the **New Customer?** slicer. This produces the chart in Figure 6.23.

*Recall that you can select multiple items in a slicer by clicking a slicer button while holding the **Ctrl** key, then clicking on each additional item you wish to select in that slicer.*

Association between Two Quantitative Variables

Thus far, we have demonstrated how to use a PivotTable and PivotChart to track a summary statistic of variable of interest over a crosstabulation of two or more categorical variables. Often a manager or decision maker is interested in the relationship between two quantitative variables. In this section, we consider methods for examining the association between two quantitative variables.

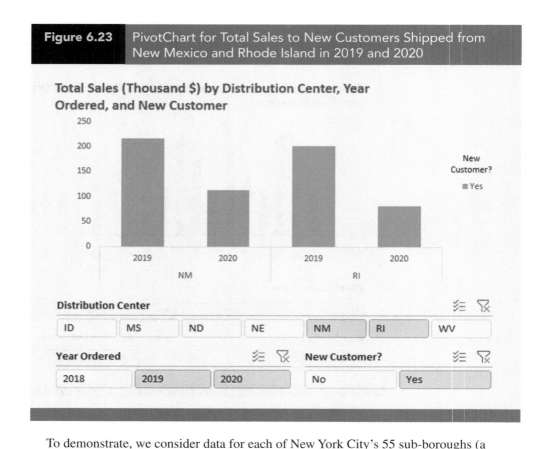

Figure 6.23   PivotChart for Total Sales to New Customers Shipped from New Mexico and Rhode Island in 2019 and 2020

To demonstrate, we consider data for each of New York City's 55 sub-boroughs (a designation of a community within New York City). Figure 6.24 contains a partial listing of these data, which tracks median monthly rent, percentage of college graduates, poverty rate, mean commute time to workplace, and borough. Suppose we want to examine the relationship between these different variables. A scatter chart is a useful graph for analyzing the relationship between two quantitative variables. Figure 6.25 displays a scatter chart of Percentage College Graduates versus Median Monthly Rent. To clearly convey meaningful patterns, the **aspect ratio** and **quantitative scales** must be appropriately set. With regard to the aspect ratio, it is generally a good idea to set the height and the width of a scatter chart to create a square plot display area that does not favor either variable. When setting the quantitative scales for a scatter chart, it is generally recommended to begin each axis at a value slightly smaller than the smallest value of the corresponding variable and end each axis at a value slightly larger than the largest value. To add the linear trendline to the scatter chart in Figure 6.25 and then format the scatter chart, we executed the following steps.

An exception to the guideline of having a square plot display area for a scatter chart occurs when the horizontal axis corresponds to time. In this case, the plot display area is often wider than it is tall.

Step 1. Select the data series by clicking on the data points
Step 2. Right click and select **Add Trendline...**
          In the **Format Trendline** task pane, under **Trendline Options** ￭￭ , select **Linear**

DATA*file*
nyc

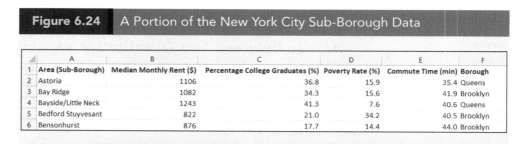

Figure 6.24   A Portion of the New York City Sub-Borough Data

	A	B	C	D	E	F
1	Area (Sub-Borough)	Median Monthly Rent ($)	Percentage College Graduates (%)	Poverty Rate (%)	Commute Time (min)	Borough
2	Astoria	1106	36.8	15.9	35.4	Queens
3	Bay Ridge	1082	34.3	15.6	41.9	Brooklyn
4	Bayside/Little Neck	1243	41.3	7.6	40.6	Queens
5	Bedford Stuyvesant	822	21.0	34.2	40.5	Brooklyn
6	Bensonhurst	876	17.7	14.4	44.0	Brooklyn

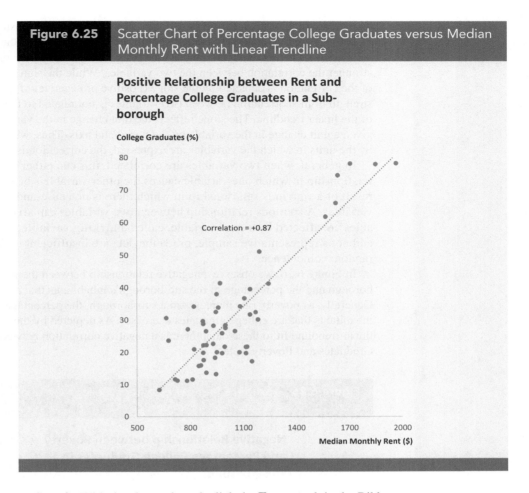

Figure 6.25 Scatter Chart of Percentage College Graduates versus Median Monthly Rent with Linear Trendline

Positive Relationship between Rent and Percentage College Graduates in a Sub-borough

College Graduates (%)

Correlation = +0.87

Median Monthly Rent ($)

*In Excel, we can set the size of the chart area in the **Size** group within the **Format** tab. However, the dimensions of the chart area, which includes the entire chart and titles, are not typically proportional to the dimensions of the plot area, which is just the graphical display, due to the space that the chart and axis titles consume. To obtain a square plot area, we must adjust the chart height and width appropriately.*

Step 3. With the chart selected, click the **Format** tab in the Ribbon

In the **Size** group, enter *6.5* in the **Height:** box and enter *5* in the **Width:** box

Step 4. Click the horizontal axis, right click and select **Format Axis…**

In the **Format Axis** task pane, under **Axis Options**, enter *500* in the **Minimum** Bound and enter *2000* for the **Maximum** Bound

Step 5. Click the vertical axis, right click and select **Format Axis…**

In the **Format Axis** task pane, under **Axis Options**, enter *0* in the **Minimum** Bound and enter *80* for the **Maximum** Bound

We observe from Figure 6.25 that generally, as median monthly rent increases in a sub-borough, the percentage of the sub-borough's inhabitants that are college graduates also increases. The positive slope of the linear trendline indicates there is a positive correlation between Percentage College Graduates and Median Monthly Rent. **Correlation** is a statistical measure of the strength of the linear relationship between variables. Values of correlation range between -1 and $+1$. Correlation values near 0 indicate no linear relationship exists between the two variables. The closer a correlation value is to $+1$, the closer the data points on the scatter chart of the two variables resemble a straight line that trends upward to the right (positive slope). The closer a correlation value is to -1, the closer the data points on the scatter chart of the two variables resemble a straight line that trends downward to the right (negative slope). We can calculate the correlation in the data for two variables using the Excel function CORREL. For example, the correlation of 0.87 between Percentage College Graduates and Median Monthly Rent is computed by placing the formula $= CORREL(C2:C56, B2:B56)$ in a cell.

The positive correlation between Percentage College Graduates and Median Monthly Rent does not imply that a change in one variable causes a change in the other variable, it only measures the degree to which an increase (decrease) in one variable corresponds to an increase (decrease) in the other variable. The strength of this positive correlation can be visually gauged by how close the data points are clustered around the linear trendline. As a collection, the less total vertical distance between the data points and the trendline, the stronger the correlation between the two variables. While the sign (positive or negative) of the correlation is depicted by the slope (positive or negative) of the linear trendline, the strength of the correlation between two variables is not related to the steepness of the slope of the linear trendline. The slope reflects the unit change in the variable on the vertical axis given a unit change in the variable on the horizontal axis. Thus, while the slope is affected by the units in which the variables are expressed, the correlation is not.

In general, when two variables are correlated, this can either indicate a causal relationship in which one variable causes the other variable's behavior, or it can be the result of a **spurious relationship** in which there is no cause-and-effect between the two variables. A spurious relationship between two variables can arise when (1) both variables are affected by a third variable, called a **lurking variable,** (2) the data are biased and not a representative sample, or (3) the data are insufficient to distinguish it from random coincidence.

In Figure 6.26, we observe a negative relationship between the poverty rate of a sub-borough and the percentage of the sub-borough's inhabitants that are college graduates. Generally, as poverty rate increases in a sub-borough, the percentage of the sub-borough's inhabitants that are college graduates decreases. As depicted by the negative slope of the linear trendline fit to these data, there is a negative correlation between Percentage College Graduates and Poverty Rate.

Figure 6.26   Scatter Chart of Percentage College Graduates versus Poverty Rate with Linear Trendline

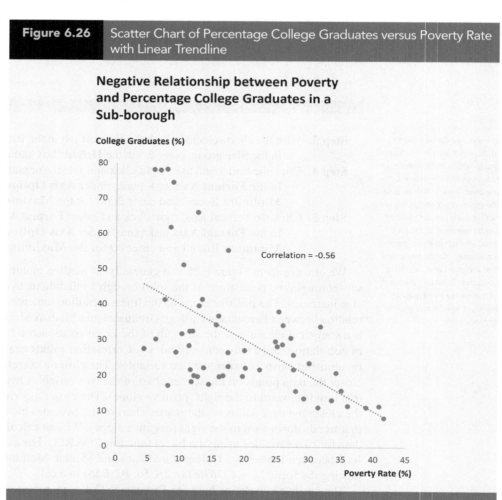

In Figure 6.27, we observe that the data points do not fit closely to the linear trendline and the correlation is near zero. This means that there is no linear relationship between Commute Time and Poverty Rate. For these data, there does not appear to be any type of relationship between Commute Time and Poverty Rate. However, we caution that a near-zero correlation only means that there is no evidence for a linear relationship between two variables, but there may be a nonlinear relationship between them.

To underscore the importance of examining the scatter charts of pairs of quantitative variables rather than just computing tables of correlation measures, we consider the scatter chart in Figure 6.28. Figure 6.28 displays data for monthly heating/cooling bills and the mean high temperature. The data points do not fit closely to the linear trendline and the correlation is near zero, suggesting there is no linear relationship between the monthly heating/cooling bill and the mean high temperature. However, it would be incorrect to conclude there is no relationship between these two variables. As the nonlinear trendline outlines, there is strong visual evidence of a nonlinear relationship between these two variables. That is, reading the chart from left to right, we can see that as the mean high temperature increases, the monthly bill first decreases as less heating is required and then increases as more cooling is required.

Consideration of a categorical variable can be added to a scatter chart displaying the relationship between two quantitative variables. Let us reconsider the relationship between a sub-borough's percentage of college graduates and its median monthly rent that was displayed in Figure 6.25. In Figure 6.25, all 55 observation pairs of Median Monthly Rent and Percentage College Graduates were plotted as a single data series. To add information about the borough to the observation pairs of Median Monthly Rent and Median Monthly

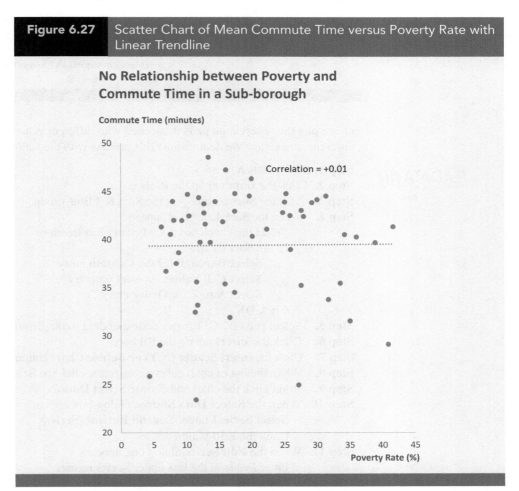

Figure 6.27 Scatter Chart of Mean Commute Time versus Poverty Rate with Linear Trendline

*The nonlinear trendline in Figure 6.28 was added by selecting **Add Trendline** and then specifying the **Polynomial** trendline option with **Order** specified as 2.*

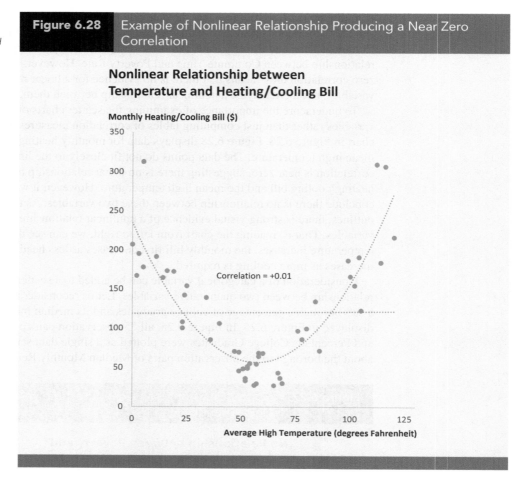

Figure 6.28   Example of Nonlinear Relationship Producing a Near Zero Correlation

Nonlinear Relationship between Temperature and Heating/Cooling Bill

Correlation = +0.01

Rent, we plot the observation pairs associated with different values of the Borough variable as different data series. We demonstrate this process with the following steps.

DATA *file*

nyc

Step 1. Select cells A1:F56
Step 2. Click the **Data** tab on the Ribbon
Step 3. Click the **Sort** button in the **Sort & Filter** group
Step 4. When the **Sort** dialog box appears:
Select the check box for **My data has headers**
In the **Sort by** row:
Select **Borough** for the **Column** entry
Select **Cell Values** for **Sort on** entry
Select **A to Z** for **Order** entry
Click **OK**
Step 5. Select cells B2:C11 (rows corresponding to the Bronx borough)
Step 6. Click the **Insert** tab on the Ribbon
Step 7. Click the **Insert Scatter (X,Y) or Bubble Chart** button in the **Charts** group
Step 8. When the list of chart subtypes appears, click the **Scatter** button
Step 9. Right click the chart and choose **Select Data...**
Step 10. When the **Select Data Source** dialog box appears:
Select **Series1** under **Legend Entries (Series)**
Click the **Edit** button
Step 11. When the **Edit Series** dialog box appears:
Enter *Bronx* in the box under **Series name:**
Click **OK**

Step 12. In the **Select Data Source** dialog box, click the **Add** button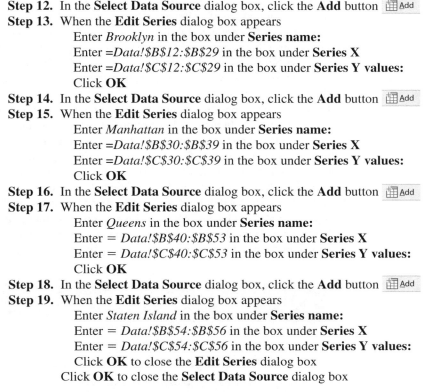
Step 13. When the **Edit Series** dialog box appears
        Enter *Brooklyn* in the box under **Series name:**
        Enter *=Data!$B$12:$B$29* in the box under **Series X**
        Enter *=Data!$C$12:$C$29* in the box under **Series Y values:**
        Click **OK**
Step 14. In the **Select Data Source** dialog box, click the **Add** button
Step 15. When the **Edit Series** dialog box appears
        Enter *Manhattan* in the box under **Series name:**
        Enter *=Data!$B$30:$B$39* in the box under **Series X**
        Enter *=Data!$C$30:$C$39* in the box under **Series Y values:**
        Click **OK**
Step 16. In the **Select Data Source** dialog box, click the **Add** button
Step 17. When the **Edit Series** dialog box appears
        Enter *Queens* in the box under **Series name:**
        Enter *= Data!$B$40:$B$53* in the box under **Series X**
        Enter *= Data!$C$40:$C$53* in the box under **Series Y values:**
        Click **OK**
Step 18. In the **Select Data Source** dialog box, click the **Add** button
Step 19. When the **Edit Series** dialog box appears
        Enter *Staten Island* in the box under **Series name:**
        Enter *= Data!$B$54:$B$56* in the box under **Series X**
        Enter *= Data!$C$54:$C$56* in the box under **Series Y values:**
        Click **OK** to close the **Edit Series** dialog box
      Click **OK** to close the **Select Data Source** dialog box

Further editing will result in a chart that matches Figure 6.29. Using color, Figure 6.29 distinguishes the 55 observations by their borough. We notice that Manhattan is characterized

Figure 6.29	Using Color in a Scatter Chart to Communicate a Categorical Variable

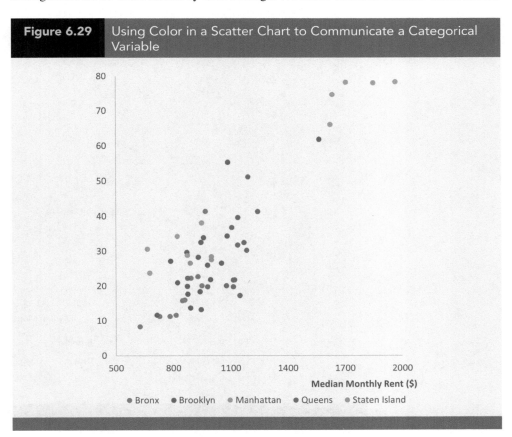

by two different types of sub-boroughs: one group with a low monthly median rent and a moderate percentage of college graduates and one group with a high monthly median rent and a high percentage of college graduates. Figure 6.29 suggests that the strength of the association between monthly median rent and percentage of college graduates may vary across boroughs. Modifying the coloration of the scatter chart, we can visualize the strength of the correlation between monthly median rent and percentage of college graduates for individual boroughs.

For example, suppose we want to highlight the sub-boroughs of Queens and Manhattan on a scatter chart. In Figure 6.30, we remove the fill color and select a subdued gray color for data points not corresponding to Queens or Manhattan. We display the correlation between these two variables for the Queens sub-boroughs in the same color (purple) as the Queens data markers. Similarly, we display the correlation between these two variables for the Manhattan sub-boroughs in the same color (green) as the Manhattan data markers. Figure 6.30 illustrates that the correlation between monthly median rent and percentage of college graduates in Queens, while positive, is not as strong as the correlation in Manhattan.

While an individual scatter chart is a great way to visualize the relationship between a single pair of individual relationships, an analyst may want to examine the pairwise

Figure 6.30	Using Color to Highlight a Specific Value of a Categorical Variable

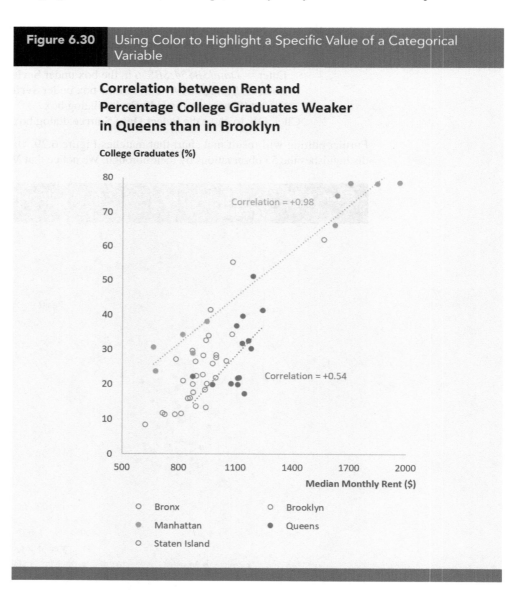

relationships between several different sets of variables. To easily see the relationships between several pairs of variables at once, a **scatter-chart matrix** provides a visual display of the scatter charts for every possible pair of quantitative variables in a data set. Figure 6.31 displays the scatter-chart matrix for the NYC data. Each column and row in the scatter-chart matrix corresponds to one categorical variable. For instance, row 1 and column 1 in Figure 6.31 correspond to the median monthly rent variable. Row 2 and column 2 correspond to the percentage of college graduates variable. Therefore, the scatter chart shown in row 1, column 2 shows the relationship between median monthly rent (on the vertical axis) and the percentage of college graduates (on the horizontal axis) in New York City sub-boroughs. The scatter chart shown in row 2, column 3 shows the relationship between the percentage of college graduates (on the vertical axis) and poverty rate (on the horizontal axis).

Figure 6.31 summarizes several interesting findings. Because the points in the scatter chart in row 1, column 2 generally get higher moving from left to right, this tells us that sub-boroughs with higher percentages of college graduates appear to have higher median monthly rents. The scatter chart in row 1, column 3 indicates that sub-boroughs with higher poverty rates appear to have lower median monthly rents. The data in row 2, column 3 show that sub-boroughs with higher poverty rates tend to have lower percentages of college graduates. The scatter charts in column 4 show that the relationships between the mean travel time and the other variables are not as clear as relationships in other columns.

A **table lens** is another way to visualize relationships between different pairs of variables. In a table lens, a table of data is highlighted with horizontal bars with lengths proportional to the values in each variable's column. A table lens can be a useful visualization tool for wide and tall data sets as the insight on the relationships between variables remains evident even if the display is "zoomed out" to show the table in its entirety or near-entirety.

The scatter charts along the diagonal in the scatter-chart matrix in Figure 6.31 (e.g., in row 1, column 1 and in row 2, column 2) display the relationship between a variable and itself. Therefore, the points in these scatter charts will always fall along a straight line at a 45-degree angle as shown in Figure 6.31.

Excel does not have a procedure for generating a scatter-chart matrix. Each scatter chart must be created individually in Excel and arranged manually.

Figure 6.31 Scatter-Chart Matrix for New York City Sub-Borough Data

The following steps demonstrate the construction of a table lens on the quantitative variables in the New York City sub-borough data.

Step 1. Select cells B2:B56
Step 2. Click the **Home** tab on the Ribbon
Step 3. Click the **Conditional Formatting** button in the **Styles** group
From the drop-down menu, select **Data Bars** and then **Blue Data Bar** from the **Solid Fill** area

nyc

*Step 4 hides the values in the selected cells of the table lens. Reformatting the cell with a different **Category:** type will make the values visible again.*

Repeat steps 1–3 for the other three quantitative variables, changing the cell range in step 1 to C2:C56, D2:D56, and E2:E56, respectively. This will result in the four quantitative variable columns being formatted with horizontal bars proportional to the values of the respective variable. To hide the numeric values in the cells, we execute the following step.

Step 4. Select cells B2:E56, then right click and select **Format Cells…**
Click the **Number** tab, then select **Custom** from the **Category:** area
In the box below **Type:**, delete General and enter ;;;
Click **OK**

To visualize relationships between variables with a table lens, we must now sort the data according to one of the quantitative variables. The next steps sort the data according to Median Monthly Rent.

Step 1. Select cells A1:F56
Step 2. Click the **Data** tab on the Ribbon
Step 3. Click the **Sort** button in the **Sort & Filter** group
Step 4. When the **Sort** dialog box appears, select the check box for **My data has headers**
In the **Sort by** row:
Select **Median Monthly Rent ($)** for the **Column** entry
Select **Cell Values** for the **Sort on** entry
Select **Largest to Smallest** for the **Order** entry
Click **OK**

Figure 6.32 displays the resulting table lens. We interpret this table lens by comparing the large values to small values pattern in the column we sorted (in this case, Median Monthly Rent) to the patterns in the columns. Because Percentage College Graduates also displays a large values to small values pattern, we can deduce that this variable has a positive association with Median Monthly Rent. Conversely, Poverty Rate displays a small values to large values pattern, so we can deduce that this variable has a negative association with Median Monthly Rent. The Commute Time column displays no pattern, so we can deduce that this variable has no relationship with Median Monthly Rent. By sorting the table on the values of a different variable, the relationships between different pairs of variables can be analyzed.

Notes + Comments

1. Excel comes bundled with a Data Analysis add-in that automates several statistical procedures. After activating this add-in, **Data Analysis** can be found in the **Analyze** group under the **Data** tab in the Ribbon. By selecting **Data Analysis** and then **Correlation**, the correlation between each pair of quantitative variables can be computed and displayed in a matrix.

2. Correlation is a measure of association between two quantitative variables. Therefore, it is inappropriate to attempt to fit a trendline between a quantitative variable and a cat-

egorical variable, even if those categories are labeled as numbers such as 1, 2, 3, … The difference between Category 1 and Category 2 may not be the same as the difference between Category 2 and Category 3, so it would be inappropriate to compute a measure such as correlation on these values.

3. For a set of n observations of two variables (x_1, y_1); (x_2, y_2); … (x_n, y_n) where $\bar{x}$ and $\bar{y}$ are the sample means for the x and y variables, respectively, the formula for computing the sample correlation between the two variables is

$$r_{xy} = \cfrac{\sqrt{\cfrac{(x_1 - \overline{x})(y_1 - \overline{y}) + (x_2 - \overline{x})(y_2 - \overline{y}) + \ldots + (x_n - \overline{x})(y_n - \overline{y})}{n - 1}}}{\sqrt{\cfrac{(x_1 - \overline{x})^2 + (x_2 - \overline{x})^2 + \ldots + (x_n - \overline{x})^2}{n - 1}} \sqrt{\cfrac{(y_1 - \overline{y})^2 + (y_2 - \overline{y})^2 + \ldots + (y_n - \overline{y})^2}{n - 1}}}$$

4. Linear trendlines are appropriate to depict correlation. Linear trendlines on a scatter chart have a constant slope that implies a change in one variable corresponds to a proportional change in the other variable regardless of the starting values of the variables. In addition to linear trendlines, Excel supports the fit of several types of nonlinear trendlines to scatter charts. An exponential trendline is appropriate when there is a positive (negative) relationship in which the slope becomes upwardly (downwardly) steeper as you move from left to right on the scatter chart. A logarithmic trendline is appropriate when there is a positive (negative) relationship in which the slope flattens as you move from left to right on the scatter chart. A polynomial trendline is appropriate when the slope changes direction as you move from left to right on the scatter chart. Figure 6.28 is an example of a polynomial trendline in which the slope changes direction once. There are other polynomial trendlines that allow the slope to change sign multiple times.

Figure 6.32   Table Lens Using File *nyc*

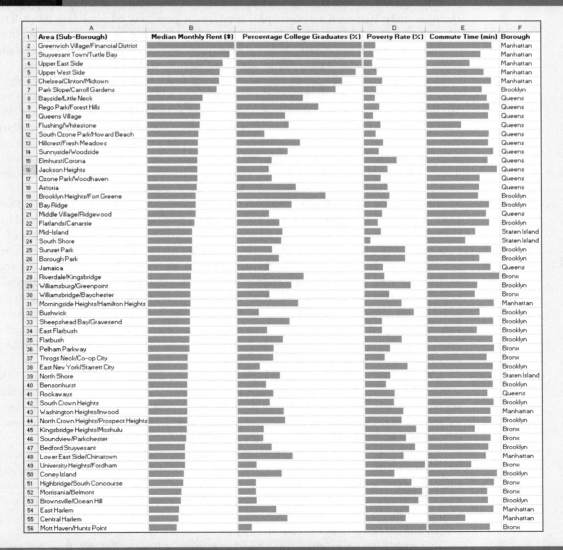

6.4 Analysis of Missing Data

Many real-life data sets suffer from missing data values. There are many reasons why data sets can contain missing values, and it is important to understand the reasons behind the missing values to know how they should be treated. In this section, we examine some of the most common forms of missing data, discuss how missing data can be addressed, and outline how to identify patterns associated with missing data.

Types of Missing Data

Data sets commonly include observations with missing values for one or more variables. In some cases, missing data naturally occur; these are called **legitimately missing data**. For example, respondents to a survey may be asked if they belong to a fraternity or a sorority and then in the next question are asked how long they have belonged to a fraternity or a sorority. If a respondent does not belong to a fraternity or a sorority, the respondent should skip the ensuing question about how long. Generally, no remedial action is taken for legitimately missing data.

In other cases, missing data occur for different reasons; these are called **illegitimately missing data**. These cases can result for a variety of reasons, such as a respondent electing not to answer a question the respondent is expected to answer, a respondent dropping out of a study before its completion, or sensors or other electronic data collection equipment failing during a study. Remedial action is considered for illegitimately missing data. After detecting illegitimately missing data, the primary options for addressing them are (1) to discard observations (rows) with any missing values, (2) to fill in missing entries with estimated values, or (3) to treat missing data as a separate category if dealing with a categorical variable.

Deciding on a strategy for dealing with missing data requires some understanding of why the data are missing and the potential impact these missing values might have on an analysis. If the tendency for an observation to be missing the value for some variable is entirely random, then whether data are missing does not depend on either the value of the missing data or the value of any other variable in the data. In such cases the missing value is called **missing completely at random (MCAR)**. For example, if a missing value for a question on a survey is completely unrelated to the value that is missing and is also completely unrelated to the value of any other question on the survey, the missing value is MCAR.

However, the occurrence of some missing values may not be completely at random. If the tendency for an observation to be missing a value for some variable is related to the value of some other variable(s) in the data, the missing value is called **missing at random (MAR)**. For data that are MAR, the reason for the missing values may determine its importance. For example, if the responses to one survey question collected by a specific employee were lost due to a data entry error, then the treatment of the missing data may be less critical. However, in a healthcare study, suppose observations corresponding to patient visits are missing the results of diagnostic tests whenever the doctor deems the patient too sick to undergo the procedure. In this case, the absence of a variable measurement actually provides additional information about the patient's condition, which may be helpful in understanding other relationships in the data.

A third category of missing data is **missing not at random (MNAR)**. Data are MNAR if there is a tendency for a missing entry of a variable to be related to its value. For example, survey respondents with extremely high or extremely low annual incomes may be less inclined than respondents with moderate annual incomes to respond to the question on annual income, so these missing data for annual income are MNAR.

Whether the missing values are MCAR, MAR, or MNAR, the first course of action when faced with missing values is to try to determine the actual value that is missing by examining the source of the data or logically determining the likely value that is missing. If the missing values cannot be determined, we must determine how to handle them. Understanding which of these three categories—MCAR, MAR, and MNAR—missing values fall into is critical in determining how to handle missing data.

If a variable has observations for which the missing values are MCAR, then discarding the observations with missing values may be a good choice if there are a relatively small number

Imputing missing data using the mode, median, or mean changes the resulting distribution for that variable. In general, the resulting distribution will have less variability than the true distribution of the variable.

of observations with missing values. When missing data are MCAR, removing observations with missing values is equivalent to randomly culling the rows of the data set. We will certainly lose information if the observations that are missing values for the variable are ignored, but the results of an analysis of the data will not be biased by the missing values. As an alternative to discarding observations with missing values that are MCAR, it may be useful to replace the missing entries for a variable with the variable's median, mean, or mode.

If missing data are MAR, then there is a relationship between the likelihood of a variable having a missing value and the value of another variable in the observation. If missing data are MAR, then discarding observations with missing values can alter the observed patterns in the remaining data. For example, suppose that missing values of blood pressure measurements are more likely to occur in younger patients. Then, discarding all records with missing blood pressure measurements would also discard a higher proportion of records with younger patients, thereby potentially distorting patterns in the remaining data. If missing values for a variable are MAR, it may be possible to estimate an observation's missing value of the variable based on the values of the other variables in the observation.

If a variable has observations for which the missing values are MNAR, the observation with missing values cannot be ignored because any analysis that includes the variable with MNAR values will be biased. Furthermore, there is no satisfactory manner to address a variable with missing data that are MNAR because it is the (unknown) values of the missing data that are causing them to be missing. If the variable with MNAR values is thought to be redundant with another variable in the data for which there are few or no missing values, removing the MNAR variable from consideration may be an option. In particular, if the MNAR variable is highly correlated with another variable that is known for a majority of observations, the loss of information may be minimal.

Exploring Patterns Associated with Missing Data

When there is a relatively small number of missing entries, an analyst may be able to research each missing entry and conjecture about the reason for its absence. When the missing entries are numerous, it may be possible to conduct exploratory data analysis to determine if there are any patterns related to the missing data. In the data from Espléndido Jugo y Batido, Inc., there are 4,977 records missing a value for Service Satisfaction Rating (24.97% of the total number of records) and 10,606 records missing a value for Product Satisfaction Rating (53.21% of the total number of records). The substantial number of records both with and without values for these variables facilitate an exploratory data analysis into patterns that may exist with respect to the missing data.

EJB notes that the entries for the Service Satisfaction Rating and Product Satisfaction Rating are retrieved from a database that contains customer responses to surveys associated with product records. As a customer response to a survey is voluntary, it is reasonable to expect some missing entries. However, it is important to examine the missing data for these variables to determine how we should handle them in the data analysis. Specifically, we would like to gain understanding on whether the missing entries are MCAR, MAR, or MNAR.

In our discussion and demonstrations, we will consider the missing data for the Service Satisfaction Rating. The only definitive way to determine whether the missing entries of Service Satisfaction Rating depend on the (unknown) values of the Service Satisfaction Rating or depend on other variables' values in the same observation would be to obtain the values of these missing entries. If possible, EJB may want to perform interviews with customers who did not provide service satisfaction ratings to ascertain that these data are missing completely at random and were not the result of a customer withholding any survey response value. For instance, it may be that customers who would otherwise report middling Service Satisfaction Ratings of 3 are more likely to skip the survey, resulting in a missing entry for this record. However, without obtaining these data, it is difficult to detect this MNAR pattern of missing data. In many cases, it may not be plausible (or reliable) to obtain the missing values. In lieu of obtaining the missing values, we use statistical summaries and charts to identify patterns in the missing data for the Service Satisfaction Rating.

We begin by considering the impact of missing data on the distribution of values for individual variables. To demonstrate, we compare the relative frequency of records by DC for records in which the Service Satisfaction Rating is reported to the relative frequency of records by DC for records in which the Service Satisfaction Rating is not reported. We begin our steps from an empty PivotTable and PivotChart using the Excel Table EJBData as the source data (as in Figure 6.13).

To clear the content of the PivotChart, click the PivotChart. From the PivotChart Fields task pane, clear the contents of the current PivotTable and PivotChart by deselecting the boxes next to the currently selected field.

DATA *file*

ejb_table

Step 1. Select any cell in the range of the empty PivotTable, for example, cell A5

Step 2. When the **PivotTable Fields** task pane appears, under **Choose fields to add to report:**
  Drag the **Order ID** field to the **Values** area
  Drag the **Distribution Center** field to the **Rows** area
  Drag the **Service Satisfaction Rating** field to the Filters area

Step 3. Click **Sum of Order ID** in the **Values** area

Step 4. Select **Value Field Settings...** from the list of options, and when the **Value Field Settings** dialog box appears:
  Click the **Summarize Values By** tab and under **Summarize value field by**, select **Count**
  Click the **Show Values As** tab and in the **Show values as** drop-down menu, select **% of Grand Total**
  Click **OK**

Step 5. In the PivotTable, click the **Filter Arrow** ▼ in cell B1 and in the drop-down menu:
  Select the check box next to **Select Multiple Items**
  Select the check boxes next to **1**, **2**, **3**, **4**, and **5**
  Deselect the check box next to the blank entry (last category)
  Click **OK**

These steps display the frequency distribution of records by DC based on records in which the Service Satisfaction Rating is reported. This output is displayed in Figure 6.33a. The next steps create the frequency distribution of records by DC based on records in which the Service Satisfaction Rating is not reported, displayed in Figure 6.33b.

Step 6. Select the worksheet containing the previously constructed PivotTable and Pivot Chart, and make a copy of this worksheet by right-clicking on the worksheet name, selecting **Move or Copy**, and selecting the **Create a copy** check box in the **More or Copy** dialog box
  Click **OK**

Step 7. In the PivotTable, click the **Filter Arrow** ▼ in cell B1 and in the drop-down menu:
  Deselect the boxes next to **1**, **2**, **3**, **4**, and **5**
  Select the check box next to the blank entry (last category)
  Click **OK**

If the tendency for a record to be missing an entry for Service Satisfaction Rating was unrelated to the DC from which the record was shipped, we would expect the frequency distribution of Figure 6.33a to be similar to the frequency distribution of Figure 6.33b. However, we observe that Mississippi was the DC for 8.75% of the orders with a service satisfaction rating, but Mississippi was the DC for 26.18% of the orders missing a service satisfaction rating. This finding suggests there may be an association between the tendency of a service satisfaction rating to be missing and whether the record was shipped from Mississippi. We should be aware that any analysis related to the service satisfaction ratings for records shipped from Mississippi may be unreliable.

For each variable in the EJB data, we can repeat the process of comparing the frequency distribution on data for which the Service Satisfaction Rating is reported to the frequency distribution on data for which the Service Satisfaction Rating is not reported. In these pairwise comparisons, we are looking for substantial differences in the distributions that may provide an indication that the missing Service Satisfaction Rating is related to the value of the variable being analyzed.

Figure 6.33	Comparing Frequency of Records by Distribution Center for Records with a Service Satisfaction Rating to Frequency of Records by Distribution Center for Records without a Service Satisfaction Rating

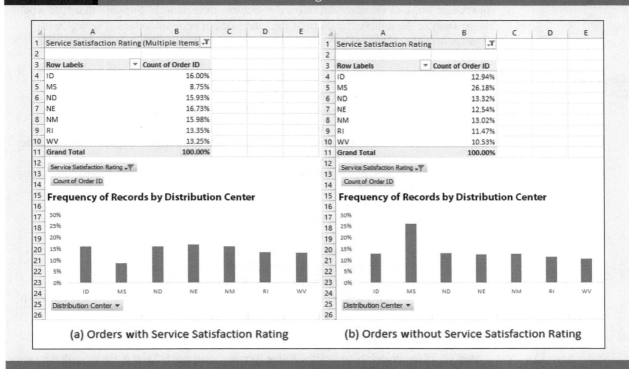

(a) Orders with Service Satisfaction Rating   (b) Orders without Service Satisfaction Rating

Similarly, by adding Service Satisfaction Rating to the Filters area of a PivotChart, we can compare the crosstabulation of two or more variables on data for which the Service Satisfaction Rating is reported to the crosstabulation on data for which the Service Satisfaction Rating is not reported. In these pairwise comparisons, we are looking for substantial differences in the crosstabulations that may provide an indication that the missing Service Satisfaction Rating is related to variables involved in the crosstabulation.

6.5 Visualizing Time Series Data

Time series data consist of observations collected at different points in time. Contrast this to **cross-sectional data**, which consist of observations collected at a single point in time. In this section, we assume that the observations are collected at regular intervals of time and ordered chronologically (which is normally the case).

In most cases, time series data should be displayed using line charts. The lines in a line chart emphasize the sequential flow and relationship between consecutive values, making visible any trend, variability, and seasonality. **Trend** is the long-run pattern in values observable over several periods of time. **Variability** in a time series is the difference in values from period to period. **Seasonality** is a pattern in time series data that recurs periodically over a regular time interval. In this section, we discuss techniques for visualizing time series data and these characteristics.

An exception to using a line chart for time series data is when we want to emphasize or compare individual values of one or more variables over time. Then, a good choice may be to use a column chart. Figure 6.22 provides an example of a stacked column chart in which total annual sales over time are being compared for different DCs and by customer status (new or existing).

Viewing Data at Different Temporal Frequencies

The Espléndido Jugo y Batido, Inc. (EJB) data that we have already seen in this chapter, are an example of a time series data. Here, we reconsider this data set to consider appropriate ways to visualize data over consecutive time periods. Suppose that EJB would like to analyze the temporal pattern of the total sales of pear smoothies. The following steps create a PivotTable and PivotChart to examine pear smoothie sales over the time period of the data in the file *ejb_table*.

DATA *file*

ejb_table

Step 1. Select any cell in the range of the data, for example, cell A3
Step 2. Click the **Insert** tab on the Ribbon
In the **Charts** group, click the **PivotChart** button PivotChart
Step 3. When the **Create PivotChart** dialog box appears:
Under **Choose the data that you want to analyze**, choose **Select a table or range** and enter *EJBData* in the **Table/Range:** box
Under **Choose where you want the PivotChart to be placed**, select **New Worksheet**
Click **OK**
Step 4. In the **PivotChart Fields** task pane, under **Choose fields to add to report:**
Drag the **Date Ordered** field to the **Axis (Categories)** area
Drag the **$ Sales** field to the **Values** area
Drag the **Flavor** field to the **Filters** area
Drag the **Category** field to the **Filters** area
Step 5. In the PivotTable, click the **Filter Arrow** ▾ in cell B1 and in the drop-down menu:
Click **Pear**
Click **OK**
Step 6. In the PivotTable, click the **Filter Arrow** ▾ in cell B2 and in the drop-down menu:
Click **Smoothies**
Click **OK**
Step 7. With the PivotChart selected, right click and select **Change Chart Type...,** and in the **Change Chart Type** dialog box, select **Line**

Further editing will result in a chart that matches Figure 6.34. Figure 6.34 displays the total sales of pear smoothies on an annual basis. Based on these three years of data, we observe a relatively steady upward trend in sales.

Figure 6.34   PivotTable and PivotChart of Annual Pear Smoothie Sales

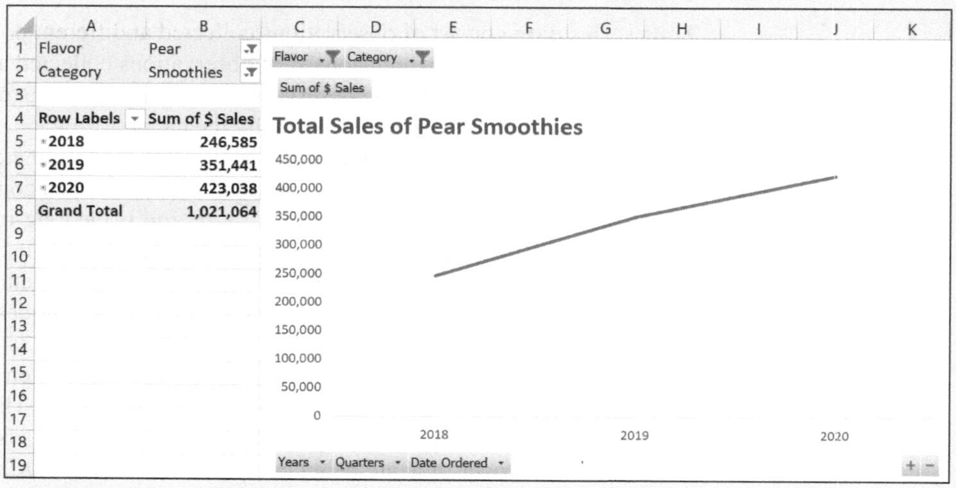

Row Labels	Sum of $ Sales
2018	246,585
2019	351,441
2020	423,038
Grand Total	1,021,064

Total Sales of Pear Smoothies

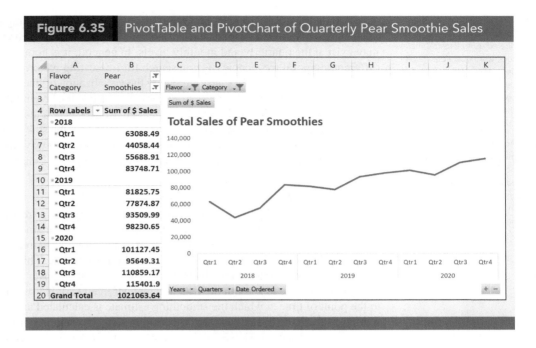

Figure 6.35 PivotTable and PivotChart of Quarterly Pear Smoothie Sales

How frequently we plot time series data can dramatically affect what we see. In a time series chart, the rate at which we display the data (typically along the horizontal axis) is called the **temporal frequency**. To demonstrate, we can view the pear smoothie sales data at different temporal frequencies by clicking the + – buttons in the bottom right-hand corner of Figure 6.34. Clicking the plus sign once results in the chart in Figure 6.35. Figure 6.35 displays the total sales of pear smoothies on a quarterly basis. As in Figure 6.34, there is still an upward trend, but now we can see the quarter-to-quarter variability and observe that quarterly sales have not always increased over time.

Clicking the plus sign again results in the chart in Figure 6.36. Figure 6.36 displays the total sales of pear smoothies on a monthly basis. The jagged lines of Figure 6.36 reveal the monthly fluctuations in sales from pear smoothies.

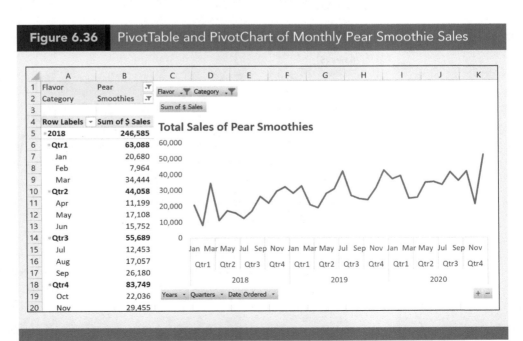

Figure 6.36 PivotTable and PivotChart of Monthly Pear Smoothie Sales

All three line charts of pear smoothie sales are useful. Aggregating pear smoothie sales at an annual level makes longer-term trends more apparent, but it conceals any patterns that may exist at the quarterly and monthly levels. In general, it is good practice to view data at different temporal frequencies as you search for interesting patterns.

The aspect ratio is another factor affecting the visualization of line series charts for time series data. As the width of the line chart increases relative to the height of the line chart, the lines flatten and the variability in the data is suppressed. Conversely, as the height of the line chart increases relative to the width of the line chart, the lines become spiky and the variability in the data is exaggerated. While there is no single aspect ratio that is always the best (as it depends on what you are trying to see), a general suggestion is to make the chart wider than it is tall.

Highlighting Patterns in Time Series Data

To visualize the trend in time series data over time, we can add a trendline. In Figure 6.37, the linear trendline highlights the upward trend in monthly pear smoothie sales over time. While such a trendline can be useful in emphasizing a long-term trend in the data, we should be aware that the entire range of data is used to fit the trendline. This has particular implications for time series data, which by nature occurs sequentially over time. In time series data, it is often desirable to smooth the data in a manner that (1) only uses observations known up to the point of time at which the smoothing estimate is calculated and (2) does not use observations from the distant past. An m-period **moving average** is computed by averaging the last m values observed. That is, at a point in time, future observations and observations from more than m periods in the past are not included in the calculation of the moving average.

The following steps add a three-month moving average trendline to the monthly pear smoothie chart.

pearsmoothie

Step 1. Select the data series by clicking on the data points.
Step 2. Right click and select **Add Trendline…**
   In the **Format Trendline** task pane, under **Trendline Options** , select **Moving Average** and enter *3* in the **Period** box

With additional editing and repeating the preceding steps to create a 6-month and 12-month moving average smoothing, we generate the **trellis display** of Figure 6.38.

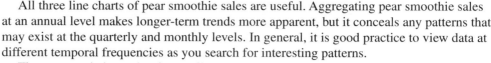

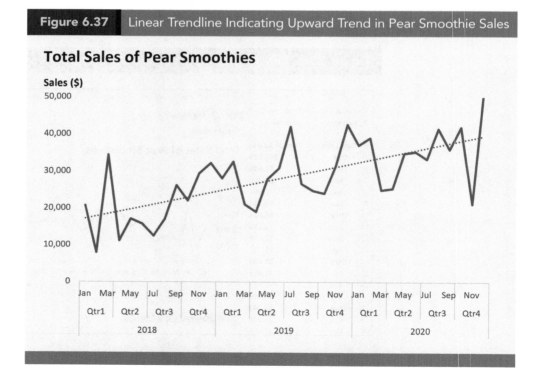

Total Sales of Pear Smoothies

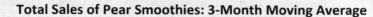

Figure 6.38 Trellis Display of Pear Smoothie Sales Smoothed by Moving Averages over 3 Months, 6 Months, and 12 Months

Total Sales of Pear Smoothies: 3-Month Moving Average

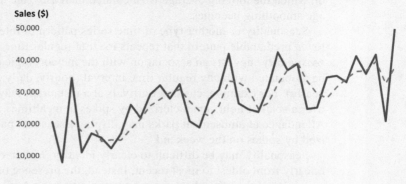

Total Sales of Pear Smoothies: 6-Month Moving Average

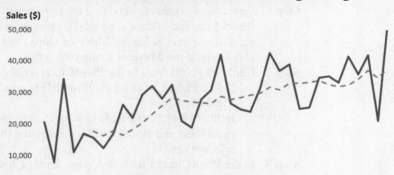

Total Sales of Pear Smoothies: 12-Month Moving Average

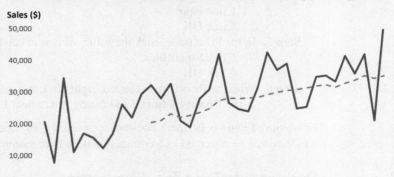

This trellis display shows monthly pear smoothie sales with three different moving averages. The top line chart is overlaid with a three-month moving average. The middle line chart is overlaid with a six-month moving average. The bottom line chart is overlaid with a 12-month moving average. As Figure 6.38 shows, as the number of periods on which the moving average is calculated increases, the more stable the moving average smoothing becomes.

Seasonality is another type of time series pattern of interest in which the values follow a predictable pattern that repeats itself at regular time intervals. Although the term *seasonality* suggests an association with the meteorological seasons, seasonality can be associated with any regular time interval (hourly, daily, weekly, monthly, quarterly, yearly). For example, customer arrivals at a restaurant may display a seasonal pattern over a span of hours characterized by spikes at mealtimes and troughs in between. Attendance at amusement parks may display a seasonal pattern over the week characterized by spikes on the weekend.

ejb_table

Seasonality may be difficult to clearly identify in charts that display all of the data linearly from oldest to most recent. Instead, the presence of seasonality recurring at a time interval is often best examined by plotting the data using multiple lines that correspond to a specific time interval. The following steps demonstrate the examination of monthly seasonality, resulting in the PivotTable and PivotChart in Figure 6.39. We assume that a PivotTable and PivotChart using the data in the Table named EJBData has previously been created (corresponding to the analysis in Figure 6.34).

Step 1. Select the worksheet containing the previously constructed PivotTable and PivotChart, and make a copy of this worksheet by right-clicking on the worksheet name, selecting **Move or Copy**, and selecting the **Create a copy** check box in the **Move or Copy** dialog box

Step 2. Click the PivotChart. In the **PivotChart Analyze** tab on the Ribbon:
Select **Field List** from the **Show/Hide** group to activate the **PivotChart Fields** task pane
In the **PivotChart Fields** task pane, clear the contents of the current PivotTable and PivotChart by deselecting the boxes next to the currently selected fields

Step 3. In the **PivotChart Fields** task pane, under **Choose fields to add to report:**
Drag the **Month Ordered** field to the **Axis (Categories)** area
Drag the **Years** field to the **Legend (Series)** area
Drag the **$ Sales** field to the **Values** area
Drag the **Flavor** field to the **Filters** area
Drag the **Category** field to the **Filters** area

Step 4. In the PivotTable, click the **Filter Arrow** in cell B1 and in the drop-down menu:
Click **Pear**
Click **OK**

Step 5. In the PivotTable, click the **Filter Arrow** in cell B2 and in the drop-down menu:
Click **Smoothies**
Click **OK**

Step 6. With the PivotChart selected, right click and select **Change Chart Type...**, and in the **Change Chart Type** dialog box, select **Line**

Examining Figure 6.39, there does not appear to be any seasonality on a monthly basis, which would be observed as a common pattern over months in each of the years.

Rearranging Data for Visualization

We have considered data sets structured in a manner that every row represents an observation of a set of variables whose respective values are recorded in columns. In a time series data set organized in this manner, each row represents an observation of the values of a set of variables at a specific point in time. However, there are multiple ways

Figure 6.39	Exploring Pear Smoothie Sales for Seasonality on a Monthly Basis

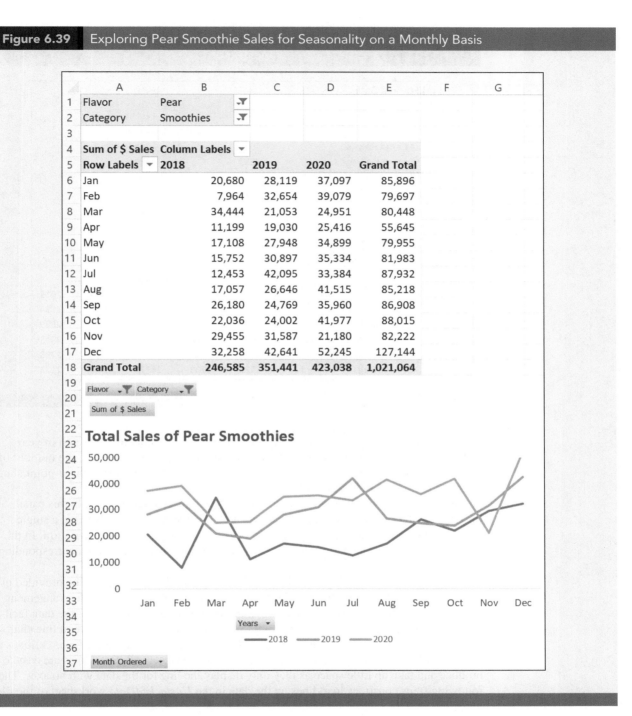

	A	B	C	D	E	F	G
1	Flavor	Pear					
2	Category	Smoothies					
3							
4	Sum of $ Sales	Column Labels					
5	Row Labels	2018	2019	2020	Grand Total		
6	Jan	20,680	28,119	37,097	85,896		
7	Feb	7,964	32,654	39,079	79,697		
8	Mar	34,444	21,053	24,951	80,448		
9	Apr	11,199	19,030	25,416	55,645		
10	May	17,108	27,948	34,899	79,955		
11	Jun	15,752	30,897	35,334	81,983		
12	Jul	12,453	42,095	33,384	87,932		
13	Aug	17,057	26,646	41,515	85,218		
14	Sep	26,180	24,769	35,960	86,908		
15	Oct	22,036	24,002	41,977	88,015		
16	Nov	29,455	31,587	21,180	82,222		
17	Dec	32,258	42,641	52,245	127,144		
18	Grand Total	246,585	351,441	423,038	1,021,064		

Flavor Category

Sum of $ Sales

Total Sales of Pear Smoothies

Years

— 2018 — 2019 — 2020

Month Ordered

to organize the data within this structure, particularly if the data contain categorical variables.

To demonstrate, consider data on the three-point shot attempts by each team in the National Basketball Association from 2015 to 2019. Figure 6.40 shows a portion of the same data arranged in two different ways. In Figure 6.40a, each row consists of three values: an observation of a team name, a year, and the number of three-point shot attempts by that team during that year. In Figure 6.40b, each row consists of six values: an observation of a team name, the number of three-point shot attempts by

Figure 6.40	A Portion of Data from the File *nba3pa* in Stacked (Panel a) and Unstacked (Panel b) Form

(a) Stacked Data

	A	B	C
1	Team	Year	Three Point Attempts
2	Atlanta Hawks	2015	2152
3	Boston Celtics	2015	2021
4	Brooklyn Nets	2015	1633
5	Charlotte Hornets	2015	1566
6	Chicago Bulls	2015	1825

(b) Unstacked Data

	A	B	C	D	E	F
1				Three Point Attempts		
2	Team	2015	2016	2017	2018	2019
3	Atlanta Hawks	2152	2326	2137	2544	3034
4	Boston Celtics	2021	2142	2742	2492	2829
5	Brooklyn Nets	1633	1508	2591	2924	2965
6	Charlotte Hornets	1566	2410	2347	2233	2783
7	Chicago Bulls	1825	1753	1831	2549	2123

that team in year 2015, the number of three-point shot attempts by that team in year 2016, the number of three-point shot attempts by that team in year 2017, the number of three-point shot attempts by that team in year 2018, and the number of three-point shot attempts by that team in year 2019.

The arrangement of data in Figure 6.40a is referred to as **stacked data**. In this panel, the data are stacked with respect to Year because all values of Year are listed in a single column. The arrangement of data in Figure 6.40b is referred to as **unstacked data**. In this panel, the data are unstacked with respect to Year because there is a column corresponding to each value of Year.

Depending on the source of the data and how it was collected, data may be provided in stacked or unstacked form. Both arrangements of data can be useful as each arrangement can facilitate different visualizations. For example, the unstacked version of the data facilitates the construction of team-specific line charts. To quickly construct several line charts to explore interesting patterns in time series data, we construct sparklines. A **sparkline** is a minimalist type of line chart directly placed into a spreadsheet cell. Sparklines are easy to produce and take up little space as they only display the line for the data with no axes. The following steps construct sparklines on the data in the *UnstackedData* worksheet of the file *nba3pa*.

DATA*file*

nba3pa

Step 1. Click the **Insert** tab on the Ribbon
Step 2. Click **Line** in the **Sparklines** group
Step 3. When the **Create Sparklines** dialog box appears:
   Enter *B3:F3* in the **Data Range:** box
   Enter *G3* in the **Location Range:** box
   Click **OK**
Step 4. Copy cell G3 to cells G4:G32

The sparklines in column G of Figure 6.41 do not indicate the magnitude of three-point shot attempts for the various teams, but they do show the overall trend for these data.

| Figure 6.41 | Sparklines on the Unstacked Three-Point Shot Attempt Data |

◢	A	B	C	D	E	F	G
1		Three Point Attempts					
2	Team	2015	2016	2017	2018	2019	
3	Milwaukee Bucks	1500	1277	1946	2024	3134	
4	Golden State Warriors	2217	2592	2562	2370	2824	
5	New Orleans Pelicans	1583	1951	2196	2312	2449	
6	Philadelphia 76ers	2160	2255	2443	2445	2474	
7	Los Angeles Clippers	2202	2190	2245	2196	2118	
8	Portland Trail Blazers	2231	2336	2272	2308	2520	
9	Oklahoma City Thunder	1864	1945	2116	2491	2677	
10	Toronto Raptors	2060	1915	1996	2705	2771	
11	Sacramento Kings	1350	1839	1960	1967	2455	
12	Washington Wizards	1381	1983	2030	2173	2731	
13	Houston Rockets	2680	2533	3306	3470	3721	
14	Atlanta Hawks	2152	2326	2137	2544	3034	
15	Minnesota Timberwolves	1223	1347	1723	1845	2357	
16	Boston Celtics	2021	2142	2742	2492	2829	
17	Brooklyn Nets	1633	1508	2591	2924	2965	
18	Los Angeles Lakers	1546	2016	2110	2384	2541	
19	Utah Jazz	1781	1956	2128	2425	2789	
20	San Antonio Spurs	1847	1518	1927	1977	2071	
21	Charlotte Hornets	1566	2410	2347	2233	2783	
22	Denver Nuggets	2032	1943	2365	2536	2571	
23	Dallas Mavericks	2082	2342	2473	2688	3002	
24	Indiana Pacers	1740	1889	1885	2010	2081	
25	Phoenix Suns	2048	2118	1854	2286	2400	
26	Orlando Magic	1598	1818	2139	2405	2633	
27	Detroit Pistons	2043	2148	1915	2373	2854	
28	Miami Heat	1659	1480	2213	2506	2658	
29	Chicago Bulls	1825	1753	1831	2549	2123	
30	New York Knicks	1614	1762	2022	1914	2421	
31	Cleveland Cavaliers	2253	2428	2779	2636	2388	
32	Memphis Grizzlies	1246	1521	2169	2152	2368	

We observe that three-point shot attempts appear to be increasing over this five-year period for almost every team. The Los Angeles Clippers are the only team who appear to have a decreasing (or at least non-increasing) trend over this period. As can be observed, sparklines provide an efficient and simple way to display basic information about a time series.

Alternatively, the stacked version of the three-point shot attempt data facilitates the construction of a box and whisker plot in which the Year variable is used as the horizontal axis. Figure 6.42 displays a box and whisker plot based on the stacked three-point shot attempt data. A box and whisker plot can be constructed in Excel from unstacked data, but the different columns are treated as different data series and differentiated by color. Figure 6.43 displays a box and whisker plot based on the unstacked three-point shot attempt data. A display like Figure 6.43 may be appropriate for cross-sectional data, but for time series data, the display in Figure 6.42 is generally preferred.

Because different arrangements of data can facilitate different visualizations, it is useful to be able to transform stacked data to unstacked data and vice versa. In the following

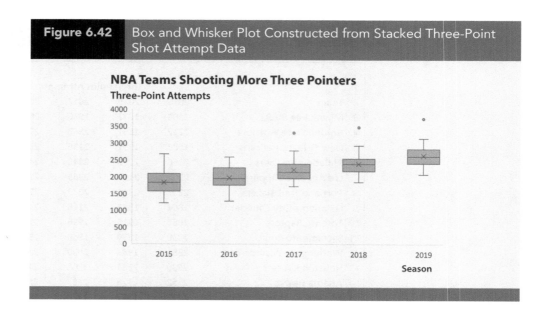

Figure 6.42   Box and Whisker Plot Constructed from Stacked Three-Point Shot Attempt Data

steps, we use the file *stackednba3pa_table* to convert the three-point shot attempt data from stacked form to unstacked form with respect to the Year variable.

DATA*file*

stackednba3pa_table

Step 1. Select any cell in the range of the Table, for example, cell A1
Step 2. Click the **Data** tab in the Ribbon
Step 3. Click **From Table/Range** in the **Get & Transform** group
Step 4. When the **Power Query Editor** window appears:
      Select the **Year** column
      Click the **Transform** tab
            Click **Pivot Column** in the **Any Column** group

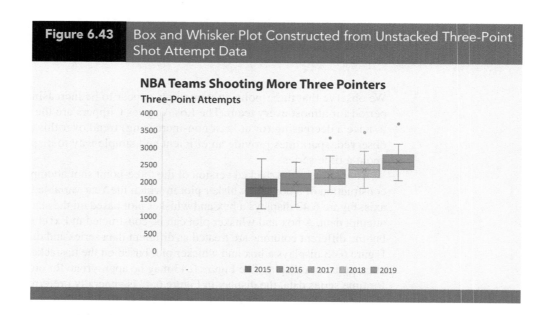

Figure 6.43   Box and Whisker Plot Constructed from Unstacked Three-Point Shot Attempt Data

When the **Pivot Column** dialog box appears, select **Three Point Attempts** in the drop-down menu for **Values Column**
Click **OK**
Click the **Home** tab and click **Close & Load** from the **Close** group

The preceding steps will create an Excel Table in a new worksheet that mirrors the unstacked data form in Figure 6.40b.

Conversely, in the following steps, we use the file *unstackednba3pa_table* to convert the three-point shot attempt data from unstacked form to stacked form with respect to the Year variable.

unstackednba3pa_table

Step 1. Select any cell in the range of the Table, for example, cell A3
Step 2. Click the **Data** tab in the Ribbon
Step 3. Click **From Table/Range** in the **Get & Transform** group
Step 4. When the **Power Query Editor** window appears:
  Select the columns corresponding to **2015**, **2016**, **2017**, **2018**, and **2019** (press the **Ctrl** key while selecting each column)
  Click the **Transform** tab
    Click **Unpivot Columns** in the **Any Column** group
  Click the **Home** tab and click **Close & Load** from the **Close** group

The preceding steps will create an Excel Table in a new worksheet that, after sorting on years, matches the stacked data form in Figure 6.40a.

6.6 Visualizing Geospatial Data

Geospatial data are data that include information on the geographic location of each record. When dealing with geospatial data, displaying them on a map can often help to discover patterns that would have been otherwise difficult to interpret. In this section, we consider two general types of geographic visualizations and discuss their use in data exploration.

Choropleth Maps

Choropleth maps are discussed in Chapters 2 and 9.

Specifically, a **choropleth map** is a geographic visualization that uses shades of a color, different colors, or symbols to indicate the values of a quantitative or categorical variable associated with a geographic region or area. A familiar example of choropleth map is a weather map, such as the one in Figure 6.44. In Figure 6.44, color is used to depict the daily high temperature, with warmer colors (on the red end of the spectrum) representing higher temperatures and cooler colors (on the purple end of the spectrum) representing lower temperatures.

While choropleth maps may provide a good visual display of changes in a variable between geographic areas, they can also be misleading. If the location data are not granular enough so the value of the displayed variable is relatively uniform over the respective areas over which it is displayed, then the values of the variable within regions and between regions may be misrepresented. The choropleth map may mask substantial variation of the variable within an area of the same color shading. Further, the choropleth map may suggest abrupt changes in the variable between regional boundaries while the actual changes across boundaries may be more gradual.

Choropleth maps are the most reliable when the variable displayed is relatively constant within the different locations to be colored. If this is not the case and a choropleth map is desired, the likelihood of the map conveying erroneous insights is mitigated when (1) variable measures are density based (quantity divided by land area or population) or (2) the colored regions are roughly equal-sized so there are no regions that are visually distracting.

For data with variables representing geographical regions (e.g., countries, states, counties, postal codes), Excel has mapping functionality that will create a choropleth map. For

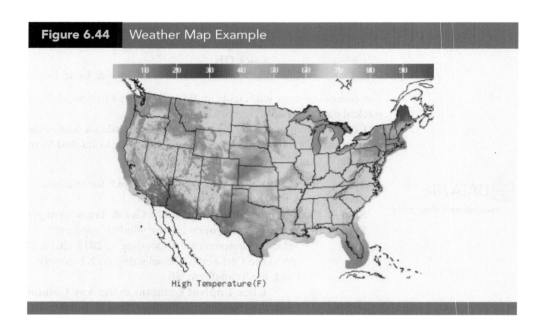

Figure 6.44   Weather Map Example

High Temperature (F)

Excel's Filled Map is powered by the Bing search engine.

DATA *file*

incomebystate

example, the file *incomebystate* contains the median income for each state in the United States (Figure 6.45). The following steps use the file *incomebystate* to create a choropleth map using shading to denote the median income in each state.

Step 1. Select cells A1:B51
Step 2. Click the **Insert** tab on the Ribbon
Step 3. In the **Charts** group, click the **Maps** button ⓜ Maps
Step 4. Select **Filled Map**

With further editing, the preceding steps produce the choropleth map in Figure 6.46.

As Figure 6.46 demonstrates, choropleth maps are typically better for displaying relative comparisons of magnitude than conveying absolute measures of magnitude. The value of median income for each state is difficult to estimate from Figure 6.46, but it is relatively easy to conclude that northeastern states have high median incomes relative to the rest of the country and that many southern states have low median incomes. Indeed, the strength of a choropleth map is the identification of the high-level characteristics of a variable with respect to geographic positioning.

We also observe in Figure 6.46 that the relative size of the states plays a role in the audience's perception. For instance, Rhode Island is barely visible while larger states dominate the audience's field of vision. Another weakness of Figure 6.46 is that it masks the income distributions within each state.

Figure 6.45   A Portion of the Data in the File *incomebystate*

⬐	A	B
1	**State**	**Median Income**
2	Alabama	49,881
3	Alaska	74,912
4	Arizona	59,079
5	Arkansas	47,094
6	California	75,250

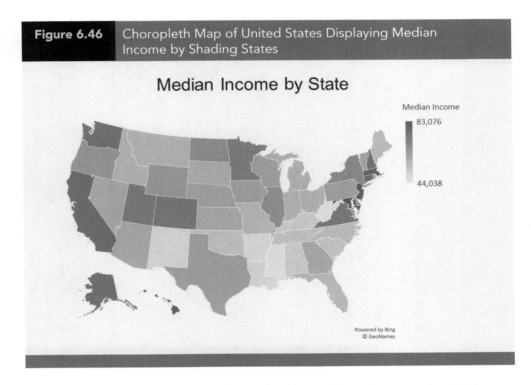

Figure 6.46   Choropleth Map of United States Displaying Median Income by Shading States

The file *incomebycounty* contains the median income data at the county level in the United States (Figure 6.47). The following steps use the file *incomebycounty* to create a choropleth map using shading to denote the median income in the counties in each state of the United States.

DATA *file*

incomebycounty

Step 1. Select cells A1:C3148
Step 2. Click the **Insert** tab on the Ribbon
Step 3. In the **Charts** group, click the **Maps** button Maps
Step 4. Select **Filled Map**

With further editing, the preceding steps produce the choropleth map in Figure 6.48.

The choice of choropleth map (state-level in Figure 6.46 or county-level in Figure 6.48) depends on the insight intended to be delivered to the audience. These two views could also be used in tandem by first showing the state-level measure and then selecting one or more states to "zoom" in on and show the county-level measure.

Cartograms

Another type of geographic display is a cartogram. A **cartogram** is a map-like diagram that uses geographic positioning but purposefully represents map regions in a manner that

Figure 6.47   A Portion of the Data in the File *Incomebycounty*

▲	A	B	C
1	State	County	Median Income
2	AL	Autauga	59,338
3	AL	Baldwin	57,588
4	AL	Barbour	34,382
5	AL	Bibb	46,064
6	AL	Blount	50,412

It may take Excel several minutes to populate the county-level choropleth map in Figure 6.48.

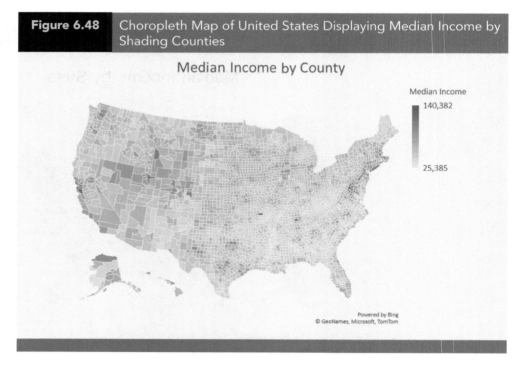

Figure 6.48 Choropleth Map of United States Displaying Median Income by Shading Counties

Median Income by County

Median Income
140,382

25,385

Powered by Bing
© GeoNames, Microsoft, TomTom

does not necessarily correspond to land area. For example, Figure 6.49 contains a cartogram of the United States in which the area of each state is based on its population. A cartogram often leverages the audience's familiarity with the geography of the displayed regions to convey its message. In Figure 6.49, we observe the tiny size of many western states (Alaska, Nevada, Idaho, Nebraska, North Dakota, and South Dakota) and the resulting white space paired with the audience's tacit knowledge of a standard U.S. map conveys the low population density in these areas.

A strength of a cartogram is that the area displayed is proportional to the variable being measured, thus avoiding any misleading impressions. A weakness of a cartogram is that the

Excel does not have the functionality to automatically generate cartograms.

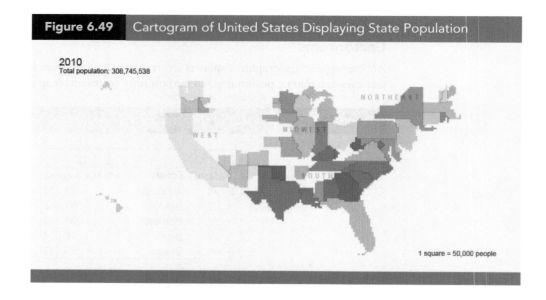

Figure 6.49 Cartogram of United States Displaying State Population

2010
Total population: 308,745,538

NORTHEAST

WEST

MIDWEST

SOUTH

1 square = 50,000 people

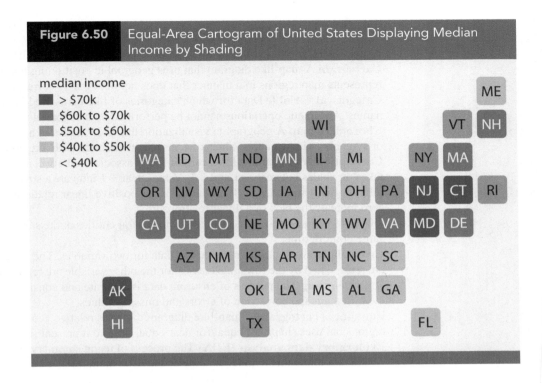

Figure 6.50 Equal-Area Cartogram of United States Displaying Median Income by Shading

sizing of the regions according to the displayed variable may distort the region enough to render the relative geographic positioning meaningless and the standard area-based geography unrecognizable.

Figure 6.50 contains a specific type of cartogram, known as an **equal-area cartogram**. In comparison to the choropleth in Figure 6.46, the equal-area cartogram provides a balanced visual representation of each state while still maintaining fidelity to relative geographic positioning.

Summary

In this chapter, we have discussed visualization techniques for conducting exploratory data analysis. We introduced Excel tools for organizing and rearranging data to facilitate the visual exploration of a data set. We discussed the challenge of missing data. We defined the types of missing data and the implications of how to potentially address missing entries.

We explained and demonstrated the process of exploring data, including the distributional analysis of individual variables and the crosstabulation of multiple variables. We visualized the association between pairs of quantitative variables with scatter charts. We introduced the concept of correlation and described how to use a trendline on a scatter chart to visualize the sign and strength of the correlation between two variables. We described how to construct a scatter chart with the consideration of a third (categorical) variable. To visualize the pairwise association between quantitative variables when dealing with data sets with several quantitative variables, we introduced the use of a scatter-chart matrix and a table lens.

In the final two sections, we discussed two particular types of data: time series data and geospatial data. For time series data, we explained the benefit of line charts to visualize trend, variability, and seasonality. We presented the use of a moving average to smooth time series data. For geospatial data, we discussed the strengths and weaknesses of choropleth maps and cartograms.

Glossary

Aspect ratio The ratio of the width of a chart to the height of a chart.

Cartogram A map-like diagram that uses geographic positioning but purposefully represents map regions in a manner that does not necessarily correspond to land area.

Categorical variable Data for which categories of like items are identified by labels or names. Arithmetic operations cannot be performed on categorical variables.

Choropleth map A geographic visualization that uses shades of a color, different colors, or symbols to indicate the values of a variable associated with a region.

Correlation A standardized measure of linear association between two variables that takes on values between -1 and $+1$. Values near -1 indicate a strong negative linear relationship, values near $+1$ indicate a strong positive linear relationship, and values near zero indicate the lack of a linear relationship.

Cross-sectional data Data collected from several entities at the same or approximately the same point in time.

Crosstabulation A tabular summary of data for two variables. The classes of one variable are represented by the rows; the classes for the other variable are represented by the columns.

Data cleansing The process of ensuring data is accurate and consistent through the identification and correction of errors and missing values.

Equal-area cartogram A map-like diagram that uses relative geographic positioning of regions but uses shapes of equal (or near-equal) size to represent regions.

Exploratory data analysis (EDA) The process of using summary statistics and visualization to gain an understanding of the data, including the identification of patterns.

Geospatial data Data that include information on the geographic location of each record.

Illegitimately missing data Missing data that do not occur naturally.

Legitimately missing data Missing data that occur naturally.

Lurking variable A third variable associated with two variables being studied that results in a correlation between the two variables, falsely implying a causal relationship between the pair.

Missing at random (MAR) Missing data for which the tendency for an observation to be missing a value for a variable is related to the value of some other variable(s) in the observation.

Missing completely at random (MCAR) Missing data for which the tendency for an observation to be missing the value for a variable is entirely random and does not depend on either the missing value or the value of any other variable in the observation.

Missing not at random (MNAR) Missing data for which the tendency for an observation to be missing a value of a variable is related to the missing value.

Moving average A method of smoothing time series data that uses the average of the most recent m values.

Multivariate analysis The examination of patterns by considering two or more variables at once.

Ordinal variable Data for which categories of like items are identified by labels or names, and there is an inherent rank or order of the categories.

Outlier An unusually small or unusually large data value.

Quantitative scales The range of quantitative values along the horizontal and vertical axes in a chart.

Quantitative variable Data for which numerical values are used to indicate magnitude, such as how many or how much. Arithmetic operations such as addition, subtraction, and multiplication can be performed on a quantitative variable.

Scatter-chart matrix A graphical presentation that uses multiple scatter charts arranged as a matrix to illustrate the relationships among multiple variables.

Seasonality A pattern in time series data in which the values demonstrate predictable changes at regular time intervals.

Sparkline A special type of line chart that indicates the trend of data but not the magnitude. A sparkline does not include axes or labels.

Spurious relationship An apparent association between two variables that is not causal but is coincidental or caused by a third (lurking) variable.

Stacked data Data organized such that the values for categorical variables are in a single column.

Table lens A tabular-like visualization in which each column corresponds to a variable, and the magnitude of a variable's values are represented by horizontal bars.

Tall data A data set with many observations (rows).

Temporal frequency The rate at which time series data is displayed in a chart.

Time series data Data that are collected over a period of time (minutes, hours, days, months, years, etc.).

Trellis display A vertical or horizontal arrangement of individual charts of the same type, size, scale, and formatting that differ only by the data they display.

Trend The long-run pattern in a time series observable over several periods of time.

Univariate analysis The examination of the data for an individual variable.

Unstacked data Data organized such that the values for a categorical variable correspond to labels for separate columns and the columns contain observations corresponding to these respective category values.

Variability Differences in values of a variable over observations.

Wide data A data set with many variables (columns).

Problems

Conceptual

1. **Choosing an Appropriate Chart**. A fitness lab is conducting an experiment in which 100 participants engage in a 30-minute period of high-intensity interval training (HIIT) and then are asked about their perceived level of exertion. They must select an answer from 1 to 4, where 1 = "did not feel challenged"; 2 = "broke a sweat but could have been pushed more"; 3 = "felt challenged but not overwhelmed"; and 4 = "extremely fatigued." In addition, each participant's body fat percentage is recorded. The following table displays a portion of the data from the experiment. **LO 4**

Participant	Body Fat Percentage	Exertion Level
1	27	3
2	31	4
3	24	1
4	21	2
5	14	4

What is a good way to show how body fat percentage is related to exertion level?
   i. Scatter chart depicting the relationship between body fat percentage and exertion level
   ii. Side-by-side box and whisker plots of the distribution of body fat percentage for participants at each exertion level
   iii. Clustered column chart of body fat percentage with different colored columns for each exertion level
   iv. Sparklines on data unstacked so columns correspond to different exertion levels

2. **Performance Evaluation.** Kiwi Analytics is assessing two different training programs for its consulting employees. One group of 50 employees used training method A for a varying number of hours and another group of 50 employees used training method B for a varying number of hours. Then, these employees were evaluated based on their performance in job-related tasks. The resulting data from this experiment are displayed in the following two scatter charts. **LO 6**

Group A Performance

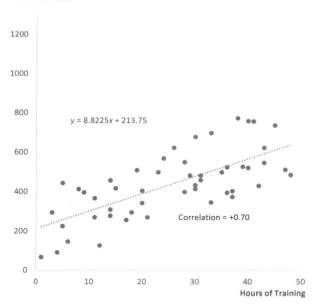

Group B Performance

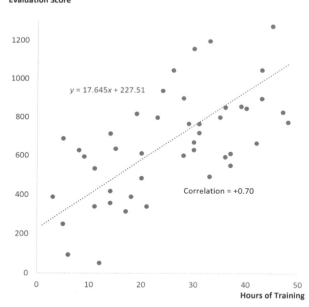

Which of the following are accurate statements based on these data? Select all that apply.

  i.   Training method A and training method B are equally effective at improving evaluation scores.

  ii. Training method A is more effective than training method B because the observations in the first scatter chart exhibit less variability around the linear trendline than the observations in the second scatter chart.

  iii. Correlation does not imply causation, and therefore, there is no meaningful conclusion from these charts.

    iv. The strength of the linear relationship between hours of training and evaluation score is the same for both training method A and training method B.

3. **Correlation Analysis of Wide Data.** Helen Wagner, a marketing analyst for Meredith Corporation, is examining a data set based on market research of potential patrons of a new social media-based e-magazine. The data set has dozens of quantitative variables measuring characteristics such as patron income, age, daily hours spent on social media, money spent based on banner ads on websites, etc.

    Helen is interested in exploring the association between these variables. What visualization would you recommend? **LO 5**

    i. Scatter-chart matrix
    ii. Table lens
    iii. Heatmap
    iv. Choropleth map

4. **Tailored Delivery.** Bravman Clothing sells high-end clothing products and is launching a service in which they use a same-day courier service to deliver purchases that customers have made by working with one of their personal stylists on the phone. In a pilot study, Bravman collected 25 observations consisting of the wait time the customer experienced during the order process, the customer's purchase amount, the customer's age, and the customer's credit score. The data for these 25 observations were used to construct the following scatter-chart matrix. **LO 6**

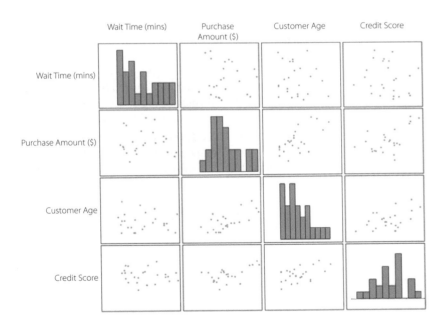

    Which of the following statements most accurately describes the insight from the scatter-chart matrix?

    i. Purchase amount, customer age, and credit score have pairwise positive relationships with each other.
    ii. Wait time has a nonlinear relationship with purchase amount.
    iii. Wait time is negatively related to customer age.
    iv. None of the variables appear to be highly correlated with each other.

5. **Wage Income Over Lifetime.** The Pew Research Center is a nonpartisan think tank that gathers information on social issues and demographic trends. It has conducted a longitudinal study in which they collected the wage income of finance professionals at various points in their lives. After accounting for inflation, the data from this study were used to create the following chart. **LO 5**

Wage Income ($1000s)

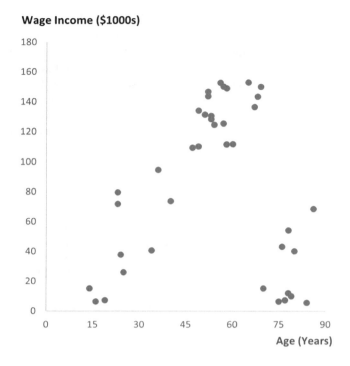

What is the best way to visually emphasize the apparent relationship between wage income and age in this chart?
  i. Add a linear trendline to the chart.
  ii. Compute the correlation between the two variables and display this on the chart.
  iii. Remove the fill color of the data points.
  iv. Add a nonlinear trendline to the chart.

6. **Wage Income Over Lifetime.** Using data from a longitudinal study that collected wage income of finance professionals at various points in their lives, an analyst has constructed the following scatter chart and placed a linear trendline on the data. **LO 5**

Wage Income ($1000s)

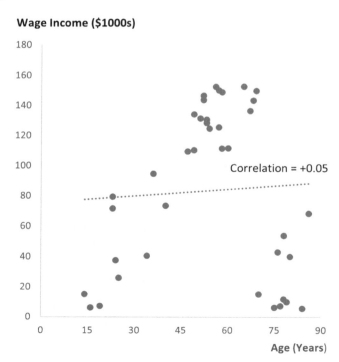

What is a reasonable conclusion from this chart?
  i. There is no relationship between a person's age and wage income.
  ii. A person's age and wage income do not appear to be linearly related, but there does appear to be a nonlinear relationship between these two variables.
  iii. A scatter chart is not the best way to view these data because they were collected over time, and therefore, a line chart should be used.
  iv. None of the variables appear to be highly correlated with each other.

7. **Types of Missing Data.** Label each of the following descriptions based on the type of missing data being described: missing completely at random (MCAR), missing at random (MAR), or missing not at random (MNAR). **LO 7**
  a. A survey is conducted that asks a sample of people their age, highest level of education completed, and preference of political party. The results indicate that many entries for highest level of education completed are missing and that respondents were more likely to omit this response if they had a high school education or less.
  b. An economic study is conducted asking people to report their profession, job title, and city of residence. Approximately 10% of the responses for job title are missing, and it is observed that men are less likely to provide their job title than women.
  c. Students at a local college are given a survey to collect data on their study habits and preferred learning styles. Students complete the survey by filling out a Scantron form on which they fill in circles to specific multiple-choice questions. Due to Scantron-reading errors, 5% of the question responses are not able to be read correctly and so are recorded as missing.
  d. A clinical study is being done to judge the efficacy of a new drug in reducing a patient's high blood pressure. Each month, study participants must each undergo a stress test where they run on a treadmill at maximum effort for 90 seconds, after which the patient's blood pressure is recorded. However, each patient is screened prior to the stress test and if their resting blood pressure is too high, they do not complete the stress test and the blood pressure reading for that patient is missing.

8. **Patterns in Missing Data.** Dr. Drake Ramoray is reviewing a patient database and has noticed that there are some missing data entries. As shown in the table below, he has highlighted these missing entries as black cells. **LO 7**

Patient	Sex	Age (yrs)	Weight (lbs)	Systolic Blood Pressure	Diastolic Blood Pressure	Cholesterol	Prostate-Specific Antigen
1	Female	60	135	110	70	75	
2	Male	50	205	115	75	150	2.4
3	Male	64	180	110	60	160	1.9
4	Male	55	225	130	80	210	3.1
5	Male	64	215	135	85	225	4.2
6	Male	18	160	100	65		
7	Female	50	140	115	75	100	
8	Female	61	145	125	80	125	
9	Male	44	180	105	65	130	0.7
10	Male	16	130	100	70		

Examine the pattern in this missing data. Which of the following classifications seems most appropriate?
  i. Missing not at random illegitimately
  ii. Missing at random
  iii. Legitimately missing data
  iv. Missing completely at random

9. **Smartphone Sales.** A manufacturer has collected the sales data for the past four years. How should the analyst team visualize these data if they are interested in exploring sales patterns over time? **LO 8**

   i. Pie chart breaking down sales by year
   ii. Heatmap to emphasize the times of the year when sales peak
   iii. A set of line charts that aggregate data at different time intervals: by year, by quarter, and by month
   iv. Radar chart to represent the cyclical nature of the business year

10. **High-Speed Rail Passengers.** Darcy Sears is a manager of a high-speed rail service between two major metro areas. Darcy is analyzing three years (36 months) of data on the number of passengers who ride the high-speed train and has created the following chart. **LO 8**

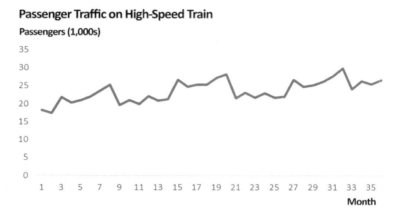

Passenger Traffic on High-Speed Train

Passengers (1,000s)

   Based on her experience with the rail service, Darcy believes there is a seasonal pattern in the amount of passenger traffic on the high-speed train. However, Darcy is disappointed that her chart does not clearly display seasonality. How should Darcy better visualize a seasonal pattern in the data?

   i. Create a different data series for each year consisting of 12 monthly observations, and plot these three separate lines on a new chart with the month labels January through December on the horizontal axis.
   ii. Aggregate the monthly observations into yearly observations, and plot the data on a new chart with Year on the horizontal axis.
   iii. Add a linear trendline to the chart above.
   iv. Add a moving average with a period equal to the length of the seasonal pattern.

11. **Comparing Moving Averages.** What is the effect of decreasing the number of periods in a moving average? **LO 8**

   i. The moving average trendline becomes smoother and less sensitive to fluctuations in the values of the data.
   ii. The value of the moving average always decreases.
   iii. The moving average trendline becomes more jagged and more responsive to recent changes in the values of the data.
   iv. There is no effect as the moving average depends on the seasonal pattern.

12. **Omaha Steaks.** As part of a marketing campaign harkening back to its company history based on Nebraska's beef industry, Omaha Steaks wants to create a visualization displaying the state's geographic distribution of beef cattle. Using data on the number of beef cattle in each county in Nebraska, the following choropleth map was created. **LO 9**

Beef Cattle Per Nebraska County

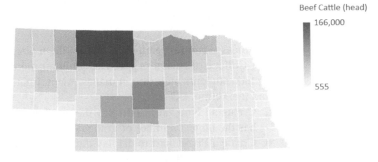

Which of the following choices best summarizes the strengths and weaknesses of this visualization?

  i. The choropleth map does a good job of depicting the geographic distribution of beef cattle in the state of Nebraska. However, the color shading does not provide a distinct enough contrast to identify the counties with the most beef cattle.

 ii. The choropleth map does a good job indicating the counties containing the most cows in absolute terms. However, there is a tendency for the largest counties to have the most cattle primarily due to their land area, and this can convey a false differentiation in the density of cows in adjacent counties.

iii. The use of color clearly shows which counties contain the most beef cattle. However, the large variance in the size of the counties makes it difficult to extract insight from the visualization for all counties.

 iv. All of these are accurate comments.

Applications

taxdata

13. **Tax Data by County.** The file *taxdata* contains information from federal tax returns filed in 2007 for all counties in the United States (3,142 counties in total). Create an Excel Table based on these data. Using Excel Table functionality, answer the following questions. **LO 1**
    a. Which county had the largest total adjusted gross income in the state of Texas?
    b. Which county had the largest average adjusted gross income in the state of Texas?

ejb_table

14. **More Univariate Analysis of EJB Data.** In the EJB example discussed within the chapter, univariate analysis was demonstrated on some of the variables. We continue this analysis in this problem. **LO 2**
    a. Using a PivotChart, construct the relative frequency distribution of records over the values of the Category variable. Describe your findings.
    b. Using a PivotChart, construct the relative frequency distribution of records over the values of the New Customer variable. In the PivotTable, relabel a "No" value for New Customer as "Existing" and a "Yes" value as "New." Describe your findings.

ejb_table

15. **Missing Data for Product Satisfaction Rating.** To understand the implications of missing data, we must explore the patterns associated with the missing entries for the Product Satisfaction Rating variable in the EJB data used within the chapter. **LO 2, 7**
    a. Construct the relative frequency distribution of records over the values of the Product Satisfaction Rating variable. What percentage of records are missing a value of Product Satisfaction Rating?
    b. Considering only records that report values of Product Satisfaction Rating, construct the relative frequency distribution of records over the different flavors.

    c. Considering records that are missing values of Product Satisfaction Rating, construct the relative frequency distribution of records over the different flavors.

    d. Compare the distributions in part (b) and part (c). What does this comparison suggest?

16. **Business Graduate Salaries.** In the file *majorsalary*, data have been collected from 111 College of Business graduates on their monthly starting salaries. The graduates include students majoring in management, finance, accounting, information systems, and marketing. **LO 2, 3**

majorsalary

    a. Create a PivotChart to display the number of graduates in each major. Which major has the largest number of graduates?

    b. Create a PivotChart to display the average monthly starting salary for students in each major. Which major has the highest average starting monthly salary?

17. **Federally Insured Bank Failures.** The file *fdic* contains data on the failures of federally insured banks between 2000 and 2012. Create a PivotChart to display a column chart that shows the total number of bank closings in each year from 2000 through 2012 in the state of Florida. Describe the pattern observed in the chart. **LO 3**

fdic

18. **Market Capitalization and Profit.** The file *fortune500* contains data for profits and market capitalizations from a recent sample of firms in the Fortune 500. Prepare a scatter chart to show the relationship between the variables Market Capitalization and Profit in which Market Capitalization is on the vertical axis and Profit is on the horizontal axis. Create a trendline for the relationship between Market Capitalization and Profit. What does the trendline indicate about this relationship? **LO 5**

fortune500

19. **Market Capitalization and Profit by Sector.** The file *fortune500sector* contains data on the profits, market capitalizations, and industry sector for a recent sample of firms in the Fortune 500. **LO 5**

    a. Differentiating observations by using a different color for each industry sector, prepare a scatter chart to show the relationship between the variables Market Capitalization and Profit in which Market Capitalization is on the vertical axis and Profit is on the horizontal axis.

    b. Emphasize the relationship between Market Capitalization and Profit within the healthcare sector by formatting all other sectors with data points in gray with no fill. Create a trendline based only on the observations in the healthcare sector. What does the trendline indicate about the relationship between Market Capitalization and Profit within the healthcare sector?

fortune500sector

20. **Table Lens on Customer Data.** Bravman Clothing sells high-end clothing products and is launching a service in which they use a same-day courier service to deliver purchases that customers have made by working with one of their personal stylists on the phone. In a pilot study, Bravman collected 25 observations consisting of the wait time the customer experienced during the order process, the customer's purchase amount, the customer's age, and the customer's credit score. The file *bravman* contains the data for these 25 observations. **LO 5**

bravman

    a. Construct a table lens on these data sorted in decreasing order with respect to the values of the Purchase Amount variable.

    b. Summarize the relationships between Purchase Amount and the other three variables.

21. **Missing Data in Marketing Survey.** The file *surveyresults* contains the responses from a marketing survey: 108 individuals responded to the survey of 10 questions. Respondents provided answers of 1, 2, 3, 4, or 5 to each question, corresponding to the overall satisfaction on 10 different dimensions of quality. However, not all respondents answered every question. **LO 7**

surveyresults

    a. To highlight the missing data values, shade the empty cells in black.

    b. For each question, which respondents did not provide answers? Which question has the highest nonresponse rate?

pixel

22. **Smartphone Sales.** The file *pixel* contains data on the monthly sales revenue for a smartphone manufacturer. **LO 8**
    a. Create a line chart to depict the sales time series at the annual level.
    b. Create a line chart to depict the sales time series at the quarterly level.
    c. Create a line chart to depict the sales time series at the monthly level.
    d. What insight does each of these three views provide?

23. **Umbrella Sales.** The file *umbrella* contains data on the quarterly sales revenue for a manufacturer of umbrellas and other weather-resistant gear. **LO 8**
    a. Create a line chart for the sales time series data. Add a four-period moving average to the chart to smooth the data.
    b. To investigate the possibility of seasonality on a quarterly basis, plot the data as a collection of five data series (one for each year). From this visualization, do you observe any indication of seasonality? If so, describe it.

umbrella

24. **Analysis of Scoring in the NFL.** The file *scoringnfl* contains the points scored by each National Football League team for 10 seasons. **LO 1, 8**
    a. NFL leadership is interested in seeing how the distribution of scoring across the league has changed over these 10 seasons. Construct a single chart that allows the audience to make these comparisons. Provide a thorough discussion of the distribution of scoring in the league over this decade.
    b. NFL leadership is also interested in the temporal patterns in scoring for individual teams. Unstack the data and use sparklines to show how scoring for each team has changed over these 10 seasons. List a team with a strong upward trend over these 10 seasons. List a team with a strong downward trend over these 10 seasons.

scoringnfl

25. **Omaha Steaks (Revisited).** In this problem, we revisit the data from Problem 12. As part of a marketing campaign harkening back to its company history based on Nebraska's beef industry, Omaha Steaks wants to create a visualization displaying the state's geographic distribution of beef cattle. Data on the number of beef cattle in each county in Nebraska and the size of each county are contained in the file *nebraskabeef*. Create a choropleth map that shades each county in Nebraska relative to the density of beef cattle (as measured by head per square mile). Compare this visualization to the choropleth map in Problem 12, and describe the strengths and weaknesses. **LO 9**

nebraskabeef

Chapter 6 Appendix

Appendix 6.1 Exploring Data with Power BI

In this appendix, we discuss in more detail how to explore data with Power BI, including crosstabulations and line charts for time series data that use filters.

Crosstabulations

Let us consider an example involving Espléndido Jugo y Batido, Inc. (EJB), a company that manufactures bottled juices and smoothies. EJB produces its products in five fruit flavors (apple, grape, orange, pear, and tomato) and four vegetable flavors (beet, carrot, celery, and cucumber), and it ships these products from distribution centers (DCs) in Idaho, Mississippi, Nebraska, New Mexico, North Dakota, Rhode Island, and West Virginia. The file *ejb* contains 19,931 order records, including the dollar amount sold, service satisfaction, and product satisfaction.

DATA *file*

ejb

Step 1. Following the steps outlined in Appendix 1.1, connect Power BI to the file *ejb*

We will first build a matrix of category sales by distribution center.

Step 2. Click **Report view** , and in the Visualizations pane, click **Build visual** to display the Build visual matrix of available charts

Select **Matrix**

In the **Data** pane, expand **Data** > Data

Drag **Distribution Center** from the **Data** pane to the **Rows** box in the **Visualizations** pane

Drag **Category** from the **Data** pane to the **Columns** box in the **Visualizations** pane

Drag **Σ $ Sales** from the **Data** pane to the **Values** box in the **Visualizations** pane

Right click **Sum of Sales** in the **Values** box, and select **Average**

The table should appear as shown in Figure P6.1.

Step 3. Right click the matrix, and select **Copy** and then select **Copy visual**

Click **Paste** under the **Home** tab in the **Clipboard** group

Click the new copy (on top of the original), and drag it to the right

In the **Visualizations** pane, click **Build visual** , and select **Clustered column chart**

Drag **Category** from the **X-axis** box to the **Legend** box

Next, we modify column chart for clarity.

Step 4. In the **Visualizations pane**, click the **Format visual** button , and click **Visual**

To edit the horizontal axis title and values, expand **X-axis** and expand **Title**

Select **Calibri** as the **Font** and **14** as the font size, and click the **Bold** button

Collapse **Title**

Expand **Values**

Select **Calibri** as the **Font** and **14** as the font size

Collapse **Values** and collapse **X-axis**

Figure P6.1	Table of EJB Average Sales by Distribution and Category

Distribution Center	Juices	Smoothies	**Total**
ID	920.47	880.29	**902.64**
MS	926.24	903.56	**915.69**
ND	866.93	864.29	**865.78**
NE	874.01	851.45	**863.86**
NM	896.43	884.26	**890.80**
RI	928.56	926.14	**927.51**
WV	895.14	914.75	**903.81**
Total	**899.86**	**887.19**	**894.18**

Step 5. In the **Visualizations** pane, click the **Format visual** button ✍ and click **Visual**
To edit the vertical axis, expand **Y-axis**
Expand **Range**
Type *750* in the **Minimum** box
Collapse **Range**, and expand **Values**
Select **Calibri** as the **Font** and **14** as the font size
Collapse **Values**
Next to **Title**, toggle the **On** button On⬤ to **Off** to hide the title
Collapse **Y-axis**

Step 6. In the **Visualizations** pane to the right of **Visuals**, click **General**
Expand **Title**. Edit the **Text** box to read *Average of $ Sales*
Select **Calibri** as the **Font** and **16** as the font size

Click the **Bold** button ⬛**B**
Collapse **Title**

Step 7 sorts the distribution centers so they appear in alphabetical order.

Step 7. In the upper right-hand corner of the chart, click **More options** ...
Select **Sort axis**, and select **Distribution Center**
Select **Sort axis**, and select **Sort ascending**

The clustered column chart should appear as shown in Figure P6.2.

Next, we add filters to the page. By clicking anywhere outside of the visuals in the Report view pane, make sure your previously created visualizations are not selected before proceeding to the following steps.

Step 8. Click **Report view** 📊, and in the **Visualizations** pane, click **Build visual** ▤
to display the **Build visual** matrix of available charts
Click outside of the current visualization so no visualizations are selected,
and select **Slicer** 🔲
Drag **Category** from the **Data** pane to the **Field** box in the **Visualizations** pane
Click outside of the current visualization so no visualizations are selected

Step 9. Click **Report** view 📊, and in the **Visualizations** pane, click **Build visual** ▤
to display the **Build visual** matrix of available charts
Select **Slicer** 🔲

Figure P6.2	A Clustered Column Chart of EJB Average Sales by Distribution and Category

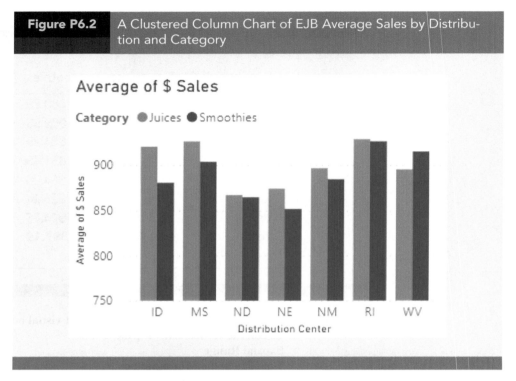

Drag **Distribution Center** from the **Data** pane to the **Field** box in the **Visualizations** pane

Steps 8 and 9 create two filters, one for Category and one for Distribution Center as shown in Figure P6.3.

Figure P6.3	Matrix and Clustered Column Chart with Filters for EJB Average Sales

Distribution Center	Juices	Smoothies	Total
ID	920.47	880.29	**902.64**
MS	926.24	903.56	**915.69**
ND	866.93	864.29	**865.78**
NE	874.01	851.45	**863.86**
NM	896.43	884.26	**890.80**
RI	928.56	926.14	**927.51**
WV	895.14	914.75	**903.81**
Total	**899.86**	**887.19**	**894.18**

Category
☐ Juices
☐ Smoothies

Distribution Center
☐ ID
☐ MS
☐ ND
☐ NE
☐ NM
☐ RI
☐ WV

CHART *file*

ejbcrosstab_chart.pbix

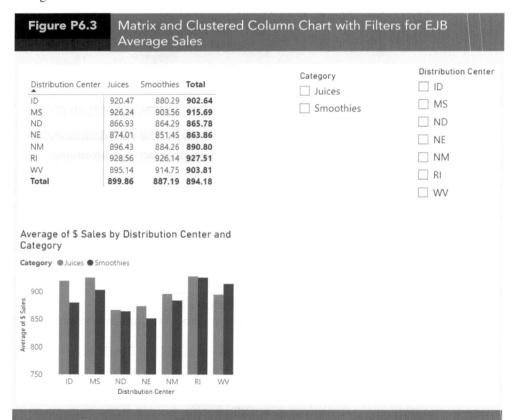

Average of $ Sales by Distribution Center and Category

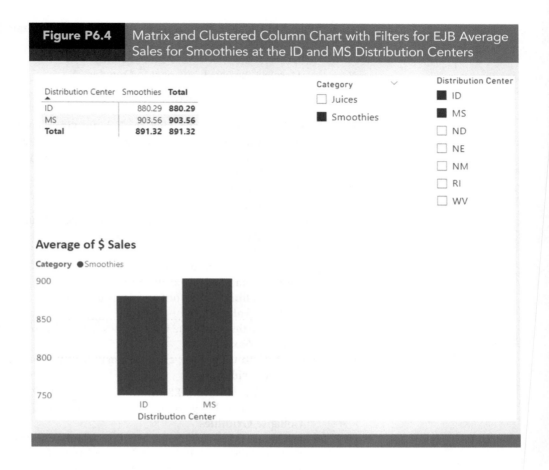

Figure P6.4	Matrix and Clustered Column Chart with Filters for EJB Average Sales for Smoothies at the ID and MS Distribution Centers

Figure P6.4 shows the results for Smoothies at the ID and MS distribution centers. This can be created by selecting the check box next to Smoothies and then selecting the check boxes next to ID and MS. Note that in a given filter, you can select multiple check boxes by holding down the **Ctrl** key.

Visualizing Time Series Data

Here, we reconsider the Espléndido Jugo y Batido, Inc. (EJB) data in the file *ejb*, which are an example of time series data. The steps below demonstrate how we can create an interactive time series chart to view the sales of pear smoothies at EJB.

DATA_file_

ejb

Step 1. Following the steps outlined in Appendix 1.1, connect Power BI to the file *ejb*

We will first build a line chart of sales over time.

Step 2. Click **Report view**, and in the **Visualizations** pane, click **Build visual** to display the **Build visual** matrix of available charts
Select **Line chart**
In the **Data** pane, expand **Data** > Data
Drag **Date Ordered** from the **Data** pane to the **X-axis** box in the **Visualizations** pane
Drag Σ **$ Sales** from the **Data** pane to the **Y-axis** box in the **Visualizations** pane

Step 3. In the **Data** pane, expand **Date Ordered**, and expand **Date Hierarchy**
  Deselect the check box next to **Day**
  Deselect the check box next to **Month**
  Deselect the check box next to **Quarter**

Next, we modify the line chart for clarity.

Step 4. In the **Visualizations** pane, click the **Format visual** button 🖐 and click **Visual**
  To edit the horizontal axis title and values, expand **X-axis**
  Next to **Title**, toggle the **On** button `On ●` to **Off** to hide the title
  Expand **Values**
  Select **Calibri** as the **Font** and **14** as the font size
  Collapse **Values** and collapse **X-axis**

Step 5. In the **Visualizations** pane, click the **Format visual** button 🖐 and click **Visual**
  To edit the vertical axis, expand **Y-axis**
  Expand **Range**
  Type *0* in the **Minimum** box
  Collapse **Range**, and expand **Values**
  Select **Calibri** as the **Font** and **14** as the font size
  Collapse **Values**
  Next to **Title**, toggle the **On** button `On ●` to **Off** to hide the title and collapse **Y-axis**

Step 6. In the **Visualizations** pane, click the **Format visual** button 🖐 and click **Visual**
  Expand **Gridlines**
  Next to **Horizontal**, toggle the **On** button `On ●` to **Off**
  Next to **Vertical**, toggle the **On** button `On ●` to **Off**
  Collapse **Gridlines**

Step 7. In the **Visualizations** pane to the right of **Visuals**, click **General**
  Expand **Title** and edit the **Text** box to read *Total Sales*
  Select **Calibri** as the **Font** and **16** as the font size

  Click the **Bold** button `B`
  Collapse **Title**

Next, we add filters to the page. By clicking anywhere outside of the visuals in the Report view pane, make sure your previously created visualizations are not selected before proceeding to the following steps.

Step 8. Click **Report view** 📊, and in the **Visualizations** pane, click **Build visual** ▦ to display the **Build visual** matrix of available charts
  Click outside of the current visualization so no visualizations are selected, and select **Slicer** 🔲
  Drag **Category** from the **Data** pane to the **Field** box in the **Visualizations** pane

Step 9. Click **Report view** 📊, and in the **Visualizations** pane, click **Build visual** ▦ to display the **Build visual** matrix of available charts
  Click outside of the current visualization so no visualizations are selected, and select **Slicer** 🔲
  Drag **Flavor** from the **Data** pane to the **Field** box in the **Visualizations** pane (you may have to drag the lower right corner to expand this slicer to display all of the flavors)

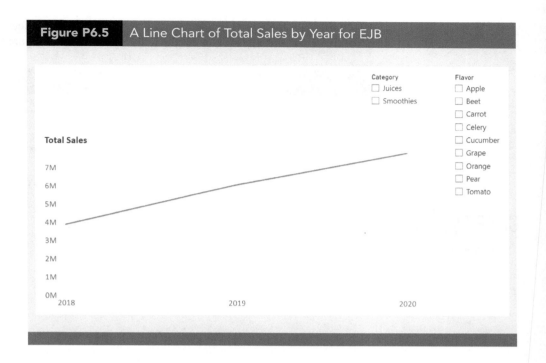

Figure P6.5   A Line Chart of Total Sales by Year for EJB

Steps 8 and 9 create two filters, one for Category and one for Flavor. The chart should now appear as shown in Figure P6.5.

To show the total sales for Pear Smoothies, we select Smoothies under Category and Pear under Flavor in their respective slicers as shown in Figure P6.6.

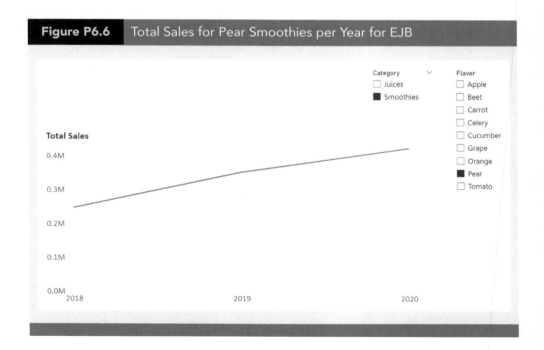

Figure P6.6   Total Sales for Pear Smoothies per Year for EJB

To show the same results by quarter, click the line chart, and select **Quarter** under **Date Hierarchy** in the **Data** pane. This results in the chart shown in Figure P6.7.

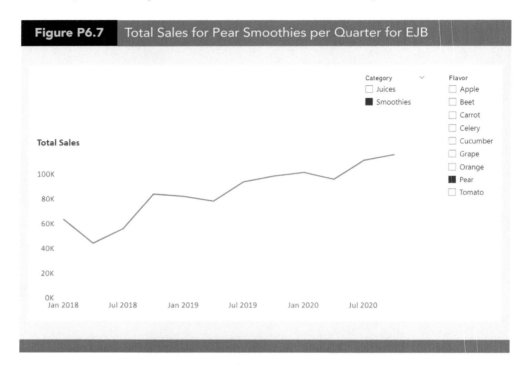

Figure P6.7   Total Sales for Pear Smoothies per Quarter for EJB

CHART *file*

ejbline_chart.pbix

Appendix 6.2 Exploring Data Visually with Tableau

In this appendix, we discuss additional ways to explore data visually using Tableau, including crosstabulations, scatter chart matrixes, and time series charts.

Crosstabulation

The file *ejb* contains data related to the company Espléndido Jugo y Batido, Inc. (EJB), a company that manufactures bottled juices and smoothies. EJB produces its products in five fruit flavors (apple, grape, orange, pear, and tomato) and four vegetable flavors (beet, carrot, celery, and cucumber), and it ships these products from distribution centers (DCs) in Idaho, Mississippi, Nebraska, New Mexico, North Dakota, Rhode Island, and West Virginia. The steps below demonstrate how to create a crosstabulation showing the sales amounts (in $) by category for each EJB distribution center.

ejb

Step 1. Following the steps outlined in Appendix 1.2, connect Tableau to the file *ejb*
Click the **Sheet 1** tab at the bottom of the Tableau Data Source screen to open the worksheet view

Step 2. In the worksheet view of Tableau, drag the pill for **Category** from the **Data** pane to the **Columns** shelf. Drag the pill for **Distribution Center** from the **Data** pane to the **Rows** shelf

Step 3. Drag the pill for **$ Sales** from the **Data** pane to the **Text** card ⊤ Text in the **Marks** area to populate the body of the crosstabulation table

Step 4. To display average sales in the table, right click the pill for **SUM($ Sales)** in the **Marks** area, click **Measure (Sum)** and select **Average**

Step 5. To add total amounts to the crosstabulation table, click the **Analysis** tab in the Ribbon, click **Totals**, and select **Show Row Grand Totals** and **Show Column Grand Totals**

The following steps modify the crosstabulation to improve clarity.

Step 6. Right click on the crosstabulation table and select **Format…**. When the **Format** pane appears:
Click next to **Worksheet:** under **Default**, and change the font size to **11**

Step 7. To modify the title of the chart, right click on **Sheet 1** at the top of the chart and select **Edit Title…**. When the Edit Title dialog box appears:
Replace **<Sheet Name>** with the title *Average Sales for Each Category by Distribution Center*
Highlight the text of the title, then change the font size to **16**, and click the

Bold button **B** to make the title bold font
Click **OK** to close the **Edit Title** dialog box

The completed crosstabulation appears in Figure T6.1.

Scatter Chart Matrix

The file *nyc* contains data on characteristics of the 55 sub-boroughs of New York City. Each observation includes the median monthly rent, percent of college graduates, poverty rate, and commute time for the sub-borough. The steps below demonstrate how to create a scatter chart matrix for these data.

nyc

Step 1. Following the steps outlined in Appendix 1.2, connect Tableau to the file *nyc*
Click the **Sheet 1** tab at the bottom of the Tableau Data Source screen to open the worksheet view

Step 2. In the worksheet view of Tableau, drag the pills for **Median Monthly Rent ($)**, **Percent College Graduates (%)**, **Poverty Rate (%)**, and **Commute Time (min)** from the **Data** pane to the **Columns** shelf. Drag the pills for **Median Monthly Rent ($)**, **Percent College Graduates (%)**, **Poverty Rate (%)**, and **Commute Time (min)** from the **Data** pane to the **Rows** shelf

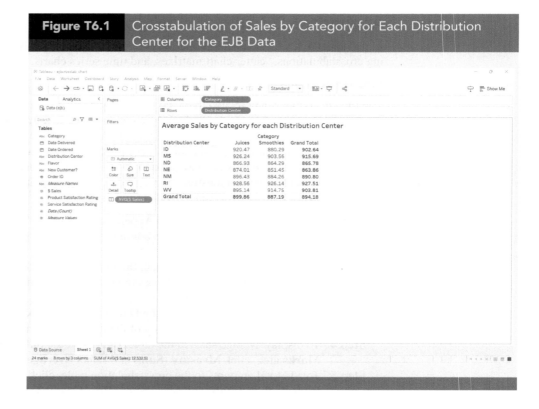

Figure T6.1   Crosstabulation of Sales by Category for Each Distribution Center for the EJB Data

CHART *file*

ejbcrosstab_chart.twbx

Step 3. Click the **Analysis** tab on the Ribbon, and deselect **Aggregate Measures** to display the individual data points

The following steps modify the scatter chart matrix to improve clarity.

Step 4. Right click the vertical axis for **Median Monthly Rent ($)**, and select **Format…**. When the **Format Median Monthly Rent ($)** pane appears:
    Click next to **Font:** under **Default**, and change the font size to **11**

Note that modifying the format of the vertical axis fonts in step 4 also modifies the format of the horizontal axis fonts for this scatter chart matrix.

Step 5. Repeat step 4 for **Percent College Graduates (%)**, **Poverty Rate (%)**, and **Commute Time (min)**

Step 6. To remove the unnecessary chart title, right click **Sheet 1** at the top of the chart and select **Hide Title**

Step 7. To remove the unnecessary grid lines in the chart, right click on the chart and select **Format…**. When the **Format** task pane opens, click on the **Lines** button ☰ , and select **None** next to **Grid Lines:**

The completed scatter chart matrix appears in Figure T6.2.

Visualizing Time Series Data

Here, we reconsider the Espléndido Jugo y Batido, Inc. (EJB) data in the file *ejb*, which are an example of time series data. The steps below demonstrate how we can create an interactive time series chart to view the sales of pear smoothies at EJB.

DATA *file*

ejb

Step 1. Following the steps outlined in Appendix 1.2, connect Tableau to the file *ejb*. Click the **Sheet 1** tab at the bottom of the Tableau Data Source screen to open the worksheet view

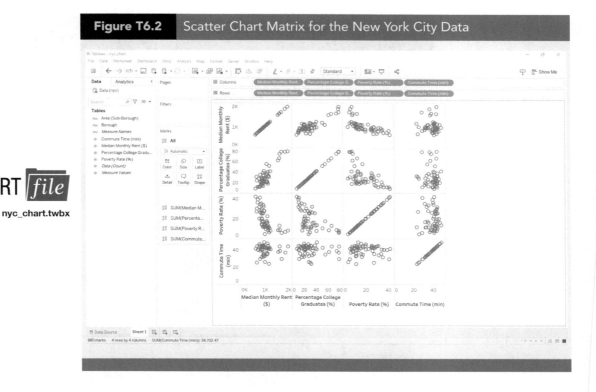

Figure T6.2   Scatter Chart Matrix for the New York City Data

CHART *file*

nyc_chart.twbx

Step 2. Drag the pill for **Date Ordered** from the **Data** pane to the **Columns** shelf

Step 3. Drag the pill for **Category** to the **Filters** area. When the **Filter [Category]** dialog box appears:

> Select the check box for **Smoothies** under **Enter Search Text**
> Click **OK** to close the **Filter [Category]** dialog box
> Right click the pill for **Category: Smoothies** in the **Filters** area and select **Show Filter**

Step 4. Drag the pill for **Flavor** to the **Filters** area. When the **Filter [Flavor]** dialog box appears:

> Select the check box for **Pear** under **Enter Search Text**
> Click **OK** to close the **Filter [Flavor]** dialog box
> Right click the pill for **Flavor: Pear** in the **Filters** area and select **Show Filter**

Step 5. Drag the pill for **$ Sales** from the **Data** pane to the **Rows** shelf

Step 6. Hover between any two horizontal axis labels and when the ⟺ appears, click and slide it right or left to widen or narrow the line chart

These steps create the line chart for the EJB time series data shown in Figure T6.3. Steps 4 and 5 add the interactive filters for Flavor and Category as shown on the right side of Figure T6.3.

The following steps modify the line chart to improve clarity.

Step 7. Right click the vertical axis for **$ Sales** and select **Format…**. When the **Format SUM($ Sales)** pane appears:

> Click next to **Font:** under **Default**, and change the font size to **11**

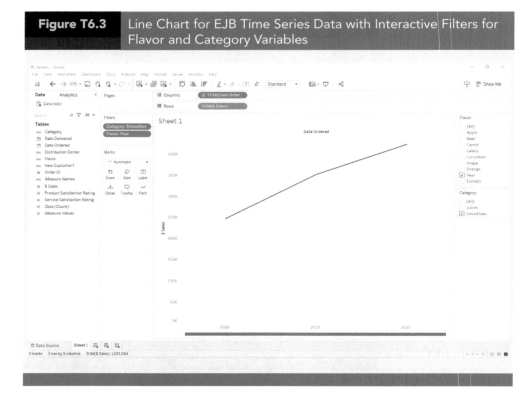

Figure T6.3   Line Chart for EJB Time Series Data with Interactive Filters for Flavor and Category Variables

Step 8. Right click the horizontal axis and select **Format…**. When the **Format YEAR(Date Ordered)** pane appears:

Click next to **Font:** under **Default**, and change the font size to **11**

Step 9. Right click the label **Date Ordered** at the top of the line chart and select **Format…**. When the **Format Field Labels** pane appears:

Click next to **Font:** under **Default**, and change the font size to **11**

Step 10. To modify the title of the chart, right click on **Sheet 1** at the top of the chart, and select **Edit Title…**. When the Edit Title dialog box appears:

Replace **<Sheet Name>** with title *Total Sales of Pear Smoothies*

Highlight the text of the title, then change the font size to **16**, and click the

Bold button ⬛B⬛ to make the title bold font

Click **OK** to close the **Edit Title** dialog box

Step 11. To remove the unnecessary grid lines in the chart, right click on the chart and select **Format…**. When the **Format** task pane opens, click on the **Lines** button ≡ , and select **None** next to **Grid Lines:**

The completed line chart appears in Figure T6.4.

We can change the temporal frequency of the time series chart using the following steps.

Step 12. Right click the pill for **YEAR(Date Ordered)** in the **Columns** shelf, and select **Quarter   Q2 2015**.

Step 12 changes the temporal frequency for these time series data from yearly to quarterly. The result of this change is shown in Figure T6.5.

The next steps change the temporal frequency for the pear smoothie sales data to monthly and add a trendline as shown in Figure T6.6

Step 13. Right click the pill for **QUARTER(Date Ordered)** in the **Columns** shelf and select **Month   May 2015**

*Note that there are two options of Quarter when you click the pill for **YEAR(Date Ordered)**. We need to select the lower option marked **Quarter Q2 2015** to display the data by quarter for all years of data.*

| Figure T6.4 | Completed Line Chart Showing Total Sales of Pear Smoothies at EJB by Year |

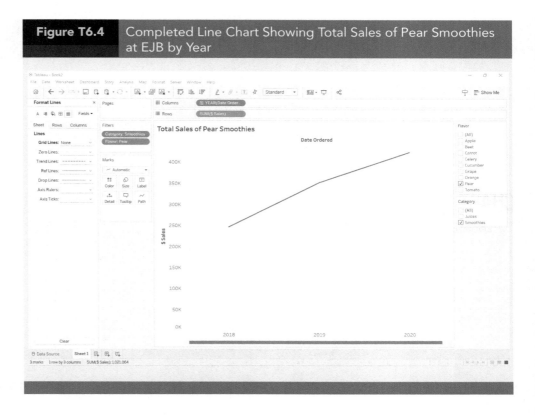

Step 14. Right click the line chart, click **Trend Lines** and select **Show Trend Lines**

Step 15. Click on the upward sloping dashed trend line to display the formula for this line, its *R*-Squared value, and its *p* value.

| Figure T6.5 | Line Chart Showing Total Sales of Pear Smoothies at EJB by Quarter |

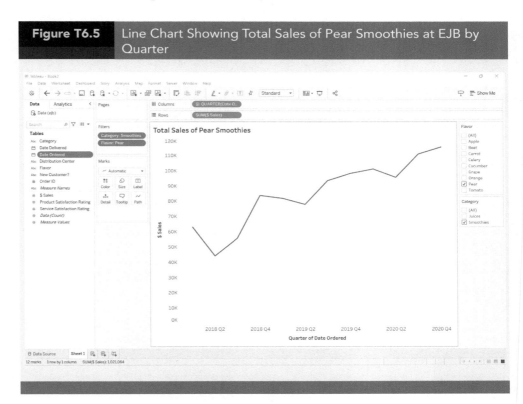

Figure T6.6	Line Chart Showing Total Sales of Pear Smoothies at EJB by Month with a Trend Line

CHART *file*

ejbline_chart.twbx

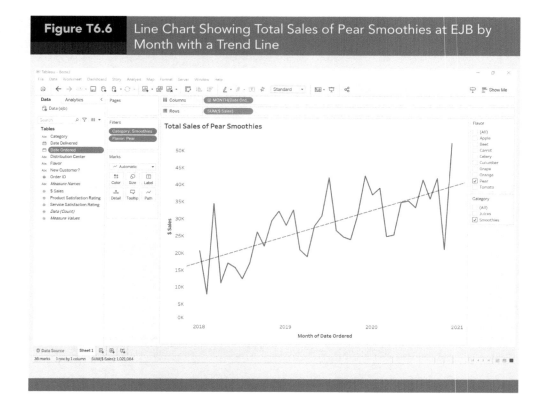

Chapter 7

Explaining Visually to Influence with Data

Contents

Learning Objectives

After completing this chapter, you will be able to

LO 1 Explain the importance of knowing your audience's needs and analytical comfort level to create an effective data visualization or presentation.

LO 2 Explain how to create the most effective message possible in your data visualization or presentation by helping the audience empathize with the data.

LO 3 List the types of data visualizations that are most appropriate to communicate specific insights and for audiences with different needs and different levels of analytical comfort.

LO 4 Effectively use dot matrix charts and big-associated numbers to give the audience a better relative understanding of large numerical values in a data visualization.

LO 5 Identify situations for which a slope chart is appropriate and be able to create a slope chart from data.

LO 6 Use preattentive attributes to emphasize certain insights for an audience and tell a story in a data visualization.

LO 7 Define Aristotle's Rhetorical Triangle and explain how it can be employed to connect with the audience to tell a story in a data visualization or presentation.

LO 8 Define Freytag's Pyramid and explain how this provides a suggested structure for telling a story in your presentation.

LO 9 Define the concept of storyboarding and explain how to storyboard a presentation using sticky notes and using PowerPoint.

LO 10 Create an effective story for a presentation that considers the needs of the audience.

Data Visualization Makeover

Increasing Youth Participation in Primary Voting[1]

A 2016 article in *The Washington Post* discussed changes in the number of young voters participating in the U.S. presidential primary elections of 2008 and 2016. One of the charts included in this article was similar to what is shown in Figure 7.1. The clustered bar chart is used to illustrate that more young voters participated in the primary election in 2016 than in 2008 for four of five states that were closely contested in the presidential election.

We can find several opportunities to improve the design of the chart in Figure 7.1. Based on concepts from previous chapters, we could change some formatting to improve this chart. However, a more substantial criticism of this chart is that it does not effectively explain the data as well as some other chart types. The goal of the chart is to communicate to the audience that youth participation in primary elections has increased in four of these five states between 2008 and 2016. It requires considerable cognitive load for the audience to understand this story from the clustered column chart. We can communicate this insight more effectively if we choose a different type of chart.

In particular, a chart known as a slope chart can communicate this story more effectively. A slope chart for these same data is shown in Figure 7.2. The slope chart makes it much easier to interpret the changes in youth participation in the primaries from 2008 to 2016. The audience can easily see that four of the states (Florida, Illinois, Missouri, and North Carolina) had increases in youth participation, but one state (Ohio) had a decrease in youth participation. Figure 7.2 also highlights the difference in the behavior of youth voters in Ohio versus the other four states using the preattentive attribute of color.

In Figure 7.2, we provide a further explanation of the data by using the descriptive title of "Four of Five Closely Contested States Saw Increased Youth Participation in Primary Elections in 2016." This explanatory title greatly reduces the cognitive load on the audience by providing a summary of the insight to be gained from this visualization. We have also added some additional explanatory information to the chart explaining the meaning of "youth voters" in this context.

Because the main insight to be conveyed in this chart for *The Washington Post* article is that most

Figure 7.1   Clustered Column Chart Showing Changes in Youth Participation in U.S. Primary Elections from 2008 to 2016

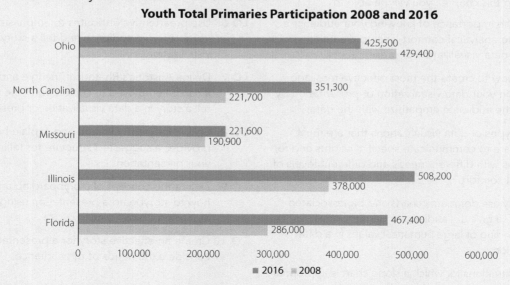

[1] This Data Visualization Makeover is inspired by an example shown here: https://www.crazyegg.com/blog/data-storytelling-5-steps-charts/ based on data and chart shown here: https://www.washingtonpost.com/news/the-fix/wp/2016/03/17/74-year-old-bernie-sanderss -amazing-dominance-among-young-voters-in-1-chart/

states have seen an increase in youth participation in primary elections between 2008 and 2016, Figure 7.2 explains this more effectively to the audience. Slope charts are very effective at showing changes over multiple variables between two different points in time, so it is a good choice for these data and audience. Using a slope chart for these data emphasizes to the audience that the important insight being communicated is the change in primary election participation between 2008 and 2016.

Figure 7.2   A Slope Chart Showing Changes in Youth Participation in U.S. Primary Elections from 2008 to 2016

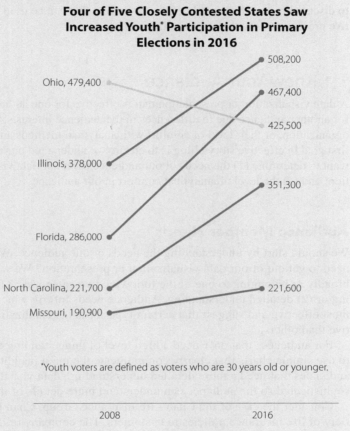

Four of Five Closely Contested States Saw Increased Youth* Participation in Primary Elections in 2016

*Youth voters are defined as voters who are 30 years old or younger.

Data visualizations are used to explore data or explain information to the audience. In this chapter, we focus on data visualizations that are being used to explain data to an audience. Our goal is to help the audience generate insights from data and to influence the audience in a way that facilitates better decision making. Explaining data to an audience through data visualization is similar to the act of storytelling. The best stories take complicated issues, themes, or ideas and convey them to the audience in a manner that is easy for the audience to understand, captures the interest of the audience, and helps the audience remember the important issues, themes, or ideas. This is true for stories presented as books, movies, or even data visualizations. Specific to stories generated from data, **storytelling** refers to the ability to build a narrative from the data that is meaningful for the audience, is memorable for the audience, and is likely to influence the audience.

To be effective at storytelling, we need to understand our audience. We also need to understand the story, or key insight(s), that we want to convey from the data. Once we know who our audience is and what story we want to tell, we can then start to think about what type of data visualization is most effective for that audience and that story. We can also think about specific design attributes and formatting that we should use in the data visualization to best convey our story to the audience.

In this chapter, we will discuss how we can understand our audience and understand the story we are trying to convey. We will consider which types of data visualizations are best for conveying the story. We will introduce several new types of charts, including the slope chart used in the Data Visualization Makeover for this chapter. We will also revisit several design issues introduced in previous chapters to illustrate how these design issues can be used to convey different stories. We conclude this chapter by bringing the concepts together to discuss broader themes related to storytelling that can be used to help you design effective presentations with data visualizations.

7.1 Know Your Audience

A data visualization or presentation that is effective for one audience may not be effective for another audience due to differences in the audience interests, their roles within the organization, or their level of comfort with analytical methods and tools. Therefore, our first goal in effective storytelling is to ensure we understand our audience. In particular, we want to determine (1) the needs of our audience from our data visualization or presentation; and (2) the level of analytical comfort in our audience.

Audience Member Needs

We should start by understanding the needs of our audience. What does the audience need to get out of our data visualization or presentation? We will classify these needs broadly as belonging to one of the following two categories: (1) high-level understanding or (2) detailed understanding. Audience needs inform which type of story will be most effective and suggest that certain types of data visualizations may be more effective than others.

For audiences that only need a high level of understanding from the data, it is best to use simple charts that clearly communicate the main insight from the data. For audiences that need a more detailed understanding, data visualizations may be more sophisticated so the audience can understand more details of the analysis.

Consider the case of the Chan Life Insurance Group. Chan Life Insurance sells a variety of life insurance policies to customers. The company relies on sales agents to sell its policies. The overall process for completing a sale is (1) the salesperson requests a quote and sends it to underwriting for pricing; (2) the underwriters perform a manual evaluation to examine the quote request, evaluate the risk, and appropriately price the policy; (3) the pricing decision made by underwriting is verified; and (4) the finalized quote is sent back to the agent who communicates this to the customer.

Chan Life Insurance's information technology (IT) department is considering investment in additional technology that would streamline the quote request and underwriting processes to reduce the delay between when an agent submits a request for a quote and when the agent receives the finalized quote. The new technology allows for faster quote request transmission, automates the underwriting process by using built-in algorithms to evaluate risk and suggest prices, and reduces the amount of time for underwriting verification.

Chan Life estimates that it will be able to install the new technology system and provide the required training to all employees by the end of August. Chan Life Insurance has been collecting data on the amount of time required to respond to requests for quotes from January through July of the current year. It has also estimated the amount of time it will take to respond to request for quotes after the new technology is installed. These data are shown in Table 7.1.

Table 7.1	Average Times to Complete Tasks Required for Responding to Request for Quote from Chan Life Insurance Sales Agents					
	Average Time to Complete Task (minutes)					
Task	**January**	**March**	**May**	**July**	**September***	**November***
Process Request for Quote	244	230	267	220	70	50
Underwrite and Generate Quote	154	167	172	168	40	20
Verify Quote	98	112	110	115	20	10
Send Quote to Agent	121	115	110	117	120	120
Total Response Time	617	624	659	620	250	200

*Projected

Chan Life Insurance would like to provide updates to its employees on this new process, but it must satisfy the needs of several different audiences. One primary audience is its sales agents. For the sales agents, the most important insight is that the time required to receive a response for an insurance policy quote request should decrease substantially after the introduction of the new technology system. The sales agents will need to adjust their routines so they can best take advantage of these decreases in response times. Therefore, the sales agents fall into the category of needing only a high-level understanding of the data shown in Table 7.1. The most effective chart for this audience is likely to be something similar to Figure 7.3, which shows a simple line chart displaying the average total response times by month. Note that here we have differentiated the portions of the line chart for the months of September and November by using a dashed line rather than a solid line to high-light the fact that these months represent projected response times after the new IT system is installed. You can easily change a portion of a line chart by double clicking an individual data point in the chart to open the **Format Data Point** task pane, then selecting the **Fill & Line** icon ⬧ and changing the **Dash type** under **Line**.

Figure 7.3	Line Chart for Chan Life Insurance Sales Agents Audience Displaying the Total Response Time for Requests for Quotes

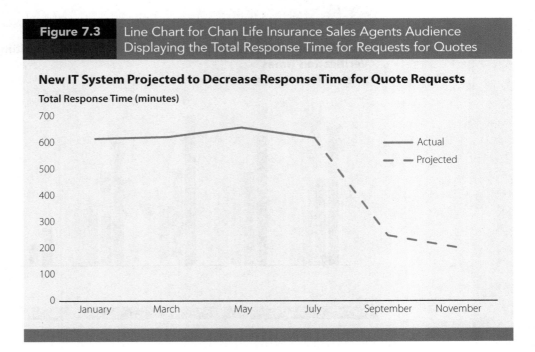

Another audience that Chan Life Insurance would like to update is its internal team of underwriters. The underwriters are likely to want to know more details on how and why the new technology system will reduce the time required to respond to requests for quotes from sales agents. This new technology will have a direct impact on the work done by the underwriters, so they are likely to want a more detailed understanding of the data shown in Table 7.1. Therefore, a clustered column chart such as the one shown in Figure 7.4 is likely to be more useful to this audience. The chart shown in Figure 7.4 shows the projected impact of the new IT system on each of the four tasks required to complete a request for a quote from a sales agent. This chart is likely to lead to further dialog and discussion so the underwriters can better understand what effect this new system is likely to have on their work and day-to-day activities.

Comparing Figure 7.3 to Figure 7.4, we also notice that the chart titles have been adjusted to provide greater meaning for the intended audience. For the sales agents, Figure 7.3 uses the chart title "New IT System Projected to Decrease Response Time for Quote Requests" to emphasize that it is important for this audience to recognize that the total time required to respond to a quote request is expected to decrease substantially after the introduction of the new IT system. Figure 7.4 uses the chart title "New IT System Projected to Decrease Processing, Underwriting, and Verification Times" to specifically indicate that the reductions in time occur in the processing, underwriting, and verification steps. Using descriptive chart titles is an effective way to highlight specific insights for the intended audience from a data visualization.

Audience Member Analytical Comfort Levels

It is also useful to understand the analytical comfort level of your audience when designing data visualizations. Some data visualizations can be overly confusing for an audience that has little experience interpreting more sophisitcated data visualizations. For audiences that have a low comfort level with analytics, it is recommended to use simple charts that can be easily explained and that highlight a single insight. For audiences that have higher levels

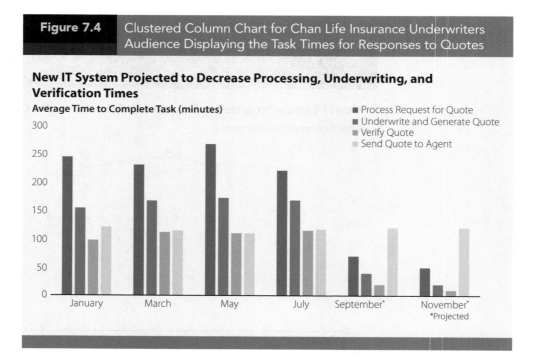

Figure 7.4 Clustered Column Chart for Chan Life Insurance Underwriters Audience Displaying the Task Times for Responses to Quotes

| Figure 7.5 | Portion of Patient Satisfaction Scores from General Hospital Data |

◢	A	B	C	D	E	F	G	H
1				Patient Satisfaction Scores				
2	Neurologic	General	Vascular	Oncology	Pediatric	Ophthalmic	Thoracic	Orthopaedic
3	1.9	3.6	3.0	2.9	3.3	3.9	4.5	4.4
4	2.8	2.5	3.5	3.7	4.6	4.0	5.0	4.5
5	2.1	2.1	1.5	3.4	3.9	4.1	4.7	4.5
6	3.2	2.8	2.6	3.8	4.1	4.0	5.0	4.4
7	2.3	3.8	1.5	3.3	3.1	3.8	4.9	4.5
8	2.7	2.6	2.2	4.3	2.9	4.2	4.4	4.6
9	2.9	3.9	2.5	3.2	4.0	3.9	4.1	4.4
10	2.0	2.4	3.1	3.2	4.6	4.1	5.0	4.4
11	2.6	2.5	2.3	4.3	4.1	4.0	4.7	4.5
12	1.6	1.6	3.1	3.5	3.8	4.1	4.5	4.5

DATA *file*

generalhospital

of comfort with analytics, it may be useful to use more sophisticated charts that provide additional details and insights.

Consider the case of General Hospital, which is located in Olympia, Washington. General Hospital tracks patient satisfaction scores for all patients that undergo surgery in its hospital. The patient satisfaction scores are based on a combination of survey responses from patients on factors such as waiting time, friendliness of staff, and effectiveness of procedure. The combined scores range between 0 and 5, and they are tracked for each surgical department in the hospital: General Surgery, Neurologic Surgery, Oncology, Opthalmic Surgery, Orthopedic Surgery, Pediatric Surgery, Thoracic Surgery, and Vascular Surgery. A portion of these data is shown in Figure 7.5 and contained in the file *generalhospital*.

General Hospital presents regular updates to its staff on the results of these patient satisfaction surveys. But it must present the results to several different audiences. One of the audiences has a low analytical comfort level, while another audience has a high analytical comfort level. For the audience with a low analytical comfort level, the column chart shown in Figure 7.6 is likely the most effective in giving a simple overview of the results of the patient satisfaction scores. Figure 7.6 is easy to interpret and makes it obvious that several surgical departments (Neurologic, General, and Vascular) have low average patient satisfaction scores, while others (Opthalmic, Thoracic, and Orthopedic) have high average patient satisfaction scores. By presenting the data as a sorted column chart, this makes relative comparisons among the surgical departments even easier for the audience.

Figure 7.7 shows the same data presented as a box and whisker chart. This type of data visualization is more appropriate for an audience with a higher analytical comfort level. Figure 7.7 takes more work for the audience to interpret than Figure 7.6, but it also provides more insights into the data. From Figure 7.7, we see that while the Thoracic and Orthopedic Surgical Departments have higher average patient satisfaction scores, the distributions of these scores are quite different from each other. The patient satisfaction scores for the Orthopedic Surgical Department are all quite similar, so there is relatively little variability in these scores. The patient satisfaction scores for the Thoracic Surgical Department have much more variability, including several outliers of very low patient satisfaction scores. Figure 7.7 also shows that the Ophthalmic Surgical Department patient satisfaction scores have little variability, while there is considerable variability in the patient satisfaction scores from Pediatric, Vascular, and General Surgery patients.

Box and whisker charts are discussed in Chapter 5.

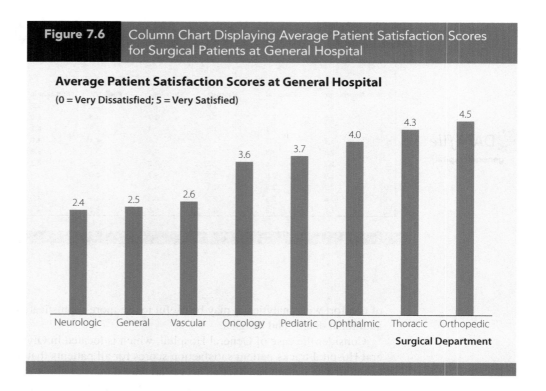

Figure 7.6   Column Chart Displaying Average Patient Satisfaction Scores for Surgical Patients at General Hospital

Average Patient Satisfaction Scores at General Hospital
(0 = Very Dissatisfied; 5 = Very Satisfied)

Neurologic: 2.4; General: 2.5; Vascular: 2.6; Oncology: 3.6; Pediatric: 3.7; Ophthalmic: 4.0; Thoracic: 4.3; Orthopedic: 4.5

Surgical Department

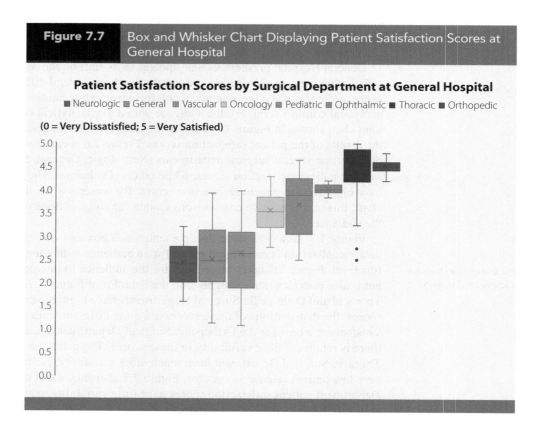

Figure 7.7   Box and Whisker Chart Displaying Patient Satisfaction Scores at General Hospital

Patient Satisfaction Scores by Surgical Department at General Hospital

■ Neurologic ■ General ■ Vascular ▢ Oncology ■ Pediatric ■ Ophthalmic ■ Thoracic ■ Orthopedic

(0 = Very Dissatisfied; 5 = Very Satisfied)

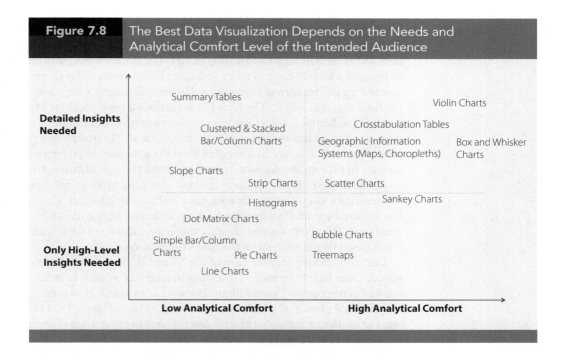

Figure 7.8 The Best Data Visualization Depends on the Needs and Analytical Comfort Level of the Intended Audience

While Figure 7.7 conveys quite a bit more information than Figure 7.6, box and whisker charts can be difficult to interpret for an audience that has a low analytical comfort level. Therefore, for such audiences, we might consider simpler data visualizations, such as the one shown in Figure 7.6 using a simple column chart. Alternatively, if we choose to use a more sophisticated chart such as the box and whisker chart shown in Figure 7.7, we must remember that we should provide additional details to explain how the audience should interpret the chart.

Figure 7.8 provides an example of recommendations for the types of charts that may be most useful for different audiences based on the level of insight needed by the audience (high level or detailed) and the analytical comfort level of the audience (low or high). Figure 7.8 shows only general recommendations that will need to be adjusted for the specific data and audience. Tables and charts can vary substantially within each type based on the formatting and amount of information contained in the table or chart.

7.2 Know Your Message

To best explain your data to an audience, you also need to ensure that you know what insight(s) you are trying to convey to the audience. This means you need to understand the data well enough that you can communicate the insights clearly and succinctly. Not only should you be able to explain what the data mean to the audience, but you should also be able to explain the limitations inherent in the data and how these limitations affect the insights drawn from the data.

In Chapter 9, we discuss additional details for how to make sure we are telling the truth with data and how to avoid confusing or misleading our audience.

To best explain the data, we need to understand what types of insights will help the decision maker. The goal of all analytical methods is to influence the audience in a way that facilitates better decisions. Examples of such decisions include how to improve patient care in a hospital, how to best communicate with voters in an election, how to allocate resources among schools in a city to effectively improve educational outcomes, which types of marketing channels to use to reach the most customers, or where to build a new store to provide the biggest boost to company sales. To know how to help our audience make better decisions, we need to understand both our audience and our data well enough to know what types of insights from the data are most likely to lead to improvements in decision making.

What Helps the Decision Maker?

To create the most effective data visualization possible, we need to make sure we understand what will help the decision maker. The decision maker is the person (or group of people) who will have to make decisions based on the analysis presented in a data visualization. The person designing a data visualization for explanatory purposes is rarely the final decision maker. The decision maker often must consider several factors (quantitative and qualitative), assess the impact on a variety of stakeholders, and execute a decision with incomplete information under time constraints. Therefore, the goal of an explanatory data visualization is to make insights from the data easy to understand in a relatively short amount of time so the decision maker can make the best decision possible.

Because most decision makers are busy and must make many decisions, it is important to create data visualizations that are clear and easy to interpret. This is another reason why it is important to create data visualizations that have high data-ink ratios and are free from chart junk. However, we also should ensure we understand what types of decisions will be made based on the analysis of the data visualization.

Let us again consider the case of the Chan Life Insurance Company. As we have stated, Chan Life Insurance is investing in a new IT system to reduce the amount of time it takes to respond to a quote request from a sales agent. However, suppose that we learn that the final choice of which new IT system to install has not yet been made. If we know that our audience includes the decision maker(s) who must choose among several alternative suppliers of IT systems, then this helps us understand what type of visualization will be most effective for this decision. We could consider creating a clustered bar chart similar to what is shown in Figure 7.9, which summarizes the performance of the three main competitors to be the supplier of the new IT system for Chan Life Insurance: YellowHat Systems, Illumination Software, and Silver Star. Figure 7.9 provides an evaluation of the three different systems on four criteria: cost, reliability, maintenance support, and ease of use. This clustered bar chart makes it easy for the decision maker to compare the different IT software vendors on the different criteria, and it can also lead to further discussion so the decision maker can ask for more details on each of the subjective evaluations. Note that we can display this clustered bar chart in multiple ways. Figure 7.9a groups the subjective evaluations by IT software vendor. Figure 7.9b groups the subjective evaluations of the different software vendors by criteria to show how vendors compare to each other on each criterion. Each of these clustered bar charts can be an effective data visualization for the decision maker, or they could be presented together. It is easy to switch between the two clustered bar chart in Excel. The following steps will change the chart shown in Figure 7.9a to the chart shown in Figure 7.9b, or vice versa.

Step 1. Right click the chart and choose **Select Data...**
Step 2. When the **Select Data Source** dialog box appears, click the **Switch Row/Column** button   Switch Row/Column

Empathizing with Data

It is also important to be able to create empathy with data. **Empathy** refers to the ability to understand and share in the feelings of others. Being able to empathize with data means remembering that data are not just numbers from a spreadsheet or database but that these data often represent real people, and the decisions made based on our analysis may have a substantial impact on real people. Therefore, it is important to consider how we can create data visualizations that can help others generate empathy. By empathizing with the data, we can create data visualizations to effectively impact decisions. Two common challenges for creating empathy with data are that audiences can lose the ability to associate meaning when considering large numerical values and that it can be difficult to consider individual cases when looking at aggregate statistics. Here, we will discuss ways of dealing with each of these challenges.

Figure 7.9 Two Possible Clustered Bar Charts to Assist a Decision Maker in Choosing among Three Competing New IT Systems for Chan Life Insurance Company

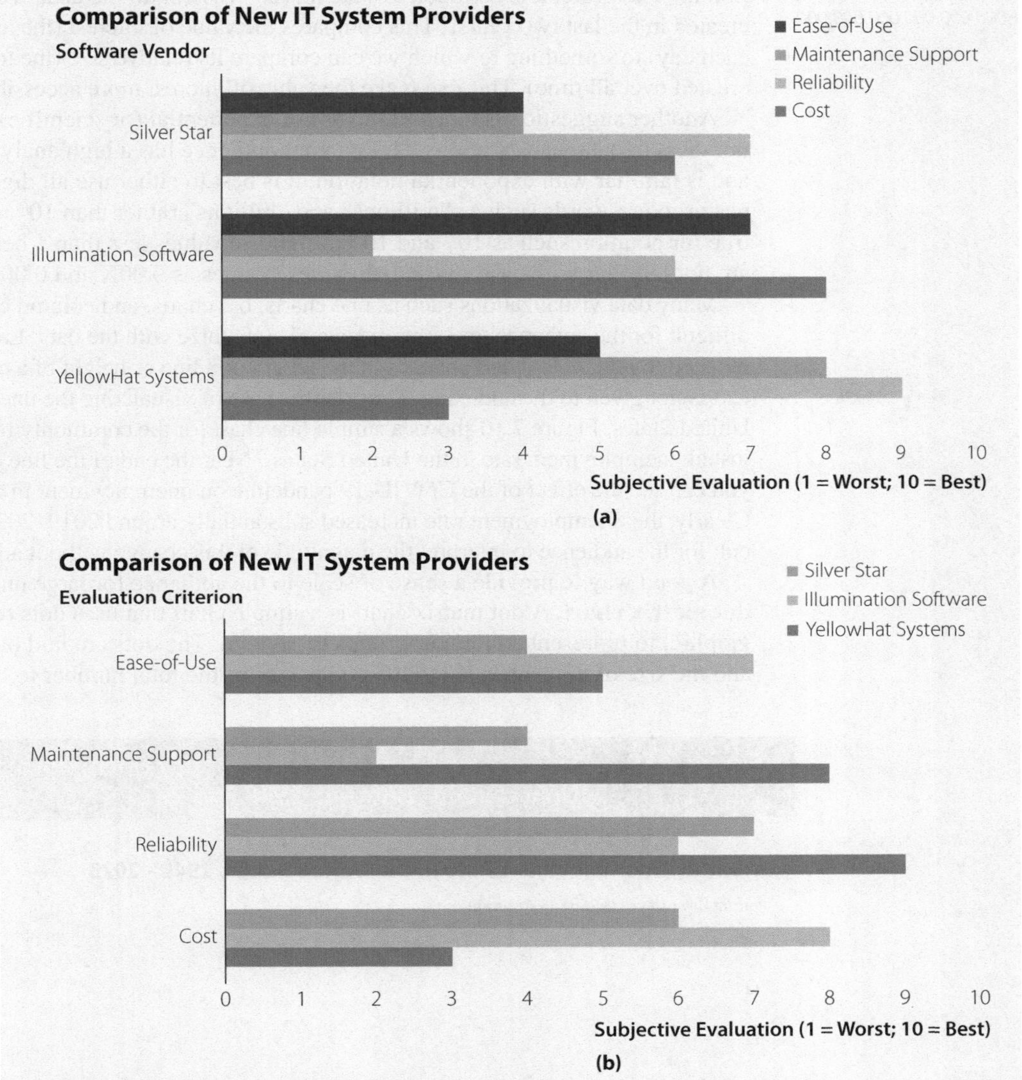
Comparison of New IT System Providers
Software Vendor
Ease-of-Use
Maintenance Support
Reliability
Cost
Silver Star
Illumination Software
YellowHat Systems
0 1 2 3 4 5 6 7 8 9 10
Subjective Evaluation (1 = Worst; 10 = Best)
(a)
Comparison of New IT System Providers
Evaluation Criterion
Silver Star
Illumination Software
YellowHat Systems
Ease-of-Use
Maintenance Support
Reliability
Cost
0 1 2 3 4 5 6 7 8 9 10
Subjective Evaluation (1 = Worst; 10 = Best)
(b)

CHART *file*
chanlife_chart

Because most of our day-to-day interactions with tangible items are with items that number less than a few hundred, it can be difficult to fully grasp the relative sizes of large numbers such as values in the millions, billions, or even larger. In general, people can visualize groups of items up to about 100 things. For larger numbers of items, it is difficult for people to easily visualize the amount.

There are several strategies for helping the audience interpret large numbers. One suggestion is to try to convert the large number into something with which the audience may be more familiar. For instance, suppose that the next payout from the Powerball Lottery is projected to be $357 million. This is a large sum of money, and most people cannot easily imagine its value relative to smaller dollar amounts. However, some simple arithmetic shows that a payout of $357 million is equivalent to receiving a payout of more than $171,000 per

1 quintillion = 1,000,000,000,000,000,000

week for the next 40 years (ignoring inflation). Most people can then compare the $171,000 per week to their own weekly income to get a quick relative calibration for this amount. Or consider the fact that it is estimated that humans are currently creating approximately 2.5 quintillion bytes of data each day. Most people have no concept of the size of a "quintillion." Therefore, it is common to state this as "90% of all the data in existence has been created in the last two years." This compares the value of interest (the amount of data created each day) to something to which we can compare its relative size (the total amount of data created over all time). This can make the value of interest more accessible to the audience.

Another suggestion is to avoid the use of exponential (or scientific) notation for large numbers in data visualizations. Unless your audience has a high analytical comfort level and is familiar with exponential notation, it is best to either use all digits in numerical values or to use words such as "millions" and "billions" rather than 10^6 and 10^9. This is also true for notation such as 10^{-3} and 10^{-6} to indicate values less than 1 because most audiences are not familiar with easily visualizing these values as 0.00X and 0.00000X.

Many data visualizations such as line charts, bar charts, and column charts also make it difficult for the audience to comprehend and empathize with the data. Large changes can be reduced to relatively small changes in the length of a line or height of a column if proper context is not given to the audience. Consider the case of visualizing the unemployment rate in the United States. Figure 7.10 shows a simple line chart for the commonly reported seasonally adjusted unemployment rate in the United States.[2] Near the end of the line chart in Figure 7.10, you can see the effect of the COVID-19 pandemic on unemployment in the United States. Clearly, the unemployment rate increased substantially around 2019–2020, but it can be difficult for the audience to interpret the magnitude of this change without additional context.

A good way to provide a sense of scale to the audience for large numbers is to use a **dot matrix chart**. A dot matrix chart is a simple chart that uses dots (or another simple graphic) to represent an item or groups of an item. The dots are laid out in a matrix form, and the size of the matrix is relative to the size of the total number to be conveyed.

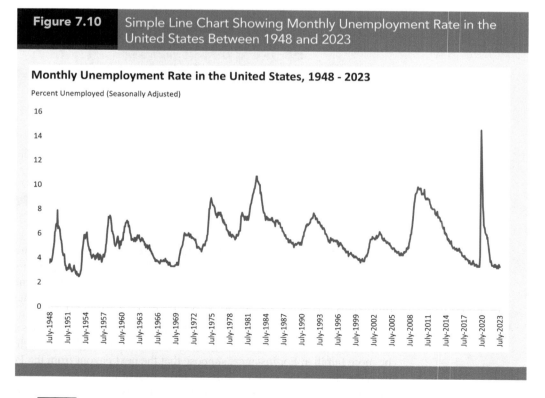

Figure 7.10   Simple Line Chart Showing Monthly Unemployment Rate in the United States Between 1948 and 2023

Monthly Unemployment Rate in the United States, 1948 - 2023

Percent Unemployed (Seasonally Adjusted)

[2] Based on data from the U.S. Bureau of Labor Statistics, https://data.bls.gov/

Consider the case of the number of jobs lost in the United States in the year 2020 due to the COVID-19 pandemic. From unemployment data, it is estimated that more than 40 million jobs were lost in 2020. This is a staggeringly large number. If we were to plot this on a simple line chart or scatter chart, the value of 40 million would be reduced to a single point on a chart where the location on the chart corresponds to 40 million. An alternative way to visualize this is to use a dot matrix chart. We can easily create a dot matrix chart in Excel using the following steps.

We will display jobs in our dot matrix chart using a simple filled dot where ● will correspond to 100,000 jobs. Because we want to visualize 40 million lost jobs, we will need to create a matrix of 40,000,000 / 100,000 = 400 dots. We will do this by creating a 20 × 20 matrix of dots. Note that we are not using the Charts function in Excel; instead, we will simply build this from a blank Excel worksheet.

Step 1. Select cell B3 in a blank worksheet in Excel
Click the **Insert** tab on the Excel Ribbon
In the **Symbols** group, click **Symbol**

Step 2. When the **Symbol** dialog box opens:
Select **Geometric Shapes** in the **Subset:** box, and click the filled dot ●
Click **Insert** to insert this dot in cell B3
Click **Close** to exit the **Symbol** dialog box

Step 3. Copy cell B3 to cells B3:U22

Step 4. Highlight Columns B:U and double-click the edge of one of the columns to reduce the spacing of the columns

Step 5. Click **View** in the Excel Ribbon and deselect the check box for **Gridlines**

Steps 1 through 5 create the dot matrix chart shown in Figure 7.11.

Figure 7.11 Initial Dot Matrix Chart Illustrating the Number of Jobs Lost in the United States During the 2020 COVID-19 Pandemic

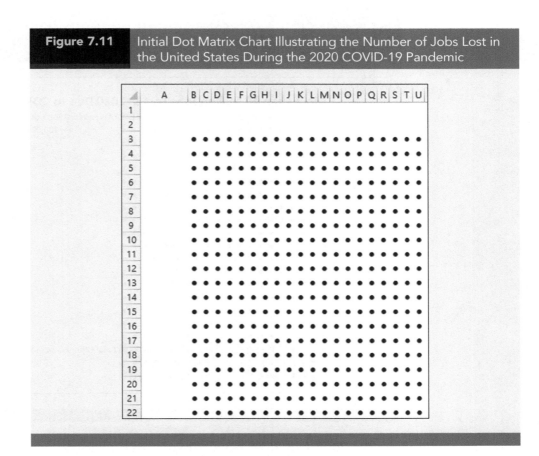

We can give additional context for these data to the audience by adding additional details to this dot matrix chart. We can use knowledge of our audience to create a meaningful reference point for the magnitude of this job loss. Suppose we are aware that our audience consists of many individuals living in the state of Ohio. According to the U.S. Bureau of Labor Statistics, the entire labor workforce in the state of Ohio was about 5.8 million jobs in 2020.[3] We will incorporate this into our dot matrix chart by using the following steps.

Because each ● = 100,000 jobs, then 5,800,000 / 100,000 = 58. So, to represent 5,800,000 jobs as the total workforce in Ohio, we shade cells D20:U20 and B21:U22 blue in Step 6, which corresponds to 58 dots.

Step 6. Change the fill color of cells D20:U20 and B21:U22 by clicking the **Home** tab on the Ribbon and then changing the **Fill Color**  to blue (see Figure 7.12)

Step 7. Select cell B1 and enter the text *More than 40 Million Jobs Lost in 2020 Due to COVID-19 Pandemic*
Select cell B1, click **Home** on the Ribbon, and change the font to **16 point Bold**

Step 8. Select cell D2 and enter the text *This is almost 7 times larger than the total labor force in the State of Ohio* using **11 point** font

Step 9. Select cell W2 and enter the text *● = 100,000 Jobs*

Step 10. Select cell V20 and enter the text *Total Labor Force in State of Ohio*

The shading used in Figure 7.12 is an example of using the Gestalt principle of enclosure introduced in Chapter 3.

The completed dot matrix chart is shown in Figure 7.12. This chart helps the audience get a relative sense of the scope of the job losses by using dots to represent groups of 100,000 jobs, by using the total labor force in Ohio as a point of comparison, and by giving a descriptive chart title. This helps the audience generate empathy with these data.

Another suggestion for helping to create empathy with the data in the audience is to include a focus on the individual rather than just presenting aggregated statistics. As an example,

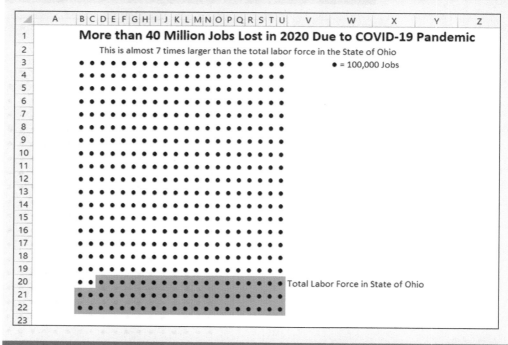

Figure 7.12   Completed Dot Matrix Chart Illustrating the Number of Jobs Lost in the United States During the 2020 COVID-19 Pandemic Relative to the Total Labor Force in State of Ohio

---

[3] See https://www.bls.gov/eag/eag.oh.htm#eag_oh.f.1.

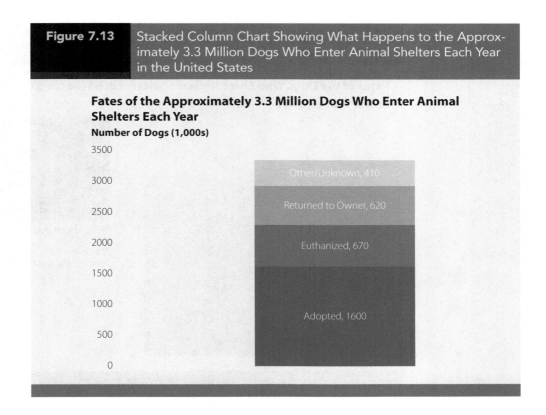

Figure 7.13   Stacked Column Chart Showing What Happens to the Approximately 3.3 Million Dogs Who Enter Animal Shelters Each Year in the United States

Fates of the Approximately 3.3 Million Dogs Who Enter Animal Shelters Each Year

consider that, according to the American Society for the Prevention of Cruelty to Animals, approximately 3.3 million dogs enter animal shelters each year. Of these 3.3 million dogs, approximately 1.6 million are adopted; 670,000 are euthanized; and 620,000 are returned to their owners. Figure 7.13 displays these data in the form of a stacked column chart.

Figure 7.13 shows that there are a lot of dogs entering animal shelters each year and that of those who enter, only some of them are returned to their original owners or adopted by new families. Clearly, there is a need to try to find more homes for dogs who enter animal shelters. However, Figure 7.13 may not influence many in the audience to take action if the audience does not empathize with the data. We can try to create more empathy with the data by focusing not just on the aggregate statistics but also including something specific that makes these numbers seem more personable and relatable. One way to do this is to include pictures in the data visualization. This is even more effective if we can include individual characteristics so the audience can relate to this specific individual. Figure 7.14 is a revision of Figure 7.13 that includes a picture and additional details.

We can add a picture to an existing chart in Excel by clicking the **Insert** tab on the Ribbon, clicking the **Pictures** button in the **Illustrations** group, and then choosing where we want to take the picture from. The picture used in Figure 7.14 is taken from **Online Pictures.**

Customer segmentation in marketing provides another example illustrating the importance of emphasizing the specific to create a story for data. Many companies use market segmentation analysis to better understand their customers. The basic idea of market segmentation is to divide a company's customers into different groups that have similar characteristics. Once the company identifies the characteristics that a particular customer group has in common, the company can design specific marketing plans, promotions, etc., to appeal

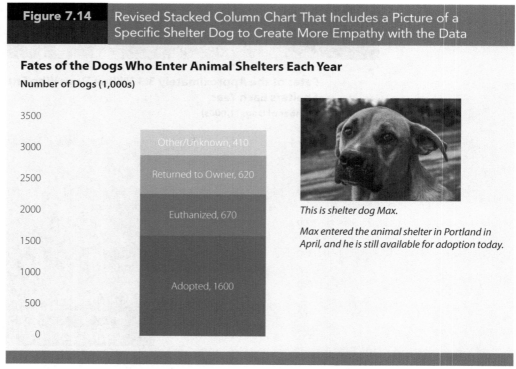

| Figure 7.14 | Revised Stacked Column Chart That Includes a Picture of a Specific Shelter Dog to Create More Empathy with the Data |

Fates of the Dogs Who Enter Animal Shelters Each Year

Number of Dogs (1,000s)

This is shelter dog Max.

Max entered the animal shelter in Portland in April, and he is still available for adoption today.

Source: Keymaster/Shutterstock.com

to that specific customer group. A common methodology that companies use to create these groups is known as clustering. Clustering algorithms use data on the characteristics of customers to form groups (or clusters) such that customers within each group share similar characteristics, but customers in separate groups are generally more different from each other.

Consider the case of Third State Bank (TSB). TSB would like to understand its banking customers better so it can create better marketing plans that appeal to specific customers. TSB's data science group has analyzed thousands of its customers using characteristics such as age, education level, marital status, number of children, home location (urban, suburban, or rural), and whether or not the customer closely follows sports and politics. TSB has used a clustering algorithm and found that one of the major clusters for its customers that is quite different from the other clusters has the characteristics shown in Table 7.2. The clustering algorithm has arbitrarily assigned this as cluster number 7.

| Table 7.2 | Summary Results from a Clustering Algorithm Used for the Customers of Third State Bank |

Customer Characteristic	Cluster #7 Results
Average Age	24
Education Level	67% college or above
Marital Status	72% unmarried
Average Number of Children	0.3
Home Location	67% urban, 21% suburban, 12% rural
Closely Follows Sports?	34% Yes, 66% No
Closely Follows Politics?	53% Yes, 47% No

To create the best story possible for these data, TSB decides to assign the name "Sophia" to represent the typical customer within this cluster. TSB defines Sophia as a single female who lives in an apartment downtown. Sophia is well-educated, follows the news closely, is likely to be politically active, and does not regularly attend sporting events.

Note that the characteristics assigned to Sophia do not match every customer within Cluster #7. In fact, these characteristics might not match any of the customers within Cluster #7. However, it is common for businesses to characterize their different clusters by giving the customers within the cluster a persona, including a name and defining characteristics. The reason for this is that it is much easier to empathize with a character persona (even when it is fictional) than to empathize with the aggregated customer characteristics shown in Table 7.2.

7.3 Storytelling with Charts

As we have discussed in this chapter, a goal of storytelling with data is to make it easy for the audience to interpret the insights from the data and compel the audience to act on those insights in some way. This starts with understanding the audience and is enabled by creating empathy with the data. Effective storytelling with data also requires you to use the correct chart for the data and the insights you are trying to convey to the audience.

Choosing the Correct Chart to Tell Your Story

Consider the case of Opening Horizons Education. Opening Horizons operates a successful chain of early-enrollment schools and daycares with five locations. The company's chief operating officer, Sandy Huggins, is interested in comparing student enrollments at each location from the start of the current year to the start of the previous year. Sandy has collected the necessary data for this analysis as shown in Figure 7.15.

In Sandy's first attempt to generate a chart to illustrate these data, she created the clustered column chart shown in Figure 7.16. Sandy will present this to the other Opening Horizons management staff and owners. What she would particularly like to point out to them is that Durango and Salida enrollments have moved in opposite directions over the last year, while other locations have remained about the same. It is possible to see this in the clustered column chart in Figure 7.16, but it might not be immediately obvious to the audience.

We introduced a slope chart in the Data Visualization Makeover at the beginning of this chapter.

An alternative chart to display these same data is a **slope chart**. A slope chart shows the change over time of a single variable for multiple entities by connecting pairs of data points for each entity. Each of the variables that we want to track is plotted on a vertical axis, and we use the horizontal axis for the dimension over which we want to see the change, or difference, for each variable. For the Opening Horizons student enrollment data, the variables are the student enrollments at each location, and the dimension is time (previous year and current year). The change, or difference, for each variable is represented by the slope of the line in the chart. The steps that follow explain how to create a slope chart for the Opening Horizons data.

DATA *file*
openinghorizons

| Figure 7.15 | Data Collected to Analyze Student Enrollment at Opening Horizons Locations |

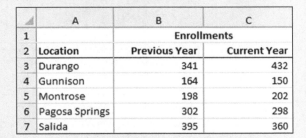

	A	B	C
1		Enrollments	
2	Location	Previous Year	Current Year
3	Durango	341	432
4	Gunnison	164	150
5	Montrose	198	202
6	Pagosa Springs	302	298
7	Salida	395	360

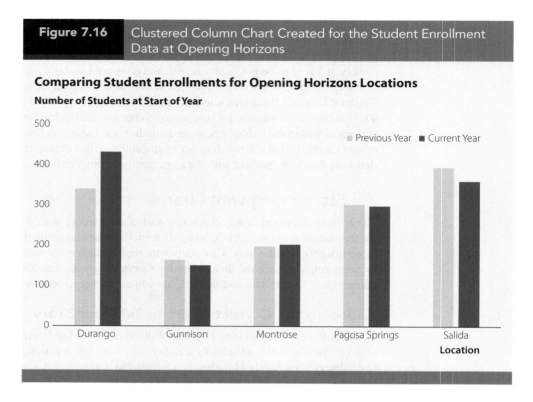

Figure 7.16   Clustered Column Chart Created for the Student Enrollment Data at Opening Horizons

Step 1. Select cells A2:C7
Step 2. Click the **Insert** tab on the Ribbon
Click the **Insert Line or Area Chart** 🔀 ▾ button in the **Charts** group
Select **Line with Markers** 📈

Steps 1–2 produce the chart shown in Figure 7.17.

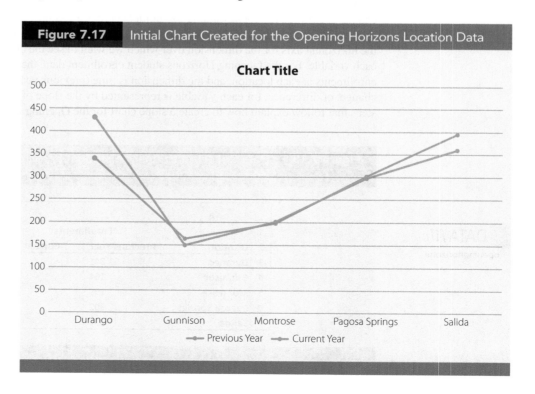

Figure 7.17   Initial Chart Created for the Opening Horizons Location Data

Step 3. When the default chart appears in Excel, right click the chart and choose **Select Data…**

When the **Select Data Source** dialog box appears, click the **Switch Row/Column** button Switch Row/Column

Click **OK**

Step 3 changes the chart from what is shown in Figure 7.17 to Figure 7.18.

Step 4. Click anywhere on the chart and click the **Chart Elements** button +

Deselect the check box for **Gridlines**

Deselect the check box for **Legend**

Select the check box for **Data Labels** and choose **Right**

Step 5. Double click the "395" data label for Salida so only this data label is selected

When the **Format Data Label** task pane appears, click the **Label Options** icon

Click **Label Options**, select the check box for **Series Name** under **Label Contains** and select **Left** under **Label Position**

In Step 5, make sure you double click to select only the "Previous Year" label; a single click will select both the "Previous Year" and "Current Year" labels.

Step 6. Repeat Step 5 for the "341," "302," "198," and "164" data labels

Step 7. Click the vertical axis values and click **Delete**

Step 8. Click the chart title box and change the title to *Comparing Student Enrollments for Opening Horizons Locations*

Click the **Home** tab on the Ribbon

Click the **Align Left** button in the **Alignment** group to left justify the chart title

Change the chart title font to **Calibri 16 pt Bold**

Drag the chart title box to align with the text to the left of the chart

Step 9. Adjust the size of the chart area and the sizes of the text boxes for the data labels so the finished chart appears similar to Figure 7.19

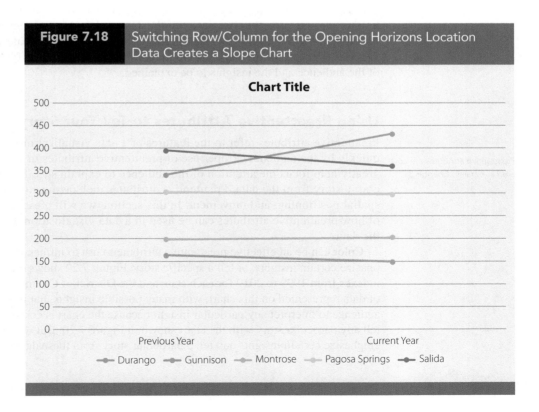

| **Figure 7.18** | Switching Row/Column for the Opening Horizons Location Data Creates a Slope Chart |

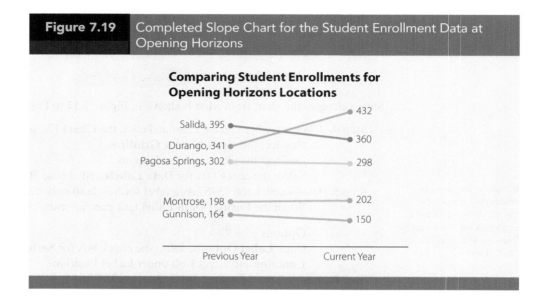

Figure 7.19   Completed Slope Chart for the Student Enrollment Data at Opening Horizons

CHART *file*

openinghorizons_chart

Comparing Figure 7.19 to Figure 7.16 shows that the slope chart makes it much more obvious to the audience that Durango has experienced an increase in student enrollment over the last year, Salida has experienced a decrease in student enrollment, and all other locations have remained relatively constant. This same insight can be seen in Figure 7.16, but it requires much more cognitive load from the audience to see this in Figure 7.16. Figure 7.19 makes this story much more obvious to the audience.

The best chart to use in a specific situation depends on the audience, the data, and the insights to be conveyed. In many cases, different charts can be used to visualize the same data. It is difficult to define exactly when specific charts will be best for different situations because this depends on things such as the needs of the audience, the analytical comfort level of the audience, the complexity of the data, and the type of decisions that will be affected by the insights from the data. In many cases, it is best to create several different draft versions of charts for the same data to judge which chart is most effective given the needs of the audience and the insights to be explained.

Using Preattentive Attributes to Tell Your Story

Preattentive attributes are covered in detail in Chapter 3.

Preattentive attributes refer to the features of a data visualization that can be processed quickly by the audience. Proper use of preattentive attributes in a data visualization can greatly help focus the attention of the audience to explain specific insights and help craft a story from the data. Preattentive attributes include the attributes of color, form, spatial positioning, and movement. In this section, we will present several examples of how preattentive attributes can be used in a data visualization to tell a story about the data.

Color can be an effective preattentive attribute to use to influence the audience, emphasize certain insights, or tell a specific story. Figure 7.20 shows quarterly house-price indexes from 1999 to 2019 for each state and the District of Columbia. There are a lot of data represented on this chart, with many possible insights, but it is difficult for the audience to interpret any particular insight because the chart is complicated. It is difficult to tell any particular story with the chart shown in Figure 7.20. But we can use color to help emphasize certain insights and tell a particular story from these data.

Figure 7.20	A Line Chart Showing Quarterly House-Price Indexes for Each State and the District of Columbia from 1999 to 2019

Quarterly House-Price Index by State

House-Price Index (Base = 1991)

houseprices_chart

houseprices_chart

Suppose we want to emphasize the fact that the state of Florida was impacted more than most other states by the subprime mortgage crisis in 2008. We can emphasize this insight in the chart by using color. Figure 7.21 colors the line corresponding to quarterly house-price indexes in Florida red while using gray for all other states and the District of Columbia. This makes it easy for the audience to compare the line for Florida to the other lines. The audience can now see that Florida experienced a large increase in house-price indexes leading up to 2008 and a large decrease after 2008. We have also changed the chart title in Figure 7.21 to emphasize this insight and tell this story.

We can modify the chart shown in Figure 7.20 to look like the chart in Figure 7.21 by using the following steps.

Step 1. Click the chart in the file *houseprices_chart*
Step 2. Double click **AK** in the chart legend so only the entry for AK is selected to open the **Format Legend Entry** task pane
Step 3. When the **Format Legend Entry** task pane opens

Click the **Fill & Line** icon

Choose a gray color for **Color** under **Border**

Step 4. Repeat Step 3 for all legend entries other than FL
Step 5. Double click **FL** in the chart legend so only the entry for FL is selected to open the **Format Legend Entry** task pane
Step 6. When the **Format Legend Entry** task pane opens

Click the **Fill & Line** icon

Choose **Red** for **Color** under **Border**

Step 7. Click on the chart legend containing the state abbreviations
Press **Delete** to delete the legend

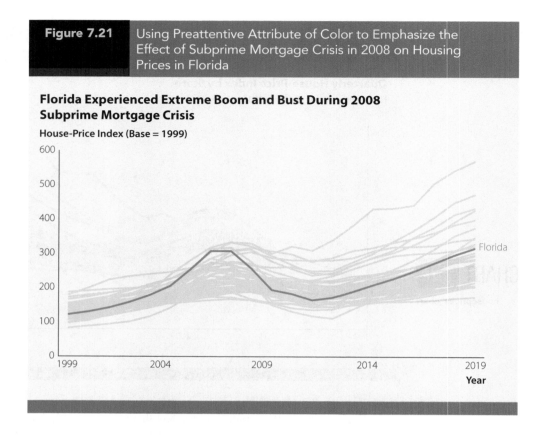

Figure 7.21   Using Preattentive Attribute of Color to Emphasize the Effect of Subprime Mortgage Crisis in 2008 on Housing Prices in Florida

Florida Experienced Extreme Boom and Bust During 2008 Subprime Mortgage Crisis

House-Price Index (Base = 1999)

Step 8.   Click the **Insert** tab on the Ribbon

Click **Text Box** [A] in the **Text** group, and click in the chart just to the right of the red line for Florida

Type *Florida* in the text box, and change the font to **Red A ˅ Calibri 10.5** (see Figure 7.21)

Size is another useful preattentive attribute that can be used in data visualizations to explain insights and tell your story. In particular, one simple but effective use of size is the use of a **big associated number (BAN)** in your data visualization. As the name implies, a BAN is simply a number associated with the visualization that is displayed in very large font. This is an exceptionally simple idea, but it can be effective in conveying meaning and directing the audience's attention for telling your story. Recall our example on the number of dogs that enter animal shelters in the United States in Figure 7.14. We can illustrate the use of a BAN to emphasize the approximate number of dogs that enter animal shelters each year as shown in Figure 7.22. In Figure 7.22, we have added "3,300,000" as a BAN to emphasize this value to the audience. We have also revised the chart title slightly to remove this redundant information from the title. The preattentive attribute of size for this text in our data visualization focuses the audience's attention on this value and then guides the story to focus on the multitude of dogs that enter shelters each year.

A BAN can be added to an existing chart in Excel by clicking the **Insert** tab on the Ribbon, clicking the **Text** button [✐ Text ˅], and selecting **Text Box** [A Text Box] to add a text box to the chart. The BAN should then be added using a large font size.

BAN is often associated with a more colloquial phrase, but we use a more formal phrase here that provides similar meaning.

Figure 7.22	Chart Incorporating the Use of a BAN to Emphasize the Number of Dogs that Enter Animal Shelters Each Year in the United States

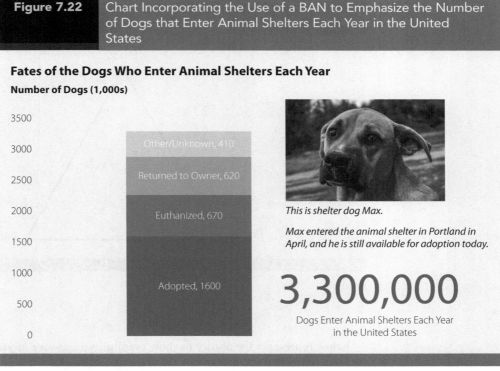

Fates of the Dogs Who Enter Animal Shelters Each Year

Number of Dogs (1,000s)

3500
3000   Other/Unknown, 410
2500   Returned to Owner, 620
2000   Euthanized, 670
1500
1000
500   Adopted, 1600
0

This is shelter dog Max.

Max entered the animal shelter in Portland in April, and he is still available for adoption today.

3,300,000

Dogs Enter Animal Shelters Each Year in the United States

Source: Keymaster/Shutterstock.com

7.4 Bringing It All Together: Storytelling and Presentation Design

The previous sections of this chapter detail how to use a single data visualization to explain insights to an audience and influence the audience through storytelling. Many of these same concepts are also applicable to a complete presentation that uses data visualizations. In this section, we expand on the concepts discussed previously to apply them to full presentations. We will introduce some general concepts for effective presentations, and then we will provide some specifics on how to create effective presentations using Microsoft PowerPoint.

Storytelling has existed for centuries in cultures throughout the world. While the subject matter of stories differs from culture to culture, there are often common traits that exist among stories. Storytelling moves beyond simply explaining something to an audience; a good story draws the audience into it. Good stories are more likely to be remembered by the audience and are more likely to persuade the audience into taking action.

Aristotle's Rhetorical Triangle

The famous Greek philosopher Aristotle was one of the earliest to notice that many stories share similar characteristics. A major requirement of storytelling is being able to connect with the audience. Aristotle proposed that there are three general areas in which a story should connect with the audience. Aristotle's basic ideas are often explained as a **Rhetorical Triangle** as shown in Figure 7.23. The Rhetorical Triangle is a visual illustration defining the three ways in which a story can connect to the audience: ethos, logos, and pathos.

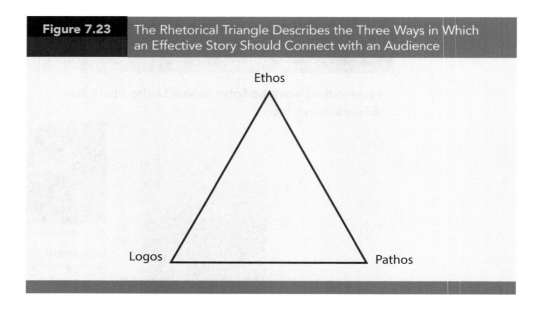

Figure 7.23   The Rhetorical Triangle Describes the Three Ways in Which an Effective Story Should Connect with an Audience

Ethos represents the ability to show credibility in a story to your audience. For stories related to data, this means that your audience trusts that you are presenting the data in a truthful manner. To be truthful requires that you use accurate data and not intentionally hide or distort the insights from that data. For example, ethos can be created through open disclosure about any data manipulation (e.g., treatment of outliers or transformation of variables). Trust with the audience can be built by clearly explaining the origin of the data used in the data visualizations, by being open about any assumptions made in the analysis, and by presenting alternative interpretations when necessary.

Logos typically refers to the logic or reasoning in the story or presentation. To connect with your audience using logos, you must present a clear argument on how the data and the analysis being presented can help the audience make better decisions. It also requires you to be clear in the logical arguments you are using to move from the underlying data to the insights you are emphasizing in your data visualizations and presentation.

The idea of **pathos** refers to connecting with the audience using emotion. For data visualizations and presentations related to analytics, you need to generate empathy in your audience for the data. This can be accomplished by trying to focus on the specific rather than just the general. Using examples of individuals rather than just talking about aggregate statistics, using pictures in your data visualizations, and creating context for large numerical values are all efforts to appeal to the audience using pathos.

Freytag's Pyramid

The Rhetorical Triangle described by Aristotle reinforces the importance of being able to connect with the audience. All good storytellers must be able to understand their audience so they can connect with them using ethos, logos, and pathos. However, effective stories often share other characteristics as well. Good stories in many forms, including novels, short stories, plays, movies, and even presentations related to data, often follow a similar recipe to involve the reader, make the insights memorable, and persuade the audience to take action. This recipe is often summarized using Freytag's Pyramid, which is shown visually in Figure 7.24.

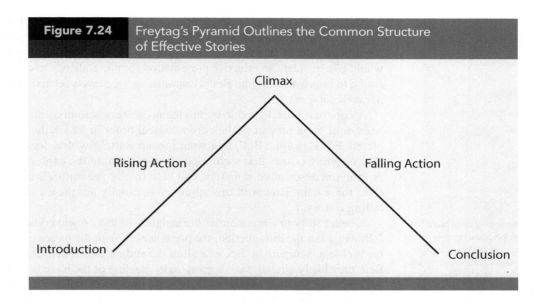

Figure 7.24 Freytag's Pyramid Outlines the Common Structure of Effective Stories

Freytag's Pyramid was developed in 1863 by the German author Gustav Freytag.

Freytag's Pyramid divides a story into five distinct elements: (1) introduction, (2) rising action, (3) climax, (4) falling action, and (5) conclusion. The introduction presents the necessary background information so the audience can understand the story to be told. This includes explanations of the major characters, the setting, and establishing the basic conflict in the story. Rising action begins to outline more details about the major conflict in the story. It explains the obstacles that are facing the protagonist. The climax is where the audience is exposed to the major conflict in the story. If the previous elements of the introduction and rising action have been well executed, the audience should feel involved enough to care about the outcome to the protagonist during the climax. A good climax has the audience hoping for a good outcome for the protagonist but also understanding why that outcome is not guaranteed. The element of falling action occurs after the climax. The protagonist's fate has usually been determined in the climax, and the audience can start to anticipate how the story will reach its conclusion during the falling action. The conclusion (sometimes referred to as the denouement or resolution) presents the end of the story. The conclusion generally resolves the conflicts presented in the story and explains the outcome for the protagonist.

Many famous works from literature and film follow the structure outlined by Freytag's Pyramid, including Shakespearean plays, the *Harry Potter* series of books, and the *Star Wars* movies. But how does this structure apply to presentations related to data?

Consider the case of Hawaiian Bell, a provider of telecommunications services for residential and business customers in the state of Hawaii. Hawaiian Bell has noticed that its customer service scores related to Internet network outages for residential customers are substantially lower than industry benchmarks. Hawaiian Bell decided to undertake an expansive data analytics effort to try to diagnose the causes of the lower customer service scores and provide recommendations to improve its customer service in this area.

Hawaiian Bell's data scientists have spent months collecting tens of thousands of records of data related to customer call logs, customer service requests, and network outages. The group has spent nearly eight weeks just reconciling the data to remove duplicate entries, resolve data inaccuracies, and link the data together from multiple sources. Several more weeks were required for exploratory data analysis to generate descriptive statistics from the data, including the average time for a customer to have connectivity restored, the most common causes of network outages, the average wait time a customer experiences when reporting an outage, etc. Hawaiian Bell's data scientists are now ready to present their results and recommendations.

The audience for this presentation includes several Hawaiian Bell vice presidents who oversee customer service and network operations. It is also expected that the chief operating officer, who has the final say on any decision, will be in attendance. The data scientists would like to create an effective presentation for this audience to convince them to take action to improve Hawaiian Bell's customer service levels related to residential Internet network outages.

A common mistake made by novice presenters is to present all the analysis that has been done for a project in the chronological order in which the analysis was completed. For Hawaiian Bell, that would mean starting with a detailed explanation of the data cleaning efforts that were used, then explaining the exploratory data analysis, presenting the descriptive statistics, and then finally presenting some aggregated findings from these data. However, this approach is usually not the most effective in terms of telling a story.

Presenting some basic facts and explanatory data during the introduction is also an example of connecting with the audience using ethos since it can help build credibility.

A better story to communicate the insights for this project could be similar to the following. For the introduction, the presenters explain the basics of the problem and why the problem is important. Because all of the audience members are executives at Hawaiian Bell, they likely already have a good understanding of the basic operations of the company, but they may not understand much about this specific problem. To help the audience connect with the story, the presenters can introduce a protagonist. In this case, the protagonist could be a fictional residential customer who purchases Internet service from Hawaiian Bell. The presenters can even create a persona and give this fictional character a name such as Liann. In the introduction, the presenters introduce Liann as a working mother whose Internet is provided by Hawaiian Bell for basic services including email and web access, as well as for accessing online schoolwork for her children. The presenters explain that Liann represents one of the more than 7,000 residential customers who contacted Hawaiian Bell in the previous year to report an Internet outage.

Using a representative protagonist to which the audience can relate is an example of using pathos because it strengthens the emotional attachment with the audience.

In the rising action section of the story, the presenters explain that Liann comes home from work one day to find that there is no Internet service available at her home. As the majority of Hawaiian Bell customers do (68% according to the data analysis), she calls the Hawaiian Bell "Contact Us" phone number. Liann waits for 12.4 minutes to speak to a live customer service representative (CSR), which is the average waiting time experienced by Hawaiian Bell residential customers over the last year. Once she speaks to a live CSR, she spends 8.9 minutes (the average for all residential customers) explaining her issue, but she can only give basic information describing the problem (which is true for nearly 84% of Hawaiian Bell customers who call to report Internet outages). Liann is completely unaware that 16 other Hawaiian Bell customers from her neighborhood have already called to report network outages at their homes. The presenters explain that this is typically the number of Hawaiian Bell customers who call to report problems during a typical network outage.

This sets up the climax of our story, which is a conflict between our protagonist, Liann, and the company in trying to diagnose and resolve an Internet outage at Liann's home. The presenters explain that Liann hangs up from her call and spends the next 14 hours with no Internet at her home, which was the 80th percentile of Internet outage durations experienced by Hawaiian Bell customers in the previous year. During this time, Liann has no access to email or the World Wide Web. Her children are not able to access their online assignments and complete their homework that evening. Liann will call twice more to get updates on the status of the Internet outage, which is actually slightly less than the average number of times (3.1) that a Hawaiian Bell customer called to get updates on Internet outages last year. After 14 hours of downtime, Hawaiian Bell restores Internet access to Liann's neighborhood, but Liann actually doesn't know that Internet service has been restored until she returns home from work the next day, 23 hours after her first phone call to Hawaiian Bell. Liann is also never made aware of the cause of the Internet outage, which, according to the data collected, is most likely due to a weather-related event (64% of outages) or to a vehicle-related accident that damages network equipment (17% of outages).

Creating a strong, logical link between the problem and the proposed solution is an example of using logos to connect with the audience.

The climax has provided an immediate resolution to the conflict that was established, but in the subsequent falling action stage, the presenters provide recommendations for improving customer service levels. The presenters explain that if Hawaiian Bell had utilized the incoming information that multiple residential customers in Liann's neighborhood had no Internet service, then it could provide an automated response that would alert other customers calling from Liann's neighborhood that "We have received reports of Internet outages in your area, and we are working on a resolution." Further, the message could ask the customers to "Press 2 if you would like to report an Internet outage at your home address." This would substantially reduce the waiting time for customers because they would not have to wait to speak to a live CSR, and they would be reassured that Hawaiian Bell knows about the issue and is working on a resolution. The presenters also explain that they are recommending that as soon as the cause of the outage is identified and an estimated time of service restoration has been determined, then the automated message should be updated to include this information. This would allow Liann to plan accordingly. Finally, once Internet service is restored, the presenters recommend that each customer that had reported an issue in that neighborhood should receive an automated call and an email alerting them that Internet access has been restored for their home and providing a reason for the outage. This would inform Liann exactly when service is restored in case she has any Internet-dependent plans and also provides closure for Liann by telling her the cause for the outage.

The conclusion section of the presentation would outline the costs and benefits of the recommendations and point out any important assumptions or any known limitations in the analysis. This provides all the necessary information for the audience to take action on the recommendations or ask clarifying questions. The conclusion section could also provide a summary of the fictional ending of the new system for our protagonist, Liann. The presenters could explain that if these changes would have been in place previously, Liann would not have wasted nearly 45 minutes of her day calling and waiting to speak to Hawaiian Bell CSRs. Furthermore, Liann would have been provided much more information during the entire episode, which is likely to improve Liann's view of the customer service provided by Hawaiian Bell.

Clearly identifying important assumptions and limitations is another example of using ethos to connect with the audience.

This story illustrates several important aspects of storytelling. First, it follows the general outline of the structure from Freytag's Pyramid. Second, it helps the audience connect with the story and empathize with the data by focusing not just on the general but also the specific. Creating the persona of Liann allows the audience to imagine a specific customer undergoing specific challenges rather than just presenting aggregated statistics such as the average customer wait time to report an outage is 12.4 minutes, 68% of customers experiencing an outage use the "Contact Us" phone number to report Internet outages, etc. Instead, the data-driven analysis is woven into the narrative to provide sufficient details for the audience to take action or to ask clarifying information.

Note that in this suggested story, we do not explicitly provide all details on the data cleaning process and exploratory data analysis. This is likely appropriate for this audience, which is made up of Hawaiian Bell executives. However, if the audience were made up of more analytically comfortable analysts who were interested in the details of how we came to our recommendations, then it could be important to include these details. It is always important to understand the needs of your audience and their analytical comfort level.

Storyboarding

To create the most effective story for your presentation, it is often useful to develop a storyboard. A **storyboard** is a simple visual organization of the main points of the story used to provide structure of the narrative that you intend to create for the audience. Storyboards are commonly used to help develop stories for movies. For presentations related to data, storyboards help to organize your thoughts and easily move things around to create the most effective story possible. There are two common methods for creating storyboards: (1) a low-tech method using sticky notes or (2) a higher-tech method using a presentation software such as Microsoft PowerPoint. We will briefly describe both methods for creating a presentation.

Many storytelling experts strongly recommend using the low-tech method of sticky notes. Sticky notes are easy to manipulate, do not require a computer, and prevent people from jumping ahead to designing the final slides for a presentation. To create a storyboard using sticky notes, all that is required is a pack of sticky notes, pens or pencils for writing, and a blank workspace. The goal is to provide a visual outline of the main points that you will communicate to the audience during the presentation. Because sticky notes can be moved around easily, it is easy to rearrange, add, and delete items from the storyboard.

A partial storyboard for the planned presentation for Hawaiian Bell using sticky notes could be something like what is shown in Figure 7.25. This storyboard would be used to craft the overall outline of the final presentation. The presenters can rearrange the sticky notes, add text to them, remove them, or add new notes to develop the outline. It is important that the presenters do not spend time at this stage developing the final visuals for the presentation. This storyboard is designed to develop the overall structure of the story, which will often change during this process.

Presentation software such as Microsoft PowerPoint can also be used to develop a storyboard, but you should be careful not to use the software to build the final slides at this stage. It is recommended that if you use PowerPoint to build your storyboard, you should make use of the Slide Sorter view in PowerPoint. This view creates a similar experience to the manual version of building a storyboard using sticky notes.

An example of creating a partial storyboard for a possible Hawaiian Bell presentation created using PowerPoint is shown in Figure 7.26. To create this storyboard, each slide is created using a blank format and the Title and Content layout. We can then view the slides in Slide Sorter view by clicking the **View** tab on the PowerPoint Ribbon and selecting **Slide Sorter** in the **Presentation Views** group. Once we are in the Slide Sorter View, we can easily rearrange slides, delete slides, and add new slides similar to what is done in the manual method of creating a storyboard using sticky notes.

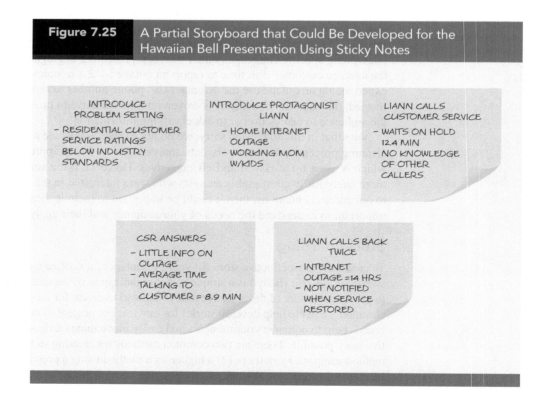

Figure 7.25   A Partial Storyboard that Could Be Developed for the Hawaiian Bell Presentation Using Sticky Notes

Figure 7.26 A Partial Storyboard that Could Be Developed for the Hawaiian Bell Presentation Using PowerPoint

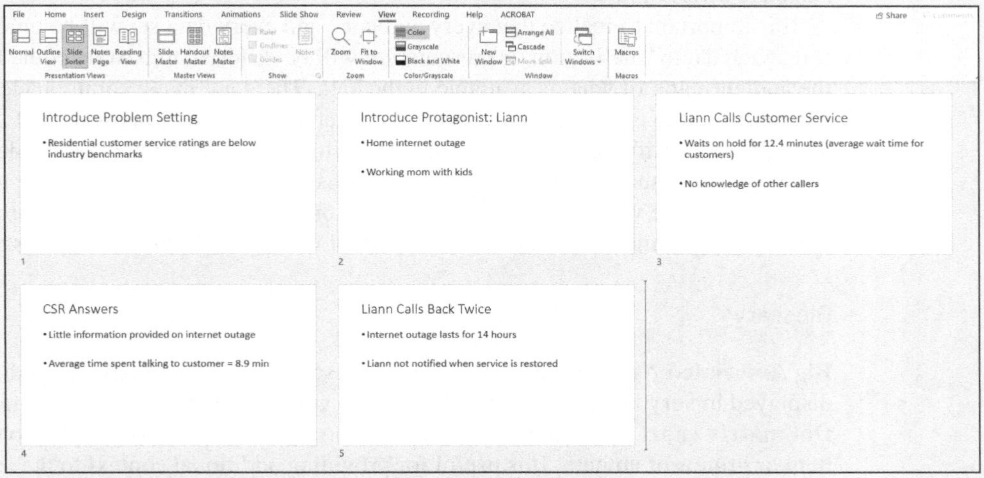

Source: Microsoft Corporation

Notes + Comments

1. For some situations, it may be appropriate to begin your presentation with the major recommendations rather than exactly following the structure outlined in Freytag's Pyramid. This alternative approach is often appropriate when the audience includes decision makers who have limited time and need to know the recommendations immediately before going into additional details.

2. You can download a Storyboard template in PowerPoint that allows for additional storyboard details by clicking **File** on the PowerPoint Ribbon, selecting **New**, typing *Storyboard* into the **Search** box, and then clicking on one of the Storyboard templates.

Summary

In this chapter, we have described methods to help explain data to an audience and to help the audience to make better decisions. This process starts with understanding the needs and analytical comfort level of the audience. We discussed how the characteristics of the audience may affect which types of data visualizations are most effective. We have also explained the importance of being able to empathize with data to create the most effective visualizations and presentations. We provided several suggestions to help create empathy in the audience with the data, including focusing on the specific rather than just the general and by helping the audience understand large numerical values by giving relative reference values for comparison. We described how preattentive attributes such as color and size can be used to highlight particular insights from data and how these can be used in a data visualization to influence the audience. We introduced two new types of data visualizations: the dot matrix chart and the slope chart.

We also expanded on our discussion of explaining and influencing by connecting these ideas to storytelling. Being a good storyteller allows you to connect with your audience and gives you the best chance at influencing the audience to make better decisions. To illustrate the importance of storytelling and provide suggestions for structuring a presentation, we introduced the concepts of the Rhetorical Triangle and Freytag's Pyramid. We also introduced storyboarding as a key element for developing an effective presentation, and we showed how storyboards can be created using either sticky notes or a presentation software such as PowerPoint.

It is important to realize that every audience and every data set will be unique. Therefore, each data visualization or presentation will be different to best meet the needs of the audience and fit what is available in the data. There are many common elements that generally lead to effective data visualizations, and the information presented in this chapter attempts to identify those common elements. However, the best method for developing effective data visualizations and presentations is practice and repetition. The more comfortable you become with creating data visualizations and presentations, the more willing you will be to experiment and find what works best for you in different scenarios.

Glossary

Big Associated Number (BAN) A number associated with a visualization that is displayed in very large font for emphasis or to guide the audience's attention.

Dot matrix chart A simple chart that uses dots or another simple graphic to represent an item or groups of an item. It is useful for providing additional context to the audience for large numerical values.

Empathy The ability to understand and share in the feelings of others.

Ethos The ability to show credibility in a story to the audience.

Freytag's Pyramid Visual illustration that defines the five common elements of the structure of an effective story: introduction, rising action, climax, falling action, conclusion.

Logos The ability to connect with the audience through logic and reasoning.

Pathos The ability to connect with the audience using emotion.

Rhetorical triangle Visual illustration proposed by Aristotle to define three general areas in which a story should connect with an audience: ethos, logos, pathos.

Slope chart A chart that shows the change of a single variable over time for multiple entities by connecting pairs of data points for each entity

Storyboard A simple visual organization of the main points of the story used to provide the structure of the narrative to be developed for the audience.

Storytelling Specific to stories generated from data, storytelling refers to the ability to build a narrative from the data that is meaningful for the audience, is memorable for the audience, and is likely to influence the audience.

Problems

Conceptual

1. **Understanding the Needs of the Audience**. For each of the following audiences, indicate whether the audience members are more likely to need a high-level understanding or a detailed understanding from a data visualization. LO 1
   a. You are presenting the results of a marketing segmentation study to a group of data scientists and the company's Chief Analytics Officer (CAO). The market segmentation study is designed to determine customer groups for the company to better target the company's marketing to specific customer segments. There are several different algorithms that can be used to perform market segmentation, and the goal of the data visualization is to get feedback from the data scientists on the different algorithms and help the CAO make a decision on which algorithm should be used.
   b. You are presenting the results of a fundraising analysis to the Board of Directors for a large nonprofit company. The fundraising analysis is designed to suggest some additional approaches for increasing the propensity of donors to financially contribute to the organization. The Board of Directors provides general oversight for the

nonprofit, but it is not involved in day-to-day decision making for the company. The board is composed of people who are known to be philanthropic and have considerable personal resources, but they have little background or expertise in analytics.

c. You are preparing a data visualization that will accompany a public-relations media release for a project that you recently completed for a startup company that does political polling and analysis. The project used data collected from likely voters in an upcoming election, and the goal was to determine the issues that are most important in terms of influencing who these voters will choose in the next election. The media release will be sent to a wide range of possible outlets including local television networks and magazines. The goal of the public-relations release is to generate publicity for the startup company and make the general public aware of the type of work this startup company does.

2. **Rainfall Amounts by Location**. Consider the following two possible data visualizations that display the results of an analysis of data collected by the meteorology department of a local university. The data collected are based on the monthly amount of rainfall received at 10 different locations (labeled as Locations A–J) over the last two years. **LO 1**

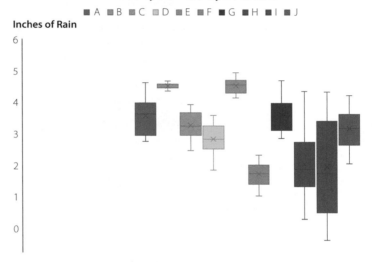

Monthly Rainfall by Location

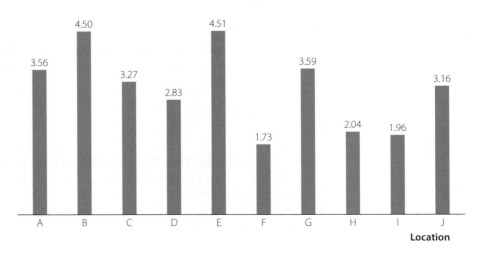

Average Monthly Rainfall by Location

Inches of Rain

a. Which of these two data visualizations (box and whisker chart or column chart) would be most appropriate for an audience that has a high comfort level with analytics and would like to understand the variability in monthly rainfall amounts at the 10 locations? Why?
b. Which location has the highest variability in monthly rainfall amounts?
c. Which location has the lowest variability in monthly rainfall amounts?

3. **Expense Report Table**. The following table shows a monthly expense report summary for an academic department at a community college located in Bethesda, Maryland. LO 1

Expense Category	Expense Amount ($)
Office Supplies	32.92
AV & Media Parts/Sup	78.90
Computing Expenses	348.71
Computer Supplies	220.39
Printer Supplies	21.55
AV Planning & Consul	1,248.50
Video Conferencing	29.98
Meeting/Seminar/Event	149.33
Refreshments & Meals	4,899.03
Travel	5,256.30
Adv & Development	3,983.75
Marketing/Promotion	3,000.00
Postage & Delivery	14.88
Memberships & Dues	3,600.00
Print/Dupl/Graphics	846.47
Parking (NonTravel)	861.50
Credit Card Process Fee	2,883.51
Services	4,136.80
Repair/Maintenance	75.00
Electric	489.00

Is this data visualization better suited for an audience that needs detailed insights or high-level insights?

4. **Chart to Provide Sense of Scale for Large Numerical Values**. Which of the following chart types is best used to provide a sense of scale for large numerical values in a data visualization? LO 4
  i. Clustered column chart
  ii. Box and whisker chart
  iii. Dot matrix chart
  iv. Slope chart

5. **Chart to Show Changes Over Time of Multiple Entities**. Which of the following chart types can be used to easily show changes to multiple entities over time? LO 3
  i. Clustered column chart
  ii. Box and whisker chart
  iii. Dot matrix chart
  iv. Slope chart

6. **Ethos, Logos, and Pathos**. Match each of the following terms with its correct explanation. LO 7

Term	Explanation
Ethos	Connecting to an audience based on logic
Logos	Connecting to an audience based on emotion
Pathos	Connecting to an audience by establishing credibility

7. **Examples of Ethos, Logos, and Pathos**. For each of the following examples, indicate whether it is an example of connecting with an audience using ethos, logos, or pathos. LO 7
   a. Providing references to all raw data used to create your data visualizations so the audience understands that the data come from reputable sources.
   b. Including pictures of specific types of people affected by the data represented in your data visualization.
   c. Explicitly listing limiting assumptions that were made in creating a particular data visualization.
   d. Using clear reasoning to connect your data visualization to a recommended action for the decision maker.
   e. Creating context for large numerical values used in a data visualization so the audience has some relative reference to understand these values.

8. **Providing a Storytelling Structure for a Presentation**. Which of the following provides a suggested structure for a story to be used for a presentation? LO 8
   i. Freytag's Pyramid
   ii. Rhetorical triangle
   iii. Preattentive attributes
   iv. Ethos, logos, and pathos

9. **Elements of Freytag's Pyramid**. Match each of the following elements from Freytag's Pyramid with the correct description of the characteristics of that element. LO 8

Freytag's Pyramid Element	Description
Introduction	Highlights the major conflict in the story and presents the outcome of the conflict
Rising Action	Presents the end of the story
Climax	Explains the obstacles that are facing the protagonist
Falling Action	Connects the resolution of the conflict to how the story will end
Conclusion	Presents the background information for the story and describes the protagonist

10. **BAN and Preattentive Attributes**. Using a BAN in a data visualization illustrates the use of which preattentive attribute? LO 4
   i. Size
   ii. Color
   iii. Shape
   iv. Motion

11. **Unemployment Rates for New England States**. The line chart below shows seasonally adjusted unemployment rates between 2010 and 2020 for states located in the New England region of the United States. The designer of this chart wants the audience to be able to easily compare the unemployment rates during this time frame for Massachusetts to the other states in the New England region. LO 6

Unemployment Rates in New England States

Percent Unemployed (Seasonally Adjusted)

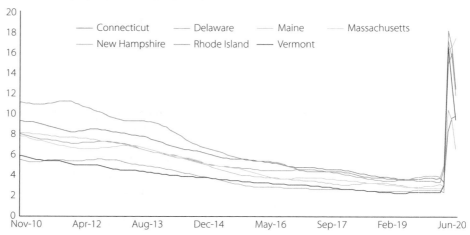

Source: https://www.bls.gov/charts/state-employment-and-unemployment/state-unemployment-rates-animated.htm

How can the designer of this data visualization use the preattentive attribute of color to make this comparison easier for the audience?

12. **Lack of Access to Improved Drinking Water**. Improved drinking water sources are defined as drinking water sources that are protected from outside contamination. According to the World Health Organization, 663 million people around the world lack access to sources of improved drinking water, which puts them at high risk for infection and illness. The bar chart below shows the number of people in each region that are estimated by the World Health Organization to lack access to improved drinking water sources. **LO 2**

Number of People Without Access to Improved Drinking Water Sources

Region

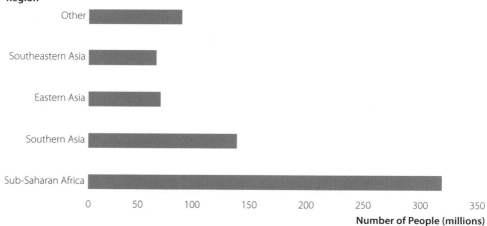

Source: Data from World Health Organization: https://apps.who.int/iris/bitstream/handle/10665/177752/9789241509145_eng.pdf;jsessionid=D7AEF25BD6C2002814352BD93FCD5607?sequence=1

Which of the following suggestions would improve this chart in terms of helping the audience empathize with the data? (Select all that are appropriate.)

   i. Add a picture showing people who lack access to improved drinking water sources.
   ii. Color each bar differently to create more excitement for the audience.

      iii. Use a dot matrix chart instead of a bar chart to give the audience a better understanding of the magnitudes of these numerical values.

      iv. Use a pie chart instead of a bar chart because pie charts create more empathy than bar charts due to the use of the preattentive attribute of shape.

      v. Use a three-dimensional (3D) bar chart because the depth dimension of a 3D chart moves an audience to feel more empathy.

13. **Sprouts Learning Academy Math Enrichment Program**. Sprouts Learning Academy helps prepare students for standardized tests in math for children in the second- through fifth-grade levels. Sprouts assesses each child by giving them a pretest when they start their math enrichment academy program and then again at the conclusion of the academy program. The test results are measured in percentiles compared to all other students taking similar tests. The clustered column chart below shows the results of these pre- and post-academy tests for each grade level. The designer of this chart would like to communicate to the audience how well the math enrichment program is doing in improving the performance of the students on this standardized test at each grade level. **LO 5**

sproutslearning_chart

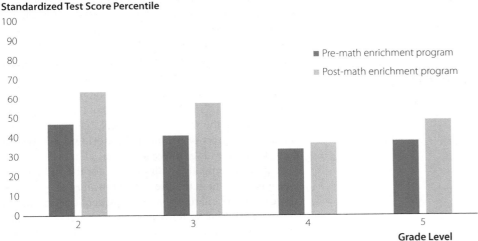

Effects of Math Enrichment Program at Sprouts Learning Academy

Which type of chart could be used to better tell the story about how well the math enrichment program is doing in improving performance on this standardized test?

      i. Pie chart

      ii. Slope chart

      iii. Dot matrix chart

      iv. Box and whisker chart

14. **Storyboard Materials**. Which of the following are recommended tools for creating a storyboard to help plan the structure of a presentation? (Select all that apply.) **LO 9**

      i. Microsoft Excel

      ii. A calculator

      iii. Sticky notes

      iv. Microsoft PowerPoint

15. **Low-Tech versus High-Tech Storyboards**. Which of the following is the foremost advantage of using a low-tech method versus a high-tech method for creating a storyboard to be used for designing a presentation? **LO 9**

      i. Low-tech methods remove the temptation of being distracted with creating final slide designs during the storyboarding process so you can concentrate on creating the structure of the story.

      ii. Low-tech methods are much faster to implement than high-tech methods.

iii. Low-tech methods make it easier to turn the finished storyboard into the final slides for the presentation.

iv. Low-tech methods make it much easier to create the final versions of extremely sophisticated data visualizations to be used in the final presentation.

16. **Storyboarding Goal.** Which of the following best describes the goal of the storyboarding process? LO 9

    i. Determine how to use design elements such as preattentive attributes in your data visualizations to best tell your story.

    ii. Create a visual outline of the structure of your presentation.

    iii. Put the finishing touches on a presentation by focusing on the format and design of the final data visualizations.

    iv. Provide an opportunity to examine the data to be used to create the data visualizations to create the most effective charts for your audience.

Applications

unemploy_chart

17. **Unemployment Rates for New England States (Revisited).** In this problem, we revisit the chart shown in Problem 11 showing seasonally adjusted unemployment rates for states in the New England region. Use the preattentive attribute of color to modify this chart so the audience can easily compare the unemployment rates during this time frame for Massachusetts to the other states in the New England region. LO 6

drinkingwater_chart

18. **Lack of Access to Improved Drinking Water (Revisited).** In this problem, we revisit the chart shown in Problem 12 showing the number of people without access to improved drinking water sources by region. LO 4, 6

    a. Approximately 663 million people do not have access to improved drinking water sources around the world. Add a BAN to the bar chart in the file *drinkingwater_chart* so the total number of people in the world who do not have access to improved drinking water sources is emphasized in this chart.

    b. To help create empathy with the data for the audience, create a dot matrix chart to represent the data in the file *drinkingwater_chart*. Use ● = 1 million people for your dot matrix chart. (*Hint:* To represent 663 million people who lack access to improved drinking water resources, you will need a matrix that contains 663 ●. You can create this by using a 25 × 26 matrix and then adding an additional partial row of 13 ●.)

    c. Differentiate the colors of the ● based on the region of the world. Include a legend on your modified dot matrix chart.

    d. The population of the United States is approximately 330 million people. To help give the audience an even better sense of scale for the number of people around the world who lack access to improved drinking water, use the Gestalt principle of enclosure by using the **Fill Color** function in Excel to shade the cells containing the number of ● that correspond to the population of the United States and label this on your chart.

sproutslearning_chart

19. **Sprouts Learning Academy Math Enrichment Program (Revisited).** In this problem we revisit the chart shown in Problem 13 for standardized test scores from the pre-math enrichment program and post-math enrichment program at Sprouts Learning Academy. LO 5, 6

    a. Create a slope chart for the data in the file *sproutslearning_chart* that compares the pre- and post-math enrichment program standardized test scores for second- through fifth-grade levels.

    b. Test scores have increased for all grade levels between pre- and post-math enrichment program tests. However, test scores for the fourth-grade level have less difference than the test scores of second-, third-, and fifth-grade levels. Use the preattentive attribute of color to emphasize the difference in the results for fourth-grade level compared to second-, third-, and fifth-grade levels.

20. **Engineering Graduate Salaries at Empire State University**. Empire State University (ESU) collects salary data for its engineering college graduates. ESU collects data on starting salaries for its graduates and then again five years post-graduation. The table below shows the median starting salaries and median salaries five years post-graduation by engineering major. Create a slope chart to display these data. LO 5

engineeringsalaries

| | Salaries ($) | |
Engineering Major	Starting	5 Years Post-Graduation
Chemical	72,500	91,400
Civil	61,000	70,300
Computer	68,400	83,600
Electrical	64,800	87,400
Industrial	57,400	74,000
Mechanical	62,900	77,100

virus_chart

21. **Measuring Viral RNA Load**. Viral RNA load measures the amount of virus in a specified volume of bodily fluid. When someone is sick due to a viral infection, the virus replicates rapidly in the body and can be measured based on the viral RNA load. Consider four possible virus vaccines that are being tested in clinical trials: Vaccines A, B, C, and D. Each vaccine is given to a group of people, and the viral RNA load of each patient is measured. The study also includes a Control group of patients who receive only a placebo vaccine. The epidemiologists running these vaccine trials would like to present the results of the studies using a box and whisker chart for an audience of clinicians who are familiar with how to interpret box and whisker charts. The epidemiologists would like to emphasize the results for Vaccine C compared to the results for the Control group. Modify the box and whisker chart found in the file *virus_chart* using the preattentive attribute of color to emphasize the results of Vaccine C and the Control group to make it easier for the audience to make the comparison between these data. LO 6

22. **Defining Freytag's Pyramid Structure for a Story**. Think of one of your favorite books, movies, or plays. Divide up the story that is told in this book, movie, or play according to the elements outlined in Freytag's Pyramid: Introduction, Rising Action, Climax, Falling Action, Conclusion. For each element, briefly describe what part of the story is included in this element and how it fits into the defined element. LO 8

23. **Storyboard for Reducing Waiting Time at General Hospital**. The Division of Performance Improvement and Analytics at General Hospital has been working on a four-month project to provide recommendations for reducing the waiting time experienced by patients who arrive to its Pediatrics Health Care Wing that provides for prescheduled clinical services such as checkups and wellness visits. The project began with an intensive six-week data collection effort that measured the waiting time for patients as well as the patient's satisfaction with their visit and any required follow-up visits. The next four weeks were spent cleaning the data and matching the data with existing patient and healthcare provider data from the hospital's IT system. The remainder of the time was spent analyzing the data, discussing findings with the clinicians, and formulating final recommendations.

   The team is now ready to present its findings and recommendations to the senior leadership of the hospital, including the hospital's Chief Operating Officer (COO) who has final decision-making power to decide which, if any, recommendations will be followed. Some of the interesting findings identified by the team from the Division of Performance Improvement and Analytics include the following:

   • Patients who were scheduled for the first or second appointment of the day experienced an average waiting time of 5.8 minutes. Patients who were scheduled for the next-to-last or last appointment of the day experienced an average waiting time of 42.3 minutes.

- Patients who responded to a reminder call about their appointment had a no-show rate (meaning they did not show up at the scheduled time of their appointment) of 8.5%. Patients who did not respond to a reminder call about their appointment had a no-show rate of 19.3%.
- Patient no-show rates were slightly higher in the afternoon than in the morning and higher on Fridays than any other weekday.
- Seventy-four percent of patients who received a text reminder responded to the reminder, while only 51% of patients who received a phone call responded to the reminder.
- When patients did not show up for their scheduled appointment time, patients who did not have a prescheduled appointment were often given priority to fill this slot. However, these patients required an average appointment duration that was 1.7 times as long as prescheduled patients because they had to complete additional tasks such as filling out medical history forms.
- There was substantial variability in the waiting times experienced by patients across different clinicians. Patients waiting to see Dr. Martinez had the highest average waiting times, which were 1.5 times as long as the average waiting times for Dr. Ahuja, whose patients had the shortest average waiting times.
- Patient waiting times are highly correlated with their satisfaction-survey scores. Patients who waited longer had substantially lower patient-satisfaction scores.
- Patients seen in the morning were 17% more likely to have a follow-up visit scheduled than those seen in the afternoon.

Based on these findings, the team would like to make the following recommendations:

- All patients should receive a text message in addition to a phone call about upcoming appointments.
- A new team should be created to examine the creation of standards for pediatric patient checkups and wellness visits to (1) reduce the variability experienced by patients waiting to see different clinicians and (2) examine the reason why patients seen in the morning are scheduled for follow-up visits more often than patients seen in the afternoon.
- Allow more time between scheduled patient visits in the afternoon than in the morning to prevent long waits for patients arriving in the afternoon.

Create a storyboard to outline the structure of the presentation for this audience of senior hospital executives, including the COO. Make sure your storyboard clearly defines the protagonist in your story and provides sufficient detail that it could be used to create a final presentation. **LO 9, 10**

Chapter 8

Data Dashboards

Contents

Learning Objectives

After completing this chapter, you will be able to

LO 1 Explain what a data dashboard is.

LO 2 Describe and explain the principles of effective data dashboards.

LO 3 List common areas of application of data dashboards.

LO 4 Describe and explain various data dashboard taxonomies.

LO 5 Describe and explain the principles of data dashboard design and development.

LO 6 Use Excel tools to build a data dashboard.

LO 7 List common mistakes made in data dashboard design and development.

Data Visualization Makeover

Washington State Transportation Improvement Board

The Washington State Transportation Improvement Board (TIB) is an independent state agency responsible for distributing and managing street construction and maintenance grants throughout Washington State. TIB selects, funds, and administers transportation projects that best address the criteria established by the Board.

The TIB has created and maintains the Transportation Improvement Board Performance Management Dashboard to provide the public with up-to-date information on the status of its various projects. A portion of the TIB *At A Glance* page of this dashboard is provided in Figure 8.1.

This dashboard shows breakdowns of the Financial Status, Project Status, and KPI (key performance indicator) Status in the pane on the left side of the dashboard. A county map of the state is provided in the pane on the right side of the dashboard. Directly above the map, there are several tabs that correspond to various factors related to the operation of the TIB (Inventory, Fund Balances, Gas Tax Revenues, Accounts Payable, and Commitment). Note that we are currently on the Inventory tab; in this discussion, we will focus on the data visualization provided on this tab as shown in Figure 8.1.

This dashboard has many positive features. The information provided on the TIB *At A Glance* page of this dashboard is easy to read. It appears to use space effectively; it is not crowded and does not appear cramped. It also uses tabs to allow for the presentation of different measures related to the operation of the TIB on separate screens. However, there is room for improvement.

Consider the information in the pane on the left side of this data visualization. This information may be useful, but it lacks the context necessary to understand and interpret it. Are these year-to-date values? If so, is the basis a calendar year or a fiscal year? If the basis is a fiscal year, how is the fiscal year defined? The numbers are also provided in rounded rectangles that are filled with red, green, gold, or white without a readily available indication of what these colors represent. Furthermore, the use of red and green as principal colors makes it difficult for colorblind members of the audience to visually process this portion of the chart, although the dashboard's inclusion of the actual numbers would mitigate this problem if context were provided.

Now consider the map in the pane on the right side of the dashboard. Each county is red, green, or gray. Again, the dashboard provides no immediate indication of what these colors represent, and the use of red and green as principal colors makes it difficult

Figure 8.1   The TIB *At A Glance* Page of the Transportation Improvement Board Performance Management Dashboard

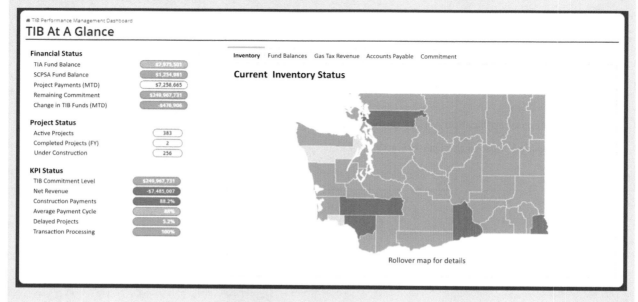

(Continued)

for colorblind members of the audience to visually process this portion of the chart. Furthermore, two of these colors (red and green) are identical to two colors used in the pane on the right side of this data visualization. Does this convey specific information, or is it an arbitrary choice?

On the positive side, we can open a popup box with the name of a county and more details on the TIB's activity in that county by rolling the cursor over the county on the map. However, this is the only way we can find the names of the individual counties on this map.

We can address these problems by making a few relatively minor modifications to this data visualization.

By adding a title to the left pane, we provide context for the information provided in that pane. By using different color schemes in the two panes and adding legends to explain the uses of these colors, we eliminate the risk of confusion that exists in the original dashboard. By avoiding the use of both red and green in either panel, we also make the dashboard easier for colorblind audience members to interpret. And by adding the county names to the map in the right pane, we make it easier for users to identify and find information on specific counties. These changes, as shown in Figure 8.2, improve this dashboard substantially.

Figure 8.2 Improved TIB *At A Glance* Page of the Transportation Improvement Board Performance Management Dashboard

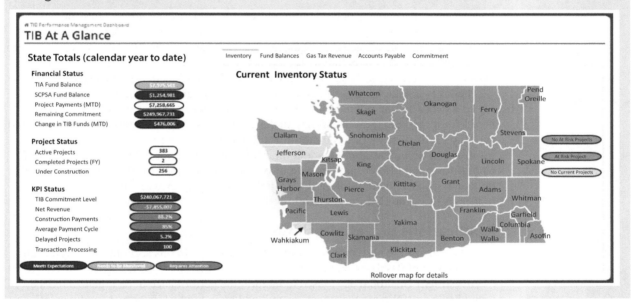

In this chapter, we discuss specific elements that can help create an effective data dashboard. We begin by discussing what data dashboards are and what they can accomplish. We then discuss various types of data dashboards, principles of good data dashboard design, and characteristics of effective data dashboards. We show how to build a data dashboard using Excel. We conclude the chapter by considering common errors made in data dashboard design and strategies for avoiding these mistakes.

8.1 What Is a Data Dashboard?

In an automobile dashboard, values such as speed, fuel level, and oil pressure are displayed to give the driver a quick overview of current operating characteristics of the vehicle. The driver can use the information provided on the dashboard to operate the vehicle effectively and efficiently. The engine coolant temperature gauge, fuel gauge, turn signal indicators, gearshift position indicator, seat belt warning light, parking brake warning light, emergency signals, and speedometer provide such information. Other information on the dashboard, such as the odometer and oil change indicator light, pertains to longer-term maintenance issues. Still other information, such as the check engine light, aids in the identification of problems that need to be addressed more immediately because they can cause serious or even irreparable damage.

Decision makers such as business managers have similar needs for information that will enable them to operate and maintain their organizations effectively and efficiently. Such values may include the organization's financial position, inventory on-hand, pending orders for raw materials, progress on projects, status of accounts, pending orders from customers, and customer service metrics. These values are referred to as **key performance indicators** (KPIs). In a healthcare setting, KPIs could refer to patient vital signs such as heart rate, respiration rate, and blood pressure. For the manager of a political campaign, KPIs could include fundraising values, recent polling results, and campaign expenditures.

Many decision makers rely on data dashboards to provide them with timely information on their organization's KPIs. A **data dashboard** is a data visualization tool that gives multiple outputs and may update in real time. The outputs provided by the dashboard are a set of KPIs for the organization that are aligned with the organization's goals and can be used to monitor current and potential future performance on a continual basis. By consolidating and presenting data from a number of sources in a data visualization designed for a specific set of purposes, data dashboards can help an organization better understand and use its data to improve decision making.

Principles of Effective Data Dashboards

Ideally, a data dashboard should present all KPIs related to some aspect of the organization's operations on a single screen that a user can easily review to understand the organization's current state of operations quickly and accurately. Rather than requiring the user to scroll vertically and horizontally to see the entire dashboard, it is better to create multiple dashboards of related KPIs so each dashboard can be viewed on a separate screen.

The KPIs displayed in the data dashboard should quickly and clearly convey meaning to its user and be related to decisions the user makes. For example, the data dashboard for a marketing manager may include KPIs related to current sales measures and sales by region. The data dashboard for a foundation officer at a university may show information on potential donors and their history of donations. The data dashboard for a chief financial officer may provide information on the current financial standing of the company. The data dashboard for a police chief may provide information on current rates of crime in different neighborhoods.

Applications of Data Dashboards

Data dashboards are used in many different applications. In this section, we describe a few common uses of dashboards in organizations.

Investment Dashboards — used to monitor the performance of an organization's or individual's portfolio of investments overall and by individual investment and type of investment. An investment dashboard supports ongoing decisions on how to best allocate invested funds, perhaps to maximize the rate of return while keeping risk at or below a certain level or to minimize risk while keeping the rate of return at or above a certain level. Information provided by these dashboards may include, but is not limited to:

- current price, recent rate of return, and the relative rate of risk of the portfolio and its individual components relative to the overall market
- current price, recent rate of return, and relative risk of investments under consideration
- share of the portfolio devoted to various industries or types of investments
- key financial data for the companies in which the investor has invested or is considering investing

Manufacturing dashboards — used to monitor a production process overall and by facility, product, individual, machine, shift, or department. A manufacturing dashboard supports ongoing decisions on how to allocate resources to produce an organization's products and/or services efficiently and effectively. Information provided by these dashboards may include, among other metrics:

- quantity produced
- quality of units produced

- rate at which the units are produced
- frequency of problems (machine downtime, returns, falling short of production targets, etc.)

Marketing dashboards — used to monitor sales and promotional efforts overall and by product or service, individual, campaign, division or department, or customer. A marketing dashboard supports ongoing decisions on how to allocate resources to design, price, promote, and distribute an organization's products and/or services efficiently and effectively. Information provided by these dashboards may include a variety of metrics, for example:

- quantity sold
- quantity delivered
- success rate/proportion of successful sales calls
- sales revenue
- prices at which products and services are sold
- advertising and promotional expenditures
- exposure and response to advertising and promotion efforts
- contact with prospective customers
- consumer satisfaction metrics

Within the category of marketing dashboards are more specific dashboards on areas such as customer service, web page utilization, and social media effectiveness.

Human resource dashboards — used to monitor the performance of an organization's workforce by individual, division, department, or shift. A human resource dashboard supports ongoing decisions on how to allocate resources to ensure an organization utilizes its workforce in an efficient and effective manner. Information provided by these dashboards may include, but is not limited to:

- number of employees
- length of employment
- employee churn (rate of employee turnover)
- reasons for leaving
- employee performance
- employee satisfaction
- absenteeism
- participation in training
- overall labor effectiveness

Technical support dashboards — used to monitor the performance of an organization's support of its technology users by individual, computer system, division or department, or location. A technical support dashboard provides information to enhance ongoing decisions on how to allocate resources to ensure an organization utilizes its workforce in an efficient and effective manner. Information provided by these dashboards may include:

- type of technical problem
- response time
- time to resolution
- outstanding issues
- persistent problems
- downtime
- scheduled maintenance
- software and hardware usage

Personal fitness/health dashboards — used to monitor aspects of an individual's physical well-being. A personal fitness or health dashboard supports ongoing decisions on how

Personal fitness/health dashboards are often populated with data collected by devices such as smartwatches, fitness monitors, and phones.

to achieve the best possible health for the individual. Information provided by these dashboards may include, but is not limited to:

- pulse
- blood pressure
- body temperature
- weight and body mass index (BMI)
- amount of exercise
- steps and distance traveled
- calories burned
- diet characteristics (calories, fat intake, carbohydrate intake, and protein intake)
- blood sugar levels

Donor dashboards — used to monitor donor/contributor activity and potential for nonprofit organizations by donor/contributor, prospective donor/contributor, or project/campaign. A donor dashboard supports ongoing decisions on how to use the organization's resources to maximize short- and long-term donor activity. Information provided by these dashboards may include, for example:

- number and dollar value of donations/contributions
- contact with new potential donors/contributors and past donors/contributors
- expenditures
- conversion rate
- cash flow
- current status of campaigns

Crime dashboards — used to monitor the occurrences of different types of crime in many cities. Crime dashboards can be used to inform the public about the current and historical rates of crime and can be used by police and other government administrators to make decisions on how best to deploy and utilize resources to increase public safety. Information provided by these dashboards may include, for example:

- number of police reports
- number and dollar value of property crimes
- number of arrests
- types of crimes reported

School performance dashboards — used to monitor the performance of schools. School performance dashboards can be used by parents to judge the relative performance of schools and by school administrators to aid in decisions related to staffing and resource allocation. Information provided by these dashboards may include, for example:

- number of students enrolled
- demographic information on students
- number of teachers and other staff employed
- student test scores
- number and types of courses offered

Data dashboards have been developed and successfully deployed for a wide variety of other applications. Any organization that needs to quickly understand a related set of rapidly changing KPIs could benefit from a well-designed data dashboard.

8.2 Data Dashboard Taxonomies

Dashboards are generally classified by whether the information they provide is updated, whether users can interact with the display, and what organizational functions they primarily support. In this section, we describe these data dashboard taxonomies.

Data Updates

A data dashboard can be classified into one of two groups based on how often the information it provides is updated. A **static dashboard** provides information on an organization's KPIs that may periodically be updated manually as new data and information are collected. These dashboards are relatively inexpensive and easy to develop, are generally updated infrequently, and are useful when the organization's KPIs change slowly.

A **dynamic dashboard** provides information on an organization's KPIs, regularly receives and incorporates new and revised data, and incorporates these data into the dashboard. These dashboards take more time and effort to develop, are generally updated frequently (perhaps continuously), and are useful when the organization's KPIs change rapidly.

User Interaction

A data dashboard can be classified into one of two groups based on whether users can customize their displays. A **noninteractive dashboard** does not allow users to customize the data dashboard display. These dashboards are useful when the data on which the dashboard is based do not change frequently.

Although interactive dashboards can be either static or dynamic, they are generally dynamic.

Conversely, an **interactive dashboard** allows users to customize the data dashboard display, effectively allowing a user to filter the data displayed to the user on the dashboard. Dashboards can allow for user interactivity in a variety of ways, including:

- **Drilling down** — a feature that provides the user with more specific and detailed information on a particular element, variable, or KPI. A drill-down can take the user to a new display with additional detailed information when the user clicks on a particular element, variable, or KPI. It can also provide a popup display with additional detailed information when the user rolls the cursor over a particular element, variable, or KPI.
- **Hierarchical filtering** — a feature that provides the user with the ability to restrict the data displayed to a specific segment of users by systematically selecting values of several categories or values of variables in a nested manner, for example, filtering the data displayed by first selecting a gender, then selecting an age group, then selecting the product purchased, etc.
- **Time interval widget** — a feature that allows the user to specify the time period to be displayed on the dashboard.
- **Customization tools** — features that allow the user to
  › select/deselect categories to be displayed on the dashboard
  › combine categories to be displayed on the dashboard
  › select/deselect variables to be displayed on the dashboard
  › add custom text and labels to the dashboard
  › add or hide various summary statistics for variables on the dashboard
  › hyperlink a particular element, variable, or KPI to related content (even an external website or resource)

Interactive dashboards can provide the user a great deal of latitude in exploring the data provided by the dashboard, finding specific relevant information, and independently learning about and finding potential solutions to the problem she or he is attempting to resolve.

Organizational Function

A data dashboard can be classified into one of four groups based on its purposes and its ultimate users.

Operational dashboards are typically used by lower level managers to monitor rapidly changing critical business conditions. Because these data usually accumulate swiftly and are critical for the daily operations of the organization, these dashboards generally update in real time or multiple times throughout the day.

Tactical dashboards are typically used by mid-level managers to identify and assess the organization's strengths and weaknesses in support of the development of organizational strategies. Because tactical dashboards usually support the development of organizational strategies, these dashboards are generally updated less frequently than an operational dashboard.

Strategic dashboards are typically used by executives to monitor the status of the KPIs' relevant overarching organizational objectives. The data that support a strategic dashboard update on a recurring basis but at less frequent intervals than tactical and operational dashboards.

Analytical dashboards are typically used by analysts to identify and investigate trends, predict outcomes, and discover insights in large volumes of data.

Some businesses use dashboards that span more than one of these categories with great success, and many organizations have developed and use dashboards that do not fall into any of these four categories. When designing a data dashboard, it is important to consider how these various types of data dashboards support the objectives of the organization for which you are designing the dashboard and meet the needs of the dashboard's end users. We explore this issue of dashboard design further in the next section.

8.3 Data Dashboard Design

Although there is a great deal of variation in the design of data dashboards, several considerations are common to successful dashboard design. In this section, we provide an overview of these considerations.

Understanding the Purpose of the Data Dashboard

At this stage, the organization assesses what the proposed data dashboard should do for its users and whether a data dashboard is the appropriate tool. The primary reason for developing a data dashboard is to support an organization's operations, decision making, and strategic planning, so the overriding consideration in designing a data dashboard is its ultimate purpose: What does the organization need to accomplish through use of the dashboard once it is operational? An organization's objectives for its data dashboard may include, for example:

- tracking KPIs
- monitoring processes
- assessing attainment of goals and objectives
- developing/enhancing insight
- sharing information
- measuring performance
- forecasting
- data exploration

Failure to consider the organization's motivations for creating a dashboard will leave the dashboard design team directionless, which can slow the development of the dashboard and potentially result in the development of a dashboard that does not address the needs of the organization.

Considering the Needs of the Data Dashboard's Users

A data dashboard should be designed to assist a particular user or group of users with specific tasks associated with the management of an organization. Thus, it is important that the dashboard design team both understands the needs of the dashboard's end users and recognizes how addressing these needs will ultimately support the organization's dashboard objectives. This knowledge, in conjunction with adherence to the principles of effective data visualization, will help the dashboard developer determine the information the dashboard should convey and the most effective manner for presenting this information to its intended audience.

Data Dashboard Engineering

Once the dashboard design team understands the organization's objectives for the dashboard and the dashboard end users' related needs, the team should turn its attention to the information that should be displayed in the dashboard. All information displayed must meet the end users' needs, and the design dashboard team should work with the end users to ensure this occurs.

After the information to be displayed is identified and organized, the dashboard design team should determine the manner in which the information will be displayed. This includes the selection of appropriate types of charts, effective use of preattentive attributes and Gestalt principles, appropriate use of color, and an effective layout that enables end users to easily find the information they need and relate information from various charts in the dashboard.

The selection of an appropriate type of chart, effective use of preattentive attributes and Gestalt principles, and appropriate use of color are discussed in Chapters 2, 3, and 4, respectively.

It is also important that the dashboard is easy to read and interpret, and that the display is not too sparse, too crowded, or overly complex. Strategies for avoiding overcrowding and unnecessary complexity include:

- avoiding inclusion of information that will not be useful to the end users
- organizing the information into subsets that each address a different need of the end users and displaying information in these subsets across multiple pages
- using interactive dashboard tools (drilling down, hierarchical filtering, time interval widget, customization tools)

In addition, at this stage, the dashboard design team should consider the environment in which the data dashboard will be used. Data dashboards are most often accessed from desktop computers. However, some data dashboards are accessed with other devices such as tablets or smartphones on factory floors or retail showrooms, in automobiles, or outdoors. It is important to consider factors such as the device being used to access the dashboard, ambient lighting, size and resolution of the display, likely distance of the user from the display, and whether a touch screen will be utilized when designing a data dashboard.

The design team should consider the most effective ways to provide context for the information presented in the data dashboard. This can be done in many ways, including:

- showing how a KPI varies over time
- comparing the value of a KPI to an organizational goal
- comparing the value of a KPI
  - internally across divisions, departments, or geographies of an organization
  - externally across customers or market segments
  - externally across competitors or organizations in the same industry

By providing appropriate context, the dashboard gives meaning to the data and enhances the dashboard user's ability to interpret and act on the data. Throughout this step, it is important that the dashboard design team collaborate with the dashboard's end users to ensure the dashboard meets their needs and doesn't incorporate extemporaneous information.

The dashboard design team must understand how the data dashboard will be used so it can organize the charts and tables on the dashboard in a way that facilitates analyses by the users. When designing the individual components of the data dashboard, the design team should be mindful of the data-ink ratio and reducing eye travel. The dashboard design team must also understand how the data dashboard will be maintained and how the data dashboard's effectiveness will be assessed. A well-designed data dashboard can quickly lose its value to its users if it is difficult to update and maintain, so the design team should consider the skills and capabilities of the individual or team that will be responsible for its maintenance and updates.

The data-ink ratio and reducing eye travel are discussed in Chapter 3.

Although the current sources of data and their format are critical considerations in dashboard design, the dashboard design team should also reflect on the future of the dashboard and discuss this issue with management. Could the organization's objectives shift in the future? If so, how will the data dashboard need to reflect these shifts? What new KPIs are likely to become important to the organization in the future? What may be the source or format of new data to be incorporated into the dashboard in the future?

Finally, errors, miscommunications, and misunderstandings occur in virtually all complex projects. These problems can result in the creation of a faulty final product that can lead to poor decisions and missed opportunities, require time-consuming and costly revisions, and damage the credibility of the data dashboard design team. It is crucial that the dashboard design team also test its work extensively at each step to ensure the dashboard functions as the team intends. At critical junctures, the dashboard design team must review its progress with the management team that initiated the development of the data dashboard to ensure the dashboard under production is meeting the management team's objectives. Finally, the data dashboard design team must provide the ultimate users with opportunities to test the dashboard extensively to ensure the dashboard is user friendly, functions in the manner expected by the users, and produces the outputs needed by its users. By following a process that adheres to these guidelines, malfunctions can be identified during the development of the data dashboard when they are easier, less expensive, and less time consuming to correct.

8.4 Using Excel Tools to Build a Data Dashboard

PivotTables, PivotCharts, and slicers are discussed in Chapter 6.

We have already reviewed several tools that are useful for constructing data dashboards. A **PivotTable** is an interactive crosstabulation that allows the user to interact with the data by applying filters to select various aspects of the data to be displayed in the table. A **PivotChart** is a chart that allows the user to interact with the data by applying filters to select various aspects of the data to be displayed in the chart. A **slicer** allows the user to filter the data to be displayed in PivotTables and PivotCharts. Because these tools provide users with the capability of interacting with tables and charts and selecting what is to be displayed, well-designed PivotTables, PivotCharts, and slicers allow the user to delve deeper into the data and learn from the data in a more focused manner.

In general, the original source of data for the dashboard should be stored separately from the dashboard, and the dashboard should not draw information directly from the original source of data. In other words, the data that are needed to create an individual chart or table on the data dashboard should be extracted from the original source data, and they should be stored separately. The dashboard's users should not be able to permanently change the dashboard. In a spreadsheet, this means the original source of data for the dashboard should be stored in its own worksheet, and the dashboard should not draw information directly from that worksheet. The data for each unique display unit (table, chart, etc.) in the dashboard should be maintained in a separate worksheet. And the components of the dashboard should be locked so the user cannot make permanent changes.

Espléndido Jugo y Batido, Inc.

Espléndido Jugo y Batido, Inc is discussed in Chapter 6.

Let us again consider Espléndido Jugo y Batido, Inc. (EJB), a company that bottles juices and smoothies in five fruit flavors (apple, grape, orange, pear, and tomato) and four vegetable flavors (beet, carrot, celery, and cucumber). EJB now wants to develop a data dashboard that its mid-level operations management team can use to track its sales over the most recent three years. By working through the data dashboard design process discussed in the previous section, the company's management team has established its objectives for this dashboard. Specifically, EJB wants to be able to track dollar sales for each of its distribution centers by year, and it wants to be able to look at these data for new and existing customers. EJB also wants to be able to track its dollar sales by year for each category (juices and smoothies), and it would like to be able to look at these data by flavor and by month. The company wants to monitor time to deliver by distribution center for each year, and it wants to be able to generate sales in dollars across category and flavor by distribution center at the year, month and date ordered levels. Finally, EJB wants this data dashboard to automatically update when new data are added to the source data.

Thus, EJB's KPIs for this dashboard are total dollar sales and average delivery times. In addition, EJB's desire to be able to specify the month ordered, year ordered, date ordered, category, flavor, distribution center, and whether new or existing customers are displayed in various charts indicates that the company needs a dynamic and interactive data dashboard.

Now that the purpose of the data dashboard, the relevant KPIs, the objectives for creating the data dashboard, and the needs of the dashboard's users have been considered, we are able to determine that we can provide EJB the functionality it desires in its data dashboard through the following charts and tables:

CHART *file*

ejb1_chart

- a stacked column chart of total sales across distribution centers and year ordered by new or existing customers
- a line chart of total sales across year and month ordered by new or existing customers
- a clustered column chart of total sales across year ordered and flavor by category
- a clustered bar chart of average time to deliver across distribution centers by year ordered
- a table of total sales across category and flavor by distribution center and year, month, and day ordered

If you click the PivotChart to open the PivotTable Fields pane, the Rows area will be referred to as the Axis (Categories) area, and the Columns area will be referred to as the Legend (Series) area.

Using PivotTables, PivotCharts, and Slicers to Build a Data Dashboard

We will use the file *ejb1_chart*, which contains the *EJBData* Excel Table in the *Data* worksheet with the fields we need and the chart and slicers provided in Figure 8.3 in the *Chart1* worksheet to create the remaining components of the EJB data dashboard.

Figure 8.3   PivotChart for Total Sales with Slicers for Distribution Center, Year Ordered, and New Customer

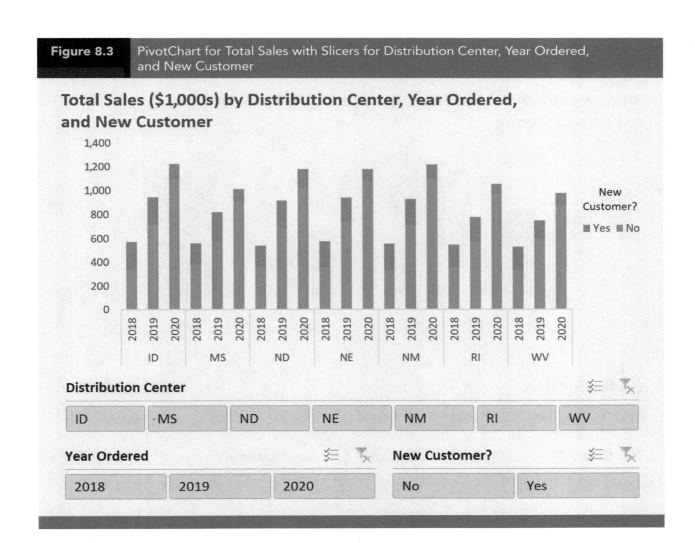

Recall that you can select multiple items in a slicer by clicking a slicer button while holding the Ctrl key, then clicking on each additional item you wish to select in that slicer.

Note that this PivotChart will allow the user to display total dollar sales for any combination of years ordered, distribution centers, and whether or not the customers are new. For example, suppose the user wants to compare sales to existing customers for the Idaho (ID) and Rhode Island (RI) distribution centers in 2019 and 2020. The user can create a chart for this purpose by selecting **ID** and **RI** in the **Distribution Center** slicer, **2019** and **2020** in the **Year Ordered** slicer, and **No** in the **New Customer?** slicer. This produces the chart in Figure 8.4.

This chart shows that total sales to existing customers increased substantially from 2019 to 2020 at both the Idaho and Rhode Island distribution centers.

Also note that Excel's tooltip feature allows the user to open a popup window with additional information for a portion of a table or chart by hovering the cursor over a portion of an Excel table or chart as shown in Figure 8.5. These popups will be active on the charts that we include in a dashboard. They provide users with some drill-down capability and can be customized to deliver a wide variety of information.

We can use PivotTables, PivotCharts, slicers, and the steps outlined in Chapter 6 to build the remaining three charts:

- a line chart of total sales across year and month ordered by new or existing customer
- a clustered column chart of sales across year ordered and flavor by category
- a clustered bar chart of average time to delivery across distribution centers by year ordered for EJB's data dashboard

Figure 8.4	PivotChart for Total Sales to Existing Customers by the Idaho and Rhode Island Distribution Centers in 2019 and 2020

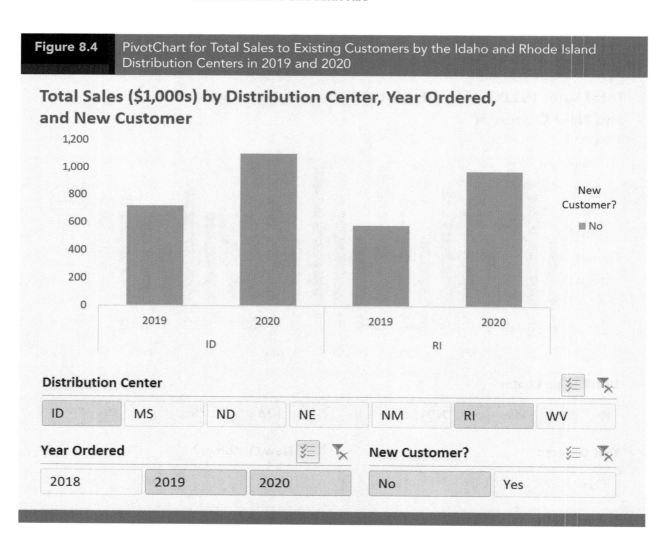

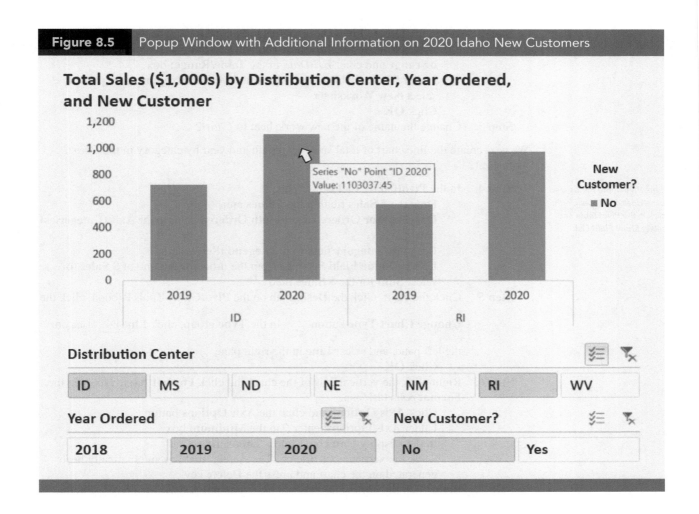

Figure 8.5 Popup Window with Additional Information on 2020 Idaho New Customers

Excel Tables are discussed in Chapter 6.

By creating an Excel Table in the *EJBData* worksheet and using this Excel Table as the source data for PivotTables and PivotCharts, we greatly simplify the process of updating the data, PivotCharts, and PivotTables. To add a new record to the existing data, we now only need to enter the record into the row adjacent to the last row of the *EJBData* table. To add a new field to the existing data, we only have to enter the field into the column adjacent to the last column of the *EJBData* table; Excel will automatically incorporate this new information into the *EJBData* table. To delete a record or a field from the existing data, we now only have to delete the entire corresponding row or column from the table.

Once new data have been added to the *EJBData* table, we can quickly refresh associated PivotTables and PivotCharts to reflect the new data (or any revisions to existing data) by clicking anywhere in a PivotTable, clicking the **PivotTable Analyze** tab on the Ribbon, clicking the **Refresh** button 🔄 in the **Data** group, and clicking **Refresh** to update the selected PivotTable or **Refresh All** to update all PivotTables in the file simultaneously. Thus, we have created a dynamic data dashboard that can be refreshed quickly to reflect recently added and revised data without updating the data range originally selected.

To create the line chart of total sales across year and month ordered by category, we use the following steps.

Step 1. In the file *ejb1_chart*, select any cell in the *EJBData* table in the *Data* worksheet
Click the **Insert** tab on the Ribbon
In the **Charts** group, click **PivotChart** and select **PivotChart & PivotTable**

CHART *file*

ejb1_chart

Step 2. When the **Create PivotTable** dialog box appears:

Under **Choose the data that you want to analyze**, choose **Select a table or range** and enter *EJBData* in the **Table/Range:** box

Under **Choose where you want the PivotTable report to be placed**, select **New Worksheet**

Click **OK**

Step 3. Change the name of the new worksheet to *Chart2*

We next create the line chart of total sales by month and year by category in the *Chart2* worksheet.

*If the **PivotTable Fields** task pane does not appear, right click in the **PivotTable** and select **Show Field List**.*

Step 4. In the **PivotChart Fields** task pane:

Drag the **$ Sales** field to the **Values** area

Drag the **Year Ordered** and **Month Ordered** fields to the **Axis (Categories)** area

Drag the **Category** field to the **Legend (Series)** area

Use the **Value Field Settings** from the drop down menu of **$ Sales** to select **Sum** for the **$ Sales** field

Step 5. Click the chart, click the **Design** tab on the **PivotChart Tools** Ribbon, click the

Change Chart Type button ▯▮ in the **Type** group, click **Line** ⋈ Line on
_{Change}
_{Chart Type}

the left pane, and select **Line** in the right pane

Click **OK**

Step 6. Right click the vertical axis of the chart and click **Format Axis…** to open the **Format Axis** task pane

Click **Axis Options** and click the **Axis Options** button

Under **Axis Options**, enter *0* in the **Minimum** box

In the **Display Units** box, select **Thousands**

Click the vertical axis title of "Thousands" that has automatically been generated on the chart and press the **Delete** key

Step 7. Right click the horizontal axis and click **Format Axis…** to open the **Format Axis** task pane

Click **Axis Options** and click the **Axis Options** button ▮▮▮

Click **Labels**, select **Specify interval unit**, and enter *1*

Step 8. Right click any **Field Button** (such as Month Ordered ▾) and select **Hide All Field Buttons on Chart**

Step 9. Click the PivotChart, click the **Insert** tab on the Ribbon, and click **Slicer** ▤
in the **Filters** group
_{Slicer}

Step 10. When the **Insert Slicers** dialog box appears:

Select the check boxes for **Category**, **Year Ordered**, and **Month Ordered**

Click **OK**

*For the chart shown in Figure 8.6, the borders have been removed from the slicers, and the number of columns has been set to 2 for the **Category** slicer, 3 for the **Year Ordered** slicer, and 6 for the **Month Ordered** slicer.*

Step 11. Click each of the slicers and use the tools in the **Slicer** tab on the Ribbon to format the slicer as appropriate

Drag the slicers to the positions they should occupy on the dashboard and resize the slicers accordingly

Some additional editing for readability to the chart created using the preceding steps results in the chart shown in Figure 8.6, which can also be found in the *Chart2* worksheet in the file *ejb_chart*. This PivotChart will allow the user to display total sales for any combination of years ordered, months ordered, and categories.

To create the clustered column chart of total sales across year ordered and flavor by category, we follow these steps.

ejb_chart

Figure 8.6   PivotChart for Total Sales with Slicers for Year Ordered, Month Ordered, and New Customer

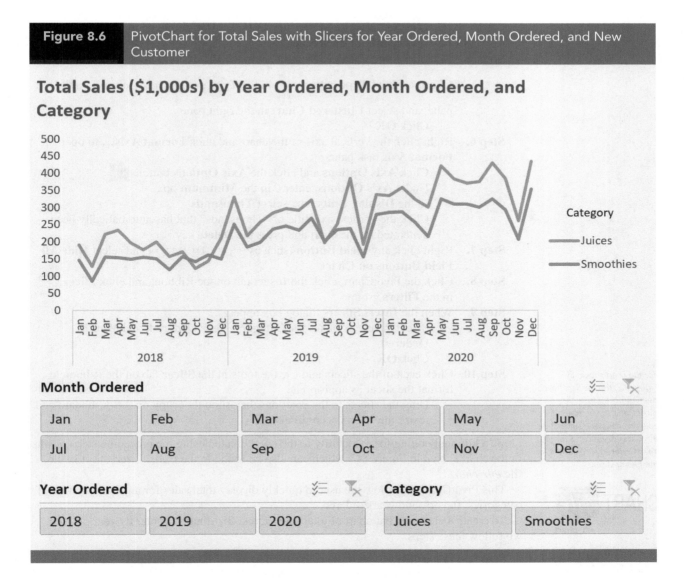

Total Sales ($1,000s) by Year Ordered, Month Ordered, and Category

ejb1_chart

Step 1.   In the file *ejb1_chart*, select any cell in the *EJBData* table in the *Data* worksheet

Click the **Insert** tab on the Ribbon

In the **Charts** group, click **PivotChart** and then select **PivotChart & PivotTable**

Step 2.   When the **Create PivotTable** dialog box appears:

Under **Choose the data that you want to analyze**, select **Select a table or range** and enter *EJBData* in the **Table/Range:** box

Under **Choose where you want the PivotTable report to be placed**, select **New Worksheet**

Click **OK**

Step 3.   Change the name of the new worksheet to *Chart3*

Step 4.   In the **PivotChart Fields** task pane:

Drag the **$ Sales** field to the **Values** area

Drag the **Year Ordered** and **Flavor** fields to the **Axis (Categories)** area

Drag the **Category** field to the **Legend (Series)** area

Use the **Value Field Settings** from the drop down menu of **$ Sales** to select **Sum** for the **$ Sales** field

Step 5. Click the chart, click the **Design** tab on the **PivotChart Tools** Ribbon, click the **Change Chart Type** button  in the **Type** group, click **Column** on the left pane, and select **Clustered Chart** in the right pane

Click **OK**

Step 6. Right click the vertical axis of the chart and click **Format Axis...** to open the **Format Axis** task pane

Click **Axis Options** and click the **Axis Options** button

Under **Axis Options**, enter *0* in the **Minimum** box

In the **Display Units** box, select **Thousands**

Click the vertical axis title of "Thousands" that has automatically been generated on the chart and press the **Delete** key

Step 7. Right click any **Field Button** (such as [Month Ordered ▾]) and select **Hide All Field Buttons on Chart**

Step 8. Click the PivotChart, click the **Insert** tab on the Ribbon, and click **Slicer** in the **Filters** group

Step 9. When the **Insert Slicers** dialog box appears:

Select the check boxes for **Category**, **Year Ordered**, and **Month Ordered**

Click **OK**

*For the chart shown in Figure 8.7, the borders have been removed from the slicers, and the number of columns has been set to 2 for the **Category** slicer, 3 for the **Year Ordered** slicer, and 4 for the **Flavor** slicer.*

Step 10. Click each of the slicers and use the tools in the **Slicer** tab on the Ribbon to format the slicer as appropriate

Drag the slicers to the positions they should occupy on the dashboard and resize the slicers accordingly

Some additional editing for readability to the chart created using the preceding steps results in the chart shown in Figure 8.7, which can also be found in the *Chart3* worksheet in the file *ejb_chart*.

This PivotChart will allow the user to quickly display total sales for any combination of categories, flavors, and years ordered.

To create a clustered bar chart of total sales across distribution center by year ordered, we follow these steps.

CHART *file*

ejb_chart

CHART *file*

ejb1_chart

Step 1. In the file *ejb1_chart*, select any cell in the *EJBData* table in the *Data* worksheet

Click the **Insert** tab on the Ribbon

In the **Charts** group, click **PivotChart** and select **PivotChart & PivotTable**

Step 2. When the **Create PivotTable** dialog box appears:

Under **Choose the data that you want to analyze**, choose **Select a table or range** and enter *EJBData* in the **Table/Range:** box

Under **Choose where you want the PivotTable report to be placed**, select **New Worksheet**

Click **OK**

Step 3. Change the name of the new worksheet to *Chart4*

We next create the clustered bar chart of total sales across distribution center by year ordered in the *Chart4* worksheet.

Step 4. In the **PivotChart Fields** task pane:

Drag the **Time to Deliver** field to the **Values** area

Drag the **Distribution Center** field to the **Axis (Categories)** area

Drag the **Year Ordered** field to the **Legend (Series)** area

Use the **Value Field Settings** from the drop down menu of **Time to Deliver** to select **Average** for the **Time to Deliver** field

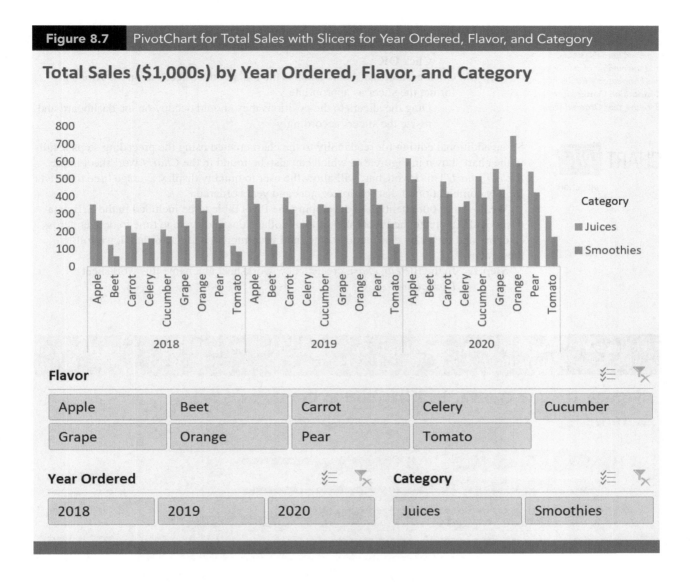

Figure 8.7   PivotChart for Total Sales with Slicers for Year Ordered, Flavor, and Category

Step 5. Click the chart, click the **Design** tab on the **PivotChart Tools** Ribbon, click the

Change Chart Type button in the **Type** group, click **Bar** Bar on

the left pane, and select **Clustered Bar** in the right pane
    Click **OK**

Step 6. Right click the vertical axis and click **Format Axis** to open the **Format Axis** pane
    Click **Axis Options** and click the **Axis Options** button
    Click **Labels**, click **Specify interval unit** and enter *1* into
    the **Specify interval unit** box
    Click **OK**

Step 7. Right click any **Field Button** (such as ⟨ Year Ordered ▼ ⟩) and select **Hide All Field Buttons on Chart**

Step 8. Click the PivotChart, click the **Insert** tab on the Ribbon, and click **Slicer** in the **Filters** group

*For the chart shown in Figure 8.8, the borders have been removed from the slicers, and the number of columns has been set to 7 for the **Distribution Center** slicer, and 3 for the **Year Ordered** slicer.*

ejb_chart

Step 9.   When the **Insert Slicers** dialog box appears:
     Select the check boxes for **Distribution Center** and **Year Ordered**
     Click **OK**

Step 10.   Click each of the slicers and use the tools in the **Slicer** tab on the Ribbon to format the slicer as appropriate
     Drag the slicers to the positions they should occupy on the dashboard and resize the slicers accordingly

Some additional editing for readability to the chart created using the preceding steps results in the chart shown in Figure 8.8, which can also be found in the *Chart4* worksheet in the file *ejb_chart*. This PivotChart will allow the user to quickly display average time to deliver for any combination of distribution centers and years ordered.

We now turn our attention to developing the PivotTable to be included in the EJB data dashboard. To create the PivotTable of total dollar sales and average time to deliver across category and flavor by distribution center and year, month, and day ordered, we follow these steps.

Step 1.   In the file *ejb_chart*, create a new worksheet and name this worksheet *Dashboard*

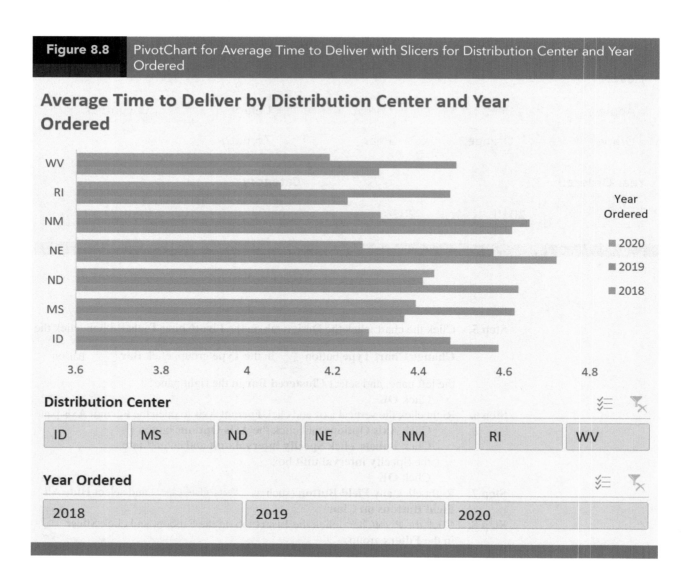

Figure 8.8   PivotChart for Average Time to Deliver with Slicers for Distribution Center and Year Ordered

Step 2 changes the fill color of cells A1:Z100 to a dark color to provide a contrasting background for the dashboard.

Step 2. Select cells A1:Z100

Click the **Home** tab on the Ribbon, and in the **Font** group, click the **Fill Color** button and select a dark blue color

Step 3. In the file *ejb_chart*, select any cell in the *EJBData* table in the *Data* worksheet

Click the **Insert** tab on the Ribbon and select **PivotTable** in the **Tables** group

Step 4. When the **Create PivotTable** dialog box appears:

Under **Choose the data that you want to analyze**, click **Select a Table or Range** and enter *EJBData* in the **Table/Range:** box

Under **Choose where you want the PivotTable report to be placed**, select **Existing Worksheet** and enter *Dashboard!B4*

Click **OK**

Step 5. In the *Dashboard* worksheet

Click the empty **PivotTable** to open the **PivotTable Fields** task pane

Step 6. In the **PivotTable Fields** pane:

Drag the **$ Sales** and **Time to Deliver** fields to the **Values** area

Drag the **Year Ordered**, **Month Ordered**, **Day Ordered**, and **Distribution Center** fields to the **Filters** area

Drag the **Category** field to the **Columns** area (make sure this is the first field listed in the **Columns** area)

Drag the **Flavor** field to the **Rows** area

Click the drop down arrow next to **Time to Deliver** in the **Values** area, click **Value Field Settings**... and change the **Summarize value field by** to **Average**

Click **OK**

Once you have completed this step, the **Drag fields between areas below:** area in the **PivotTable Fields** pane should look like Figure 8.9. Note that the order in which the fields are listed in each area determines the layout of the resulting PivotTable.

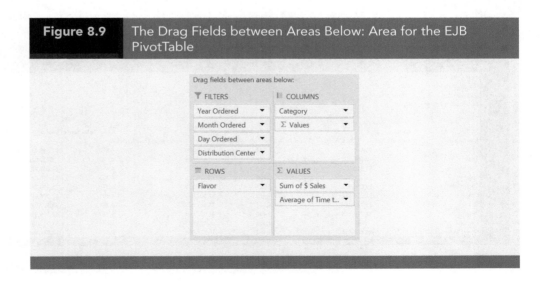

Figure 8.9   The Drag Fields between Areas Below: Area for the EJB PivotTable

Step 7. Right click any cell in the PivotTable and select **PivotTable Options...**

Step 8. When the **PivotTable Options** dialog box opens:

Click the **Layout & Format** tab

Deselect the check box for **Autofit column widths on update**

CHART *file*

ejbdashboard1_chart

This creates the PivotTable shown in Figure 8.10, which can also be found in the *Dashboard* worksheet in the file *ejbdashboard1_chart*.

This PivotTable will allow the user to find total dollar sales and average time to deliver for any combination of categories, flavors, and distribution centers for any years, months, or dates ordered.

Now that we have created each of the data dashboard's components, we can assemble the data dashboard. We start by considering the relative positioning of each of these charts on the dashboard. Our objective is to minimize eye travel by putting charts that are likely to be used together in proximity to each other.

- The chart of total sales by distribution center, year ordered, and new customer? (in the *Chart1* worksheet) and the chart of total sales (thousand $) by year ordered, flavor, and category (in the *Chart3* worksheet) will both be used in analyses of EJB's sales history by year and should be adjacent to each other.
- The chart of total sales by distribution center, year ordered, and new customer? (in the *Chart1* worksheet) and the chart of average time to deliver by distribution center and year ordered (in the *Chart4* worksheet) will both be used in analyses at the distribution center level and should be adjacent to each other.
- The chart of total sales by year ordered, month ordered, and category (in the *Chart2* worksheet) and the chart of total sales by year ordered, flavor, and category (in the *Chart3* worksheet) will both be used in analyses at the category level and should be adjacent to each other.
- The table of total sales across category and flavor by distribution center and year, month, and day ordered should be at the top of the dashboard for easy access.

Figure 8.10 PivotTable for EJB Data Dashboard

| Row Labels | Column Labels | | | | Total Sum of $ Sales | Total Average of Time to Deliver |
| | Juices | | Smoothies | | | |
	Sum of $ Sales	Average of Time to Deliver	Sum of $ Sales	Average of Time to Deliver		
Apple	$1,436,632	4.481	$1,116,500	4.318	$2,553,132	4.409
Beet	$606,708	4.449	$352,319	4.583	$959,026	4.502
Carrot	$1,110,233	4.345	$932,670	4.417	$2,042,903	4.378
Celery	$724,257	4.806	$826,358	4.313	$1,550,615	4.548
Cucumber	$1,080,531	4.325	$899,259	4.376	$1,979,790	4.348
Grape	$1,269,622	4.411	$1,007,050	4.301	$2,276,672	4.362
Orange	$1,740,004	4.437	$1,387,955	4.381	$3,127,959	4.412
Pear	$1,278,248	4.438	$1,021,064	4.469	$2,299,312	4.452
Tomato	$648,656	4.419	$383,834	4.344	$1,032,489	4.389
Grand Total	$9,894,891	4.447	$7,927,008	4.379	$17,821,899	4.416

Year Ordered (All)
Month Ordered (All)
Day Ordered (All)
Distribution Center (All)

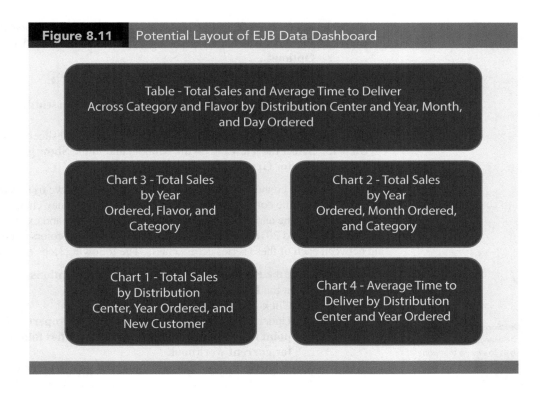

Figure 8.11 Potential Layout of EJB Data Dashboard

One configuration that satisfies these criteria is provided in Figure 8.11.

We will complete construction of the EJB data dashboard in this layout using the following steps.

Step 1. Click the PivotChart in *Chart1* worksheet

Step 2. Click the **Analyze** tab on the **PivotChart Tools** Ribbon, and click the **Move Chart** button ▦ in the **Actions** group

Step 3. When the **Move Chart** dialog box appears:
Select **Object in:** and choose **Dashboard**
Click **OK**

Step 4: In the *Chart1* worksheet, click the **Distribution Center** slicer
Click the **Home** tab on the Ribbon
Click **Cut** in the **Clipboard** group

Step 5. In the *Dashboard* worksheet
Click the **Home** tab on the Ribbon
Click **Paste**

Step 6. Position the PivotChart and slicer where you want them on the dashboard

Step 7. Repeat Steps 1–6 to move the charts and slicers in the *Chart2*, *Chart3*, and *Chart4* worksheets to the *Dashboard* worksheet and position these objects where you want them on the dashboard

Step 8. Double click one of the PivotCharts in the *Dashboard* worksheet to open the **Format Chart Area** task pane
Click **Chart Options**, then click the **Size & Properties** button ▦
Click **Properties**, then select **Don't move or size with cells**

Step 9. Repeat Step 8 for the remaining charts on the *Dashboard* worksheet

Step 10. Right click one of the slicers in the *Dashboard* worksheet, then select **Size and Properties...** to open the **Format Slicer** dialog box
Click **Properties**, then select **Don't move or size with cells**

Step 11. Repeat Step 10 for the remaining slicers on the *Dashboard* worksheet

Step 12. Right click any chart on the *Dashboard* worksheet and select **PivotChart Options...**

Step 13. When the **PivotTable Options** dialog box opens:
  Click the **Layout & Format** tab
  Deselect the check box for **Autofit column widths on update**
  Click **OK**

Step 14. Adjust the positioning and size of the charts and slicers so they align as desired

Step 15. Select the **View** tab on the Ribbon, and in the **Show** group, deselect the check box for **Gridlines**

The dashboard created to this point looks great, but when we use a slicer to filter out some series on a chart, the colors assigned to the remaining series may change. Furthermore, this dashboard uses blue and orange to differentiate between new and existing customers, juices and smoothies, and 2018 and 2019 if we use different sets of colors to consistently differentiate between each of these series across charts. The following steps address both concerns.

Step 16. Click the **File** tab on the Ribbon, then select **Options**

Step 17. When the **Excel Options** dialog box appears:
  Click **Advanced**
  Under **Chart**, select the check boxes for **Properties follow chart data point for all new workbooks** and **Properties follow chart data point for current workbook**

*Use **Format Data Series** to check each series on each chart to ensure that none of the colors assigned to the series in any of the charts in the dashboard are reassigned automatically by Excel when the slicers are used to filter the data.*

Step 18. Assign the specific colors below to different chart elements by right clicking on that chart element, then clicking **Fill** and selecting **More Fill Colors...**
  Blue to existing customers and Orange to new customers
  Purple to juices and Red to smoothies
  Brown to 2018, Pink to 2019, and Green to 2020

Step 19. Change the fill color of cells A1:AL80 to dark blue to create a contrasting background

Step 20. Type *Espléndido Jugo y Batido, Inc. Sales Dashboard* into cell A2
  Change the font to white **48 pt. Brush Script MT** font

Step 21. Select cells A2:AF2, select the **Home** tab on the Ribbon, and in the **Alignment** group, click **Merge & Center**

ejbdashboard1_chart

Some additional editing for readability to the table created using the preceding steps results in the dashboard shown in Figure 8.12, which can also be found in the *Dashboard* worksheet in the file *ejbdashboard1_chart*.

You can change the style and settings for any slicers by clicking the slicer, clicking **Options** on the Ribbon, and using the various tools such as those in the **Slicer Styles** group.

Linking Slicers to Multiple PivotTables

The data dashboard in Figure 8.12 allows the user to filter each chart separately using the associated slicer(s). This is a definite advantage of this dashboard design for users who need this level of control over the charts on their dashboard. However, users may prefer to use a single slicer that controls multiple related charts. For example, a single Distribution Center slicer that simultaneously controls the Distribution Centers that are displayed on all relevant charts on the dashboard might be preferable.

We will illustrate with Distribution Center. Start by deleting all but one of the Distribution Center slicers from the EJB dashboard as shown in Figure 8.13. The following steps will connect the remaining Distribution Center slicer to the PivotTables in the *Chart1* and *Chart4* worksheets.

Step 1. Select the remaining **Distribution Center** slicer on the *Dashboard* worksheet
  Click the **Slicer** tab on the Ribbon
  Click the **Report Connections** button   in the **Slicer** group

| **Figure 8.12** | EJB Data Dashboard |

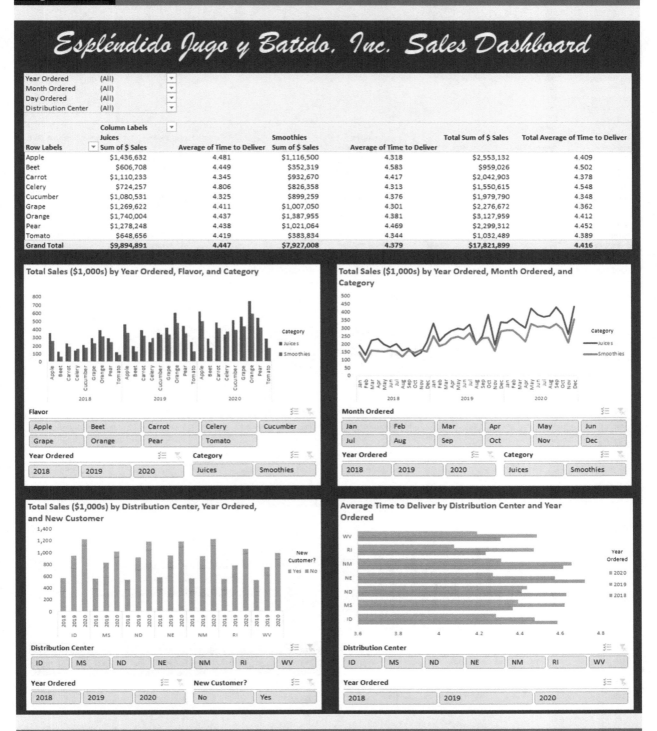

Figure 8.13 EJB Data Dashboard after Deleting All but One of the Distribution Center Slicers

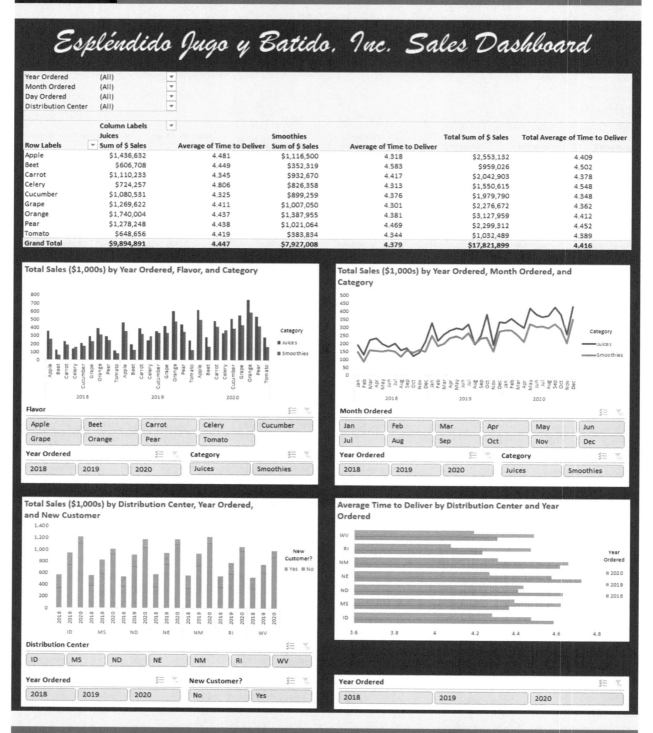

Step 2.   Select both the PivotTables created in the *Chart1* worksheet and the *Chart4* worksheet
Click **OK**

Because the PivotCharts created in the *Chart1* and *Chart4* worksheets are linked to the corresponding PivotTables in the *Chart1* and *Chart4* worksheets, the single **Distribution Center** slicer now controls the value(s) of Distribution Center that are displayed in both of these charts.

Step 3.   Repeat Steps 1 and 2 to link the PivotTables created in the *Chart2* and *Chart3* worksheets to a single **Category** slicer and to link the PivotTables created in the *Chart1*, *Chart2*, *Chart3*, and *Chart4* worksheets to a single **Year Ordered** slicer

With fewer slicers to display, we can rearrange and resize the charts in a manner that is more visually appealing and easier to read while still meeting the criteria we established for which charts should be adjacent to each other, leading to the result shown in Figure 8.14.

In addition to allowing for simultaneous filtering of related charts and providing EJB with easy access to the information it desires, the dashboard now appears less cluttered. Note, however, that only PivotTables that are generated from the same data can be filtered simultaneously by a single slicer. For the EJB data dashboard, we generated each PivotTable from the *EJBData* table on the *Data* worksheet to ensure that any slicer we create could be used to filter every chart we created.

Protecting a Data Dashboard

Finally, we need to prevent users from altering the dashboard while still allowing them to interact with the dashboard through the slicers and filters. We will do so through the following steps.

Step 1.   Right click any slicer on the *Dashboard* worksheet, then click **Size and Properties...**

Step 2.   When the **Format Slicer** task pane appears:
Under **Position and Layout**, select the check box for **Disable resizing and moving**
Under **Properties**, select **Don't move or size with cells** and deselect the check box for **Locked**

*After selecting one slicer, you can hold down the **Ctrl** key and select additional slicers to execute Steps 1 and 2 on multiple slicers simultaneously*

Step 3.   Repeat Steps 1 and 2 for each remaining slicer on the *Dashboard* worksheet

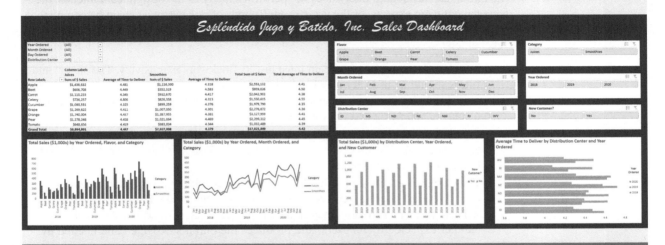

Figure 8.14   EJB Data Dashboard with Connected Slicers

Step 4.   Select the range of cells that contains the PivotTable in the *Dashboard* worksheet (this is cells B4:H21 on our *Dashboard* worksheet)
Click the **Review** tab on the Ribbon
In the **Protect** group, click the **Allow Edit Ranges** button

Step 5.   When the **Allow Users to Edit Ranges** dialog box appears:
Click the **New...** button

Step 6.   When the **New Range** dialog box appears:
Enter *DashboardPivotTable* in the **Title:** box
Click **OK**

Step 7.   When the **Allow Users to Edit Ranges** dialog box returns:
Click the **Protect Sheet...** button

Step 8.   When the **Protect Sheet** dialog box opens:
Deselect the check box for **Select locked cells**
Select the check box for **Use PivotTable & PivotChart**
Enter a password in the **Password to unprotect sheet:** box
Renter the same password in the **Reenter password to proceed** box of the **Confirm Password** dialog box (recall that we used the password TRIAL to protect the dashboard in the file *ejbdashboard2_chart*)
Click **OK**

Step 9.   Select the *Chart1* worksheet tab, then hold the **Ctrl** key down and select the *Chart2*, *Chart3*, *Chart4*, and *Data* worksheet tabs so all worksheet tabs in the *EJB2Dashboard* file except the *Dashboard* worksheet are selected
Right click the *Chart1* worksheet tab and select **Hide**

*The **Protect Sheet** button toggles to the **Unprotect Sheet** button when the sheet is protected and back to the **Protect Sheet** button when the sheet is not protected.*

CHART *file*

ejbdashboard2_chart

The complete dashboard with linked slicers is in the *Dashboard* worksheet of the file *ejbdashboard2_chart*.

A user can now use the slicers and filters on the dashboard but cannot otherwise alter or move the PivotCharts, the PivotTable, or the slicers. Each of the worksheets other than the *Dashboard* worksheet is also hidden from the user, preventing unwanted changes from being made to the raw data and PivotCharts that have been used to create the data dashboard.

When you need to revise the dashboard, use the following steps to unprotect the *Dashboard* worksheet and unhide the *Chart1*, *Chart2*, *Chart3*, *Chart4*, and *Data* worksheets.

Step 1.   Right click the *Dashboard* worksheet tab
Step 2.   Click **Unhide...**
Select the hidden worksheet you wish to unhide

Final Review of a Data Dashboard

The initial data dashboard likely does not perform exactly as the design team intends, the management team expects, or the users need. Rounds of reviews must again be completed to ensure the final product works properly from the perspectives of all the dashboard's stakeholders:

- The data dashboard design team must test its final work extensively. The slicers and filters should be used at many levels, and the results in the PivotCharts and PivotTables should be reviewed at these levels to ensure the information is accurate and the display is appealing and informative.

- The design team must also review the final data dashboard with the management team that authorized the development of the data dashboard to ensure the data dashboard meets the management team's objectives.

- The design team must provide the ultimate users with opportunities to test the final data dashboard extensively in the environment(s) in which the dashboard will ultimately be used to ensure the dashboard is user friendly, functions in the manner expected by its users, and produces the outputs expected and needed by its users.

In addition, the design team must work with the management team and the users to create a process for ongoing monitoring and revision of the data dashboard to ensure it continues to effectively meet the organization's needs. Following a process that adheres to these guidelines ensures the data dashboard will generate value for the organization throughout its life.

Notes + Comments

1. One important limitation of Excel PivotTables is that they can only be used to create column, bar, line, pie, and radar PivotCharts.

2. Slicers filter PivotTables, so data tables with user control can be included on a data dashboard if that will be useful to the users.

3. Borders can be removed from each slicer by clicking the slicer, clicking the **Slicer Tools Options** tab on the Ribbon, right clicking the current style in the **Slicer Styles** group, clicking **Duplicate**, selecting **Whole Slicer** and clicking the **Format** button in the **Modify Slicer Style** dialog box, then clicking the **Border** tab and selecting **None**. This creates a new style for **Slicer Styles** in the **Slicer Tools Options** tab on the Ribbon that you can apply to any slicer in your workbook.

4. Excel's **Timeline** works the same way a slicer works, but the timeline works exclusively with date fields to provide a way to filter and group the dates in a PivotTable. The **Timeline** button can be found adjacent to the **Slicer** button in the **Filters** group on the **Insert** tab.

5. Excel's **Developer Tab** is another set of tools that can be used to allow the user to interact with a data dashboard. The functionality of several of the **Developer Tab** tools can be incorporated into dashboards through slicers, and other **Developer Tab** tools require macros to be written. The Developer Tab is generally hidden and must be activated in order to be added to the Ribbon.

6. A variety of commercial products for developing data dashboards are available. Products such as Tableau, Domo, Qrvey, GROW, Microsoft Power BI, and ClicData can be used to create complex data dashboards.

8.5 Common Mistakes in Data Dashboard Design

Although there are many types of mistakes one can make in designing and developing a data dashboard, a few of these types of mistakes are common. These include:

- Not considering the reason the organization wants to develop a data dashboard, i.e., the organization's needs and objectives. This includes:
  › neglecting information that is important with respect to the objectives of the organization
  › focusing on information that is not meaningful with respect to the objectives of the organization

- Neglecting to obtain sufficient input from the actual users throughout the data dashboard design process
- Not considering the environment(s) in which the data dashboard will be used
- Failing to position complimentary components (charts, tables, etc.) on the data dashboard in a manner that facilitates their simultaneous use
- Using an inappropriate or ineffective type of chart for the data and its message
- Neglecting the principles of good chart and table design when creating the individual components of the data dashboard
- Creating a data dashboard that is too cluttered
- Designing an unattractive visual display
- Not considering the organization's and users' potential future needs

Summary

In this chapter, we have discussed how data dashboards can help users understand and investigate data and ultimately make better decisions. The process of developing a data dashboard starts with understanding the principles of effective data dashboards, common applications of data dashboards, and various types of data dashboards.

We reviewed various aspects of data dashboard design. We discussed the need to understand the purpose of the data dashboard and consider the needs of the data dashboard's users. We explained the importance of considering the information to be displayed and how it is to be displayed in the data dashboard. We showed how to use PivotTables, PivotCharts, and slicers to build a data dashboard in Excel. We discussed how to link slicers to multiple PivotTables and how to protect a data dashboard so users cannot make permanent changes. We emphasized the importance of a final review of a data dashboard and consideration of future needs. We concluded by listing several mistakes commonly made in data dashboard design and development.

Glossary

Analytical dashboard A dashboard typically used by analysts to identify and investigate trends, predict outcomes, and discover insights in large volumes of data. Because analytical dashboards usually support exploration of long-term issues, these dashboards are generally updated less frequently than operational, strategic, or tactical dashboards.

Customization tool A feature that allows the user to tailor the dashboard to specific needs.

Data dashboard A data visualization tool that gives multiple outputs and may update in real time.

Drilling down A feature that provides the user with more specific and detailed information on a particular element, variable, or KPI.

Dynamic dashboard A dashboard that automatically receives and incorporates new data into the dashboard as the new data become available.

Hierarchical filtering A feature that provides the user with the capability to restrict the data displayed to a specific segment by systematically selecting values of several categories or values of variables in a nested manner.

Interactive dashboard A dashboard that allows users to customize the data dashboard display, effectively allowing a user to filter the data displayed on the dashboard.

Key performance indicator A value a manager uses to operate and maintain their businesses effectively and efficiently. Also known as a KPI.

Noninteractive dashboard A dashboard that does not allow users to customize the data dashboard display.

Operational dashboard A dashboard typically used by lower level managers to monitor rapidly changing critical business conditions.

PivotChart A chart that allows the user to interact with the data by applying filters to select various aspects of the data to be displayed in the chart.

PivotTable A table that allows the user to interact with the data by applying filters to select various aspects of the data to be displayed in the table.

Slicer A tool that allows the spreadsheet user to filter the data to be displayed in PivotTables and PivotCharts.

Static dashboard A dashboard that may periodically be updated manually as new data and information are collected.

Strategic dashboard A dashboard typically used by executives to monitor the status of KPIs relevant to overarching organizational objectives.

Tactical dashboard A dashboard typically used by mid-level managers to identify and assess the organization's strengths and weaknesses in support of the development of organizational strategies.

Time interval widget A feature that allows the user to specify the time period to be displayed on a data dashboard.

Problems

Conceptual

1. **Definition of a Data Dashboard**. Which of the following is true with regard to a data dashboard? **LO 1**
    i. It is a data visualization tool that gives multiple outputs and may update in real time.
    ii. Its outputs are often a set of KPIs for the company or some unit of the company that are aligned with organizational goals.
    iii. It can help an organization better understand and use its data.
    iv. All of the above are true with regard to a data dashboard.

2. **Understanding the Objectives of Effective Data Dashboards**. Ideally, a data dashboard for an organization should do which of the following? **LO 2**
    i. Present all KPIs to provide the broadest information possible.
    ii. Present unrelated KPIs to provide the most contrasting information possible.
    iii. Present both unrelated and related KPIs to provide the broadest information possible.
    iv. Present KPIs related to some aspect of the organization's operations to provide information relevant to a specific problem or concern.

3. **Understanding Principles of Effective Data Dashboards**. Which of the following is true when designing a data dashboard? **LO 2**
    i. One does not need to be concerned with adhering to the principles of effective data visualization for the dashboard or any of its components (charts, tables, etc.).
    ii. One should adhere to the principles of effective data visualization for all components (charts, tables, etc.) of the dashboard but not necessarily for the overall dashboard.
    iii. One should adhere to the principles of effective data visualization for the overall dashboard but not for any of the components (charts, tables, etc.) of the dashboard.
    iv. One should adhere to the principles of effective data visualization for the dashboard and each of its components (charts, tables, etc.).

4. **Common Areas of Application for Data Dashboards**. Which type of dashboard is used to monitor the performance of an organization's workforce by individual, division or department, or shift? **LO 3**
    i. Technical support
    ii. Marketing
    iii. Human resource
    iv. Investment

5. **Common Areas of Application for Data Dashboards**. Which type of dashboard is used to monitor contributor activity and potential for nonprofit organizations by contributor, prospective contributor, or project/campaign? **LO 3**
    i. Technical support
    ii. Donor
    iii. Marketing
    iv. Manufacturing

6. **Data Dashboard Taxonomies**. Which type of dashboard might provide information on a user's pulse, blood pressure, weight, body-mass index, and calories consumed in a day? **LO 4**
    i. Technical support
    ii. Manufacturing
    iii. Investment analytics
    iv. Personal fitness

7. **Data Dashboard Taxonomies**. Which of the following most accurately describes a dynamic dashboard? **LO 4**
   i. It regularly receives and incorporates new and revised data and incorporates these data into the dashboard.
   ii. It provides information in a lively manner.
   iii. It incorporates animation.
   iv. It is most useful when the organization's KPIs change slowly.

8. **Characteristics of an Interactive Data Dashboard**. Which of the following most accurately describes an interactive dashboard? **LO 4**
   i. It regularly receives and incorporates new and revised data and incorporates these data into the dashboard.
   ii. It allows a user to permanently alter the data displayed on the dashboard.
   iii. It allows a user to filter the data displayed to her or him on the dashboard.
   iv. It incorporates audio responses to the user.

9. **Restricting User Interaction in a Data Dashboard**. Which of the following features allow the user to restrict the data displayed to a specific segment of users by systematically selecting values of several categories or values of variables in a nested manner? **LO 4**
   i. Hierarchical filtering
   ii. Data cleansing
   iii. Information sifting
   iv. Methodical selection

10. **Data Dashboard Taxonomies**. Identify which type of data dashboard is best described by each of the following descriptions. **LO 4**
    a. Dashboards typically used by executives to monitor the status of KPIs relevant to overarching organizational objectives.
       i. Operational
       ii. Tactical
       iii. Strategic
       iv. Analytic
    b. Dashboards typically used by analysts to identify and investigate trends, predict outcomes, and discover insights in large volumes of data.
       i. Operational
       ii. Tactical
       iii. Strategic
       iv. Analytic
    c. Dashboards typically used by mid-level managers to identify and assess the organization's strengths and weaknesses in support of the development of organizational strategies.
       i. Operational
       ii. Tactical
       iii. Strategic
       iv. Analytic
    d. Dashboards typically used by lower level managers to monitor rapidly changing critical business conditions.
       i. Operational
       ii. Tactical
       iii. Strategic
       iv. Analytic

11. **Overcrowding and Unnecessary Complexity in a Data Dashboard**. Which of the following is not a valid strategy for avoiding overcrowding and unnecessary complexity in data dashboard design? **LO 5**
    i. Using as many different colors as possible on the charts and tables used in the dashboard

ii. Using interactive dashboard tools (drilling down, hierarchical filtering, time interval widget, customization tools)

iii. Organizing the information into subsets that each address a different need of the end users and displaying information in these subsets across multiple pages

iv. Avoiding inclusion of information that will not be useful to the end users

12. **Providing Effective Context in a Data Dashboard**. Which of the following is an effective way to provide context for the information provided by the data dashboard? **LO 5**

    i. Comparing the value of a KPI to an organizational goal
    ii. Showing how a KPI varies over time
    iii. Comparing the value of a KPI across customers
    iv. All of the above.

13. **The Data Dashboard Testing Process**. Which of the following is not an important part of the process of testing a data dashboard throughout its development? **LO 5**

    i. Reviewing progress with the management team that authorized the development of the data dashboard at critical junctures to ensure the dashboard under production is meeting the management team's objectives
    ii. Allowing the general public to use and comment on the data dashboard at various stages of development to ensure the dashboard can be used by anyone
    iii. Allowing the ultimate users to test and comment on the data dashboard at various stages of development to ensure the dashboard is user friendly, functions in the manner expected by the users, and produces the outputs expected and needed by its users
    iv. Testing of the dashboard at each step by the dashboard design team to ensure the dashboard functions as the team intends

14. **Excel Tools for Filtering Data in a Data Dashboard**. Which of the following is an Excel tool that allows the dashboard user to filter the data to be displayed in PivotTables and PivotCharts? **LO 6**

    i. Screener
    ii. Dicer
    iii. Slicer
    iv. Strainer

15. **Excel Tables and Building Data Dashboards**. What is the advantage of creating an Excel Table from the raw data in Excel? **LO 6**

    i. You can add a new record to the existing data by entering the record into the row adjacent to the last row of the table.
    ii. You can add a new field to the existing data by entering the field into the column adjacent to the last column of the table.
    iii. You can give the table a name and refer to the table by that name instead of its range of cells.
    iv. Each of the above is an advantage of creating a table from the raw data in Excel.

16. **Common Mistakes in Data Dashboard Design**. Which of the following is a common mistake in designing and developing a data dashboard? **LO 7**

    i. Using copious amounts of animation to engage and entertain the user
    ii. Using a different type of chart for each display in a data dashboard to provide the user with visual variety
    iii. Not giving careful consideration to the environment(s) in which the data dashboard will be used
    iv. Randomly providing unrelated but interesting trivia about the organization at the bottom of the data dashboard to encourage the user to return often

Applications

17. **Evaluating the Design of a Data Dashboard**. An alternative version of the Espléndido Jugo y Batido data dashboard shown in Figure 8.12 follows. How would you modify this alternative to improve the dashboard? **LO 2**

18. **Evaluating the Choice of Charts in a Data Dashboard**. An alternative version of the Espléndido Jugo y Batido data dashboard shown in Figure 8.12 follows. How would you modify this alternative to improve the dashboard? **LO 2**

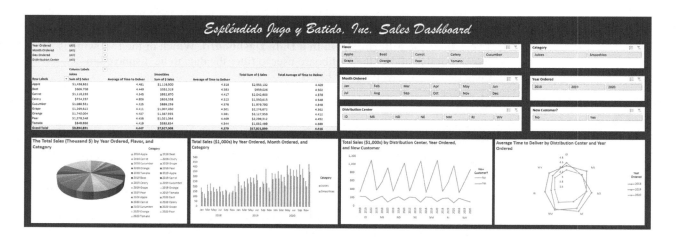

19. **Adding a Chart to a Data Dashboard**. In addition to the information provided on the data dashboard shown in Figure 8.12, Espléndido Jugo y Batido management has decided it would like to include a series of charts that show the relationship between average service satisfaction rating and average product satisfaction rating across the distribution centers for each of the past three years. EJB Management would also like to include a table that provides the average service satisfaction rating and average product satisfaction rating by distribution center across years. **LO 2**

   a. What type of chart(s) would you recommend to show the relationship between the average of the service satisfaction rating and the average of the product satisfaction rating across the distribution centers for each of the past three years? Explain why you would suggest such chart(s)?

   b. How would you revise the data dashboard in Figure 8.12 to incorporate the chart or charts you suggested in part a?

20. **Building a Technical Support Data Dashboard**. Bogdan's Express, a chain of sporting goods stores in Washington, wants to construct a technical support data dashboard to monitor how effectively its technical support group deals with IT problems. Management is primarily interested in the time it takes the IT support group to respond once a problem has been reported (response time) and how long it takes the group to resolve the issue after the initial response by the IT support group (time to resolution) over the most recent four months. They would like to be able to review the IT group's performance by date, type of technical problem (email, hardware, or Internet), and office (Bellingham, Olympia, Seattle, or Spokane).

Each reported problem is immediately logged and issued a case number, and the data collected by Bogdan from its relational database includes the case number, date, office, type of technical problem, response time (in minutes), and time to resolution (in minutes). They have also created a new field for the month during which the problem was reported. Note that both Response Time and Time to Resolution only include time that elapses during normal business hours.

Bogdan's staff has already created the following components for the data dashboard in Excel. **LO 6**

- A line chart of average response time across months by office (in the *Chart1* worksheet)
- A line chart of average time to resolution across months by office (in the *Chart2* worksheet)
- A clustered bar chart of average time to resolution across offices by type of technical problem (in the *Chart3* worksheet)
- A stacked cluster column chart of number of problems reported across office by type of technical problem (in the *Chart4* worksheet)

bogdan_chart

The data and these charts are available in the file *bogdan_chart*, and the name of the worksheet in which each chart can be found is given with the descriptions of the charts Bogdan has developed.

a. Create the following slicers for the charts created by Bogdan.
- A slicer for month and a slicer for office for the chart in the *Chart1* worksheet
- A slicer for month and a slicer for office for the chart in the *Chart2* worksheet
- A slicer for office and a slicer for type of technical problem for the chart in the *Chart3* worksheet
- A slicer for office and a slicer for type of technical problem for the chart in the *Chart4* worksheet

b. Create the data dashboard by creating a new worksheet and naming it *Dashboard*; moving the charts and slicers from the *Chart1*, *Chart2*, *Chart3*, and *Chart4* worksheets to the *Dashboard* worksheet; repositioning these charts and slicers on the *Dashboard* worksheet; and adding a title to the dashboard and doing whatever formatting and editing is necessary to make the dashboard functional and visually appealing.

c. Amend the data dashboard you created in part b in the following ways.
- Create a single slicer to filter month for the charts created in the *Chart1* and *Chart2* worksheets
- Create a single slicer to filter office for the charts created in the *Chart1*, *Chart2*, *Chart3*, and *Chart4* worksheets
- Create a slicer to filter type of technical problem for the charts created in the *Chart3* and *Chart4* worksheets

Once you have amended the data dashboard, rearrange the charts and slicers to create an effective and visually appealing dashboard. Test each slicer to ensure it works on the appropriate charts.

d. Protect the data dashboard in part c from being revised by users. Ensure that the slicers cannot be resized or moved, password protect the *Dashboard* worksheet (use the password Problem820), and hide all worksheets except the *Dashboard* worksheet.

e. The following seven entries for April 29–30 in the following table were not logged. Add these data to the *BogdanData* table, and refresh all PivotTables and PivotCharts. Comment on the differences between the resulting dashboard and the dashboard from part d.

Case Number	Date	Month	Office	Type of Technical Problem	Response Time (Minutes)	Time to Resolution (Minutes)
1990	29-Apr	Apr	Olympia	hardware	59.9	23.1
1994	29-Apr	Apr	Spokane	hardware	15.8	64.1
2000	29-Apr	Apr	Bellingham	hardware	26.7	53.4
2005	29-Apr	Apr	Bellingham	Internet	41.4	12.8
2011	30-Apr	Apr	Olympia	hardware	96.1	14.6
2012	30-Apr	Apr	Spokane	hardware	125.6	55.0
2019	30-Apr	Apr	Spokane	email	4.5	45.9

21. **Building a Donor Data Dashboard**. The American Retriever Foundation (ARF) is a not-for-profit organization dedicated to health issues faced by the six distinct retriever dog breeds (Chesapeake Bay, curly-coated, flat-coated, golden, Labrador, and Nova Scotia duck tolling). ARF needs to develop a data dashboard to monitor its donor activity and its interactions with potential donors. Management is concerned primarily with the number and dollar value of donations, the number of legacy donors (those who have donated in the past twelve months) and new potential donors solicited, and the number of solicitations that result in donations. They want to compare these results across ARF's four development officers (Randall Shalley, Donna Sanchez, Marie Lydon, and Hoa Nguyen) by date and mode of contact (telephone, email, or personal meeting).

    ARF has collected data for each solicitation initiated last year from its relational database. These data include the solicitation number, development officer, date of solicitation, mode of solicitation, whether the solicitation resulted in a donation, and whether the solicited potential donor was a legacy donor. ARF also added a field for month in which the solicitation was made.

    ARF's staff has already created the following components for the data dashboard in Excel.

    - A stacked bar chart of the number of solicitations across development officer by whether the solicitation resulted in a donation (in the *Chart1* worksheet)
    - A stacked bar chart of the percentage of successful solicitations across mode of solicitation by whether the solicitation resulted in a donation (in the *Chart2* worksheet)
    - A stacked bar chart of total donations (in $1,000s) across development officer by legacy designation (in the *Chart3* worksheet)
    - A cluster bar chart of total donations (in $1,000s) across mode of solicitation by legacy designation (in the *Chart4* worksheet)

CHART *file*

arf_chart

The data and these charts are available in the file *arf_chart*, and the name of the worksheet in which each chart can be found is given with the descriptions of the charts ARF has developed. **LO 6**

a. Create the following for the charts created by ARF.
   - A slicer for development officer, a slicer for whether the solicitation resulted in a donation, and a slicer for the month of solicitation for the chart in the *Chart1* worksheet
   - A slicer for mode of solicitation, a slicer for whether the solicitation resulted in a donation, and a slicer for development officer for the chart in the *Chart2* worksheet
   - A slicer for development officer, a slicer for the legacy status of the donor, and a slicer for the month of solicitation for the chart in the *Chart3* worksheet
   - A slicer for the mode of solicitation, legacy status, and month of donation for the chart in the *Chart4* worksheet

b. Create a data dashboard by creating a new worksheet and naming it *Dashboard*; moving the charts and slicers from the *Chart1*, *Chart2*, *Chart3*, and *Chart4* worksheets to the *Dashboard* worksheet; repositioning the charts and slicers on the *Dashboard* worksheet; and adding a title to the dashboard and doing whatever formatting and editing is necessary to make the dashboard functional and visually appealing.

c. Amend the data dashboard you created in part b in the following ways.
   - Create a single slicer to filter month for the charts created in the *Chart1*, *Chart2*, and *Chart4* worksheets
   - Create a single slicer to filter development officer for the charts created in the *Chart1*, *Chart2*, and *Chart3* worksheets
   - Create a single slicer to filter whether or not a solicitation resulted in a donation for the charts created in the *Chart1* and *Chart2* worksheets
   - Create a single slicer to filter legacy status for the charts created in the *Chart3* and *Chart4* worksheets
   - Create a single slicer to filter mode of solicitation for the charts created in the *Chart2* and *Chart4* worksheets

   Once you have amended the data dashboard, rearrange the charts and slicers to create an effective and visually appealing dashboard. Test each slicer to ensure it works on the appropriate charts.

d. Protect the data dashboard in part c from being revised by users. Ensure that the slicers cannot be resized or moved, password protect the *Dashboard* worksheet (use the password Problem821), and hide all worksheets except the *Dashboard* worksheet.

DATA *file*
arfnewdata

e. The file *arfnewdata* contains 15 entries for the past year that were not originally entered into the relational data base before the data for this dashboard was retrieved. Add these data to the *ARFData* table, and refresh all pivot tables and pivot charts. Comment on the differences between the resulting dashboard and the dashboard from part d.

22. **Building a Personal Fitness Data Dashboard**. Late last year, Veronica Camp learned she is pre-diabetic. Her physician recommended that she immediately begin exercising regularly and limiting her calorie intact to approximately 1,500 calories per day. Her physician also advised her to monitor her systolic and diastolic blood pressure, heart rate, and blood glucose daily.

On January 1, Veronica began exercising three times a week for approximately 30 minutes, and she started monitoring her calorie intake at meals with an app she downloaded. She also started monitoring her systolic and diastolic blood pressure, heart rate, and blood glucose daily. She has created a database with these data recorded on a daily basis through November, and she has generated the following charts. **LO 6**

CHART *file*
veronica_chart

   - A line chart of monthly average systolic blood pressure (in the *Chart1* worksheet)
   - A line chart of monthly average diastolic blood pressure (in the *Chart2* worksheet)
   - A line chart of monthly average heart rate (in the *Chart3* worksheet)
   - A line chart of monthly average blood glucose level (in the *Chart4* worksheet)
   - A line chart of monthly total minutes of exercise (in the *Chart5* worksheet)
   - A line chart of average daily calorie intake for each meal across months (in the *Chart6* worksheet)

a. Create a data dashboard for Veronica by creating a new worksheet and naming it *Dashboard*; moving the charts from the *Chart1*, *Chart2*, *Chart3*, *Chart4*, *Chart5*, and *Chart6* worksheets to the *Dashboard* worksheet; and repositioning the charts on the *Dashboard* worksheet, adding a title to the dashboard, and doing whatever formatting and editing is necessary to make the dashboard functional and visually appealing.

b. Create a single slicer in the data dashboard you created in part a that filters day of the week for all charts on the dashboard. Once you have amended the data dashboard, rearrange the charts and slicers to create an effective and visually appealing dashboard. Test the slicer to ensure it works on the appropriate charts.

c. Create the new field Total Calories in column L of the *VeronicaData* Excel Table by summing Breakfast Calories, Lunch Calories, Dinner Calories, and Dessert Calories for each day. Refresh all PivotTables and PivotCharts, then add average daily total calories to the line chart of average daily calorie intake for each meal across months. Comment on the differences between the resulting dashboard and the dashboard from part b.

d. Protect the data dashboard in part c from being revised by users. Ensure that the slicer cannot be resized or moved, password protect the *Dashboard* worksheet (use the password Problem822), and hide all worksheets except the *Dashboard* worksheet.

23. **Building a Baseball Statistics Data Dashboard**. The Springfield Spiders, a baseball team in the All American Baseball Association, wants to create a data dashboard for its fans. Spiders management would like the fans to be able to review the runs scored and allowed by game and review the number of wins and losses and the average per game attendance by opponent and by day of the week. They would also like for the fans to be able to filter each of these displays by home and away games.

The Spiders have collected data on the date, opponent, whether the game was played at home or away, how many runs the Spiders scored, how many runs the Spiders allowed their opponent to score, whether the Spiders won or lost, and the attendance for each game of the previous season. They also added a field for the day of the week and have created the following charts for inclusion in its data dashboard. **LO 6**

CHART *file*

spider_chart

- A line chart of runs scored and runs allowed by game (in the *Chart1* worksheet)
- A clustered column chart of number of wins and losses by month (in the *Chart2* worksheet)
- A clustered bar chart of average per game attendance across months for home and away games (in the *Chart3* worksheet)
- A clustered bar chart of average per game attendance across days of the week for home and away games (in the *Chart4* worksheet)

a. Create a data dashboard for the Spiders by creating a new worksheet and naming it *Dashboard*; moving the charts from the *Chart1*, *Chart2*, *Chart3*, and *Chart4* worksheets to the *Dashboard* worksheet; and repositioning the charts on the *Dashboard* worksheet, adding a title to the dashboard, and doing whatever formatting and editing is necessary to make the dashboard functional and visually appealing.

b. Amend the data dashboard you created in part b in the following ways.
- Create a slicer to filter day of the week for the charts created in the *Chart1*, *Chart2*, *Chart3*, and *Chart4* worksheets
- Create a slicer to filter opponent for the charts created in the *Chart1*, *Chart2*, *Chart3*, and *Chart4* worksheets
- Create a slicer to filter month for the charts created in the *Chart1*, *Chart2*, *Chart3*, and *Chart4* worksheets
- Create a slicer to filter home and away games for the charts created in the *Chart1*, *Chart2*, *Chart3*, and *Chart4* worksheets

Once you have amended the data dashboard, rearrange the charts and slicers to create an effective and visually appealing dashboard. Test each slicer to ensure it works on the appropriate charts.

c. Create an alternative display of the Runs Scored and Runs Allowed by game through the following steps.

Step 1.   Create the new field Run Differential in Column I of the *SpidersData* table by subtracting Runs Allowed from Runs Scored for each game
Refresh all PivotTables and PivotCharts

Step 2.   Create a new worksheet and rename the worksheet *Chart1A*
Create a new pivot table and pivot chart in the *Chart1A* worksheet
Drag the **Date** field to the **Rows** area and the **Run Differential** field to the **Values** area in the **PivotFields Table** pane to create a column chart

Right click the horizontal axis and click **Format Axis...** to open the **Format Axis** pane, click the **Axis Options** button and click **Labels**, then select **Low** from the **Label Position** dropdown menu to position the horizontal axis at the bottom of the chart

While still in the **Format Axis** task pane, click the **Axis Options** button and click **Fill & Line**, then in the **Line** area, change the color of the axis to black and increase its width to 2 pt

Click any bar in the chart and click **Format Data Series**, click the **Fill & Line** button, and in the **Fill** area, click the **Invert if Negative** box and select the colors to be applied to the positive and negative bars

Step 3. Replace the line chart on the dashboard that was originally created in the *Chart1* worksheet with the chart you created in the *Chart1A* worksheet

Comment on differences between the resulting dashboard and the dashboard from part b.

d. Protect the data dashboard in part c from being revised by users. Ensure that the slicers cannot be resized or moved, password protect the *Dashboard* worksheet (use the password Problem823), and hide all worksheets except the *Dashboard* worksheet.

spidersnewdata

e. Data for the first month of the new season is available in the file *spidersnewdata*. Add this new data to the *SpidersData* table and delete the data for the previous season in the *SpidersData* table in the *Data* worksheet of the dashboard from part c so the dashboard displays only the new season data. What does the resulting data dashboard communicate? What alternative approach to incorporating the new data into the existing data dashboard would you suggest?

Chapter 8 Appendix

Appendix 8.1 Building a Data Dashboard with Power BI

In this appendix, we discuss how to build a dashboard in Power BI.

Let us consider an example involving Espléndido Jugo y Batido, Inc. (EJB), a company that manufactures bottled juices and smoothies. EJB produces its products in five fruit flavors (apple, grape, orange, pear, and tomato) and four vegetable flavors (beet, carrot, celery, and cucumber), and it ships these products from distribution centers (DCs) in Idaho, Mississippi, Nebraska, New Mexico, North Dakota, Rhode Island, and West Virginia. The file *ejb* contains 19,931 order records including the dollar amount sold, service satisfaction, and product satisfaction over the years 2018–2020.

We provide the steps required to build a sales dashboard for EJB that contains the following table and charts: a table of total sales and average delivery time for each flavor, a clustered bar chart for average delivery time by distribution center, a clustered column chart of sales by flavor and year, and total sales by month and year. Note that we will have to create a new variable called Time to Deliver, defined as the Date Delivered – Date Ordered. Finally, we also want to be able to filter the dashboard by category.

DATA*file*

ejb

Step 1. Following the steps outlined in Appendix 1.1, connect Power BI to the file *ejb*

We will first create a new variable called *Time to Deliver*.

Step 2. Click the **Table view** ⊞ on the left side of the canvas

Under the **Table tools** tab, click **New column** in the **Calculations** group

Next to **Column 1 =**, type *Data*, and select **Data[Date Delivered]**. Type one space, and type –, type a space, and then type *Data* and select **Data[Date Ordered]**
Press **Enter**
Click **Column tools** on the Ribbon, and in the **Structure** group, select **Whole number** from the dropdown menu next to **Data type**
When the **Data type change** dialog box appears, click **Yes** for **Do you want to continue?**
Right click the **Column** header, select **Rename**, and type *Time to Deliver*
Press **Enter**

The following steps build a matrix of total sales and average deliver time by flavor.

Step 3. On the left side of the canvas, click **Report view** 📊, and in the **Visualizations** pane, click **Build visual** to display the **Build visual** matrix of available charts

Select **Matrix** ⊞

In the **Data** pane, expand **Data** > ⊞ Data
Drag **Flavor** from the **Data** pane to the **Rows** box in the **Visualizations** pane

Drag **Category** from the **Data** pane to the **Columns** box in the **Visualizations** pane

Drag **Σ $ Sales** from the **Data** pane to the **Values** box in the **Visualizations** pane

Drag **Time to Deliver** from the **Data** pane to the **Values** box in the **Visualizations** pane

Step 4. In the **Values Box** in the **Visualizations** pane, right-click **Sum of Time to Deliver**, and select **Average**

In the **Values Box** in the **Visualizations** pane, right-click **Sum of $ Sales**, select **Rename for this visual**, and edit to read *$ Sales*

Click and drag the lower right-hand corner, and expand until all of the columns are revealed

The matrix appears in Figure P8.1

The following steps build a clustered bar chart of average time to deliver for each distribution center.

Step 1. Click the canvas. In the **Visualizations** pane, click **Build visual** ▦, and select **Clustered bar chart** 🗠

In the **Data** pane, expand **Data** ❭ ▦ Data

Drag **Distribution Center** from the **Data** pane to the **Y-axis** box in the **Visualizations** pane

Drag **Time to Deliver** from the **Data** pane to the **X-axis** box in the **Visualizations** pane

In the **X-axis** box in the **Visualizations** pane, right-click **Sum of Time to Deliver** and select **Average**

In the **Data** pane, expand **Date Ordered**, and expand **Date Hierarchy**

Drag **Year** from the **Data** pane to the **Legend** box in the **Visualizations** pane

Click the border of the chart, and expand and shape as needed

Step 2. In the **Visualizations** pane, click the **Format visual** button 🖌, and click **Visual**

Expand **X-axis**

Next to **Title**, toggle the **On** button `On●` to **Off**

Expand **Values**

Select **Calibri** as the **Font**, and collapse **Values**

Collapse **X-axis**

Figure P8.1	Matrix of $ Sales and Average Time to Deliver

| Category | Juices | | Smoothies | | Total | |
Flavor	$ Sales	Average of Time to Deliver	$ Sales	Average of Time to Deliver	$ Sales	Average of Time to Deliver
Apple	1,436,632.35	4.48	1,116,499.52	4.32	2,553,131.87	4.41
Beet	606,707.52	4.45	352,318.62	4.58	959,026.14	4.50
Carrot	1,110,232.99	4.34	932,670.17	4.42	2,042,903.16	4.38
Celery	724,256.93	4.81	826,358.09	4.31	1,550,615.02	4.55
Cucumber	1,080,530.73	4.32	899,259.39	4.38	1,979,790.12	4.35
Grape	1,269,622.16	4.41	1,007,050.22	4.30	2,276,672.38	4.36
Orange	1,740,004.28	4.44	1,387,955.21	4.38	3,127,959.49	4.41
Pear	1,278,248.10	4.44	1,021,063.64	4.47	2,299,311.74	4.45
Tomato	648,655.77	4.42	383,833.62	4.34	1,032,489.39	4.39
Total	**9,894,890.83**	**4.45**	**7,927,008.48**	**4.38**	**17,821,899.31**	**4.42**

Expand **Gridlines**
Next to **Vertical**, toggle the **On** button 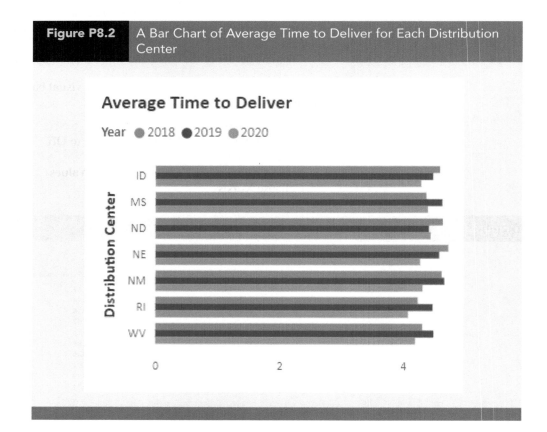 to **Off**
Collapse **Gridlines**

Step 3. In the **Visualizations** pane, click the **Format visual** button ⬇, and click **Visual**

Expand **Y-axis**, and expand **Title**
Select **Calibri** as the **Font**, and click the **Bold** button B
Collapse **Title**
Expand **Values**
Select **Calibri** as the **Font**
Collapse **Values**, and collapse **Y-axis**

Step 4. In the **Visualizations** pane, click the **Format visual** button ⬇, and click **Visual**

Expand **Legend**, and expand **Text**
Select **Calibri** as the **Font**
Collapse **Text**, and collapse **Legend**

Step 5. In the **Visualizations** pane to the right of **Visuals**, click **General**

Expand **Title**. Edit the **Text** box to read *Average Time to Deliver*
Select **Calibri** as the **Font**
Click the **Bold** button B
Collapse **Title**

The bar chart is shown in Figure P8.2.

Figure P8.2   A Bar Chart of Average Time to Deliver for Each Distribution Center

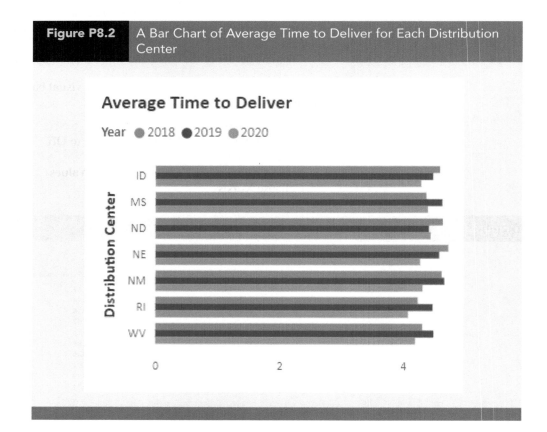

Next, we create a clustered column chart of sales by flavor and year.

> **Step 1.** Click the canvas. In the **Visualizations** pane, click **Build visual** ▦, and select
>
>   **Clustered column chart** ⬚
>
>   In the **Data** pane, expand **Data** > ▦ Data
>   Drag **Σ $ Sales** from the **Data** pane to the **Y-axis** box in the **Visualizations** pane
>   Drag **Category** from the **Data** pane to the **Legend** box in the **Visualizations** pane
>   Expand **Date Ordered**, and expand **Date Hierarchy**
>   Drag **Year** from the **Data** pane to the **X-axis** box in the **Visualizations** pane
>   Drag **Flavor** from the **Data** pane to the **X-axis** box in the **Visualizations** pane
>
> **Step 2.** In the **Visualizations** pane, click the **Format visual** button ⬚, and click **Visual**
>
>   Expand **X-axis**
>   Next to **Title**, toggle the **On** button `On●` to **Off**
>   Expand **Values**
>   Select **Calibri** as the **Font**, and collapse **Values**
>   Collapse **X-axis**
>
> **Step 3.** In the **Visualizations** pane, click the **Format visual** button ⬚, and click **Visual**
>
>   Expand **Y-axis**
>   Next to **Title**, toggle the **On** button `On●` to **Off**
>   Expand **Values**
>   Select **Calibri** as the **Font**
>   Collapse **Values**, and collapse **Y-axis**
>
> **Step 4.** In the **Visualizations** pane, click the **Format visual** button ⬚, and click **Visual**
>
>   Expand **Legend**
>   Expand **Text**
>   Select **Calibri** as the **Font**
>   Collapse **Text**, and collapse **Legend**
>
> **Step 5.** In the **Visualizations** pane, click the **Format visual** button ⬚, and click **Visual**
>
>   Expand **Gridlines**
>   Next to **Horizontal**, toggle the **On** button `On●` to **Off**
>
>   Next to **Vertical**, toggle the **On** button `On●` to **Off**
>   Collapse **Gridlines**
>
> **Step 6.** In the **Visualizations** pane, click the **Format visual** button ⬚, and click **General**
>
>   Expand **Title**
>   Edit the **Text** box to read *Annual Sales*
>   Select **Calibri** as the **Font**
>   Click the **Bold** button B
>   Collapse **Title**

The clustered column chart is shown in Figure P8.3.

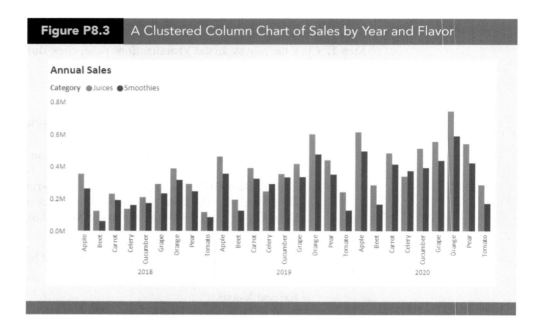

Figure P8.3   A Clustered Column Chart of Sales by Year and Flavor

The following steps build a line chart with monthly total sales by year and by category.

Step 1. Click the canvas. In the **Visualizations** pane, click **Build visual** ▦ , and select **Line chart** 〽️

> In the **Data** pane, expand **Data** ❯ ▦ Data
> Expand **Date Ordered**, and expand **Date Hierarchy**
> Drag **Year** from the **Data** pane to the **X-axis** box in the **Visualizations** pane
> Drag **Month** from the **Data** pane to the **X-axis** box in the **Visualizations** pane
> Drag **Σ $ Sales** from the **Data** pane to the **Y-axis** box in the **Visualizations** pane
> Drag **Category** from the **Data** pane to the **Legend** box in the **Visualizations** pane

Step 2. In the **Visualizations** pane, click the **Format visual** button ✍️ , and click **Visual**

> Expand **X-axis**
> Expand **Title**
> Select **Calibri** as the **Font**, and click the **Bold** button B
> Collapse **Title**
> Expand **Values**
> Select **Calibri** as the **Font**, and collapse **Values**
> Collapse **X-axis**

Step 3. In the **Visualizations** pane, click the **Format visual** button ✍️ , and click **Visual**

> Expand **Y-axis**
> Next to **Title**, toggle the **On** button On⬤ to **Off**
> Expand **Values**
> Select **Calibri** as the **Font**
> Collapse **Values**, and collapse **Y-axis**

Step 4. In the **Visualizations** pane, click the **Format visual** button, and click **Visual**

    Expand **Legend**
    Expand **Text**
    Select **Calibri** as the **Font**
    Collapse **Text**, and collapse **Legend**

Step 5. In the **Visualizations** pane, click the **Format visual** button, and click **Visual**

    Expand **Gridlines**
    Next to **Horizontal**, toggle the **On** button to **Off**

    Next to **Vertical**, toggle the **On** button to **Off**
    Collapse **Gridlines**

Step 6. In the **Visualizations** pane, click the **Format visual** button, and click **General**

    Expand **Title**. Edit the **Text** box to read *$ Sales*
    Select **Calibri** as the **Font**
    Click the **Bold** button B
    Collapse **Title**

The line chart is shown in Figure P8.4.
    Use the following steps to create a slicer for category and a title for the dashboard.

Step 1. Click the canvas. In the **Visualizations** pane, click Build visual, and select **Slicer**

    In the **Data** pane, expand **Data** > Data
    Drag **Category** from the **Data** pane to the **Field** box in the **Visualizations** pane

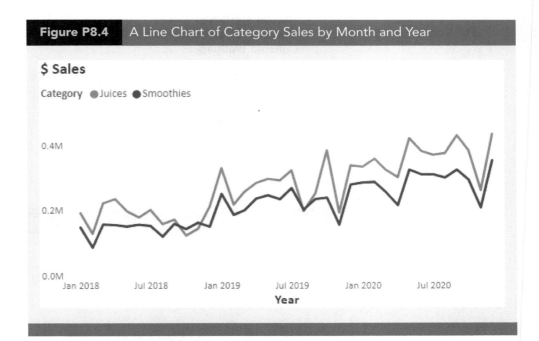

Figure P8.4   A Line Chart of Category Sales by Month and Year

Step 2. In the **Visualizations** pane, click the **Format visual** button ✍, and click
Visual

Expand **Values**

Choose **Calibri** as the **Font**

Collapse **Values**

Grab the border of the slicer and size, and move to the upper right corner of
the canvas

Step 3. Click the canvas

Click the **Insert** tab on the Ribbon in the **Elements** group, and click **Text**

$\boxed{\text{A}}$
Text
box box , which results in the dialog box shown in Figure P8.5

Click inside the box on the left, and type *Espléndido Jugo y Batido Inc.
Sales Dashboard*

Highlight *Espléndido Jugo y Batido Inc. Sales Dashboard*, and select

Calibri as the font, **28** as the font size, and click the italics button *I*

Click **Center** ▤ to center the dashboard title

Expand the text box by grabbing the edges to get the shape that reveals the
entire title, and move it to the top of the canvas

Step 4. In the **Format** pane on the right, click **General**

Expand **Effects** and expand **Background**

Choose a light blue color for **Color**

Collapse **Background**, and collapse **Effects**

To select a background color for the canvas of the dashboard and put a border on each
chart:

Step 5. Click the canvas. In the **Visualizations** pane on the right, click the

Format page button 🖉

Expand **Wallpaper**

Choose a dark blue color for **Color**

Collapse **Wallpaper**

For each chart (and the matrix, slicer, and title) to create a consistent border:

Step 6. Click the chart (or matrix, slicer, or title)

In the **Visualizations** pane, click the **Format visual** button ✍

Click **General**

Expand **Effects**, and expand **Visual border**

Figure P8.5	The Text Box Dialog Box

Figure P8.6 The Completed EJB Sales Dashboard

ejbdashboard.pbix

Toggle the **Off** button ⬤Off to **On**
Choose black as the **Color**
Set **Rounded corners** to **5 px**
Collapse **Visual border**, and collapse **Effects**

By clicking on each object in the canvas, shaping as needed, and moving it to the appropriate location, position the elements of the dashboard as shown in Figure P8.6.

The slicer in the upper right-hand corner of the dashboard allows the user to filter the data to show data only for one of the categories. For example, choosing **Smoothies** in the slicer creates the results shown in Figure P8.7.

Figure P8.7 The EJB Sales Dashboard Filtering on Smoothies

The dashboard also allows the user to drill down by clicking on a piece of any visual, and all visuals will adjust to just the piece selected. For example, if in the Average Time to Deliver bar chart, the user clicks on the ID 2019 bar, the other charts in the dashboard will adjust based on the value selected. This case is shown in Figure P8.8. The matrix now displays values for sales only at the ID Distribution Center in 2019. These sales are also highlighted in the Annual Sales clustered column chart, and the $ Sales line chart only shows sales over time from the ID Distribution Center in 2019.

Figure P8.8   The EJB Dashboard with a Drill Down on ID and 2019

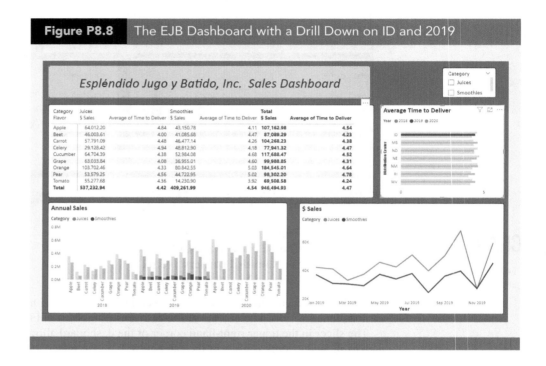

Appendix 8.2 Building a Data Dashboard with Tableau

In this appendix, we discuss how to build a dashboard in Tableau.

Let us consider an example involving Espléndido Jugo y Batido, Inc. (EJB), a company that manufactures bottled juices and smoothies. EJB produces its products in five fruit flavors (apple, grape, orange, pear, and tomato) and four vegetable flavors (beet, carrot, celery, and cucumber), and it ships these products from distribution centers (DCs) in Idaho, Mississippi, Nebraska, New Mexico, North Dakota, Rhode Island, and West Virginia. The file *ejb* contains 19,931 order records including the dollar amount sold, service satisfaction, and product satisfaction over the years 2018–2020.

We provide the steps required to build a sales dashboard for EJB that contains the following table and charts: a table of total sales and average delivery time for each flavor, a clustered bar chart for average delivery time by distribution center, a clustered column chart of sales by flavor and year, and total sales by month and year. Note that we will have to create a new variable called Time to Deliver, defined as the Date Delivered – Date Ordered. Finally, we also want to be able to filter the dashboard by category.

DATA *file*

ejb

Step 1. Following the steps outlined in Appendix 1.2, connect Tableau to the file *ejb*
Click the **Sheet 1** tab at the bottom of the Tableau Data Source screen to open the worksheet view.

We will first create a new variable called *Time to Deliver*.

Step 2. Right click in the **Data** pane, and select **Create Calculated Field….** When the dialog box opens:
Type *Time to Deliver* as the title of the field
Drag the pill for **Date Delivered** from the **Data** pane to the dialog box
Type a minus sign, **-** , in the dialog box
Drag the pill for **Date Ordered** from the **Data** pane to the dialog box
(see Figure T8.1)
Click **Apply** in the dialog box
Click **OK** to close the dialog box

The result of step 2 is a new column in the data file called "Time to Deliver" that calculates the difference between the date delivered and the date ordered in days.

Figure T8.1	Dialog Box to Create New Field of Time to Deliver

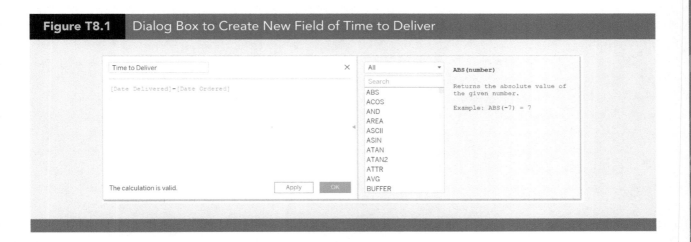

The following steps build a matrix of total sales and average time to deliver by flavor.

Step 3. Drag the pill for **Category** from the **Data** pane to the **Columns** shelf, and drag the pill for **Flavor** from the **Data** pane to the **Rows** shelf

Step 4. Drag the pill for **$ Sales** from the **Data** pane to the body of the table, and drag the pill for **Time to Deliver** from the **Data** pane to the body of the table

Step 5. Right click on the pill for **SUM(Time to Deliver)** in the **Measure Values** area, select **Measure (Sum)**, and click **Average**

Step 6. Right click the pill for **Avg (Time to Deliver)** and select **Format…**. When the **Format AVG(Time to Deliver)** pane appears:

Select **Number (Custom)** for **Numbers** under **Default**

Set **Decimal Places** to **2**

Click ✕ to close the **Format AVG(Time to Deliver)** pane

Step 7. Move the pill for **Measure Names** from the **Rows** shelf to the **Columns** shelf

Step 8. Click the **Analysis** tab on the Ribbon, click **Totals**, and select **Show Column Grand Totals**

Step 9. To modify the column title, right click the **Avg. Time to Deliver** title, and select **Format…**. When the **Format Measure Names** pane appears:

Click next to **Alignment:** under **Default**, and select the button for **On** under **Wrap**

Step 10. To remove the title of the chart, right click on **Sheet 1** at the top of the chart and select **Hide Title**

The resulting table appears in Figure T8.2.

Figure T8.2   Table of $ Sales and Average Time to Deliver for EJB Data

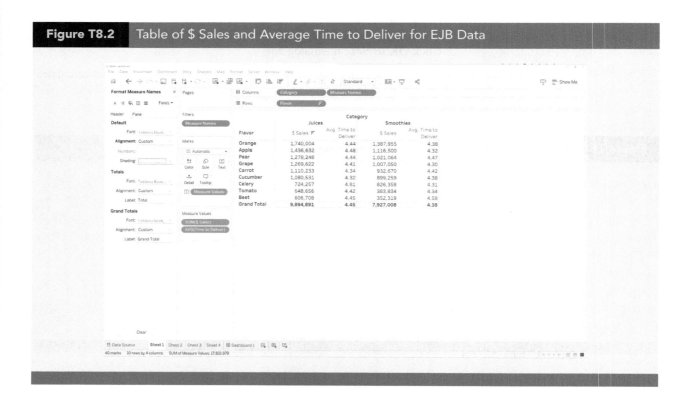

The following steps build a clustered bar chart of average time to deliver for each distribution center. In step 1, we first create a new Worksheet for this new visualization.

Step 1. Click the **Worksheet** tab on the Ribbon, and select **New Worksheet**

Step 1 creates a new **worksheet** in Tableau with the title "Sheet 2."

Step 2. In the new Worksheet, drag the pill for **Time to Deliver** from the **Data** pane to the **Columns** Shelf
Right click the pill for **SUM(Time to Deliver)** in the **Columns** shelf, select **Measure (Sum)**, and click **Average**

Step 3. Drag the pill for **Distribution Center** from the **Data** pane to the **Rows** shelf, and drag the pill for **Date Ordered** from the **Data** pane to the **Rows** shelf

Step 4. Click the dropdown arrow in the **Marks** area and change the visualization type to **Bar**

Step 5. Drag the pill for **Date Ordered** from the **Data** pane to the **Color** card Color in the **Marks** area

Step 6. To change the colors used for the bar chart, right click the legend, and **select Edit Colors…**. When the **Edit Colors [Year of Date Ordered]** dialog box appears:
Set the **Select Color Palette:** by clicking the dropdown arrow and selecting **Blue** Blue
Click the **Assign Palette** button
Click **OK** to close the **Edit Colors [Year of Date Ordered]** dialog box

Step 7. To edit the title of the chart, right click **Sheet 2** at the top of the chart and select **Edit Title…**. When the **Edit Title** dialog box appears:
Replace **<Sheet Name>** with *Average Time to Deliver*
Highlight the text of the title, then change the font size to **16**, and click the **Bold** button β to make the title bold font
Click **OK** to close the **Edit Title** dialog box

Step 8. To hide the unnecessary legend, click the dropdown arrow in the upper right of the legend and select **Hide Card**

The completed bar chart appears in Figure T8.3.
Next, we create a clustered column chart of sales by flavor and year.

Step 1. Click the **Worksheet** tab on the Ribbon, and select **New Worksheet**

Step 1 creates a new worksheet in Tableau with the title "Sheet 3."

Step 2. Drag the pill for **Date Ordered** from the **Data** pane to the **Columns** shelf, drag the pill for **Flavor** from the **Data** pane to the **Columns** shelf, and drag the pill for **Category** from the **Data** pane to the **Columns** shelf.

Step 3. Drag the pill for **$ Sales** from the **Data** pane to the **Rows** shelf

Step 4. Drag the pill for **Category** from the **Data** pane to the **Color** card Color in the **Marks** area

Step 5. To remove the unnecessary category labels, right click the category labels at the bottom of the chart and deselect **Show Header**

Step 6. To remove the unnecessary horizontal axis title, right click **Date Ordered / Flavor** at the top of the chart and select **Hide Field Labels for Columns**

Step 7. To edit the flavor labels, right click one of the flavor labels at the top of the chart (e.g., **Apple**), and select **Rotate Label**

Figure T8.3   Bar Chart of Average Time to Deliver for Each Distribution Center for EJB Data

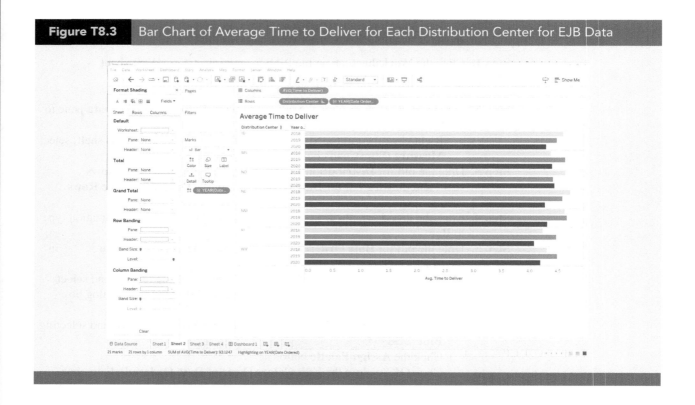

Step 8. To edit the title of the chart, right click **Sheet 3** at the top of the chart and select **Edit Title…**. When the **Edit Title** dialog box appears:
Replace **<Sheet Name>** with *Annual Sales*
Highlight the text of the title, then change the font size to **16**, and click the **Bold** button Β to make the title bold font
Click **OK** to close the **Edit Title** dialog box

Step 9. To edit the title of the legend, right click on the legend in the upper right of the chart and select **Edit Title…**. When the **Edit Legend Title** dialog box appears:
Highlight the text of the title, then change the font size to **11**, and click the **Bold** button Β to make the title bold font
Click **OK** to close the **Edit Title** dialog box

Step 10. To remove the unnecessary horizontal grid lines in the chart, right click on the chart and select **Format…**. When the **Format Font** task pane opens, click on the **Lines** button ≡ and select **None** next to **Grid Lines:** to remove the grid lines in the chart

The completed clustered column chart appears in Figure T8.4.
The following steps build a line chart with monthly total sales by year and by category.

Step 1. Click the **Worksheet** tab on the Ribbon, and select **New Worksheet**

Step 1 creates a new worksheet in Tableau with the title "Sheet 4."

Step 2. Drag the pill for **Date Ordered** from the **Data** pane to the **Columns** shelf
Right click the pill for **YEAR(Date Ordered)** in the **Columns** shelf and select **Month   May 2015**

Step 2 formats the horizontal axis to contain values by month.

Figure T8.4   Clustered Column Chart of Sales by Year and Flavor for EJB Data

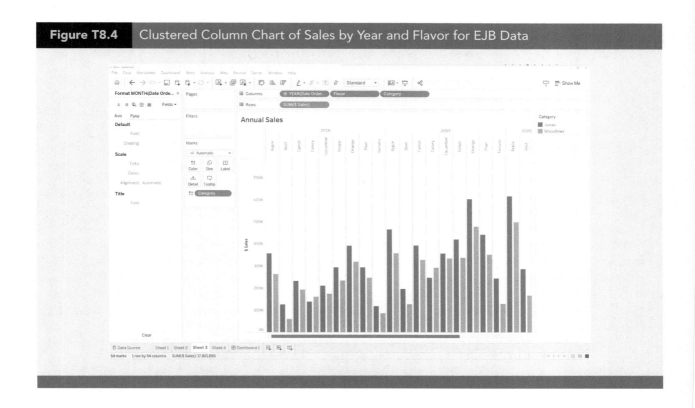

Step 3. Drag the pill for **$ Sales** from the **Data** pane to the **Rows** shelf

Step 4. Drag the pill for **Category** from the **Data** pane to the **Color** card ⬚ Color in the **Marks** area

Step 5. To edit the title of the horizontal axis, right click **Month of Date Ordered** at the bottom of the chart, and select **Edit Axis…**. When the **Edit Axis [Month of Date Ordered]** dialog box appears:

Select **Custom** under **Axis Titles** and change the title to *Date Ordered*

Click ✕ to close the **Edit Axis [Month of Date Ordered]** dialog box

Step 6. To remove the unnecessary chart title, right click **Sheet 4** at the top of the chart and select **Hide Title**

Step 7. To remove the unnecessary grid lines in the chart, right click on the chart and select **Format…**. When the **Format** task pane opens, click on the **Lines** button

☰ and select **None** next to **Grid Lines:** to remove the grid lines in the chart

The completed line chart appears in Figure T8.5.

The following steps create a dashboard using the charts created previously.

Step 1. Click the **Dashboard** tab on the Ribbon, and select **New Dashboard**

Step 1 opens a new tab in Tableau called "Dashboard 1" (see Figure T8.6). Note the area at the top right of the Dashboard pane in Figure T8.6 that includes the Device Preview button ⬚ Device Preview . This allows you to view how the dashboard will appear on different screens, including on a phone.

Step 2. Select the **Tiled** button at the bottom left of the **Dashboard 1** tab under **Objects**

Selecting **Tiled** in step 2 allows Tableau to automatically position the visualizations in the specific areas in the dashboard canvas called "containers." Selecting **Floating** allows the user to drag the visualizations anywhere in the dashboard canvas.

Figure T8.5   Line Chart of Category Sales by Month for EJB Data

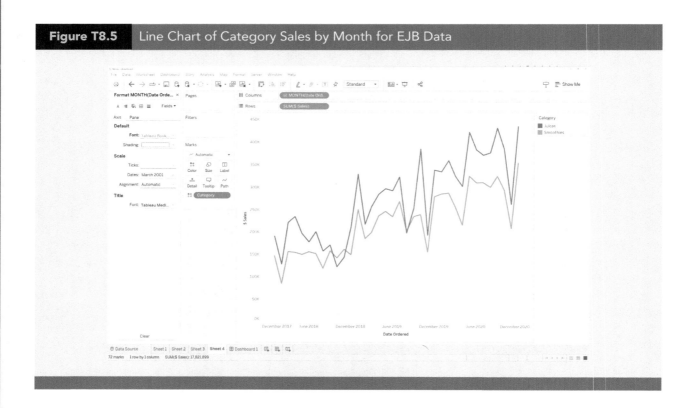

Figure T8.6   New Dashboard Tab in Tableau

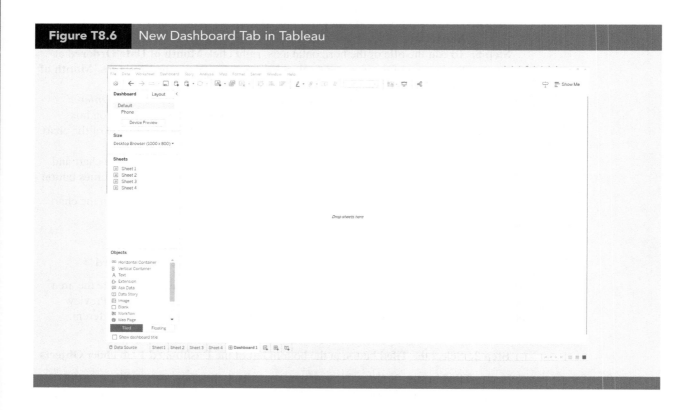

When dragging a sheet into the canvas, the container into which the sheet will be dropped is shaded. Dragging to different areas of the canvas will select (shade) different containers.

Step 3. Drag **Sheet 1** from the **Sheets** area to the top left container of the canvas that says *Drop sheets here*

Step 4. Drag **Sheet 2** from the **Sheets** area to the top right container of the canvas

Step 5. Drag **Sheet 3** from the **Sheets** area to the bottom left container of the canvas

Step 6. Drag **Sheet 4** from the **Sheets** area to the bottom right container of the canvas

Step 7. To add a title for the dashboard, drag **Text**  from the **Objects** area at the bottom left of the screen to the top container of the canvas. When the **Edit Text** dialog box appears:

*To create the é character in the dashboard title, use the alt code for this character by pressing the **ALT** key, and typing **0232** while holding down the **ALT** key.*

  Type *Espléndido Jugo y Batido, Inc. Sales Dashboard*
  Highlight the text of the title, then change the font size to **20**, click the
  Bold button B to make the title bold font, and click the **Center** button
  to center the text
  Click **OK** to close the **Edit Title** dialog box
  Resize the dashboard title by dragging the border to the appropriate size

Step 8. Move the legend for **Category** by right clicking on legend, and selecting **Floating**
  Drag the **Category** legend into the line chart in the Canvas
  Remove the container where the **Category** legend was located by right clicking in this area and selecting **Remove Container**

Step 9. Resize the charts in the dashboard for best readability by dragging the borders separating charts

Step 10. Click the **Window** tab on the Ribbon, and select **Presentation Mode** to view the dashboard in full screen

CHART *file*

ejbdashboard.twbx

Figure T8.7 shows the completed dashboard.

Figure T8.7	Completed EJB Sales Dashboard

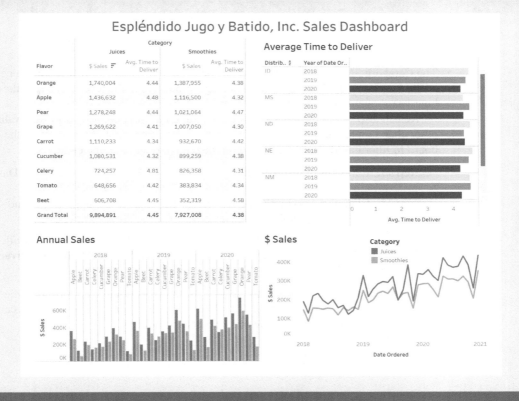

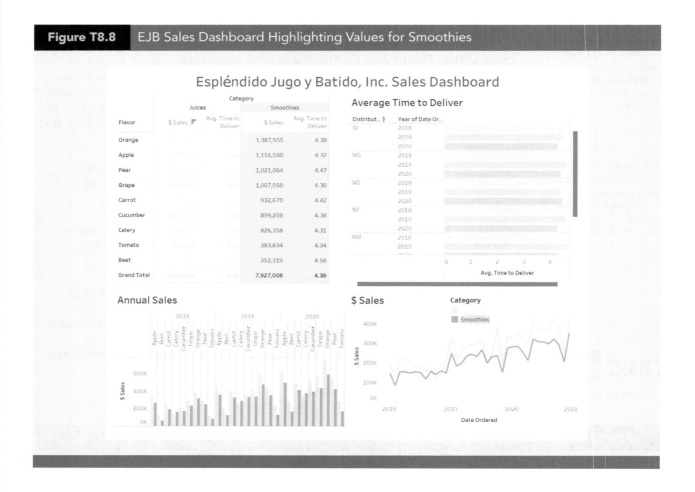

The Category legend in the line chart can be used to highlight values for the Juices or the Smoothies category. For example, choosing **Smoothies** in the legend changes the dashboard as shown in Figure T8.8.

We can also set up the dashboard so clicking on a value in one chart filters values in all other charts on the dashboard. The following steps demonstrate how to set up the dashboard to filter based on values chosen in the bar chart and the line chart.

Step 11. Exit **Presentation Mode** by pressing the **ESC** key to return to the Dashboard 1 tab

Step 12. Click the **Average Time to Deliver** bar chart in the upper right, and select the **Filter** button ▽ to the right of the bar chart

Step 13. Click the **Window** tab on the Ribbon, and select **Presentation Mode**

Step 14. Click **ID** under **Distribution Center** in the **Average Time to Deliver** bar chart

Step 14 filters the other charts in the dashboard to display only data related to the ID distribution center as shown in Figure T8.9. Clicking values for other distribution centers or years in the bar chart will filter the other charts accordingly.

Figure T8.9 EJB Sales Dashboard Filtered for Values Related to ID Distribution Center

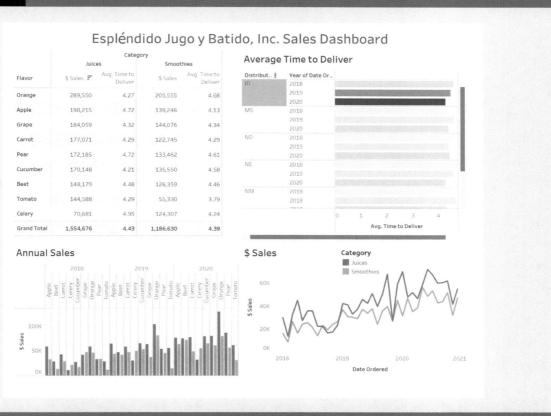

Chapter 9

Telling the Truth with Data Visualization

Contents

Learning Objectives

After completing this chapter, you will be able to

LO 1   Identify missing data and data errors using Excel.

LO 2   Define the meaning of biased data and explain the concepts of selection bias and survivor bias.

LO 3   Define Simpson's paradox and explain how a scatter chart can be used to identify some instances of Simpson's paradox.

LO 4   Explain the importance of adjusting for inflation in time series data that represent long time periods and use a price index to adjust nominal values to account for inflation.

LO 5   Identify deceptive design practices related to the axes used in charts and suggest ways to improve the axes in these charts to communicate insights to the audience more clearly.

LO 6   Explain why dual-axis charts are often confusing and misleading for audiences and suggest an alternative to using a dual-axis chart that is less confusing for the audience.

LO 7   Explain how the range of data and the temporal frequency of data included in a chart affects the insights conveyed to the audience.

LO 8   Explain why some geographic maps can result in misleading data visualizations and provide recommendations for how to improve these types of maps.

Top-10 Movies of All Time

Many lists of the top movies of all time can be found on the Internet. Some of these lists are subjective and based on movie ratings or opinions. Other lists are based on quantitative data such as revenues earned, tickets sold, or profit generated. Box Office Mojo is a website that collects data on box office revenue and makes these data available to the public. Box Office Mojo is owned by the Amazon.com subsidiary IMDb. The website boxofficemojo.com contains a great deal of data for movies and box office revenue. The website continuously tracks the top movies based on box office revenue, and it has collected data for many movies made in the United States over the last 100 years.

Figure 9.1 shows the all-time[1] top-10 movies made in the United States based on box office revenues earned by movies in North American theaters. In Figure 9.1, the horizontal axis shows the year the movie was released, and the vertical axis shows the total box office gross revenue earned in North America. Interestingly, we see that all of the top-10 movies were made recently; the oldest movie in the top 10 is *Titanic*, which was released in 1997. The nine other movies shown here were released since 2009.

Based on Figure 9.1, we might conclude that the most recent years have produced all of the top movies in terms of greatest box office revenue in North America. From this figure, it appears that movies prior to 1997 were not as popular at the box office as movies in recent years.

In examining the design of Figure 9.1, we see few obvious errors. The chart has an explanatory title, the axes are well labeled, there is no obvious evidence of clutter, and the chart is relatively simple with a high data-ink ratio. However, we still must take great care in interpreting this chart. A common problem arises when examining monetary units such as revenues, costs, or profits at different points of time. This is because $500,000 earned in box office revenue in 1951 is different than $500,000 earned in box office revenue in 2020. This difference is due to inflation. According to IMDb,[2] the average price of a movie ticket in 1951 was $0.53, while the average

Figure 9.1   Scatter Chart Showing the Top-10 Movies of All Time Based on Lifetime North America Box Office Gross Revenues

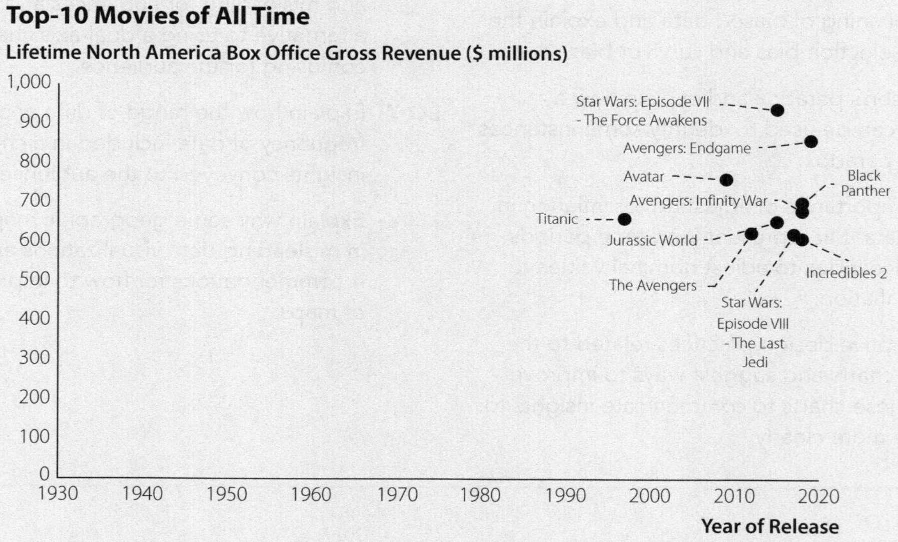

Top-10 Movies of All Time

Lifetime North America Box Office Gross Revenue ($ millions)

Figure 9.2 Scatter Chart Showing the Top-10 Movies of All Time Based on Inflation-Adjusted Lifetime North America Box Office Gross Revenue

Top-10 Movies of All Time

Lifetime North America Box Office Gross Revenue, Adjusted for Inflation ($ millions)

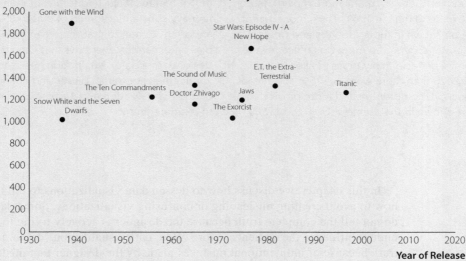

price of a movie ticket in 2020 was $9.37. Therefore, to earn $500,000 in revenue in 1951, a movie would need to sell $500,000 / $0.53 = 943,396 tickets at the box office. To earn $500,000 in revenue in 2020, a movie would only need to sell $500,000 / $9.37 = 53,362 tickets. In other words, selling 5.6% as many tickets for a movie in 2020 as a movie in 1951 generates the same amount of box office revenue. This means it is difficult for older movies to appear on this chart of top-10 movies because older movies would have to sell many more tickets at the box office than more recent movies. This effectively biases our data to more heavily weight box office ticket sales of newer movies.

To help remove the bias in these data, we can measure the top-10 movies of all time based on *inflation-adjusted* box office gross revenue. Later in this chapter, we will explain in more detail how to adjust for inflation, but for now we explain the concept as simply that we measure the box office gross revenue in terms of 2020 dollars. This allows us to compare movies released in different years as if all the box office revenue was earned in the year 2020. Figure 9.2 shows the top-10 movies based on inflation-adjusted box office gross revenue.

From Figure 9.2, we see that many older movies generated some of the highest values of box office gross revenue in North America after adjusting for

inflation. *Gone with the Wind*, which was released in 1939, actually generated the all-time highest box office gross revenue in North America when we adjust for inflation. We also see from Figure 9.2 that no movie released after the year 2000 is in the top 10 of box office gross revenue after adjusting for inflation. Comparing Figure 9.1 to Figure 9.2, we see that only one movie, *Titanic*, which was released in 1997, appears in both figures.

Figures 9.1 and 9.2 illustrate the importance of adjusting for inflation when visualizing monetary values that occurred at different points of time. It is generally not important to adjust for inflation when all monetary values are from similar time periods (usually within a few years), but failing to adjust for inflation when monetary values occur across wide spans of time can produce extremely biased visualizations. The insight provided by Figure 9.1 is that all of the highest box office revenue producing movies were released fairly recently, with only one movie in the top 10 being released prior to the year 2000. However, by showing values adjusted for inflation, Figure 9.2 provides a drastically different insight—all of the top-10 highest box office revenue producing memories were released prior to the year 2000.

It is also important to note that inflation is only one potential cause of bias for these data. When

(continued)

comparing data from different points in time, there are many other factors that could affect the data. For instance, the population of North America has increased substantially between 1951 and 2020. As the population has increased, so has the number of movie theaters. This means there are many more movie theaters in existence in 2020 than in 1951. Thus, more recent movies can be shown in more theaters and possibly sell more tickets to generate more box office revenue. However, there are also many more movies being released in 2020 than there were in 1951. This means that there is more competition and more movies competing to be shown in the theaters. Until the 1950s, movies also did not have meaningful competition for an audience from television. The COVID-19 pandemic also contributed to changes in viewers' movie-watching habits, and many more people now expect to watch new release movies at home rather than in a movie theater. Adjusting for inflation removes one potentially substantial source of bias in the data, but it is important to realize that there can be other sources of bias and changes over time that can affect data. The designer of a data visualization needs to consider the impact these potential biases and changes may have on their visualization and what steps should be taken to mitigate them.

In this chapter, we discuss how to design data visualizations to tell the truth and how to avoid creating misleading or confusing visualizations. Some data visualizations do not tell the complete truth because the designer is actively trying to mislead or unduly influence the audience. More often, data visualizations do not tell the complete truth because of unintentional mistakes made by the designer that mislead or cause confusion for the audience. As shown in the Data Visualization Makeover for this chapter, considerations as simple as not adjusting for inflation can completely change the resulting data visualization and the insights drawn from the visualization. The issues covered in this chapter will help you create data visualizations that are clear and truthful for the audience.

All data visualizations begin with data. If we use wrong, incomplete, or biased data, then our visualization will not tell the complete truth. Therefore, we begin this chapter by talking about common issues with data, such as missing data and biased data, that can cause misleading or confusing data visualizations. We discuss deceptive data visualization designs that should be avoided when creating visualizations. These deceptive designs often involve improper choices related to the design of chart axes or choices on which data to include in the visualization. We also discuss issues that can arise when creating geographic maps, and we provide recommendations for how to avoid misleading charts when creating these types of maps.

9.1 Missing Data and Data Errors

Many real-life data sets suffer from missing data values and data errors. There are many reasons why data sets may contain missing values and data errors, and it is important to understand the reasons behind the missing values to know how they should be treated. Removing or replacing missing data values and errors in data affects all subsequent analysis of that data, including the creation of data visualizations. In this section, we examine some common methods of identifying missing data and data errors, and we discuss methods for dealing with missing data and data errors.

Types of missing data are discussed in Chapter 6.

Identifying Missing Data

Consider the case of Blakely Tires, a producer of automobile tires located in the United States. In an attempt to learn about the conditions of its tires on automobiles in the state of Texas, the company has obtained information for each of the four tires from 116 automobiles with Blakely brand tires that have been collected through recent state automobile inspection facilities in Texas. The data obtained by Blakely includes the position of the tire on the automobile (left front, left rear, right front, right rear), age of the tire, mileage on the tire, and depth of the remaining tread on the tire. Before Blakely management attempts to learn more about its tires on automobiles in Texas, it wants to assess the quality of these data. The first few rows of the data collected by Blakely are shown in Figure 9.3.

The tread depth of a tire is a vertical measurement between the top of the tread rubber to the bottom of the tire's deepest grooves, and it is measured in 32nds of an inch in the United States. New Blakely brand tires have a tread depth of 10/32nds of an inch, and a tire's tread depth is considered insufficient if it is 2/32nds of an inch or less. Shallow tread depth is dangerous as it results in poor traction and makes steering the automobile more difficult. Blakely's tires generally last for four to five years or 40,000 to 60,000 miles.

We begin assessing the quality of these data by determining which (if any) observations have missing values for any of the variables in the Blakely Tires data. We can do so using Excel's COUNTBLANK function. The following steps show how to count the missing observations for each variable in the file *blakelytires*.

DATA *file*

blakelytires

Step 1. Enter the heading *# of Missing Values* in cell G2
Step 2. Enter the heading *Life of Tire (Months)* in cell H1, the heading *Tread Depth* in cell I1, and the heading *Miles* in cell J1
Step 3. Enter the formula *=COUNTBLANK(C2:C457)* in cell H2
Copy cell H2 to cells I2 and J2

The result in cell H2 shows that none of the observations in these data is missing its value for Life of Tire. By repeating this process for the remaining quantitative variables in the data (Tread Depth and Miles) in columns I and J, we determine that there are no missing values for Tread Depth and one missing value for Miles. The first few rows of the resulting Excel spreadsheet are provided in Figure 9.4.

Next, we sort all of Blakely's data on Miles from smallest to largest value to determine which observation is missing its value of this variable. Excel's sort procedure will list all observations with missing values for the sort variable, Miles, as the last observations in the sorted data.

Figure 9.3   Portion of Excel Spreadsheet Showing Blakely Tires Data

	A	B	C	D	E
1	ID Number	Position on Automobile	Life of Tire (Months)	Tread Depth	Miles
2	13391487	LR	58.4	2.2	2805
3	21678308	LR	17.3	8.3	39371
4	18414311	RR	16.5	8.6	13367
5	19778103	RR	8.2	9.8	1931
6	16355454	RR	13.7	8.9	23992
7	8952817	LR	52.8	3	48961
8	6559652	RR	14.7	8.8	4585
9	16289814	LR	6.2	10.1	5221

Figure 9.4 Portion of Excel Spreadsheet Showing Number of Missing Values for Variables in Blakely Tires Data

	A	B	C	D	E	F	G	H	I	J
1	ID Number	Position on Automobile	Life of Tire (Months)	Tread Depth	Miles			Life of Tire (Months)	Tread Depth	Miles
2	13391487	LR	58.4	2.2	2805		Number Missing Values	=COUNTBLANK(C2:C457)	=COUNTBLANK(D2:D457)	=COUNTBLANK(E2:E457)
3	21678308	LR	17.3	8.3	39371					
4	18414311	RR	16.5	8.6	13367					
5	19778103	RR	8.2	9.8	1931					
6	16355454	RR	13.7	8.9	23992					
7	8952817	LR	52.8	3	48961					
8	6559652	RR	14.7	8.8	4585					
9	16289814	LR	6.2	10.1	5221					

	A	B	C	D	E	F	G	H	I	J
1	ID Number	Position on Automobile	Life of Tire (Months)	Tread Depth	Miles			Life of Tire (Months)	Tread Depth	Miles
2	13391487	LR	58.4	2.2	2805		Number Missing Values	0	0	1
3	21678308	LR	17.3	8.3	39371					
4	18414311	RR	16.5	8.6	13367					
5	19778103	RR	8.2	9.8	1931					
6	16355454	RR	13.7	8.9	23992					
7	8952817	LR	52.8	3.0	48961					
8	6559652	RR	14.7	8.8	4585					
9	16289814	LR	6.2	10.1	5221					

Chapter 6 provides step-by-step directions for how to use Excel's Conditional Formatting tool to find missing values.

We can also use the Excel Conditional Formatting tool to quickly explore the data and use visualization to help us identify any missing values. Figure 9.5 indicates that the value of Miles is missing from the left front tire of the automobile with ID Number 3354942. Because only one of the 456 observations is missing its value for Miles, we may be able to salvage this observation by logically determining a reasonable value to substitute for this missing value. It is sensible to assume that the value of Miles for the left front tire of the automobile with the ID Number 3354942 would be identical to the value of miles for the other three tires on this automobile, so we sort all the data on ID number and highlight data values with ID Number 3354942 to find the four tires that belong to this automobile (see Figure 9.6).

Figure 9.5 Using Excel Conditional Formatting Tool to Highlight Missing Values in Blakely Tires Data

	A	B	C	D	E
19	12277878	LF	8.1	9.8	2390
20	20420626	RF	24.4	6.6	672
21	1383349	RF	25.9	7.1	6094
22	21514254	LR	17.8	8.3	5161
23	10363514	RR	31.9	6.2	57694
24	6427178	RR	13.3	9	6858
25	11980523	LF	21.3	7.8	28108
26	6465679	RR	18.4	8.3	43751
27	11320872	RR	12.9	9.1	27143
28	9091771	RF	1.8	10.8	2917
29	3354942	LF	17.1	8.5	
30	19783520	RR	45	4.2	356
31	10363514	RF	31.9	6.3	57694

Figure 9.6	Portion of Excel Spreadsheet Showing Blakely Tires Data Sorted from Lowest to Highest by ID Number with ID 3354942 Highlighted

	A	B	C	D	E
52	2253516	LF	26.2	7.1	55231
53	2253516	RR	26.2	7.1	55231
54	3121851	LR	17.1	8.4	21378
55	3121851	RR	17.1	8.4	21378
56	3121851	RF	17.1	8.4	21378
57	3121851	LF	17.1	8.5	21378
58	3354942	LF	17.1	8.5	
59	3354942	RF	21.4	7.7	33254
60	3354942	RR	21.4	7.8	33254
61	3354942	LR	21.4	7.7	33254
62	3574739	RR	73.3	0.2	57313

Figure 9.6 shows that the value of Miles for the other three tires on the automobile with the ID Number 3354942 is 33,254, so this may be a reasonable value for the Miles of the left front tire of the automobile with the ID Number 3354942. However, before substituting this value for the missing value of the left front tire of the automobile with ID Number 3354942, we should attempt to ascertain (if possible) that this value is valid—there are legitimate reasons why a driver might replace a single tire. In this instance, we will assume that the correct value of Miles for the left front tire on the automobile with ID Number 3354942 is 33,254 and substitute that number in the appropriate cell of the spreadsheet.

Identifying Data Errors

Many data sets include errors. These errors could be introduced because of manual entry mistakes, miscalibration of sensors that automatically collect data, or a variety of other reasons. Examining the variables in the data set by use of summary statistics, frequency distributions, histograms, scatter charts, and other tools can uncover data quality issues and outliers. For example, finding the minimum or maximum value for Tread Depth in the Blakely Tires data may reveal unrealistic values—perhaps even negative values—for Tread Depth, which would indicate a problem for the value of Tread Depth for any such observation.

It is important to note here that many software, including Excel, ignore missing values when calculating various summary statistics such as the mean, standard deviation, minimum, and maximum. However, if missing values in a data set are indicated with a unique value (such as 9999999), these values may be used by software when calculating various summary statistics such as the mean, standard deviation, minimum, and maximum. Both cases can result in misleading values for summary statistics, which is why many analysts prefer to deal with missing data issues prior to using summary statistics to attempt to identify erroneous outliers and other erroneous values in the data.

We again consider the Blakely Tires data. We calculate the mean and standard deviation of each variable (age of the tire, mileage on the tire, and depth of the remaining tread on the tire) to assess whether the values of these variables are reasonable in general.

Return to the file *blakelytires,* and complete the following steps:

Step 1. Enter the heading *Mean* in cell G3
　　　　　Enter the formula *=AVERAGE(C2:C457)* in cell H3
　　　　　Copy cell H3 to cells I3 and J3
Step 2. Enter the heading *Standard Deviation* in cell G4
　　　　　Enter the formula *=STDEV.S(C2:C457)* in cell H4
　　　　　Copy cell H4 to cells I4 and J4

The results in cells H3 and H4 show that the mean and standard deviation for the life of tires are 23.8 months and 31.83 months, respectively. These values appear to be reasonable for the life of tires in months. The mean and standard deviation for tread depth are 7.64/12ths of an inch and 2.51/12ths of an inch, respectively, and the mean and standard deviation for miles are 25,834.54 and 24,143.38, respectively. These values appear to be reasonable for tread depth and miles. The results of this analysis are provided in Figure 9.7.

While the summary statistics of mean and standard deviation are helpful in providing an aggregate perspective on the data, we also need to attempt to determine if there are any erroneous individual values for our three variables. We start by finding the minimum and maximum values for each variable. Return again to the file *blakelytires,* and complete the following steps:

Step 3. Enter the heading *Minimum* in cell G5
　　　　　Enter the formula *=MIN(C2:C457)* in cell H5
　　　　　Copy cell H5 to cells I5 and J5
Step 4. Enter the heading *Maximum* in cell G6
　　　　　Enter the formula *=MAX(C2:C457)* in cell H6
　　　　　Copy cell H6 to cells I6 and J6

The results in cells H5 and H6 show that the minimum and maximum values for Life of Tires (Months) are 1.8 months and 601.0, respectively. The minimum value of life of tires in months appears to be reasonable, but the maximum (which is equal to slightly over 50 years) is not a reasonable value for Life of Tires (Months). To identify the automobile with this extreme value, we sort the entire data set on Life of Tire (Months) from smallest to largest and scroll to the last few rows of the data.

We see in Figure 9.7 that the observation with Life of Tire (Months) value of 601.0 is the left rear tire from the automobile with ID Number 8696859. Also note that the left rear tire of the automobile with ID Number 2122934 has a suspiciously high value for Life of Tire (Months) of 111. Sorting the data by ID Number and scrolling until we find the four tires from the automobile with ID Number 8696859, we find the value for Life of Tire (Months) for the other three tires from this automobile is 60.1. This suggests that the decimal for Life of Tire (Months) for this automobile's left rear tire value is in the wrong place. Scrolling to find the four tires from the automobile with ID Number 2122934, we find the value for Life of Tire (Months) for the other three tires from this automobile is 11.1, which suggests that the decimal for Life of Tire (Months) for this automobile's left rear tire value is also misplaced. Both of these erroneous entries can now be corrected.

By repeating this process for the remaining variables in the data (Tread Depth and Miles) in columns I and J, we determine that the minimum and maximum values for Tread Depth are 0.0/12ths of an inch and 16.7/12ths of an inch, respectively, and the minimum and maximum values for Miles are 206.0 and 107,237.0, respectively. Neither the minimum nor the maximum value for Tread Depth is reasonable; a tire with no tread would not be drivable, and the maximum value for tire depth in the data actually exceeds the tread depth on new Blakely brand tires. The minimum value for Miles may be reasonable, but the maximum value is not. A similar investigation should be made into these and other extreme values to determine if they are in error and, if so, what the correct value might be.

Not all erroneous values in a data set are extreme; these erroneous values are much more difficult to find. However, if the variable with suspected erroneous values has a

Note that rows 8 to 451 are hidden in Figure 9.7.

Figure 9.7	Portion of Excel Spreadsheet Showing the Blakely Tires Data Sorted on Life of Tires (Months) from Lowest to Highest Value and with Calculated Summary Statistics

◢	A	B	C	D	E	F	G	H	I	J
1	ID Number	Position on Automobile	Life of Tire (Months)	Tread Depth	Miles			Life of Tire (Months)	Tread Depth	Miles
2	9091771	RR	1.8	10.7	2917		Number Missing Values	0	0	0
3	9091771	LF	1.8	10.7	2917		Mean	23.76	7.64	25834.54
4	9091771	RF	1.8	10.8	2917		Standard Deviation	31.83	2.51	24143.38
5	7712178	LR	2.1	10.6	2186		Minimum	1.8	0.0	206.0
6	7712178	LF	2.1	10.7	2186		Maximum	601.0	16.7	107237.0
7	7712178	RR	2.1	10.7	2186					
452	3574739	RR	73.3	0.2	57313					
453	3574739	RF	73.3	0.2	57313					
454	3574739	LF	73.3	0.2	57313					
455	3574739	LR	73.3	0.2	57313					
456	2122934	LR	111.0	9.3	21000					
457	8696859	LR	601.0	2.0	26129					

relatively strong relationship with another variable in the data, we can explore the data set through data visualization tools such as scatter charts to help us identify data errors. Here, we will consider the variables Tread Depth and Miles. Because more miles driven should lead to less tread depth on an automobile tire, we expect these two variables to have a negative relationship. A scatter chart will enable us to see whether any of the tires in the data set have values for Tread Depth and Miles that are counter to this expectation.

The red ellipse in Figure 9.8 shows the region in which the points representing Tread Depth and Miles would generally be expected to lie on this scatter plot. The points that lie outside of this ellipse have values for at least one of these variables that are inconsistent with the negative relationship exhibited by the points inside the ellipse. If we position the cursor over the point outside the ellipse that corresponds to relatively high values of Miles and Tread Depth, Excel will generate a pop-up box that shows that the values of Tread Depth and Miles for this point are 9.7 and 104658, respectively. The tire represented by this point has very high Tread Depth for this many Miles, which suggests that the value of one or both of these two variables for this tire may be inaccurate and should be investigated. Note that the other two data points outside the red ellipse in Figure 9.8 represent the previously identified likely data errors for Tread Depth.

Closer examination of outliers and potential erroneous values may reveal an error or a need for further investigation to determine whether the observation is relevant to the current analysis. A conservative approach is to create two different data visualizations, one with and one without outliers and potentially erroneous values. If the insights being conveyed by the two data visualizations are very different, then you should spend additional time tracking down the cause of the outliers.

Notes + Comments

1. Excel's Data Validation tool can be used to control what a user can enter into a cell, limiting the ability to create data errors from manual entries. Data validation is implemented in Excel by clicking on the **Data** tab on the Ribbon and then clicking the **Data Validation** icon ▧ ˅ in the **Data Tools** group. This opens the **Data Validation** dialog box that allows you to create rules that define what types of inputs are valid and prevents the user from entering invalid inputs.

2. Outliers should only be removed after careful consideration of their cause and on their effect on the insights drawn from the data. If an outlier is due to an obvious data error, then it can be removed or replaced by a corrected value. If outliers that are not due to obvious data errors are removed, it is generally recommended that this removal be noted in the data visualization or associated documentation so the audience knows that the outliers have been removed.

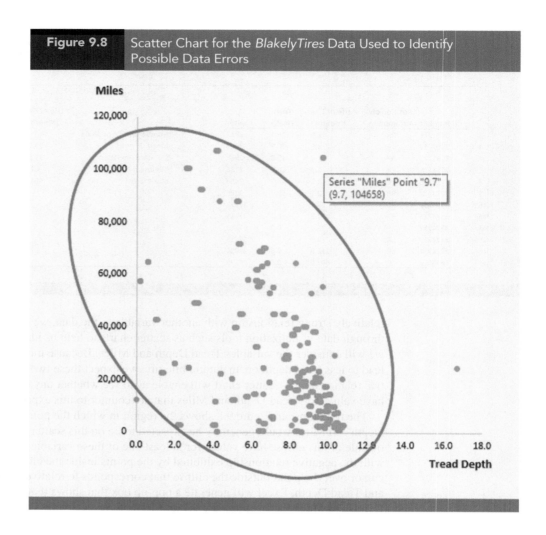

Figure 9.8 Scatter Chart for the *BlakelyTires* Data Used to Identify Possible Data Errors

9.2 Biased Data

Another data issue that can lead to misleading or incorrect data visualizations is bias. **Biased data** exist when the sample data are not representative of the population data that are under study. There are many causes for biased data, and we will discuss some of the more common causes of biased data in this section as well as ways that data exploration can identify potentially biased data.

Selection Bias

Selection bias is a common source of bias in data that can lead to misleading data visualizations and incorrect insights. **Selection bias** occurs when data for a sample are not drawn randomly from a population, resulting in a sample that fails to represent the intended population. Selection bias occurs frequently in many different fields, including political science. Consider a political polling firm that wants to poll likely voters in the United States to determine their preference among candidates in an upcoming election. If the polling firm attempts to contact potential voters using only landline phone numbers, then the resulting sample is likely to be biased in terms of the age of respondents. Older people are much more likely to have landline phones in their homes and to answer them when called by a political polling firm. In this case, selection bias occurred due to how the sample was collected, resulting in a sample consisting of potential voters likely to be much older than the voter population. Therefore, the polling firm must be careful about using this sample to infer insights about candidate preference among the population of all likely voters.

Consider a related but slightly different challenge faced by a research group in the Economics Department at Empire State University. This group of researchers is trying to analyze factors that affect annual incomes in the United States. The researchers have gathered sample data from 106 respondents that include many factors, such as the respondent's age, place of residence, and annual income for the most recent year. A portion of these data are shown in Figure 9.9.

Trendlines are introduced in Chapter 6.

To check their data, the researchers generate a simple scatter chart to explore the relationship between age and annual income for this sample data. This scatter chart is shown in Figure 9.10. The researchers also fit a simple linear trendline to these data as shown in Figure 9.10. Surprisingly, the researchers find that there is a negative relationship between age and annual income in these sample data. This seems to contradict the expectation that annual incomes rise as someone becomes older due to more years of work experience and advancing in their career.

However, further investigation indicates that this negative relationship is caused by a specific form of selection bias. The researchers investigate how the data were collected, and they find that the data were collected from residents of three different cities in the United States: San Francisco, California; Dallas, Texas; and Naples, Florida. These three different cities are geographically distant from each other with San Francisco in the west, Dallas in the middle, and Naples in the east. However, this does not necessarily make them representative of the entire population of the United States. Figure 9.11 shows a scatter plot similar to Figure 9.10 for the same data.

Figure 9.9 Portion of Data Used to Examine Relationship between Age and Income

ageincome

	A	B	C
1	Age	Income	Location
2	52	$ 72,600	Dallas
3	58	$ 53,802	Naples
4	70	$ 50,405	Naples
5	52	$ 109,522	San Francisco
6	42	$ 131,709	San Francisco
7	32	$ 52,338	Dallas
8	67	$ 58,456	Naples
9	44	$ 75,024	Dallas
10	67	$ 67,999	Naples
11	55	$ 45,096	Naples
12	42	$ 54,324	Dallas
13	33	$ 110,072	San Francisco
14	58	$ 40,349	Naples
15	65	$ 41,118	Naples
16	54	$ 48,012	Naples
17	53	$ 178,806	San Francisco
18	46	$ 67,913	Dallas
19	36	$ 144,141	San Francisco
20	28	$ 106,496	San Francisco

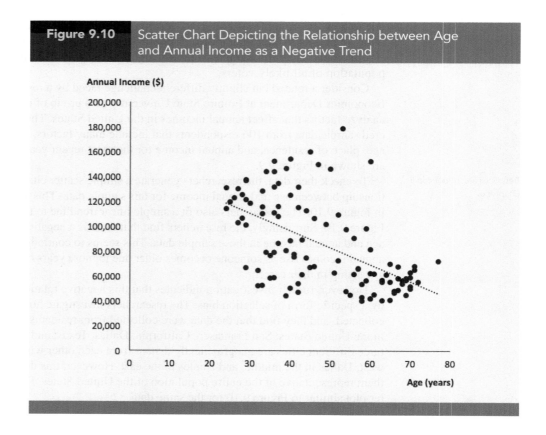

Figure 9.10 Scatter Chart Depicting the Relationship between Age and Annual Income as a Negative Trend

In Figure 9.11, we have used color to differentiate among the locations of the respondents. The researchers have also fit simple linear trendlines to the relation between age and annual income for each of the different cities.

Figure 9.11 shows that the relation for the data within each city is a positive trend: as age increases, annual income also increases. However, when we aggregate all the data together, as in Figure 9.10, the relation between age and annual income appears to be the opposite in that annual income decreases as age increases. This is because the ages and annual incomes from the respondents in each of the three different cities are quite distinct. These demographic differences become apparent when we color the scatter chart by location in Figure 9.11. Respondents in San Francisco tend to be younger and have higher incomes, respondents in Naples tend to be older with lower annual incomes, and respondents in Dallas tend to be somewhere in between.

The effect shown in Figures 9.10 and 9.11 is known as Simpson's paradox. Simpson's paradox occurs when a specific trend that appears in subsets of data disappears or reverses when the subsets are aggregated. In this example, there is a positive trend between age and annual income within the data from each city, but this trend appears to reverse when we aggregate the data across all three cities. Simpson's paradox is also a form of selection bias because we have chosen a sample (in this case using only respondents from three cities) that does not represent the population (the entire United States).

Survivor Bias

Survivor bias is another common source of bias that can lead to misleading data visualizations and incorrect insights. **Survivor bias** occurs when a sample data set consists of a disproportionately large number of observations corresponding to positive

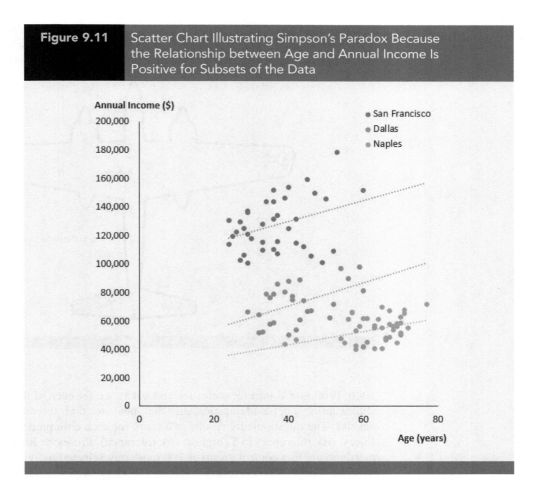

Figure 9.11 Scatter Chart Illustrating Simpson's Paradox Because the Relationship between Age and Annual Income Is Positive for Subsets of the Data

Chapter 6 shows how to create a scatter chart in Excel using multiple colors to differentiate data points.

outcomes for a particular event. It is closely related to selection bias because, similar to selection bias, the sample data are not representative of the population that is being studied.

One of the earliest examples of survivor bias was identified in World War II. The common version of this story is that the U.S. military was experiencing heavy losses to its aircraft due to antiaircraft fire and enemy fighters. The U.S. military studied the damage sustained by returning aircraft to identify where planes were most likely to be damaged. They found that most damage occurred to certain sections of the tail and wings of the aircraft similar to what is shown in Figure 9.12. One suggested action from this analysis was to add armor to these sections of the tail and wings to protect these parts of the aircraft. However, the mathematician Abraham Wald argued that this was the opposite of the correct course of action. Because the only data being examined were from planes that had survived the observed damage, it was likely that damage to these areas of the wings and tail were actually the least harmful to the aircraft. Therefore, armor should be added to the areas where surviving planes did not show damage as it was likely that damage to these areas is what may have caused the non-surviving planes to crash and not return.

For a more recent example of survivor bias, consider the case of Professor Raturi, a business school professor who studies entrepreneurship and risk behaviors. Professor Raturi hypothesizes that entrepreneurs are more likely to have a greater risk tolerance than non-entrepreneurs. To study this hypothesis, Professor Raturi collects data on 87 entrepreneurs who guided their companies from start-up to initial public offering

Figure 9.12	Depiction of Common Areas of Damage to Returning Planes in World War II

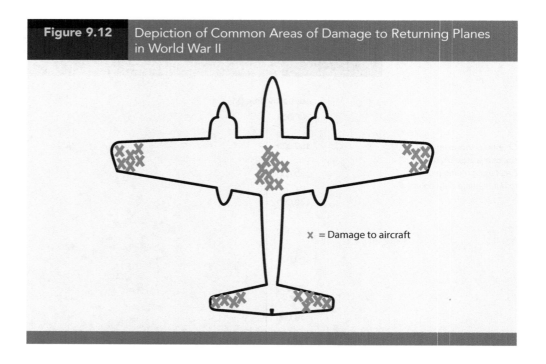

x = Damage to aircraft

(IPO). Professor Raturi measures the risk tolerance for each of these entrepreneurs by administering a detailed questionnaire that measures their tolerance to take on financial risk. The questionnaire results in a score for each entrepreneur that ranges from 1 (lowest risk tolerance) to 5 (highest risk tolerance). Professor Raturi gives this same questionnaire to a control group of 100 randomly selected individuals who are not entrepreneurs. The results of Professor Raturi's research are summarized in Figure 9.13.

Figure 9.13	Comparing Average Risk Tolerance of Entrepreneurs to a Control Group of Non-Entrepreneurs

Risk Tolerance Comparison for Entrepreneurs and Non-Entrepreneurs
Average Financial Risk Tolerance (1 = Lowest; 5 = Highest)

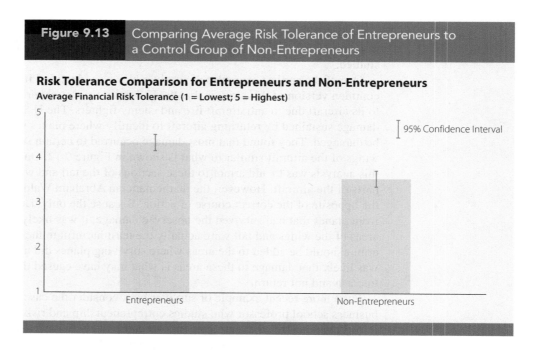

Figure 9.13 clearly shows that the entrepreneurs have a higher average risk tolerance than the control group, even when we compare the 95% confidence intervals. So, can we conclude that entrepreneurs have higher risk tolerance than non-entrepreneurs? Not necessarily. Our results here suffer from survivor bias. The only data we have are for successful entrepreneurs—those that survived and made it to an IPO. We have no data for unsuccessful entrepreneurs—those whose companies failed prior to IPO. It is possible that entrepreneurs, whether they are successful or not, have higher risk tolerances than the general public. But because we have no data on unsuccessful entrepreneurs, we cannot conclude that entrepreneurs have a higher risk tolerance than non-entrepreneurs.

The visualization of confidence intervals on sample statistics is discussed in Chapter 5.

9.3 Adjusting for Inflation

Time series data are discussed in Chapter 5.

Many data visualizations use time series data related to monetary units such as revenues, costs, and profits. When the time interval over which the data are collected becomes long, prices are increasing rapidly, or we are comparing monetary units from different countries, it can be important to adjust for inflation to avoid misleading visualizations and incorrect insights. **Inflation** refers to the general increase in prices over time, and it is measured by tracking the changes in the price of a standard set of products and services referred to as a **price index**. Inflation, and hence the price index, varies over time and also by country or region due to changes in the prevailing economic conditions. There are many popular price indexes that are tracked by economic organizations and used for adjusting for inflation including the consumer price index (CPI) and the producer price index (PPI). It is appropriate to use the price index that is most closely associated with the type of products being analyzed.

In the Data Visualization Makeover at the beginning of this chapter, we illustrated the importance of adjusting for inflation when attempting to identify the top movies of all time based on box office revenues. In this section, we will present an additional example to illustrate this point and explain one way to adjust time-series data for inflation. Consider the price of gasoline in the United States over time. Figure 9.14 displays a simple time series chart showing the price of gasoline between 1978 and 2017. From this chart, it appears that gasoline prices in the United States have increased substantially between 1978 and 2017. The data used to create this chart are contained in the file *pricegasoline*. Examining these data shows that the price of gasoline increased from $0.65 per gallon in 1978 to $2.47 per gallon in 2017. However, these prices represent the **nominal values**, meaning that the values have not been adjusted for inflation.

To allow for meaningful comparisons of the prices of gasoline, we need to adjust the nominal values for inflation. Figure 9.15 shows a portion of the nominal values of the average price of gasoline between 1978 and 2017 as well as the average annual price index for each year. To adjust for inflation, we need to calculate the price of gasoline in each year as if the gasoline was being sold in one common year, known as the **base year**. Here we will define the base year to be the year 2017. Therefore, to adjust for inflation for the price of gasoline in 1978, we use the following calculation:

$$\text{Inflation-Adjusted Price of Gas in 1978} = \text{Nominal Gas Price in 1978} \times \frac{\text{Price Index in 2017}}{\text{Price Index in 1978}}$$

$$= \$0.65 \times \frac{211.8}{51.9} = \$2.66.$$

This result shows us that although the price of gasoline in 1978 was only $0.65 per gallon, this is equivalent to a price of $2.66 per gallon in 2017. The general formula used to find the inflation-adjusted value of a good or service in year y from the nominal value given in year y is the following.

*Inflation adjusted values are also known as **real values**.*

$$\text{Inflation-Adjusted Value in Year } y = \text{Nominal Value in Year } y \times \frac{\text{Price Index in Base Year}}{\text{Price Index in Year } y}$$

Figure 9.14	Non-inflation Adjusted Price per Gallon of Gasoline in the United States between 1978 and 2017

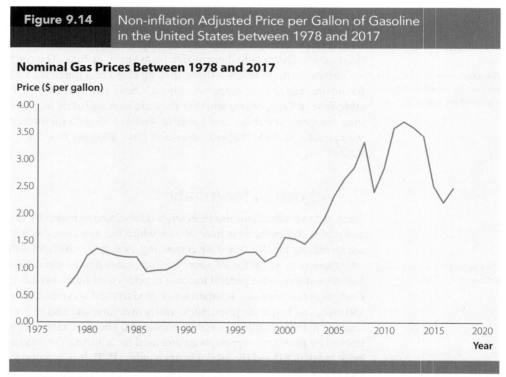

Nominal Gas Prices Between 1978 and 2017

Source: Data from https://www.usinflationcalculator.com/gasoline-prices-adjusted-for-inflation/

Figure 9.15	Portion of Data that Contains Nominal Prices and Price Index Values for a Gallon of Gasoline in the United States between 1978 and 2017

	A	B	C
1	Year	Nominal Gas Price (per gallon in $)	Price Index
2	1978	0.65	51.9
3	1979	0.88	70.2
4	1980	1.22	97.5
5	1981	1.35	108.5
6	1982	1.28	102.8
7	1983	1.23	99.4
8	1984	1.20	97.8
9	1985	1.20	98.6
10	1986	0.93	77.0
40	2016	2.20	187.6
41	2017	2.47	211.8

pricegasoline

Note that rows 11 through 39 are hidden.

Figure 9.16 shows the calculations used in Excel to convert the nominal gasoline prices into the inflation-adjusted gasoline prices using 2017 as the base year. These values are then used to create Figure 9.17, which shows the nominal values and the inflation-adjusted values of the price of gasoline between 1978 and 2017. From Figure 9.17, we see that when we adjust for inflation, the insight from these time-series data is very different

Figure 9.16	Adjusting Nominal Gasoline Prices for Inflation in Excel

Note that rows 11–39 are hidden.

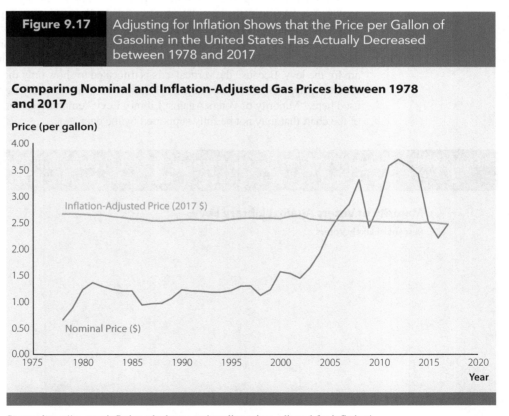

	A	B	C	D
1	Year	Nominal Gas Price (in $)	Price Index	Inflation Adjusted Price (in 2017 $)
2	1978	0.652	51.9	=B2*($C$41/C2)
3	1979	0.882	70.2	=B3*($C$41/C3)
4	1980	1.221	97.5	=B4*($C$41/C4)
5	1981	1.353	108.5	=B5*($C$41/C5)
6	1982	1.281	102.8	=B6*($C$41/C6)
7	1983	1.225	99.4	=B7*($C$41/C7)
8	1984	1.198	97.8	=B8*($C$41/C8)
9	1985	1.196	98.6	=B9*($C$41/C9)
10	1986	0.931	77	=B10*($C$41/C10)
40	2016	2.204	187.602	=B40*($(
41	2017	2.469	211.77	=B41*($(

	A	B	C	D
1	Year	Nominal Gas Price (in $)	Price Index	Inflation Adjusted Price (in 2017 $)
2	1978	0.65	51.9	2.66
3	1979	0.88	70.2	2.66
4	1980	1.22	97.5	2.65
5	1981	1.35	108.5	2.64
6	1982	1.28	102.8	2.64
7	1983	1.23	99.4	2.61
8	1984	1.20	97.8	2.59
9	1985	1.20	98.6	2.57
10	1986	0.93	77.0	2.56
40	2016	2.20	187.6	2.49
41	2017	2.47	211.8	2.47

Figure 9.17	Adjusting for Inflation Shows that the Price per Gallon of Gasoline in the United States Has Actually Decreased between 1978 and 2017

Comparing Nominal and Inflation-Adjusted Gas Prices between 1978 and 2017

Price (per gallon)

[Chart showing Inflation-Adjusted Price (2017 $) remaining roughly constant around 2.50–2.66 and Nominal Price ($) rising from ~0.65 in 1978 to peaks above 3.50 around 2010–2012, then declining.]

Year

Source: https://www.usinflationcalculator.com/gasoline-prices-adjusted-for-inflation/

than Figure 9.15. The inflation-adjusted price of gasoline in the United States has not increased between 1978 and 2017; in fact, it has slightly decreased.

We can adjust nominal values to account for inflation using any year in the time series as the base year. The specific base year to choose generally depends on the comparisons that are to be made.

9.4 Deceptive Design

Effective data visualizations convey insights from data to the audience clearly and accurately. We want to avoid deceptive designs that do not accurately communicate insights from the data. It is easy to create deceptive data visualizations—even when the analyst is not actively trying to deceive the audience. The previous sections in this chapter emphasize the importance of ensuring the data are as accurate as possible. In this section, we will show how decisions related to the design of the chart can also greatly affect the insights conveyed to the audience and how to avoid deceptive design choices for data visualizations.

Design of Chart Axes

Choices related to the axes used in many different types of charts can greatly affect the insights conveyed to the audience. Changing the lower and upper limits of either the vertical or horizontal axes can completely change what the audience perceives from the chart. Even changes to the vertical and horizontal size of some charts can change the insights communicated to the audience. Therefore, the chart designer must be extremely careful when making decisions related to the chart axes to avoid deceptive design practices.

It is common for political polling firms to gather data related to the way likely voters plan to vote on proposed ballot issues. Consider the case in Franklin County, Maryland, where voters in the next election will be asked to vote on a library levy. If approved, the levy will provide funds from a property tax increase to rehabilitate two aging libraries in Franklin County. A local political polling firm conducts a poll of likely voters in Franklin County to determine whether voters are "For" or "Against" the levy. The results of the poll are shown in Figure 9.18 as a column chart. This column chart appears to convey that many more voters are "Against" the levy than "For" the levy. However, it is important to note that the vertical axis ranges only between 48% and 52%. In fact, Figure 9.18 shows that 51% of likely voters are against the levy while 49% are for the levy. Because the vertical axis is truncated to show only the range of 48–52%, this difference appears to be much larger in Figure 9.18 than it actually is. Notice also that the title used here, "Majority of Voters Against Library Levy," emphasizes one particular interpretation of the chart that may not be fully supported by the data.

Figure 9.18 Column Chart that Exaggerates the Difference in Proportion of Likely Voters Against the Library Levy and the Proportion of Likely Voters for the Library Levy

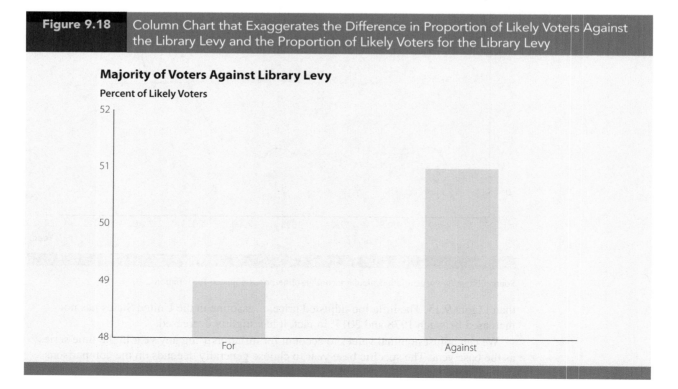

Figure 9.19 shows a revised column chart for these data. There are several differences between Figure 9.19 and Figure 9.18. The vertical axis now has a range of 0–60%, we have added data labels on each column showing their value, and because these polling results represent an estimated proportion from a sample, we have added errors bars to the figure. Figure 9.19 more accurately conveys that there is little difference between the proportion of voters who are against the levy and the proportion of voters who are for the levy. Figure 9.19 also shows that the 95% confidence intervals on the two proportions overlap, so we cannot claim that these results are statistically different at a 95% level of confidence.

Confidence intervals are discussed in more detail in Chapter 5.

Generally, column (and bar) charts should begin with zero as the minimum value on the vertical (and horizontal) axis. Exceptions to this recommendation include cases where the measure being displayed has some minimum value other than zero such as cash flows that can take on negative values or scores on a standardized test where 400 is the minimum score.

The title used in Figure 9.19, "Fate of Library Levy Uncertain," also presents a different insight than what is shown in Figure 9.18. Figures 9.18 and 9.19 illustrate the importance of the chart title in determining which insights from the data are communicated to the audience.

The minimum and maximum values used on the vertical axis of line charts can also greatly influence the insights conveyed to the audience. Consider a researcher who is examining changes to the global surface temperature of the earth over time. Figure 9.20 displays the average annual surface temperature for the earth from 1880 to 2016 in degrees Celsius (°C).

The insight communicated about these data to the audience appears to be that average annual global surface temperatures have basically remained unchanged between 1880 and 2016. However, Figure 9.21 displays the same data as Figure 9.20, but the range of the vertical axis has been changed to have a minimum value of 13.5°C and maximum value of 14.5°C.

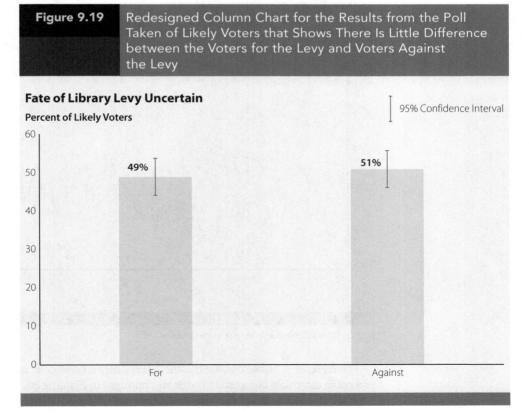

Figure 9.19 Redesigned Column Chart for the Results from the Poll Taken of Likely Voters that Shows There Is Little Difference between the Voters for the Levy and Voters Against the Levy

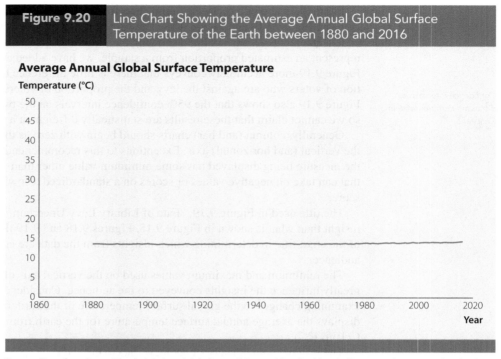

Figure 9.20   Line Chart Showing the Average Annual Global Surface Temperature of the Earth between 1880 and 2016

Source: Data from https://datahub.io/core/global-temp#data and inspired by similar example on page 65 of Cairo, A., *How Charts Lie: Getting Smarter About Visual Information*

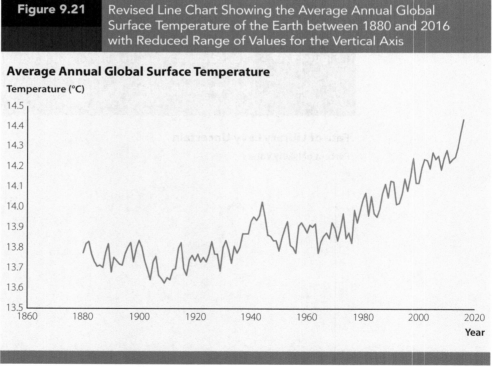

Figure 9.21   Revised Line Chart Showing the Average Annual Global Surface Temperature of the Earth between 1880 and 2016 with Reduced Range of Values for the Vertical Axis

Source: https://datahub.io/core/global-temp#data

From Figure 9.21, we can see that there is actually a substantial amount of variability present in these data compared to what was apparent in Figure 9.20. Figure 9.21 also shows what appears to be an upward trend in the data after around 1920 that is not apparent in Figure 9.20.

Preattentive attributes are discussed in detail in Chapter 3.

For charts that use the preattentive attributes of length and width such as bar and column charts, it is generally recommended that the vertical axis start at 0 unless there is a different relative minimum value for the variable being used on the vertical axis. However, for charts that use preattentive attributes related to orientation or spatial positioning such as line charts and scatter charts, it is not always recommended to start the vertical axis at zero or the relative minimum value. To communicate the information in the data through orientation or spatial positioning, it may be necessary to use a smaller range on the vertical axis to illustrate the variability, trend, or correlation in the data.

Figure 9.22 shows two additional possible line charts to display the average annual global surface temperatures over time. The charts in Figure 9.22 have identical ranges for the axes, but they have different aspect ratios. The **aspect ratio** refers to the ratio of the width of a chart to the height of a chart. In Figure 9.22a, the line chart is tall but not very wide. Figure 9.22b shows the same data in a line chart that is short but wide. In other words, Figure 9.22a has a smaller aspect ratio than Figure 9.22b. Comparing these two different line charts shows that using a line chart that is tall and narrow (smaller aspect ratio) can exaggerate trends in the data, while using a line chart that is short and wide (larger aspect ratio) can disguise trends in the data even when we have the same minimum and maximum vertical axis values.

The aspect ratio is discussed in Chapter 6.

Figure 9.22 demonstrates the importance of considering the aspect ratio used in creating data visualizations when showing them to an audience as well as the importance of the audience to consider the effect of the aspect ratio on the data visualizations when viewing them. This can be particularly important, and challenging, when designing multiple data visualizations that will be dynamically updated, such as for data dashboards.

Figure 9.22	Two Different Line Charts for the Average Annual Global Surface Temperature Data Showing the Effect of the Size of the Line Chart on the Insights Conveyed to the Audience

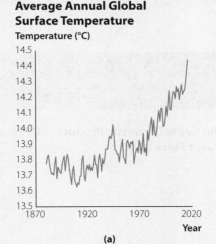

(a)

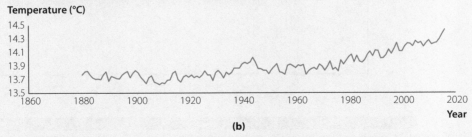

(b)

Source: https://datahub.io/core/global-temp#data

Dual-Axis Charts

Sometimes it is necessary to display two different variables from a data set to the audience where each variable has different units and/or different magnitudes. A common approach to creating a chart for such a situation is to use what is known as a dual-axis chart. A **dual-axis chart** makes use of a secondary axis to represent one of the variables so both variables can be shown on the same chart. However, in most cases, dual-axis charts are difficult for the audience to interpret, and there is often a better way to present the data.

Consider a case in which the audience is interested in comparing the gross domestic product (GDP) and unemployment rate of the United States since the year 2000. The GDP of the United States is measured in the trillions of dollars, while the unemployment rate is specified as a percentage value of the eligible workforce. Figure 9.23 shows the data for both variables on the same chart using the same vertical axis. Clearly this chart is not particularly informative for the audience. The unemployment rate appears to be a flat line at zero because the vertical axis must extend much higher even when the unit is expressed in billions of U.S. dollars. Further, with only a single axis, it can be confusing for the audience to understand the units of measure for the vertical axis because GDP and unemployment rate are measured in different units.

A common alternative to the chart shown in Figure 9.23 is a dual-axis chart. The dual-axis chart makes use of a secondary vertical axis to represent one of the variables. In this case, the secondary axis will represent the unemployment rate. The resulting dual-axis chart is shown in Figure 9.24. Because we can now use two different vertical axes, the unemployment rate no longer appears as a flat line. We can now see changes in both the U.S. GDP and the unemployment rate on the chart and compare the two lines.

However, dual-axis charts can still be misleading and difficult for the audience to interpret. Because the lines in Figure 9.24 appear together on the same chart, it is natural for the audience to compare them to each other. At first glance, it can appear that the unemployment rate is higher than the GDP in certain years. The audience must correctly match each line to the corresponding vertical axis, which requires considerable cognitive load.

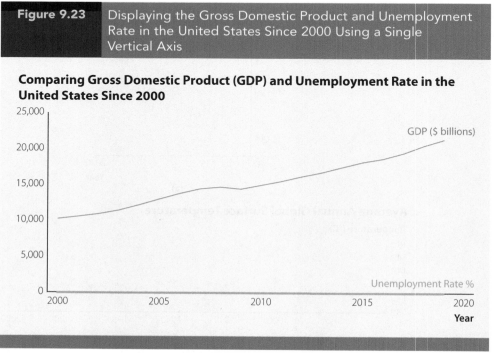

Figure 9.23 Displaying the Gross Domestic Product and Unemployment Rate in the United States Since 2000 Using a Single Vertical Axis

Source: U.S. Bureau of Labor Statistics and World Bank

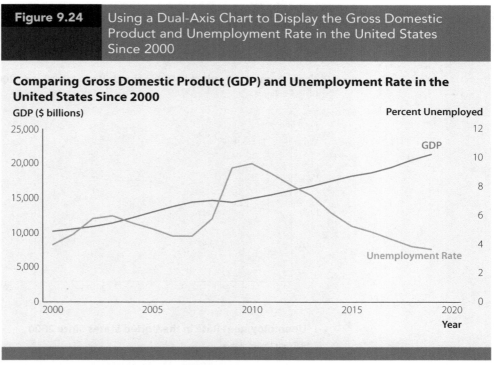

| Figure 9.24 | Using a Dual-Axis Chart to Display the Gross Domestic Product and Unemployment Rate in the United States Since 2000 |

Source: U.S. Bureau of Labor Statistics and World Bank

It is also incorrect to interpret meaning from a comparison of the slopes of the lines shown in Figure 9.24. To create a dual-axis chart in Excel similar to the chart in Figure 9.24, first create a scatter line chart for the GDP and Percent Unemployed data. Then click

Chart Design on the Ribbon and select **Change Chart Type** ⬚ in the **Type** group. When the **Change Chart Type** dialog box opens, click **Combo** Combo, then select **Line** Line for the **Chart Type** for both Series and click the check box for **Secondary Axis** for the Percent Unemployed data.

Because each line in Figure 9.24 is scaled to a different vertical axis, the audience cannot directly compare the slopes of the lines. What appears to be a rapid increase in unemployment rates cannot be directly compared to the corresponding increase or decrease in GDP because the scales of the vertical axes are different. As shown previously in this chapter, the slopes of the lines are dependent on the ranges chosen for the vertical axes. In general, the magnitudes of the representation of the data for the different variables cannot be compared directly because the audience must adjust each representation of the data by the scale of the appropriate vertical axis.

Another possible point of confusion with dual-axis charts is that the audience is typically drawn to places where lines intersect. The natural inclination is to assume that the two variables are equal at these points of intersection in Figure 9.24. However, this is incorrect in a dual-axis chart since each variable is represented on a different vertical axis. In reality, the lines do not intersect at all if they are shown on the same vertical axis as in Figure 9.23.

A simple alternative to using a dual-axis chart is to replace the dual-axis chart with two charts where each variable is shown on a different chart. An example of this is shown in Figure 9.25. Using two different charts to display the data helps the audience understand that each variable uses a different vertical axis and that the magnitudes and slopes cannot be compared directly. Because the horizontal axis is the same for each of these charts, it can be helpful to stack the charts vertically so that the horizontal axes align. The downside of using two charts is that it takes more space to display both charts.

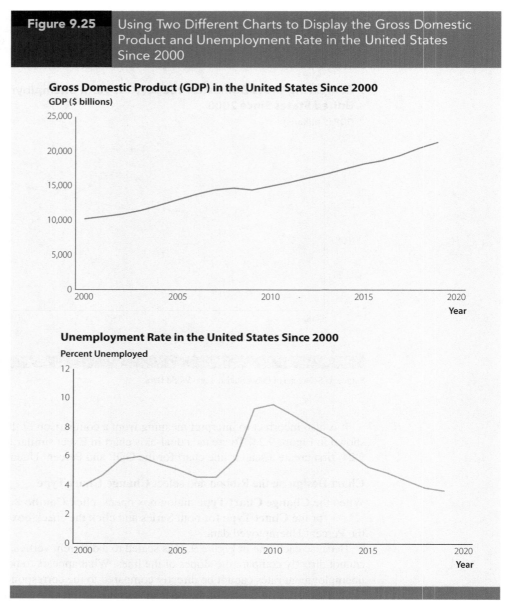

Figure 9.25   Using Two Different Charts to Display the Gross Domestic Product and Unemployment Rate in the United States Since 2000

Source: U.S. Bureau of Labor Statistics and World Bank

Data Selection and Temporal Frequency

Choosing which data to include in a chart greatly affects the insights conveyed to the audience. This is particularly true for time series data collected over successive points in time.

Time series data are discussed in Chapter 6.

Stock prices in finance, inventory levels at a retail store, water flow rates in a river, patient occupancy levels in a hospital, political polling data collected over time, and many other applications often rely on the use of time series data.

Consider the charts shown in Figure 9.26, which appear to represent the share prices of two stocks (A and B) for potential investment. Trendlines have also been added to these charts to show the general linear trend in the data. The stock prices shown in Figure 9.26a appear to be highly variable with a trendline that is basically flat. The stock prices shown in Figure 9.26b appear to be more stable and have an increasing trend and so may be perceived as a superior potential investment. However, both charts actually represent the same stock; both charts in Figure 9.26 have the same ending date, but the start dates are different. Figure 9.26a shows the data for the last 90 days, and Figure 9.26b shows the data for the last

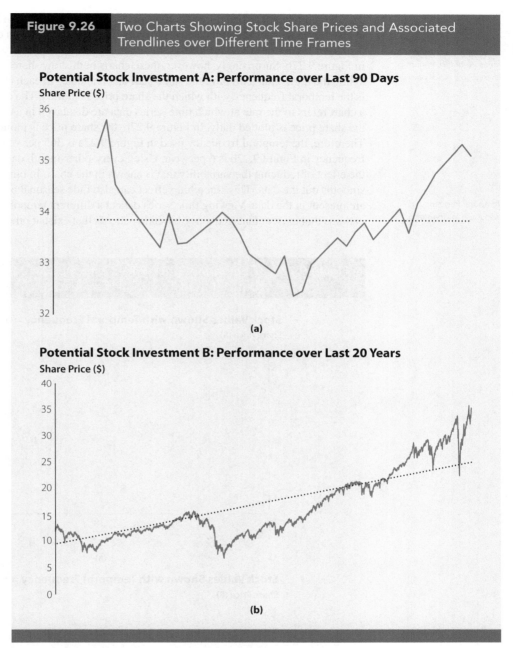

Figure 9.26   Two Charts Showing Stock Share Prices and Associated Trendlines over Different Time Frames

Potential Stock Investment A: Performance over Last 90 Days

(a)

Potential Stock Investment B: Performance over Last 20 Years

(b)

Source: Yahoo Finance, https://finance.yahoo.com/quote/%5EGSPC?p=^GSPC&.tsrc=fin-srch

20 years. The audience would likely feel differently about the possibility of investing in a stock whose price behaved as shown in Figure 9.26a than in a stock whose price has behaved as shown in Figure 9.26b. This illustrates how changing the range of the dates on the horizontal axis can greatly affect the insights conveyed to the audience. Figure 9.26 also reinforces the importance of labeling vertical and horizontal axes. Without the horizontal axis labels in Figure 9.26, it can be easy for an audience to misinterpret the insights from these charts.

Whether Figure 9.26a or Figure 9.26b is more appropriate depends on the needs of the audience. If the audience does not intend to hold the stock for very long and is only interested in short-term performance of the share price, Figure 9.26a may be more relevant. However, if the audience intends to invest for the long term, Figure 9.26b may be more appropriate.

Volatility is a common measure of the amount of change in a stock price.

Next, compare the share prices of the stocks shown in the charts in Figure 9.27. In these charts, the same start and end dates are used for the horizontal axis in each chart. The stock displayed in Figure 9.27a appears to have much higher price volatility than the stock displayed in Figure 9.27b. Surprisingly, however, these charts both show share prices for the same stock. While the horizontal axes have the same start and end dates in each chart, what varies here is the temporal frequency with which the share price is plotted. The **temporal frequency** in a chart refers to the rate at which time-series data are displayed in a chart. In Figure 9.27a, the share price is plotted daily. In Figure 9.27b, the share price is plotted every other month. Therefore, the temporal frequency used in Figure 9.27a is 365 per year while the temporal frequency in Figure 9.27b is 6 per year. Using every-other-month data in Figure 9.27b has the effect of reducing the variability that is shown in the chart. In other words, Figure 9.27b smooths out the data. This smoothing effect can also hide seasonal or cyclical effects that are present in the data. Viewing time series data at a different temporal frequency can reveal patterns that exist at that frequency but hide patterns that exist at other frequencies.

Temporal frequency is discussed in Chapter 6.

Figure 9.27 Comparing Stock Prices with the Same Start and End Dates but Different Temporal Frequencies

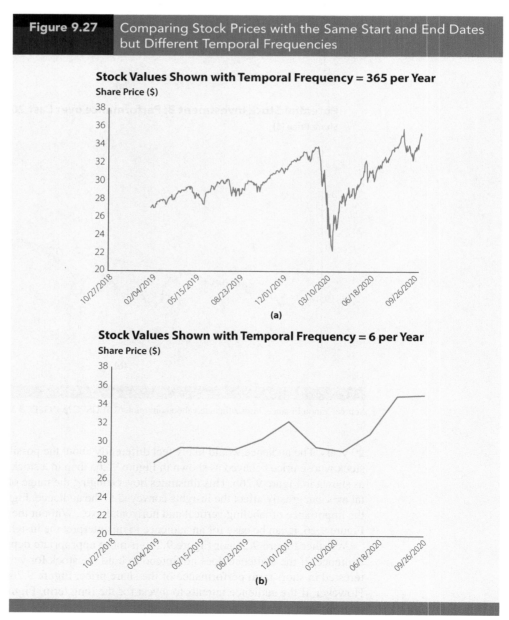

Source: Yahoo Finance, https://finance.yahoo.com/quote/%5EGSPC?p=^GSPC&.tsrc=fin-srch

Figure 9.27 shows that even when time series charts have the same start and end dates on the horizontal axes, the insights conveyed in the chart can still differ based on the temporal frequency with which the data are shown. Charts that use a lower temporal frequency will tend to reduce the apparent variability shown in the chart.

A general recommendation for time series is to collect the data at the highest possible temporal frequency. That is, data should be collected at as frequent time intervals as possible. This is because it is easy to aggregate data, but it is usually difficult, or even impossible, to disaggregate it. If we have data that are measured at the daily level, it is easy to aggregate these data to weekly, monthly, quarterly, or annual levels. However, if the data only exist at the annual level, it may be impossible to disaggregate to the quarterly, monthly, weekly, or daily level.

Issues Related to Geographic Maps

Choropleth maps and other geographic maps are discussed in Chapters 2 and 6.

The use of geographic maps for data visualization introduces additional possibilities for misleading the audience. Choropleth maps that use different shades of a color to represent quantitative variables are a common type of data visualization for exploring and examining data related to different geographic regions. Choropleth maps are commonly used to examine the differences in many different economic and health variables such as employment rates, income levels, cancer rates, political support, and average life spans across geographic regions such as counties, states, regions, and countries.

Consider the choropleth map shown in Figure 9.28 in which color shading is used to denote the estimated number of individuals living below the poverty line in each state in the United States. This map appears to show that states such as California (CA), Texas (TX), Florida (FL), and New York (NY) have the most poverty of any of the states. While it is true in an absolute sense that these states have the highest number of people living below the poverty line, it is also true that these states also have the highest populations. Compare Figures 9.28 to 9.29, which shows a choropleth map that represents the population in each state. Figure 9.28 and Figure 9.29 are extremely similar. In fact, many choropleth maps that show the absolute number of people in almost

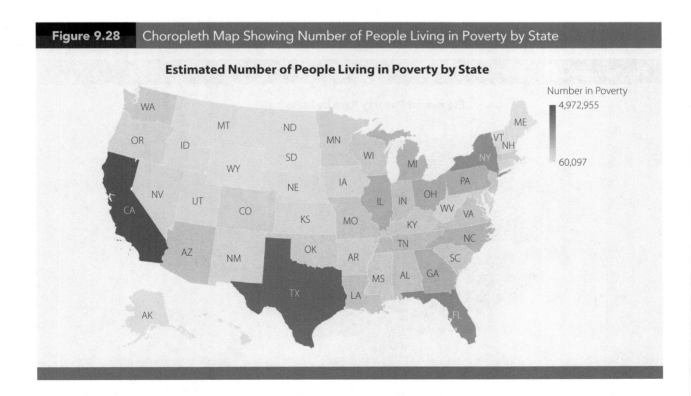

Figure 9.28 — Choropleth Map Showing Number of People Living in Poverty by State

Estimated Number of People Living in Poverty by State

Number in Poverty
4,972,955

60,097

Figure 9.29   Choropleth Map Showing Population by State

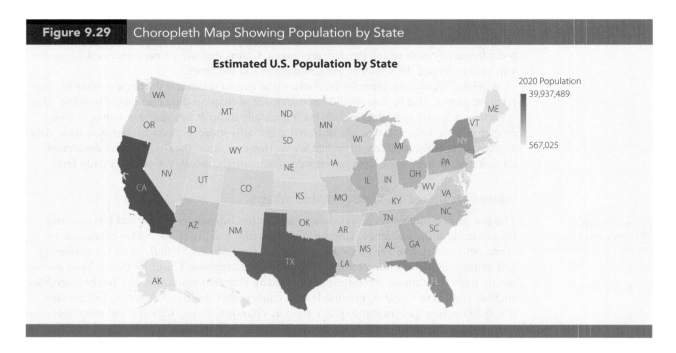

any particular category will appear similar to Figure 9.29. Figure 9.28 does not provide much insight into which states have the greatest challenges with poverty, because it is really only showing which states have the largest populations.

Figure 9.30 is a better choropleth map for communicating which states have the highest number of people living in poverty relative to the overall state population. Figure 9.30 uses the poverty rate rather than the total number of people living in poverty. The poverty rate for each state is defined as shown in the equation below.

$$\text{Poverty rate in a state} = \frac{\text{Number of people in poverty in a state}}{\text{Total population in a state}} \times 100\%$$

Figure 9.30   Choropleth Map Showing Poverty Rate by State

In other words, the poverty rate measures the percentage of each state's population that is living in poverty. In Figure 9.30, we see that states such as Mississippi (MS), New Mexico (NM), and Louisiana (LA) have the highest rates of poverty, while California (CA), Texas (TX), Florida (FL), and New York (NY) have lower poverty rates. In most cases, it is best to use a value relative to the population of the region when creating choropleth maps.

Notes + Comments

1. The book *How Charts Lie: Getting Smarter about Visual Information* by Alberto Cairo contains many additional examples of deceptive chart designs and how these deceptions can be remedied.

2. Dual-axis charts can be created in Excel by clicking the **Insert** tab on the Ribbon, clicking the **Insert Combo Chart** button ⬛ ˅ in the **Charts** group, and then selecting ⬛ Create Custom Combo Chart... . To create a dual-axis chart, select a **Chart Type** for each variable to be shown in the chart, and then select the check box under **Secondary Axis** for one of the variables. The dual-axis chart can be a single type of chart, such as the line chart shown in the example in this chapter, or it can combine chart types such as a column chart and a line chart.

3. The proper aspect ratio for a chart depends on the exact chart and how it will be displayed to the audience.

In general, we recommend that charts used to show correlation between variables such as a scatter chart use an aspect ratio of 1:1 where the width is equal to the height. For most other charts, it is recommended that the width is larger than the height, but there are exceptions to this such as for slope charts, introduced in Chapter 7, where the width is usually smaller than the height.

4. Data labels can be added to a map in Excel by clicking on the map, clicking on the **Chart Elements** button ⊞ , clicking the arrow next to **Data Labels** ▶ and selecting **More Data Label Options...** to open the **Format Data Labels** task pane. Then select the appropriate option under **Label Options** to add data labels to the map.

Summary

In this chapter, we have covered several common issues in data visualizations that can lead to confusing and misleading interpretations. The goal of effective data visualization is to convey insights accurately and truthfully in a way that requires as little cognitive load from the audience as possible. Deceptive data visualizations are sometimes created intentionally to mislead an audience, but more often they are caused by a lack of understanding of the needs of the audience, poor data quality, or poor data visualization design choices.

Creating truthful data visualizations begins with having complete and accurate data. We began this chapter with a description of some simple methods for identifying missing data and data errors. The exact nature of missing data and data errors is specific to the type of data and problem setting being analyzed. However, the methods introduced here are simple enough to complete in Excel and can help mitigate some obvious cases of missing data and data errors.

We discussed the importance of adjusting for inflation when dealing with time series data that have been collected over long time periods. Failing to adjust for inflation can easily lead to incorrect insights and misleading data visualizations. We discussed the importance of considering choices related to the design of axes in charts. Using different ranges of values for the axes, and even simply using different sizes for the chart, can greatly affect the insights conveyed to the audience for the same data. We explained why the use of dual-axis charts is often confusing or misleading for the audience, and we suggested the use of two separate charts that each show a single variable instead. We also discussed how the selection and frequency of time series data can change the insights conveyed to the audience. Finally, we covered some issues related to the use of geographic maps and how to prevent misleading the audience when using these types of charts.

There are many other data visualization design decisions that can lead to misleading charts. Decisions as simple as the wording used in the title of the chart can sometimes mislead the audience. There is a fine line between influencing the audience by highlighting specific insights from the data and misleading the audience using deceptive design.

However, the goal of an effective data visualization is to convey insights to the audience as truthfully as possible. The material covered in this chapter, and throughout this textbook, should help create more truthful and more effective data visualizations.

Glossary

Aspect ratio The proportion between the chart's width and its height.
Base year Arbitrary year chosen to be the common year to measure economic values such as costs and prices to adjust for inflation.
Biased data Sample data that are not representative of the population that is under study.
Dual-axis chart A type of data visualization that makes use of a secondary axis to represent one of the variables so both variables can be shown on the same chart.
Inflation The general increase in prices over time.
Nominal values Raw values that have not been adjusted for inflation or other important factors.
Price index Measure of the relative change in the price of a standard set of products and services over time.
Real values Values that have been adjusted for inflation.
Selection bias Bias that occurs when data for a sample are not drawn randomly from a population, resulting in a sample that fails to represent the intended population.
Simpson's paradox Subsets of data show a specific trend that either disappears or reverses when the data are aggregated.
Survivor bias Bias that occurs when a sample data set consists of a disproportionately large number of observations corresponding to positive outcomes for a particular event.
Temporal frequency The rate at which time-series data are displayed in a chart.

Problems

Conceptual

1. **Identifying Missing Data** Which of the following Excel methods can be used to help identify missing data? **LO 1**
   i. Conditional formatting to highlight missing data values
   ii. Using the COUNTIF() function to find the number of missing data values
   iii. Sorting the data to find missing data values
   iv. All of the above

2. **Data Errors**. Which of the following is true regarding data errors? **LO 1**
   i. A data error is always identified by a unique numerical value such as 9999999.
   ii. Any data that are determined to be outliers should be considered data errors and should be removed.
   iii. Identifying outliers in a data set can be helpful in uncovering data errors.
   iv. Data errors occur only when data are collected manually.

3. **Types of Data Bias**. Match each of the following types of data bias with the correct description. **LO 2, 3**

Type of Data Bias	Description
Selection bias	Occurs when subsets of data show a specific trend, but that trend disappears, or reverses, when the data are aggregated.
Simpson's paradox	Occurs when a data set is made up of a disproportionately high number of observations corresponding to positive outcomes from a particular event.
Survivor bias	Occurs when data are drawn from a sample that had not been properly randomized to represent the intended population.

4. **Potential Bias in Weight-Loss Study**. A clinical trial has been conducted to evaluate the efficacy of a new drug to enable weight loss for obese patients. A pool of 249 obese individuals are chosen for the study. Study participants must track their weight at home daily to compute their body-mass index (BMI) and have a clinical evaluation once per week at a local hospital over six months to complete the clinical trial. At the end of six months, it is found that 47% of those who received the new drug completed the clinical trial. Those who completed the clinical trial are found to have reduced their BMI by 3.2 kg/m^2, on average, over six months. Explain how these results could be affected by bias and how that could affect the data. **LO 2**

5. **Simpson's Paradox in Baseball**. In the sport of baseball, batting average is calculated by dividing the number of hits a player achieves by the number of official at bats. The following table shows the batting performance for Mike Legg and Edison Vasquez over two consecutive seasons. **LO 3**

	Season 1		Season 2	
Player	Hits	At Bats	Hits	At Bats
Mike Legg	14	56	192	589
Edison Vasquez	112	418	57	149

   a. Calculate the batting average for Mike Legg and Edison Vasquez in Season 1. Which player has a higher batting average in Season 1?
   b. Calculate the batting average for Mike Legg and Edison Vasquez in Season 2. Which player has a higher batting average in Season 2?
   c. Calculate the batting average for Mike Legg and Edison Vasquez over the combined Seasons 1 and 2. Which player has the higher batting average over Seasons 1 and 2?
   d. Explain how the results in parts a through c illustrate Simpson's paradox.

6. **Average Nominal Hourly Earnings**. An economist is examining wage growth in the United States. She has collected data on average nominal hourly earnings for workers in the United States between 2006 and 2020, which are shown in the following chart. Her conclusion is that hourly earnings for workers in the United States have been steadily growing since 2006. How might this conclusion be incorrect, and how can she modify these data to investigate the appropriateness of this conclusion? **LO 4**

Nominal Earnings in the United States between 2006 and 2020

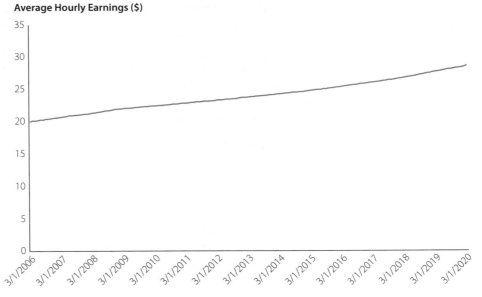

7. **Meaning of Inflation**. Which of the following are accurate statements regarding inflation? (Select all that apply.) **LO 4**
   i. Inflation refers to the tendency of prices to increase over time.
   ii. Inflation only occurs in economies that are experiencing destabilizing events like war or famine.
   iii. Prices that are not adjusted for inflation are referred to as nominal prices.
   iv. Failing to adjust for inflation in time series data that relates to monetary units can lead to misleading data visualizations.
   v. When creating a line chart for cost data over time, it does not matter if the data are adjusted for inflation or not.

8. **Political Polling Results in County Commissioner Election**. Two candidates are running for county commissioner in Bell County, Texas: Lisa Adamek and Rosemary Andrews. The local newspaper has conducted a poll of likely voters to see where the candidates stand in regards to the election. The local newspaper has analyzed the results of its poll and posted the following chart to its website. **LO 5**

Poll for Bell County Commissioner Election

Percent of Likely Voters in Favor

   a. Why might this chart be misleading for the audience?
   b. How could this chart be improved to be less misleading for the audience?

9. **COVID-19 Positivity Rates in Ohio**. An epidemiologist has collected data on positivity rates for COVID-19 testing in the state of Ohio. The positivity rate is defined as the number of tests that come back positive for the COVID-19 virus divided by the total number of COVID-19 tests completed. The epidemiologist has created the following chart showing positivity rates in Ohio between April and October 2020. The audience for this chart is interested in trying to gain insights into any overall increasing or decreasing trends in the positivity rate for COVID-19 during this time period. **LO 5**

Positivity Rate for COVID-19 in Ohio

Percent Positive Tests

Source: Data from https://covidtracking.com/data/download

How can this chart be improved to meet the needs of the audience?

10. **Dual-Axis Charts**. Which of the following statements are true of dual-axis charts? (Select all that apply.) **LO 6**
    i. Dual-axis charts use a secondary vertical axis to represent one of the variables shown in the chart.
    ii. Dual-axis charts require two different horizontal axes and two different vertical axes for each variable displayed in the chart.
    iii. Dual-axis charts can be used to display two different types of data visualizations, such as a line graph and a column graph, on the same chart.
    iv. Dual-axis charts can be difficult for the audience to interpret because the magnitudes of the representation of the data cannot be compared directly without adjusting for the scale of each vertical axis.
    v. Dual-axis charts can only be created for pie charts and column charts.

11. **Headcount and Revenue at Maximus Fashion**. Maximus Fashion is a high-end clothing store in Naperville, Illinois. The store manager would like to create a data visualization that shows trends in the store's headcount of retail associates and revenues. For the last eight quarters, the manager has collected data on the store's headcount of retail associates (expressed in terms of full-time equivalent [FTE] employees) and the store's revenues. The manager has chosen to display these data as the dual-axis chart that follows. The audience for this chart is an informal advisory group for the store who has considerable experience in fashion but little experience with financial analysis or data visualization in general. **LO 5, 6**

maximus_chart

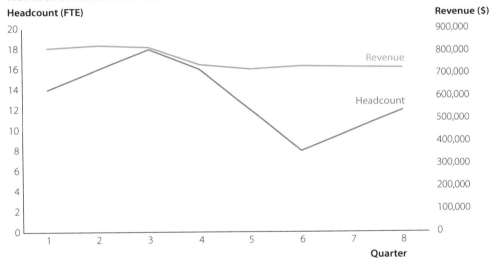

a. What possible confusion could the use of this chart create for the audience?
b. How could the store manager redesign this chart to better present these data to the audience?

12. **Investing in Amazon.com Stock**. Marisha Ray is a 30-year-old software engineer. Marisha is considering investing in a large amount of Amazon.com stock that she plans to hold until her retirement around age 60. Consider the following charts. Each chart shows the performance of Amazon.com stock but over different time periods. One chart shows the performance of Amazon.com stock over the last five days, and the other chart shows the performance of Amazon.com stock over the last five years. Which chart would be the best chart to show to Marisha as she considers investing in Amazon.com stock for her retirement savings? Why? **LO 7**

Performance of Amazon.com Stock over Last 5 Days

Source: https://finance.yahoo.com/quote/AMZN/history?period1=1445472000&period2=1603324800&
interval=1d&filter=history&frequency=1d&includeAdjustedClose=true

Performance of Amazon.com Stock over Last 5 Years

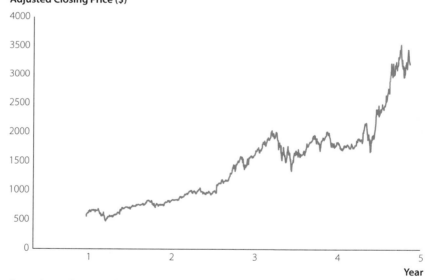

Source: https://finance.yahoo.com/quote/AMZN/history?period1=1445472000&period2=1603324800&
interval=1d&filter=history&frequency=1d&includeAdjustedClose=true

13. **Communicating Insights with Time Series Charts**. Which of the following properties
    of a time series chart can influence the insights communicated to the audience? **LO 7**
    i.   The temporal frequency with which the data are shown
    ii. The start and end date used on the horizontal axis for the chart
    iii. The range of values displayed on the vertical axis
    iv. All of the above

14. **Poverty and Millionaires Choropleth Maps**. The following choropleth maps show
    the number of people living in poverty by state and the number of millionaires by state,
    respectively. Interestingly, these choropleth maps appear to be similar; states with a
    high level of millionaires also appear to be the same states with high levels of poverty.
    One possible insight from comparing these two choropleth maps is that poverty and
    high wealth appear to be positively correlated. **LO 8**

Estimated Number of People Living in Poverty by State

Number of Millionaires by State

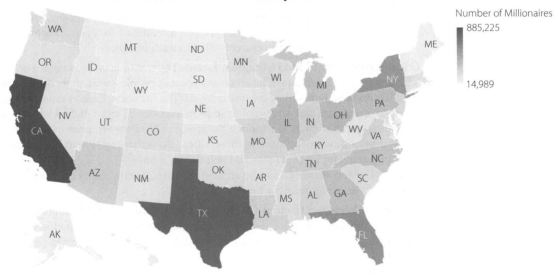

a. Why might it be incorrect to conclude that higher rates of poverty occur in states that have higher rates of wealth based on these two choropleth maps?

b. How would you improve these choropleth maps to provide a better comparison between poverty rates and rates of high wealth by state?

Applications

javacup

15. **Java Cup Taste Data**. Huron Lakes Candies (HLC) has developed a new candy bar called Java Cup that is a milk chocolate cup with a coffee-cream center. In order to assess the market potential of Java Cup, HLC has developed a taste test and follow-up survey. Respondents were asked to taste Java Cup and then rate Java Cup's taste, texture, creaminess of filling, sweetness, and depth of the chocolate flavor of the cup on a 100-point scale. The taste test and survey were administered to 217

randomly selected adult consumers. Data collected from each respondent are provided in the file *javacup*. **LO 1**

a. Are there any missing values in HLC'S survey data? If so, identify the respondents for which data are missing and indicate which values are missing for each of these respondents.

b. Are there any values in HLC'S survey data that appear to be erroneous? If so, identify the respondent for which data appear to be erroneous and indicate which values appear to be erroneous for each of these respondents.

attendmlb

16. **Major League Baseball Attendance**. Marilyn Marshall, a professor of sports economics, has obtained a data set of home attendance for each of the 30 major league baseball franchises for each season from 2010 through 2016. Dr. Marshall suspects the data, provided in the file *attendmlb*, is in need of a thorough cleansing. You should also find a reliable external source of Major League Baseball attendance for each franchise between 2010 and 2016 to use to help you identify appropriate imputation values for data missing in the *file attendmlb*. (*Hint*: ESPN.com contains attendance data for Major League Baseball franchises.)

a. Are there any missing values in Dr. Marshall's data? If so, identify the teams and seasons for which data are missing and which values are missing for each of these teams and seasons. Use the reliable external source of Major League Baseball Attendance for each franchise between 2010 and 2016 to find the correct value in each instance.

b. Are there any values in Dr. Marshall's data that appear to be erroneous? If so, identify the teams and seasons for which data appear to be erroneous and indicate which values appear to be erroneous for each of these teams and seasons. Use the reliable external source of Major League Baseball attendance for each franchise between 2010 and 2016 to find the correct value in each instance.

unemployrate

17. **Unemployment Rate and Delinquent Loans.** The rate of unemployment is often correlated with the amount of delinquent loans because people have a more difficult time repaying loans on time if they are unemployed. The file *unemployrate* contains data on unemployment rates and percent of delinquent loans for 27 cities in the United States. **LO 2**

a. Create a scatter chart to examine the relationship between unemployment rate and percent of delinquent loans in these cities. Does there appear to be a relationship between unemployment rate and delinquent loans?

b. Based on the scatter chart you created in part a, are there any data points that would cause concern as possibly being a data error?

guaraldi

18. **Amount of Vacation Used at Consulting Firm**. Guaraldi and Associates is a management consulting firm located in Manhattan. The firm is interested in examining the relationship between the amount of vacation their consultants use per year and how long the consultant has been with the firm. All consultants at Guaraldi and Associates, other than the Managing Partners, are considered either Junior Consultants or Senior Consultants based on their skills and expertise. The file *guaraldi* contains data on all Junior and Senior Consultants at Guaraldi and Associates, including the years of service the consultant has at the firm and the number of hours that the consultant took as vacation last year. **LO 4**

a. Create a scatter chart and add a trendline to examine the relationship between years of service and amount of vacation time used for all consultants at Guaraldi and Associates. Based on the scatter chart, what appears to be the relationship between years of service and amount of vacation time used?

b. Create a scatter chart for the same data, but this time, differentiate the points in the scatter chart based on whether the consultant is junior or senior. Do you see the same relationship in this scatter chart individually for junior and senior consultants as you saw in part a for all consultants?

c. Do the results in parts a and b provide an example of Simpson's paradox? Why or why not?

nominalwages

19. **Average Nominal Hourly Earnings (Revisited).** In this problem, we revisit the data used in Problem 6. The file *nominalwages* contains the data that were used to create the line chart shown in Problem 6. This file also contains price index data that can be used to adjust the nominal hourly earnings in the file for inflation. Use the price index data to adjust the nominal hourly earnings data for inflation using 3/1/2006 as the base period. Create a line chart for the inflation-adjusted hourly earnings and compare it to the line chart in Problem 6. What do the inflation-adjusted hourly earnings data suggest about the growth of hourly wages between 2006 and 2020? **LO 5**

commissioner_chart

20. **Political Polling Results in County Commissioner Election (Revisited).** In this problem, we revisit the chart from Problem 8. The chart shown in Problem 8 could be misleading for an audience comparing the polling results for the candidates Lisa Adamek and Rosemary Andrews. Redesign this chart using the data in the file *commissioner_chart* to be a more effective data visualization for the polling results for these two candidates. **LO 6**

positivityohio_chart

21. **COVID-19 Positivity Rates in Ohio (Revisited).** In this problem, we revisit the chart from Problem 9. The chart in Problem 9 could mislead an audience about trends related to the positivity rate for COVID-19 tests in Ohio between April and October 2020. Use the data in the file *positivityohio_chart* to redesign the chart to present a more effective data visualization for an audience trying to gain insights into the positivity rate of COVID-19 testing in Ohio. **LO 6**

maximus_chart

22. **Headcount and Revenue at Maximus Fashion (Revisited).** In this problem, we revisit the chart from Problem 11. The dual-axis chart used in Problem 11 is likely not an effective chart for an audience with little experience in finance and data visualization. Using the data in the file *maximus_chart*, redesign this dual-axis chart to be more effective for the audience. **LO 7**

povertymillionaires

23. **Poverty and Millionaires Choropleth Maps (Revisited).** In this problem, we revisit the charts from Problem 14. The choropleth maps in that problem show the number of people living in poverty by state and the number of millionaires by state, respectively. However, these charts could be misleading for an audience. The file *povertymillionaires* contains data on the number of people living in poverty in each state, the number of millionaires in each state, and the population of each state. **LO 8**
    a. Create a choropleth map that shows the poverty rate as a percent of the total state population in each state. Which states have the highest poverty rates?
    b. Create a choropleth map that shows the rate of millionaires as a percent of the total state population. Which states have the highest rate of millionaires?
    c. Compare the choropleth maps in parts a and b with the maps in Problem 14. Do you see the same relationship in the maps in parts a and b between the poverty rate and rate of millionaires as is seen in the maps in Problem 14? Why or why not?

Case 1: Piedmont General Hospital

Piedmont General Hospital (PGH) is a large healthcare facility located in the southeastern United States, renowned for its commitment to quality care of its patients. Megan Avery is the Vice President of Quality for PGH. Megan manages the team responsible for implementing and overseeing all quality and risk control programs.

PGH has recently noticed an uptick in the readmission rate. A readmission is when a discharged patient returns to the hospital for the same or related care within 30 days of being discharged from the hospital. Readmissions strain resources and negatively impact patient outcomes and patient satisfaction. Furthermore, for patients on Medicare, the Hospital Readmissions Reduction Program passed by Congress financially penalizes hospitals by reducing the amount paid for services when the hospital exceeds their expected number of readmissions. PGH has, to date, never exceeded its expected number of readmissions, and Megan wants to ensure that PGH continues to have fewer readmissions than expected.

Megan has asked her team to investigate factors that lead to higher readmission rates. Megan believes that if factors that seem related to higher readmission rates can be identified from the analysis of patient records, the team will be able to create strategies to mitigate the number of readmissions. To that end, David Moore, a data analyst on Megan's team, has collected a sample of 500 records for patients admitted for congestive heart disease.[1] The data set in the file *readmissions* includes the following variables:

DATA *file*
readmissions

- Patient ID Number – patient identification numbers from 1 to 500 to protect the privacy of the patient
- Age – the age of the patient at the time of the original admission to the hospital
- Comorbidities – health conditions other than congestive heart failure present in the patient
- Length of Stay – duration of the stay in the hospital in the original admission
- Discharge Instructions – instructions given to the patient when discharged (exercise and/or medication)
- Compliance – how well the patient complied with the discharge instructions (scored as low, medium, or high)
- Readmission status – whether or not the patient was readmitted for congestive heart failure within 30 days of discharge (1 = yes and 0 = no)

Now, David needs to analyze the data and develop a report for Megan. **LO 2.1, 2.2, 2.3, 2.4, 6.3, 6.5**

Summary Report

David's goal is to develop a report that shows which factors (if any) seem to be related to patient readmission. Your job is to conduct the analysis and help David with the report. Begin by investigating each of the following relationships with an appropriate chart:

1. How is readmission rate related to age? Consider age as a categorical variable with categories 40–49, 50–59, 60–69, and 70–80, and construct a column chart to answer this question.
2. How is readmission rate related to length of stay?
3. Is readmission rate higher for certain comorbidities?
4. How is readmission rate related to compliance?

---

[1]The data in this case are simulated.

    5. Construct a clustered column chart with readmission rates for the comorbidities by age category.

Based on your analysis, what are the characteristics of patients that should be targeted first for interventions and/or special follow-up care?

    Your report should include the charts and tables generated to answer the questions posed and a brief description and conclusion of each.

Case 2: Bayani Bulb Bases

Bayani Bulb Base, Inc (BBB) produces and sells Edison screw bases that are used by its wholesale customers as inputs into the production of LED (light-emitting diode) bulbs. The six light bulb bases BBB produces are:

- E11 - Miniature Candelabra/Sconce (11 mm)
- E12 - Candelabra/Sconce (12 mm)
- E14 - European (14 mm)
- E17 - Intermediate (17 mm)
- E26 - Standard/North American (26 mm)
- E39 - Mogul/High Lumen (39 mm)

BBB manufactures its light bulb bases in Appleton, Wisconsin; Greenville, South Carolina; and Henderson, Nevada. These modern factories are completely automated; all functions are performed by robots, so BBB factories are capable of production 24 hours per day and seven days per week. When BBB receives an order, it is immediately shipped from one of BBB's warehouses to the customer, and one of BBB's factories is immediately assigned to produce replacements and ship them to that warehouse to replenish BBB's inventory.

The finished bases are packed in cases of 244, and BBB's factories each have limited capacity to temporarily store cases of finished bases before they are shipped to BBB's warehouses in Boise, Idaho; Scranton, Pennsylvania; Jackson, Mississippi; and Sante Fe, New Mexico. The limited storage capacity at the factories compels BBB's factories to ship cases of finished bases within 2.5 days of manufacturing and packing on average. Once the cases of finished bases arrive at the warehouses, robots automatically unload and store them as directed by BBB's inventory control system.

In addition to BBB management's concern about the length of time cases of finished bases remain in temporary storage at each of its factories, BBB management also wants to determine whether any factory tends to produce cases of finished bases at slower or faster rates than the other two factories and whether any factory tends to ship cases of finished bases at slower or faster rates than the other two factories. Additionally, for each type of light bulb base, BBB management wants to monitor its monthly productivity by factory and the monthly number of cases of finished bases shipped from each factory to each warehouse.

Members of the BBB executive team asked Marisa Vallejo, Directory of Information Technology (IT), to develop a tool that will enable them to quickly gain insight into the status of each of these issues. Marisa decided that her staff could design a dashboard that would effectively and quickly provide these insights in a visual manner that would be easy for BBB's management to assimilate.

Marisa's first step was to task her staff with identifying and collecting the data necessary to support the development of this data dashboard. The IT staff collected the following data for each order placed with BBB over the past 36 months.

- Order Number
- Product Ordered
- Cases Ordered
- Factory in which the Order is Produced
- Warehouse to which the Order is Shipped
- Date Ordered
- Date Manufactured by Factory
- Date Shipped by Factory to Warehouse

These data are available in the file *bbb*. Because each row in these data represents an order of cases that has been fulfilled (produced and shipped), the field Cases Ordered also corresponds to the number of cases produced and the number of cases shipped. **LO 2.1, 2.3, 2.4, 2.5, 4.3, 4.5, 8.6**

DATA*file*

bbb

Summary Report

Marisa's objective is to develop a data dashboard that provides BBB executives with insight into the time cases of finished bases remain in temporary storage in each of its factories, the time to produce cases of finished bases in each of its factories, and the time to ship cases of finished bases from each of its factories. For each type of light bulb base, the dashboard should also enable BBB executives to determine the monthly number of cases of finished bases produced by each factory and the monthly number of cases of finished bases shipped from each factory to each warehouse.

Assist Marisa by first determining and creating the most appropriate chart of:

- Monthly average time to produce finished bases for each of its factories by product and year
- Monthly average time cases of finished bases remain in temporary storage in each of its factories by product and year
- Monthly average time to ship cases of finished bases for each of its factories by product and year
- Monthly number of cases of finished bases produced by each factory by product and year
- Monthly number of cases of finished bases shipped from each factory to each warehouse by product and year

Use these charts to build a dashboard that will enable the user to view them and select the factory, product, year, and warehouse for display. The dashboard should allow the user to control the selected factory, year, and product simultaneously.

Based on your results, your report should include discussions of the following questions:

1. Is the monthly average time to produce finished cases of bases for any BBB product(s) by any BBB factory substantially higher or lower than the other BBB factories?
2. Is any BBB factory systematically storing cases of finished bases of any BBB product(s) in temporary storage in excess of BBB's standard of an average of no more than 2.5 days?
3. Is the monthly average time to ship finished cases of bases for any BBB factory substantially superior or inferior to the other BBB factories for any BBB product(s)?
4. Is the monthly average cases of finished bases produced by any BBB factory systematically greater or less than the other BBB factories for any BBB product(s)?
5. Is the monthly number of cases of finished bases shipped for any factory-to-warehouse combination systematically greater or less than the other combinations of BBB factories and warehouses?

Case 3: International Monetary Fund Housing Affordability[1]

The International Monetary Fund (IMF) was formed in 1944 near the end of World War II. The IMF is headquartered in Washington, D.C., and it represents 190 member countries. The stated mission of the IMF is to work "to foster global monetary cooperation, secure financial stability, facilitate international trade, promote high employment and sustainable economic growth, and reduce poverty around the world (see https://www.imf.org/en/About)." The IMF often assists countries suffering financial crises by making loans using its resources of more than 600 billion US dollars, which are collected from member countries.

The IMF is also a leading global economic data and research organization, charged with watching over the global economy and calling attention to potential economic risks and major events. The IMF publishes many research reports, including the annual *World Economic Outlook* and more specialized working papers and visualizations based on world economic data and specific issues.

DATA *file*

imf

Gita Kotrangada is a research assistant for the IMF. Gita has been asked to compare housing affordability in the United States with Germany between the years of 1985 and 2020. Gita needs to create a single chart that best compares housing affordability for the United States and Germany over this time period. The data Gita has available to create this chart are median residential non-apartment home prices, median per capita incomes, and consumer price index values for both the United States and Germany during the years from 1985 to 2020 in the file *imf*. All home prices and income values are provided as nominal values (not adjusted for inflation). **LO 2.1, 2.2, 2.3, 2.4, 9.4, 9.5, 9.6**

Summary Report

Gita's goal is to create a single chart that best compares housing affordability in the United States and Germany during the years from 1985 to 2020. To help understand the best way to visualize these data, perform the following analysis.

1. Create a combo line chart displaying nominal home prices and nominal median per capita income in the United States. Create a similar combo line chart for Germany.
2. Create a line chart that compares the nominal home price in the United States to the nominal home price in Germany. Create a similar line chart comparing nominal incomes in the United States and Germany.
3. Create a nominal housing affordability metric by using the ratio of home prices to income for each country and create a line chart comparing these housing affordability metrics in the United States to Germany.
4. Create a chart comparing the housing affordability metrics for the United States and Germany that adjusts for inflation.
5. Based on the charts created in parts (1)–(4), which chart do you think presents the best comparison for these data? Why?

---

[1]The data provided for this case are drawn from similar data collected by the St. Louis Federal Reserve Bank and the World Bank.

Case 4: Short-Term Rental Market

Unlike traditional hotels, short-term rentals typically involve renting private residences for stays ranging from a single night to a few weeks. Fostered by the emergence of platforms such as Vrbo (Vacation Rentals by Owner) and Airbnb, the short-term rental market has become a robust sector of the lodging industry. These platforms provide a centralized online marketplace for property owners to list their properties and for travelers to conduct highly personalized searches for lodging options.

Short-term rentals offer travelers opportunities for more unique travel experiences at properties with their choice of amenities while also appealing to the notion of the sharing economy. Short-term rentals are also often a more economical choice for larger family groups that wish to stay in one house rather than split across multiple hotel rooms. In many cases, the rental host serves as a local guide, providing recommendations for dining, entertainment, and recreation.

Simone Douglas, an intern with the local Chamber of Commerce, has been asked to explore patterns in short-term rental bookings in the Santa Barbara area. The file *airbnb* contains a sample of the number of daily short-term rental bookings for the 731 days from July 2, 2021, to July 2, 2023. In addition, the file *airbnb* contains daily forecast information for July 3, 2023, to January 1, 2024. Specifically, for each of the 183 days spanning July 3, 2023, to January 1, 2024, there is a predicted number of bookings as well as a lower bound and upper bound (reflecting a 95% prediction interval for the forecast). **LO 4.5, 5.8, 6.8, 9.7**

DATA*file*

airbnb

Summary Report

Simone has been asked to develop data visualizations that explain the patterns in daily short-term rental bookings. Simone's goal is to create a series of charts that display the historic short-term rental booking data and forecast information at different temporal frequencies.

1. Plot the time series data with a chart that displays the number of daily bookings averaged annually.
2. Plot the time series data with a chart that displays the number of daily bookings averaged quarterly. Plot the historic and forecasted data on the same chart.
3. Plot the time series data with a chart that displays the number of daily bookings averaged monthly. Plot the historic and forecasted data on the same chart.
4. Plot the time series data with a chart that displays the number of bookings on a daily basis. Plot the historic and forecasted data on the same chart.
5. Create a column chart that displays the average number of daily bookings on the seven days of the week.
6. Based on the five charts in parts (1)–(5), what patterns do you observe in the short-term rental bookings?
7. Noting that there is not an entire year's worth of data for 2021 and 2023, explain how the trend in the chart displaying the number of daily bookings averaged annually may be misleading.
8. For the chart that displays the number of daily bookings averaged quarterly, explain why there appears to be a large discrepancy between the historic data for Quarter 3 and the forecasted data for Quarter 3.

Appendix

Data Wrangling: Preparing Data for Visualization

Contents

Analytics in Action

Wrangling Data at Procter & Gamble*

Procter & Gamble (P&G) is one of the largest consumer packaged goods companies in the world. P&G serves consumers around the world with a portfolio of trusted brands including Charmin, Crest, Gillette, Olay, Oral-B, Pantene, and Tide. To operate at the speed and efficiency required by today's market, P&G must process large volumes of new data daily. Before any data set is used to produce business insights at P&G, it goes through a complex data governance and data wrangling process. After legal and information security aspects of data acquisition and data usage are clarified, a dedicated team takes responsibility for the data and enters relevant information into P&G's data catalog. Before data are used for downstream applications such as data visualization, the data are validated and loaded into the data model, which meets company standards and is easier to understand by subscribers of the data.

To meet the unique needs of each downstream analysis, the data are filtered and aggregated to ensure that only relevant data are processed in further steps. An analysis is rarely performed on data from a single source, so these steps are executed for all data sets. Next, related data sets are combined so they can be presented in a single view or fed into an algorithm. Because the data wrangling process can be very complex, a data expert or an automated data quality algorithm validates the data before it is published to the wider audience. Once the data receive approval from the data expert, they are made available to the users, and notifications are sent, if necessary, to any downstream applications.

---

*The authors are indebted to Jacek Tokar, Michal Antkowiak, and David Dittmann of Procter & Gamble for providing this Analytics in Action.

It is good practice to always maintain a copy of the original raw data and data set produced at intermediate steps of the data wrangling process.

Raw data, which are sometimes called source data or primary data, are data that have not been processed or prepared for data visualization and other analysis. **Data wrangling** is the process of cleaning, transforming, and managing raw data so they are more reliable and can be more easily accessed and used for data visualization and other analysis, This process, which is also sometimes referred to as data munging or data remediation, involves transforming raw data into a new data set that is designed specifically to support visualization and analysis.

Data wrangling activities include:

- Merging multiple data sources into a single data set
- Identifying missing values in data and either filling or deleting the record or observation
- Identifying erroneous values in data and replacing them with the correct values
- Identifying and deleting duplicate observations or records in data
- Identifying extreme values in data, determining whether they are legitimate, and taking appropriate action
- Subsetting data to facilitate displays and comparisons of subgroups of the raw data

The data wrangling process can be manual or automated, or it can be a combination of manual and automated. The process can also be ad hoc or systematic. As the size, complexity, and importance of the raw data increases, an automated and systematic approach to data wrangling becomes more necessary. No matter how it is accomplished, the objective of data wrangling is to facilitate the efforts of data scientists and analytics professionals to focus on their visualization and analysis tasks and the extraction of meaningful information from the data.

Although each data wrangling project is unique, the objective is to produce a final data set that is accurate, reliable, and accessible. This objective leads to a series of steps that are commonly taken in the data wrangling process:

- **Discovery:** The goal of the discovery phase is for the analyst to become familiar with the raw data to be able to conceptualize how it might be used. During this step, the analyst often discovers potential issues that will need to be addressed later in the data wrangling process. Just as data wrangling is a precursor to meaningful visualization

If new raw data are added to the existing raw data set in the enriching step, the new raw data should be subjected to the discovery, structuring, and cleaning steps. Also, it is good practice to always maintain a copy of the enriched raw data.

and analysis, discovery is a precursor to the data wrangling steps that follow, and this step should not be overlooked or neglected.

- **Structuring:** In the structuring phase, the analyst arranges the raw data so it can be more readily displayed and analyzed in the intended manner.
- **Cleaning:** The goal of the cleaning phase is to find and correct errors in the raw data that might distort the ensuing visualization and analysis. This can include addressing missing or incorrect values.
- **Enriching:** In this step, the analyst may augment the raw data by incorporating values from other data sets and/or applying transformations to portions of the existing data to ensure that all data required for the ensuing visualization and analysis will be included in the wrangled data set.
- **Validating:** In the validating phase, the analyst verifies that the wrangled data are accurate and reliable and that they are ready for the ensuing visualization and analysis.
- **Publishing:** In this step, the analyst creates a file containing the wrangled data and documentation of the file's contents and makes these available to their intended users in a format they can use.

The quality of any data visualization is limited by the quality of the source data. Data that are incomplete, inaccurate, unreliable, or inaccessible may limit the insights that can be gained from their visual representation or even result in erroneous conclusions and poor decisions. By properly wrangling the raw data, the analyst reduces these risks by ensuring data are reliable and accessible before they are represented visually. Although data wrangling can be time-consuming and resource intensive, it is critical that organizations methodically and conscientiously follow the steps of the data wrangling process before moving on to the visual representation of the data. Likewise, before data are used in more sophisticated models, accuracy of the data is of paramount importance. The old adage "garbage in = garbage out" rings true in data visualization. In the ensuing sections of this chapter, we will discuss each of the steps of the data wrangling process in more detail.

A.1 Discovery

Data wrangling starts with discovery, as the analyst becomes familiar with and understands the raw data with an eye toward how the data should be organized to facilitate its use and visualization. The analyst should come to this step with a thorough understanding of how these data may be displayed and consider this as the discovery process proceeds. This understanding includes how the raw data can be accessed, the structure of the raw data, whether the data are numerical or text, how they are arrayed or arranged, and the types of file(s) that contain the raw data.

In this section, we will consider issues that arise in the wrangling of raw data to ultimately be used in the creation and maintenance of a database for Stinson's MicroBrew Distributor, a licensed regional independent distributor of beer and a member of the National Beer Wholesalers Association. Stinson's provides refrigerated storage, transportation, and delivery of premium beers produced by several local microbreweries. The company's facilities include a state-of-the-art temperature-controlled warehouse and a fleet of temperature-controlled trucks. Stinson's employs sales, receiving, warehousing/inventory, and delivery personnel. When making a delivery, Stinson's monitors the retailer's shelves, taps, and keg lines to ensure the freshness and quality of the product. Because beer is perishable and because microbreweries often do not have the capacity to store, transport, and deliver large quantities of the products they produce, Stinson's holds a critical position in this supply chain.

Accessing Data

Accessing the data involves importing the raw data into whatever software is to be used to wrangle the raw data. Raw data can come in many formats, including:

- Delimited text (txt) files, comma separated value (csv) files, JavaScript Object Notation (JSON) files, XML files, Excel (xlsx) files, and HTML files

- Databases such as ACCESS, SQL, or ORACLE
- Web pages/HTML files

sdeliveries.csv

Stinson's routinely receives a csv file that contains information on each delivery the company received from its supplier microbreweries during a given week. These data for one week, as stored in the csv file *sdeliveries.csv*, are shown in Figure A.1. The names of the fields are shown in the first row of the data. In Figure A.1, we see that the file *sdeliveries.csv* contains:

SOrderNumber: Stinson's internal number assigned to each order placed with a
    microbrewery
BrewerID: Stinson's internal identification number assigned to the microbrewery with
    which the order has been placed
EmployeeID: The identification number of the Stinson's employee who received the delivery
Date of SDelivery: The date on which Stinson's received the delivery
SQuantity Delivered: The quantity (in units) received in the delivery

A csv file is a file that is in comma separated values format.

Each ensuing row in the file *sdeliveries.csv* represents one record or delivery, and tags or markers called **delimiters** indicate how to separate the raw data into various fields when they are read. Commas are used to delimit the fields in each record in the file *sdeliveries.csv*.

Many of the tools that can be used for data wrangling, such as Excel, R, Python, SQL, and Access, can import raw data from a csv file. Excel can automatically open and import a csv file, so if Stinson's wants to import the raw data into Excel, it can do so through the following steps once Excel is open:

Step 1. Click the **File** tab on the Ribbon and select **Open**

Figure A.1	Display of the CSV File *sdeliveries* That Contains Information on Deliveries Received by Stinson's from Various Microbreweries During a Recent Week

SOrderNumber,BrewerID,EmployeeID,Date of SDelivery,SQuantity Delivered
17351,3,94,11/5/2023,3
17352,9,9,11/5/2023,6
17353,7,135,11/6/2023,2
17354,3,94,11/6/2023,3
17355,2,135,11/6/2023,2
17356,6,135,11/6/2023,5
17358,9,135,11/7/2023,3
17359,4,135,11/7/2023,2
17360,3,94,11/8/2023,8
17361,2,135,11/8/2023,1
17362,7,94,11/8/2023,2
17363,9,94,11/9/2023,4
17364,6,135,11/8/2023,2
17365,2,94,11/9/2023,5
17366,3,94,11/9/2023,4
17366,7,135,11/10/2023,4
17366,9,94,11/9/2023,4
17367,4,94,11/9/2023,3

Step 2. Click **Browse**, select **All Files (*)** in the **File Type** dropdown list in the **Open** dialog box, and navigate to the location of the file *tblpurchaseprices.txt*

Step 3. Select the file and click **Open**

Stinson's also maintains a txt file that contains the prices charged by each microbrewery that supplies Stinson's with beer. These data, as stored in the file *tblpurchaseprices.txt*, are shown in Figure A.2. The names of the fields are shown in the first row of the data. In Figure A.2, we see that the file *tblpurchaseprices.txt* contains:

BrewerID: Stinson's internal identification number assigned to the microbrewery with which the order has been placed

KegPurchasePrice: The price the microbrewery associated with the record charges for a keg of its beer

CasePurchasePrice: The price the microbrewery associated with the record charges for a case of its beer

Each ensuing row in the file *tblpurchaseprices.txt* represents one microbrewery, and the information in the records is tab delimited.

Many data wrangling software packages import delimited raw data that utilize tabs or other delimiters. If Stinson's wants to import the raw data in the file *tblpurchaseprices.txt* into Excel, it can do so through the following steps once Excel is open:

Step 1. Click the **File** tab on the Ribbon and select **Open**

Step 2. Click **Browse**, select **All Files (*)** in the **File Type** dropdown list in the **Open** dialog box, and navigate to the location of the file *tblpurchaseprices.txt*

Step 3. Select the file and click **Open**

Step 4. In the **Text Import Wizard—Step 1 of 3** dialog box (shown in Figure A.3)

Select **Delimited** in the **Original data type: Chose the file type that best describes your data** area

Indicate that the delimited raw data to be imported (*tblpurchases.txt*) has headers

Click **Next**

Step 5. In the **Text Import Wizard—Step 2 of 3** dialog box (shown in Figure A.4)

Select **Tab** in the **Delimiters** area

Review the raw data in the **Data preview** area to ascertain that the data will import correctly

Click **Finish**

DATA *file*

tblpurchaseprices.txt

You can use the Text Import Wizard to import data from files that use other delimiters by indicating the appropriate delimiter in the **Text Import Wizard—Step 2 of 3** *dialog box.*

| Figure A.2 | Display of File *tblpurchaseprices.txt* Containing Information About the Price Charged by Each Microbrewery That Supplied Stinson's with Beer During a Recent Week |

BrewerID	KegPurchasePrice	CasePurchasePrice
1	$158.00	$43.00
2	$227.00	$62.00
3	$214.00	$59.00
4	$156.00	$43.00
5	$248.00	$68.00
6	$191.00	$52.00
7	$179.00	$49.00
8	$237.00	$65.00
9	$245.00	$67.00
10	$181.00	$50.00
11	$236.00	$65.00

| Figure A.3 | Text Import Wizard—Step 1 of 3 Dialog Box |

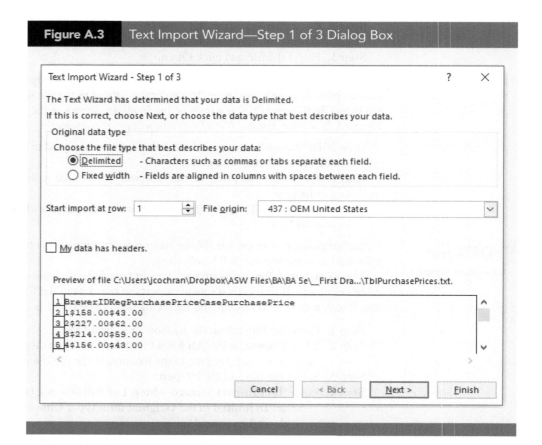

| Figure A.4 | Text Import Wizard—Step 2 of 3 Dialog Box |

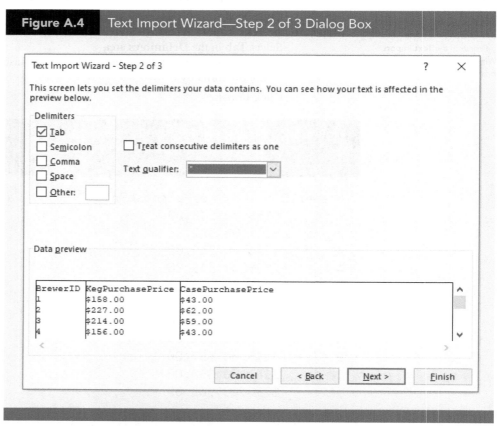

Table A.1	Structured Data from the File tblbrewersaddresses		
BrewerID	**Brewery Name**	**Address**	**Phone Number**
3	Oak Creek Brewery	12 Appleton St, Dayton, OH, 45455	937-449-1212
6	Gonzo Microbrew	1515 Marlboro Lane, Dayton, OH, 45429	937-288-2651
4	McBride's Pride	425 Dry River Rd, Miamisburg, OH, 45459	937-441-0123
9	Fine Pembrook Ale	141 Dusselberg Ave, Trotwood, OH, 45426	937-852-8752
7	Midwest Fiddler Crab	844 Small Hills Ave, Kettering, OH, 45453	937-633-7183
2	Herman's Killer Brew	912 Highlite Dr, Fairborn, OH, 45442	937-883-2651

The Format of the Raw Data

The format of the raw data determines how the data are wrangled. Each **record** in a data set is a grouping of characteristics for a particular observation, and each **field** is a characteristic of the observations in a data set. **Structured data** refers to data that are arrayed in a predetermined pattern that make them easy to manage and search. The most common pattern in which structured data are arrayed as a rectangle, with each row representing an observation or record and each column representing a variable or field. A file that is arrayed in this manner is often referred to as a **flat file**. Table A.1 provides an example of structured data from the file *tblbrewersaddresses*, which contains contact information about each microbrewery that supplies Stinson's with beer.

The simple and orderly arrangement and formatting of structured data make them relatively easy to process. However, this also imposes constraints on what structured data can contain.

Unstructured data are databases that are not arranged in a predetermined pattern and, therefore, in their raw form cannot be stored in a manner similar to that of a flat file. Text, multimedia, email messages, social media posts, chats, photographs, satellite images, medical scans, Internet of Things (IoT) sensor data, webpages, and video and audio files are common examples of files that contain unstructured data. Figure A.5 provides an example of unstructured data from responses to an open-ended survey question dealing with why respondents do not purchase or use Ship-Shape Basin bathroom cleaner.

Because of its complex arrangement and formatting, raw unstructured data can be difficult to process and analyze. Although unstructured data are more difficult to search and use than structured data, they are abundant. Experts estimate that over 80% of the world's data is unstructured. Unstructured data can also be useful, as it often contains unique data that can be harvested for deep and novel insights.

Figure A.5	Unstructured Data from Responses to an Open-Ended Survey Question: "Why Respondents Do Not Purchase or Use Ship-Shape Basin Bathroom Cleaner?"

Ship-Shape smells terrible—like a doctor's office—and the smell lingers for days after I have used it.

The bright neon lime green color of the foam is nauseating.

The smell is extremely mediciney—it gives me a headache. And the product doesn't get my sinks and toilets very clean—it is too much work to clean with Ship-Shape.

Ship-Shape leaves big streaks on whatever I use it to clean—then I have to use something else to clean the streaks!!!

Figure A.6	Semi-Structured Data from an Internet Browsing Session in Microsoft Edge

Structured Data

```
<head data-client-settings="{"aid":"EA362BF547C44186AF14F1F726D9834A", "static_page":"fals
e", "queryparams":"?locale=en-US&market=US&enableregulatorypsm=0&enablecpsm=0&ishostisolat
ionenforced=0&targetexperience=enterprise", "apptype":"edge", "pagetype":"ntp", "configRoo
tUrl":"https://assets.msn.com/config/v1/", "feedBaseDomain":"", "deviceFormFactor":"deskto
p", "pageGenTime":"2021-11-21T01:11:46Z", "pcsInfo":{"v":"20211117.18_master", "env":"pro
d"}, "featureFlags":{ "wpoEnabled": "true" }, "market":{}, "locale":{"language":"en", "scr
ipt":"", "market":"us"}, "servicesEndpoints":{"staticConfig": {"domain": "https://assets.m
sn.com", "path": "/config/v3/", "v": ""},"crs": {"domain": "", "path": "/resolver/api/reso
lve/", "v": "v3"},"feedService": {"domain": "https://assets.msn.com", "path": "", "v":
""},"enterpriseFeedService": {"domain": "https://ent-api.msn.com/", "path": "", "v": ""}},
"bundleInfo":{"v":"20210726.374", "alias":"latest", "hash":"56a8d611e7c96e8f053923720a1f8e
bf", "configsHash":"e2a6614aa036bd627142880173cba606", "locConfigsHash":"6617e75fe53f1a919
1bf689ca5c19cfd"}, "os":"windows", "browser":{"browserType":"edge", "version":"18", "ismob
ile":"false"}, "domain":"www.msn.com", "detection":{"ip":"68.63.102.156"}, "geo_countr
y":"US", "geo_countryname":"United States", "geo_subdivision":"Alabama", "geo_zip":"3547
3", "geo_city":"Northport", "geo_lat":"33.2623", "geo_long":"-87.5397"}" data-info="f:msna
llexpusers,rrotbn,muidflt11cf,muidflt12cf,muidflt16cf,prg-trvl-wce,muidflt47cf,muidflt48c
f,muidflt261cf,mmxandroid1cf,mmxios1cf,blockdedupmsanc,bingcollabedge1cf,starthp2cf,starth
p3cf,ads-artbtoho,platagyhz1cf,artgly3cf,artgly4cf,1s-bing-news,vebudumu04302020,bbh202005
21msncf,shophp1cf,grocmit4,groceriesmit4,prg-bingshopmit,1s-brsagedsdc,1s-brsagel3urac2,pr
g-1sw-bluesm-c,prg-1sw-contcol-c,prg-1sw-nmkt2,prg-1sw-revtr,prg-1sw-qucg,prg-1sw-noreacth
over,prg-1sw-enads,prg-1sw-ucb10,prg-1sw-spvdo,prg-1sw-nobkplate-c,btrecenus,iframeflex,pr
g-adspeek,csmoney6cf,1s-br30min,1s-winauthservice,prg-1sw-n-api1,prg-1sw-api1,1s-winsegser
vice,1s-fqrc1s,prg-1sw-alertinfov,prg-hprewflyout-c,prg-wf-sky-re,prong2c,prg-1s-brcrwtch-
a1,f-rel-allc,prg-winwtchads3-c,prg-wincom-on,1s-pagesegservice,prg-ias,prg-1sw-weameta,ro
utentpring2t,prg-wf-v33-ba,prg-1sw-pdt31,prg-1sw-pdtg,prg-sh-tabthc,prg-1sw-hldynobg,prg-1
sw-wxnrt36,prg-sh-mitcartg-cf;;userOptOut:false;userOptOutOptions:">…</head>
<body>
```

Unstructured Data

Semi-structured data does not have the same level of organization as structured data, but it does contain elements that allow for the isolation of some elements of the raw data when they are imported. An example of a semi-structured file is the record of an Internet browsing session shown in Figure A.6. Some elements of the file do not have a pre-defined structure, but other elements (such as "locale," "apptype," "os," and "pageGenTime") have a structure that allows them to be easily identified and isolated.

Raw data in each of these formats can be valuable, and businesses commonly collect and need to analyze structured, unstructured, and semi-structured data.

A.2 Structuring

Once the analyst understands the raw data and how it should be organized to facilitate its visualization, the focus turns to structuring the raw data file so it can be more readily displayed in the intended manner. This may include the formatting of the data fields, how the data are to be arranged, splitting one field with several important pieces of information into several fields, and merging several fields into a single more meaningful field.

Data Formatting

The two primary forms of data are numeric and text. **Numeric data** are data that are stored in a manner that allows mathematical operations to be performed on them. Data of this type generally represent a count or measurement.

Software can often be used to apply specific formats to fields in raw data. For example, Excel offers several formats that can be applied to numerical data, including Currency, Accounting, Long Date, Short Date, Time, Percentage, and Scientific Notation. For example, we may want to use a different format for the date field in the csv file *sdeliveries.csv* (shown in Figure A.1). To change the format of this field in Excel, we apply the following steps after importing the file *sdeliveries.csv* into Excel:

Step 1. Select cells D2:D19 (the range of cells to format)
Step 2. Right click one of the highlighted cells and select **Format Cells . . .**
Step 3. When the **Format Cells** dialog box opens:
  Select **Date** in the **Category** pane and click **March 14, 2012** (the desired format for this field) in the **Type** pane as shown in Figure A.7
  Click **OK**

The data in the Date field are now shown in the new format.

Text data are data that are words, phrases, sentences, and paragraphs. This kind of data includes characters such as alphabetical, numerical (when the numbers are not to be used in mathematical calculations, such as with a field for which 1 corresponds to YES and 2 corresponds to NO), and special symbols. Brewery Name and Address in the file *tblbrewersaddresses.csv* (shown in Figure A.2) are examples of text data.

DATA*file*

sdeliveries.csv

Arrangement of Data

We have considered data sets that are arrayed in a manner such that every row (record) represents an observation on a set of variables (fields), and the values of those variables

---

Figure A.7   The Excel Format Cells Dialog Box

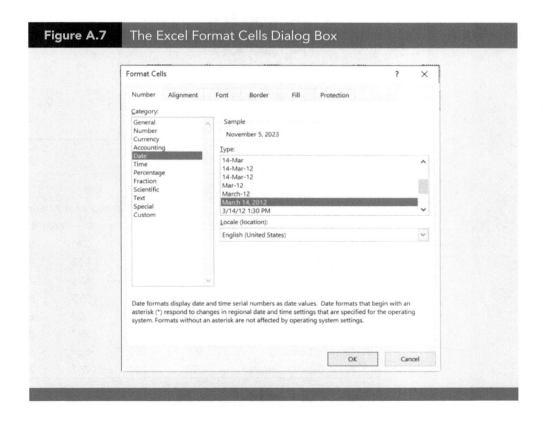

are listed in the columns. However, there are multiple ways to organize the data within this structure, particularly if the data contain categorical variables.

Consider data on three-point shot attempts by each team in a high school basketball conference for the past six years. Figure A.8a and Figure A.8b show the same portion of these data arranged in two different ways. In Figure A.8a, each record (row) consists of values in three fields (columns): a team name, a year, and the number of three-point shot attempts by that team during that year. In Figure A.8b, each record (row) consists of values in seven fields (columns): a team name, and then in the next six columns, the number of three-point shot attempts by that team in each of six years.

Figure A.8   A Portion of Data from the File hs3pa in Stacked (Panel a) and Unstacked (Panel b) Form

(a) Stacked Data

	A	B	C
1	Team	Year	Three Point Attempts
2	Gamaliel Gremlins	1	602
3	Fitzgerald Hawks	1	713
4	Delano Demons	1	647
5	Ulysses Gazelles	1	711
6	Milhous Rams	1	800
7	Birchard Spiders	1	682
8	Quincy Bobcats	1	800
9	Knox Golden Bears	1	650
10	Gamaliel Gremlins	2	918
11	Fitzgerald Hawks	2	755
12	Delano Demons	2	759
13	Ulysses Gazelles	2	873
14	Milhous Rams	2	890
15	Birchard Spiders	2	762
16	Quincy Bobcats	2	631
17	Knox Golden Bears	2	794
18	Gamaliel Gremlins	3	776
19	Fitzgerald Hawks	3	808
20	Delano Demons	3	653
21	Ulysses Gazelles	3	919

(b) Unstacked Data

	A	B	C	D	E	F	G
1		Three Point Attempts					
2	Team	Year 1	Year 2	Year 3	Year 4	Year 5	Year 6
3	Gamaliel Gremlins	602	918	776	590	600	559
4	Fitzgerald Hawks	713	755	808	841	831	628
5	Delano Demons	647	759	653	779	626	826
6	Ulysses Gazelles	711	873	919	676	775	645
7	Milhous Rams	800	890	506	695	775	764
8	Birchard Spiders	682	762	587	800	903	773
9	Quincy Bobcats	800	631	626	910	894	670
10	Knox Golden Bears	650	794	737	772	642	717

The arrangement of data in Figure A.8a is referred to as stacked data. **Stacked data** are data organized so the values for each variable are stored in a single field. The arrangement of data in Figure A.8b is referred to as unstacked data. **Unstacked data** are data organized so the values for one variable correspond to separate fields. The data in Figure A.8a are stacked with respect to Year because all values of Year are listed in a single field; each record corresponds to a unique combination of team and year. The data in Figure A.8b are unstacked with respect to Year because there is a field corresponding to each value of Year; each record corresponds to a single team for each of several years. The same data are contained in both versions, but the data are arranged differently.

In Chapter 6, we compare data visualizations constructed from stacked and unstacked data.

Depending on the source of the data and how it was collected, data may be provided in stacked or unstacked form. Both arrangements of data can be useful as each arrangement can facilitate different visualizations. For example, the unstacked version of the raw data facilitates the display of individual team performances across multiple years, and the stacked version of the raw data facilitates the display of the performances in individual years across multiple teams. Some software packages also require the data be in stacked or unstacked form, so it is useful to be able to transform stacked data to unstacked data and transform unstacked data to stacked data. In the following steps, we use Excel to convert the three-point shot attempt data from stacked form in the file *stackedtablehs3pa* (shown in Figure A.8a) to unstacked form with respect to the Year variable.

stackedtablehs3pa

Step 1. Select any cell in the range of the Table, for example, cell A1
Step 2. Click the **Data** tab on the Ribbon
Step 3. In the **Get & Transform** group, click **From Table/Range**
Step 4. When the **Power Query Editor** window appears:
  Select the **Year** column
  Click the **Transform** tab
  In the **Any Column** group, click **Pivot Column**
  When the **Pivot Column** dialog box appears, select **Three Point Attempts** in the dropdown menu for **Values Column**
  Click **OK**
  Click the **Home** tab and in the **Close** group, click **Close & Load**

The preceding steps create an Excel Table that contains the same fields and records in a new worksheet that are arranged in the same manner as the unstacked data form in Figure A.8b.

Conversely, in the following steps we convert the three-point shot attempt data from unstacked form in the file *unstackedtablehs3pa* (shown in Figure A.8b) to stacked form with respect to the Year variable:

unstackedtablehs3pa

Step 1. Select any cell in the range of the Table, for example, cell A3
Step 2. Click the **Data** tab on the Ribbon
Step 3. In the **Get & Transform** group, click **From Table/Range**
Step 4. When the **Power Query Editor** window appears
  Select the columns corresponding to **Year1**, **Year 2**, **Year 3**, **Year 4**, **Year 5**, and **Year 6** (press the **Ctrl** key while selecting each column)
  Click the **Transform** tab
  In the **Any Column** group, click **Unpivot Columns**
  Click the **Home** tab and in the **Close** group, click **Close & Load**

The preceding steps create an Excel Table in a new worksheet that, after sorting on years, matches the stacked data form in Figure A.8a.

Splitting a Single Field into Multiple Fields

Sometimes one field in the raw data contains several pieces of information that would be more useful if divided into separate fields. For example, dates, addresses, and times often contain multiple pieces of information that may be more useful if divided into separate fields. Consider the Address field in the file *tblbrewersaddresses* shown in Figure A.2. The information contained in this field might be easier to use if the street address, city, state, and zip code were each in its own field. Such an arrangement would allow us to sort on City or Zip Code and display the data in that manner.

Many data wrangling software packages provide tools for splitting a single field into multiple fields. In Excel, on the **Data** tab in the **Data Tools** group, the **Text to Columns** button invokes the **Convert Text to Columns Wizard** that can be used for this purpose. Useful operations that can be performed using the **Convert Text to Columns Wizard** include:

- Splitting names into the first name and last name
- Splitting email addresses into username and domain name
- Extracting the first *n* characters of a string

We will illustrate splitting one field into multiple fields by applying the **Convert Text to Columns Wizard** tool to raw data in the file *tblbrewersaddresses*. We will separate the field Address as shown in Figure A.9 into the individual fields Street Address, City, State, and Zip Code.

tblbrewersaddresses

Once the file *tblbrewersaddresses* is open:

Step 1. Select columns D, E, and F by clicking on the heading of column D and dragging the cursor across the headings of columns E and F
Step 2. Right click anywhere in the selected columns and select **Insert** to insert three columns immediately to the right of the Address column to provide space for the new columns to be generated (the four columns generated for the new Address, City, State, and Zip Code fields will fill the column now occupied by the Address field and the three new columns)
Step 3. Select cells C2:C7 (the range of the field to be separated)
Step 4. Click the **Data** tab on the Ribbon
Step 5. In the **Data Tools** group, click **Text to Columns**
Step 6. When the **Convert Text to Columns Wizard—Step 1 of 3** dialog box appears (as shown in Figure A.10)
    Select **Delimited** (because the data in the Address field that is to be put into individual columns is separated by commas)
    Click **Next**
Step 7. When the **Convert Text to Columns Wizard—Step 2 of 3** dialog box appears (as shown in Figure A.11)
    In the **Delimiters** pane, select **Comma** and deselect all other delimiter options
    Click **Next**

Figure A.9   Data from the File *tblbrewersaddresses*

◢	A	B	C	D
1	BrewerID	Brewery Name	Address	Phone Number
2	3	Oak Creek Brewery	12 Appleton St, Dayton, OH, 45455	937-449-1212
3	6	Gonzo Microbrew	1515 Marlboro Lane, Dayton, OH, 45429	937-288-2651
4	4	McBride's Pride	425 Dry River Rd, Miamisburg, OH, 45459	937-441-0123
5	9	Fine Pembrook Ale	141 Dusselberg Ave, Trotwood, OH, 4542(	937-852-8752
6	7	Midwest Fiddler Crab	844 Small Hills Ave, Kettering, OH, 45453	937-633-7183
7	2	Herman's Killer Brew	912 Highlite Dr, Fairborn, OH, 45442	937-883-2651

Figure A.10	Convert Text to Columns Wizard—Step 1 of 3 Dialog Box

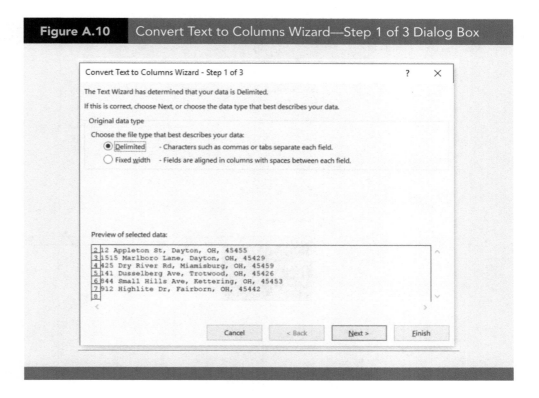

Figure A.11	Convert Text to Columns Wizard—Step 2 of 3 Dialog Box

Figure A.12 Convert Text to Columns Wizard – Step 3 of 3 Dialog Box

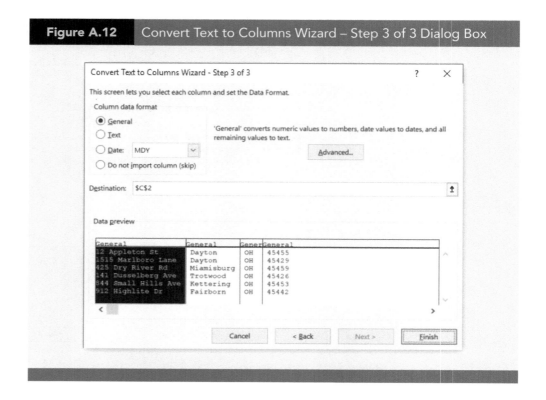

Step 8. When the **Convert Text to Columns Wizard—Step 3 of 3** dialog box appears (as shown in Figure A.12)

In the **Column data format** pane, click the first column in the **Data preview** area

Select **General** in the **Column data format** area

Repeat this process for each column

Click **Finish**

We have created the worksheet in Figure A.13.

We can now add appropriate headers to columns C, D, E, and F and save the file under the name *tblbrewers*.

Figure A.13 Contents of the File *tblbrewersaddresses* with the Address Field Split into Four Fields

	A	B	C	D	E	F	G
1	BrewerID	Brewery Name	Address				Phone Number
2	3	Oak Creek Brewery	12 Appleton St	Dayton	OH	45455	937-445-1212
3	6	Gonzo Microbrew	1515 Main St	Dayton	OH	45429	937-278-2651
4	4	McBride's Pride	425 Mad River Rd	Miamisburg	OH	45459	937-439-0123
5	9	Fine Pembrook Ale	141 Dusselberg Ave	Trotwood	OH	45426	937-837-8752
6	7	Midwest Fiddler Crab	844 Far Hills Ave	Kettering	OH	45453	937-633-7183
7	2	Herman's Killer Brew	912 Airline Dr	Fairborn	OH	45442	937-878-2651

Figure A.14	Excel Spreadsheet Showing the Names Data

	A	B	C	D	E
1	Prefix	First Name	Middle Name	Last Name	Suffix
2	Dr.	Zuri	G	Leseoana	
3	Ms.	Donna		Spicoli	
4	Mr.	Juan	Mateo	Rivera	Jr.
5		Donny	John	Moroni	
6	Mr.	Albert		Levy	III
7	Mr.	Haneul		Seong	
8		Meera		Bhatt	
9	Ms.	Jasmine	D	Belcher	

Combining Multiple Fields into a Single Field

Sometimes, several fields in the raw data contain information that would be more useful if combined into a single field. For example, if we received the data shown in Figure A.14 but needed the prefix, first name, middle name, and last name all in a single field (perhaps to facilitate the creation of shipping labels), we would want to combine these four fields into a single field.

*After entering Dr. Zuri G Leseoana in cell F2, you can also use the Flash Fill functionality to automatically fill the remaining records in column F by clicking the **Data** tab on the Ribbon, then clicking **Flash Fill** 🔲 in the **Data Tools** group.*

Many data wrangling software packages provide tools for combining multiple fields into a single field. In Excel, the Flash Fill functionality will quickly combine multiple fields into a single field. If we enter *Dr. Zuri G Leseoana* in cell F2, and then start typing *Ms.* in cell F3, Excel will fill in column F for each ensuing record. Figure A.15a shows the Flash Fill function filling the remainder of cell F3 as well as all of cells C4:C7.

Note that Flash Fill replicates the pattern it observes in the first entry, so for each record it will add a blank space for each missing field in ensuing records. Thus, for the Names data, Flash Fill adds a blank space in front of the first name for the entries it creates for Donny John Moroni and Meera Bhatt (because these records do not include a prefix). Flash Fill also adds a blank space between the first name and last name in the entries it creates for Ms. Donna Spicoli, Mr. Albert Levy, and Mr. Haneul Seong (because these records do not include a middle name or initial). Also note that Flash Fill will not pick up the suffixes in the Names data because there is no suffix in the entry in cell F2 (the cell that was used to establish the pattern to be replicated).

Figure A.15a	Excel Flash Fill Function Filling the Remainder of Cell F3 and All of Cells C4:C7

	A	B	C	D	E	F	G
1	Prefix	First Name	Middle Name	Last Name	Suffix		
2	Dr.	Zuri	G	Leseoana		Dr. Zuri G Leseoana	
3	Ms.	Donna		Spicoli		Ms. Donna Spicoli	
4	Mr.	Juan	Mateo	Rivera	Jr.	Mr. Juan N	
5		Donny	John	Moroni		Donny Jo	
6	Mr.	Albert		Levy	III	Mr. Alber	
7	Mr.	Haneul		Seong		Mr. Haneu	
8		Meera		Bhatt		Meera Bh	
9	Ms.	Jasmine	D	Belcher		Ms. Jasmi	

Figure A.15b	Excel Spreadsheet Showing the Names Data with the Fields Prefix, First Name, Middle Name, Last Name, and Suffix Combined in a Single Field

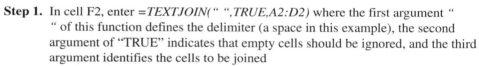

◢	A	B	C	D	E	F	G
1	Prefix	First Name	Middle Name	Last Name	Suffix		
2	Dr.	Zuri	G	Leseoana		Dr. Zuri G Leseoana	Dr. Zuri G Leseoana
3	Ms.	Donna		Spicoli		Ms. Donna Spicoli	Ms. Donna Spicoli
4	Mr.	Juan	Mateo	Rivera	Jr.	Mr. Juan Mateo Rivera	Mr. Juan Mateo Rivera, Jr.
5		Donny	John	Moroni		Donny John Moroni	Donny John Moroni
6	Mr.	Albert		Levy	III	Mr. Albert Levy	Mr. Albert Levy, III
7	Mr.	Haneul		Seong		Mr. Haneul Seong	Mr. Haneul Seong
8		Meera		Bhatt		Meera Bhatt	Meera Bhatt
9	Ms.	Jasmine	D	Belcher		Ms. Jasmine D Belcher	Ms. Jasmine D Belcher

We can resolve these problems and combine the fields Prefix, First Name, Middle Name, Last Name, and Suffix into a single field for each record with Excel's TEXTJOIN function. We illustrate combining multiple fields into a single field by applying the TEXTJOIN function to the raw data in the file *names* (shown in Figure A.14) to create a single field containing the contents of the Prefix, First Name, Middle Name, Last Name, and Suffix fields.

Because we want to delimit the fields Prefix, First Name, Middle Name, and Last Name with spaces and delimit the combination of these fields and the field Suffix with a comma in the final result, we will work in two steps.

DATA *file*

names

Step 1. In cell F2, enter *=TEXTJOIN(" ",TRUE,A2:D2)* where the first argument " " of this function defines the delimiter (a space in this example), the second argument of "TRUE" indicates that empty cells should be ignored, and the third argument identifies the cells to be joined

Step 2. Copy cell F2 into cells F3:F9

Step 3. In cell G2, enter *=TEXTJOIN(", ",TRUE,F2,E2)* where the first argument "," of this function defines the delimiter (a comma in this example), the second argument "TRUE" indicates that empty cells should be ignored, and the third argument identifies the cells to be joined

Step 4. Copy cell G2 into cells G3:G9

The results of these steps appear in Figure A.15b. Using Excel's TEXTJOIN function, we have created a new field in column G that contains the contents of the fields Prefix, First Name, Middle Name, Last Name, and Suffix for each record with no extraneous blank spaces.

Notes + Comments

1. In addition to numeric and text data, Excel also supports logical data, which returns the value TRUE or FALSE as the product of a test or comparison, and error data, which occurs when Excel recognizes a mistake or missing information while processing an entry.

2. Excel's CONCAT function can also be used to combine the contents of multiple fields into a single field. As with Flash Fill, the CONCAT function does not ignore empty fields. However, the CONCAT function does allow the user to control the fields to be combined.

A.3 **Cleaning**

Once the discovery and structuring phases of data wrangling are complete, the analyst moves on to cleaning the raw data. This step includes identifying missing data, erroneous data, duplicate records, and outliers and determining the best actions for addressing these issues. Although our focus here is on preparing data for data visualization, it is important to note that data cleaning makes heavy use of descriptive statistics and data-visualization methods to identify missing data, erroneous data, and outliers.

Missing Data

Data sets commonly include observations with missing values for one or more variables, and addressing these instances may be necessary to facilitate an accurate display of the data. In some cases, there is an appropriate reason for a value of a field to be missing; these are called **legitimately missing data**. For example, respondents to a survey may be asked if they belong to a fraternity or a sorority, and then in the next question are asked how long they have belonged to a fraternity or a sorority. If a respondent does not belong to a fraternity or a sorority, they should skip the ensuing question about how long. Generally, no remedial action is taken for legitimately missing data.

We discuss the use of data visualization to identify missing values in Chapter 6. In Chapter 9, we discuss how to use Excel's COUNTBLANK function to identify missing values.

In other cases, there is not an appropriate reason for the value of a field to be missing; these are called **illegitimately missing data**. These cases can result from a variety of reasons, such as a respondent electing not to answer a question that they are expected to answer, a respondent dropping out of a study before its completion, or sensors or other electronic data collection equipment failing during a study. Remedial action is considered for illegitimately missing data. If possible, the original source of the data should be checked for all instances of illegitimately missing data to establish whether the values that are missing can be determined. If the missing value can be found in the source of the data, the verified value from the source of the data should be used to replace the missing value. The primary options for addressing missing data if the missing value cannot be found at its source are: (1) to discard records (rows) with any missing values, (2) to discard any field with missing values, or (3) to fill in missing entries with estimated values.

Identification of Erroneous Outliers, Other Erroneous Values, and Duplicate Records

Examining the variables in the data set by use of summary statistics, frequency distributions, bar charts and histograms, z-scores, scatter charts, correlation coefficients, and other tools can uncover data quality issues and outliers. For example, finding the minimum or maximum value for a variable may reveal unrealistic values which could indicate a problem for that value of the variable.

It is important to note here that many software packages, including Excel, ignore missing values when calculating various summary statistics such as the mean, standard deviation, minimum, and maximum. However, if missing values in a data set are indicated with a unique value (such as 9999999), these values may be included by software packages in calculations of various summary statistics such as the mean, standard deviation, minimum, and maximum. Both cases can result in misleading values for summary statistics, which is why many analysts prefer to deal with missing data issues prior to using summary statistics to attempt to identify erroneous outliers and other erroneous values in the data.

Once we have resolved the erroneous outlier and other erroneous value issues in the raw data to the best of our ability, we move on to identification of illegitimate duplicate records. In some raw data, duplicate records legitimately occur. But in other raw data, each record is likely unique. Here, we demonstrate in Excel how to identify duplicate records with conditional formatting and remove duplicate records with the **Remove Duplicates** tool. As an example, let us consider Blakely Tires, a U.S. producer of automobile tires. To learn about the conditions of its tires on automobiles in Texas, the company has obtained information for each of the four tires from 116 automobiles with Blakely

DATA *file*

treadwear

brand tires that have been collected through recent state automobile inspection facilities in Texas; these data are provided in the file *treadwear*. The data obtained by Blakely includes the position of the tire on the automobile (left front, left rear, right front, right rear), age of the tire, mileage on the tire, and depth of the remaining tread on the tire. Before Blakely management attempts to learn more about its tires on automobiles in Texas, it wants to assess the quality of these data.

Blakely Tires has now obtained information for each of the four tires from 116 additional automobiles with Blakely brand tires that have been collected through recent state automobile inspection facilities in Texas. The data, contained in the file *treadwearnew*, include the same information as the file *treadwear*. However, the *treadwearnew* data are suspicious because they should contain records for 116 sets of four tires or $116 \times 4 = 456$ records, but actually the data include records for 457 tires. We will therefore look for duplicate records in the *treadwearnew* data.

We begin by searching for duplicate records using the IF and COUNTIFS functions and conditional formatting in Excel. Excel's IF function allows you to make a logical comparison between the value in a cell and a target value by testing for a condition and returning one result if the condition is true and a different result if the condition is false. The general form of the IF function is

=IF(condition, result if condition is true, result if condition is false)

Excel's COUNTIFS function counts the cells in one or more ranges that satisfy one or more conditions. The general form of the COUNTIFS function is

=COUNTIFS(condition_range1, result if condition 1 is true, condition_range2, result if condition 2 is true, …)

After opening the file *treadwearnew*:

DATA *file*
treadwearnew

Step 1. Enter *Duplicate Record?* in cell F1
Step 2. Enter *=IF(COUNTIFS($A$2:$A$458,$A2,$B$2:$B$458,$B2,$C$2:$C$458, $C2,$D$2:$D$458,$D2,$E$2:$E$458,$E2)>1, "Duplicate record", " ")* in cell F2

By nesting the COUNTIFS function inside the IF function in step 2, we will determine if each record in the range A2:A458 is a duplicate on the criteria in ranges B2:B458, C2:C458, D2:D458, and E2:E458, and we enter *Duplicate record* in the corresponding cell in column F if the corresponding record is a duplicate on all of these four ranges.

Step 3. Copy cell F2 to cells F3:F458

Each cell in the range F2:F458 that corresponds to a range that contains a duplicate record will now contain the phrase Duplicate record, and all other cells in this range will remain blank.

Step 4. Select cells A2:F458
Step 5. Click the **Data** tab on the ribbon
Step 6. Click the **Sort** button in the **Sort & Filter** group
Step 7. In the **Sort** dialog box
    Select **Duplicate Record?** in the **Sort by** window
    Select **Z to A** in the **Order** window
    Click the **Add Level** button
    Select **ID Number** in the new **Sort by** window
    Select **Smallest to Largest** in the **new Order** window
    Click **OK**

As Figure A.16 shows, the duplicate records, sorted by ID Number, appear in the first rows of the data in the worksheet.

We can now see that the vehicle with ID Number 81518 has duplicate records for its right rear tire and unique records for each of the other three positions on the automobile. We also

Figure A.16	Identification of Duplicate Records in the New Blakely Tires Data

▲	A	B	C	D	E	F
1	ID Number	Position on Automobile	Life of Tire (Months)	Tread Depth	Miles	Duplicate Record?
2	81518	RR	20.6	8.6	37408	Duplicate record
3	81518	RR	20.6	8.6	37408	Duplicate record
4	13391952	LR	58.5	2.2	3007	
5	21679618	LR	17.2	8.0	39084	
6	18414342	RR	15.0	9.8	13709	
7	19778015	RR	7.3	10.9	2002	
8	16356967	RR	13.3	8.5	24334	
9	8951784	LR	53.0	3.2	49033	
10	6558415	RR	14.0	8.4	4296	
11	16289891	LR	5.4	10.4	5647	
12	8698313	LF	61.1	1.6	26190	
13	8919904	LF	11.4	10.1	19490	

see that these data do not have any other duplicate records. We can now delete one of the two records for the right rear tire of the vehicle with ID Number 81518 and save the file.

Once they are identified, manual deletion of duplicate records is simple. But if there are many duplicate records, a more automated approach will be more efficient. In Excel, we can accomplish this task by using the **Remove Duplicates** tool. With the file *treadwearnew* open:

Step 1. Select cells A2:E458
Step 2. Click the **Data** tab on the ribbon
Step 3. In the **Data Tools** group, click the **Remove Duplicates** button
Step 4. When the **Remove Duplicates** dialog box (Figure A.17) opens:
    Click the **Select All** button to indicate you want to find rows that are
        duplicates on all columns
    Click **OK**

Figure A.17	Remove Duplicates Dialog Box

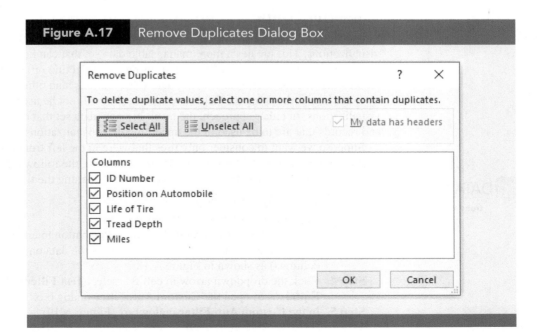

This action will delete all but one record from each set of duplicate records. This deletes one of the two duplicate rows for the vehicle with ID Number 81518.

Note that although you can skip the steps to detect duplicate records and proceed directly to deletion of duplicate records, this is a risky strategy. You should always identify and examine duplicate records to determine whether they are legitimately separate records before deleting them from the data.

Notes + Comments

1. Bar charts, histograms, scatter charts, and other data visualization tools that can be used to uncover data quality issues and outliers are discussed in Chapter 2.

2. Summary statistics, frequency distributions, z-scores, correlation coefficients, and other statistical tools that can be used to uncover data quality issues and outliers are discussed in statistics textbooks such as the authors' *Statistics for Business and Economics*.

3. Many practitioners will consider a value of a potential outlier worthy of investigation if the absolute value of its z-score exceeds 3.0.

4. Many software packages used for analyzing data, such as R and Python, can be used to clean data. The exact steps for doing this depend on the software tool that is used.

A.4 Enriching

The discovery, structuring, and cleaning steps of the data wrangling process provide a deeper understanding of the raw data. In the enriching step, we use this understanding in thinking about what information will be useful to have in the data set. Here, we consider how we might want to simplify the data by selecting the subset of fields or records that will be useful for the ensuing visualization, supplement the raw data with additional data, or enhance the raw data through transformations on its fields. Although enriching the data is an optional step, it can be an extremely important step if the raw data does not meet the requirements for the ensuing visualization.

Subsetting Data

Subsetting is the extraction of fields and records that will be useful for ensuing data visualizations. This creates a more manageable data set that can be processed and visualized more efficiently. Some software subsets data by selecting or retaining the fields and records that will be useful for ensuing data visualizations, and other software subsets data by excluding or dropping the fields and records that will not be useful for ensuing data visualizations. In either approach, the result is a new data set that contains only the fields and records that are to be used in the upcoming data visualizations.

Suppose we want to consider only tires that were in the left front position and had tread depth of no more than 2/32nds of an inch. We could use the following steps to produce the subset of records that satisfy these conditions. After opening the file *treadwear*:

treadwear

Step 1. Select cells A1:E458

Step 2. Click the **Data** tab on the Ribbon

Step 3. In the **Sort & Filter** group click the **Filter** button to enable the filters (these can be used to sort and filter the records of the data on values of their respective columns) as shown in Figure A.18

Step 4. Click the dropdown arrow in cell B1, select **Test Filters**, then select **Equals...** to open the **Custom AutoFilter** dialog box

Step 5. In the **Custom AutoFilter** dialog box (Figure A.19)

Figure A.18   The Blakely Tires Data with Filters Enabled

	A	B	C	D	E
1	ID Number ▾	Position on Automobile ▾	Life of Tire (Months) ▾	Tread Depth ▾	Miles ▾
2	13391487	LR	58.4	2.2	2805
3	21678308	LR	17.3	8.3	39371
4	18414311	RR	16.5	8.6	13367
5	19778103	RR	8.2	9.8	1931
6	16355454	RR	13.7	8.9	23992
7	8952817	LR	52.8	3.0	48961
8	6559652	RR	14.7	8.8	4585
9	16289814	LR	6.2	10.1	5221

Figure A.19   The Custom AutoFilter Dialog Box for Position on Automobile

	A	B	C	D	E
1	ID Number ▾	Position on Automobile ▾	Life of Tire (Months) ▾	Tread Depth ▾	Miles ▾
	A↓ Sort A to Z		58.4	2.2	2805
			17.3	8.3	39371
	Z↓ Sort Z to A		16.5	8.6	13367
	Sort by Color >		8.2	9.8	1931
	Sheet View >		13.7	8.9	23992
			52.8	3.0	48961
	⅄x Clear Filter From "Position on Autom..."		14.7	8.8	4585
	Filter by Color >		6.2	10.1	5221
	Text Filters >		60.1	2.0	26129
			11.7	9.2	19237
	Search 🔍		10.9	9.3	6211
	◼ (Select All)		7.7	9.6	11708
	☑ LF		17.1	8.4	21378
	☐ LR		7.7	9.8	14423
	☐ RF		69.0	0.6	64742
	☐ RR		19.5	8.1	11903
			21.9	7.6	44929
			8.1	9.8	2390
			24.4	6.6	672
			25.9	7.1	6094
	OK Cancel		17.8	8.3	5161
			31.9	6.2	57694

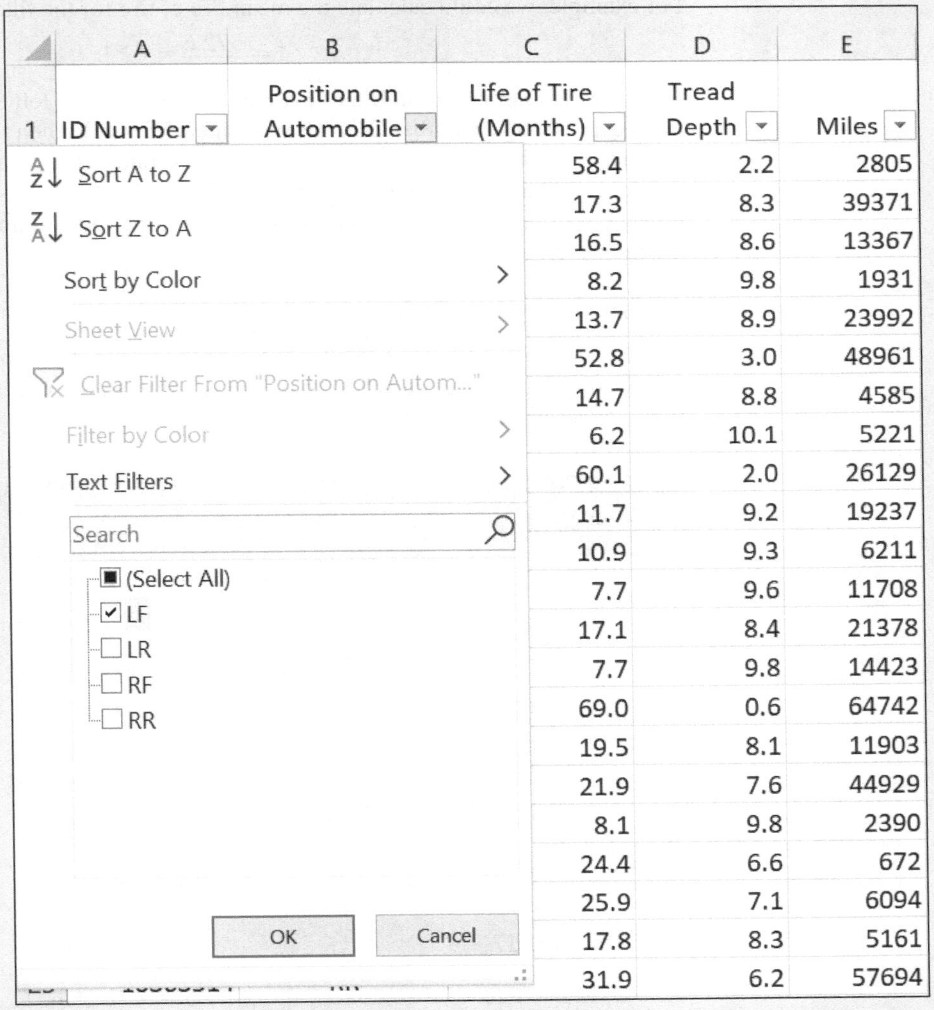

In the top box under **Show rows where: Position on Automobile**, click the
    down arrow and select equals
In the adjacent box, click the down arrow and select LF
Click **OK**

Step 6. Click the dropdown arrow in cell D1, select **Number Filters**, then select **Less than or equal to** to open the **Custom AutoFilter** dialog box

Step 7. In the **Custom AutoFilter** dialog box
In the top box under **Show rows where: Tread Depth**, click the down arrow
    and select **is less than or equal to**
In the adjacent box, enter *2*
Click **OK**

The resulting display as shown in Figure A.20, includes only records that correspond to tires that were on the left front position and had tread depth of no more than 2/32nds of an inch.

*To restore all data to our view, click the **Home** tab on the Ribbon, then click the Filter button in the **Sort & Filter** group to disable the filters on the worksheet.*

Note that all 458 records are still present on this worksheet, but all are hidden except those that satisfy the filters we applied. To perform data visualization on only the filtered data in Excel, we must select the cells with the filtered data, copy the filtered data and paste them into a new worksheet, and then create the visual display of the data in the new worksheet.

Subsetting can also be used to support visualizations of groups of interest in a data set. For example, we could calculate the mean life of tire for the filtered data:

$$\bar{x} = \frac{372.6}{6} = 62.1$$

This is the sample mean life of tire data that were in the left front position and had tread depth of no more than 2/32nds of an inch. We could then follow the same process to produce the sample mean for records that correspond to tires that were on the right front position and had tread depth of no more 2/32nds of an inch to assess the difference in mileage for tires that were on the two front positions and had tread depth of no more than 2/32nds of an inch.

Supplementing Data

We often identify additional data that we want to add to the records in the raw data or receive raw data in multiple files. In these instances, these data must be combined into a single data set if they are all potentially relevant to the ensuing visualization.

Figure A.20   The Blakely Tires Data Filtered to Include Only Left Front Tires with Tread Depth of No More than 2/32nds of an Inch

	A	B	C	D	E
1	ID Number	Position on Automobile	Life of Tire (Months)	Tread Depth	Miles
10	8696859	LF	60.1	2.0	26129
70	14922617	LF	39.6	0.0	12346
159	16691383	LF	66.5	1.1	42632
294	10395904	LF	69.0	0.6	64742
401	3574739	LF	73.3	0.2	57313
436	21817569	LF	64.1	1.3	22618
458					

If we have different data for individual records in multiple files, we combine the data from these files by appending fields. If each record occurs no more than once in each data set, we combine the data for each unique record by using a **one-to-one merger** of the data sets. If we have different data for individual records in multiple locations and at least one record occurs more than once in at least one of the data sets, we combine the data for each unique record by using a **one-to-many merger** of the data sets. These operations are generally similar.

The file *treadwearmodels* contains information on the model for each vehicle in the *treadwear* data by ID Number as shown in Figure A.21. Here, we want to append the appropriate value for the field Model in the file *treadwearmodels* to each record in the *treadwear* data. This is an example of a one-to-many merger since four records are associated with each ID Number. In the following steps, we demonstrate how to do this using Excel's XLOOKUP function. The XLOOKUP function allows the user to pull a subset of data from a larger table of data based on some criterion. The general form of the XLOOKUP function is

= XLOOKUP(*lookup_value, lookup_array, return_array, [if not found], [match mode], [search_mode]*)

Required arguments:

lookup_value	=	The value to search for; it can be an actual value or a cell location containing the value
lookup_array	=	The range to search for the *lookup_value*
return_array	=	The range from which to return a value based on the *lookup_value*

Optional arguments:

[if not found]	=	when a valid match is not found, return the text you supply in *[if not found]*
		The default return if a valid match is not found and this option is missing is #N/A

Figure A.21   A Portion of the Blakely Tires Model Data

	A	B
1	ID Number	Model
2	80441	Volkswagen
3	95990	Chevrolet
4	202372	Cadilac
5	238850	Dodge
6	292849	Kia
7	662056	Chevrolet
8	852812	Chevrolet
9	888432	Toyta
10	1064251	Chevrolet
11	1086054	Ford
12	1383349	Mercedes
13	2122934	Dodge

[match mode]	=	0 means search for an exact match, if none is found, return #N/A (this is the default)
	=	−1 means search for an exact match, if none is found, return the next smaller item
	=	1 means search for an exact match, if none is found, return the next larger item
[search_mode]	=	1 means start the search at the first item in the list
	=	−1 means start the search at the last item in the list (a reverse search)
	=	2 means perform a search that relies on *lookup_array* being sorted in ascending order. If not sorted, invalid results will be returned.
	=	−2 means perform a search that relies on *lookup_array* being sorted in descending order. If not sorted, invalid results will be returned.

DATA *file*

treadwear

DATA *file*

treadwearmodels

In earlier versions of Excel, VLOOKUP allowed the user to search a data range that is set up with fields in columns, and HLOOKUP allowed the user to search a data range that is set up with fields in rows. XLOOKUP is capable of searching a data range that is set up with the fields in columns or rows.

After opening the files *treadwear* and *treadwearmodels*,

Step 1. Enter *Model* in cell F1 of the DATA worksheet in the file *treadwear*

Step 2. Enter =*XLOOKUP(A2,[treadwearmodels.xlsx]Sheet4!$A$2:$A$115, [treadwearmodels.xlsx]Sheet4!$B$2:$B$115)* in cell F2 of the *treadwear* spreadsheet where
- A2 is the cell that contains the value to be matched
- [treadwearmodels.xlsx]Sheet4!$A$2:$A$115 identifies the cells that will be searched for a matching value
- [treadwearmodels.xlsx]Sheet4!$B$2:$B$115 identifies the cells that contain the values to be transferred if a match is found

Step 3. Copy cell F2 into cells F3:F457 of the *treadwear* spreadsheet

Figure A.22 shows partial results of the one-to-many merger of the *treadwearmodels* data with the *treadwear* data. Note that the XLOOKUP function can merge data from multiple worksheets or from multiple workbooks.

Figure A.22	A Portion of the Blakely Tires Data with the Field Model Appended to Each Record

	A	B	C	D	E	F
1	ID Number	Position on Automobile	Life of Tire (Months)	Tread Depth	Miles	Model
2	13391487	LR	58.4	2.2	2805	Hyundai
3	21678308	LR	17.3	8.3	39371	Mercedes
4	18414311	RR	16.5	8.6	13367	Volkswagen
5	19778103	RR	8.2	9.8	1931	Volvo
6	16355454	RR	13.7	8.9	23992	Volkswagen
7	8952817	LR	52.8	3.0	48961	Chrysler
8	6559652	RR	14.7	8.8	4585	Chevrolet
9	16289814	LR	6.2	10.1	5221	Acura
10	8696859	LF	60.1	2.0	26129	Volkswagen
11	8921457	LF	11.7	9.2	19237	Chevrolet
12	7505467	LF	10.9	9.3	6211	Chevrolet
13	18307885	RR	7.7	9.6	11708	Acura

We sometimes have multiple data sets that each contains unique records. This often happens with time series data. For example, we may have three separate files that each contain quarterly sales data for one of the past three years as shown in Figure A.23.

DATA *file*

qtrsalesbyear

In Excel, we deal with cases such as this by cutting and pasting the raw data from these files into a new file in which each record represents a unique record from one of the ten original raw data files. The result of combining the three years of quarterly sales data in Figure A.23 into a single worksheet is shown in Figure A.24.

Other software packages can deal with this issue in a more direct and less manual manner.

Enhancing Data

When we make a transformation on one or more fields in a data set, we change the format, structure, or values of data in a well-defined, systematic manner. This is sometimes done for presentation; for example, an analyst may reformat a field to show as a percentage because that will communicate more effectively with the target audience. However, transformations on fields are also frequently used to facilitate insights that can be derived from data visualization. In this section, we will discuss transforming quantitative fields and transforming categorical fields.

In Chapter 1, we define types of data, including quantitative variables.

We define quantitative data as data for which numerical values are used to indicate magnitude, such as how many or how much. Recall that arithmetic operations such as addition, subtraction, and multiplication can be performed on quantitative data. This allows us to create new quantitative fields as functions of existing quantitative fields using these mathematical operations. Most data wrangling software packages provide tools for making functional transformations of quantitative fields.

Figure A.23	Three Years of Quarterly Sales Data in Separate Files

Year	Quarter	Sales
1	1	$3,000,023
1	2	$3,028,816
1	3	$3,383,280
1	4	$3,241,443

Year	Month	Sales
2	1	$3,106,613
2	2	$3,172,476
2	3	$3,453,856
2	4	$3,277,489

Year	Month	Sales
3	1	$3,168,071
3	2	$3,174,391
3	3	$3,585,522
3	4	$3,403,250

Figure A.24	Three Years of Quarterly Sales Data in a Single Worksheet

	A	B	C	D	E
1	Year	Quarter	Sales		
2	1	1	$3,000,023		
3	1	2	$3,028,816		
4	1	3	$3,383,280		
5	1	4	$3,241,443		
6	2	1	$3,106,613		
7	2	2	$3,172,476		
8	2	3	$3,453,856		
9	2	4	$3,277,489		
10	3	1	$3,168,071		
11	3	2	$3,174,391		
12	3	3	$3,585,522		
13	3	4	$3,403,250		

Year 1 | Year 2 | Year 3 | **Combined Years**

Data sets often contain quantitative fields that, considered separately, are not particularly insightful but that when appropriately combined, result in a new field that may be useful in the ensuing data visualizations. For example, suppose an analyst wanted to use the miles per months achieved by each tire in the Blakely tires data shown in Figure A.22. The analyst could use the following steps in Excel to do so. With the file *treadwear* open:

Step 1. Enter *Miles per Month* in cell G1 of the DATA worksheet
Step 2. Enter *=E2/C2* in cell F2
Step 3. Copy cell F2 into cells F3:F457

Figure A.25 shows a portion of the Blakely Tires data with the Miles per Month Field added.

In other instances, a functional transformation of an existing field may result in a new field that reveals an important relationship that may be useful in the ensuing visualization. We can apply a wide variety of functional transformations, such as a logarithmic transformation, to an existing quantitative field to create a new quantitative field that may be relevant to visualization of the data. Here, we demonstrate how to apply a natural logarithmic transformation to the field Tread Depth. With the file *treadwear* open:

Step 1. Enter *LN Tread Depth* in cell H1 of the DATA worksheet
Step 2. Select cell H2

The Excel function LN calculates the natural logarithm of a number.

Step 3. Click the **Formulas** tab and click the **Insert Function** button f_x to open the **Insert Function** dialog box
In the **Or select a category** dropdown menu, select **Math & Trig**
In the **Select a function** area, scroll down to **LN**
Select **LN**
Click **OK**

Figure A.25 A Portion of the Blakely Tires Data with the Miles per Month Field Added

	A	B	C	D	E	F	G
1	ID Number	Position on Automobile	Life of Tire (Months)	Tread Depth	Miles	Model	Miles per Month
2	13391487	LR	58.4	2.2	2805	Hyundai	48.03
3	21678308	LR	17.3	8.3	39371	Mercedes	2275.78
4	18414311	RR	16.5	8.6	13367	Volkswagen	810.12
5	19778103	RR	8.2	9.8	1931	Volvo	235.49
6	16355454	RR	13.7	8.9	23992	Volkswagen	1751.24
7	8952817	LR	52.8	3.0	48961	Chrysler	927.29
8	6559652	RR	14.7	8.8	4585	Chevrolet	311.90
9	16289814	LR	6.2	10.1	5221	Acura	842.10
10	8696859	LF	60.1	2.0	26129	Volkswagen	434.76
11	8921457	LF	11.7	9.2	19237	Chevrolet	1644.19
12	7505467	LF	10.9	9.3	6211	Chevrolet	569.82
13	18307885	RR	7.7	9.6	11708	Acura	1520.52

Step 4. When the **Function arguments** dialog box appears, enter *D2* into the **Number** box

   Click **OK**

Step 5. Copy cell H2 into cells H3:H457

Figure A.26 shows a portion of the *treadwear* data with the LN Tread Depth field added.

In Chapter 1, we define types of data, including categorical variables.

Next, we will create supplementary data for a field that is a categorical variable. We define categorical data as data for which categories of like items are identified by labels or names. Recall that arithmetic operations cannot be performed on categorical data (even if numbers are used as the labels).

Dummy variables are used extensively for analytics, including regression models and data mining applications.

It is sometimes necessary to create a **dummy variable**, or a field that takes values of 0 or 1 to indicate the absence or presence of some categorical effect, from the values of an existing field in the raw data. This is usually done by defining a new field as a function of the values of an existing field in the raw data. We proceed with a few examples from Excel for the data in the file *airportconditions*, which contains daily information on several weather conditions for a regional airport in the Midwest for February. These data are shown in Figure A.27.

We will first use Excel's IF function to create a dummy variable for a quantitative variable; this dummy variable will indicate whether the temperature dropped below freezing each day. The dummy variable, which we will name Below32, will equal 1 if the low temperature at the airport was below 32 on each date and 0 otherwise. Once the file *airportconditions* is open in Excel:

DATA*file*

airportconditions

Step 1. Enter *Below32* in cell F1
Step 2. Enter *=IF(C2<32,1,0)* in cell F2
Step 3. Copy cell F2 into cells F3:F29

We have created our dummy variable Below32 in column F.

	A	B	C	D	E	F	G	H
1	ID Number	Position on Automobile	Life of Tire (Months)	Tread Depth	Miles	Model	Miles per Month	LN Tread Depth
2	13391487	LR	58.4	2.2	2805	Hyundai	48.03	0.7884574
3	21678308	LR	17.3	8.3	39371	Mercedes	2275.78	2.1162555
4	18414311	RR	16.5	8.6	13367	Volkswagen	810.12	2.1517622
5	19778103	RR	8.2	9.8	1931	Volvo	235.49	2.2823824
6	16355454	RR	13.7	8.9	23992	Volkswagen	1751.24	2.1860513
7	8952817	LR	52.8	3.0	48961	Chrysler	927.29	1.0986123
8	6559652	RR	14.7	8.8	4585	Chevrolet	311.90	2.1747517
9	16289814	LR	6.2	10.1	5221	Acura	842.10	2.3125354
10	8696859	LF	60.1	2.0	26129	Volkswagen	434.76	0.6931472
11	8921457	LF	11.7	9.2	19237	Chevrolet	1644.19	2.2192035
12	7505467	LF	10.9	9.3	6211	Chevrolet	569.82	2.2300144
13	18307885	RR	7.7	9.6	11708	Acura	1520.52	2.2617631
14	3121851	LR	17.1	8.4	21378	Kia	1250.18	2.1282317

Figure A.26   A Portion of the Blakely Tires Data with the LN Tread Depth Field Added

We will next create a series of separate dummy variables for a categorical variable that has multiple values. These dummy variables will indicate whether runway conditions were rainy, icy, or dry for each date.

Step 1. Enter *Rainy* in cell G1, *Icy* in cell H1, and *Dry* in cell I1
Step 2. Enter =IF(D2="Rainy",1,0) in cell G2
Step 3. Enter =IF(D2="Icy",1,0) in cell H2
Step 4. Enter =IF(D2="Dry",1,0) in cell I2
Step 5. Copy cells G2:I2 into cells G3:I29

We have created our dummy variables Rainy, Icy, and Dry in columns G, H, and I that are equal to 1 if the associated condition (Rainy, Icy, Dry) was present on a particular date and 0 otherwise.

Next, we will create a dummy variable based on the values of two variables, one quantitative and one categorical. If runway conditions are icy and the windspeed is at least 20 MPH, hazardous landing conditions exist. The dummy variable we will create here indicates whether runway conditions were rainy and there was high wind for each date.

Step 1. Enter *Hazardous Conditions* in cell J1
Step 2. Enter =IF(D2="Icy",IF(E2>=20,1,0),0) in cell J2
Step 3. Copy cell J2 into cells J3:J29

We have created our dummy variable in column J that is equal to 1 if hazardous landing conditions exist on a particular date and 0 otherwise

Finally, we will create a categorical variable that represents a reduction in the number of categories for the field Conditions. The airport communications system automatically sends a text message to the crew of an outbound flight if the airport is experiencing

Figure A.27	Weather Conditions for a Regional Airport in the Midwest During February of Last Year

	A	B	C	D	E
1	Date	High Temperature	Low Temperature	Conditions	Wind Speed (mph)
2	2/1	43	21	Rainy	21
3	2/2	66	48	Rainy	27
4	2/3	58	43	Rainy	15
5	2/4	49	8	Dry	15
6	2/5	65	45	Dry	12
7	2/6	42	21	Dry	10
8	2/7	48	30	Icy	23
9	2/8	42	40	Rainy	6
10	2/9	46	42	Dry	5
11	2/10	37	31	Dry	13
12	2/11	20	16	Icy	15
13	2/12	33	0	Dry	24
14	2/13	44	22	Rainy	5
15	2/14	38	24	Dry	0
16	2/15	50	40	Rainy	5
17	2/16	53	46	Rainy	10
18	2/17	46	38	Rainy	4
19	2/18	45	29	Dry	15
20	2/19	42	29	Icy	26
21	2/20	35	11	Icy	19
22	2/21	34	20	Dry	15
23	2/22	44	16	Dry	1
24	2/23	34	16	Dry	23
25	2/24	39	38	Rainy	8
26	2/25	50	41	Dry	14
27	2/26	51	47	Dry	7
28	2/27	49	30	Rainy	18
29	2/28	25	5	Dry	15

precipitation (Rainy or Icy) on the date of the flight. The categorical variable we will create here indicates whether runway conditions were rainy or icy (Precipitation) or dry (No Precipitation) for each date.

Step 1. Enter *Precipitation?* in cell K1
Step 2. Enter *=IF(D2="Icy","Precipitation",IF(D2="Rainy","Precipitation", "No Precipitation"),"No Precipitation")* in cell K2
Step 3. Copy cell K2 into cells K3:K29

We have created our categorical variable in column K that is equal to Precipitation if conditions are rainy or icy on a particular date and No Precipitation otherwise. Figure A.28 shows the resulting Excel worksheet with the additional dummy variables and categorical variable.

Figure A.28	Weather Conditions Data with Dummy Variables

4	A	B	C	D	E	F	G	H	I	J	K
1	Date	High Temperature	Low Temperature	Conditions	Wind Speed	Below32	Rainy	Icy	Dry	Hazardous Conditions	Precipitation?
2	2/1	43	21	Rainy	21	1	1	0	0	0	Precipitation
3	2/2	66	48	Rainy	27	0	1	0	0	0	Precipitation
4	2/3	58	43	Rainy	15	0	1	0	0	0	Precipitation
5	2/4	49	8	Dry	15	1	0	0	1	0	No Precipitation
6	2/5	65	45	Dry	12	0	0	0	1	0	No Precipitation
7	2/6	42	21	Dry	10	1	0	0	1	0	No Precipitation
8	2/7	48	30	Icy	23	1	0	1	0	1	Precipitation
9	2/8	42	40	Rainy	6	0	1	0	0	0	Precipitation
10	2/9	46	42	Dry	5	0	0	0	1	0	No Precipitation
11	2/10	37	31	Dry	13	1	0	0	1	0	No Precipitation
12	2/11	20	16	Icy	15	1	0	1	0	0	Precipitation
13	2/12	33	0	Dry	24	1	0	0	1	0	No Precipitation
14	2/13	44	22	Rainy	5	1	1	0	0	0	Precipitation
15	2/14	38	24	Dry	0	1	0	0	1	0	No Precipitation
16	2/15	50	40	Rainy	5	0	1	0	0	0	Precipitation
17	2/16	53	46	Rainy	10	0	1	0	0	0	Precipitation
18	2/17	46	38	Rainy	4	0	1	0	0	0	Precipitation
19	2/18	45	29	Dry	15	1	0	0	1	0	No Precipitation
20	2/19	42	29	Icy	26	1	0	1	0	1	Precipitation
21	2/20	35	11	Icy	19	1	0	1	0	0	Precipitation
22	2/21	34	20	Dry	15	1	0	0	1	0	No Precipitation
23	2/22	44	16	Dry	1	1	0	0	1	0	No Precipitation
24	2/23	34	16	Dry	23	1	0	0	1	0	No Precipitation
25	2/24	39	38	Rainy	8	0	1	0	0	0	Precipitation
26	2/25	50	41	Dry	14	0	0	0	1	0	No Precipitation
27	2/26	51	47	Dry	7	0	0	0	1	0	No Precipitation
28	2/27	49	30	Rainy	18	1	1	0	0	0	Precipitation
29	2/28	25	5	Dry	15	1	0	0	1	0	No Precipitation

A.5 Validating and Publishing

We conclude the steps in the data wrangling process by ensuring the data are accurate and accessible. This is accomplished through validating and publishing.

Validating

In the validation step, the analyst checks the accuracy and consistency of data before it is made available for data visualization or used for other business operations. This includes (i) checking that the information in the wrangled data correctly represents the information provided by the raw data and (ii) determining that the fields in the data sets (particularly new fields created in the data wrangling process) are defined in the same manner for all records in the data.

Many data wrangling software packages allow for the identification of values of a field that are outside of the known minimum and maximum values for that field. If you know the minimum and maximum values of a field, these tools can allow you to identify such invalid values in a more direct and efficient manner. In Excel, this is done using the Data Validation tool. We demonstrate the use of the Excel Data Validation tool using the Tread Depth field in the Blakely Tire data. We know that no tire can have a nonpositive value or a value greater than 10 (the tread depth of new Blakely brand tires). Once the file *treadwear* is open, complete the following steps:

DATA *file*

treadwear

Step 1. Select cells C2:C457
Step 2. Click the **Data** tab on the Ribbon
Step 3. In the **Data Tools** group, click the **Down Arrow** on the Data **Validation** button ⧉ ˅ and select **Data Validation** (note that clicking the **Data Validation** button rather than its **Down Arrow** will open the **Data Validation** dialog box directly)

Step 4. When the **Data Validation** dialog box opens:
Select **Decimal** in the **Allow** box
Select **Between** in the **Data** box
Enter *0.1* in the **Minimum** box
Enter *10* in the **Maximum** box
Click **OK**

Step 5. In the **Data Tools** group, click the **Down Arrow** on the **Validation** button and select **Circle Invalid Data** (do not click the **Validation** button rather than its **Down Arrow** as this will open the **Data Validation** dialog box directly)

We immediately note that the cell showing Tread Depth for the left rear tire with ID Number 16289814 is circled as shown in Figure A.29. Scrolling through the data reveals several other tires with Tread Depth values outside of the valid range we specified for the field.

Note that the circles created by Excel's **Data Validation** tool are static; if you sort the data, the circles will remain in their original locations and will no longer be meaningful. Thus, if you want to use this tool to identify extreme values on data sorted in a particular order, you must sort the data so they are in the desired order prior to applying the Excel's **Data Validation** tool. To remove the circles, click the **Down Arrow** on the **Data Validation** button in the **Data Tools** group and select **Clear Validation Circles** (do not click the **Data Validation** button rather than its **Down Arrow** as this will open the **Data Validation** dialog box directly).

The validation step is similar to the cleaning step, and we can use the same tools we used for cleaning and validating the data (summary statistics, frequency distributions, bar charts and histograms, *z*-scores, scatter charts, correlation coefficients, and Excel's Data Validation and Remove Duplicates tools).

As with the cleaning step, the validation step may need to be repeated several times to ensure the accuracy and consistency of the data. Validation is the final step in preparing the

Figure A.29 Portion of Excel Spreadsheet for the Blakely Tire Data Showing an Extreme Value of Tread Depth Circled

	A	B	C	D	E
1	ID Number	Position on Automobile	Life of Tire (Months)	Tread Depth	Miles
2	13391487	LR	58.4	2.2	2805
3	21678308	LR	17.3	8.3	39371
4	18414311	RR	16.5	8.6	13367
5	19778103	RR	8.2	9.8	1931
6	16355454	RR	13.7	8.9	23992
7	8952817	LR	52.8	3.0	48961
8	6559652	RR	14.7	8.8	4585
9	16289814	LR	6.2	10.1	5221
10	8696859	LF	60.1	2.0	26129
11	8921457	LF	11.7	9.2	19237
12	7505467	LF	10.9	9.3	6211
13	18307885	RR	7.7	9.6	11708

raw data for data visualization, so this is the last opportunity for the analyst to identify and address issues with the data that are to be analyzed.

It is often the case that anomalies in the data persist after the initial wrangling of the data. These anomalies might only be discovered once the data visualization is under way and unexpected results occur. In these cases, the data wrangling and data visualization might take several iterations.

Publishing

Once the raw data have been wrangled into a high-quality data set that is ready for data visualization, we enter the publishing step of data wrangling. At this point, we make the newly wrangled data available in a location that makes it easy to access and in a format that is easy to use. If we fail to accomplish either of these goals in the publishing step, all the work we performed in the first five steps of the data wrangling process is fruitless.

Software packages used for data wrangling are generally capable of exporting wrangled data in a wide variety of formats, including:

- Delimited text (txt) files, comma separated value (CSV) files, JavaScript Object Notation (JSON) files, XML files, Excel (xlsx) files, and HTML files
- Databases such as ACCESS, SQL, or ORACLE
- Web pages/HTML files

In addition to making the wrangled data available in a format suitable for data visualization, a data dictionary must be created for the data in the publishing step. The **data dictionary** documents characteristics of the data such as names and definitions of the fields, units of measure used in the fields, the source(s) of the raw data, relationship(s) of the wrangled data with other data, and other attributes. Thus, an effective data dictionary is critical because it ensures that everyone who uses the wrangled data can understand the data and use them in appropriate ways across various data visualizations.

Summary

In this appendix, we have introduced data wrangling. We discussed the importance of data wrangling to the quality and meaningfulness of visual displays to be produced using the data and the consequences of devoting insufficient time and effort into wrangling the data. We then proceeded to a detailed discussion of the six steps in data wrangling, beginning with the discovery step and consideration of accessing the raw data and the format of the raw data. We then proceeded to the structuring step of the data wrangling process and consideration of formatting the data, the arrangement of data, splitting a single field into multiple fields, and combining multiple fields into a single field.

In our discussion of the cleaning step, we dealt with finding and dealing with missing data, including methods for data imputation. In this step, we also discussed identification of erroneous values, outliers, and duplicate records. We considered subsetting, supplementing, and enhancing the raw data in our discussion of the enriching step of the data wrangling process. Here, we also considered creating new quantitative fields and new categorical fields. We concluded with a discussion of the validating and publishing steps of the data wrangling process.

Glossary

Cleaning The data wrangling step in which errors in the raw data are corrected.

Data dictionary Documentation of characteristics of the wrangled data such as names and definitions of the fields, units of measure used in the fields, the source(s) of the raw data, relationship(s) of the wrangled data with other data, and other attributes.

Data wrangling The process of cleaning, transforming, and managing data so it is more reliable and can be more easily accessed and used for data visualization.

Delimiter A tag or marker that separates structured data into various fields.

Discovery The data wrangling step in which the analyst becomes familiar with the data to conceptualize how it might be used and potentially discovers issues that will need to be addressed later in the data wrangling process.

Dummy variable A field that that takes a value of 0 or 1 to indicate the absence or presence of some categorical effect.

Enriching The data wrangling step in which the raw data are augmented by incorporating values from other data sets and/or applying transformations to portions of the existing data to ensure that all data that will be required for the ensuing visualization will be included in the resulting data set.

Field A characteristic of the observations in a data set.

Flat file A data file in which structured data are arrayed as a rectangle, with each row representing an observation or record and each column representing a unique variable or field.

Illegitimately missing data Instances for which there is not an appropriate reason for the value of a field to be missing.

Legitimately missing data Instances for which there is an appropriate reason for the value of a field to be missing.

Numeric data Data that are stored in a manner that allows mathematical operations to be performed on them. Data of this type generally represent a count or measurement.

One-to-one merger Combining multiple data sets that each have different data for individual records, when each record occurs no more than once in each data set.

One-to-many merger Combining multiple data sets that each have different data for individual records, when at least one record occurs more than once in at least one of the data sets

Publishing The data wrangling step in which a file containing the wrangled data and documentation of the file's contents are made available to its intended users in a format they can use.

Raw data Data that have not been processed or prepared for data visualization or analysis.

Record A grouping of characteristics for a particular observation in a data set.

Semi-structured data Data that do not have the same level of organization as structured data but that allow for the isolation of some elements of the raw data when they are imported.

Stacked data Data organized so the values for each variable are stored in a single field.

Structured data Data sets that are arrayed in a predetermined pattern that make them easy to manage and search.

Structuring The data wrangling step in which the raw data file is arranged so it can be more readily analyzed in the intended manner.

Subsetting The extraction of fields and records that will be useful for the ensuing data visualization.

Text data Data that are words, phrases, sentences, and paragraphs.

Unstacked data Data organized so the values for one variable correspond to separate fields, each of which contains observations corresponding to these respective fields.

Unstructured data Databases that are not arranged in a predetermined pattern and, therefore, in their raw form cannot be stored in a manner similar to a flat file.

Validating The data wrangling step in which the accuracy and reliability of the wrangled data are confirmed so they are ready for the ensuing data visualization.

References

Benton, C. J. *Excel Pivot Tables and Introduction to Dashboards: The Step-by-Step Guide Paperback.* Amazon Digital Services, 2019.

Berengueres, J., Fenwick, A., and Sandell, M. *Introduction to Data Visualization and Storytelling: A Guide for the Data Scientist.* Independently published, 2019.

Berinato, S. *Good Charts: The HBR Guide to Making Smarter, More Persuasive Data Visualizations.* Harvard Business Review Press, 2016.

Berinato, S. *Good Charts Workbook: Tips, Tools, and Exercises for Making Better Data Visualizations.* Harvard Business Review Press, 2019.

Cairo, A. *How Charts Lie.* W. W. Norton and Company, 2019.

Cairo, A. *The Truthful Art: Data, Charts, and Maps for Communication.* Pearson Education, 2016.

Camm, J. D., Cochran, J. J., Fry, M. J., and Ohlmann, J. W. *Business Analytics.* 5th ed., Cengage, 2024.

Camm, J. D., Fry, M. J., and Shaffer, J. A. Practitioner's Guide to Best Practices in Data Visualization. *Interfaces,* 47:6, 473–488, 2017.

Choy, E. *Let the Story Do the Work: The Art of Storytelling for Business Success.* AMACOM, 2017.

Duarte, N. *DataStory: Explain Data and Inspire Action through Story.* Ideapress Publishing, 2019.

Edwards, B. *Color: A Course in Mastering the Art of Mixing Colors.* Penguin, 2004.

Evergreen, S. D. *Effective Data Visualization: The Right Chart for the Right Data.* 2nd ed., SAGE Publications, 2019.

Few, S. *Information Dashboard Design: Displaying Data for At-a-Glance Monitoring.* Analytics Press, 2013.

Few, S. *Information Dashboard Design: The Effective Visual Communication of Data.* O'Reilly Media, 2006.

Few, S. *Now You See It: Simple Visualization Techniques for Quantitative Analysis.* Analytics Press, 2009.

Jones, B. *Avoiding Data Pitfalls.* Wiley, 2020.

Gallo, C. *The Storyteller's Secret: From TED Speakers to Business Legends, Why Some Ideas Catch On and Others Don't.* St. Martin's Publishing Group, 2016.

Goldmeier, J., and Duggirala, P. *Dashboards for Excel.* Apress, 2015.

Knaflic, C. N. *Storytelling with Data: A Data Visualization Guide for Business Professionals.* John Wiley and Sons, 2019.

Knaflic, C. N. *Storytelling with Data: Let's Practice!* John Wiley and Sons, 2019.

Knaflic, C. N. *Storytelling with You: Plan, Create, and Deliver a Stellar Presentation.* John Wiley and Sons, 2023.

Kriebel, A., and Murray, E. *#MakeoverMonday: Improving How We Visualize and Analyze Data, One Chart at a Time.* John Wiley and Sons, 2018.

Mollica, P. *Color Theory: An Essential Guide to Color—From Basic Principles to Practical Applications.* Walter Foster Publishing, 2013.

Page, S. E. *The Model Thinker: What You Need to Know to Make Data Work for You.* Basic Books, 2018.

Reynolds, G. *Presentation Zen: Simple Ideas on Presentation Design and Delivery.* Pearson Education, 2009.

Rowell, K., Betzendahl, L., and Brown, C. *Visualizing Health and Healthcare Data.* John Wiley and Sons, 2021.

Schwabish, J. *Data Visualization in Excel: A Guide for Beginners, Intermediates, and Wonks.* CRC Press, 2023.

Tufte, E. R. *The Visual Display of Quantitative Information.* Graphics Press, 1983.

Tufte, E. R. *Visual Explanations.* Graphics Press, 1997.

Tufte, E. R. *Envisioning Information.* Graphics Press, 1998.

Wexler, S., Shaffer, J., and Cotgreave, A. *The Big Book of Dashboards: Visualizing Your Data Using Real-World Business Scenarios.* John Wiley and Sons, 2017.

Wilke, C. O. *Fundamentals of Data Visualization: A Primer on Making Informative and Compelling Figures.* O'Reilly, 2019.

Index

W

Y